MANAGERIAL FINANCE FOR THE SEVENTIES

McGRAW-HILL SERIES IN FINANCE

Professor Charles A. D'Ambrosio University of Washington, Consulting Editor

Committe: Managerial Finance for the Seventies
Curran: Principles of Financial Management
Dobrovolsky: The Economics of Corporation Finance
Hastings and Mietus: Personal Finance
Francis: Investments Analysis and Management
Sharpe: Portfolio Theory and Capital Markets
Troelstrup: The Consumer in American Society

MANAGERIAL FINANCE FOR THE SEVENTIES

T. C. COMMITTE

Chairman, Department of Finance and Accounting
University of West Florida

with contributions by
Dr. Charles D. McQuillen, Furman University
Dr. Thomas C. Richey, The University of West Florida
Dr. Allen Schwadron, University of Eastern Michigan

McGRAW-HILL BOOK COMPANY

New York
St. Louis
San Francisco
Düsseldorf
Johannesburg
Kuala Lumpur
London
Mexico
Montreal
New Delhi
Panama
Rio de Janeiro
Singapore
Sydney
Toronto

MANAGERIAL FINANCE FOR THE SEVENTIES

Library of Congress Catalog Card Number 72-39287

07-012371-3

2 3 4 5 6 7 8 9 0 KPKP 7 9 8 7 6 5 4 3 2

This book was set in News Gothic by The Maple Press Company, and printed and bound by Kingsport Press, Inc. The designer was Anne Canevari Green; the drawings were done by Vantage Art, Inc. The editors were Jack R. Crutchfield, Cynthia Newby, and Joseph F. Murphy. Peter D. Guilmette supervised production.

CONTENTS

Preface xv

Chapter One | INTRODUCTION 1

THE ROLE AND SCOPE OF THE FINANCIAL EXECUTIVE 1
Functions of the Financial Executive 1
Treasurer's Function 4
Controller's Function 4
The Interdisciplinary Nature of the Finance Function 5
THE GOAL OF FINANCIAL MANAGEMENT 6
THE APPROACH TO FINANCIAL DECISION MAKING 11
Summary 14
References 15

Chapter Two | THE LEGAL AND TAX FRAMEWORK 17

LEGAL IMPLICATIONS OF THE INDIVIDUAL PROPRIETOR 17
Individual Income Tax Considerations 21
Significance of Marginal and Average Tax Rates 24
LEGAL AND TAX IMPLICATIONS OF A PARTNERSHIP 26
Authority, Duties, Rights, and Remedies of Partners 27
Dissolution and Termination of Partnerships 28
Other Types of Partnerships or Associations 28
LEGAL IMPLICATIONS OF A CORPORATION 29
Types of Corporate Stock 32
Par Value and No-par Value Stock 32
Transfer of Ownership through the Sale of Shares 33
Regulation of the Issuance of Corporate Shares 34
Corporate Management 35
THE FRAMEWORK OF CORPORATE TAXES 36
Significance of Capital Gain and Loss Considerations 37
Net Operating Loss 40
Installment Sales 41

Dividends Received **44**
Payment of Income Taxes **44**
Investment Tax Credit **45**
Improper Accumulation of Earnings **46**

ARTICLES OF INCORPORATION **48**
Summary **50**
Questions for Discussion **51**
Problems **52**
References **54**

Chapter Three | SOME ANALYTICAL TOOLS AVAILABLE 57

SUPPLY AND COST **57**
Fixed and Variable Costs **59**
Function and Significance of Economic Cost Curves **60**
Economies of Scale **62**
Diseconomies of Scale **62**

MATHEMATICS OF FINANCE **66**
Compound Interest and Present-value Concepts **66**
Compound Sum of an Annuity **69**
Present Value of a Single Sum **73**
Present Value of an Annuity **75**
Summary **79**
Questions for Discussion **80**
Problems **81**
References **83**

Chapter Four | MARGINAL ANALYSIS AND THE SUPPLY DECISION 85

CONTRIBUTION OF FINANCIAL STATEMENTS TO THE SUPPLY DECISION **86**

THE FLEXIBLE BUDGET **88**
Cost Curves and the Flexible Budget Reconciled **89**

MARGINAL COST OR DIFFERENTIAL COST **93**

BREAKEVEN ANALYSIS **94**

COST-PROFIT-VOLUME RELATIONSHIP **95**

SIGNIFICANCE OF FIXED-VARIABLE COST RELATIONSHIP **96**
The *b* Formula **99**
Regression Analysis and Least Squares **101**

OPERATING LEVERAGE **104**
Summary 105
Questions for Discussion **106**
Problems **107**
References **109**

Chapter Five | CAPITAL BUDGETING 111

CAPITAL BUDGETING DEFINED **113**
Generation of Proposals **114**
Estimation of Costs and Benefits **114**
Evaluation of Risk **114**
Selection of Proposals **115**
Reevaluation **116**
Postaudit **116**

CAPITAL BUDGETING APPLIED **116**
Alternative 1 **118**
Alternative 2 **120**
Alternative 3 **120**

PROJECT SELECTION **122**
Payback Period **122**
Average Return on the Average Annual Investment **123**
The Internal Rate of Return **125**
The Net Present Value **127**
Sensitivity Analysis **140**
A 25 Percent Increase in Variable Costs **143**
A Change in Sales Volume and Weighted Price **143**
A 25 Percent Increase in Average Variable Cost and a 20 Percent Increase in Total Sales Together with a Change in Sales Mix from 3 to 1 to 6 to 4 **144**
Probability Analysis **145**
Sensitivity and Probability Combined **145**
Summary **152**
Questions for Discussion **154**
Problems **154**
References **156**

Chapter Six | INTERMEDIATE-TERM FINANCING 159

SOURCE OF FUNDS **159**

BANK FINANCING **164**
Alternative 1—Manufacturer Financing **167**
Use of Present-value Concepts **168**
Alternative 2—Add-on Interest **170**
Alternative 3—Interest on Unpaid Balance **171**

LEASING **173**

BUY VERSUS LEASE **175**
Summary **181**
Questions for Discussion **182**
Problems **182**
References **183**

Chapter Seven | THE DEPRECIATION METHODS AND THE FLOW OF FUNDS 185

TAX IMPLICATIONS **186**

GENERALLY ACCEPTED DEPRECIATION METHODS **187**

Straight-line Method **188**

Evaluation of the Straight-line Method **188**

Service-life Methods **190**

Service-hours **190**

Productive Output **191**

Evaluation of Service-life Methods **192**

Accelerated Methods **192**

Declining Balance **192**

Sum of the Years Digits **194**

Evaluation of Accelerated-depreciation Methods **195**

THE TAX SHIELD AS A SOURCE OF FUNDS WITH EMPHASIS ON EARNINGS PER SHARE **195**

Straight-line Method **195**

Service-life Methods **196**

Accelerated-depreciation Methods **196**

THE TAX SHIELD APPLIED **198**

THE EFFECT OF DEPRECIATION METHOD ON THE BUY-VERSUS-LEASE DECISION **202**

Analysis of Effect on EPS of the Jones Buy-versus-Lease Decision **204**

Summary **206**

Questions for Discussion **207**

Problems **208**

References **209**

Chapter Eight | THE INTERNAL CONTROL AND MANAGEMENT OF CASH 211

THE LIQUIDITY RESPONSIBILITY **211**

THE PROFITABILITY OF CASH **214**

INTERNAL CONTROL OF CASH **216**

MANAGEMENT OF SHORT-TERM INVESTMENTS **221**

United States Government Marketable Debt **223**

Prime Sales Finance Paper **223**

Dealer Paper—Industrial **223**

Bankers' Acceptances **223**

Dealer Paper—Finance **224**

Negotiable Certificates of Deposit **224**

Short-term Tax-exempt Bills **225**

Repurchase Agreements **226**

CASH-FLOW ANALYSIS **227**

STATEMENT OF SOURCE AND APPLICATION OF FUNDS **234**

CREDIT AND BILLING PROCEDURES **236**
Lockbox System **237**
Float Time **237**
Effect of Cash Discounts **238**
Summary **242**
Questions for Discussion **244**
Problems **244**
References **246**

Chapter Nine | MANAGEMENT OF ACCOUNTS RECEIVABLE AND INVENTORIES 251

ACCOUNTS RECEIVABLE POLICY **252**
To Whom Should Credit Be Offered and How Much Should Be Offered to a Single Customer **254**
Character **254**
Capacity **254**
Capital **254**
Collateral **254**
Conditions **254**
Sources of Credit Information **255**
Credit Extension **258**
Step 1 **258**
Step 2 **258**
Collection Expenditures **260**

CONTROL OF INVENTORIES **262**

INVENTORIES AND COSTS **264**
Economic Order Quantity **265**

INVENTORY TURNOVER RATIOS **269**

RECONCILIATION OF INVENTORY POLICY WITH SALES AND PRODUCTION BUDGETS **272**
Production Costs **275**
Sales Forecast and Sales Pattern **275**
Lead Time and Safety Stock **276**
Stock-out Costs **276**

INTERNAL CONTROL OF INVENTORIES **277**

VALUATION OF INVENTORIES **278**

SIGNIFICANCE OF VALUATION METHODS **279**
Summary **281**
Questions for Discussion **282**

Problems **283**
References **284**

Chapter Ten | THE FINANCIAL EXECUTIVE AND THE ECONOMIC ENVIRONMENT 287

ECONOMIC ENVIRONMENT **289**
MARKET STRUCTURE AND PRICES **296**
Monopolistic Competition **297**
Oligopoly **298**
Types of Oligopoly **299**
Monopoly **300**
PRICING **300**
The Price-Volume Relationship **301**
Marginal and Average Revenue **303**
ADMINISTERED PRICES **306**
MARKET SUMMARY **308**
Questions for Discussion **310**
Problems **311**
References **312**

Chapter Eleven | FINANCIAL STATEMENT ANALYSIS 315

A FRAMEWORK FOR ACQUISITIONS **316**
ANALYSIS OF FINANCIAL STATEMENTS **320**
Ratio Analysis **321**
Liquidity Ratios **321**
Leverage Ratios **322**
Activity Ratios **324**
Profitability Ratios **325**
Value of Internal Data **327**
Industry Data Usefulness **327**
ADDITIONAL ANALYSIS **327**
Analysis of Retained Earnings **329**
Significance of Asset Appraisals **333**
PRESENT VALUE AND PURCHASE PRICE **334**
ADDITIONAL ANALYSIS (Continued) **336**
Summary **338**
Questions for Discussion **339**
Problems **340**
References **342**

Chapter Twelve | THE COST OF CAPITAL 343

CLASSICAL THEORY OF INTEREST **344**
SIGNIFICANCE OF INTEREST RATE ON THE SOURCE OF FUNDS **347**
Purchasing-power Risk **351**

Interest-rate Risk **351**
Financial Risk **352**
Market Risk **354**
Significance of Investment Risks to Cost of Capital **355**

COST OF CAPITAL **356**
The Firm as Represented by Professional Management **356**
The New Equity Investor **357**
The Investor in Debt **357**

PROBABLE VALUE OF FIRM'S STOCK **358**
Comparison with Other Firms **359**
Probable Value to Earnings Group **363**
Significance of Financing Mix on Cost of Debt and Equity Capital **366**

INVESTOR ANTICIPATION AND COMMON STOCK PRICES **369**
Significance of Increased Sales Volume to Earnings per Share **374**

SIGNIFICANCE OF PRESENT-VALUE ANALYSIS TO MARKET VALUE OF STOCK **375**
Probable Market Value to Earnings-Dividends Group **378**
Significance of Stock Splits and Stock Dividends on Market Value of Stock **379**
Summary **380**
Questions for Discussion **382**
Problems **383**
References **385**

Chapter Thirteen | LONG-TERM FINANCING 389

CHARACTERISTICS OF LONG-TERM FINANCING **389**
Secured Bonds **390**
Unsecured Obligations—The Debenture **392**
Public versus Private Placement **396**
Significance of Trust Indenture Act of 1939 **397**
Mortgage Bonds **398**
Equipment Trust Certificates **398**
Collateral Trust Bonds **399**
Income Bonds **399**
Convertible Bonds **399**

EFFECT OF LONG-TERM FINANCING ON RETURN TO EQUITY—LEVERAGE **405**

MARGINAL COST OF DEBT **408**
Summary **418**
Questions for Discussion **419**
Problems **421**
References **422**

Chapter Fourteen | Mergers AND ACQUISITIONS 425

GUIDELINES FOR MARKET RESEARCH **426**
Company Sales in Units **429**
Company Sales in Dollars **430**
Company Costs and Expenses **431**
The Diversification Gap **432**
INTERNAL DIVERSIFICATION **434**
DIVERSIFICATION THROUGH MERGERS AND ACQUISITION **434**
TYPES OF MERGERS **435**
Significance of Antitrust Laws **436**
THE MERGER CANDIDATE **440**
MECHANICS OF MERGERS AND ACQUISITIONS **440**
Depreciation Recapture **441**
Tax Consequences **442**
Tax-free Reorganizations **442**
Taxable Transaction **443**
Significance of the Accounting Method **444**
Purchase Accounting **444**
Pooling Accounting **445**
THE TOOLS OF ACQUISITIONS AND MERGERS **446**
FORMS OF PAYMENT AND RESULTANT EPS **446**
Acquisition by Common Stock **447**
Acquisition by Cash **448**
Acquisition by Convertible Debentures **448**
THE SEARCH FOR ACQUISITION CANDIDATES **450**
DESCRIPTION OF KIDCO **452**
ACQUISITION OF KIDCO (PURCHASE) **454**
ACQUISITION OF KIDCO (POOLING) **457**
Summary **459**
Questions for Discussion **460**
References **461**

Chapter Fifteen | REORGANIZATION AND BANKRUPTCY 463

THE LEGAL RIGHTS OF INTERESTED PARTIES **464**
THE EFFECT OF HIGH DEBT-TO-EQUITY RATIO **466**
VOLUNTARY BANKRUPTCY **468**
INVOLUNTARY BANKRUPTCY **469**
ACTS OF BANKRUPTCY **469**
THE VALUATION PROBLEM **471**
ALTERNATIVES TO BANKRUPTCY **478**

Summary **481**
Questions for Discussion **482**
References **483**

Appendix
Table A-1: Compound Sum of $1 **486**
Table A-2: Present Value of $1 **488**
Table A-3: Sum of an Annuity of $1 for N Years **490**
Table A-4: Present Value of an Annuity of $1 for N Years **492**

Glossary **493**

Index **503**

PREFACE

The biggest problem in any problem is knowing what the problem is. It is, therefore, vital that a student learn to identify, analyze, and diagnose problems. This is the very essence of quality education. What a college or university graduate knows is important. But what he does not know can be far more important. It is within this frame of reference that *Managerial Finance for the Seventies* was conceived.

To the Student: This text offers you both an introduction to the world of finance and a framework for further planning and study as you develop your career pattern. The author will certainly not guarantee that you will wind up as the president or chief financial officer of General Motors, Chrysler, Ford, or International Harvester. However, it is significant that the president or chief financial officer of these companies and of many others *did* rise to the top via the finance route.

The "continuous case method" has been adopted to present an overall view of the dynamics of the financial decision-making process and to eliminate unrelated chapters and abstract presentations. You will be confronted with real world problems and will have to live with the results of practical decisions. You will become a participant in the learning process, a situation the author regards as the basis for a meaningful educational experience. The author sincerely hopes that you will find this experience worthwhile.

To the Instructor: In general, and in the final analysis, all managerial decisions are financial decisions. Financial decisions involve applied economics with accounting and statistics supplying the decision-making data. Historical data may also be necessary or helpful. However, the executive is always dealing with the risks and uncertainties of tomorrow. Decisions must be made, and they must be made in the context of an ever-changing world. To expose the student to descriptive, isolated, and unrelated chapters dealing with the subject matter of management finance is clearly not enough. Many textbooks available today do not, in the author's view, give students a sufficiently realistic and flexible view of the role of today's financial executive. Even more significant, today's financial executive must understand that he will be involved with professional people who have been trained in other disciplines and that together they will form a team in the managerial decision-making process. The "continuous case method" employed in this book seeks to meet these needs.

Plan of the Book After a brief treatment of some of the analytical tools available to the financial manager, including the economics of marginal analysis, the mathematics of finance, and the tax and legal frameworks of business (Chapters 2 and 3), the student is placed in his first position as an employee of a single proprietor. (The proprietorship soon incorporates.) No prior knowledge of any discipline is assumed. The brief treatment of the analytical tools is designed either to focus the knowledge acquired in prior courses toward a business frame of reference or to enable the student who has not been exposed to the related areas to approach his future studies with a *raison d'etre.*

After the student reports to his new position (Chapter 4), he learns that he is the only member of the firm with training in the area of managerial finance. His first decision involves accepting or rejecting a substantial order from a new customer at a reduced selling price. This specific problem is first examined from the economist's point of view. The student soon discovers that the economic cost curves and the accountant's flexible budget give exactly the same answer, and, in fact, the cost curves are nothing more than the flexible budget plotted. After detailed analysis, this problem is solved with the student and the order is accepted. The finished product of this chapter serves as the raw material for the next chapter. This same format is followed throughout the text. This technique keeps the student continually involved with the material, and as progress is made through the chapters the entire picture of financial management unfolds. Thus, at the end of Chapter 4, a second order is received from the same customer that is twice as big as the first order. It is at this point that the chapter ends.

In analyzing the financial implications of this second order, the student consults the cost curves and flexible budget prepared in the previous chapter, and it becomes obvious that the order cannot be accepted at the stated price without additional production capacity. The student is then confronted with a capital budgeting problem, which is the subject matter of Chapter 5. After considerable study of the capital budgeting material and application to the problem at hand (see Table of Contents), the student finds himself with an intermediate-term financing problem (Chapter 6).

Significantly, Chapter 6 relates back to Chapters 4 and 5 in that the text material is presented and the immediate problem solved only after a thorough examination of alternative financing methods. Thus institutional, descriptive material is presented in an analytical framework. The student absorbs this material as he is seeking a solution to his problem. The solution finally involves a buy-versus-lease analysis. Present-value and compound interest concepts are utilized throughout as well as the tax implications of the decision. However, the solution assumes a given method of depreciation. What, the student is asked, would have been the results of his analysis had alternative depreciation methods been used. The question appropriately enough deals with the effect the financing will have on earnings per share, and a hint is given as to the significance of the cost of capital. However, it is only a hint because we are not ready to tackle that subject at this point.

As you might surmise, Chapter 7 deals with alternative depreciation methods, with emphasis on the buy-versus-lease question. This question is expanded to include the funds made available by the tax shield provided by depreciation and, again, the effect on earnings per share. Again, present-value, compound interest, and tax considerations are woven into the analysis. The needed equipment is leased.

Chapter 8 builds upon the profit projections prepared in Chapter 5 where the material was prepared from the cost curves and flexible budget developed in Chapter 4 to test the investment alternatives as the student was considering capital budgeting. The student at first considers the liquidity and profitability responsibilities associated with the internal control and the management of cash. He is delighted with the profit projections and undertakes to determine the optimum way to invest the excess cash that is apparent. He is suddenly brought up short when a cash-flow analysis, which is prepared with considerable detail, indicates that the firm could well be out of business at the end of 120 days because of a liquidity problem. He has forcefully learned the difference between liquidity and profitability. This experience focuses his attention on short-term financing, which is covered in the same chapter. While analyzing the implications of the cash-flow analysis he becomes concerned with the management of accounts receivable and inventory policy.

Needless to say, these two problems dominate Chapter 9. They are overcome only after various alternatives and quantitative techniques have been thoroughly examined. Increased sales volume has caused a profit squeeze, and some consideration must be given to an adjustment in the selling price. Chapter 10 examines the various types of economic market within which the firm is selling, and the parameters of a pricing decision are developed. Again, earnings per share is the focal point. The same chapter finds our successful student being promoted to financial vice-president and demands that he examine the macroeconomic environment within which he must operate. He relates forecasting, government activity in the money markets, purchasing power, and the like to the economics of *his* firm.

In Chapter 11 he is faced with the problem of analyzing financial statements in general and specifically the statements of a firm which his organization is contemplating purchasing, merging with, or selling out to. The analysis is quite exhaustive and includes the tax implications of operating losses, capital gains, and "transfer prices" along with other considerations. The decision is made not to merge, not to sell, but to purchase the other firm. A long-term financing problem is thus created.

As a preparation for the matter of long-term financing (Chapter 13), Chapter 12 deals with the "cost of capital" to the firm, to the debt investor, and to the new equity investor. This examination includes a consideration of interest rates and the supply and demand for loanable funds, the establishment of a theoretical probable market value for the firm's closely held stock, and an analysis of the contribution the to-be-acquired firm could make to earnings per share as related to the cost of the firm's debt and equity capital. These examinations are made in considerable detail.

After this background is obtained, the long-term financing problem is approached head-on by an examination of alternative debt financing instruments (Chapter 13). Various financing combinations are extensively reviewed, and a convertible bond is finally utilized to acquire the stock of a $5 million corporation by a firm with an equity capitalization of only $250,000. This accomplishment is examined in true "conglomerate style," utilizing the pre-1969 tax reform laws to illustrate how it has been done, and then the terms of the agreement are changed to reflect the provisions of the 1969 Tax Reform Act. By this time, the term is over and a solid background has been laid for further study.

Chapter 14 finds that the firm's rate of growth in earnings per share is leveling off. The theory and mechanics of mergers and acquisitions are examined. Purchase versus pooling is a focal point. Chapter 15 deals with bankruptcy. The student is consulted by an attorney for advice concerning subordinate debentures in a firm on the edge of bankruptcy. Alternatives are examined, and the matter is worked out.

Some General Points This text has proved to be highly motivating to some 900 to 1,000 students who have participated in a three-year pretest of the manuscript. Lively classroom discussions have ensued. The student has been involved from the first day of the term until the end. Participating professors have found it unnecessary to rehash the case as it develops. Students have had the responsibility of studying the text material. The style of the text is sometimes subtle, which has encouraged discussion. Therefore, the discussion questions at the end of each chapter are designed to serve as a lesson plan. This approach will ensure that when all the questions have been covered, the professor will have ample opportunity to make a significant contribution as he elaborates on the basis of his own experience and special skills.

For the professor who would prefer to take the analytical approach, there are adequate problems at the end of each chapter. These problems are related and keyed to the class discussion questions for exactly the same purpose. Some professors have preferred both the class discussion questions and the analytical problems.

In short, the analytical style stimulates the student by presenting a continuous application of otherwise abstract financial concepts. The text is not fragmented by conceptual boundaries. The consequences of one managerial decision provide the basis for new problems, just as the finished goods of one department become the raw material for another.

Acknowledgments The author has received significant help from Drs. Charles McQuillen, Furman University; Allen Schwadron, University of Eastern Michigan; and Professor Thomas C. Richey, The University of West Florida. Any one of these gentlemen could have written this text, or a similar text, in their own right. Valuable assistance was received from Dr. Charles D'Ambrosio of the University of Washington, Consulting Editor for the McGraw-Hill Series in Finance; from the thousand-odd students who have participated in the development of this text over the past four years; and from Mrs. Carolyn Mengers, Mrs. Lois Bolling, and Mrs. Jonnetta Cook as the manuscript was worked and reworked, typed and retyped.

The mistakes that remain are my own. However, these would have been many more without the expertise of the McGraw-Hill editorial staff—especially Mr. Jack Crutchfield, Miss Cynthia Newby, Mr. Joseph Murphy, and Mrs. Marjorie Appert.

It has been a challenging experience over the past four years, and the author sincerely hopes and trusts that the student will enjoy and learn as he has enjoyed and learned in preparing this manuscript.

T. C. Committe

MANAGERIAL FINANCE FOR THE SEVENTIES

Chapter One
INTRODUCTION

THE ROLE AND SCOPE OF THE FINANCIAL EXECUTIVE

Functions of the Financial Executive

The biggest problem in any problem is knowing what the problem is. Therefore, the very essence of quality education lies in training the student to diagnose, analyze, and define problems. This is the primary concern of all professional people. The medical doctor, using whatever diagnostic aids are appropriate, for example, x-ray, cardiogram techniques, and laboratory tests, diagnoses the problem. Lawyers must define the issues of the case before the matter can be heard by the court. Engineers must analyze basic material problems before construction or before further plans can be made.

The financial executive, if he is to be effective and if he is to make a substantial contribution to the management team, must likewise be able to diagnose, analyze, and define problems. His problems, however, may be considerably more complex and considerably more involved than those problems identified with any single profession. This is so because, in fulfilling his role on the management team, he is dealing with many different types of professional people. Each of these professions will bring a different approach to the solving of a common problem.

The very nature of the financial executive's total responsibility will make it relatively easy for him to become involved in the decision-making process. Keeping him involved, however, may be quite another matter. The financial executive must interact with the various experts from other areas who also participate in the decision-making process. When subject matters come up about which he knows absolutely nothing, he has only two things to do: back up and shut up! When this happens too often, his effectiveness is lost, and the decision-making process flows around rather than through him. More than likely, the paycheck will soon likewise flow around him! It is at this precise point that what we do not know can be far more important than what we do know.

What, then, is the responsibility of the financial executive? What is it that we must be certain that he does know? Will the answers to these questions vary with the size and type of the business organization? We will examine the last question first. As we all know, our economy and our business entities have moved a long way from the time when business was generally owner-operated. By this we mean that generally business decisions are no longer made by and are no longer the responsibility of one man. The process of group decision making is itself an outgrowth of the evolution of business enterprises from simple to complex.

The smaller the business entity, the more knowledgeable the financial executive must be, in perhaps a less sophisticated way. That is, the problems may be less complex, and expert help more than likely will not be available from the immediate staff. However, the basic skills required to recognize the problem and to be familiar, at least in a general way, with the courses of action available to solve the problem are common to all firms. Expert help would, no doubt, be available to the small business on a consulting basis. However, in view of the cost of such services the financial manager must use such help sparingly. The larger enterprise facing a number of problems which demand a high level of expertise for their solution will be in a position to employ full-time staff members to function in these areas on a day-to-day basis. Nevertheless, the types of problems faced by financial managers in large and small firms will be essentially the same.

We can now turn to the question of the financial executive's responsibilities as he fulfills his role as a significant member of the management team. What is his function?

There are three basic finance functions that are common to all business. In the first instance, funds must be acquired and provisions must be made for their safekeeping. Essentially, the business entity will acquire funds as individuals invest in the firm for a stock interest. These funds we will term *equity funds.* The business entity may also acquire funds by borrowing. Funds acquired in this manner we will term *debt financing.* By "safekeeping" we mean the depositing of funds in banks or depositories and the release of funds only after proper authorization for business needs. Second, data must be collected and records must be maintained. These data and records are the raw material for financial statements and reports that will be used as the focal point in management's decision-making process. Finally, available funds must be "effectively utilized" to meet the goals and objectives of the business entity. The total responsibility of the financial executive embraces all three of these functions and more.

Quite often in a relatively small owner-operated business the acquisition of funds is simply the process of moving from one financial crisis to another. The control of funds is often the equivalent of periodic cash deposits and the required signature on a check. The effective utilization of funds is often the product of the owner's day-to-day judgment, or perhaps lack of judgment, as he carries on his business activities. (We will learn that there is a big difference between profitability—the ability to earn a profit—and liquidity—the ability to pay obligations as they become due. Without liquidity, the opportunity to earn a profit may be lost. The effective use of funds includes both—profitability and liquidity.) It has been clearly established that the number one cause of small-business failures has not been the lack of good ideas, products, or services, but either the lack of working capital or the ineffective use of funds. A lack of attention to these vital requirements may be symptomatic of a serious, if not fatal, defect in the management's approach to business problems. This is perhaps just another way of saying that the number one cause of business failures has been the lack of ability to acquire adequate capital or the lack of proper attention to adequate capital requirements. Running a close second as a cause of business failures has been the matter of inadequate data and records and internal control. Adequate performance data and internal control are essential if these records are to be used effectively as a bench mark in testing the "effective utilization" of funds which have been committed by the enterprise. Without adequate internal control, we are not managing; we are drifting along as victims of fate rather than its master.

The success or failure of a "one-man operation" must be one man's responsibility. However, as business entities grow larger, and the corporation emerges as a business institution, there is a distinct division of financial responsibility between the acquiring and safeguarding of the funds on one hand and the providing of records and data to be used in the decision-making process on the other. The acquisition and safeguarding duties are assumed by the treasurer. The duties associated with the records and other data are assumed by the controller, or the comptroller, as he is sometimes called.

Treasurer's Function

As an example, the treasurer of the business entity normally assumes the following responsibilities:

1. He establishes and executes programs dealing with the procurement of the capital needed by the firm, including both debt and equity.
2. He receives, has custody of, and disburses company monies and securities.
3. He is responsible for company credit and collection policies.
4. He invests company funds and is responsible for pension plans and other company trust obligations.
5. He handles the financial aspects of property sales and insurance coverage.

In short, the treasurer has total responsibility within the parameters of his defined functions.

Controller's Function

The controller's function has been defined by the Planning Committee of the Controller's Institute of America, in essence, as follows:

1. The controller will establish, coordinate, and administer, plans to facilitate the forecasting of sales, expense budgets, and cost standards that will permit profit planning, capital budgeting, and financing.
2. The controller will formulate accounting policy and procedures. Operating data and special reports must be prepared so that performance can be compared with plans and standards, and any variance between actual operations and the predetermined standards can be analyzed for corrective action by management.
3. The controller will be responsible for tax policies and procedures and will supervise and coordinate the reports required by governmental agencies.
4. The controller will be responsible for the protection of the business assets to the extent possible by internal control, internal auditing, and insurance coverage.
5. The controller must continually be aware of economic and social forces as well as the effect of governmental policy and action on business activities.

In short, the controller has the operational responsibilities. He is a consultant to management with reference to the effectiveness of policies and the attainment of objectives.

Standing astride both of these functions like the "jolly green giant" is the corporate financial executive. He is vitally interested in the effective use of the funds provided by the treasurer and so must receive significant aid in the form of reports and statements prepared by the controller's office. This is so because the procurement and the effective use of the funds are obviously interrelated. The ability or inability to acquire funds in the first instance may, if not will, set the financial limits within which the firm must operate. Likewise, after operations have begun, the efficiency with which the firm has used available funds may, and probably will, have a direct bearing on the ability to acquire additional funds as they are needed. Therefore, the well-prepared financial executive cannot afford to recognize an artificial division of duties between the treasurer and controller and must, by necessity, be knowledgeable in both the areas administered by these executives.

The Interdisciplinary Nature of the Finance Function

In addition, the financial executive must have a broad interdisciplinary education. This type of education is not easily attained because the various scholastic disciplines, economics, accounting, statistics, and finance, have been rushing to develop a separate "body of knowledge" for each discipline. In so doing, often we have overlooked or left blurred and clouded the simple fact that, in many instances, we are talking about the same thing. We have built walls and barriers between the several disciplines in our feverish efforts to formalize our knowledge in this discipline or that.

As an example, many accountants insist that all economists are "eggheads," that is, impractical theorists. Likewise, many economists insist that all accountants are "bookkeepers," that is, account keepers. (In many instances, both these accusations may be true!) However, if either or both of the above observations are true, it is generally the result of one or two things—lack of education on one side or the other and perhaps both!

Often the various disciplines deal with a common problem. Solutions offered by the various disciplines may be relatively the same although the tools applied to solve the problem may appear to be 180 degrees apart. In addition, the analytical concepts of one discipline may be dependent upon the possible alternative solutions offered by another discipline. Neither discipline may recognize this simple (or complex) fact.

As a student, you have no doubt been subjected to repetition and overlap of subject matter in various courses you have taken. The obvious fact that there is overlap in the various disciplines, implicitly or explicitly, forcefully illustrates the points we have just discussed. It is clear that the education of the financial executive must be interdisciplinary and broad indeed. He must be concerned with the acquisition and control of the company funds. He must be concerned with the availability of reliable records and reports. In addition, the financial executive must coordinate and at times guide and direct the various disciplines represented on the management team toward a common goal. As indicated earlier, the larger the business entity the more likely it is that specialized experts will be available to contribute to or to confuse the recognition of and the solution of problems. In these organizations the financial manager must bridge the gaps. When we adopt the point of view that the financial manager has a responsibility, directly or indirectly, in all business decisions and, further, that all such decisions affect the efficient utilization of funds, the role of the financial executive becomes quite sophisticated.

Experts can and do make significant contributions in determining alternative courses of action. However, more often than not, the experts may be extremely knowledgeable in their given discipline, but they likewise may lack the insight and knowledge to deal with other problems related to the capabilities and/or limitations of the total business entity. For example, the expert may design an excellent production unit. The new unit may be nothing more than an engineering exercise if the cost implications have not been examined, and if the project is not financially feasible. As an example, a feasibility study may involve the use of the Internal Revenue Code carry-back and carry-forward provisions, accelerated depreciation, or capital gain opportunities. Our tax expert may have all these provisions at his fingertips, but not have the faintest idea about production problems. Alternative production methods may be available to take advantage of the tax provisions, or the tax provisions may indicate the alternatives.

This is not to say that our financial executive must be an expert in all these areas. However, the biggest problem is knowing what the problem is! Our financial executive must have the appreciation and insight, the trained instinct, if you will, to recognize the interdisciplinary problems. If he is, in fact, to be concerned with the effective use of funds, he must be able to diagnose, analyze, and define problems.

THE GOAL OF FINANCIAL MANAGEMENT

We have discussed the role of the financial manager and briefly described the scope of his activities. Obviously, the role he plays and the scope of his responsibilities are related to the achievement of some corporate goal. We have thus far alluded to this goal only as the effective and efficient use of funds entrusted to the business. Although it is difficult to be more specific, it is possible to be substantially more descriptive.

Let us assume momentarily that you are the owner-operator of a small charter airline. Your goal as an entrepreneur is, of course, to make your business as valuable as your resources and talents permit. What exactly is meant by valuable? What actions would you take with respect to this business in order to make it valuable? The first answer which comes to mind is probably related to the earnings of the airline. Let's look at these earnings and see how they are related to the value of the enterprise.

We will call call your annual gross earnings G, and from this figure we will make the required deductions in order to discover what the net earnings of your firm are.

What deductions will have to be made? At least annually you will have to overhaul your aircraft in order to keep it flying and generating the gross earnings figure mentioned above. We will call this deduction O. O, then, is your annual reinvestment required to maintain the gross income flow G.

In all likelihood, you will also have certain payments to make to people outside your own organization, for example, an interest payment to the bank which financed your purchase of the plane. These payments we will call P.

Finally, and of no surprise to any of us, you must pay taxes on your earnings. These tax payments can be termed T.

The net earnings or profits which will accrue to you are then G minus the deductions which we have described. By substituting some numbers in a simple equation, net earnings will be calculated to be $15,000 as follows:

$$G - (O + P + T) = E$$

or

Gross income − (annual reinvestment + payments + taxes) = net earnings

or

$28,000 − ($1,000 + $7,000 + $5,000) = $15,000 net earnings

We have now a figure which is your net earnings or profits. However, we still have not determined the value of your business, nor can we yet rate your ability as a financial manager with respect to maximizing the value of that business. You may disagree. You may say that the value of the firm is simply its earnings, and we have already calculated that figure. Let's see if you are correct. Suppose a gentleman appears in the hangar one day and tells you that he would like to purchase your firm and asks you to set a price. Would you simply set the price at a figure corresponding to *E*, or the $15,000 calculated above? No, you would rather ask for some multiple of this figure. In other words, you would set a price at 5 times ($75,000) or 10 times ($150,000) this single year's earnings. The result of this multiplication would, perhaps, yield the value of the business. A value thus determined would be a function of or the result of (1) the actual net earning and (2) the quality or sureness of those earnings as reflected in the multiple which the buyer is willing to accept. If the earnings were relatively certain, the buyer might be willing to pay 10 times the annual earnings. If the annual earnings were not so certain, he would more than likely offer less.

Let's test this last observation. Let us take two very different enterprises and illustrate this concept of quality. Consider two firms. One firm is a public utility company and the other is a manufacturer of ladies' swimsuits, and both firms have net earnings of $1 million in a given year. The earnings are equivalent in amount, but are they of equal quality and sureness? In other words, would a prospective buyer pay the same multiple for the earnings of each of these firms? Instinctively, we suspect not. The sales of electricity from one year to the next are highly predictable, as are the earnings derived from such sales. Sales of high-fashion swim wear, on the other hand, are dependent on any number of unpredictable factors. Will women accept our styles over those of a competitor? Will the retailers purchase and push our lines? Will the summer be a warm one in our sales area? We could go on and on, but the point is clear. The chances of the utility's earnings changing radically are much lower than the chances for a radical alteration in the sales and earnings pattern of the swim-wear manufacturer. Consequently, despite the fact that this year's earnings are equal in amount for both firms, the value of the firms will differ. The utility might sell for 10 times its earnings, while the swim-wear firm might sell at only 5 times its earnings. Thus, the former could be considered twice as valuable as the latter.

With this background, we can now restate the goal of financial management in terms of maximizing the value of the enterprise. This maximization will be reflected in the market value of the firm's stock.

The value of the firm as represented by its shares of stock, like the value of your airline, is usually described in terms of some multiple of the earnings stated on a per-share basis. For example, if a corporation earns $5 per share and if the multiplier is 10 at this particular time, then the price of the shares is $50 each. In market terminology, the share would be said to have a price-earnings ratio of 10 to 1. In short, a value of $10 is ascribed to every dollar of earnings. This is, of course, only a different way of describing the multiple of 10. For example,

$P =$ price of shares
$E =$ earnings
$M =$ multiple

$$\begin{aligned} P &= E(M) \\ &= 5(10) \\ &= \$50 \end{aligned}$$

A more usual way of saying the same thing uses a capitalization rate rather than a multiplier. They are related. The capitalization rate K is simply the reciprocal of the multiplier. That is, the earnings of $5 will equal 10 percent of the market price because the multiplier is 10. If the multiplier were 5 times the earnings, the capitalization rate would be 20 percent. Again, if the multiplier were 12 times, the capitalization rate would be 8.333 percent (100 percent ÷ 12 = 8.333 percent). We can then rewrite the above equation and show the relationship between price and earnings in the following manner:

$$P = \frac{E}{K}$$

where K is the reciprocal of the multiplier, or 0.10. Thus,

$$\begin{aligned} P &= \frac{5}{0.10} \\ &= 50 \end{aligned}$$

From the owner's or individual shareholder's viewpoint, the task of the financial manager is to maximize the price at which these shares trade. This is, for all intents and purposes, synonymous with maximizing the value of the business.

If the financial manager is to achieve the highest possible price for the shares of the firm, he must obviously be in a position which will enable him to influence both *earnings* and the *quality* of those earnings (the capitalization rate). Any decisions he makes which result in an increase in earnings will increase the value of the shares held by the owners; likewise, any action he takes which improves the quality of those earning will lower the capitalization rate (that is, increase the multiple) and so cause an increase in the price at which the shares of stock sell.

This last paragraph is quite significant. Earnings can be influenced by changes in cost, changes in selling price, and changes in volume sold. Therefore, any decision that will affect the cost, the selling price, or the volume sold will be of concern to the financial executive. The last paragraph is likewise significant because, obviously, the reported earnings of $5 per share were based on last year's operation. The assumption here is that the investor anticipates that the $5 per share earnings will continue indefinitely. He will then weigh the risk involved in this assumption and arrive at his capitalization rate. Therefore, as indicated, any change in earnings or the capitalization rate will change the market price. (If we are not careful, we will be trying to solve all the problems involved in Chapter 12. However, as you can see, the well-educated financial executive is a professional indeed.)

To sum up, then, the goal of the financial executive is to maximize the value of the outstanding shares of stock which represent the ownership interest in the firm. It can be readily seen that if he is to achieve this goal, the scope of his activities is extensive.

One final word of caution, however, is called for. We have established a goal for the financial executive, but we are still hard pressed to rate his success on the basis of this single criterion. That is to say, if the price of the shares of a particular firm is falling, can we be sure that the financial executive of the firm has failed to make proper decisions relating to the commitment of the funds entrusted to him by the owners? Such a judgment cannot be fairly made in some instances. In order to illustrate this point, we have only to consider the recent price performance of the stocks of leading conglomerate enterprises. In 1968, the stocks of conglomerates like Litton Industries and Ling-Temco-Vought sold at high earnings multiples. In less than a year, the value of these stocks fell. Conglomerate stocks dropped 53 percent as a group in 1969–1970 from their 1968 highs despite a generally rising earnings trend.[1] Was the financial executive at fault? He could have been if he were in complete control of all the variables which were causal to this precipitous price decline. However, in this case, many of the contributory factors were beyond his control. Some of these factors were:

1. A new and tougher government stand on conglomerate mergers and a heightened enforcement of existing antitrust laws
2. New accounting techniques relating to the calculations of the earnings per share (EPS), that is, techniques requiring that EPS be stated on a fully converted basis[2]
3. A general disenchantment on the part of buyers with those stocks
4. An overall decline in stock prices generally
5. General economic conditions

[1] See *Wall Street Transcript*, Sept. 1, 1969, p. 17,756.

[2] Opinion #15 of the Accounting Principles Board of the American Institute of Certified Public Accountants ruled that firms with convertible securities (that is, stocks, bonds, or other securities that can be converted into common stock at the owner's option) which were deemed to be common stock equivalents should include these residual shares in the calculation of earnings per share.

None of these factors could have been effectively controlled by the financial managers of the firms in question, but the interaction of these factors prevented these executives from reaching their goal of maximizing the value of the firm's common stock.

Up to this point we have been describing the role of the financial executive. Now, you are about to be one!

THE APPROACH TO FINANCIAL DECISION MAKING

As you assume the role of the financial executive in the chapters to follow, you will no doubt agree that the function of the financial executive cannot be simply categorized as one, two, three, . . . this, or one, two, three, . . . that. As we develop our subject, we cannot afford to assume anything, and we will not; that is, we will make no assumption about the beginning finance student's background. We will be dealing with the disciplines of economics, accounting, elementary statistics, business law, taxes, and other related fields in order to emphasize the total function and the total responsibility of the financial executive. Over the years, this assumption of "no assumptions" has proved again and again to be a wise one indeed.

This is not to say that the student did not learn the theoretical aspects of, for example, microeconomics in the first instance. Rather, it is to say that sometimes theory and application can be two quite different "cups of tea." In any event, it takes only a few pages to provide an adequate review, and then no assumptions are necessary.

As we move through our study, we will be interested in projecting an estimate of the resources needed to carry out operating plans. It will be necessary for us to determine what proportion of the required resources can be generated by the business itself, and what proportion we must obtain elsewhere. It will be necessary for us to determine the best sources and/or means of obtaining the outside funds. There will always be alternative courses of action. You as the financial manager must be prepared to recognize and evaluate these alternatives.

We will be deeply involved in planning. It is not a question of simply feeding definite, precise data and instructions into a computer in order to receive precise answers. We know that 2×2 is always equal to 4, 4×4 is always equal to 16. and on and on. However, in order to arrive at an answer of 4 via multiplication, our input must be precisely 2×2 or 4×1. As we plan for the future, we do not always have this precise information or input data. In fact, generally we do not. As we know, the future is clouded with uncertainty.

How, then, do we go about this planning process? Our first problem is to identify our goals. Even this identification may not be definite.

As an example, we may be planning for a given rate of return on investment, sometimes called a "target return on investment" (for example, 8 percent after taxes), perhaps a growth rate in terms of sales volume or earnings per share (for example, 15 percent annual growth in sales or a 10 percent increase in earnings per share). We may be interested in liquidity, or our ability to meet outside obligations. Liquidity in turn may affect our profitability, stability, and growth. It is quite clear that each of these goals may have a definite influence on the attainability of a second and equally desirable goal.

A second type of decision may involve the type of product or products we will manufacture or sell. Should we plan to develop vertically; that is, should we produce or manufacture the raw material for our product as well as strive to ultimately operate our own retail or wholesale outlets? Should we develop horizontally and operate more of the same type of plants or stores than we do at present? It is quite clear that in any event our problem will be the effective use of our funds to accomplish an unending list of possible goals.

No doubt, as you made the decision to study managerial finance, you had no reason to appreciate the fact that the responsibilities of the financial executive were so broad and all-encompassing. We must hasten to add that many times and in many firms, they are not! However, you can reasonably anticipate that a well-educated finance student can become involved relatively quickly and easily in a firm's decision-making process. You may start as someone's third assistant someplace. But in order to progress, you need do only two things.

First, you must understand the basic input with which you are working, which means you must be familiar with the sources of your information, who is giving it to you, what they are giving you, what they think they are giving you, and—more important—what they should be giving you! Secondly, you must understand the significance of what you have when you have it! Good decision making requires at least this much.

As we start your year's adventure as a financial executive, it would be helpful to review some elementary accounting. You should understand what a balance sheet and a profit and loss statement are and how they are prepared. However, even more important, perhaps, it would be well to recognize that just to look at an accounting statement can be a relatively meaningless exercise.

If someone were to hand you a balance sheet and a profit and loss statement for a firm, they could mean very little to us. This is not to say that they are incorrect, but that they might mean very little to you. There is a significant difference! As an example, one asset on the balance sheet could be entitled accounts receivable—$17,924.62. But that number really doesn't mean very much unless you are familiar with the judgment or lack of judgment that was used in arriving at it. The significant question is, Did the firm set up an adequate reserve to take care of bad debts as they arise? If the reserves are too high, the accounts receivable number, as reported, is too low. If the reserves are too low, the accounts receivable are overstated. We could make similar observations about the inventory figures and the valuation placed on the fixed assets. (There are several ways of valuing inventory: first in first out, last in first out, weighted average, moving average, and others. Depreciation can be reported on a straight-line basis or on an accelerated basis.) The various methods, when applied consistently, may be quite proper, as we shall see. However, each of the various methods will reflect quite different valuations as reported on the accounting statements.

Therefore, while it is not necessary for you to be proficient in the preparation of accounting statements, you must understand the significance of what you have when you have it! We must have some familiarity with the judgment factors involved. (Do not be alarmed; we will assume very little about the student's accounting background.)

In order to provide a common frame of reference, we must define some parameters and recall certain basic concepts and analytical tools. In our judgment, it is better and easier to do so now; it will make our subsequent analysis much smoother. We will be able to follow the analysis step by step without losing the continuity of these steps. We will define these parameters and review the basic concepts and analytical tools in Chapters 2 and 3. We will soon begin by assuming that your college days are over (there is an assumption!) and that you have been employed for the first time by Jones Electronic Corporation. Your employer asks your opinion on a rather important matter. The problem involves a decision as to whether or not Jones Electronic should accept an order from a new customer for 20,000 units (total present sales, 100,000 units) at a price of $5 per unit (present selling price is $6 per unit). The general production manager says the answer is *no!* You don't know! As you sit behind your desk, you may feel a bit inadequate to answer such an important question. You do not have experts available in economics, accounting, or statistics. You must solve the problem. However, you have learned a long time ago, or will soon learn, that what appears to be a big problem is really only a series of little problems.

We will make the necessary decisions together as we guide a small, single proprietorship step by step into a sophisticated giant of industry. We will continually examine alternative courses of action. We will not always be correct in our choice of alternatives, but we will examine carefully the rationale for our decision and, perhaps, will learn from our mistakes.

SUMMARY

This initial chapter introduces the basic financial functions which occur within all business firms:

1. The acquisition of funds
2. The custody and safekeeping of funds
3. The utilization of funds to finance ongoing business activity

Historically, these functions have been performed by two distinct corporate officers, the treasurer and the controller. The treasurer's responsibilities normally involve:

1. The procurement of funds from external sources
2. The custody of funds and the disbursement of corporate monies and securities
3. The investment of excess funds
4. The establishment of corporate credit and collection policies
5. The disposal of corporate property or assets

The controller, on the other hand, has a more internal orientation. His functions will usually include:

1. The establishment, coordination, and administration of both capital and operating budgets
2. The formulation of accounting policy and procedure
3. The filing of reports with federal regulatory agencies, including the Internal Revenue Service
4. The initiation of internal audits for the purpose of asset identification and control

In more recent years, these functions of the treasurer and controller have become coordinated under the supervision of the financial executive. This individual is the general financial officer of the firm. Consequently, it is he who directs the financial management functions and is responsible for the overall financial success or failure of the enterprise.

The financial executive stands astride both the treasurer's function and the comptroller's function like the "jolly green giant." All managerial decisions, sooner or later, in one way or another, are financial decisions. The financial executive, therefore, must have a broad interdisciplinary education if he is to be the coordinator, the leader, and if he is to bridge the gap between the various disciplines involved in the decision-making process.

It is often said implicitly and explicity that an executive can always hire the accountant, statistician, or economist as he is needed. This may or may not be true. However, assume for the moment that it is true. Many a man has been indeed sorry, if not unemployed, because an expert made a decision without the knowledge of the broader implications of that decision on other aspects and/or facets of the total business entity; and the executive has to pick up the check.

The financial executive's first and foremost obligation is to maximize the value of the firm's equity. This function may include the minimizing of unavoidable losses. Value is a function of earnings and the quality of those earnings. Quality of earnings is a function of predictability—the future. It is quite clear that a financial executive must be well educated. He must be knowledgeable.

REFERENCES

Curtis, Edward T.: "Company Organization of the Finance Function," AMA Research Study LV, American Management Association, New York, 1962.

Marris, Robin: A Model of the "Managerial" Enterprise, *Quarterly Journal of Economics,* vol. LXXVII, pp. 185–209, May, 1963.

Marting, Elizabeth, and Robert E. Finley (eds.): "The Financial Manager's Job," American Management Association, New York, 1964.

Moag, Joseph S., Willard T. Carleton, and Eugene M. Lerner: Defining the Finance Function: A Model-systems Approach, *Journal of Finance,* vol. XXII, pp. 543–556, December, 1967.

Moore, John R.: The Financial Executive in the 1970's, *Financial Executive,* vol. XXXV, pp. 28–29, 32–34, 36, January, 1967.

Solomon, Ezra: What Should We Teach in a Course in Business Finance? *Journal of Finance,* vol. XXI, pp. 411–415, May, 1966.

Vance, Jack O.: The Changing Role of the Corporate Financial Executive, *Financial Executive,* vol. XXXI, no. 3, pp. 27–29, March, 1963.

Weston, J. Fred: The Finance Function, *Journal of Finance,* vol. IX, pp. 265–282, September, 1954.

Weston, J. Fred (ed.): The New Power of the Financial Executives, "Financial Management in the 1960's: New Challenges and Responsibilities," pp. 2–8, Holt, Rinehart and Winston, Inc., New York, 1966.

Weston, J. Fred: "The Scope and Methodology of Finance," Prentice-Hall, Inc., Englewood Cliffs, N.J., 1966.

———: The State of the Finance Field, *Journal of Finance,* vol. XXII, no. 4, pp. 539–540, December, 1967.

Chapter Two

THE LEGAL AND TAX FRAMEWORK

You reported to your first job at a fortuitous time! The very first morning Mr. Jones invited you to accompany him to a meeting with the firm's attorney and accountant. The reason for the meeting was to discuss the implications of changing the form of the Jones business organization from a single proprietorship to a corporation. Mr. Jones is an electrical engineer. The Jones organization had its beginning in an oversized garage, and Jones operated the business on a part-time basis. Within six months, Jones resigned his former position and began designing electrical components for experimental aircraft and space hardware. As developments in his work passed the experimental stage, Jones sold his home to raise cash and borrowed more to finance the equipment needed to manufacture the components he had designed. His success, on a small scale, was almost immediate. He now has some 80 employees at work in leased premises.

LEGAL IMPLICATIONS OF THE INDIVIDUAL PROPRIETOR

As a sole owner (single proprietorship) it was relatively easy to get into business from a legal point of view. He simply (1) applied for the Federal Employer Social Security and Federal and State Unemployment

Insurance Identification numbers and (2) paid the appropriate state and local business license fees. A single proprietorship, like any other form of business organization, is obligated to withhold social security and income tax amounts from employees and to make the proper employer contributions. Having complied with these requirements and having achieved some degree of financial success (net profit $60,000 last year on $600,000 gross sales), Jones was concerned about other matters such as the following:

1. He has unlimited personal liability as a single proprietor for all business obligations and legal actions. Most of the latter matters can be covered by adequate insurance protection, but not so the personal liability for business obligations.
2. He further realized that the business would most likely terminate upon his death or retirement. His family does not have the capacity to continue the business without outside assistance. At best, it could be difficult to transfer to outsiders a part of the business and to get anything near fair value for it.
3. His ability to attract debt capital was likewise limited by the form of organization he had selected. It had been suggested by several bankers that the business be incorporated to make it easier to attract debt capital. He felt that these factors restrict the size of the enterprise and tend to retard its growth.

Mr. Jones then expressed concern about the tax status of the corporate form of organization versus the sole proprietorship form, which he was currently using. It was obvious that not all his points were well taken, but there was considerable merit in what he was saying. You were taking notes, which can be summarized as follows:

He was concerned about the income tax implications of the sole proprietorship. He understood that the personal income tax rates are higher at his present level of income ($60,000 annually) than they would be if the business were incorporated. He stressed his lack of flexibility in leveling income and accumulating capital. The individual does not always have the opportunities of the corporation, to spread the same income among various taxable entities. Profits of a corporation can be spread among the shareholders in the form of salary, rent, interest, deferred profit-sharing plans, and pension arrangements if the shareholders are in fact officers or employees of the corporation.

Because of the graduated individual income tax rates, it is difficult for the individual proprietor to accumulate capital. The maximum corporate marginal tax rate has been rather steady at a few percentage points above or below the 50 percent level. As we will see, the maximum individual income tax rates clearly exceed this percentage by a significant margin except on an individual's "earned taxable income," for example, compensation for personal services.[1]

He was quite disturbed this past year because he had to pay income tax on approximately $50,000 (after $10,000 deductions for personal interest expense and other personal deductions) when, in fact, he withdrew only $12,000 during the year. He commented that the tax payment was more than the $12,000 he withdrew from his business for personal use!

While he did file a joint return with Mrs. Jones, thus getting a reduction in his tax bill, he was disturbed because he could not transfer additional income to his children. He reasoned that if he were to give his four boys shares of stock, the income would be taxable to them at a lower marginal tax rate.

Jones receives very little in the way of fringe benefits that normally are granted to corporate employees. He has no pension plan, medical coverage, or group insurance that can be considered as an expense of his business. One of the major disadvantages of the single proprietorship is that the owner is not considered an employee.

Under the corporate form, the stockholder-executive may obtain the tax benefits of pension and profit-sharing plans. These plans give the employee considerable tax advantage in excess of these same plans when they are set up by self-employed individuals. Under a qualified plan, corporate employers can currently deduct the contributions made to such a plan on behalf of their employees and claim the same as a tax deduction. The employees receiving the benefits under the plan are not taxed on this income until they or their beneficiaries actually receive the income. In many cases, this will be some time in the future when the retired employee or the beneficiary is in a much lower marginal tax bracket.

Further, normally the premiums paid by a corporation on group term life insurance of its employee are considered as income to him. This is so because, in effect, the corporation is paying the personal expenses of the employee if the employee designates the beneficiary of the policy. However, special provisions of the Internal Revenue Code provide that these premiums, when paid by the corporation, up to $50,000 coverage are not taxable to the employee. A stockholder-executive can be included in the group insurance plan.

Jones was also concerned about the difficulty that he has as a sole proprietor in transferring the ownership of his business to his family in order to minimize estate taxes. He has been told by his attorney and accountant that the corporate form of operation is generally preferable to the single proprietorship for estate planning purposes. During

[1] For the calendar year 1971, the maximum marginal tax rate (that is, the highest tax bracket) may not exceed 60 percent on an individual's earned taxable income. For the calendar year 1972 and thereafter, the marginal rate may not exceed 50 percent.

the lifetime of the owner, the ownership of the business can be transferred to members of his family through gift or sale of stock in the corporation. The size of the estate tax will thus be reduced. (Income taxes during his lifetime will likewise normally be reduced.) There may or may not be a gift tax involved as the transfer is made. However, there will usually remain an overall tax saving because the gift tax rates are significantly lower than the estate tax rates.

On the other hand, the ownership of a proprietorship cannot be

TABLE 2-1: MARGINAL AND AVERAGE TAX RATES OF THE INDIVIDUAL INCOME TAX
1970 Rates
(Married Persons Filing Separate Returns)

	TAX CALCULATION				
Taxable Income	Base Amount	+ Marginal Tax Rate	=	Tax*	Average Tax Rate (Individual)
$0–$500	$0	14%		$70	14.0%
500–1,000	70	15		145	14.5
1,000–1,500	145	16		225	15.0
1,500–2,000	225	17		310	15.5
2,000–4,000	310	19		690	17.3
4,000–6,000	690	22		1,130	18.8
6,000–8,000	1,130	25		1,630	20.4
8,000–10,000	1,630	28		2,190	21.8
10,000–12,000	2,190	32		2,830	23.5
12,000–14,000	2,830	36		3,550	25.3
14,000–16,000	3,550	39		4,330	27.0
16,000–18,000	4,330	42		5,170	28.7
18,000–20,000	5,170	45		6,070	30.3
20,000–22,000	6,070	48		7,030	31.9
22,000–26,000	7,030	50		9,030	34.7
26,000–32,000	9,030	53		12,210	38.1
32,000–38,000	12,210	55		15,510	40.8
38,000–44,000	15,510	58		18,990	43.1
44,000–50,000	18,990	60		22,590	45.2
50,000–60,000	22,590	62		28,790	48.0
60,000–70,000	28,790	64		35,190	50.3
70,000–80,000	35,190	66		41,790	52.2
80,000–90,000	41,790	68		48,590	54.0
90,000–100,000	48,590	69		55,490	55.5
100,000–150,000	55,490	70		90,490	60.3
150,000–200,000	90,490	70		125,490	62.7
200,000–500,000	125,490	70		335,490	67.1
500,000–1,000,000	335,490	70		685,490	68.5
1,000,000–5,000,000	685,490	70		3,485,490	69.7
5,000,000–100,000,000	3,485,490	70		69,985,490	70.0

* Based on upper limit of each class interval.

TABLE 2-2: MARGINAL AND AVERAGE TAX RATES OF THE PERSONAL INCOME TAX
1970 Rates
(Joint Returns)

	TAX CALCULATION			Average
Taxable Income	Base Amount +	Marginal Tax Rate =	Tax*	Tax Rate (Individual)
$0–$1,000	$0	14%	$140	14.0%
1,000–2,000	140	15	290	14.5
2,000–3,000	290	16	450	15.0
3,000–4,000	450	17	620	15.5
4,000–8,000	620	19	1,380	17.4
8,000–12,000	1,380	22	2,260	18.8
12,000–16,000	2,260	25	3,260	20.4
16,000–20,000	3,260	28	4,380	21.9
20,000–24,000	4,380	32	5,660	23.6
24,000–28,000	5,660	36	7,100	25.4
28,000–32,000	7,100	39	8,660	27.1
32,000–36,000	8,660	42	10,340	28.7
36,000–40,000	10,340	45	12,140	30.4
40,000–44,000	12,140	48	14,060	32.0
44,000–52,000	14,060	50	18,050	34.7
52,000–64,000	18,060	53	24,420	38.2
64,000–76,000	24,420	55	31,020	40.8
76,000–88,000	31,020	58	37,980	43.2
88,000–100,000	37,980	60	45,180	45.2
100,000–120,000	45,180	62	57,580	48.0
120,000–140,000	57,580	64	70,380	50.3
140,000–160,000	70,380	66	83,580	52.2
160,000–180,000	83,580	68	97,180	54.0
180,000–200,000	97,180	69	110,980	55.5
200,000–300,000	110,980	70	189,980	60.3
300,000–400,000	180,980	70	250,980	62.7
400,000–1,000,000	250,980	70	670,980	67.1
1,000,000–10,000,000	670,980	70	6,970,980	69.7
10,000,000–100,000,000	6,970,980	70	69,920,980	70.0

* Based on upper limit of each class interval.

transferred during the lifetime of the owner without creating a partnership or a leaseback situation. Both of these arrangements may be undesirable.

Individual Income Tax Considerations

The meeting with the attorney and accountant took place the following morning. They began the discussion by indicating that an individual, as the sole owner of an enterprise, does not file a tax return for the business, per se. Rather, business profits and losses are added to or subtracted from the owner's other taxable income and losses reportable on an individual tax return (Form 1040) which he is required to file. Form 1040 has as a part of the total return a separate schedule (Schedule C) that is used to summarize the business operation. Married taxpayers have the option of filing individual or joint returns with their spouses. This option is available even though the spouse did not have taxable income to report. As you examine the tax rates, it will be observed that there is an advantage to filing a joint return. However, when a joint return is filed, both the husband and wife are personally liable for any errors, omissions, or fraud involved in the preparation of the tax return.

Included in Table 2-1 and 2-2 are representative individual income tax rates (exclusive of the income tax surcharge of 2.5 percent for 1970) for married taxpayers filing separate returns and married couples filing joint returns.

The rate schedule for unmarried individuals (other than surviving spouses and heads of households) for 1970 is the same as for married persons filing separate returns. For 1971 and thereafter the rate schedule for unmarried individuals (other than surviving spouses and heads of households) follows:

If the Taxable Income Is:		**The Tax Is:**	
Not over $500		14% of the taxable income	
Over:	**But Not Over:**		**Of Excess Over:**
$500	$1,000	$70 + 15%	$500
1,000	1,500	145 + 16	1,000
1,500	2,000	225 + 17	1,500
2,000	4,000	310 + 19	2,000
4,000	6,000	690 + 21	4,000
6,000	8,000	1,110 + 24	6,000
8,000	10,000	1,590 + 25	8,000
10,000	12,000	2,090 + 27	10,000
12,000	14,000	2,630 + 29	12,000
14,000	16,000	3,210 + 31	14,000
16,000	18,000	3,830 + 34	16,000
18,000	20,000	4,510 + 36	18,000
20,000	22,000	5,230 + 38	20,000
22,000	26,000	5,990 + 40	22,000
28,000	32,000	7,590 + 45	26,000
26,000	38,000	10,290 + 50	32,000
43,000	44,000	13,290 + 55	38,000
43,000	50,000	16,590 + 60	44,000
50,000	60,000	20,190 + 62	50,000
60,000	70,000	26,390 + 64	60,000
70,000	80,000	32,790 + 66	70,000
80,000	90,000	39,390 + 68	80,000
90,000	100,000	46,190 + 69	90,000
100,000		53,090 + 70	100,000

It should be noted that for unmarried individuals who qualify as heads of households there is a separate rate schedule. The rates are halfway between the rates for single persons and the rates for married couples filing joint returns.

As you examine the tax tables, it is significant to note that they provide the tax rates based on *taxable income. Taxable income* consists of adjusted gross income less (1) itemized non-business deductions (or the standard deduction) and (2) personal and dependency exemptions. Adjusted gross income is defined by the Internal Revenue Code as gross income minus certain deductible "business" expenses. Detailed definitions are as follows:

The total income received from the sources listed below represents the taxpayer's gross income:

Business
Wages and salaries earned
Annuities and pensions
Reimbursed expenses
Dividends received
Commissions, bonuses, tips
Rents and royalties
Prizes
Alimony
Gains from sales of property
Farm income
Any other remuneration in property or money

The deductions that can be subtracted from the gross income in arriving at adjusted gross income include the following:

Business expenses
Travel expenses
Employees' reimbursed expenses
Outside salesmen's expenses
Depreciation
Expenses attributed to rent and royalty income
Loss from sales or exchanges
Net operating loss
Farm expenses
Long-term capital gains deductions
Self-employment retirement plan payments
Moving expenses

At this point, the individual taxpayer (for 1970) has the choice of taking a standard deduction for non-business expense of 10 percent of adjusted gross income, with a maximum of $1,000 for taxpayers filing a joint return ($500 for each married spouse filing separate returns), or itemizing the allowable deductions.

The standard deduction climbs from 10 percent of adjusted gross income to 15 percent over a three-year period as follows:

Taxable Year Beginning in	**Applicable Percentage**	**Maximum Amount**
1971	13	$1,500
1972	14	2,000
1973 and thereafter	15	2,000

If he elects to itemize expenditures, some of the more important expenses allowed as deductions from the adjusted gross income are:

Charitable contributions (subject to limitations)
Real estate, state income taxes
Interest paid
Casualty losses
Alimony
Medical expenses
Child care expenses
Union dues

After the standard or itemized deductions are subtracted from adjusted gross income to arrive at net income, an individual taxpayer is permitted a deduction for personal and dependency exemptions. These exemptions for the calendar year 1970 are $625 each for the taxpayer, the spouse, and each dependent. A special provision allows an additional exemption for a blind taxpayer or a blind spouse or both. An additional exemption is likewise permitted if the taxpayer and/or a spouse reaches the age of 65 before the end of the taxable year. The personal exemption (for taxpayer and spouse) and the dependency exemption increase to $750 as follows:

Taxable Year Beginning in	Amount Allowed for Each Exemption
1971	$650
1972	700
1973 and thereafter	750

When the personal exemptions have been subtracted from net income, the resulting figure is taxable income.

There can be, and generally is, a substantial difference between gross income and taxable income. Therefore, and most significantly, a general statement cannot be made as to how much income tax must be paid on the profits earned by a businessman operating his business as a sole proprietorship. This is so because business profits may constitute only a part of total gross income. The businessman may have additional income and/or losses from other sources which will be included in total gross income, as well as the personal deductions and exemptions that must be deducted to determine taxable income.

Significance of Marginal and Average Tax Rates

In addition, the accountant and the attorney stressed the significance of distinguishing between the average tax rate and the marginal tax rate.

The marginal tax rate is the tax rate on "one more dollar." The average tax rate is the total tax payable divided by the total taxable income. The attorney illustrated by examining in detail a $10,000 taxable income for a married couple filing separate returns. He noted that the initial tax rate is 14 percent for the married taxpayer filing a separate return on all taxable income from 0 to $500. Thus, the average and the marginal tax rate are 14 percent on the first $500, or any part thereof. He pointed out that when income exceeds this initial bracket, the marginal rate increases faster than the average tax rate. This is so because, regardless of the total taxable income, the first $500 is always taxed at 14 percent, the next $500 is taxed at the marginal rate of 15 percent, the next $500 at the marginal rate of 16 percent, and so on up the ladder until the marginal rate on the last step is reached. The marginal and average tax rates on a taxable income of $10,000 would be calculated as follows without the benefit of Table 2-1, which summarizes the tax liability on taxable income between $8,000 and $10,000.

	Taxable Income	Marginal Tax Rate	Marginal Amount	Total Tax	Average Tax Rate
First	$ 500	14%	$ 70	$ 70	14.0%
Next	500	15	75	145	14.5
Next	500	16	80	225	15.0
Next	500	17	85	310	15.5
Next	2,000	19	380	690	17.3
Next	2,000	22	440	1,130	18.8
Next	2,000	25	500	1,630	20.4
Next	2,000	28	560	2,190	21.8
Totals	$10,000			$2,190	21.8%

The attorney reemphasized the significance of the marginal tax rate, asking you to assume you now have a taxable income of $10,000 and have an opportunity to earn $2,000 additional income. What would be your additional income after income tax? In essence, what is the marginal tax or the tax to be paid on the additional $2,000 income? Consulting the tax table for married persons filing separate returns (Table 2-1), you will find that the marginal tax rate on taxable income between $10,000 and $12,000 is 32 percent. When you multiply 32 percent times the $2,000, you find that the marginal tax is $640. After-tax income would be $1,360 on the additional income of $2,000. The average tax rate on the total income of $12,000 would be 23.5, an overall average tax increase of 1.7 percent. It was the increase in the marginal rate from 28 to 32 percent that caused the overall average tax increase of

1.7 percent! Clearly, for decision-making purposes, the marginal tax rate is the more significant. We will greatly expand this point later in our study.

When you examine the tax table for married taxpayers filing joint returns (Table 2-2), you will note that the various tax brackets are doubled in amount while the marginal tax increments remain the same as those in Table 2-1. This is an obvious advantage for married couples who elect to file a joint return. You continue with your notes as the attorney discusses the partnership form of business entity.

LEGAL AND TAX IMPLICATIONS OF A PARTNERSHIP

While the single proprietorship is the most common form of business organization, many businesses have two or more owners. This type of business entity is commonly known as a partnership. A partnership, then, is a legal relationship created by the voluntary association of two or more persons (individuals, corporations, trusts) as co-owners to carry on a business for profit. If profit is not the objective, the group will commonly be called an unincorporated association. Our interest here is the voluntary association for profit.

The essence of a partnership is simply that the partners agree to the ground rules for conducting a business owned by more than one person. The law is concerned with the intent of the parties. Generally, the agreement may be written or unwritten. However, to avoid later controversies concerning the original intent of the parties and to satisfy other legal requirements, a written agreement is desirable. The significant point to recognize, however, is that partnership agreements, although in written form, very often do not spell out all the intentions of the parties. However, the intentions of the parties are the significant factor in interpreting partnership agreements. When these intentions are not expressly spelled out, there is room for conflicting interpretations. Therefore, great care should be exercised in the preparation of a partnership agreement.

Partners may be classified as follows:

1. A *general partner* is one who actively and publicly engages in the firm's activities.
2. A *nominal partner* shares in neither the management nor the profits, but publicly represents himself or permits others to represent him as a partner. The legal significance is that he may be held liable for the activities of the partnership just as though he were, in fact, a partner.
3. A *silent partner* is one who takes no active part in the management of the business, but may be publicly known as a partner.

4. A *secret partner* is one who takes an active part in partnership management but is not publicly known as a partner.
5. A *dormant partner* is one who neither takes an active part in the business nor is known to the public. His contribution is normally associated with the initial financing of the business venture.

Authority, Duties, Rights, and Remedies of Partners

Unless a written or unwritten agreement requires the contrary, decisions on business matters are made by majority vote. No action can be taken if an even number of partners are deadlocked. The written agreement or a majority of the partners may expressly state that a partner has authority to do certain acts. In addition, a partner has authority to perform those acts which are customary for a member of a particular type of association. The scope of these "customary" powers not only will vary with the nature of the partnership but also will include the "customary" acts of partners engaged in similar businesses.

The partners may agree expressly to limit the "customary" power of each or all partners to act for the partnership. However, innocent third parties are not bound by this limitation unless public notice of the limiting agreement has been given. An innocent third party may lose this protection if he blindly assumes that the limited partner has the authority he purports to have. The third party must exercise reasonable care. However, should any partner cause damage to the partnership by exceeding his authority, he may be held liable by the other partner or partners.

On the other hand, there are certain transactions which must be entered into by the partnership as a unit. Below are some examples:

1. A partner cannot agree to accept liability for the firm. All partners have the right to defend themselves.
2. A partner cannot bind the firm to the terms of a contract that would make it impossible for the firm to continue its normal business.
3. A partner cannot trade his personal obligations in return for the discharge of claims the firm may have.

Each partner owes to the other members of the firm his loyalty and good faith. He must carry out his obligations and duties to the firm in a manner consistent with the partnership agreement or majority vote. He must exercise reasonable care in all firm transactions and has a duty to truthfully and fully inform all partners concerning partnership matters.

Unless the partners agree to the contrary, all partners have equal rights to participate in partnership profits. The partners, on the other hand, may agree to distribute the profits and other compensation in any lawful manner and in unequal proportions.

Each partner is liable for all debts and obligations of the partnership, but is entitled to recover from his copartners their proportionate share. Some states have statutes limiting the liability of each partner to his proportionate share.

Dissolution and Termination of Partnerships

A partnership is dissolved by the voluntary agreement of the parties, the withdrawal of a partner, or the expulsion of a partner. A partnership is automatically dissolved by the operation of law upon the death of one of the parties or bankruptcy of the firm, or when any event occurs which makes it illegal for the business of the partnership to be conducted.

A partner may obtain a court decree of dissolution upon the insanity, incapacity, or misconduct of another partner. When a partnership is dissolved for any reason, the partnership with all the rights, duties, and obligations of the individual partners continues until the process of winding up partnership business has been completed. As an example, upon the death, insanity, or incapacity of a partner, his partnership rights and obligations pass on to his estate until all partnership business in process has been completed and the partnership affairs have been concluded.

If a partnership is to be terminated or has been terminated, notice must be given explicitly to the remaining partners and to interested third parties. This includes, of course, persons or firms that have had business transactions with the partnership. An advertisement in a generally read local newspaper is sufficient notice to all others.

When a partnership is dissolved for any reason, creditors have first claim on the partnership assets. Each partner is entitled to receive next any loans or advances he has made to the partnership. Then each partner is entitled to his share of the profits and must assume responsibility for his share of the losses, if any. If a partner cannot contribute to the firm any amount he owes as his share of partnership losses, the other partners will share this additional loss according to their profit-sharing ratio.

Other Types of Partnerships or Associations

The attorney briefly touched on certain other types of partnership arrangements, such as the following:

A *limited partnership* can be created in most states by statutory authorization only. Certain members known as *limited partners* can limit their liability for the firm's debts to the amount of capital they have contributed without assuming any additional personal liability. A duly executed agreement must be filed for public notice in the proper state office designated to receive and record such papers. To establish this type of partnership, the provision of the particular state statute must be followed with care.

A *joint venture* is the combination of two or more persons, including corporations, to undertake a single business project or objective. When this project or objective is completed, the association may be terminated.

A *syndicate* is generally an association of individuals, including corporations, formed to conduct a particular business transaction. This usually involves a transaction of a financial nature. A syndicate may or may not be incorporated. If a corporation is formed, the partnership characteristics cease. If it is not incorporated, it is for the most part treated as a normal general partnership.

What is known as a *Massachusetts trust, common-law trust*, or a *business trust* is created when property is transferred to trustees for management purposes for the benefit of the original owners. Trust certificates are issued to the former owners of the property in return for the legal title. Profits are distributed to the holders of the trust certificates. Generally, this type of business organization must be treated as a corporation for tax purposes. Most states do not hold the owners of the trust certificates liable for trust business transactions if they have no control over the actions of the trustees.

A *joint stock company* resembles a combination of a partnership, a corporation, and a business trust. Its shares may be transferred without dissolving the company, and the new owner of the shares becomes a partner without the consent of the other shareholders or partners. Normally, the number of shareholders is considerably larger than that of an ordinary partnership. Therefore, active management is usually delegated to a management group.

Mr. Jones clearly indicated that he was not interested in any type of partnership in the foreseeable future. His interest noticeably quickened when his attorney began to discuss the corporate form of organization.

LEGAL IMPLICATIONS OF A CORPORATION

A corporation is a legal person created by a sovereign power which in most cases is a state government. It is legally recognized and empowered to perform those acts and to conduct such affairs as outlined in its corporate charter. The federal government is not expressly granted power to create corporations, but may do so to carry out powers granted by it. An example is the Federal Deposit Insurance Corporation.

All assets and liabilities of the corporation are the property and responsibility of the corporation rather than the property and responsibility of the owners of the corporation. Therefore, an investor (a shareholder) in a corporation cannot be held personally liable for the corporate debts, nor can he claim ownership in the corporate property.

Many, but not all, state governments follow the Model Business Corporation Act promulgated by the American Bar Association. In general, the various states grant corporate charters when the following requirements or conditions are met:

1. Three or more persons of full age file an application for a corporate charter. Some states require that the applicants be shareholders in the proposed organization. Other states do not have this requirement.
2. The application must set forth the proposed name, object, and capital stock structure. The capital stock structure must include the number and value of the shares into which the proposed corporation is to be divided, the class and type of stock, and the relative rights of each class. A *minimum* of \$1,000 in money or services or a combination of both must be received by the corporation before it can commence business. (However, \$1,000 is only a minimum. The charter as proposed by the original incorporators may require a significantly larger amount.)
3. The place of business or principal office of the corporation must be set forth.
4. Most states permit a perpetual life for the entity, but others limit this life to a stated number of years.
5. The names and addresses of the responsible officers for at least the first year may be required.
6. Names and addresses of the incorporators must be given. Individual commitments to subscribe to the stock may also be required.

Upon approval by the proper state authority, a charter authorizing the corporation to do those things enumerated in the application is generally granted. The granting of a corporate charter is automatic in most instances unless a new corporation has adopted a name already in use by another corporation that has been granted a charter by the same state. In the event that not all legal requirements are met and the proposed corporation proceeds to conduct the affairs of the business, the incorporators may be held personally liable as partners.

If the charter indicates a stated period of existence, the corporation automatically ceases to exist upon the expiration of this period. The corporation may also dissolve itself by surrendering its charter after satisfying all its outstanding obligations and responsibilities. The governmental unit may forfeit the charter for good cause. Should a corporation reorganize under federal bankruptcy laws, the corporation does not terminate but merely exchanges old obligations for new ones as determined by the court in the reorganization process.

When two or more corporations consolidate, the old corporations cease to exist and the new entity succeeds to the rights and duties of the original consolidating entities. A merger of two or more corporations results in the loss of identity and existence of the corporations absorbed. The remaining entity continues and preserves its original charter. (This item may be of considerable interest to Jones. He has had some overtures concerning merger possibilities.)

Corporations are owned by shareholders in proportion to the number of shares owned. Fifty-one percent of the outstanding stock constitutes a majority. Shareholders elect a board of directors, which in turn appoints the managing officers. Directors and officers may or may not be shareholders. The shareholders themselves have inherent powers to make bylaws that set forth the ground rules which provide a framework for the operation of corporate affairs.

Corporations have the implied power to borrow the money necessary to conduct normal business affairs unless expressly forbidden to do so by restriction in the charter, bylaws, or state law.

This power includes the right to issue or endorse debt and various types of bonds. Still subject to possible state law and/or charter or bylaw restrictions, the corporation can lease, buy, or sell both personal and real property as is reasonably necessary to carry out corporate functions. Modern state corporation codes generally permit one corporation to acquire the stock of other corporations. Should a corporation own controlling interest in one or more corporations, it is known as a parent or holding company. The corporations so controlled are known as subsidiary or operating companies.

Generally, a solvent company is permitted to hold and purchase shares of its own stock. Reacquired stock that is not retired is known as treasury stock. It has the characteristics of outstanding stock on an inactive basis and neither votes nor receives dividends.

Subject to state restrictions and requirements, a corporation has the inherent right to engage in business in other states. An act that goes beyond the corporate powers is known as an ultra vires act. In all states a stockholder may bring a legal action for damages for the loss caused by such unauthorized acts against the person or persons who made or approved the act. A stockholder may obtain an injunction (a court order) to stop the ultra vires act, or the state itself may bring a legal action to revoke the corporate charter for serious or repeated violations of this nature.

Types of Corporate Stock

Various types of stock may be issued by a corporation subject to any limitations and/or authorization contained in the corporate charter. The usual types of stock issued may be described as follows:[1]

1. *Common stock.* Several types of common stock are used in financing modern corporations. As an example, common stock may be designated voting and nonvoting. Normally, each share of the voting common stock carries with it the right to one vote at stockholders' meetings. All common stock has a right to share in profit distribution, known as dividends, when and if the board of directors declares such a distribution, and to participate in the distribution of capital upon liquidation of the company.
2. *Preferred stock.* Preferred stock, likewise, may be of several classes and have a priority of rights as designated for each class. Preferred stock has priority over common stock with respect to dividend distribution. Generally, ordinary preferred stock will indicate a percentage return (such as 6 percent) which represents both the minimum and the maximum the preferred stockholder will receive on the par value of such stock as a dividend on his share. It has been held by court decision that without the express provision that preferred stock is noncumulative, this type of stock will be cumulative, with characteristics and rights as indicated below. Other courts have ruled that to be cumulative the preferred stock certificate must so state.
3. *Cumulative preferred stock.* This type of stock carries the right to accumulate annual dividends whether or not the board of directors declares them and to receive all back and current dividends before the common stock receives anything. A definite percentage return on par value is usually stipulated, just as it is for ordinary preferred stock.
4. *Participating preferred stock.* This type of stock gives the preferred stockholder the right to receive an additional share of the profit after the common stockholder has received an amount agreed upon. The amount of the additional profit participation will be set forth by the provisions of the participating preferred stock certificate.

Par value and no-par value stock. Stock is sometimes issued by the corporation at a price specified as the par value on the face of the stock certificate. Subscribers and purchasers must pay at least the par value per share into the corporation in return for the stock in money or services.

[1] This discussion will be extended in a later and more appropriate section of this text.

Failure to do so creates liabilities—and risk for the purchasers. For example, under certain circumstances one who pays $90 for a share of stock, issued by the corporation, that carries a par value of $100 may be liable to creditors for the additional $10.

In order to avoid such contingencies, some corporations issue low-par or no-par shares. No-par value stock may be purchased from the corporation at a price per share determined by the board of directors. Generally, no-par stock avoids the possibility of additional liability referred to above in connection with par value stock.

In addition to discussing these forms of stock, the attorney also explained some of the terminology associated with capital stock. He first mentioned legal capital. The *capital* of the corporation refers to the value of the assets after all liabilities have been subtracted. It signifies subscribed and paid-in capital plus or minus all gains, profits, or losses.

> *Capital stock* refers to the number and the value of the various shares of stock outstanding.
>
> *Market value* is the price at which the stock can be voluntarily bought and sold on the open market.
>
> *Book value* is the value found by dividing the net assets (assets minus liabilities) by the number of shares outstanding.

In the absence of restrictions contained in state statutes, the corporate charter, bylaws, or other agreement, a shareholder may transfer his or its shares to anyone. A common restriction in smaller, closely held corporations would provide that existing shareholders or the corporation itself must be given first option to purchase the shares before they can be transferred to another. This option is known as the preemptive right. Restrictions must be reasonable, as defined by the circumstances and surrounding facts.

Transfer of Ownership through the Sale of Shares

A transfer of a share of stock is effected upon delivery of the share properly endorsed as one would ordinarily endorse a check. However, as far as the corporation is concerned, the transfer is not effective until proper transfer has been made on corporate records.

To effect a transfer, it is generally necessary to present or cause to be presented the properly endorsed certificate to the corporation or its duly authorized transfer agent. It is generally assumed that the new stock certificate will be issued to the purchaser within a five-day period.

Regulation of the Issuance of Corporate Shares

Just as the formation of corporations is regulated by the 50 states, so too is the sale of the securities we have just discussed. These regulations are set down on both the state and the federal level. At the federal level several agencies are involved in such regulation.

"Blue-sky laws" have been enacted by many states to protect the investor from the sale of worthless securities or securities from nonexistent corporations. State statutes vary in the methods used to provide this public protection. Some states require governmental commission approval, others require the licensing of security dealers, and still others attach criminal and/or civil liability to such sales. State laws apply only to intrastate transactions.

The federal government adopted the Federal Securities Act in 1933 to provide protection to investors involved in interstate security transactions. All securities or a prospectus for securities sent through the mails or interstate commerce must be registered with the Securities and Exchange Commission. This registration requires full disclosure of information pertaining to the stock issue and is available to private investors. This registration does not constitute an implicit or explicit approval or guarantee by the Securities and Exchange Commission of any representation contained in the prospectus. The act does not apply when the total stock to be issued is less than $300,000. Such issues are not registered but are regulated under the provisions of Regulation A of the 1933 act.

Other safeguards to limit market manipulation are set forth by the Federal Securities Exchange Act of 1934. This act declares it to be unlawful for any dealer, broker, or exchange to make use of, directly or indirectly, the mails or other means of communication to effect any transaction in a security that is not registered with the SEC unless that security is exempt from registration.

Trading activities and the manipulation of the securities markets are also regulated by the SEC. (As an example, certain manipulation devices are used in an attempt to create the impression of great trading activity, such as the buying and selling of a stock simultaneously or the manipulation of buying and selling orders.) Likewise, the circulation of false rumors and tips is made unlawful and is prohibited.

Proxy solicitations, or the request of one or more individuals for the right to vote for the stockholder at stockholders' meetings, are also regulated. The name of the solicitor and the action to be voted upon must be set forth in the request. Regulations have been promulgated that prohibit corporate officers and other "insiders" from gaining a profit as a result of corporate information not available to the general public. The Federal Reserve Board regulates the down payment (margin requirements) and controls the credit financing of stock sales. Interstate utilities and utility holding companies are also regulated and are required to register with and report to the Federal Power Commission.

Corporate Management

A corporation is managed and its business is conducted through its board of directors, the officers, and the employees of the corporation. A stockholder, while he may be an owner, cannot bind a corporation by contract, nor can he participate in management while acting solely in the capacity of stockholder. Stockholders elect the board of directors, as indicated, and thus may exercise indirect control of management or may participate as officers or employees of the corporation.

Corporate actions requiring stockholder approval must take place at a duly constituted stockholders' meeting at the time designated by the charter or bylaws or at special meetings called by the board of directors. Special meetings, generally, can be called at the request of a designated percentage of the outstanding stock. Explicit notice must be given concerning all special meetings. However, notice is not necessary for meetings required by the corporate charter or bylaw provisions.

Corporate action by directors can likewise take place only at duly authorized meetings of the board. A director must personally attend to the business of the corporation. He cannot vote by proxy. Subject to charter and bylaw restriction, a majority of the board must normally be present to constitute a proper meeting. Directors are not permitted to exercise a vote on matters with which they may have a conflict of interest. Courts will not interfere with the prerogative of management decisions in the absence of fraud or illegal conduct. When courts do question managerial prerogatives, it is usually the result of a so-called derivative suit filed by a shareholder in behalf of the corporation itself.

Directors are fiduciaries entrusted with corporate management. When they have acted in good faith with due diligence and reasonable care, they are not liable for losses caused by managerial decisions. They are, however, held strictly accountable for willful or negligent acts. Directors are not personally liable for wrongs committed by the corporation unless they have ratified or authorized such act or have participated in the wrong.

The officers of the corporation act as its agents. Courts have held that the president of a corporation has, by virtue of his office, implied authority to act on behalf of the corporation within the scope of corporate business. Other courts have held that the president has these broad powers only when he is acting in the capacity of the general manager. Other officers are limited to the duties of their office. An unauthorized act of an officer may be ratified or accepted by the corporation. The officer, like the director, has a fiduciary responsibility and is subject to that obligation in the same manner as a director of the corporation.

Mr. Jones found no fault with these general provisions. However, he was exceedingly interested in the tax implications of incorporation.

THE FRAMEWORK OF CORPORATE TAXES

An incorporation of an existing sole proprietorship business (that is, the owner's transfer of the business assets to the corporation in exchange for the corporation's stock) generally is tax-free.

The analysis of the corporate income tax rate structure is relatively simple. There are only two basic rates of tax involved. The first $25,000 of taxable income is currently taxed at the rate of 22 percent. All taxable income above this amount is taxed at the current marginal rate of 48 percent. For 1970, there is also a 2.5 percent surcharge rate which will be disregarded in this discussion. These rates are subject to change by the Congress from time to time. The average rate of tax will lag behind the marginal rate until the corporation reaches an income of $100 million. Above this amount the marginal and average rates will be the same.

TABLE 2-3: MARGINAL AND AVERAGE TAX RATES OF THE CORPORATION INCOME TAX
(In Percentages)

Corporate Income (In Dollars)	Marginal Tax Rate	Average Tax Rate*
0–25,000	22	22.00
25,001–26,000	48	23.00
26,001–32,000	48	27.69
32,001–38,000	48	30.89
38,001–44,000	48	33.23
44,001–50,000	48	35.00
50,001–60,000	48	37.17
60,001–70,000	48	38.71
70,001–80,000	48	39.88
80,001–90,000	48	40.78
90,001–100,000	48	41.50
100,001–150,000	48	43.67
150,001–200,000	48	44.75
200,001–500,000	48	46.70
500,001–1,000,000	48	47.35
1,000,001–5,000,000	48	47.87
5,000,001–10,000,000	48	47.94
10,000,001–100,000,000	48	47.99
100,000,001–500,000,000	48	48.00

* Applied to the upper limit of each class interval.

Significance of Capital Gain and Loss Considerations

This particular topic is significant. However, it is also complex. (Mertens' "Law of Federal Income Tax" devotes one entire volume, 951 pages, to "Capital Gains and Losses.") We will make no attempt to summarize the various conflicting legal definitions, descriptions, and ramifications. However, when one understands that it is possible for one corporate taxpayer to pay 48 percent while another corporate taxpayer earning a similar amount of income pays a *maximum* tax of less than 48 percent, he can see that it is worthwhile for the financial executive to become familiar, in a general way, with the capital gain and loss provisions. It is significant to note that some capital gains and losses are also taxed at a lesser rate than ordinary income in the case of individual taxpayers.

In general, the provisions with respect to capital gains and losses apply basically to capital assets such as property held for investment purposes. There are some exceptions to this rule. One exception is the applicability of the capital gain provisions to Section 1231 property, that is, depreciable property and real estate used in a trade or business that have been held for more than six months. (When the occasion arises, we will discuss the details with our tax man.)

In order to appreciate the significance of the capital gains and losses provisions of the Internal Revenue Code, however, we must understand certain basic rules and definitions.

I. Capital gain definitions and classifications
   - A. A short-term capital gain or loss may be incurred by the sale or exchange of a capital asset held for six months or less.
   - B. A long-term capital gain or loss may be incurred by the sale or exchange of a capital asset held for more than six months.
   - C. 1. In a taxable year, short-term capital gains are combined with short-term capital losses and short-term capital loss carry-overs to arrive at net short-term capital gain or net short-term capital loss.
     2. Long-term capital gains are combined with long-term capital losses and long-term capital loss carry-over to arrive at net long-term capital gain or net long-term capital loss.

Mr. Jones' position with respect to capital gains and losses as an individual taxpayer would be quite different from the treatment accorded his corporation.

II. Individual taxpayers
   - A. A net short-term capital gain is taxed at the taxpayer's marginal income tax rate. An excess of net short-term loss over

net long-term capital gain may be deducted from ordinary income up to a maximum of $1,000 for a taxable year. The balance of the net short-term loss is carried forward as a short-term capital loss until it is used up.

B. A net long-term gain must be applied against a net short-term loss. An excess of a net long-term capital gain over a net short-term loss is taxed under either of the following methods, depending on which method produces the lesser tax:
   1. Fifty percent of the excess is added to the taxpayer's ordinary income and will thus be taxed at the taxpayer's marginal income tax rate.
   2. An alternative tax of 25 percent on the first $50,000 plus, for taxable years beginning in 1970, 29½ percent[1] of the excess over $50,000; for taxable years beginning in 1971, 32½ percent of the excess over $50,000; for taxable years beginning in 1972, 35 percent of the excess over $50,000.

      It should be noted that the 25 percent alternative tax rate will apply to all capital gains, without exception, received before January 1, 1975, from sales under binding contracts entered into on or before October 9, 1969.

C. A net long-term capital loss must be applied against a net short-term capital gain. Only one-half of the excess of net long-term capital loss over a net short-term gain up to a maximum of $1,000 per taxable year may be deducted from ordinary income. The excess of net long-term capital loss over net short-term capital gain that is not deducted from ordinary income can be carried over to future years until it is used up. Thus, if the excess of a net long-term loss over a net short-term gain is $1,500, up to one-half of $1,500 ($750) is available as a deduction for a taxable year; if the excess is $6,000, up to 50 percent of $2,000 ($1,000) out of the $6,000 is available as a deduction for a taxable year, and $4,000 can be carried over as a long-term capital loss until it is used up.

D. If a taxpayer realizes both a net long-term capital loss and a net short-term capital loss, the amount deductible from ordinary income up to a maximum of $1,000 comes first out of the net short-term capital loss of that year and the balance from the net long-term capital loss.

   Example 1. If a taxpayer realizes a net long-term loss of $2,000 and a net short-term loss of $4,000, $1,000 of the $4,000 net short-term loss can be deducted from ordinary income. There would be an unused long-term capital loss

[1] Excluding the tax surcharge.

carry-over of $2,000 and an unused short-term capital loss carry-over of $3,000 which can be carried forward until used up.

Example 2. If a taxpayer realizes a net long-term loss of $3,600 and a net short-term loss of $700, the latter amount would be available as a deduction. The other $300, to bring the deduction to the maximum of $1,000, must come from $600 of the $3,600 net long-term loss (50 percent of $600 = $300). There could be an unused long-term capital loss of $3,000 which could be carried over to subsequent years as a long-term capital loss until used up.

E. Net capital losses can be carried over indefinitely.

The rules for capital gains and losses of corporations are the same as for individuals, with these exceptions:

1. A corporation is not allowed a special deduction from ordinary income of one-half of the excess of a net long-term capital gain over a net short-term capital loss.
2. However, the alternative capital gains tax applicable to individuals also applies to corporations, with some modifications.

   A corporation's effective tax rate on the excess of a net long-term capital gain over a net short-term capital loss is limited to 28 percent[1] for years beginning in 1970, and to 30 percent in years beginning in 1971 and thereafter.

   Until 1975, the alternative capital gains tax is 25 percent on gains from binding contracts entered into on or before October 9, 1969; liquidating distributions made before October 10, 1970, and under a plan of complete liquidation adopted on or before October 9, 1969, are likewise taxed at 25 percent.
3. Unlike individuals, corporations are allowed a three-year capital loss carry-back for net capital losses.
4. Unlike individuals, who can carry over net capital losses indefinitely, corporations are limited to a five-year carry-over period. (Corporate capital loss carry-backs and carry-forwards are treated as short-term capital losses.)

Several illustrations are in order at this time.

1. Suppose a taxpayer has $7,000 taxable income without regard to capital gains or losses (ordinary income $10,000 less $3,000 personal deductions and exemptions). In addition, the taxpayer has a recognized long-term capital gain of $3,100 and a short-term capital loss of $1,600 during the taxable year. The basic problem

[1] Exclusive of the tax surcharge.

is how will these capital gain and loss transactions affect taxable income? You must first find out whether the taxpayer is an individual or a corporation.

a. If the taxpayer is an individual, the short-term capital loss of $1,600 is offset against the long-term capital gain of $3,100, leaving a net long-term capital gain of $1,500. *One-half* of $1,500 can be added to the taxpayer's other income, making taxable income $7,750. The net capital gain thus increases the taxable income from $7,000 to $7,750. Consulting Table 2-2, we see that the marginal tax rate from $4,000 to $8,000 is 19 percent. The tax payable as a result of the capital gain is $142.50 (19 percent × $750). The alternative tax of 25 percent of the long-term capital gain is of no use since this method would result in a higher tax.
b. If the taxpayer is a corporation, the *entire* net capital gain of $1,500 will be taxed at 22 percent (marginal tax rate), resulting in a tax of $330. The alternative tax rate does not apply because it is greater than the marginal tax rate. Note that the corporation must take 100 percent of the capital gain into ordinary income, and the marginal tax is 22 percent.

2. Assume the same set of facts as in situation 1 above except that the long-term capital gain is $1,600 and the short-term capital loss is $3,100.
   a. If the taxpayer is an individual, he will deduct the $1,600 long-term gain from the short-term $3,100 capital loss, resulting in a net short-term capital loss of $1,500. The taxpayer can deduct from ordinary income $1,000 of this net short-term capital loss. This $1,000 is deductible in the year in which the above events occur; the remaining $500 short-term capital loss can be carried forward as a short-term capital loss to be deducted from capital gains and ordinary income in the same manner as that used in the current taxable year until exhausted.
   b. If the taxpayer is a corporation, the net capital loss cannot be used as a deduction from income but must be carried back three years as a short-term capital loss and carried forward five years. The amount of the carry-over that is not absorbed by capital gains during the eight-year period is lost forever as a deduction.

Net Operating Loss

The financial executive should be particularly interested in the net operating loss provisions of the Internal Revenue Code. This type of loss generally occurs when losses and expenses exceed income in a given taxable year. The net loss can be carried back three years and carried forward five years. The excess taxes paid in three prior years as a result of deducting the net operating loss carry-back may be recovered by filing amended tax returns for these years. Thus, a net operating loss for 1970 would be subtracted first from the income reported in 1967; second, from the income reported for 1968; and then, from the income for 1969. If the income for these three years is less than the 1970 loss, the unused portion of the 1970 loss may be carried forward to reduce the income for the succeeding five years.

As an example, assume income and losses as follows:

Year	Taxable Income	Tax Paid	Refund (plus Interest)
1967	+$30,000	$ 7,900	$ 7,900
1968	+ 70,000	27,100	27,100
1969	0	0	0
1970	−300,000	0	0
1971	+100,000	0	41,500*
1972	+50,000	0	17,500*
1973	+20,000	0	4,400*
1974	+15,000	0	3,300*
1975	+10,000	0	2,200*

*These amounts are not refunds, per se. They represent the yearly income tax savings resulting from deduction of the 1970 net operating loss carry-forward.

You will note that only $295,000 of the $300,000 1970 loss was absorbed over the eight-year period. The unused loss of $5,000 can no longer be used as a tax deduction.

Installment Sales

The financial executive may be interested in knowing that special tax provisions exist with respect to installment sales at a profit. The installment method applies only to sales at a profit. If a loss is incurred, it must be deducted in full in the year of sale.

Four types of sales may be reported on the installment basis if certain conditions are met:

1. A casual sale of real property
2. Personal and real property regularly sold on the installment basis by dealers in such property
3. A casual sale of personal property for a price exceeding $1,000
4. Revolving credit plans (special rules apply)

The gross profit on the installment sale is deferred and reported ratably as the installment payments are received.

As an example, assume a new corporation engaged in the retail jewelry business adopts the installment method with regard to sales of merchandise. In the first year, gross sales are $50,000. No payments are received during the year of the sale. The cost of the merchandise amounts to $25,000, leaving a gross profit of $25,000 (50 percent of sales). Other business expenses amount to $4,000 for each year of operation. A total of $15,000 is paid on the contracts the following year (1971). On the installment basis the net profit when reportable for 1970 and 1971 is calculated as follows:

1970	Gross income	none
	Other business expense	$4,000
	Net loss for year	($4,000)
1971	*1970 Installment Sale*	
	Gross sales	$50,000
	Cost of goods sold	25,000
	Gross profit	$25,000
	Cash collections in 1971 and 1970 installment sales	$15,000
	Gross profit percentage	×50%
	Gross profit to be reported	$ 7,500
	Less other business expense	4,000
	Net profit to be reported in 1971	$ 3,500*

* Can the $4,000 net operating cost for 1970 be carried forward to 1971? The answer is yes, and $500 of the 1970 loss will be available as a net operating loss deduction in 1972.

The installment method of reporting income can be extremely valuable to dealers engaged exclusively in installment sales (such as retail jewelry or retail furniture dealers). This method of reporting income is also available to nondealer corporations and individuals who realize gains on casual sales of real and personal property on the installment basis. The most important aspect of an installment-sale method of reporting income is that the taxpayer realizing the gain need not pay the income taxes on the gain until he receives the proceeds of the sale.

In the case of a casual sale, it should be noted that the installment method of reporting the income on the sale is permitted only if (1) no payments are received in the taxable year of the sale (exclusive of evidences of indebtedness of the purchaser) or (2) the payments received in the year of sale do not exceed 30 percent of the selling price. Moreover, there must be more than one installment payment.

For example, an individual sells in 1970 some of his machinery and equipment used in his sole proprietorship business. He receives from the buyer $10,000 in cash in 1970 and two notes, one for $25,000 due one year later at 8 percent interest and one for $15,000 due two years later at 8 percent interest.

The cost of the assets in 1965 was $40,000. He received an ordinary deduction of $25,000 for depreciation on these assets from 1965 to the date of the sale, so that the adjusted basis of the property at the time of sale was $15,000.

Whether the individual is on a cash or accrual basis for reporting his business income, he is required to report in 1970 the entire gain of $35,000 (selling price of $50,000 less adjusted basis of the property of $15,000) unless he can and does elect the installment method of reporting the gain on the sale.

Since, in the year of sale, the taxpayer receives less than 30 percent of the sale price of $50,000 (he receives $10,000—30 percent of $50,000 is $15,000) and since the balance of the sales price is payable in two installments, the taxpayer can elect the installment method. Should he so elect and if the notes are paid off, $7,000 of the $35,000 gain would be reportable in 1970, $17,500 in 1971, and $10,500 in 1972, computed as follows:

	Total	Percentage	1970	1971	1972
Sales price	$50,000	100	$10,000	$25,000	$15,000
Adjusted basis	15,000	30	3,000	7,500	4,500
Gross profit	$35,000	70	$ 7,000	$17,500	$10,500
			All ordinary income	All ordinary income	$500 ordinary income; $10,000 long-term capital gain

It should be noted that since the machinery and equipment are property used in the trade or business and held over six months, they are treated like capital assets under Section 1231 of the Internal Revenue Code. The gain is a long-term capital gain except to the extent of the depreciation taken on the property, which has been deducted from ordinary income. Thus, the first $25,000 of the total gain of $35,000 is ordinary income, and $10,000 is long-term capital gain.

If in the above example the taxpayer were a corporation, the same results would generally follow.

Dividends Received

Again, there is a significant difference between the individual and corporate tax treatment of dividend income.

1. Dividend income is ordinary income taxed at the taxpayer's marginal rate. Individual taxpayers are permitted an exemption up to $100 for dividends received from domestic corporations. If the stock is owned by husband and wife jointly, each spouse is allowed the maximum $100 exemption.
2. Eighty-five percent of all dividends received by one domestic corporation from another domestic corporation are exempt from taxation (subject to limitation). If the receiving corporation owns 80 percent or more of the stock of the corporation paying the dividend, under certain conditions, 100 percent of the dividends received by the parent corporation are exempt from taxation. This is a significant point.

Payment of Income Taxes

Lower-bracket individual taxpayers who receive all their income from employment pay all their income taxes via withholding from the source by the employer. This type of taxpayer is not our concern here.

An individual taxpayer must file a declaration of estimated tax if:

1. The employed taxpayer anticipates income of more than $200 that is not subject to withholding.
2. The gross income from employment plus other income not subject to withholding exceeds $10,000 for a married individual filing a joint return, or $5,000 for a single individual.
3. An additional income tax of $40 or more will be due above the amount withheld.

The filing of an estimated tax requires the taxpayer to estimate in advance of April 15 of the taxable year what his income will be for that taxable year, then estimate the tax thereon and subtract the amount of income taxes which he estimates the employer will withhold from his wages; the balance represents the amount which he will be required to pay in four installments on April 15, June 15, and September 15 of the current year and January 15 of the following year. These provisions are especially significant to Mr. Jones since he is not an employee of the Jones Electronic organization and he receives no wages subject to withholding.

Again, there is a significant difference in the treatment of the estimated tax liability for corporations. A corporation's estimated tax is its expected tax liability less allowable tax credits, such as the foreign tax credit, and the statutory exemptions. The statutory exemptions consist of a basic exemption of $5,500 and an exemption based on the $100,000 exemption that was allowed prior to 1968. This latter exemption is usually referred to as the "transitional" exemption because the Internal Revenue Code has been changed so as to gradually phase out the $100,000 exemption so that after 1971, only the basic exemption of $5,500 will be allowed in estimating corporate tax payments. For 1970, the transitional exemption is 40 percent of $94,500 ($100,000 less $5,500 basic exemption); for 1971, the transitional exemption is 20 percent of $94,500; for 1972 and thereafter, only the basic exemption of $5,500 will be available in estimating corporate tax payments.

Corporations must file estimated returns and pay the estimated tax in equal installments. The payment dates for a calendar-year corporation are April 15, June 15, September 15, and December 15 of the current year. The payment dates of a fiscal-year corporation are the fifteenth day of the fourth, ninth, and twelfth months of the taxable year. All these dates are significant to the financial executive, who must arrange to have sufficient funds on hand for payment of the tax liability.

Investment Tax Credit

The investment tax credit was conceived in 1962 as a method of encouraging investment by business entities to stimulate or sustain the national economic growth. The credit was suspended in 1966 because it was considered a stimulus to inflation. It was then reinstated by Congress in 1967 when the President concluded that the inflationary pressures had eased. In 1969, the administration decided that the credit was detrimental to the nation's economy, and the Tax Reform Act of 1969 repealed the credit provisions entirely.

The 1969 Repealing Act, however, allows the credit with respect to property that had not been put into service at the cutoff date (April 18, 1969), but substantial commitment to do so had been made prior to the cutoff date. However, no credit will be allowed for property placed in service after 1975.

In general, the investment-credit provisions provided that a business enterprise could reduce its income tax due for a taxable year because it invested in certain new property. A specified percentage of the new investment (depending on the useful life of the investment) constituted the credit allowed to reduce the enterprise's tax liability as follows (note that the provision operates as a credit against the tax, reducing the tax liability, rather than a deduction from income):

Amount of Credit	Useful Life of Investment
7%	Eight years or more
$4\frac{2}{3}$%	Six or seven years
$2\frac{1}{3}$%	Four or five years
None	Less than four years

Improper Accumulation of Earnings

A corporation may be inclined to accumulate earnings rather than pass through the earnings to the stockholders as dividends. This may be especially true if the corporation is relatively small or has a relatively small number of stockholders whose marginal tax rates are high. As an example, if Jones Electronic were incorporated and had earnings that could be distributed to Jones as dividends in the amount of $200,000 and if Jones were in the 70 percent marginal tax bracket, he would retain after taxes only $60,000 of the dividends so received. His decision might be not to declare the dividend and to leave the funds in the corporation. The Internal Revenue Code provides a penalty in the amount of 27.5 percent on the first $100,000 of "improperly" accumulated taxable income and 38.5 percent on such taxable income over this amount.

Funds are determined to be "improperly" accumulated "if the purpose of the accumulation is to enable the stockholders to avoid the personal income tax." Earnings are, however, validly retained to finance plant expansion, unexpected demands for funds, and general growth. If the corporation files a statement justifying the earnings accumulation, the burden is on the U.S. Treasury Department to prove the retention is unjustified. There is a big difference between avoiding personal taxes and providing funds for expansion and growth. However, for tax purposes, it may be a very fine line. On the other hand, there may be times when the financial executive will make the decision to pay the penalty tax and avoid a higher marginal tax rate.

It was a long and difficult afternoon. However, there simply was no way to avoid the legal and tax implications of your future profession as a financial executive. It is true, as so many have said, "I can hire or retain all the accountants or tax experts I will need. These details are unnecessary." This statement may or may not be so. However, it is a very sad situation when we hear from our legal and/or tax experts the following statement: "I could have been of considerable help to you if I had been in on the planning stage. Now, all I can do is try to pick up the pieces." It is not necessary that the financial executive be knowledgeable in all the details of the tax implications, but he certainly must be able to recognize the problem! It is difficult indeed to imagine a financial decision (or almost any managerial decision) that does not have tax implications.

As a final statement, the attorney added that certain incorporated businesses may elect to be taxed somewhat like proprietorships or partnerships. For emphasis, he repeated that under certain conditions some corporations may elect to be taxed somewhat like proprietorships or partnerships. In such a case, the corporation is not taxed (except on certain capital gains), but the shareholders are taxed their pro rata shares of the corporation's net profit or loss. He cited three main requirements and mentioned that other details should be investigated. The basic requirements are as follows:

1. The firm must be a domestic corporation and not part of a group eligible to file consolidated returns.
2. There must be no more than 10 stockholders, all of whom must be individuals (a corporate shareholder would thus eliminate this possibility).
3. The business must not earn more than 20 percent of its gross income from rents, royalties, interest, dividends, or annuities or from gains on the sales of securities.

That's enough! I'm going to the golf course—care to join me? My handicap is 20. This means I need more than an extra stroke each hole to come close to par.

After dinner, you received a phone call. Mr. Jones requested that you meet him at the office in 30 minutes. When you arrived, Mr. Jones, Mrs. Jones, the attorney, and the accountants were already there. Mr. Jones announced that the attorney had been instructed to draw up the proper papers to incorporate the business under the name of Jones Electronic Corporation. President Jones was to be named president and treasurer, and Mrs. Jones was to be secretary. Authorized capital stock was to consist of 500,000 shares of no-par common stock. All existing assets and liabilities were to be transferred and assumed by the corporation. Mr. Jones was to be issued 49,998 shares of no-par common, Mrs. Jones was to receive one share, and the eldest Jones son (the Joneses have four boys) was to receive one share. These three people were to be the incorporators.

You wondered what you were doing there, but certainly didn't ask! President Jones later indicated to you that you had been invited so you would know all the details. This was a nice gesture, but was really unnecessary. You could have learned everything there was to know from the incorporation papers after they had been returned from the secretary of state (state of incorporation).

ARTICLES OF INCORPORATION

These papers were duly received about a week later and appeared as follows (this application for a charter is just an example; each state has its own specific requirements):

ARTICLES OF INCORPORATION
of
JONES ELECTRONIC CORPORATION

The undersigned subscribers to these articles of incorporation, each a natural person competent to contract, hereby associate themselves together to form a corporation under the laws of the state of ___________.

ARTICLE I. NAME
The name of this corporation is: Jones Electronic Corporation.

ARTICLE II. NATURE OF BUSINESS
The general nature of the business to be transacted by this corporation is to engage in the design, manufacture, and sale of any product or products approved by the board of directors and any other activity approved by the board of directors.

ARTICLE III. CAPITAL STOCK
The maximum number of shares of stock that this corporation is authorized to have outstanding at any one time is 500,000 shares no-par common stock.

ARTICLE IV. INITIAL CAPITAL
The amount of capital with which this corporation will begin business is Eighty-five Thousand, Eight Hundred Thirty-Three ($85,833) Dollars.

ARTICLE V. TERM OF EXISTENCE
This corporation is to exist perpetually.

ARTICLE VI. ADDRESS
The initial post office address of the principal office of this corporation in the state of _____________ is ______________________________. The board of directors may from time to time move the principal to any other address in ____(state)____.

ARTICLE VII. DIRECTORS
This corporation shall have three (3) directors, initially. The number of directors may be increased or diminished from time to time, by bylaws adopted by the stockholders, but shall never be less than three.

ARTICLE VIII. INITIAL DIRECTORS

The names and post office addresses of the members of the first board of directors are:

Name	*Address*
James Thomas Jones	——
Susan Jones	——
James Thomas Jones, Jr.	——

ARTICLE IX. SUBSCRIBERS

The name and post office address of each subscriber of these articles of incorporation, the number of shares of stock each agrees to take, and the value of the consideration therefore are:

Name	*Address*	*Shares*	*Consideration*
James Thomas Jones	——	49,998	
Susan Jones	——	1	
James Thomas Jones, Jr.	——	1	

ARTICLE X. AMENDMENT

These articles of incorporation may be amended in the manner provided by law. Every amendment shall be approved by the board of directors, proposed by them to the stockholders, and approved at a stockholders' meeting by majority of the stock entitled to vote thereon, unless all the directors and all the stockholders sign a written statement manifesting their intention that a certain amendment of these articles of incorporation be made.

____
James Thomas Jones

____
Susan Jones

____
James Thomas Jones, Jr.

STATE OF ______________
COUNTY OF ______________

I hereby certify that on this day, before me, a Notary Public duly authorized in the state and county named above to take acknowledgments, personally appeared *James Thomas Jones, Susan Jones,* and *James Thomas Jones, Jr.,* to me known to be the persons described as subscribers in and who executed the foregoing articles of incorporation, and acknowledged before me that they subscribed to those articles of incorporation.

Witness my hand and official seal in the county and state named above this ______________ day of ______________, 19__.

____
Notary Public.
My commission expires: (Date)

The legal and tax framework we have established has indeed been a thorough one. Clearly, it will be unnecessary for us to carry all these details at our fingertips. However, if the biggest problem is always knowing what the problem is—and it is—then we certainly have available sufficient material to recognize many problems.

It's been a long week and your secretary is quite exhausted from transcribing your notes. For a while, let's forget it. I'm going to the golf course and would like for you to come along; however, you decline (you just don't realize what a real duffer I am). After you rest a bit, go back and review these details so that you will be able to recognize the problem when it arises. If you need help, call me at the clubhouse. See you later.

SUMMARY

Your study of the material contained in Chapter 1 made you aware of the general goal of the financial manager. Chapter 2 introduced the first of many constraints which make the achievement of that original goal somewhat more complicated. Mr. Jones and his new financial manager were exposed to the several potential forms of business organization and became aware of the tax implications which flow from the selection of any one form of organization.

The firm was organized as a sole proprietorship. While this form had certain initial advantages for Mr. Jones, its inherent disadvantages were becoming evident. The primary limitations of the sole proprietorship are:

1. The lack of a legal personality apart from that of its owner
2. The limited ability to attract investment funds in significant amounts
3. The unlimited personal liability of owners for debts of the business
4. The difficulties inherent in the transfer of ownership
5. The unfavorable marginal tax rates paid by the sole proprietor when profits (income to the owner) are high

In your search for a more congenial form of organization you next investigated the partnership. The partnership, you will recall, was defined as a voluntary association of two or more individuals, as co-owners, to carry on a business for profit. Various types of partnership agreements were then described and the terms *general partner, nominal partner, silent partner,* etc., were defined. The major point of emphasis concerned the importance of a written agreement among the partners in order to delimit the rights and the responsibilities of the individuals and those of the partnership itself. In addition, procedures covering the termination or dissolution of the written agreement were explained.

The next form of business organization which was explained by the attorney was the corporation. The corporation is itself a legal person created by the state. In its capacity as a legal person the corporation may own property, incur debts, and otherwise perform those activities which are necessary to its business purpose. It has a life apart from its owners and in most cases a perpetual existence. Corporate ownership is evidenced by shares of interest or stock certificates. The owners of a majority of the outstanding shares elect the corporate officers and through these representatives control the activities of the firm. Stock certificates can take a variety of forms, and the basic aspects of several types of stock were briefly outlined for both Mr. Jones and you. In addition, the attorney explained the legal aspects of issuance and transfer of corporate stock and the duties and responsibilities of corporate directors.

In response to your inquiry, the tax implications of incorporation were then explained. The tax rates which the corporation is required to pay on taxable income were considered in their marginal and average contexts. Special reference was made to the treatment of capital gains and losses, operating losses, installment sales contracts, dividends, and other corporate tax matters.

As a financial executive you are not required to be a tax expert; however, you must be tax-conscious. That is to say, you should recognize that there are tax implications to almost all business decisions. The financial executive, at a minimum, must be able to converse with the tax expert and understand the "tax man's" viewpoint and potential contribution. You should, for example, understand that certain corporations may elect proprietorship tax treatment. Your tax man will tell you whether or not your firm is qualified to be considered under the provisions of Subchapter S and what the implications of such an election would be.

The author will be the first to admit that after twenty years in tax law practice and as a corporate executive, he does not carry all of the details in his head. However, he can recognize a problem when he sees one. This is the significant thing. Of equal significance is the distinction between the marginal and the average tax rate. All managerial decisions are marginal, and thus the marginal tax rate is significant.

QUESTIONS FOR DISCUSSION

1. What are the characteristics of a single proprietorship?
2. How does the single proprietorship differ from the partnership?
3. What are the outstanding advantages and disadvantages of these two forms of business organizations?

4. a. What is the difference between the average tax rate and the marginal tax rate?
   b. How are the two related?

5. Distinguish between gross income, adjusted gross income, and taxable income with respect to individual tax returns.

6. Under what circumstances is a partnership automatically dissolved?

7. What is the significance of the fact that a corporation is a legal person?

8. How does the liability for the debts of a corporation differ from the liability of partners for the debts of the partnership?

9. If you were going to incorporate a business, what general requirements would you have to meet in states which pattern their incorporation laws after the Model Business Corporation Act?

10. What is the significance of the corporate charter?

11. What is the essence of the fiduciary relationship which exists between corporate directors and the shareholders who have elected them?

12. What are capital gains and losses?

13. a. Is the tax treatment of such gains and losses the same for individuals and corporations?
    b. If not, how does the treatment differ?

14. a. Are dividends received by individuals and corporations subject to the same tax treatment?
    b. If they are treated differently, describe the differences.

15. a. Who must file a declaration of estimated tax?
    b. Under what circumstances must such a filing be made?

16. Under what circumstances would a financial manager choose to pay an improper accumulations tax rather than pay out corporate earnings in the form of dividends?

PROBLEMS

1. A single taxpayer, age 30 with no dependents, has the following sources of income:

Annual salary	\$9,500
Dividend income	200
Commissions	1,000

He has incurred legitimate interest expenses in the amount of \$500, and his charitable contributions total another \$200.

a. What is his gross income?
b. What is his adjusted gross income?

c. According to the appropriate tax schedule presented in the chapter, determine his required tax payment.

2. Assume the same facts as above except that the taxpayer is age 67 and is filing a joint return with his wife, who is 65 years of age. Determine his tax liability in this situation.

3. A single taxpayer, age 30 with no dependents, has the following sources of income:

Annual salary	$35,000
Dividend income	1,000
Rent from real estate	2,000

During the taxable year he has made charitable contributions and paid interest in the amounts of $500 and $700, respectively. In addition, he has incurred short-term capital losses of $3,000 and a short-term capital gain of $2,500.

Utilizing the appropriate tax tables, determine this individual's taxes due.

Recalculate the above figure, using the same information as before, but this time assume the capital gains and losses to be long-term rather than short-term.

4. A corporation shows its earnings before taxes to be $45,000. Calculate its tax liability.

When would these payments be due if the corporation reported on a calendar-year basis?

When would the payments be due if the corporation ended its fiscal year on September 30 rather than December 31?

5. Each of the following situations concerns a married couple, with two dependents, filing joint returns. What is the amount of the standard deduction, and should the standard deduction be claimed?

Gross Income	**Adjusted Gross Income**	**Total Itemized Deductions**
$ 4,000	$ 3,500	$ 150
5,500	4,900	300
8,000	7,000	700
11,000	10,500	1,300

6. During 1971 J. Jones had the following transactions:
   a. January 6—Bought 500 shares of XYZ stock at $100 per share.
   b. February 9—Sold 100 shares of XYZ stock at 110 and bought 100 shares of ABC stock at 90.
   c. June 10—Sold 400 shares of XYZ stock at 98 and sold 100 shares of ABC stock at 102.

   What would be the capital gains tax for the year resulting from these transactions?

7. T. Carroll filed his tax returns on a cash and calendar-year basis. During 1971 he sold 100 shares of the capital stock of XYZ that he held as an investment to J. Jones for $100 per share. The stock had cost Jones $50 five months earlier. Jones agreed to pay $5,000 during 1971, $3,000 in 1972, and $2,000 in 1973. What would the taxable income be each year if each deferred payment earned interest at the rate of 8 percent per year? Accrued interest would be paid on the deferred payments at the time the deferred payments were made.

8. Calculate the taxable income resulting from the following transactions:

	A-Individual	B-Corporation
Taxable income before capital gains	$60,000	$60,000
Long-term capital gain	30,000	30,000
Short-term capital gain	5,000	5,000
Long-term capital loss	42,000	42,000
Short-term capital loss	3,000	3,000

REFERENCES

Ballantine, H. W.: "Ballantine on Corporations," rev. ed., chap. 1, Callaghan & Co., Chicago, 1946.

Bittker, Boris I., and James S. Eustice: "Federal Income Taxation of Corporations and Shareholders," 2d ed., Federal Tax Press, Hamden, Conn., 1966.

Friend, Irwin, James R. Longstreet, Morris Mendelson, Ervin Miller, and Arleigh P. Hess, Jr.: "Investment Banking and the New Issues Market," The World Publishing Company, Cleveland, 1967.

Guthmann, Harry G., and Herbert E. Dougall: "Corporate Financial Policy," 4th ed., chaps. 2, 3, Prentice-Hall, Inc., Englewood Cliffs, N.J., 1962.

Hazard, John W., and Milton Christie: "The Investment Business," Harper & Row, Publishers, Incorporated, New York, 1964.

Holyman, Robert S.: "Tax Basis for Managerial Decisions," Holt, Rinehart and Winston, Inc., New York, 1965.

McCarthy, Clarence F., Billy M. Mann, Byrle M. Abbin, William H. Gregory, and John P. Lindgren: "The Federal Income Tax: Its Sources and Applications," Prentice-Hall, Inc., Englewood Cliffs, N.J., 1968.

"Opinion of the Accounting Principles Board, No. 11, Accounting for Income Taxes," American Institute of Certified Public Accountants, New York, 1967.

Raby, William L.: "The Income Tax and Business Decisions," Prentice-Hall, Inc., Englewood Cliffs, N.J., 1964.

Reeves, James Patrick: "Tax Aspects of Corporate Mergers, Exchanges, Redemptions, Liquidations, and Reorganizations," Vantage Press, New York, 1967.

Robbins, Sidney: "The Securities Markets," The Free Press, New York, and Collier-Macmillan Limited, London, 1966.

Shultz, Birl E.: "The Securities Market—And How It Works," rev. ed. (revision by Albert P. Squires), Harper & Row, Publishers, Incorporated, New York, 1962.

Smith, Don Throop: "Tax Factors in Business Decisions," Prentice-Hall, Inc., Englewood Cliffs, N.J., 1968.

Van Arsdell, Paul M.: "Corporation Finance, Policy, Planning, Administration," chaps. 2, 3, The Ronald Press Company, New York, 1968.

Weston, J. Fred, and Eugene F. Brigham: "Managerial Finance," 3d ed., chap. 2, Holt, Rinehart and Winston, Inc., New York, 1969.

Willett, Edward R.: "Fundamentals of Securities Markets," Appleton-Century-Crofts Division of Meredith Corporation, New York, 1968.

Winter, Elmer L.: "A Complete Guide to Making a Public Stock Offering," Prentice-Hall, Inc., Englewood Cliffs, N.J., 1962.

Chapter Three

SOME ANALYTICAL TOOLS AVAILABLE

You still have a few days left before officially taking over your duties as the financial executive of the Jones Electronic Corporation. You can put this time to good use by sharpening up the tools of your profession, with special emphasis on those areas in which your first decisions are likely to be made. We recall that during our initial interview with Mr. Jones he made references to several areas of the firm's operation which presented special problems and which would require immediate attention. As you could easily see, there was then little financial expertise within the organization. One of the problem areas was product cost analysis. We may be familiar with the microeconomic definitions of marginal cost, differential cost, etc., involved in product analysis, but we would nevertheless be well advised to review these and related concepts.

SUPPLY AND COST

We know that the supply of a particular commodity is directly related to the cost of producing that commodity. It is necessary, then, that we understand what is meant by the term *cost*.

In our understanding of the economic framework within which the financial executive must operate, the term *cost* includes all costs that are necessary to bring about production. In general, we speak about rent to land, wages to labor, interest to capital, and profits to owners as costs of production. It is sometimes said that only when all four of these "factors of production" are paid an amount equal to what they could earn engaged in another activity, will they continue to be committed to a particular industry and to produce a given product. This statement is not entirely accurate. A man might choose to operate his own business and, in fact, earn less in profits as an owner than he could earn in wages as an employee.[1] However, the fact remains that part of the cost he is paying to operate his own business is the wages he is giving up. This is known as *opportunity cost.* In this sense, then, opportunity costs are the wages, profits, or income one gives up or forgoes because he chooses one course of action rather than another. Total cost does include this opportunity cost. We must emphasize this last sentence. It will be significant as we begin to examine alternative courses of action in the decision-making process. There will always be income or benefits that are given up as we choose one alternative rather than another.

As an example, suppose that you owned an undeveloped piece of property that a soft-drink manufacturer wanted to lease from you for parking facilities for his employees and equipment. The company was willing to pay you $650 per month rental for the property. However, parking space was at a premium and you decided to quit your job and operate a public parking lot at that location. You resigned your job, which paid a monthly salary of $500, built an inexpensive office, and opened for business as a parking-lot operator.

During the first month you collected $900 in parking fees. Your real estate taxes on the property amounted to $150 per month. Did you earn $750 profit? Really, you did not when all economic costs are considered. You lost $250! Why? What economic costs must be considered? The answer is *opportunity costs,* sometimes called *implicit costs.* Your opportunity cost, as related to this example, would be $1,000. You could have rented the property for a net income of $500 after real estate taxes ($650 rent less $150 real estate taxes), and your former position paid you $500. Your income would have been $1,000. Your net income from the parking business was $750. You lost $250!

Part of the cost of attending school for a student is the loss of income that could be earned during school and study hours. For some this cost may be high; for others the cost is quite low. It is the expectation over a longer period of time that makes education financially worthwhile. However, opportunity costs are costs nevertheless.

[1] Some authorities would hold that even this man is fully compensated since being his own boss is a form of psychic income which is the equivalent of the wages sacrificed.

Fixed and Variable Costs

In almost any business, some costs will be fixed and some will be variable. *Fixed costs* are those costs which are not within management's control, in the short run, and are unrelated to the amount of production. The contractual rental payment that the soft-drink company was willing to make for 12 months would have represented a fixed cost to that company each month. The company was obligated to pay the monthly rental fee whether or not the property was actually used. This period of one year is the short run as far as the lease payments are concerned. The short run, as we use the term, is that period of time during which the factors of production are fixed and cannot be changed.

A closer look at the parking-lot example reveals that in this example, for all practical purposes, all costs are fixed. *Total fixed costs,* then, equal $1,150 (lost wages, $500; lost rent, $500; and taxes, $150). Let us examine fixed costs a little more explicitly.

If the lot had a capacity of 200 cars per day for 25 days each month, *the fixed cost per car* would depend directly upon the total number of cars that used the lot. If the lot were full every minute of every day in the month, there would be the equivalent of 5,000 cars using the lot. Various cars might go in and out, but the net result would be 5,000 equivalent full-time cars. On the basis of 5,000 equivalent cars, the fixed cost would be 23 cents per car (total fixed cost divided by the number of cars, or $1,150 ÷ 5,000). If the lot averaged 2,500 full-time equivalent cars, the fixed cost per car would be 46 cents. If the lot averaged one-fourth occupancy, the fixed cost per car would increase to 92 cents. If the lot had 1,000 full-time equivalent cars during the month, the fixed cost per car would increase to $1.15. See Figure 3-1.

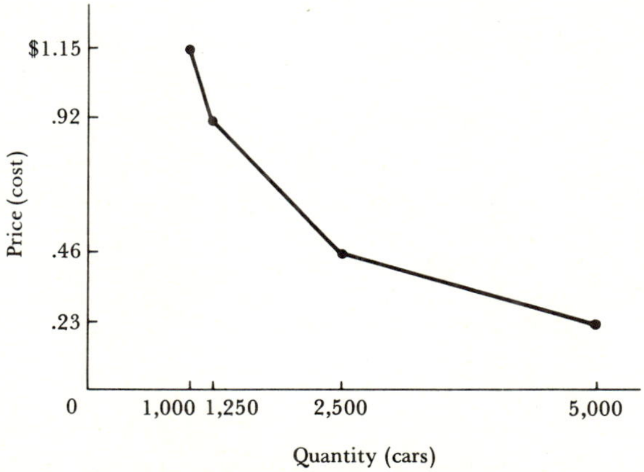

Figure 3-1 Average fixed cost per car.

These simple truths concerning fixed cost do appear to be rather obvious, and they are. However, bear them firmly in mind. Many problems that appear to be sophisticated and complex will be solved or greatly simplified as we identify fixed costs and remember that average fixed cost per unit will decrease or increase as total production or sales volume increases or decreases.

Variable costs are those costs which are within the control of management in the short run and do vary in total with the amount of production. All costs are variable in the long run. Direct raw material expense and direct labor expense, as illustrated by production workers who are paid in accordance with the number of hours of work performed or units produced, are good examples of variable cost. The assumption is that we will hire only as many men as are needed to produce the desired quantity of production. (When labor is paid on a weekly or monthly salary basis for a given period of time, irrespective of the amount of production, these wages can be considered as fixed, and represent a fixed cost for the period.)

Average variable cost per unit will "typically" decrease as units of production increase to a point and then sharply increase as additional units are produced. However, we must be extremely careful about making this assumption. Not all variable costs may behave in a "typical" fashion. The average variable cost per unit may, for all practical purposes, remain constant as total production or sales increase significantly within a fairly wide range. This latter observation may be especially applicable for the various levels of production or sales under investigation at any given time.

As an example of the typical analysis of variable costs, assume that the equipment used to manufacture a soft drink requires four separate operations as follows: (1) the bottles must be washed and prepared for a conveyor; (2) the bottles must then be carried from the washer to the conveyor; (3) the bottles then move along the conveyor and are filled, capped, and delivered to the loading table; (4) the bottles are then put into cases and hauled to the warehouse. For maximum efficiency, four men should operate the machinery. Let's check this operation with various numbers of workmen and prepare a schedule (Table 3-1) to show the average variable cost per case. Average variable cost per case is obtained by dividing total variable cost by total cases produced (column 4 ÷ column 2 = column 5). Each man is $12 per day.

Function and Significance of Economic Cost Curves

As we examine the first two columns of Table 3-1, we will see that if we use only one machine and add more workmen, total production will, at first, increase rapidly; then, as additional men are used, the rate

TABLE 3-1

(1) Number of Workmen	(2) Total Production, Cases	(3) Average Production per Man	(4) Total Labor Cost	(5) (Col. 4 ÷ Col. 2) Average Variable Cost per Case
1	50	50	$ 12	$0.24
2	200	100	24	0.12
3	600	200	36	0.06
4	1,400	350	48	0.034
5	1,500	300	60	0.04
7	1,610	230	84	0.052
8	1,625	203	96	0.059
9	1,650	183	108	0.065
10	1,675	167	120	0.072
20	1,675	83¾	240	0.143

of increase in total production will decline. We could continue to hire men, beyond the maximum of 20 illustrated in Table 3-1, to the point where they would get into each other's way and total production might eventually cease altogether.

In our example of the bottling process it can be easily seen that when only one employee is hired he must perform each of the four production steps. However, when four are hired, each becomes a specialist in one of the four production phases. The additional three employees should and do add to the efficiency of the production line.

Because of the *economies of scale,* the average variable cost per case line (see Figure 3-2) will slope downward as quantity produced increases, but only to a point. Costs will then increase beyond this point because of the *diseconomies of scale.* What is meant by these two terms?

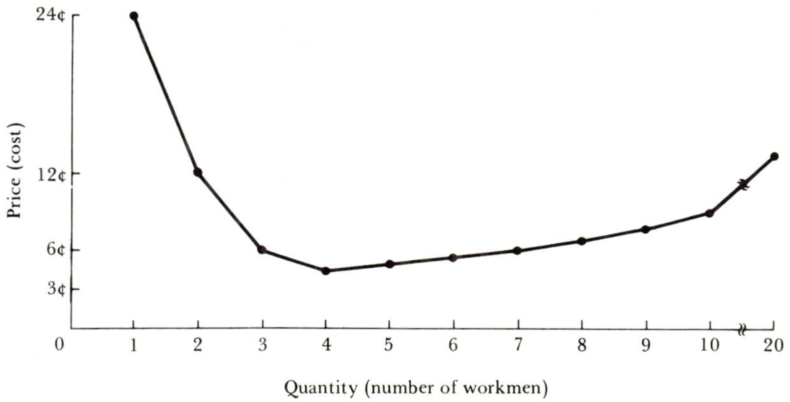

Figure 3-2 Average variable cost per case.

Economies of scale. These economies are those which are related to increased labor productivity caused by the increase in the size of the organization as well as the cost savings resulting from quantity purchases, more efficient use of material (for example, less waste), and a wider distribution of overhead expense.

Diseconomies of scale. These diseconomies are the additional costs that are related to the growth of the business entity. These additional costs, while perhaps necessary, do not produce additional units. Thus, the cost per unit will be increased to reflect these additional expenses. For example, accounting and statistical data are necessary to furnish the decision-making information. Paper work and red tape add to the per-unit cost. In our soft-drink-plant example, the increased average variable cost per unit was caused by employing more than the optimum number of workmen to operate the machinery available. Table 3-1 clearly shows the reduction of average variable cost per case as production increases from 50 cases to 1,400 per day.

Now, if we understand these concepts and those of fixed and variable costs, we are ready to draw a composite picture that will show *average total* cost per case at different levels of production. We will reduce our numbers to facilitate understanding and draw up some cost information. Suppose our costs are as indicated in Table 3-2.

TABLE 3-2

(1) Total Production, Cases	(2) Change in Total Production	(3) Total Fixed Costs	(4) Total Variable Costs	(5) Total All Costs	(6) Change in Total Cost	(7) (Col. 6 ÷ Col. 2) Average Cost of Producing One More Unit (Marginal Cost)
12		$20	$ 60	$ 80		
	12				$30	$\frac{30}{12} = \$2.50$
24		20	90	110		
	16				30	$\frac{30}{16} = 1.875$
40		20	120	140		
	10				45	$\frac{45}{10} = 4.50$
50		20	165	185		
	10				51	$\frac{51}{10} = 5.10$
60		20	216	236		
	5				44	$\frac{44}{5} = 8.80$
65		20	260	280		

TABLE 3-3

(1) Total Production	(2) Total Fixed Cost Divided by Total Production	(3) Average Fixed Cost per Case	(4) Total Variable Cost Divided by Total Production	(5) Average Variable Cost per Case	(6) Average Total Cost
12	$\frac{20}{12} =$	$1.67	$\frac{60}{12} =$	$5.00	$6.67
24	$\frac{20}{24} =$	0.84	$\frac{90}{24} =$	3.75	4.59
40	$\frac{20}{40} =$	0.50	$\frac{120}{40} =$	3.00	3.50
50	$\frac{20}{50} =$	0.40	$\frac{165}{50} =$	3.30	3.70
60	$\frac{20}{60} =$	0.33	$\frac{216}{60} =$	3.60	3.93
65	$\frac{20}{65} =$	0.30	$\frac{260}{65} =$	4.00	4.30

Did you read carefully the last column that designates marginal cost? Marginal cost indicates the average cost of producing "one more case" at different levels of production.[1] This is significant, as we shall see. All managerial decisions are marginal. They are concerned with the effect and the results of producing and selling "one more unit." Marginal cost was obtained by dividing the change in total cost as production moved from one level to another by the increase in case production between these same levels. A note of caution: Do not pass over the concept of marginal cost too lightly. Examine the illustration carefully.

From the cost data illustrated in Table 3-2, the average fixed cost, average variable cost, and average total cost per case at each level of production can be determined, as shown in Table 3-3.

Average total cost is nothing more than average fixed cost plus average variable cost. We can then superimpose marginal cost, and the picture we draw will be quite significant with respect to managerial decision making. See Figure 3-3.

As we have seen, the marginal cost curve depicts the addition to total cost caused by the production of "one more unit." For our analysis, the phrase "one more unit" is not quite accurate. Rather, our marginal cost curve shows the average addition to total cost caused when we move from one level of production to another. As an example,

[1] Strictly speaking, we have increased production by an amount larger than a single case, but this is due to the mechanics of our production line. The economic principle, however, remains the same.

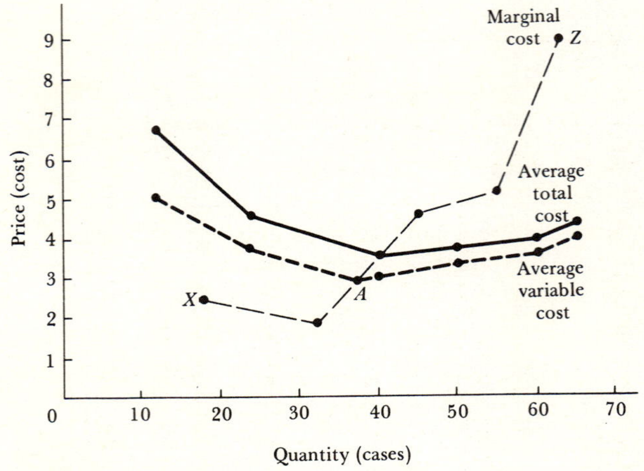

Figure 3-3 Cost curves.

when we increased production from 12 to 24 cases, the addition to total cost was $30. We can then divide the $30 by the additional units produced, 12, and arrive at an average additional cost per case of $2.50. This is the average marginal cost for all units from 12 through 24.

If a more detailed analysis would serve any good purpose, it would be possible to refine our cost figures to show the cost of "one more unit" instead of the average between production levels. Generally, such an explicit determination of marginal cost is neither desirable nor practical.

Let us now prepare a table (3-4) showing average cost per unit at different levels of production. We will use this table as a reference later in our discussion.

TABLE 3-4*

Production:	**12**	**24**	**40**	**50**	**60**	**65**
Average fixed cost	$ 1.67	$ 0.84	$ 0.50	$ 0.40	$ 0.33	$ 0.303
Average variable cost	5.00	3.75	3.00	3.30	3.60	4.00
Average total cost per case	$ 6.67	$ 4.59	$ 3.50	$ 3.70	$ 3.93	$ 4.303
Total manufacturing costs (ex., 12 × $6.67)	80.04	110.16	140.00	185.00	235.80	279.70
Difference in total cost		30.12	29.84	45.00	50.80	43.90
Increase in units produced		12	16	10	10	5
Average marginal cost between production levels (ex., $30.12 ÷ 12)		2.50	1.87	4.50	5.10	8.80

* Several figures have been rounded because of fractions of cents.

The significance of the cost data we have developed can be summarized as follows:

1. Average fixed cost per case will continue to decrease as the quantity manufactured increases.
2. Average variable cost per case will decrease to a point and will then increase as the quantity manufactured increases.
3. Marginal cost will initially fall and then increase rapidly as the quantity manufactured increases.
4. The marginal cost curve is the supply curve for the firm, if our goal is to maximize our profits. Supply is directly related to cost.

An examination of our picture and supporting cost schedules will clearly support the first three observations. Let us test item 4. (We must keep in mind that a profit to owners equal to what could be earned in an alternative economic activity (opportunity cost) should be included in our cost figures. This amount would be added to fixed cost and be spread over the units of production in the same manner that our fixed cost was distributed. Profit was not included in our cost figures in order not to complicate your understanding of the data.)

With reference to the picture of average cost per unit, Figure 3-3, we can see that the portion of the marginal cost line between the points *X* and *A* lies below the average variable cost per unit. The significance of this portion of the marginal cost line is that it indicates that a selling price of $3 per unit for 37 units will recover only the variable costs, not the fixed costs. A selling price of less than $3 per unit will not recover even the variable costs.

As indicated above, when we produce and sell 37 units at $3 each, we still are not recovering any of our fixed cost. In the very short run and in anticipation of price increases, we may be willing to absorb the fixed cost that would have to be paid if we did not produce any quantity at all. (When selling price is approximately $3.50 and the quantity sold is 40, we are recovering both fixed and variable cost. The owner's profit is included in fixed cost.) The quantity of 37 can be termed both the startup point and the shutdown point; that is, we will not produce any quantity if we cannot recover at least our variable costs, or we will discontinue production if sales fall below 37 unless we anticipate that the price will go up as indicated.

Our willingness to produce begins when the selling price is equal to average variable cost. Marginal cost represents the minimum price we will accept for each additional unit. Perhaps—we are willing to concede this point—but what about the marginal cost from point *A* to point *Z*? Does this portion of our marginal cost curve represent our willingness to supply? The answer is clearly yes, if we want to maximize our profits. Let us try an example.

Assume that we are selling 40 cases of soft drink at a price of $4 each. Referring to our cost curves, we can see that average total cost is $3.50. We are earning 50 cents per case with total earnings of $20. Would we not be willing to sell an additional 10 cases for $4 each? The answer is no, not if we did not want to lose 50 cents per case on the additional 10 cases. Total earnings would be reduced by $5. The total earnings would be $15. Why? Average total cost when we sell 50 units is $3.70. It would appear that we would earn 30 cents per case on the additional 10 cases. It may appear so, but you are not considering marginal cost. Our cost curves indicate that when production increases from 40 to 50 cases, the average marginal cost per case is $4.50. Selling price is only $4. We would lose 50 cents per case on the additional 10 cases. Another way of recognizing the same thing is to look at the change in total cost. The total cost to manufacture 40 cases is $140, or 40 times $3.50. The total manufacturing cost for 50 cases is $185, or an increase in total cost of $45. The additional revenue is $40. Loss on the sale of the additional 10 cases is $5. Do not brush! This is significant!

Marginal cost, then, is our supply curve for all quantities above the startup and shutdown points.

MATHEMATICS OF FINANCE

During your original interview, President Jones indicated that he was thinking about replacing some of his present production equipment. In addition, he mentioned the possibility of selling stocks or bonds. We recall that our elementary mathematics of finance course approached these types of problems via compound interest and present-value analysis. You'll be starting with Jones Electronics in a few days. Let's review.

Compound Interest and Present-value Concepts

Mathematicians and statisticians have developed many quantitative techniques that can be useful to the financial executive. We will examine several. It will not be our purpose to prove the validity of the techniques. Rather, we will examine the basic assumptions that are necessary to make them work and determine the significance of what we have when we have it. A mathematical computation within itself is precise and will give a precise answer. However, on most occasions, as indicated earlier, the financial executive is not dealing with precise data. On the contrary, more often than not, the data are of uncertain validity. However, regardless of their inherent quality, the data available must be used.

Quantitative techniques, even when based on rigid, precise assumptions, can furnish a "point of departure" for further inquiry. Mathematical models are not intended to make managerial decisions directly. Rather, they are used to analyze possible results of alternative courses of action. The emphasis in the last sentence is on the word "possible." This is so because, in general, the data we use are not precise because of forecasting difficulties. As an example, we cannot be certain that a stream of income dependent on business operations will remain constant during future periods. (We are really back to uncertainty again!) However, this does not mean that we should add to our difficulties by using illogical or incorrect methods of analysis. In short, the significant aspect of any decision is the informed judgment of management based upon a review of the best data available. We will start the examination by reviewing the mathematics of compound interest and present value.

There are two types of interest, *simple interest and compound interest.* Simple interest is that interest which is calculated once to cover the invested capital for the entire period. For example, $1,000 left at simple interest of 6 percent per year for a period of two years will amount to $1,120. At the end of the two-year period, the total interest earned amounts to 12 percent of $1,000, or $120. Compound interest is the interest that accrues on unpaid interest and principal. For example, $1,000 at 6 percent compound annual interest for three years will amount to $1,191.02. This total is calculated as follows:

Sum left at interest	$1,000			
Interest	60			
Amount end first year		$1,060		
Interest (6 percent)		63.60		
Amount end second year			$1,123.60	
Interest (6 percent)			67.42	
Amount end third year				$1,191.02

In essence, we earned interest not only on the principal of $1,000 all these years, but also on the unpaid interest earned each year.

You no doubt notice that we used the term *amount.*[1]

[1] We could have used the term *future value of a dollar.* You will undoubtedly see this term used in other texts.

When we speak of an amount or the compound amount, we mean the value of a sum left to earn interest for a given period of time. It is unnecessary to perform the multiplication for each year as we did in the example just presented. We can use compound interest tables. To facilitate our understanding of these tables, let's build a compound interest table using $1 as an amount and 4 percent as the rate of interest earned by that dollar.

Periods	
1	$1.000 × $1.04 = $1.040 amount of $1 for 1 period at 4%
2	1.040 × 1.04 = 1.082 amount of $1 for 2 periods at 4%
3	1.082 × 1.04 = 1.125 amount of $1 for 3 periods at 4%
4	1.125 × 1.04 = 1.170 amount of $1 for 4 periods at 4%
5	1.170 × 1.04 = 1.217 amount of $1 for 5 periods at 4%
6	1.217 × 1.04 = 1.265 amount of $1 for 6 periods at 4%

We could build a table at any rate of interest if we wanted to do it, but this is unnecessary. These tables, being mathematically precise, were developed many years ago and are found in the Appendix. Mathematicians express what we have done by the following formula: $a = 1 + i$. They are simply saying that the amount of $1 = $1 + interest compounded as many times as you wish. Thus, $a = (1 + i)^5$ would simply mean that we do exactly as we did above when we constructed the table. As an example, the compound amount of $1 at 4 percent for five periods is $1.2167 (1.04 × 1.04 × 1.04 × 1.04 × 1.04 = 1.2167). Assume we want to know the compound of $1,528 compounded annually at 4 percent for five periods. The answer would be $1,528 × 1.217, or $1,859.046. In essence, if $1 will grow to $1.217 when compounded at 4 percent for five periods, any number of dollars (and cents) will do likewise![1]

[1] When more than a single year is involved in such calculations and interest is compounded on something other than an annual basis, a few additional steps are required to secure the answer. The stated annual interest rate must be divided by the number of compounding periods which occur in a single year, and the number of years must be multiplied by the number of times compounding occurs in a single year.

For example, if a single sum of $10,000 is deposited today to earn interest at a stated rate of 6 percent compounded semiannually for a period of five years, what will be the final value of this deposit?

Step 1. Divide the stated rate 6 percent by 2, the number of times compounding occurs, 0.06/2 = 0.03, or 3 percent.

Step 2. Multiply the number of periods or years, 5, by the number of times compounding occurs in a given year, 2. Now you are dealing with 3 percent and 10 periods. In the compound amount table A-1 you will see the figure 1.344.

You now know that in the circumstances described $1 would have increased in value to $1.344, and the $10,000 would have become $10,000(1.344) = $13,440.

Conversely, if we are interested in the compound interest, we know it is simply the difference between the sum originally deposited and the total amount available at the end of the interest earning period. For example, if we are interested in the compound interest to be earned or paid on $1,528 over five periods, we can multiply the $1,528 by 1.217 and subtract the original sum of $1,528; or we can multiply the $1,528 by the interest factor 0.217 and arrive at the same answer.

Mathematicians would write the equation $i = (1 + i)^5 - 1$, which means the compound interest is equal to ($1 + 0.04) to the fifth power less the original sum of $1, or $0.217.

Compound sum of an annuity. A series of equal payments at regular intervals with interest compounded at a given rate is called an *annuity.* As an example, if we deposit $1 each year at interest and leave the deposits for a given number of periods, the total amount deposited plus the interest is the compound sum of an annuity. The equal payments are sometimes called *rents.*[1] The regular payments may be made at any given interval such as a month, three months, six months, or a year. The secret is to calculate the proper interest rate for the given period of time. For example, an interest rate of 6 percent per year is ½ percent per month, 1½ percent for three months, 2 percent for four months, 3 percent for six months, and 4 percent for nine months. Any number of months can be calculated by adding ½ percent interest for each month.

There are two types of annuities. The first is called an *ordinary annuity,* and the second is called an *annuity due.* If the amount is to be determined *immediately* after the last payment, it is an *ordinary annuity.* If the *interest continues* for one period after the last deposit is made, the total amount is known as an *annuity due.* For example:

1st deposit of $1.00	2d deposit of $1.00	3d deposit of $1.00	4th deposit of $1.00	5th deposit of $1.00	
/	/	/	/	/	/
Dec. 31 1968	Dec. 31 1969	Dec. 31 1970	Dec. 31 1971	Dec. 31 1972	Dec. 31 1973

If we want to know the compound amount of the annuity on December 31, 1972, we are talking about an *ordinary annuity.* If we wait until one year after the last payment or deposit was made, until December 31, 1973, we are talking about an *annuity due.*

[1] Do not confuse this terminology with the economic definition of the word "rent."

An example of a compound sum of an *ordinary annuity* at 4 percent interest for five periods is as follows:

Interest Earning Periods:	**1**	**2**	**3**	**4**	**5**			
Deposits	$1	$1	$1	$1	$1			Dates
						Earns no interest	$1.000	12-31-68
						Earns interest for 1 period	1.040	12-31-69
						Earns interest for 2 periods	1.082	12-31-70
						Earns interest for 3 periods	1.125	12-31-71
						Earns interest for 4 periods	1.170	12-31-72
Compound amount of an ordinary annuity at 4% for 4 periods							$5.417	

We have calculated the amount of this ordinary annuity by using compound interest table A-1. We have observed the number of periods each deposit will earn compound interest, recorded the compound amount for each deposit, totaled the compound amounts, and arrived at the amount of an ordinary annuity of five deposits compounded at 4 percent per period. Once we have calculated the amount of the ordinary annuity for $1 for any number of periods, we can multiply this factor by *X* dollars, representing equal rents for the same number of periods, and arrive at the compound amount of an annuity of *X* dollars.

We really went about this problem the hard way. Our solution involved looking up the interest factor for each deposit. This could be cumbersome and time-consuming if, say, 20 deposits were involved.[1] Fortunately, this is unnecessary. The multiplication will give exactly the same answer every time. We can, therefore, use the permanent table that has been constructed to give the compound amount of an ordinary annuity of $1 at selected interest rates for a limited number of periods. Table A-2 is such a table. In order to become completely familiar with table A-1 or A-2, it might be helpful to take table A-2 apart and see just how it has been constructed.

[1] In the case of annual payments which are unequal in amount, we are not dealing with real annuities as defined earlier. In such cases the cumbersome method of compounding single sums each year must be used, as in the example on the previous page.

COMPOUND AMOUNT OF AN ***ORDINARY ANNUITY*** **(4%)**

Interest Earning Periods:	**0**	**1**	**2**	**3**	**4**
Deposits (5)	$1	$1.04	$1.082	$1.125	$1.170
		1.00	1.040	1.082	1.125
Periodic deposits of $1		$2.04	1.000	1.040	1.082
			$3.122	1.000	1.040
				$4.247	1.000
Notice amount is determined immediately after last deposit (*Ordinary annuity*)					$5.417

The table clearly indicates that the $1 deposits will accumulate compound interest for the number of periods on deposit. Notice that each deposit grows as per Table A-1 at 4 percent. Table A-2 is nothing more than a combination of Table A-1 calculations! Check Tables A-1 and A-2 and, except for possible rounding adjustments, note the relationship of the two tables. Master these tables now, if you have not done so, and much time and confusion will be saved later. We use these tables constantly throughout our study.

Our next task is to calculate the amount of an *annuity due*. Definition is crucial, and lack of understanding of the distinction between an ordinary annuity and an annuity due can be fatal! Again, an annuity due remains on deposit at the appropriate interest rate one period after the last deposit was made. The annuity due is illustrated as follows:

COMPOUND AMOUNT OF AN ***ANNUITY DUE*** **(4%)**

Interest Earning Periods:	**0**	**1**	**2**	**3**	**4**	**5**
Deposits (5)	$1	$1	$1	$1	$1	
					Earns 1 period	$1.040
				Earns 2 periods		1.082
			Earns 3 periods			1.125
		Earns 4 periods				1.170
	Earns 5 periods					1.217
Notice amount is determined one period after last deposit *(Annuity due)*						$5.634

Again, we have constructed the illustration above the hard way. We used the compound interest table (A-1), and looked up each factor for each rent. Fortunately, this detailed type of calculation is not necessary. We know, however, that Table A-2 has been constructed to give us the answer for an *ordinary annuity* for any number of periods at various rates of interest. Now we are not dealing with an ordinary annuity; rather, we are dealing with an annuity due.

Therefore, we must convert the *ordinary annuity* table for use in calculating an *annuity due.* We can convert Table A-2 by using one more period and subtracting $1. This conversion is necessary because, as you will notice, Table A-2 starts with the figure $1 at the end of the first period. This indicates that the last rent or payment draws no interest (an ordinary annuity).

The distinction between an ordinary annuity and an annuity due, as indicated, is the fact that the last deposit does earn interest for one period before the total value of the annuity due is calculated. Thus, our answer of 5.634, which we calculated by using the factors contained in Table A-1 for the five individual deposits, will be found on Table A-3 for six periods at 4 percent interest less $1. When we subtract the $1, we eliminate the last deposit, which was not made! We are thus able to convert an ordinary annuity table into a table to be used for an annuity due. Why? Simply because when we are dealing with an annuity due, all deposits earn interest one more period, but there is no deposit the final period.

COMPOUND AMOUNT OF AN ***ANNUITY DUE***
Five deposits at 4%

Interest Earning Periods:	**0**	**1**	**2**	**3**	**4**	**5**
Deposits (5)	$1	$1.04	$1.082	$1.125	$1.170	$1.217
		1.00	1.040	1.082	1.125	1.170
		$2.04	1.000	1.040	1.082	1.125
			$3.122	1.000	1.040	1.082
				$4.247	1.000	1.040
					$5.417	
						$5.634

Once we have determined the annuity factor for an annuity of $1, we can multiply this factor times any number of dollars involved in the annuity problem. As an example, assume we want to know the amount of an annuity due when equal payments of $500 are made for five periods at 5 percent. We would multiply our factor 5.634 × $500 to arrive at the amount.

Mathematicians would express what we have done as follows:

1. Compound amount $= (1 + i)^n$
2. Compound interest $= (1 + i)^n - 1$
3. Compound amount of an ordinary annuity $= \dfrac{(1 + i)^n - 1}{i}$
4. Compound amount of an annuity due $= \dfrac{(1 + i)^{n+1}}{i}(1 + i)$

Examples of these formulas, where n is equal to five periods and the given sum is \$2,000, would appear as follows (the appropriate tables are used):

1. Compound amount of \$2,000 at 4 percent for five periods $= \$2{,}000 \times 1.217 = \underline{\underline{\$2{,}434}}$

2. Compound interest

$$
\begin{aligned}
&= \$2{,}000(1.217 - 1)\\
&= \$2{,}434 - \$2{,}000\\
&= \underline{\underline{\$434}}
\end{aligned}
$$

3. Compound amount of an ordinary annuity

$$
\begin{aligned}
&= \$2{,}000\,\frac{1.04^5 - 1}{0.04}\\
&= \$2{,}000\,\frac{1.217 - 1}{0.04}\\
&= \$2{,}000\,\frac{0.217}{0.04}\\
&= \$2{,}000(5.425)\\
&= \$10{,}850
\end{aligned}
$$

4. Compound sum of an annuity due

$$
\begin{aligned}
&= \$2{,}000\left[\frac{(1.04)^{5+1} - 1}{0.04} - 1\right]\\
&= \$2{,}000\left[\frac{(1.04)^6 - 1}{0.04} - 1\right]\\
&= \$2{,}000\left(\frac{1.265 - 1}{0.04} - 1\right)\\
&= \$2{,}000\left(\frac{0.265}{0.04} - 1\right)\\
&= \$2{,}000(6.634 - 1)\\
&= \$2{,}000 \times 5.634\\
&= \$11{,}268
\end{aligned}
$$

Present Value of a Single Sum

We have seen that a sum deposited and left to accrue interest will grow to a larger amount. We will now reverse the process. The present value of \$1 at a given rate of interest is equivalent to the amount that must be deposited now and left at the given rate of interest for a given period of time in order to grow to \$1 over the time period.

Mathematicians would write a formula to express the present value of $1 as follows:

$\text{P.V.} = \frac{\$1}{(1+i)^n}$ which means the present value of $1 to be received *n* periods in the future,

if money is worth 1 interest per period $= \frac{\$1}{1. + \text{interest rate}}$.

We can illustrate a 4 percent interest rate as follows:

$\frac{\$1}{1.04} =$ $1.000 ÷ 1.04 = $0.962 = present value of $1 discounted for 1 period at 4 percent

$\frac{1}{(1.04)^2} =$ 0.962 ÷ 1.04 = 0.925 = present value of $1 discounted for 2 periods at 4 percent

$\frac{1}{(1.04)^3} =$ 0.925 ÷ 1.04 = 0.889 = present value of $1 discounted for 3 periods at 4 percent

$\frac{1}{(1.04)^4} =$ 0.889 ÷ 1.04 = 0.855 = present value of $1 discounted for 4 periods at 4 percent

$\frac{1}{(1.04)^5} =$ 0.855 ÷ 1.04 = 0.822 = present value of $1 discounted for 5 periods at 4 percent

$\frac{1}{(1.04)^6} =$ 0.822 ÷ 1.04 = 0.790 = present value of $1 discounted for 6 periods at 4 percent

Therefore, the present value of $1 discounted for six periods at 4 percent is equal to 79 cents, which means that if we could deposit 79 cents to earn compound interest at 4 percent per period for six periods, we would have a total of $1 at the end of the sixth period. This calculation can be illustrated further by starting with 79 cents and adding 4 percent interest each period for six periods.

End of Interest Earning Periods:	**6**	**5**	**4**	**3**	**2**		
Deposit	$0.79						
Int. 4%	0.032						
Total		$0.822					
Int. 4%		0.032					
Total			$0.854				
Int. 4%			0.034				
Total				$0.888			
Int. 4%				0.036			
Total					$0.924		
Int. 4%					0.037		
Total						$0.961	
Int. 4%						0.038	
Total							$0.999

Stated another way, $1 is 1.265 percent of 79 cents. Does the number 1.265 look familiar? It is the compound interest factor from Table A-1 for six periods at 4 percent! In short, we have proof that the answer to the question of the present value of $1 discounted for six periods at 4 percent is 79 cents. We can multiply our 79-cent present-value figure by the compound interest factor for six periods at 4 percent, 1.265, and the result is $1. This proof clearly illustrates, we hope, the distinction between the compound interest concepts and the present-value concept.

Compound interest starts with a sum and builds forward to an amount.

Now Six periods at
4% compound interest
79¢ ——→——→ | = $1

The present-value concept starts with an amount to be received six periods in the future and discounts or removes the interest to be earned during the six periods to arrive at a present value!

Six periods at
4% discount
79¢ = | ←——←—— | $1

Discount factors for several periods at various rates of interest have been calculated for us and can be found on Table A-3. To illustrate the interrelationships which exist between compounding and discounting, we may use the following example.

Question: What is the maximum price which you would pay now to an insurance company for its promise to give you $1 six years from today? The maximum amount which you can earn on your available funds is 4 percent.

Answer: Seventy-nine cents. This is the maximum which you would pay, since you could place your 79 cents in the bank at 4 percent and in six years it would have grown to $1. If the insurance company had asked 85 cents for its promise, you would naturally have rejected its offer, taken your 85 cents, put it in the bank at 4 percent for six years, and watched it grow to $1.075.

$85(1.265) = 1.075$, or $\$1.07\frac{1}{2}$

Present Value of an Annuity

The present value of an annuity is the sum that must be deposited at interest now to permit regular periodic *equal withdrawals.* When we examined the *compound amount* of an annuity earlier, we were talking about regular periodic deposits left at interest until the end of a term. Now when we speak of the *present value of an annuity,* we are talking about regular periodic withdrawals.

If the first withdrawal is not made until the amount deposited earns interest for one period, we are dealing with the present value of an *ordinary annuity.* If the first withdrawal is made at the same time as the first deposit is made, we are dealing with the present value of an *annuity due.* This is a parallel concept to our ordinary annuity and the annuity due.

Note carefully the difference between the term "ordinary annuity" when we are speaking of compound sums and the term "ordinary annuity" when we are dealing with present values. The lack of understanding of this distinction can be fatal! Compare the two concepts immediately!

The present value of an ordinary annuity at 4 percent that will permit the withdrawal of $1 for six periods is calculated as follows:

PRESENT VALUE OF AN ORDINARY ANNUITY DISCOUNTED SIX PERIODS AT 4%

Present Value of Each Dollar	Periods:	Dec. 31, 1967	Dec. 31, 1968 1	Dec. 31, 1969 2	Dec. 31, 1970 3	Dec. 31, 1971 4	Dec. 31, 1972 5	Dec. 31, 1973 6
$\frac{1}{1.04} = \$0.962$			$0.962					
$\frac{1}{(1.04)^2} = 0.925$				0.925				
$\frac{1}{(1.04)^3} = 0.889$					0.889			
$\frac{1}{(1.04)^4} = 0.855$						0.855		
$\frac{1}{(1.04)^5} = 0.822$							0.822	
$\frac{1}{(1.04)^6} = 0.790$								0.790
$5.243 Present value of an ordinary annuity of six payments of $1 at 4%.								

The example illustrated above shows that if we deposit $5.243 now to earn interest at 4 percent, we can withdraw $1 for six periods. After the last withdrawal of $1, the balance will be zero. In other words, if I owe you $1 per period for six periods, I could deposit $5.243 to earn interest at 4 percent per period now and withdraw $1 each period for six periods and pay my total obligation of $6. Again, consider the insurance company example previously cited, and determine what is the maximum amount which you would pay for their promise to pay you an annuity of $1 per year for six years. As a further illustration, consider the following: An amount is deposited. This total amount will earn interest at the specified rate for the first period. A withdrawal is then made to lower the amount. The balance earns interest until the next regular withdrawal. This process is repeated until, when the final withdrawal is made at the end of the given period, the balance of the fund after the last withdrawal is zero.

	Deposit Now	First Period	Second Period	Third Period	Fourth Period	Fifth Period	
	$5.243						
Add 4% int.	0.209	$5.452					
Less		—1.000	$4.452				
Add 4% int.			0.178				
Bal.			$4.630				
Less			—1.000	$3.630			
Add 4% int.				0.145			
Bal.				$3.775			
Less				—1.000	$2.775		
Add 4% int.					0.111		
Bal.					$2.886		
Less					—1.000	$1.886	
Add 4% int.						0.075	
Bal.						$1.961	
Less						—1.000	$0.961
Add 4% int.							0.038
Bal.							$0.999
Less							—1.000
Bal.							0
Amount deposited	$5.243						
Interest earned	0.756						
Total available	$5.999						

Did you notice when the first withdrawal was made in the illustration above? What type of annuity are we dealing with?

The present value of *annuity due* can be calculated exactly the same way, except that the amount withdrawn on the date of the initial deposit will earn no interest. One dollar must be deposited in full to cover the first withdrawal.

PRESENT VALUE OF AN ANNUITY DUE DISCOUNTED SIX PERIODS AT 4%

	Present Value of Each Dollar	Periods:	Dec. 31, 1967 1	Dec. 31, 1968 2	Dec. 31, 1969 3	Dec. 31, 1970 4	Dec. 31, 1971 5	Dec. 31, 1972 6
	\$1.000	Earns no interest						
$\frac{1}{1.04} =$	0.962	Earns interest 1 year						
$\frac{1}{(1.04)^2} =$	0.925	Earns interest 2 years						
$\frac{1}{(1.04)^3} =$	0.889	Earns interest 3 years						
$\frac{1}{(1.04)^4} =$	0.855	Earns interest 4 years						
$\frac{1}{(1.04)^5} =$	0.822	Earns interest 5 years						
	\$5.453							

The above illustration shows the calculations for the present value of an annuity due at 4 percent of six rents of \$1. If the amount of \$5.453 were deposited at 4 percent, it would be possible to withdraw \$1 on the date of deposit and \$1 thereafter for five periods. The present-value factors for an ordinary annuity are found in Table A-4. To convert the present value of an ordinary annuity table for us in calculating the present value of an annuity due, find the factor at the appropriate discount rate for one period less than the number of payments or withdrawals required and add \$1 for the first payment that is deposited and immediately withdrawn before interest is earned.

What is the amount to be deposited on January 1, 1971, to earn interest at 5 percent so that seven equal withdrawals of \$1,000 can be made at the end of each year? The first withdrawal is to be made on January 1, 1971. Stated another way—what is the present value of an annuity due discounted seven periods at 5 percent?

Present-value factor from Table A-4, six periods at 5 percent	\$5.076
Add \$1 for withdrawal 1/1/71	1.000
Present value of an annuity due of \$1 for seven periods at 5 percent	\$6.076
Required annual withdrawal	× 1,000
	\$6,076

This has been quite a review! I've had enough—so I'm going to the golf course. *I would invite you to go* with me, but I really think you should work the problems at the end of the chapter. If you master these concepts now, we will breeze along later. In addition, you report for work Monday! Call me if you are free Saturday or Sunday afternoon and we'll try at least nine holes!

SUMMARY

The goal of this chapter was to arm the financial manager with two more of the basic tools of his trade. The economic concepts of supply and cost were introduced, and the financial manager and the economist were found to be not worlds apart, but only words apart.

You should be especially mindful of the fact that each of the factors of production requires compensation. Thus, the availability of land, labor, and capital to the firm will depend upon the firm's ability to compensate those factors at a level which is at least equal to the level of compensation available to them elsewhere. In short, the firm must meet the opportunity costs of the various factors of production if it hopes to attract them.

Cost analysis, then, is a fundamental activity of the financial manager. For the purposes of analysis, costs are normally categorized as fixed or variable. Fixed costs are those which are largely beyond the control of management, in the short run, and are unrelated to the firm's level of production. These costs, however, can be diagrammatically expressed in relation to production levels. Thus, fixed costs when expressed on a per-unit basis give rise to the downward-sloping cost curve developed in the chapter.

Variable costs, on the other hand, are those costs which do vary with production levels and are largely within management's control, in the short run. Variable costs, when expressed on a per-unit basis, normally produce a cost curve which falls initially and then gradually begins to rise. The characteristic shape of the variable cost curve can be explained with reference to the economies and the diseconomies of scale. For example, in our illustration of the bottling plant, you will note that as the number of workers increased from one to two, total production rose from 50 to 200 cases. This more-than-proportionate increase in production can be explained with reference to the increasing specialization and division of labor within our work force. These are economies of scale. Diseconomies of scale would be realized at that point when increases in the size of our labor force no longer cause increases in total production. Thus, in our bottling plant we can envision the situation in which our work force has grown so large that employees are tripping over one another and all production ceases.

The concepts of average total cost and marginal cost were then introduced. Average total cost is simply a combination of average fixed cost and average variable cost. The marginal cost or the cost of producing one more unit received extended treatment. Marginal cost is a critical concept, and the financial executive must appreciate its implications. If you are at all unsure of marginal analysis, go back now and build your competence in this area. Your first decision in Chapter 4 requires an understanding of this concept.

The final decision-making tool introduced in this chapter was the mathematics of finance. The discounting and compounding of a single sum or a series of equal payments or receipts is a daily activity for most financial executives. Almost any financial problem which can be envisioned entails compounding or discounting or some combination of the two. That is to say, almost all financial decisions involve our answers to one or more of the following questions:

1. What is the future or compound value of a single sum deposited or employed to earn a specified return over a certain period of time?
2. What is the future or compound value of a series of equal sums deposited or employed to earn a specified return over a certain period of time?
3. What is the present or now value of a single sum to be received at some future date?
4. What is the present or now value of a series of equal sums to be received over some future period of time?

Manufacturing corporations, commercial banks, life insurance companies, etc., are all faced with decisions which involve answers to questions very much like those posed above.

You should know and understand the techniques of present-value analysis. You should also be fully aware of the assumptions upon which the tables are founded. Once you know them and appreciate the circumstances of a particular problem, the task of adjusting a table so that its assumptions and the circumstances of the problem are compatible becomes quite easy.

QUESTIONS FOR DISCUSSION

1. What is the significance of the term "cost"?
2. Distinguish between fixed and variable cost. Illustrate.
3. Describe the "typical" fixed and variable cost curves.
4. What is marginal cost?
5. What is your opportunity cost of attending school?

6. Why (or why not) is the marginal cost curve the supply curve for the firm in the short run?

7. What is the "startup" or "shutdown" point?

8. What is the significance of the startup or shutdown point?

9. What are the economies and diseconomies of scale?

10. Why does the marginal cost curve cut the average variable and average total cost curves at their lowest points?

11. Distinguish between "simple interest" and "compound interest." Illustrate.

12. What is an ordinary annuity? Illustrate.

13. What is an annuity due? Illustrate.

14. Distinguish between the compound sum of an annuity due and the present value of an annuity due.

15. Examine Tables A-1 to A-4 and distinguish between them.

16. Why would you not be able to use Table A-3 or A-4 to calculate the compound sum or present value of the following annual payments or withdrawals?

First period	$1.00
Second period	1.25
Third period	1.50
Fourth period	1.75

PROBLEMS

1. The accountant for J. T. Jones Corporation has prepared the following information for you:

Output	Total Variable Cost
1	$ 2,000
2	2,500
3	3,000
4	4,000
5	5,000
6	6,000
7	10,010
8	16,000

Total fixed cost is 50 percent of the variable cost when the output is 1. President Jones has requested that you advise him the number of units that can be manufactured and sold if the selling price is set at $2,000 each.

2. XYZ Airlines has consulted with you concerning the feasibility and profitability of adding another flight to their regular schedule. The additional flight will originate at Pensacola, Florida, and fly nonstop to New Orleans.

   What information would you need to answer the question of profitability?

3. The production manager has estimated that average variable cost is $1 per unit when the plant is operating at 50 percent capacity and is producing 50,000 units. Further data reveal that average variable cost per unit will increase 10 cents per unit for each 10,000-unit increase in production. Likewise, the average variable cost will decrease 10 cents for each 10,000-unit decrease in production. Fixed costs at the present level of production are $1 per unit.

   He has requested that you prepare the cost curves with supporting schedules at 10,000-unit intervals up to 80,000 units. Beyond this point, he feels, additional production is not practical at the present level of prices.

4. A deposit of $10,000 is made in a savings bank and allowed to accumulate interest for four years.

   Determine the amount of the deposit at the end of this four-year period under each of the following conditions:
   a. Interest is compounded annually at a rate of 4 percent.
   b. Interest is compound semiannually at an annual rate of 4 percent.
   c. Interest is compounded monthly at an annual rate of 12 percent.

5. You are planning to make five equal annual deposits to a fund so that so you can accumulate $10,000. The deposits will earn interest at the rate of 5 percent annually. The first deposit will be made on December 31, 1971. How much must the deposits be if you want the $10,000 on:
   a. December 31, 1975
   b. December 31, 1976
   c. December 31, 1980

6. Suppose that you saved $100 per quarter for a period of five years and invested these savings at 8 percent compounded quarterly. Thereafter your accumulated funds drew interest at 4 percent compounded semiannually for a period of three years. At this time you drew down your balance for a house payment. How large a payment could you make?

7. What single sum would you have to deposit today in order to have $20,000 at the end of 20 years under the following conditions?
   a. The interest rate is 4 percent compounded annually.
   b. The interest rate is 4 percent compounded semiannually.

8. A relative left an estate that included an inheritance for you. You are to receive $10,000 on December 31, 1971. You plan to deposit this

amount to earn interest at 5 percent compounded annually. You further plan to make five equal withdrawals beginning on:

a. December 31, 1971
b. January 1, 1972
c. January 1, 1975

What would be the amount of each withdrawal in each of the three cases above?

9. William Gillespie is 10 years old today. His father desires to know what single sum deposited today will provide William with an annuity of $1,000 per year for each of his four years in college. William will enter college on his eighteenth birthday, and funds will earn 5 percent compounded annually over the entire time period.
   a. What is the amount required when William is 18 years of age?
   b. What is the amount to be deposited today by William's father?
   c. Compile a payout table showing the growth and withdrawal of the funds while William is in college.

10. Rework Problem 9 with the assumption that William's father desires to accumulate the required sum in (a) above by making annual deposits rather than depositing a single sum on William's tenth birthday.

11. You are entitled to an annuity of $1,000 per year for 10 years beginning at the end of one year. You have no pressing need for these funds and so you accumulate them. Following the final payment you plan to purchase a 10-year annuity. All funds earn 4 percent. What is the maximum 10-year annuity you can purchase?

12. A businessman is entitled to an annuity of $5,000 per year payable at the end of each year. The annuity has been computed on a 2 percent yield basis. He can earn 6 percent on the funds if he invests them in the business. Therefore, he asks for and receives the present value of the annuity and employs the funds in his own business for 10 years. At the end of this period he draws down the funds and purchases a 10-year retirement annuity. All interest is compounded annually.
   a. What is the present value of the first annuity?
   b. What amount will be accumulated during the first 10 years in which funds are employed in his business?
   c. What retirement annuity can he purchase?

REFERENCES

Bain, Joe S.: "Industrial Organization," pp. 145–169, John Wiley & Sons, Inc., New York, 1959.

Blodgett, Ralph: "Principles of Economics," chaps. 5–8, Rinehart & Company, Inc., New York, 1946.

Dorfmany, Robert: "Prices and Markets," chap. 3, Prentice-Hall, Inc., Englewood Cliffs, N.J., 1967.

Ferguson, C. E.: "Microeconomics Theory," chap. 7, Richard D. Irwin, Inc., Homewood, Ill., 1966.

Hart, William L.: "Mathematics of Investment," 4th ed., chaps. 1–9, D. C. Heath and Company, Boston, 1958.

Hilborn, C. E.: "Mathematics for Use in Business," chaps. 7, 8, 12–18, Houghton Mifflin Company, Boston, 1948.

Hummel, Paul M., and Charles L. Seebeck, Jr.: "Mathematics of Finance," 2d ed., McGraw-Hill Book Company, New York, 1956.

Johnston, J.: "Statistical Cost Analysis," McGraw-Hill Book Company, New York, 1960.

Leftwich, Richard H.: "An Introduction to Economic Thinking," chaps. 7, 8, Holt, Rinehart and Winston, Inc., New York, 1969.

Lloyd, Cliff: "Microeconomic Analysis," part II, Richard D. Irwin, Inc., Homewood, Ill., 1967.

Viner, J.: Cost Curves and Supply Curves, in S. J. Stigler and K. Boulding (eds.), "Readings on Prime Theory," Richard D. Irwin, Inc., Homewood, Ill., 1952.

Watson, Donald S.: "Price Theory and Its Uses," 2d ed., chaps. 9, 10, Houghton Mifflin Company, Boston, 1968.

Chapter Four

MARGINAL ANALYSIS AND THE SUPPLY DECISION

We have now examined several frameworks within which the financial manager must operate. Our frameworks are not all-inclusive. We will add more elements as our study continues. However, we have established a solid point of departure. Let's go to work.

When you reported to J. T. Jones, president of the Jones Electronic Corporation, for your first day of real work as the only financial executive in his relatively small business enterprise, he explained that he manufactures electrical components for television, aviation, and space hardware. Without a doubt, he is an engineering genius, but he has a problem. He has received an offer from Allied Electronics Co. for the purchase of 20,000 units at a price of $5 each. He asked you to outline the financial implications involved if he accepts the offer. He explained further that he knows absolutely nothing about financial matters and couldn't care less. He returned to his laboratory after he simply announced that—"the financial problem is your baby!"

As you settled back into your chair, you began to realize the tremendous responsibility that President Jones had just placed upon your shoulders. You sat silently for a few moments. Slowly, you began to gather your thoughts. It became quite clear that to analyze the financial implications of this decision, it would be necessary for you to be directly involved with the fundamental relationships of supply and cost. More explicitly, you would be concerned with marginal cost or "the cost of producing one more unit." You would be concerned with the effect this sale to Allied might or might not have on normal sales. You might or might not be concerned with the reaction of competitors. In short, you would be concerned with the practicability of the Jones Corporation's manufacturing the additional units to sell at a price of $5 each. Therefore, while the final answer might involve a simple arithmetical calculation, subtracting cost from selling price, the total analysis might be a bit more complex. The "financial problem" that you were examining clearly requires a more explicit and thorough understanding of the entire Jones operation. It will always be so. How, then, would you proceed to analyze the immediate problem in a meaningful manner?

CONTRIBUTION OF FINANCIAL STATEMENTS TO THE SUPPLY DECISION

First, we must build a decision-making framework which will contain only meaningful and pertinent information. Let's start with the financial statements of the organization. At our request, the accountant and his assistants furnish us with last year's balance sheet:

J. T. Jones
Balance Sheet as of December 31, 1970

Current Assets			**Current Liabilities**		
Cash		$27,000	Accounts Payable		0
Accounts Receivable		15,000	Notes Payable (6½%)		$ 4,500
Inventories			Other Current Liability		0
Finished Goods	$ 2,500				
Raw Materials	500	3,000			
Total Current Assets		$45,000	Total Current Liability		$ 4,500
Fixed Assets	$50,000		Long-term Liabilities		None
Less Accumulated					
Depreciation	25,000	25,000	Capital 1/1/70	$ 51,500	
			Add Profit, 1970	60,000	
				$111,500	
			Less Withdrawal*	46,000	
			J. T. Jones, Capital 12/31/70		65,500
Total Assets		$70,000	**Total Liabilities and Capital**		$70,000

* Includes Jones personal income tax.

The balance sheet indicates to us the assets that are available at this time to produce both the requirements for what we will term our normal sales and the additional order for Allied. The liability section of the balance sheet indicates that Jones Electronic has outstanding one obligation, the 6½ percent note payable. The capital section indicates that Jones started the year with $51,500 in capital, earned $60,000 during 1970, and withdrew $46,000, providing the accounts receivable, inventories, and fixed assets were valued correctly.

In short, the left-hand side of the balance sheet shows the value of the assets of the firm as represented by the book figures, while the right-hand side shows how the claims on those assets are divided between creditors and owners. *We have stated "the value of the assets as represented by the book figures." In reality, as we shall see later, the real "value" of the assets may, and probably will, be something else indeed.* This is to suggest that the "value" of the assets as shown by the records may be quite unrealistic. We will deal directly with this matter in Chapter 11. On the other hand, the creditors' claims against the assets should represent actual claims. In the Jones situation the only creditor of the firm is the bank, which holds our 6½ percent promissory note. The remaining or residual claims against the assets of the corporation are the claims of the owners, in this case the stockholders, Jones and his family.

As we review the balance sheet, it is obvious that it doesn't contribute very much toward the solution of our immediate problem—the additional order by Allied for 20,000 units at $5 each. On the other hand, the balance sheet does indicate that the company owes very little and may be in a position to borrow additional funds when and if necessary. It also shows us the progress President Jones has made since June 20, 1968. It was on this date that he resigned his position as a research engineer and started Jones Electronic in an oversized garage. We next examined the profit and loss statement.

Jones Electronic Corporation Profit and Loss Statement for Year Ended 12/31/70

Sales ($6 per unit on 100,000 units)	$600,000	
Cost of Goods Sold	500,000	
Gross Profit		$100,000
Administrative, General, and Selling Expense		40,000
Net Profit for Year		$ 60,000

The profit and loss statement adds little more. It does, however, indicate the normal selling price and the number of units sold last year.

In short, it is immediately apparent that the statements furnished by the accounting department are nothing more than historical records. The profit and loss statement represents a summary of the financial results of last year's operations. The balance sheet indicates the accumulated results since June 20, 1968, when J. T. Jones started his electronics manufacturing enterprise.

Clearly, as indicated, this type of historical data furnished to date by the accounting department has not been of much assistance except to establish the following:

1. Jones Electronic Corporation is making a profit at the current level of operations.
2. Its liquidity (that is, ability to pay current obligations) is excellent.

We now must request the accounting department to furnish additional data which is more directly related to our current discussion. We are concerned with the details of the cost of goods sold. The following statement is presented:

Jones Electronic Corporation Cost of Goods Sold for Year Ended 12/31/70

	Total	**Per Unit**
Material	$100,000	$1.00
Labor	200,000	2.00
Overhead	200,000	2.00
	$500,000	$5.00

You will perhaps note that we said the statements show that the corporation is making a profit and its liquidity position is excellent at the *current level of production.* We must not pass over this qualifying phrase too lightly. It is quite significant! If we decrease the level of production, and if the corporation sells less than the number of units it is now selling, perhaps, you may think it may not earn as much total profit as it is now earning. This may or may not be true! Would you be surprised if we said—it *may* earn less total profit if it sells more units at $6 each than it is currently selling? This is the essence of our present problem—except that the only price offered for the additional units is $5 per unit!

THE FLEXIBLE BUDGET

Your next step after receiving the financial statements indicated above is to request the accounting department to prepare a *flexible budget* that will represent estimated manufacturing costs based on historical data adjusted for all known changes in factor costs at various levels of plant capacity. The Jones enterprise has never had a flexible budget prepared before, and just the term you used caused mixed emotions in the accounting department. Your request sounded both complex and complicated. In reality it is not. Let's look at a flexible budget. Examine it carefully. Determine the type of information this statement provides, because it is a significant step forward toward the solution of our immediate problem. It is not absolutely necessary that you understand all the details needed for the preparation of a flexible budget. However, it is imperative that you understand what you have now that you have it. And, when you "understand what you have now that you have it," in the future you will be in a position to know whether or not your accounting colleagues have provided you with adequate data for the decision-making process!

As we examine the corporation's flexible budget, we can readily see that it is nothing more than a series of operating budgets based on different levels of productive activity. You will notice that operating expenses are classified and tabulated as fixed cost and variable cost. The flexible budget may appear in more detail as each operating item is examined to determine the fixed and variable portion. This determination is not always easy. Accountants by study and observation can make this determination. However, the cost of obtaining the information precisely by this method can be prohibitive.

We are not concerned here with proficiency in making the fixed cost–variable cost determination. However, it is essential that we understand the significance of the determination and have some familiarity with normal methods of determination and presentation. Certain quantitative techniques are available that may give a reasonably accurate picture of the division between the fixed and variable components of cost. We will review one such technique, known as the *b* formula, later in this chapter.

As we examine the flexible budget that has been prepared for the corporation, we see that total fixed cost is constant at $170,000 at all levels of production. Variable expenses do, in fact, vary at different levels of production. That is all there is to it. We simply determine the fixed and variable costs at different levels of production. In fact, it is nothing more than an elementary arithmetical exercise, once the fixed cost–variable cost determination has been made. The significance of the flexible budget lies not in the mechanical preparation but rather in what can be done with it once we have it. The problem of determining changes in variable and fixed expenses at different levels of production is discussed subsequently.

Cost Curves and the Flexible Budget Reconciled

Let's see what we can do with it. First a question: Does the flexible budget serve as an aid in determining the financial implications of ac-

JONES ELECTRONIC CORPORATION FLEXIBLE BUDGET

Units of Production: **% of Plant Capacity:**	**80,000** **45%**	**90,000** **50%**	**100,000** **55%**	**110,000** **60%**	**120,000** **65%**	**130,000** **70%**	**140,000** **75%**	**150,000** **80%**	**160,000** **85%**	**170,000** **90%**
Variable expense										
Direct material	$ 89,000	$ 99,000	$100,000	$110,000	$120,000	$130,000	$160,000	$200,000	$ 230,000	$ 330,000
Direct labor	185,000	190,000	200,000	220,000	240,000	270,000	294,000	450,000	625,000	850,000
Overhead										
Supplies										
Heat, Light, Power										
Adm., gen., and selling										
Total overhead, adm., gen., and selling	30,000	49,000	70,000	77,000	84,000	93,000	104,000	125,000	160,000	200,000
Total variable expense	$304,000	$338,000	$370,000	$407,000	$444,000	$493,000	$558,000	$775,000	$1,015,000	$1,380,000
Fixed expense										
Overhead	$150,000	$150,000	$150,000	$150,000	$150,000	$150,000	$150,000	$150,000	$ 150,000	$ 150,000
Adm., gen., and selling	20,000	20,000	20,000	20,000	20,000	20,000	20,000	20,000	20,000	20,000
Total fixed expense	$170,000	$170,000	$170,000	$170,000	$170,000	$170,000	$170,000	$170,000	$ 170,000	$ 170,000
Total cost	$474,000	$508,000	$540,000	$577,000	$614,000	$663,000	$728,000	$945,000	$1,185,000	$1,550,000

Units of Production:	**80,000**	**90,000**	**100,000**	**110,000**	**120,000**	**130,000**	**140,000**	**150,000**	**160,000**	**170,000**
% of Plant Utilization:	**45%**	**50%**	**55%**	**60%**	**65%**	**70%**	**75%**	**80%**	**85%**	**90%**
Total cost	$474,000.00	$508,000.00	$540.000,00	$577,000.00	$614,000.00	$663,000.00	$728,000.00	$945,000.00	$1,185,000.00	$1,550,000.00
Difference in total cost		34,000.00	32,000.00	37,000.00	37,000.00	49,000.00	65,000.00	217,000.00	240,000.00	365,000.00
Average marginal or differential cost per unit (difference in total cost ÷ change in units produced)*		3.40	3.20	3.70	3.70	4.90	6.50	21.70	24.00	36.50
Average variable cost per unit†	3.80	3.75+	3.70	3.70	3.70	3.79+	3.98	5.16	6.34+	8.11
Average fixed cost per unit‡	2.12+	1.88+	1.70	1.54+	1.41+	1.30+	1.21+	1.13+	1.06	1.00
Average total cost per unit §	5.92	5.63	5.40	5.24+	5.11+	5.09+	5.19	6.29+	7.40	9.11+

* We have found the average marginal cost at various levels of production by taking the difference in total cost between the several levels of production and dividing it by the increase in production between levels (for example, $508,000 — $474,000 = $34,000, and 34,000/10,000 units = $3.40 per unit).
† We have determined the average variable cost per unit at different levels of production by dividing total variable cost by total number of units produced at that level (for example, $304,000/80,000 units = $3.80 per unit).
‡ We have obtained the average fixed cost per unit at different levels of production by dividing total fixed cost by the number of units to be produced (for example, $170,000/80,000 units = $2.12 per unit).
§ Average total cost per unit = average variable cost per unit plus average fixed cost per unit.

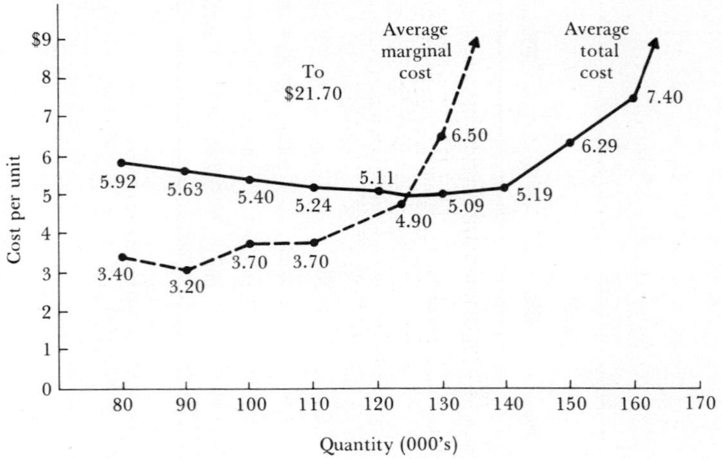

Figure 4-1

cepting the additional order of 20,000 units? Yes, it does. Take the same information, rearrange it, add a few elementary arithmetical calculations, and see what you have.

With specific reference to our supply-cost framework developed in Chapter 3, let's develop our average total cost and marginal cost curves from the data just obtained from the flexible budget. Let's focus or zero in on the marginal cost curves, as shown in Figure 4-1.

Can you determine whether or not it would be profitable to accept the order after examining the cost curves? Let's leave this approach momentarily and examine the same question from another point of view.

As a point of departure, we need a detailed analysis of the cost data presented earlier. Notice that we have added the administrative, general, and selling expenses. Notice also that we are using our *present level* of production (100,000 units).

	Total	Total Fixed Cost	Fixed Cost per Unit (100,000 Units)	Total Variable Cost	Variable Cost per Unit (100,000 Units)
Cost of goods sold:					
Material	$100,000			$100,000	$1.00
Labor	200,000			200,000	2.00
Overhead	200,000	$150,000	$1.50	50,000	0.50
Adm., gen., and selling	40,000	20,000	0.20	20,000	0.20
Totals	$540,000	$170,000	$1.70	$370,000	$3.70

The total unit cost is \$5.40 (\$1.70 fixed cost plus \$3.70 variable cost). The \$6 selling price indicates a profit of 60 cents per unit (60 cents per unit × 100,000 units = \$60,000 reported profit).

At first blush, it would appear that if average total cost is \$5.40 per unit, then the sale of 20,000 additional units at \$5 each would result in a loss of 40 cents per unit (a total loss of \$8,000). The general manager of the Jones organization is taking exactly this position. His recommendation is to decline the offer of \$5 per unit. He would insist that the price cover the average total cost of \$5.40 as calculated earlier.

The significance of the analysis to follow is that it clearly indicates that if the financial executive does not understand the supply-cost framework within which the firm is operating, then considerable income from this offer and like offers may be lost. Let us reexamine the cost-per-unit data presented by the accounting department and recall certain other information presented in the accounting statements.

1. The Jones organization is operating at a profit. Therefore, fixed costs are covered.
2. Based on the information from the flexible budget and/or cost curves, the variable cost should be \$3.70 per unit. Should Jones' cost factors (labor, material, overhead) change during the contract period, then the \$3.70 per unit variable cost will have to be adjusted upward or downward. For our purposes, and for the moment, the variable costs will remain constant. That is, the price we pay for labor, materials, and other expense items will not change.

Let us now combine our supply-cost framework with some basic economic and/or accounting information and watch the \$8,000 loss turn into a \$26,000 profit.

MARGINAL COST OR DIFFERENTIAL COST

As indicated earlier, economists call the concept we are about to discuss *marginal cost.* Accountants term this concept *differential cost.* The fact that each discipline calls the concept by a different name is immaterial. The significant thing is to know that they are both talking about the same thing.

The general manager could have arrived at his total cost per unit from our flexible budget and/or cost curves as follows:

Variable cost per unit	\$3.70
Fixed cost per unit	1.70
Total cost per unit	\$5.40

Total fixed costs have been covered by our present sales volume of $600,000 or 100,000 units. We know this to be the case because a profit is indicated.[1] We now have only variable costs to be concerned with as we anticipate the additional order. Therefore:

Selling price—additional order	$5.00
Less variable cost per unit	3.70
Contribution to profit per unit	$1.30

Total additional profit if order accepted: $1.30 × 20,000 units = $26,000

We have established that as a first approximation, one of the financial implications of the additional order of 20,000 units could be an increase in profit of $26,000, when only incremental costs are correctly computed. As indicated earlier, in addition to the profit consideration of the Allied offer, we must investigate the following questions:

1. Will the sale of 20,000 units to Allied disturb our present markets and the present selling price in such markets?
2. Is there any problem with possible retaliation from other manufacturers?

Our examination of these questions indicates:

1. That the additional order will not disturb our present market. Allied will not be reselling to our present customers.
2. That we have excess capacity and that labor and material costs will remain constant.
3. That no other manufacturer can violate our patent protection.

President Jones was quite pleased with your analysis. He asked one further question. "At our present level of production (100,000 units), how many units must we sell to cover all costs—in essence, to break even?"

BREAKEVEN ANALYSIS

When total fixed cost, average variable cost per unit, and selling price per unit are known, breakeven analysis is a simple grade school calculation. Our breakeven point will be that level of sales at which all costs are covered. At the breakeven point we will be neither earning a profit nor incurring a loss.

[1] As you know, profit will appear at a particular sales level only after fixed and variable costs are completely covered.

Jones Electronic Corporation Breakeven Analysis for Year Ended 12/31/70

Unit selling price	$6.00
Less average variable cost	−3.70
Contribution per unit (contribution toward fixed cost and then profit)	$2.30

1. You will notice that we have eliminated the variable cost by subtracting the unit variable cost from the unit selling price.
2. Total fixed costs as indicated by our flexible budget are $170,000.
3. The breakeven point occurs when all costs are covered—variable and fixed.
4. Therefore, if each unit "contributes" $2.30 toward fixed cost, it is a simple matter to divide $2.30 into $170,000 and arrive at the number of units that must be sold to cover all cost, to break even!

$$\frac{\$170{,}000}{\$2.30} = \underline{\underline{73{,}913}} \text{ units (rounded)}$$

Total sales volume of 73,913 units × $6 yields an approximate total dollar sales volume of $443,478 to break even.

COST-PROFIT-VOLUME RELATIONSHIP

Every additional unit sold after 73,913 units will "contribute" $2.30 each toward total profit. To test this example further:

Total units sold by Jones	100,000
Breakeven volume	73,913
Units sold beyond breakeven point	26,087
	× $2.30
Reported profit	$60,000.10 (approx.)

When you presented your illustration in the conference room, the general manager challenged your calculations. He noted that every unit after the breakeven point, 73,913 units, sold for $6, not $2.30! Therefore, he said, total profit should be 26,087 units × $6, not $2.30. He was quickly reminded that each one of the additional 26,087 units still had a variable cost of $3.70 and therefore the "contribution" to profit after 73,913 units were sold was $2.30 per unit, not $6!

The general manager replied that this type of analysis was fine if the selling price remained constant at $6 per unit throughout the year. "What would we do if the selling price did change one or more times throughout the year? Then we could not subtract the variable cost per unit from the selling price per unit and get the contribution to profit." The general manager is correct. However, if the selling price should change, we would simply resort to averages with the following formula:

$$\text{Breakeven} = \frac{\text{total fixed cost}}{1 - \dfrac{\text{total variable cost}}{\text{total sales volume}}}$$

Let's look at the formula a little closer. Isn't it doing exactly the same thing we did before, only this time we are dealing with totals and averages? Let's test this second approach to breakeven analysis.

$$\text{Breakeven point} = \frac{\$170{,}000 \text{ (total fixed cost)}}{1 \text{ (or } 100\%) - \dfrac{\$370{,}000 \text{ (total variable cost)}}{\$600{,}000 \text{ (total sales volume)}}}$$

As we divide \$600,000 into \$370,000, we are really determining the percentage total variable cost is of total sales, or \$370,000/600,000 = $61\frac{2}{3}$ percent. If total variable cost is $61\frac{2}{3}$ percent, total "contribution" per sales dollar is $38\frac{1}{3}$ percent (100 percent — $61\frac{2}{3}$ percent). Therefore, if total fixed cost (\$170,000) is equal to $38\frac{1}{3}$ percent of the total dollar sales necessary to break even, we can divide \$170,000 by $38\frac{1}{3}$ percent and calculate the sales volume in dollars at the breakeven point, or \$170,000/0.38$\frac{1}{3}$ = \$443,472!!!

We have seen that breakeven analysis gives management a clear picture of the cost-profit-volume relationship. It presents, in a clear and concise manner, a picture that could require voluminous accounting reports and statements. However, knowledge implies at least two significant things. They are, first, a clear understanding of the basic data necessary to achieve the goal of our analysis and, second, an understanding of the significance of what we have when we have it. Clearly, breakeven analysis is an analytical tool that can be helpful in analyzing past experience in a meaningful manner and can provide a point of departure for planning in the immediate future.

SIGNIFICANCE OF FIXED-VARIABLE COST RELATIONSHIP

In our analysis of the offer made to the corporation, we have used certain basic assumptions based upon experience and historical data. These assumptions were that variable cost would remain constant at \$3.70 per unit and total fixed cost would remain constant for the increase in production. As a general rule, accountants adopt these assumptions on the basis that any cost change within the time period involved will be insignificant within relative ranges of production. Of course, if the changes in costs are significant as production moves from one level to another, these changes must be recognized. When factor costs or economies of scale change significantly, causing the variable cost per unit to change significantly, then the analysis is more sophisticated.

Using the cost-profit-volume relationship developed earlier for the enterprise as a point of departure, let us relax the rigid assumptions and decrease the variable cost per unit while permitting total fixed cost to increase. Let us assume that the additional production of the 20,000 units will increase fixed cost in the amount of $5,000 and, because of the economies of scale developed in a supply-cost framework, variable cost per unit will fall from $3.70 to $3.20.

The method of analysis will be the same.

Selling price	$5.00	
Less average variable cost per unit	—3.20	
Contribution to additional fixed cost and profit	$1.80	
	×20,000	additional units
	$36,000	
Less additional fixed cost	—5,000	
Profit accruing from the additional order of 20,000 units	$31,000	

But, is this all? No, it is not! If the increase in production levels results in a decrease in *average* variable cost per unit equal to 50 cents, we will earn an additional 50 cents per unit on all units sold, including the first 100,000! *Total* additional profit as a result of the new order will be $81,000! Do you understand the significance of this last sentence?

Now, assume that diseconomies of scale cause the *average* variable unit cost to increase to $4 and total fixed cost increases by $5,000.

Selling price	$5.00
Less average variable unit cost	—4.00
Contribution to additional fixed cost and profit	$1.00
	×20,000
	$20,000
Less additional fixed cost	—5,000
Income accruing from new order	$15,000

But, is this all? What about the additional 30 cents in average variable cost for the first 100,000 units? We will lost $30,000 on "normal" sales!

We have seen that a very significant point in our analysis of cost data is the distinction between fixed cost and variable cost. An effective way to illustrate the significance of the relationship between fixed and variable cost is to prepare what is known as a "breakeven chart." Using the data we have just developed for Jones Electronic, we will develop this chart for the next meeting of the executive committee. While we really have no quarrel with the general manager, our "breakeven chart" should eliminate all doubt about the validity of our position. Our accountant agreed to prepare it for us, and he did so, using the following information. Hopefully, this graphic presentation (see Figure 4-2) will enable those members of the executive committee who are unfamiliar with accounting concepts to visualize both the problem and our solution. Having the right answer is one thing, but selling it to the executive committee may be quite another.

Total fixed cost	$170,000
Variable cost per unit	$3.70
Price per unit	$6.00

The breakeven chart looks beautiful—but in this instance it may not be correct! You examine the chart carefully; does it really reflect your data? The general manager said the chart was incorrect. Was he in error?

We were quite pleased with the general manager's observation that the breakeven chart prepared by the accountant was in error. It was! In the competitive business world, and especially where a small firm is involved, one cannot always be right. Conversely, one cannot con-

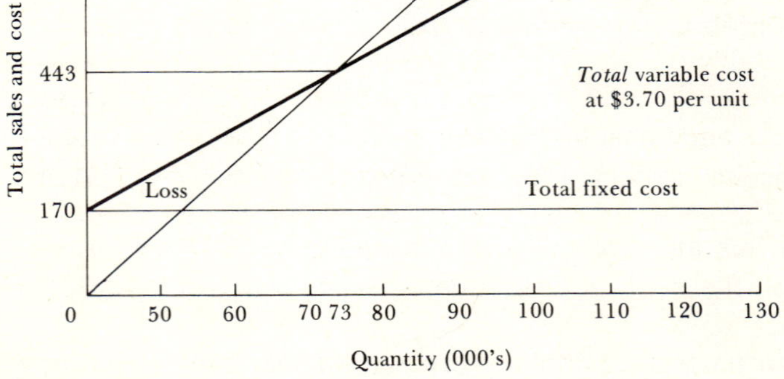

Figure 4-2

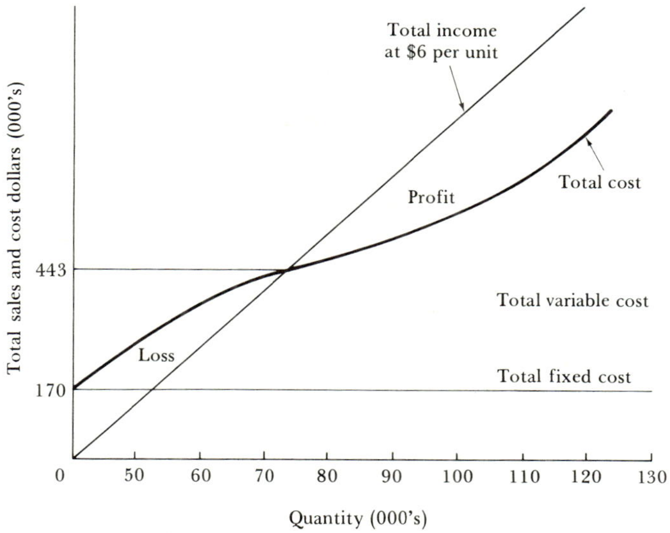

Figure 4-3

tinually point out that the other fellow is wrong. We must operate as a team, with each of us making a contribution to the firm's policies, if possible. Therefore, when one continually points out that another person is wrong, this action in itself—even though quite correct—is not politic. In other words, we can be dead right, and yet so wrong!

The general manager pointed out that we went through careful preparation and made a detailed examination of fixed and variable cost at different levels of production when we prepared our flexible budget and cost curves. He then presented the breakeven chart shown in Figure 4-3. Does his chart more clearly reflect the Jones operation? It certainly does, and you were delighted.

It has not been our purpose to make the financial executive proficient in all the uses of breakeven and marginal or differential analysis. However, not only must he be able to recognize a problem in which this type of analysis may be helpful, but he must realize that in general all management decisions are marginal. Management is almost always weighing the effect of "one more unit" of labor, material, sales, or equipment. Variable cost is therefore quite significant after sales have passed the breakeven point. We have referred to the *b* formula earlier. Let's pause a moment and assess its potential briefly.

The *b* Formula

In the preparation of the flexible budget for the Jones organization we accepted certain elements of cost as fixed and other elements as variable.

It was pointed out then that this determination is not always easy to make. This is especially true in large organizations. Several problems arise. The first problem is the matter of definition. As a point of departure, we must keep in mind that the well-educated financial executive, as well as any other well-educated man, must "never let his education interfere with his common sense." As an example, a given assembly-line operation may require 10 men to operate the line efficiently. Economists and accountants may literally consider the wages paid to men as a variable cost. It is probably quite true that the entire assembly line could be operated with one, two, or three men, and the wage cost could be considered as being within the control and discretion of management and would, in fact, vary with the volume of production. This assembly-line operation would thus come within our definition of the variable cost as defined in Chapter 3. However, if management always uses 10 men to operate the assembly line, then for all practical purposes, the wages of these 10 men could be considered as fixed. This last observation assumes, of course, that the assembly-line employees work a standard work week and are paid on an hourly or weekly basis.

Consider another problem. Let us assume we are analyzing the firm's electricity expense for a given period of time. We know that a certain amount of electricity is necessary simply to light the working premises. In addition, we know that if additional electricity is used in the working process, such as for the operation of high-speed or low-speed motors, the additional expense for electricity may be related to the number of direct labor hours incurred during any given period of time. By direct labor hours, we mean those hours which workmen actually spend operating these particular machines. If this is so, then our monthly electricity expense must be allocated between fixed cost and variable cost. This type of expense is termed *semivariable.* A large number of expense items generally fall into this latter category. The fixed portion of a given expense is usually necessary in order to maintain either a minimum organization or a given level of capacity. By strict definition a given cost factor can be variable. However, for purposes of cost analysis it will be considered fixed.

This is exactly the problem we encountered as we prepared the flexible budget to indicate the variable cost as we moved from one level of production to another.

Several techniques are available to aid us in determining the variable element of a given cost factor. Most, if not all, of these techniques require that we first determine an *independent* variable and a *dependent* variable. Direct labor hours in our electricity expense example given above would be termed the *independent* variable. The electricity expense would be termed a *dependent* variable. That is to say, the amount of electricity used beyond the amount necessary to light the working area would be dependent upon the number of direct labor hours used during the period of time under analysis. In short, we are trying to correlate the electricity expense with direct labor hours. The selection of the proper independent variable for any given expense item is not always easy. The degree of correlation between a given independent variable and a given dependent variable can be determined by statistical methods (however, we will leave the details of this determination to your statistics class).

Regression analysis and least squares. Let us assume that you have made the determination that there is a high correlation between the

CALCULATIONS USING *b* FORMULA

Month	(1) Direct Labor Hours Used	(2)* Monthly Difference from Average (35,000 hr.)	(3) Total Electrical Expense	(4)* Monthly Difference from Average ($650)
January	27,000	−8,000	$ 550	−100
February	32,000	−3,000	640	−10
March	27,000	−8,000	560	−90
April	42,000	+7,000	720	+70
May	46,000	+11,000	725	+75
June	32 000	−3 000	645	−5
July	27,000	−8,000	560	−90
August	28,000	−7,000	555	−95
September	33,000	−2,000	645	−5
October	47,000	+12,000	765	+115
November	48,000	+13,000	755	+105
December	31,000	−4,000	680	+30
Total	420,000	0	$7,800	0
Monthly Av.	35,000		$ 650	

* Column 2 = *X*; column 4 = *Y*.

Month	X	Y	X^2	XY
January	−8,000	−100	64,000,000	800,000
February	−3,000	−10	9,000,000	30,000
March	−8,000	−90	64,000,000	720,000
April	+7,000	+70	49,000,000	490,000
May	+11,000	+75	121,000,000	825,000
June	−3,000	−5	9,000.000	15,000
July	−8,000	−90	64,000,000	720,000
August	−7,000	−95	49,000,000	665,000
September	−2,000	−5	4,000,000	10,000
October	+12,000	+115	144,000,000	1,380,000
November	+13,000	+105	169,000,000	1,365,000
December	−4,000	+30	16,000,000	120,000
			762,000,000	7,140,000
			ΣX^2	ΣXY

direct labor hours used in a given operation and the expense for electricity for that operation. Once this determination has been made, the allocation between fixed cost and variable cost is relatively easy. One widely used technique to allocate fixed and variable cost is known as the *method of least squares.* (This method of least squares is used for many other types of analyses, as we will discover later in our study.) This technique is likewise sometimes called *regression analysis.*

The method of least squares uses the equation for a straight line, $Y = a + bX$. For our purposes here, the Y represents the total electrical expense, a equals the fixed portion of the electrical expense, X is equal to the direct labor hours, and b represents the degree by which the electricity expense varies with the direct labor hours, expressed as a percentage. Our main concern here is the b factor. We are interested in knowing how much the electrical expense increases or decreases as the number of direct labor hours increases or decreases. Fortunately, there is a formula that can be used to solve for b:

$$\frac{\Sigma XY}{\Sigma X^2}$$

Our next problem is to determine what we mean by $\Sigma XY/\Sigma X^2$. Perhaps the easiest way to illustrate the use of our formula would be to provide an example at this point. Using historical data for the past 12 months, we can compile the information as shown on page 101. (Note: The letters X and Y represent month-to-month deviation from the average values of X and Y.)

Therefore,

Average Historical Annual Variable Rate

$$\frac{\Sigma XY}{\Sigma X^2} = \frac{7{,}140{,}000}{762{,}000{,}000} = \$0.00937 \text{ per direct labor hour}$$

Applying the regression formula $Y = a + bX$, where Y = total electrical expense; X = independent variable, in this case direct labor hours; and b = variable cost (dependent variable) relationship to direct labor hours:

$$\text{Total electrical expense} = \text{fixed portion} + (\$0.00937 \times 35{,}000 \text{ hr})$$
$$\$650 = \text{fixed portion} + \$327.95$$
$$\text{Fixed portion} = \$650 - \$327.95$$
$$\text{Fixed portion} = \$322.05$$

We must clearly recognize that we have arrived at an average figure which represents the fixed portion of the total electrical expense. For all practical purposes in our planning, this average figure is quite adequate. It might be well to make certain that you have a working knowledge of the *b* formula. We will have occasion to refer to it in later chapters.

As we shall see later in our study of the corporation's development, the type of analyses we have just completed will be helpful in decisions involving new property acquisitions, loan and dividend payments, expansions of plant facilities, cash-flow analysis, capital structure, and other problems.

As a further example of the significance of fixed and variable cost, let's look ahead a bit. For example, we can hypothesize two firms, one of which has a high percentage of fixed cost to total cost, and the other evidencing a low percentage of fixed cost to total cost.

Firm A		**Firm B**	
Sales	$1,000,000	Sales	$1,000,000
Fixed cost	800,000	Fixed cost	100,000
Variable cost	100,000	Variable cost	800,000
Before-tax earnings	$ 100,000	Before-tax earnings	$ 100,000

Suppose that each of these firms experiences a 50 percent increase in sales. For ease of computation we will assume that each unit of output sells for $1.

Firm A		**Firm B**	
Sales	$1,500,000	Sales	$1,500,000
Fixed cost	800,000	Fixed cost	100,000
Variable cost	150,000	Variable cost	1,200,000
Before-tax earnings	$ 550,000	Before-tax earnings	$ 200,000

Notice that for each firm fixed cost remains constant and variable cost varies directly with sales and increases 50 percent in each firm. However, for Firm A a 50 percent increase in unit sales resulted in a 450 percent increase in earnings, while for Firm B a 50 percent increase in unit sales resulted in a 100 percent increase in earnings. In financial terms we have shown the difference in operating leverage between two firms. We can then say that a firm has high *operating leverage* when percentage increases in earnings far exceed percentage increases in sales. We could show the same information for Firm A and Firm B on an earnings-per-share basis. (Assume no taxes.)

If each firm had 100,000 shares outstanding, Firm A would have increased its earnings from $1 per share to $5.50 per share. The increase for Firm B would have been from \$1 to \$2 per share. Thus, the importance of the relationship between fixed and variable cost and/or operating leverage can be clearly seen. Our flexible budget highlights this relationship at various sales levels.

OPERATING LEVERAGE

If we desire to measure the degree of operating leverage at any particular level of sales, we have simply to compare the percentage increase in earnings before tax with the percentage increase in units sold.

$$\frac{\text{Degree of operating leverage at}}{\text{1,000,000 units of production}} = \frac{\text{\% of increase in earnings before tax}}{\text{\% of increase in units produced}}$$

$$\text{Firm A operating leverage} = \frac{450\%}{50\%} = 9$$

$$\text{Firm B operating leverage} = \frac{100\%}{50\%} = 2$$

For Firm A, earnings will then increase at a rate nine times the rate of increase in sales. For Firm B, the leverage factor is 2.

Returning to the Jones problem, we must be aware that thus far, we have prepared only a forecast of future events based on experience and historical information. This is not planning per se. It is perhaps a first step. Planning is the process of deciding future action as a result of our forecast. Our plan of action, once it has been formulated, not only must be consistent with the short-range and the long-range goals of the Jones organization but also must be within the organization's financial capability.

Really, this is our next question. What are the short-range and the long-range goals of the Jones Corporation? If you examine the cost curves or the flexible budget we prepared, you will see some obvious problems looming in the not-too-distant future if sales volume continues to increase. Like most small or even medium-sized businesses, in the early years, the Jones organization had enough of a problem just staying in business without worrying about philosophical goals in the short or the long run!

At the moment, we are too pleased with ourselves and the apparent success we had in analyzing our first problem to worry about anything else. President Jones invited you to have lunch with him. (You went; I couldn't make it—had a golf date.) Just as a point of conversation, but yet perhaps more, you inquired, "President Jones, where do we go from here?"

He replied, "You know, that's the first time anyone has ever asked me that question, young man. I never really gave it much thought. I will! For now, however, enjoy your lunch."

SUMMARY

Probably the most significant thing we learned in this chapter was the factor that "all managerial decisions are marginal." That is, management is almost always concerned about the addition (and at times just as important, the reduction) of "one more" of this or "one more" of that. Management faces such questions as "Should we add one more man to the sales force or open up an entirely new sales territory? (It is understood—*bien entendu*—that "one more" as used here really does not mean "one more." Rather, we may be talking about three or five more.) Other marginal decisions may relate to "one more" piece of equipment for the assembly line, "one more" accountant or secretary for the office force, or perhaps an entirely new product line. All of these decisions have marginal implications. (Reason for us to learn well our microeconomics.)

When we discuss marginal problems, as used herein, we must think about the distinction between fixed and variable cost. In a "typical" firm,

1. Average variable cost per unit will fall to a point as production increases because of the economies of scale. After production passes a certain level, average variable cost per unit will increase.
2. Marginal cost or the cost of producing one more unit will likewise fall considerably more rapidly and then will increase in the same manner.
3. Average fixed cost per unit will continue to decrease as units of production increase. Total fixed cost will remain constant until additional fixed cost is added to the factors of production.

The significance of the fixed and variable cost determination can be emphasized by the fact that if a firm has passed the breakeven point, that is, if all costs are covered, the only cost involved as additional units are produced is variable cost per unit. As was seen in the chapter, this is significant.

As illustrated in the chapter, the cost factors are clearly evident as the economic cost curves or the accounting flexible budget is prepared and analyzed. Both disciplines arrive at the same result using different techniques. The key to the entire analysis is the economist's "marginal cost" and/or the accountant's "differential cost." Again, the words are different, but the concept and results obtained are the same.

The mathematician and the statistician offer the regression analysis technique as a method of determining the average fixed and average variable cost relationships over a period of time. The significant thing to remember here is that the result is an average. Generally speaking, this latter degree of accuracy is more than adequate for this purpose.

Your discussions relating to the acceptance of the additional order unavoidably involved you in the technique of breakeven analyses. The breakeven point was defined to be that level of sales at which the firm is neither making a profit nor incurring a loss. You developed the concept of contribution margin and formulas for the determination of the firm's breakeven point, both in sales dollars and in units of production. Next, you approached the same topic with a graphical presentation of breakeven analysis.

The standard format which the accountant prepared was found to be inappropriate in that it:

1. Failed to recognize the true nature of variable costs.
2. Assumed that selling price was constant.
3. Assumed that at zero sales, revenues were zero.

The revised breakeven chart which you drew did:

1. Recognize the true nature of variable costs.
2. Show a constant selling price only for the first 100,000 units.
3. Continue to make the assumption of zero revenues at zero sales. (This assumption is appropriate for this firm, since our income statement shows that sales are our only source of revenues.)

This discussion of the nature of costs unavoidably involved you in the *b* formula. You had assumed in your flexible budget that all costs were either fixed or variable. An inspection of our own plant, however, has shown us that certain costs are semivariable. That is, they have both a fixed and a variable component. The *b* formula can be used to isolate the variable cost component of such semivariable costs as electricity and heat.

The final cost-volume-profit relationship with which the chapter deals is operating leverage. While all firms have some degree of operating leverage, certain types of firms have a high degree of leverage.

High operating leverage was defined to exist when percentage increases in earnings far exceeded the percentage increases in sales, giving rise to those earnings. If you have a complete understanding of breakeven analysis, you should be able to understand the cost structure which gives rise to high operating leverage. (Note the different cost structures of the firms used to illustrate high and low operating leverage.)

QUESTIONS FOR DISCUSSION

1. What information does the balance sheet present?
2. Does the balance sheet purport to show the value of the business?

3. What information does the profit and loss statement present?
4. Of what use is the breakdown of costs into fixed and variable components?
5. What is a flexible budget and how is it used?
6. What is operating leverage and how is it related to the composition of fixed and variable costs?
7. How are marginal and differential costs related?
8. What is the breakeven point?
9. Once sales have passed the breakeven point, why is marginal cost the most important variable in a pricing decision?
10. What assumptions does breakeven analysis make about factor costs?

PROBLEMS

1. Given the following data, calculate the breakeven point in units and dollars for the Jones organization. For the purpose of this problem assume that expenses are a function of sales. Selling price is $6 per unit.

Sales, Units	Total Expense
80,000	$474,000
90,000	503,000
100,000	540,000
110,000	577,000
120,000	614,000

2. Reconcile your answer in Problem 1 with the breakeven point as calculated in the text material. Why is your answer the same as the text, or why did you arrive at a different answer?

3. Given the following data, prepare a flexible budget for the Jones organization.

Production, Units
80,000
90,000
100,000
110,000
120,000

Fixed cost at the 100,000-unit level is $140,000 and will decrease $5,000 for each 10,000-unit decrease in production and will increase $2,000 for each 10,000-unit increase in production.

Variable cost at the 100,000-unit level of production is a total of $350,000 and will increase 20 cents per unit for each 10,000-unit decrease in production and will increase 10 cents per unit for the first 10,000-unit increase in production and an additional 30 cents per unit as production moves from 110,000 units to 120,000 units.

4. Construct the economic cost curves based on the data in Problem 3 and then answer the following questions if the company policy is to set the selling price at 25 cents above cost.
   a. What is the breakeven point in units and dollar sales?
   b. What is the price the company must charge at the 110,000-unit level to be consistent with the stated policy?
   c. The company has received an opportunity to sell Allied 4,000 additional units at a price of $5. Should Jones accept the offer if present sales volume is (1) 90,000 units? (2) 100,000 units? (3) 110,000 units?

5. Earlier in the Jones organization's history they were operating at about 15 percent capacity. Total fixed costs at that time were $75,000, and total variable costs were $60,000. They were producing and selling 20,000 units per year. These sales were made at a price of $6 per unit.

   Several proposals were made at that time.

   Allied made their first request to buy an undetermined number of units at $5. How many units must Jones contract to sell Allied in order to earn a total company profit of $10,000 for the year?

6. Use the data given in Problem 5, but instead of a lower price for the Allied sale, another alternative was presented. It was proposed that the advertising budget be increased $20,000, the price be maintained at $6, and the Allied offer not be accepted.
   a. How many additional units must the advertising campaign sell in order to produce a total company profit of $10,000 for the year?
   b. Lower the selling price 10 percent and increase the advertising budget $10,000. How will this change your answer?

7. President Jones invited you to spend a weekend at the Mountain View Lodge. While there you learned that he owned the facility. You also learned that the lodge is open only from December through March of each year. The lodge has 50 rooms and is 90 percent occupied on the average during this period. President Jones expressed a desire to keep the lodge open all year. He asked you to determine the minimum price he could charge per room, calculated on a 50 percent occupancy rate based on a 360-day year. President Jones has a total investment of $50,000. A summary of the information you asked for and received is as follows:
   a. Real estate insurance, real estate taxes, and depreciation amount to $17,000 per year.
   b. Salaries for the staff amount to $100 per day.
   c. Utilities, materials, and room supplies are equal, on the average, to $1.33⅓ per day per occupied room. During the off-season months these costs would be reduced 25 percent.
   d. The fishing is excellent and the scenery delightful.
   e. The lodge earned an excellent net profit, after taxes, of 50 percent last year. You gave him the answer in five minutes. What was it?

REFERENCES

Arcus, Albert L., and William H. Dietsch: Planned Performance and The Product Cost Controversy, *Management Accounting,* September, 1970, p. 9.

Crowningshield, Gerald R., and George L. Battista: Cost-Volume-Profit Analysis in Planning and Control, *N.A.A. Bulletin,* vol. XLV, pp. 3–15, July, 1963.

Helfert, Erich A.: "Techniques of Financial Analysis," rev. ed., chap. 2, Richard D. Irwin, Inc., Homewood, Ill., 1967.

Jaedicke, Robert K., and Alexander A. Robichek: Cost-Volume-Profit Analysis under Conditions of Uncertainty, *Accounting Review,* vol. XXXIX, October, 1964, reprinted in James Van Horne (ed.), "Foundations for Financial Management," pp. 11–24, Richard D. Irwin, Inc., Homewood, Ill., 1966.

Johnson, Robert W.: "Financial Management," 3d ed., chap. 10, Allyn and Bacon, Inc., Boston, 1966.

Mecimore, Charles D.: Locating and Evaluating Unprofitable Products or Segments of a Business Firm, *Management Accounting,* July, 1970, p. 57.

Miller, Robert D., and Terry L. Robinson: Performance Reports Based on Direct Costing: A Case Study, *Management Accounting,* April, 1970, p. 43.

Mock, Edward J., Robert E. Schultz, Raymond G. Schultz, and Donald Hart Shuckett: "Financial Decision Making," chap. 4, International Textbook Company, Scranton, Pa., 1968.

Raun, D. L.: Limitations of Profit Graphs, Breakeven Analysis, and Budgets, *Accounting Review,* vol. XXXIX, pp. 927–945, October, 1964.

Robbins, Sydney M.: Emphasizing the Marginal Factor in the Breakeven Analysis, *N.A.A. Bulletin,* vol. XLI, pp. 53–60, June, 1960.

Soldofsky, R. M.: Accountant's vs. Economist's Concepts of Breakeven Analysis, *N.A.A. Bulletin,* vol. XLI, pp. 5–18, December, 1959.

"Statement of the Accounting Principles Board, No. 4, Basic Concepts and Accounting Principles Underlying Financial Statements of Business Enterprises," American Institute of Certified Public Accountants, New York, 1970.

Weiner, Julius: To Better Results through a More Accurate Breakeven Formula, *N.A.A. Bulletin,* vol. XLI, pp. 5–18, July, 1960.

Weston, J. Fred, and Eugene F. Brigham: "Essentials of Managerial Finance," chap. 4, Holt, Rinehart and Winston, Inc., New York, 1968.

Willson, James D.: Practical Applications of Cost-Volume-Profit Analysis, *N.A.A. Bulletin,* vol. XLI, pp. 5–18, March, 1960.

Chapter Five
CAPITAL BUDGETING

At the weekly executive committee meeting, President Jones indicated that the corporation had made considerable progress and that more progress was anticipated. He was pleased that the Allied sales finally produced an additional $22,000 in net income. Variable costs did exceed our predictions and, consequently, we did not earn quite as much as we had anticipated. (A problem we will examine soon will be to determine why our anticipations were unrealized. We will not, however, abandon our budget figures until we determine the cause of the variance from the budgeted figures.)

Sales prospects for the coming year indicated that the Jones organization not only would hold firm by selling the normal 100,000 units but could anticipate a 12 to 15 percent increase. In addition, there was a request from Allied Electronics to increase their order of 20,000 units (purchased during the current year at $5 per unit) to 40,000 units next year at the same price. President Jones stated that he would sign the agreement that afternoon. The general manager immediately expressed disapproval. You recommended to President Jones that he delay signing the new contract for a day or so. (What you really meant was a week or more.)

After the meeting, President Jones came immediately to your office. He expressed surprise at your reaction to what he thought was good news—the proposed annual increase in Allied's order from 20,000 to 40,000 units. You explained to President Jones that before this particular decision could be made, it would be necessary to define the company's short-range and long-range goals. You were quite aware of the cost and production problems that made the general manager seem so definite in his disapproval of the new order. The present plant has production limitations, and as we press against those limitations, costs will rise.

The basic question concerns the marginal cost of the additional production of 12,000 to 15,000 units of normal sales and the additional 20,000-unit order from Allied. The answer to this question can be quickly determined if you will reexamine the flexible budget and/or the cost curves presented earlier. Do it! Now!

Did your examination of the cost curves and/or flexible budget, based upon present capacity to produce, confirm that there are problems associated with any increase in Allied's order? If not, look again!

The problem is summarized below:

	Jones	**Allied**	**Total**
Present sales, units	100,000	20,000	120,000
Marginal cost = \$3.70. Average total cost = \$5.11+ per unit.			
Anticipated sales, units	115,000	40,000	155,000

What happens to marginal cost when production moves from 120,000 to 155,000 units? Is it quite obvious to you that additional plant capacity is needed if we are to continue to accept the Allied orders and still provide growth capacity without an increase in price?

You reviewed with the president the significance of marginal cost in any plans to increase production. He reviewed the cost curves and flexible budget with you and quickly pointed out that even at average cost per unit, we cannot accept the new order with our existing plant capacity. An increase in price is out of the question. Do you see the problem now? If you do not, go back and reexamine the economic framework developed earlier in Chapter 4 for the Jones Corporation.

In broad perspective, we are concerned with the question of how large our company should be and how fast it should grow. Can we or should we attempt to raise additional funds to finance capital improvements that will enable us to grow by increasing our sales to Allied and our other customers? If it is decided that we should raise additional funds to permit this expansion, the next question is how we should raise these funds, debt or equity, that is, by borrowing or by additional investments by the owners. We are concerned with defining the goals for our firm and the formulation of plans for implementing action to attain these goals.

President Jones quickly indicated his confidence in Allied's ability to expand and grow. He indicated further that if possible, we should supply Allied with all their requirements if only to make it difficult for competitors to gain a foothold with this customer. The forecast is clear. We cannot meet a 155,000-unit production demand with our present production capacity. We will lose our current profitability position (that is, we will suffer a loss) if we attempt to fill Allied's additional order. It may be necessary to cut back the more profitable Jones sales at $6 per unit to supply Allied at $5 per unit. This entails the possible loss of present customers. President Jones has indicated a short-run decision that has long-run implications! Time is of the essence. Allied needs an answer to their offer.

On the basis of your discussion with President Jones, you recognized that he is primarily concerned with sales and organizational growth. So are you. However, you realize that such growth requires systematic planning. You also recognized that the decision to expand capacity will require increased investment by the firm. You are, in fact, involved in an area of finance which is known as capital budgeting. Let's take a moment and discuss capital budgeting in isolation from our immediate problem. What is capital budgeting? What do capital budgeting systems do, and finally, why are they important?

As we know, any firm grows in size and scope on the basis of its success in carrying out its current operations and its ability to expand these operations and add new ones. As a firm grows, it must increase its asset size by making new investments. The Jones Corporation has already done this in the past. The resources which were required to finance this growth stemmed from profits of the firm which were retained and used by the business rather than taken out of the business by its stockholders. We also have increased assets by borrowing the necessary funds. The funds were used to increase the size of our asset base, making it possible to increase production.

CAPITAL BUDGETING DEFINED

A budget is an investment plan expressed in financial terms. Capital budgeting is a planned procedure used by the firm to allocate funds which are available for capital investment. In a conventional sense the word "investment" is taken to mean the expenditure of funds by the firm at one point in time in order to secure returns (profits) during successive time periods. For example, a firm may commit $1 million to the purchase of a new machine in anticipation of the fact that this expenditure will result in annual profit inflows of $30,000 for the next five years. If this sounds reminiscent of some of the material in Chapter 3, it should, since capital budgeting systems involve an application of the mathematics of finance which you reviewed earlier.

In its capital budgeting procedures, the firm becomes involved in weighing the merits of an expenditure of cash or credit in order to secure the cash flows which that expenditure promises. Jones Electronic's investment problem is little more than this. If new orders are to be filled, expenditures for additional assets will be required. The obvious question which arises concerns the justification of that expenditure. Will the anticipated added sales produce cash flows which justify the proposed expenditure?

A capital budgeting system must involve at least these basic components. It should:

1. Generate proposals for capital expenditures.
2. Estimate the costs to be incurred and benefits which can be expected from each of the series of proposals generated.
3. Evaluate the risks associated with each of the proposals.
4. Select or reject proposals from among those generated.
5. Reevaluate the entire procedure on the basis of operational experience with those proposals which have been selected and adopted in the past.

Let's look now specifically at each of the system's components.

Generation of Proposals

In the Jones organization the proposal with which we are dealing was generated by the president himself. This is not a typical procedure for most large firms. For example, when Sears Roebuck entered the insurance field by creating Allstate Insurance, considerable planning at all levels preceded the commitment of funds. Such planning is most normally the responsibility of specialized staffs within the firm. The planning group investigates areas which may provide the firm with attractive investment opportunities. The same group evaluates present operations and assesses the effectiveness of prior capital commitments made by the firm.

Estimation of Costs and Benefits

This activity requires a translation of plans or proposals into budgetary figures and cash flows. The concept of cash flows will be explained later with particular reference to the Jones Electronic Corporation. Generally, we can say that this stage of the capital budgeting process will ascribe to each proposal a cash cost and delineate a level of cash returns which may be expected from the adoption of the proposal.

Evaluation of Risk

During this phase of the process the planning committee must attempt to differentiate between the investment proposals with respect to the inherent risks of each. For example, it is obvious that there is a difference in risk between a proposal regarding a commitment of funds to an area in which the firm is already knowledgeable and a like commitment to an area in which the firm has no prior operating experience. To illustrate, we can again turn to our example of Sears, Roebuck & Co. Assume that two different proposals are generated; each requires the expenditure of $10 million, and the estimated cash flows from each of these proposals are identical in size and duration. *Question:* Is the firm indifferent as to which one it selects, assuming that it is unable to finance both? The answer will depend on the risks associated with each proposal. If the two proposals were (1) the building of additional retail stores and (2) the creation of an insurance subsidiary (Allstate), Sears would probably not be indifferent between the two. The first proposal represents the commitment of funds to an area in which the firm has great experience and an ability to estimate with accuracy those predicted cash flows. The second proposal, a commitment to the Allstate Insurance subsidiary, represents a quite different situation with respect to the firm's ability to predict cash flows with accuracy.

Thus, the capital budgeting procedure must not simply generate proposals and estimate costs and cash flows; it must also evaluate proposals with respect to the risks involved.

Selection of Proposals

Once proposals have been generated and cash flows estimated and evaluated, certain of the projects proposed must be selected and others rejected. You may wonder why the firm will not take advantage of all the proposals which the planning committee has examined. Proposals are usually unacceptable on one or more of the following grounds:

1. Proposals may represent alternative ways of accomplishing the same goal. They are then mutually exclusive since the adoption of one will preclude the acceptance of the other. For example, proposal 302 may concern the use of a computer to handle payrolls, and proposal 303 might suggest that this work be subcontracted to an outside firm at a stipulated cost. If we accept 302, we will automatically reject 303.

   The other side of this coin concerns proposals which are independent. That is, the selection of one in no way affects the selection or rejection of the other. Thus, our acceptance of proposal 302 has no effect on our selection or rejection of proposal 401 (building a new office building).

   The final relationship which may exist among proposals is that of dependency. For example, project 302, our in-house computerized payroll system, would be dependent on the acceptance of another project—let's call it project 107—involving the purchase of a computer system. We cannot fruitfully consider proposal 302 until we have accepted or rejected proposal 107.

2. Proposals may be rejected on the basis of the fact that the firm lacks the financial resources which are required for acceptance. If the total capital budget were $10 million for a particular year, a project which demanded the expenditure of $20 million would not be feasible and would probably be rejected. Thus, the firm may not be able to accept all nonconflicting proposals simply because capital is momentarily limited.
3. Finally, projects must be screened and accepted or rejected based upon the return which they promise to deliver. The firm will have certain standards or performance criteria which are related to the cost of the funds to be committed to the investment. If a project fails to meet these standards, it will be rejected.

   The bulk of the material which will be presented in this chapter deals with the selection process, and so little more will be said at this point with respect to the establishment of investment criteria or the methods of evaluation employed in the selection and rejection phase of the capital budgeting procedure.

Reevaluation

The final phase of the capital budgeting procedure demands that the firm reevaluate the effectiveness of its investment effort. At this point questions like the following should be answered. Are we generating an adequate number of proposals, and are they of significant scope? Have we accurately assessed both the cash flows and the risks associated with those flows? If not, why not? Has our selection process functioned to maximize the value of the firm's new investment? This reevaluation is an important self-critique and, as such, demands that those involved view the activity objectively. It would serve no purpose to disregard mistakes or errors. The reevaluation process must provide for the correction of these mistakes in the future.

Post audit

Finally, after the project has been completed and is operational, the budgeting process demands that a review of actual operations be made to determine whether or not the project has met expectations. The significant questions at this point are why or why not.

CAPITAL BUDGETING APPLIED

We have thus far discussed what capital budgeting is and what components are basic to the system. Now we must assess the importance of the capital budgeting activity to the firm.

The importance of capital budgeting is threefold:

1. Large annual expenditures are involved.
2. Its consequences are long-term.
3. Successful capital allocation contributes to the maximization of the value of the firm.

The size of capital budgeting expenditures can be substantial indeed. As an example, from 1956 to 1965 the Jones and Laughlin Steel Corporation made an expenditure of $750 million on new plant and equipment. Clearly, the capital expenditures were large. Once the $750 million investment is made, the firm is forced to live with the investment decision for a significant period of time in the future and is dependent on the investment for a large percentage of total corporate profitability.

How are capital budgeting activities related to the financial manager's goal of maximizing the value of the enterprise? We have only to return to our discussion in Chapter 1 of the goal of financial management to appreciate this interrelationship. If you recall, we demonstrated at that time the relationship which exists between corporate earnings and the value of the enterprise. With reference to a single share of stock, we also showed that its current value was simply the present value of an anticipated earnings stream discounted at some rate.

$$P_0 = \frac{EA \text{ (estimated earnings)}}{K \text{ (discount rate)}}$$

The capital budgeting process affects each of the components of our valuation equation. Estimated earnings and the discount factor K are directly influenced by our success or failure in the area of capital budgeting. If the firm consistently generates and selects those proposals which promise the highest possible returns, for a given level of risk, this growing stream of earnings will be translated into increased prices for the common shares. In short, effective capital budgeting is required if the financial executive is to realize his goal of wealth maximization.

Our current capital budgeting problem, then, is really three problems. First, we must search for possible alternatives that will provide the additional production capacity needed to supply Allied and our own increased sales. Second, we must analyze the cost and income data concerning possible alternatives. (We must keep in mind the lessons we have learned about breakeven analysis as well as marginal and differential cost.) Third, we are interested in other capital budgeting constraints, such as the supply of and cost of funds necessary to implement the alternative which is finally selected. Most important of all, we are concerned about our ability to attract available funds to the Jones Electronic Corporation.

We must keep in mind that we are dealing with an area of uncertainty that may involve considerable risk to the firm. We are not certain about cost factors, and we may ultimately have little control over them. Current material and labor costs are unlikely to remain constant for the next 15 years. We cannot predict with absolute accuracy the productive life of machinery and equipment. Wear and tear allowances are a matter of judgment, and obsolescence is a function of unpredictable technological change. The cost of funds and tax rates in future years are at best an estimate. In addition, we are not certain about possible reactions by our competition and many other significant matters which will bear on estimated cash flows and the risks associated with them.

However, the uncertainty and risk must be met with the best possible analysis. It would be much easier to do nothing; however, business operates in a dynamic setting. There is no standing still. It is either grow or retrogress! We must face and solve our problem. How do we secure the additional production capacity? What are the alternatives?

After considerable discussion with the executive committee, there appear to be three alternative methods of increasing our productive capacity.[1]

1. Add another unit to our production machinery.
2. Replace all the present machinery with more efficient, higher-capacity units.
3. Build an entirely new, larger, and more efficient plant.

These alternatives are "mutually exclusive." Making such a choice is a very serious undertaking. Once we have committed our funds in a given direction, there may be no turning back without considerable loss! Therefore, we must test the relative advantages and disadvantages of each possibility and select our course of action very carefully.

Alternative 1

Let us begin by generating data with respect to alternative 1, the acquisition of an additional production unit. Information and data, requested and received from our production foreman, plant superintendent, purchasing agent, accountant, and others, provided the following information:

1. Practical capacity will increase from 120,000 to 156,000 units. This increase in capacity will provide our immediate needs.

Projected regular sales	=	$115,000
Projected sales to Allied	=	40,000
		$155,000

[1] In view of the president's decision to grow with Allied, the alternative of doing nothing is not a viable one.

2. The new production unit will cost $22,000 installed and will have an estimated life of 15 years with a salvage value of $2,000 at the end of that time. Annual depreciation charges will be $1,333. [Cost less salvage ($20,000) divided by 15 years = $1,333.]
3. The executive committee believes that no commitment of corporate funds should be made unless the firm can realize a 10 percent return on this commitment. This standard or hurdle rate has been selected without any real analysis of what is the lowest rate the firm should accept. We will use this standard for now, but later we will investigate its validity.
4. Income tax will be assumed to be 50 percent for convenience.

We must now prepare a statement that will project the additional profit that will accrue to the Jones organization if the new machine is purchased. New cost curves and a new flexible budget have been prepared by the accounting department to reflect the installation and utilization of the additional machine. The cost curves constructed to include the new production unit indicate that variable cost between the 120,000- and the 155,000-unit level of production will be $3.80 per unit. We have been extremely careful. We know that our cost figures are only as reliable as the accuracy of our new flexible budget and cost curve calculations.

Additional revenue:				
Jones' sales = 15,000 units at $6		$ 90,000		
Allied sales = 20,000 units at $5		100,000		
Total additional revenue				$190,000
Additional costs:				
Variable = $3.80 × 35,000 units =			$133,000	
Fixed costs:				
Added depreciation	$ 1,333			
Foreman's salary[1]	10,667			
Miscellaneous[2]	1,000		13,000	
Total additional costs				146,000
Additional income before taxes				$ 44,000
Less income tax (50 percent)				22,000
Estimated annual additional income per year for 15 years				$ 22,000

[1] A new foreman must be hired to supervise the additional production.
[2] Estimated power requirements resulting from installation of the new machines.

As we review this projection, we note that we are dealing only with the *incremental income* to be provided by the additional machine. *Incremental income* may be defined as the additional income generated less the additional costs incurred.

Alternative 2

Alternative 2 is to replace all the present equipment with new and more efficient production machinery. The new machinery will increase our total annual practical capacity to 225,000 units. The following data have been compiled with respect to this alternative.

1. The new equipment will cost $332,100 and will have an estimated useful life of 10 years with an estimated salvage value of $32,100. Annual depreciation expense will be $30,000.
2. All units produced with the new equipment at the 155,000 annual unit level of production will have an average total cost, excluding depreciation, of $3.30. Depreciation at this level of production is approximately 20 cents per unit. Marginal cost at this level of production will be $2 per unit.
3. Present equipment can be sold at this time for $10,000.

Again, we must prepare a projection of the additional income that will be provided if we replace all the present equipment under alternative 2. The selling price will remain the same, $6 per unit for those normally sold by Jones and $5 per unit for those sold to Allied. Quite significantly, additional income will be provided by the reduction in the cost per unit for the present sales (120,000 units) as well as by the anticipated additional sales (15,000 units by Jones, 20,000 units by Allied). We can now summarize the anticipated results:

First 120,000 units:			
Average total cost with present equipment		$5.11	(See flexible
Average total cost with new equipment		—3.50	budget in
Savings per unit		$1.61	Chapter 4)
Multiplied by present sales		×120,000 units	
Total savings present volume			$193,200
Additional 35,000 units anticipated:			
Jones, 15,000 at $6 =	$ 90,000		
Allied, 20,000 at $5 =	100,000		
		$190,000	
Average total cost, 35,000 units at $3.50		—122,500	
Income provided by new sales			67,500
Total additional income before taxes			$260,700
Less income taxes (50 percent)			130,350
Additional annual income after taxes for 10 years			$130,350

We will now examine the third alternative:

Alternative 3

Alternative 3 is to design, build, and equip a completely new, modern, semiautomated plant that would have an annual practical capacity of

750,000 units. The following data on the project have been compiled:

1. Total cost is estimated to be $1,250,000 (building, $250,000; equipment, $1,000,000). The building will have an estimated life of 25 years with no salvage value. Annual depreciation of the building will be $10,000. Developments in equipment design have been quite rapid, and other firms are conducting extensive research in the equipment area. Early obsolescence is a distinct possibility. However, these are unknown factors at the moment. To be conservative, however, an eight-year useful life will be estimated for the equipment with a salvage value of $100,000.[1] Depreciation on the equipment will be $112,500 per year. Total annual depreciation will be $122,500.
2. All units produced at the 155,000 annual unit level of production will have an average total cost, excluding depreciation, of $2.13. Depreciation at this level of production will be 73 cents per unit.[2] Average total cost will thus be $3 per unit. Marginal cost at this level of production will be $1 and will decrease to 50 cents at the 500,000-unit level of production and then increase quite rapidly. Average total cost will follow a similar pattern.
3. Present equipment will be sold for $10,000.

We will prepare another projection to indicate the expected additional income if alternative 3 is adopted:

First 120,000 units:

Average total cost with present equipment	$5.11	
Average total cost with new plant	−3.00	
Savings per unit	$2.11	
Multiplied by present sales	×120,000 units	
Additional income on present volume		$253,200

Additional units anticipated:

Jones, 15,000 at $6 = $ 90,000		
Allied, 20,000 at $5 = 100,000		
Additional gross income	$190,000	
Less cost—35,000 at $3	105,000	
		85,000
Total additional income before taxes		$338,200
Less income taxes (50 percent)		169,100
Additional annual income after taxes for eight years		$169,100

[1] The equipment itself may be serviceable for 25 years.

[2] $\frac{\$112{,}500}{155{,}000 \text{ units}}$ = 73 cents per unit (approx.)

PROJECT SELECTION

We can now use these data and like data for each of the alternatives in the selection process. For each alternative four selection standards will be applied. These tests are known as:

1. Payback period
2. Average-return method
3. Rate of return
4. Net present value

Two of these tests will yield correct choices from among our three alternattives. As you will see, the other two tests will lead to decisions which are inconsistent with our goal of maximizing the value of the firm. Let us consider first the payback test and apply it to the solution of our capital budgeting problem.

Payback Period

The payback period is the period of time necessary so that the annual earnings from the investment after taxes plus the annual depreciation allowance will equal the original investment. According to our earlier projection of alternative 1, we will recover our total additional investment in less than one year.[1] However, even though we will recover the original investment in less than one year, we will not have provided production capacity for additional growth. (Unfortunately, we will not be able to add more machines in the future as we did in this case because of the technological requirements of the production methods.) We will now examine the second alternative.

The payback period under alternative 2, purchasing all new equipment, will be approximately 2.07 years.[2] The installation of this equipment will provide for additional growth up to an annual practical capacity of 225,000 units. Our cost data show that average total cost will fall to $3 when we reach 190,000 units of production. Variable cost at this point will be approximately $1.80. Above this level, average marginal cost and average cost per unit will increase at first slowly and then quite rapidly.

[1] $$\frac{\text{Cost}}{\text{Annual earnings after taxes} + \text{depreciation}} = \frac{\$22{,}000}{\$22{,}000 + \$1{,}333} = 0.94 \text{ year}$$

[2]

Estimated annual income	$130,350
Add depreciation allowance	30,000
	$160,350

$$\frac{\$332{,}100}{\$160{,}350} = 2.07 \text{ years}$$

The payback period for alternative 3 will be approximately 4.28 years.[1] Additional growth capacity will be provided up to an annual *practical capacity* of 750,000 units.

We have now started to build a framework within which to make a decision concerning the three alternatives. A summary of our present framework would be as follows:

Alternative	Practical Capacity, Units	Estimated Equipment Life, Years	After Taxes Additional Annual Earnings	Payback Period, Years	Original Cost of Investment
1	156,000	15	$ 22,000	0.94	$ 22,000
2	225,000	10	130,350	2.07	332,100
3	750,000	8	169,100	4.28	1,250,000

If we were to apply the "payback" test, it is clear that alternative 1 would be the best choice. We would be quite content with this selection if we were sure that the payback period is a valid measure of the desirability of the several investment alternatives. Is it in fact a valid test? The answer is no, since the payback period emphasizes the least important criterion of investment worth. That is to say, the payback period confines itself to a consideration of the return *of* investment rather than the return *on* investment. The latter truly measures investment value. Secondly, the payback method of selection fails to take into account the cash returns which occur after the payback period is complete. Lastly, this system fails to consider the timing of returns. That is to say, it fails to distinguish between cash flows which occur five or ten years from now and those which occur today.

Average Return on the Average Annual Investment

Let us, therefore, apply a second criterion that is often used when choices among competing alternatives must be made in the capital budgeting process. This test is known as the "average annual return on the average annual investment." To apply this system, simply divide the average annual earnings after depreciation by the average annual investment.

$$\frac{\text{Average annual earnings after depreciation}}{\text{Average annual investment}} = \text{average annual return on average annual investment}$$

The average investment is equal to the total investment divided by the estimated life.

[1] You check this one!

$$\text{Alternative 1} = \frac{\$22{,}000}{\$22{,}000/15} = \frac{\$22{,}000}{\$1{,}467} = 15 \text{ times (approx.)}$$

$$\text{Alternative 2} = \frac{\$130{,}350}{\$332{,}100/10} = \frac{\$130{,}350}{\$33{,}210} = 4 \text{ times (approx.)}$$

$$\text{Alternative 3} = \frac{\$169{,}100}{\frac{\text{(Bldg.) } \$250{,}000}{25} + \frac{\$1{,}000{,}000 \text{ (equip.)}}{8}} = \frac{\$169{,}100}{\$10{,}000 + \$125{,}000} = \begin{array}{l}1.25 \text{ times} \\ \text{(approx.)}\end{array}$$

What we are saying, in substance, is that when we use the "average annual return on average annual investment" test as defined above, alternative 1 will return the original investment to the Jones Company 15 times each year over the estimated life of the equipment. Alternative 2 will return the average annual investment approximately four times each year. Alternative 3 will return the original investment 1.25 times each year. You should note that the "average annual rate of return" test does not consider the difference in dollar value of the annual earnings over the life of the various alternatives. What does this mean? This is significant. Would you rather earn $22,000 for 15 years, $130,350 for 10 years, or $169,100 for eight years, after taxes annually?

You will notice that your calculation above was the "average annual return on average annual investment." Quite often, you will see this test applied to give the average return on average investment calculated as follows:

Average investment:

Alternative 1 = $ 22,000 ÷ 2 = $ 11,000
Alternative 2 = $ 332,100 ÷ 2 = $166,050
Alternative 3 = $1,250,000 ÷ 2 = $625,000

The original investment is divided by 2 to indicate that the original investment will decline in value to zero over its estimated life. Therefore, the average investment will be the original investment divided by 2.

$$\text{Alternative 1} = \frac{\$22{,}000}{\$11{,}000} \text{ or 2 times}$$

$$\text{Alternative 2} = \frac{\$130{,}350}{\$166{,}050} \text{ or 0.78 time}$$

$$\text{Alternative 3} = \frac{\$169{,}100}{\$625{,}000} \text{ or 0.270 time}$$

What is the significance of this information? Based on our projected annual earnings, we will earn two times our average investment, as defined, each year under alternative 1, 0.78 time under alternative 2, and 0.270 time under alternative 3. (We personally prefer our original calculations when we use the average *annual* investment. The data provided are more meaningful to us—take your choice,)

The Internal Rate of Return

We have thus far applied two popular tests to aid us in our selection, but we have been disappointed by both. We are really looking for some test which emphasizes the return which will be earned by the firm on the initial cash outlay. A third criterion of investment worth, the internal rate of return method, does, in fact, focus its attention in the latter area. This method will enable us to calculate a rate of return for each investment proposal and then rank each proposal based on its projected rate of return.

What exactly is a rate of return? If a friend told us that he had received an annual interest payment of $6 on a deposit made in the local bank which paid an annual rate of interest of 6 percent, we would know immediately that the size of his deposit was $100. In order to get that answer, we unconsciously had capitalized his $6 return at the stated interest rate of 6 percent.

$$\text{Deposit} = \frac{\$6}{0.06}$$

$$= \$100$$

The rate of return on an investment can be defined as that rate of interest which will discount the cash proceeds or cash inflow over the life of the investment and make them equal to the cost of the investment.[1] Let's prove it. Suppose that a firm invests $997.50 in a machine and that as a result of this investment the firm realizes cash flows of $250 per year for the next five years. (Is the $250 anything more than an annuity as we have learned to use the term?) What is the rate of return on this particular investment? It is that rate of interest which will discount the cash proceeds and make them equal to the cost of the investment. To find it, enter your present value of $1 per period table at five years. Now select any interest rate that strikes your fancy,

[1] Cash inflow for capital budgeting purposes is defined to be net profit after tax plus depreciation. Thus, the cash-flow figure contains both a return on investment and a return of investment.

for example, 6 percent. In the 6 percent five-year column the figure 4.212 appears. Will this factor multiplied by $250 equal $997.50?

$250(4.212) = $1,053

This interest rate of 6 percent was not sufficiently high to discount the cash proceeds and make them equal to the cost of the investment. Let's try 10 percent, which means we will use the factor 3.790.

$250(3.790) = $947.50

This 10 percent rate was too high since its use produced a figure which is lower than our cost of the investment. We now know that the true rate of return lies between 6 and 10 percent. Let's try 8 percent, using the factor 3.990.

$250(3.990) = $997.50

In the case of this particular investment we can say that it offers a rate of return of 8 percent, which means that you could deposit $997.50 now and let this sum earn interest one year at 8 percent. At the end of one year you could withdraw $250 and leave the balance to earn interest at 8 percent for a second year, and then withdraw $250 again. You could follow this same procedure for five years. After the fifth withdrawal of $250 the balance in the original fund would be zero. Has your investment not earned 8 percent per year?

If we were to calculate a rate of return for each investment proposal offered by our capital budgeting committee, we could rank-order them on the basis of their internal rates of return and finally select those offering the highest rates. For example, assume the following proposals and their respective rates of return:

Proposal Number	Rate of Return
92	38%
71	32%
302	29%
307	28%
408	26%
22	22%
.	.
.	.
.	.

In order to maximize the value of its investment effort, the firm would simply proceed down the list, starting with proposal 92 and continuing to select those investments which offered a rate of return higher than the cost of the funds to be employed.

Graphically, the process can be shown in the following manner:

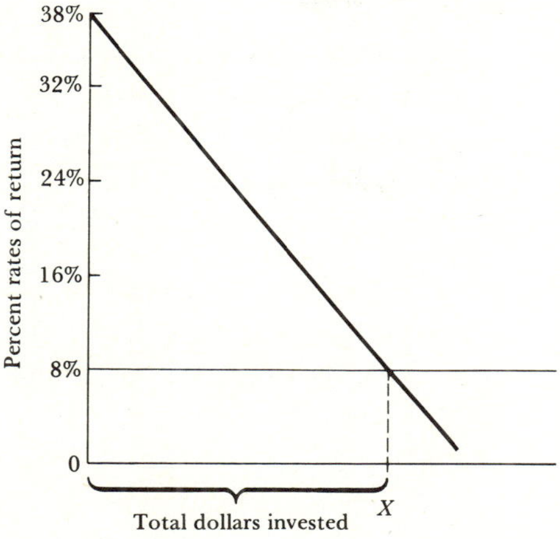

If the funds which were to be committed to the capital budget cost the firm 8 percent, the firm would accept all nonconflicting proposals offering a return of 8 percent or more and commit an amount of money *OX* to the capital budget. At that point the firm would have invested in all projects whose returns were equal to or exceeded their costs. In so doing, the firm would also maximize its earnings and, at least theoretically, its value.

With respect to our particular problem at Jones Electronic, we are faced with three mutually exclusive proposals. We, therefore, can accept that alternative which offers the highest rate of return. However, let's postpone these calculations briefly and consider a fourth and related test of investment worth known as the net present value method.

The Net Present Value

The selection technique employed in this test of investment worth is directly related to the internal rate of return method discussed above. That particular test, you will recall, calculated a definite rate of return for each proposal and then compared that return with the cost of funds expressed as a rate percent. Projects were then selected based upon their explicit rates of return.

The net present value method accomplishes much the same selection process but avoids the laborious procedure of calculating a specific rate of return for each proposal. Cash flows are discounted for each proposal at the rate of discount which is equal to the firm's cost of funds expressed as a rate percent. If the discounted value of the cash flows is equal to or greater than the cost of the investment, the project is acceptable. Why is this so? Suppose that a new machine will cost $5,000 and this machine will produce net cash flows of $2,000 annually for eight years. (This annual flow is also an annuity.) The cost of funds for the firm is 10 percent.

If you enter the table which gives the present value of a $1 per period at 10 percent and eight years, you will see the number 5.334. This tells us that the present value of eight payments of $1 discounted at 10 percent is $5.334. The annual payments produced by this machine are not $1, but $2,000. The present value of this annual flow is

$$\$2,000 \times 5.334 = \$10,668$$

The net present value of this investment would be the present value of the cash inflow less the cost of the investment, or the present value of the cash outflow.

$10,668	Present value of cash inflow
—5,000	Present value of the cost (cash outflow)
$ 5,668	Net present value

How does this relate to the internal rate of return offered by the proposal? Think of our definition for the internal rate of return. You will recall that it is that rate of interest which will discount the value of the cash proceeds and make them equal to the cost of the investment. In our example above, was 10 percent the rate of return of this proposal? Obviously not, since it failed to discount the cash proceeds sufficiently to make them equal to the cost of the investment. The true rate of return would have to be higher than 10 percent since it must be a rate which is capable of discounting the proceeds and making them equal to the cost of the investment. In this case that rate would approximate 36 percent.

The discount factor for 36 percent for eight periods, as shown on your present worth of an annuity table, is 2.540.

$$\$2,000 \times 2.540 = \$5,080$$

Therefore, the rate of return would be slightly more than 36 percent per year.

The relationship between the two systems should now be clear. The internal rate of return system compares calculated rates of return for various projects with the firm's cost of funds. The net present value method discounts anticipated cash flows at the firm's cost of funds and reveals indirectly whether or not the proposal under consideration has

Deposit Now	End of First Year	End of Second Year	End of Third Year	End of Fourth Year	End of Fifth Year	End of Sixth Year	End of Seventh Year	End of Eighth Year	
$10,668									
	$10,668								
Add 10%	1,067								
	$11,735								
Less	2,000	$ 9,735							
	Add 10%	973							
		$10,708							
	Less	2,000	$8,708						
		Add 10%	871						
			$9,579						
		Less	2,000	$7,579					
			Add 10%	758					
				$8,337					
			Less	2,000	$6,337				
				Add 10%	634				
					$6,971				
				Less	2,000	$4,971			
					Add 10%	497			
						$5,468			
					Less	2,000	$3,468		
						Add 10%	347		
							$3,815		
						Less	2,000	$1,815	
							Add 10%	182	
								$1,997	
							Less	2,000	
								0	Oops, we rounded too much!

a rate of return equal to or greater than the firm's cost of funds. Under either system, maximization of the investment effort will occur when the firm accepts all proposals which offer rates of return equal to or greater than the cost of funds employed.

While the payback and average return methods of calculation were unacceptable on several grounds, both the internal rate of return and the net present value system of capital allocation are acceptable because both of these techniques (1) value all returns, (2) explicitly consider the time value of money, and (3) maximize the effectiveness of the firm's investment activity.

Let us now return to our own capital budgeting problems at Jones Electronic and employ the net present value method of calculation. For now, we will assume that the firm's cost of funds is 10 percent. Using this discount rate and the information we already possess, we can calculate the net present value of each of our alternatives.

	Alternative 1			Alternative 2		Alternative 3	
	(1)	(2)	(3)	(4)	(5)	(6)	(7)
Year	P.V. "at" 10%	Est. Annual Cash Flows* after Taxes	Present Value	Est. Annual Cash Flows* after Taxes	Present Value Col. 1 × Col. 4)	Est. Annual Cash Flows* after Taxes	Present Value Col. 1 × Col. 6)
1	0.909 ×	$ 23,333	$ 21,210	$ 160,350	$145,758	$ 291,600	$ 265,064
2	0.826 ×	23,333	19,273	160,350	132,449	291,600	240,862
3	0.751 ×	23,333	17,523	160,350	120,423	291,600	218,991
4	0.683 ×	23,333	15,936	160,350	109,519	291,600	199,163
5	0.621 ×	23,333	14,490	160,350	99,577	291,600	181,084
6	0.564 ×	23,333	13,160	160,350	90,437	291,600	164,462
7	0.513 ×	23,333	11,970	160,350	82,260	291,600	149,591
8	0.467 ×	23,333	10,896	160,350	74,883	291,600	136,177
9	0.424 ×	23,333	9,893	160,350	67,988		
10	0.386 ×	23,333	9,007	160,350	61,895		
11	0.350 ×	23,333	8,167				
12	0.319 ×	23,333	7,443				
13	0.290 ×	23,333	6,767				
14	0.263 ×	23,333	6,137				
15	0.239 ×	23,333	5,577				
	7.605	$349,995	$177,449	$1,603,500	$985,189	$2,332,800	$1,555,394

Total annual factors for 8 years = 5.334

Total annual factors for 10 years = 6.145

Total annual factors for 15 years = 7.605

* Cash flow includes income after taxes plus depreciation.

The present values of the projected cash flows for the three alternatives were purposely calculated the hard way in order to reemphasize the relationships of the present-value tables A-2 and A-4. We could have arrived at the same total present values by using Table A-4 in the first instance. You will notice that we have added the various present-value factors that we have taken from Table A-2 for the 15-year period for alternative 1, 7.605; the 10-year period for alternative 2, 6.145; and the 8-year period for alternative 3, 5.334. Now you check the factors given in table A-4 for 15 periods at 10 percent, 10 periods at 10 percent, and 8 periods at 10 percent. Table A-4 is nothing more than the cumulative totals for Table A-2 for any number of periods contained in the table. (Larger and more comprehensive tables are available to cover almost any number of periods at any discount rate.)

By calculating the present value of the income for the three alternatives, what have we really accomplished? We are saying that under alternative 1, if we now had $177,449 to deposit in a bank, or to invest under some other plan, to earn compound interest at 10 percent, we would be able to withdraw our projected income under alternative 1, $23,333 annually for a 15-year period. In order to withdraw $160,350 annually for 10 years, the projected income provided by alternative 2, we would have to deposit $985,189 now to earn compound interest at 10 percent. It would require a deposit now of $1,555,394 at 10 percent to have available $291,600 annually for the eight-year-period life of alternative 3. Let's summarize these figures:

	Investment required now to produce at compound interest rate of 10 percent the anticipated flow of funds under each alternative
Alternative 1	$ 177,449
Alternative 2	985,189
Alternative 3	1,555,394

Do you see the significance of our analysis thus far? If your rich uncle offered you your choice of the three investments, which would you take? Clearly, the returns offered by alternative 3 are higher and, consequently, require the largest investment now. You would, therefore, since you were the beneficiary, take alternative 3.

You will notice we have been talking about the investment required now to supply the required annual earnings plus depreciation under the three alternatives. (These are the "inflows" from our investment.) What we have really discovered, then, is that alternative 3 would be more attractive—*if* the actual initial investment of all three alternatives were equal. That is, if all three alternatives required an initial investment of

$100,000, clearly alternative 3 gives a superior return. But, what about the actual initial investment? (Let's call the actual investment our "outflows.") Consideration of our actual investment adds a new dimension to our thinking. Let's calculate the cash cost and cash proceeds for each of our alternatives.

You will note that in previously arriving at our income after taxes for all three alternatives, we have included the annual depreciation expense. Because depreciation is a book entry and a noncash item, it must be added back to the projected income to arrive at the cash flow. In short, then, we desire to compare the present value of the cost of the investment with the present value of the cash flows which are anticipated as a result of making the investment in question. This calculation can be illustrated in the following manner:

ALTERNATIVE 1

	Amount before Taxes	Amount after Taxes	Year Event Occurs	Present-value Factor at 10%	Present Value
Net present cash outflow:					
1. Investment in new equipment	$22,000	$22,000	0	1.00	$ 22,000
Net cash outflow					$ 22,000
Anticipated funds inflow:					
2. Annual incremental funds generated	45,333	23,333	1–15	7.605	$177,447
3. Salvage value of new equipment	2,000	2,000	15th	0.239	478
Cash inflow					$177,925
Excess present value of inflows over outflows					$155,925

Profitability index* $\frac{\$177{,}925}{\$\ 22{,}000} = 8.08$

* The profitability index is calculated by dividing the present value of the cash inflows by the present value of the cash outflows.

Let's examine each step in the presentation above.

1. *Investment in new equipment.* There are no immediate tax implications at the time the investment is made. Net cash outflow is $22,000. The cash investment of $22,000 that must be made now obviously has a present value of $22,000. This is the present value of the cash cost of the investment.
2. *Annual incremental funds generated.* The word profit was not used! In order to convert the accounting profit before taxes, the $44,000 reported earlier, to a cash flow, we must add back the noncash

deduction that had been made for depreciation. Depreciation expense was a cost of production, but not a cash cost. We did not write a check payable to the order of depreciation expense. We still have the cash inflows that have been called accumulated depreciation. In order to include all cash flows, we must add the annual depreciation accumulation back to the project.

Estimated annual income after depreciation and before taxes	\$ 44,000
Add annual depreciation provision	1,333
Total funds generated before taxes	\$ 45,333
Less income tax (50% of \$44,000)	\$ 22,000
Total funds generated	\$ 23,333
Multiplied by P.V. of an annuity factor at 10%, 15 years	7,605
Present value of funds generated from incremental investment	\$177,447

3. *Salvage value.* At the end of the 15-year period the new machine is estimated to have a \$2,000 salvage value. This will be a cash inflow at that time. The present value of \$2,000 is calculated by multiplying this sum by the present-value factor at 10 percent for 15 years (\$2,000 × 0.239 = \$478.)

There are several basic assumptions implicit in the use of the present-value factor of 10 percent that we should recognize.

1. When we arrive at the present value of the inflows, we are saying that if we invested \$177,925 now to earn interest at 10 percent, we could withdraw \$23,333 (annual funds generated after taxes) each year for 15 years and then withdraw the salvage value, \$2,000, at the end of the 15-year period and come out exactly even. The assumption is that 10 percent will be the rate of earnings over the 15-year period. This figure may remain at 10 percent during the 15-year period or change to 8 percent or 12 percent! The 10 percent was an assumption!

   We could approach the 10 percent assumption from a second angle.
2. The Jones Corporation, or any business entity, would not be expected to make any capital investment unless the investment promises a return in excess of its "cost of funds." This phrase "cost of funds" is indeed complex and involved. For now let's just agree that a 10 percent return is President Jones' best estimate of the return that could be earned if the funds were invested elsewhere (the opportunity cost!). We will define the term "cost of funds" in more detail as we study Chapter 12.

3. The salvage value at the end of the 15-year period, and thus the rate of depreciation during the 15-year period, is an assumption. This assumption is not too serious, if it is reasonable. The worst that can happen is an adjustment to our earnings in the fifteenth year (and here we are assuming we keep the new machine that long). *For tax purposes, the tax law provides that any gain on the sale of depreciable personal property held for over six months will be treated as ordinary income to the extent of the depreciation previously allowed (or allowable) as a tax deduction.* The tax law also provides that gain on the sale of commercial depreciable real property held over six months will be ordinary income to the extent of the excess of the accelerated depreciation previously taken as a tax deduction over the straight-line depreciation that would have been allowed on the property sold had that method been used. *That portion of any gain that exceeds the depreciation recaptured as ordinary income in the two previous situations will be treated as a Section 1231 gain.* This might result in a long-term capital gain, depending on the other Section 1231 transactions during the taxable year. However, all this will take place many years hence and will have little effect on the present value as calculated. Check your table to see why!

ALTERNATIVE 2

	Amount before Taxes	Amount after Taxes	Year Event Occurs	Present-value Factor at 10%	Present Value
Net present cash outflow:					
1. Investment in new equipment	$332,100	$332,100	0	1.00	$332,100
2. Loss on sale of old equipment	(10,833)*	(5,417)	0	1.00	(5,417)
Present value of net outflows					$326,683
Anticipated funds inflow:					
3. Incremental funds generated	290,700*	160,350†	1–10	6.145	$985,350
4. Depreciation lost from old equipment	(4,166)	(2,083)	1–5	3.791	(7,897)
5. Salvage value of new equipment	32,100	32,100	10th	0.386	12,390
Excess present value of inflows over outflows					$989,843
					$663,160

Profitability index $\frac{\$989,843}{\$326,683} = 3.33$

* Original cost	$50,000
Less accumulated depreciation	29,167
Book value	20,833
Selling price	10,000
Loss on sale	$10,833

† How did we arrive at these figures?

As a result of the introduction of all these contingencies, one might be inclined to question the validity of this or any analysis! This would indeed be an error. The fact that the basic assumptions are significant forcefully points up the necessity of being extremely careful when the basic data are being compiled. The management function is always surrounded with uncertainty and characterized by risk. However, as will be repeated over and over, decisions must be made. Analytical tools are helpful, but are no substitute for informed managerial judgment.

We can now prepare the same type of analysis for alternatives 2 and 3.

Net present cash outflows:

1. Present cash outflow, the purchase price of the equipment.
2. Reduction is federal income tax during year of purchase because of loss on sale of equipment.

Anticipated incremental funds generated:

3. Estimated annual income after depreciation and

before taxes	$260,000
Add annual depreciation expense	30,000
Total funds generated before taxes	$290,700
Less income tax (50% of $260,700)	130,350
Total funds generated after taxes	$160,350
Multiplied by present value of an annuity factor at 10% for 10 years	6.145
	$985,350

4. We have been dealing with incremental income, or the additional income that will accrue as a result of the purchase of the new machinery. You will notice that in our calculations of this income in item 3 above we included for tax purposes 100 percent of the depreciation on the new equipment. This resulted in an annual tax saving of $15,000 (50 percent of $30,000 annual depreciation). However, with the sale of the old equipment we will lose the tax savings we would have received from the depreciation on the old equipment over the remaining five-year period. The book value of the old equipment was $20,833. The loss in annual tax saving would be 50 percent of the annual depreciation $4,166, or $2,083.

We must reduce the incremental funds by this amount. In essence, the tax saving will be:

	\$15,000	tax saving because of depreciation on new equipment
Less	(2,083)	tax saving because of depreciation on old equipment for five years
	\$12,917	net tax saving depreciation for first five years

5. Salvage value—same rationale as alternative 1.

ALTERNATIVE 3*

	Amount before Taxes	Amount after Taxes	Year Event Occurs	Present-value Factor at 10%	Present Value
Net present cash outflow:					
Investment in new plant	\$1,250,000	\$1,250,000	0	1.00	\$1,250,000
Tax loss on sale	(10,833)	(5,417)	0	1.00	(5,417)
Total outflows					\$1,244,583
Anticipated funds inflow:					
Incremental funds generated	460,700	291,600	1–8	5.335	\$1,555,686
Anticipated salvage value of new equipment	100,000	100,000		0.467	46,700
Depreciation on old equipment	(4,166)	(2,083)	1–5	3.791	(7,897)
Annual income from rental value + depreciation of bldg. after eight years	60,000	35,000	9–25	8.022 and 0.467	~~131,119†~~ 131,119†
Total inflows					\$1,725,608
Excess present value of inflows over outflows					\$ 481,025

Profitability index $\frac{\$1{,}725{,}608}{\$1{,}244{,}583} = 1.38$

* No explanations; how did we arrive at the figures?

† \$35,000
8,022 (17 years at 10%)
\$280,770

\$280,770
0.467 (back 8 years to present)
\$131,119

(You will notice that we included the rental value of the building for the estimated 17 years of useful life beyond the life of the equipment at an arbitrary rental of \$50,000 per year, plus annual depreciation of \$10,000.)

President Jones immediately eliminated any further consideration of alternative 1 because of the limited capacity provided. He stated that alternative 3 just involved too much money at this time. Alternative 2 appeared to him to be an excellent investment.

We quickly reminded the president that our present-value calculations as presented for alternatives 2 and 3 were limited to sales at the

155,000-unit level; and we pointed out the additional capacity provided by alternative 3 and the cost differentials between 2 and 3 beyond the 155,000 annual unit level. These considerations are very significant, as we shall see as we continue to build our framework for a decision.

He stated that while he realized we had to project and plan for the future, he was not willing to accept the risk involved in alternative 3 when alternative 2 gave evidence of satisfactory anticipated results.

In view of the fact that we can no longer fruitfully consider either alternative 1 or 3, let us concentrate on the second alternative and calculate its internal rate of return.

It is extremely unfortunate that we cannot reach for a formula that will equate the present value of the outflows and the present value of the inflows, thus giving us the "internal rate of return" for our investment under alternative 2. There is none. We must simply, by trial and error, find the interest factor that will equate the present value of the outflows with the present value of inflows. This interest factor will, as you recall, tell us the rate of return we are earning on our investment.

Alternative 2:	
Present value of net outflows	$326,683[1]
Present value of inflows after taxes, 10 years at 10%	$985,350
Depreciation lost on old equipment	(7,897)
Excess present value of net outflows over present value of inflows	$663,160

[1] Totals from page 134.

As indicated above, our problem now is to find that rate of discount which will equate the present value of the estimated inflows with the present value of the net outflows.

Assuming that we may not always have the present-value tables available, we will develop the present-value factors at 47 percent. We will use our present-value formula:

$$\text{P.V.} = \frac{1}{(1+i)} \text{ or } \frac{1}{(1+0.47)} \text{ or } \frac{1}{1.47}$$

$$1 \text{ year} = \frac{1}{1.47} = 0.68$$

$$2 \text{ years} = \frac{0.68}{1.47} = 0.462$$

$$3 \text{ years} = \frac{0.462}{1.47} = 0.314$$

$$4 \text{ years} = \frac{0.314}{1.47} = 0.213$$

$$5 \text{ years} = \frac{0.213}{1.47} = 0.144 \text{ Total 5 years} = 1.813$$

$$6 \text{ years} = \frac{0.144}{1.47} = 0.098$$

$$7 \text{ years} = \frac{0.098}{1.47} = 0.066$$

$$8 \text{ years} = \frac{0.066}{1.47} = 0.044$$

$$9 \text{ years} = \frac{0.044}{1.47} = 0.029$$

$$10 \text{ years} = \frac{0.029}{1.47} = \frac{0.019}{2.069}$$

The factor 2.069 is the present value of an annuity of $1 discounted at 47 percent for 10 years. The factor 0.019 is the present value of $1 discounted at 47 percent for 10 years. The factor 1.813 is the present value of an annuity of $1 discounted for five years at 47 percent.

Using the discount factors just developed, we can calculate that the internal rate of return for alternative 2 is approximately 47.80 percent.

	Amount after Taxes	**Year Event Occurs**	**Discount Factor at 47%**	**Present Value**
Present value of net outflows:				
Net investment	$326,683	1	1	$326,683
Present value of net inflows:				
Incremental funds generated	160,350	1–10	2.069	$331,764
Salvage value	32,100	10th	0.019	610
Less depreciation on old equipment	(2,083)	1–5	1.813	(3,776)
				$328,598
Excess P.V. inflows over outflows				$ 1,915

Other data given:

P.V. of inflows at 48% = $324,312
By interpolation:

$$\frac{(47\%)\quad 328{,}598 - 326{,}683}{(48\%)\quad 324{,}312 - 326{,}683} = 0.80$$

(Column heads: P.V. inflows, P.V. outflows)

Internal rate of return = 47.67%

President Jones was delighted! An internal rate of return of 47.80 percent is excellent indeed. However, we made some very rigorous assumptions implicitly and explicitly which affected the calculation of this rate of return.

1. Selling price would remain constant at $6 per unit for normal sales and $5 per unit for Allied sales!
2. Average total cost would remain constant at $3.50 per unit!
3. Implicit in item 2 above is the assumption that production would remain constant at the 155,000 units annual level!

As we reexamine these assumptions in reverse order, it appears highly unlikely that sales will remain at the present level. (In fact, it is quite obvious that we do not anticipate that sales will remain at this level. One reason we did not seriously consider alternative 1 was that the additional machine would provide production capacity only up to the 155,000-unit level.) We know that production costs will not remain at $3.50, average total cost, as production surpasses the 155,000 level. In addition, selling prices may or may not remain at $6 and $5, respectively.

As we begin to relax these assumptions and to deal with possible changes in selling price and/or changes in production-factor costs (material, labor, and overhead), it is significant that we recall our cost curves. First, we know that if all dollar costs remain constant, as production exceeds the anticipated 155,000 units annually, average total cost will fall until production reaches 190,000 units annually. Therefore, we know that average total cost per unit will fall below the present $3.50 per unit because of the economies of scale. Why are we so certain? If you can answer this question, it is clear that you have grasped the problem. If you cannot, do you recall that alternative 2 provides that average total cost will fall until production reaches the 190,000 level?

In essence, we are saying that average total cost per unit will decrease as production increases and we move downward on our cost curves to the 190,000-unit level. We could easily recalculate the profitability of alternative 2 at any level on our cost curves, which would be specifically constructed for this purpose. We could and should likewise prepare new present value and internal rates of return tests based on different production estimates. Should we follow these procedures, we would be examining a range of possibilities rather than a single result based on the rather rigid assumptions of constant quantity and constant cost. (The computer will do this task easily and quickly.)

We have likewise been assuming that the price we must pay for the production cost factors will remain stable for the estimated 10-year life of alternative 2! If the price we pay for material, labor, and/or overhead costs does not remain constant over the estimated life of the equipment, our cost curves will shift, causing corresponding changes in profitability and resulting in corresponding changes in present values and internal rates of return! (Prior to this point we have considered only cost changes caused by the movement along the cost curves prompted by variations in production.)

To make things more realistic and somewhat more complicated, let's assume that selling price, quantity sold, and factor costs all change and, perhaps, change in different directions! As an example, selling price could go up or down as the costs of labor and material and other overhead items increase and decrease at different rates. At this point one might perhaps wonder why we went through the exercise of making the capital budgeting analysis at all! We did attempt to project profitability over the next eight or ten years without considering the possibility of changes in selling price and in the dollar price we pay for the factors of production! However, all has not been in vain. If we thoroughly understand the concepts as outlined, we have made considerable progress. We just can't learn everything in "one easy lesson." In short, prior capital budgeting analysis can be used as a bench mark against which to judge the usefulness of future analyses.

President Jones has taken a calculated risk. What are the risk factors? We know we are earning a reasonable profit at the present time. We know likewise that our projected profits are excellent. However, as indicated, selling price and the several factor costs can move in all directions and at different rates over the life of the investment. In addition, Allied, our best customer, may or may not grow and may or may not continue to buy our product! Bench marks are fine, but offer little more than a basis for hindsight if our estimated income and cost factors have been grossly in error! We may or may not be able to absorb a relatively large loss. We know Jones Electronic cannot absorb a substantial loss. Most of the additional funds necessary to finance the equipment acquisition must come from external sources.[1] This could involve a chattel mortgage or other credit instrument, fixed charges (interest), and possible foreclosure and loss of the entire business. One cannot help appreciating the uncertainty involved in investing $332,000 from a capital base of one-fourth that size![2] One cannot help recognizing the risk. However, this is an integral part of the game. Decisions must be made.

Sensitivity Analysis

What we really should do at this point is to develop a sensitivity analysis. (We have been discussing some basic elements of this type of analysis.)

[1] Since the demand for investment action is immediate, we cannot wait for the profits from existing operations to provide the required funds.

[2] In effect, you have bet your company on the outcome of a single decision.

This type of analysis is designed to show the effect on profitability of changes or variation in price of cost factors. Let's examine this idea in more detail by bringing forward some figures from a flexible budget that we assume has been prepared for alternative 2.[1]

		Normal	Allied
1.	Percent of total sales[2]	75% (approx.)	25% (approx.)
	Selling price	\$6.00	\$5.00
	Average variable cost at 155,000-unit level with new equipment	2.00	2.00
	Contribution	\$4.00	\$3.00
2.	Total fixed cost \$232,500		
	For our purposes, assume percent of total sales	75%	25%
	or	3 × \$4 = \$12	1 × \$3 = \$3
	Weighted present contribution	\$12.00	+ \$3.00 = \$15.00

$$\frac{\$15}{4 \text{ units}} = \$3.75 \text{ per unit} = \text{average contribution per unit}$$

3\. $$\text{Breakeven point} = \frac{\text{Total fixed cost}}{\$3.75} = 62{,}000 \text{ units}$$

4.	Total estimated sales, first year	155,000 units
	Breakeven point with current ratio of sales between "normal" and Allied	62,000 units
	Sales beyond breakeven point	93,000 units
	Average contribution per unit	\$ 3.75
	Estimated profit before taxes	\$348,750
	Estimated income tax (50%)	174,375
	Estimated profit after taxes	\$174,375

There are certain things that can be derived from this information. As quantity produced increases, the downward movement on our cost curves will reduce average total cost per unit a maximum of 50 cents until we reach the 190,000-unit level.

Average total cost at 155,000 level	\$3.50
Average total cost at 190,000 level	3.00
Reduction in total cost per unit	\$0.50

[1] A flexible budget was not prepared for alternative 2. To do so would be a repetition of Chapter 4.

[2]

Allied sales	\$ 40,000 = 25.8%
Normal sales	115,000 = 74.2%
Total sales	\$155,000 = 100%

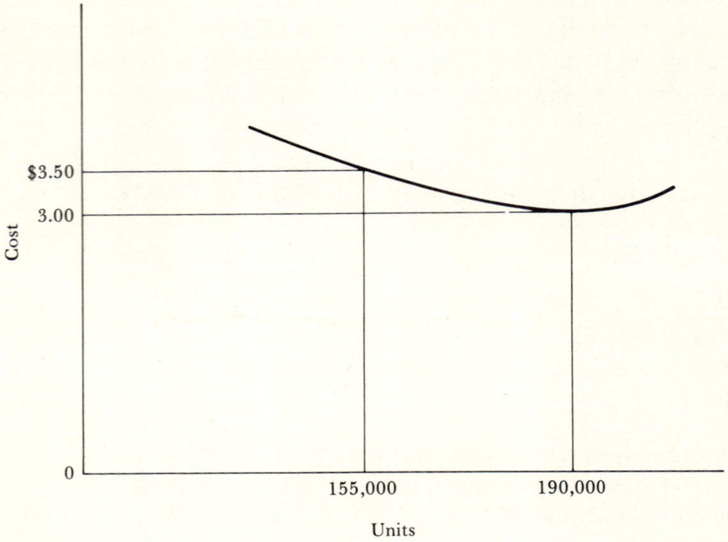

Note carefully:

$$\frac{\text{Total fixed cost } \$232{,}500}{\text{Units } 155{,}000} = \$1.50 \text{ (average fixed cost per unit)}$$

$$\frac{\$232{,}500}{190{,}000} = \$1.22 + \text{(average fixed cost per unit)}$$

AFC at 155,000 units	$1.50
AFC at 190,000 units	1.22
Reduction in fixed cost per unit	$0.28
Reduction in average total cost	0.50
Reduction in average fixed cost	—0.28
Reduction in variable cost per unit	0.22

In addition, we know the following:

1. If total fixed costs will remain fixed, including such items as insurance, taxes, and salaries, the variable cost factors can increase approximately 50 cents per unit without changing our projected profit. Average variable costs will have been reduced 22 cents per unit, and average fixed cost will have declined approximately 28 cents per unit. (How do you know that!)
2. If fixed costs increase, the total cost increase must not exceed 50 cents per unit.

3. We, therefore, have a built-in cushion of 50 cents per unit to absorb factor dollar cost increases as we move into the future and production and sales increase from the 155,000-unit level of production to the 190,000-unit level of production. We could likewise calculate the cushion at any level of production.

We can now relax the rigid assumptions that the weighted selling price and factor costs will remain constant.

A 25 percent dollar increase in variable costs. A 25 percent dollar increase in factor costs ($2.00 to $2.50) will cause a 13⅓ percent decrease in the contribution at the 155,000-unit level. Sales ratio remains 3 to 1.

Normal selling price	$6.00	Allied	$5.00
Average variable cost	2.50		2.50
Contribution	$3.50		$2.50

Weighted: $3.50 × 3 = $10.50 and $2.50 × 1 = $2.50
$13.00 ÷ 4 = $ 3.25 weighted price

Former weighted contribution	$3.75	
New weighted contribution	3.25	$\frac{0.50}{3.75} = 13.3\%$
Reduction in contribution	$0.50	

The breakeven point will increase from 62,000 to 71,538 units:

$$\frac{\text{Total fixed cost}}{\text{Weighted contribution}} \quad \frac{\$232{,}500}{\$3.25} = 71{,}538 \text{ units to breakeven}$$

Gross profit before taxes will decrease from $348,750 to $271,251:

Sales	155,000 units	155,000 units
Units to breakeven	62,000	71,538
	93,000	83,462
Weighted contribution	$3.75	$3.25
Gross profit	$348,750	$271,251

A change in sales volume and weighted price. Assume that sales increase 20 percent from 155,000 units to 186,000 and that the ratio of normal sales to sales to Allied has changed to 60 to 40 percent. In essence, Allied sales have grown at a faster rate than normal sales, and the sales mix has changed from 75 to 25 percent to 60 to 40 percent. What effect will this change have on profitability?

Normal sales price	$6 × 6 = $36
Sales to Allied	$5 × 4 = 20
Weighted price per unit	$56 ÷ 10 = $5.60

Weighted price per unit	$5.60
Average variable cost	2.00
Contribution per unit	$3.60

$$\frac{\text{Total fixed cost}}{\text{Contribution per unit}} \quad \frac{\$232{,}500}{\$3.60} = 64{,}583 \text{ units to breakeven}$$

Total unit sales	186,000
Breakeven point	64,583
	121,417 × $3.60 = $437,137 gross profit

A 25 percent increase in average variable cost and a 20 percent increase in total sales together with a change in sales mix from 3 to 1 to 6 to 4

Weighted price as calculated	$5.60
Average variable cost	2.50
Weighted contribution per unit	$3.10

$$\frac{\text{Total fixed cost}}{\text{Weighted contribution per unit}} \quad \frac{\$232{,}500}{\$3.10} = 75{,}000 \text{ units to breakeven}$$

Total sales	186,000 units
Breakeven point	75,000 units
Gross profit	111,000 × $3.10 = $344,100

As a first approximation, it would appear that we would earn less gross profit at the 186,000-unit level of sales ($344,100) than we calculated earlier for the 155,000-unit level. However, we have considered only the increase in *dollar cost* in average variable cost ($2.00 to $2.50). We have not given consideration to the *economies of scale* (the cushion calculated earlier) as we move from the 155,000 units to the 186,000-unit level! Therefore the average variable cost will be reduced 22 cents per unit below the $2.50 level. Why do we use 22 cents instead of 50 cents as mentioned earlier?

If you review the cushion discussion earlier, you recall that the 50 cents cushion was made up of two factors, 22 cents average variable cost per unit and 28 cents average fixed cost per unit.

Therefore, when we approach our problem via selling price, variable cost, and contributions to fixed cost and profit, we are interested only in the change in variable cost. This is so because we are dealing with *total* fixed cost and not average fixed cost per unit. Thus, we can say that *because of the economies of scale,* the average variable cost was reduced 22 cents per unit, resulting in an additional increase in gross profit of $40,920 (186,000 units × 22 cents)! Total gross profit would then be

As calculated	$344,100
Add	40,920
	$385,020

Let's test this observation.

Income from sales:			
Normal:		111,600 units at $6 =	$ 669,600 (60%)
Allied:		74,400 units at $5 =	372,000 (40%)
			$1,041,600 (100%)
Cost of goods sold:			
Average variable cost ($2.50 – $0.22)	$2.28		
Average fixed cost	1.25[1]		
Total	$3.53	× 186,000 units =	656,580
Gross profit			$ 385,020

[1] Total fixed cost:

$$\frac{232{,}500}{186{,}000 \text{ units}} = \$1.25 \text{ fixed cost per unit}$$

In essence, a complete sensitivity analysis will indicate how much the after-tax income, and therefore the present value and/or the rate of return, will differ from our original estimates if selling price and/or factor costs do not follow the initially projected pattern. This type of analysis will reflect all reasonably anticipated price and cost variations. (Our analysis here will be limited to alternative 2. However, it is quite possible that an analysis of all alternatives might indicate that President Jones should switch to alternative 3!)

Probability Analysis

We have just indicated that all reasonably anticipated cost and/or price variances should be included. This raises the question of the probability of price and/or cost changes. In essence, we are talking about a type of "risk analysis." Quite often, this question is answered by combining the sensitivity analysis with a probability analysis. This latter analysis has been presented several ways. The simplest way is to project two estimates of profitability—a pessimistic estimate and an optimistic estimate. An alternative involves projecting high, low, and middle estimates. This analysis will present a range of present values and rates of return rather than the single one which we have predicted.

Sensitivity and Probability Combined

A more sophisticated risk analysis builds into the sensitivity analysis a probability that each particular variation of price and cost will occur. (It is not our purpose at this point to provide proficiency in either sensitivity or probability analysis. Rather, it is our purpose to provide familiarity with the total process.) In general, a simplified analysis would involve the following steps:

1. Careful study would be made of the key variable items; perhaps selling price, quantity sold, and detailed material, labor, and overhead costs. We would need estimates of future changes in the prices to be paid for those items and an estimate of the probability of these changes. We must become as knowledgeable as possible in each of the key areas.
2. We would then develop a probability diagram, as illustrated below in simplified form. The computer, properly programmed, would handle the many possible combinations of variables quickly and easily.
3. We would then calculate rates of return and/or present values of the possible outcomes.
4. Finally, we would prepare a weighted average of the probable results.

For illustrative purposes, let's assume that a detailed study of our markets, the estimated price we must pay for our factors of production, and the estimates of the quantity that would be sold indicate the following:

Chance of Occurring:	**25%**	**50%**	**25%**
Selling price (weighted average)	$5.75*	$5.60†	$6.10‡
Quantity sold	178,250	186,000	193,750
	(Up 15%)	(Up 20%)	(Up 25%)
Chance of Occurring:	**5%§**	**80%§**	**15%§**
Total variable production cost per unit	$2.00	$2.50	$3.00
	(No change)	(Up 25%)	(Up 50%)

* Assuming a continuation of the 75 percent normal sales and 25 percent sales to Allied:
Normal: $6 × 3 = $18
Allied: $5 × 1 = 5
$23 ÷ 4 = $5.75

† Assuming a change in sales pattern to 60 percent normal sales and 40 percent to Allied:
Normal: $6 × 6 = $36
Allied: $5 × 4 = 20
$56 ÷ 10 = $5.60

‡ Assuming a continuation of the 60 to 40 percent ratio but a 50-cent increase in selling prices:
Normal: $6.50 × 6 = $39
Allied: $5.50 × 4 = 22
$61 ÷ 10 = $6.10

§ Would normally be broken down into individual components if significant.

The above analysis indicates that the Jones organization anticipates that there is a 25 percent chance that the weighted price will remain at $5.75 per unit and that the quantity sold will increase 15 percent from 155,000 to 178,250 units. There is a 50 percent chance that the weighted price will drop to $5.60 per unit while volume sold increases 20 percent from 155,000 to 186,000 units. There is another 25 percent chance that the weighted price will increase to $6.10 per unit while volume sold increases 25 percent from 155,000 to 193,750 units.

At the same time that the weighted price and volume are moving, there is also a 5 percent chance that there will be no change in the dollar price Jones must pay per unit of variable production cost (VPC). There is likewise an 80 percent chance that VPC will increase in dollar cost 25 percent from $2 to $2.50 per unit, and there is a 15 percent chance that VPC will increase 50 percent from $2 to $3 per unit.

Therefore, for each of our three price combinations, there are three possible variable factor production costs. This is a total of nine possibilities. We can visualize these possibilities as an umbrella containing the probability of each of the nine possible combinations, as follows:

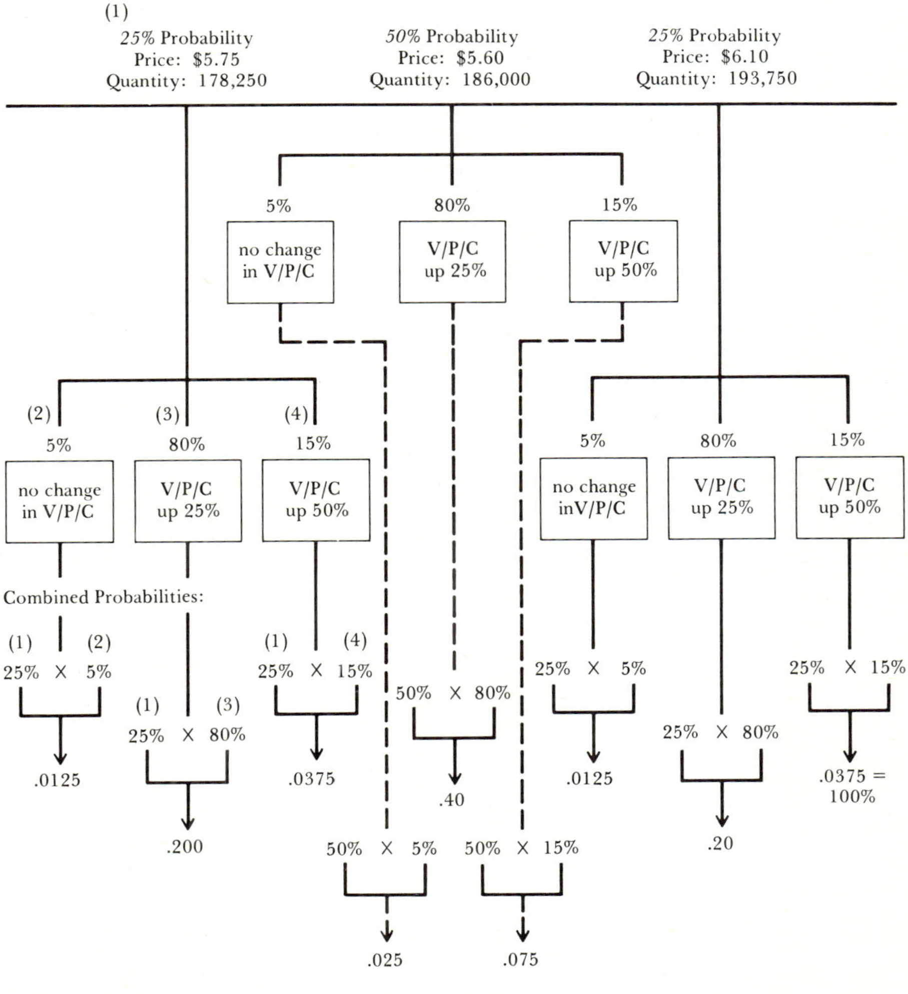

(V/P/C = Variable factor price change)

The analysis presented above indicates that we have accounted for 100 percent of the sensitivity-probability possibilities based on the nine discrete alternatives selected. Each of the possibilities is a combination of the probability of price-quantity change and the change in variable factor cost. As an example, there is a 25 percent probability that the weighted price will remain at $5.75 per unit and the quantity sold will amount to 178,250 units (probability 1 above). There is a 5 percent chance that there will be no change in variable factor price (probability 2 above). Thus, 25 percent × 5 percent = 0.0125 percent. Thus, there is a $1\frac{1}{4}$ percent chance that this combination will occur. On the other hand, when the same 25 percent with respect to price and quantity is combined with the 80 percent chance that variable factor prices will increase as indicated by probability 3 above, there is a 20 percent chance that this combination of price, quantity, and variable factor cost will occur (25 percent × 80 percent = 20 percent). Likewise, a combination of 25 percent and 15 percent (1 and 4) indicates that there is a 0.0375 percent chance that 1 and 4 will occur together.

Based upon our best estimate at this time, a probability profile of alternative 2 would appear as follows:

Volume, Units	Weighted Price	Average Variable Cost	Probability
186,000	$5.60	$2.50	40%
178,250	5.75	2.50	20
193,750	6.10	2.50	20
186,000	5.60	3.00	$7\frac{1}{2}$
178,250	5.75	3.00	$3\frac{3}{4}$
193,750	6.10	3.00	$3\frac{3}{4}$
186,000	5.60	2.00	$2\frac{1}{2}$
178,250	5.75	2.00	$1\frac{1}{4}$
193,750	6.10	2.00	$1\frac{1}{4}$
			100%

We could and should prepare a sensitivity-probability analysis for alternative 3. However, in view of the financial constraints (President Jones has indicated that he would be unable and unwilling at this time to raise the $1,250,000 for alternative 3), there would be little point in doing so. We cannot pass over the data we have developed too lightly. We have learned again and again that every analysis contains some basic assumptions. An understanding of these assumptions is essential as we test the significance of "what we have now that we have it"!

A very significant assumption involved the increase in estimated average variable production costs. However, this increase in average variable production cost was based entirely on an anticipated increase in production factor dollar costs, for example, increased cost of material, labor, and overhead items. This factor is most significant! Dollar cost for material, labor, and overhead may increase, but, as illustrated earlier, we must not overlook our economies of scale. The facts of the Jones case indicate that we will operate on a downward-sloping cost curve until we reach the 190,000-unit production level. This is the "cushion" referred to earlier. This is significant. Review if necessary.

Therefore, as long as factor prices do not increase more than 50 cents per unit, our economies of scale will balance out the increase in dollar costs and will prevent factor prices from becoming a major problem.

There is more analysis that could be done at this time. The additional work would include the following:

1. Recalculate the additional income provided by alternative 2, using each of the nine selling price–cost combination probabilities indicated by our probability diagram.
2. Recalculate the internal rate of return and/or the present-value analysis made earlier for each probability.
3. For the purpose of simplicity, we have assumed that no additional working capital is necessary as sales volume increases. As we will learn later in our study, this omission could be a fatal error. The net cost of investment figure should be increased to include any additional working capital requirements.

However, for the Jones Electronic analysis, perhaps it will be sufficient to make the following observations. Of the nine selling price–cost combinations, there is an 80 percent probability that one of three will actually occur.

Volume, Units	**Weighted Price**	**Average Variable Cost**	**Probability**
186,000	$5.60	$2.50	40%
178,250	5.75	2.50	20
193,750	6.10	2.50	20

Wouldn't it be great to relax our probability assumptions, which admit to only three possibilities for price changes and three possibilities for factor dollar cost changes, and have the computer print out for us a large "rainbow" of possibilities. Can you visualize that rainbow projected on a large screen or white wall?

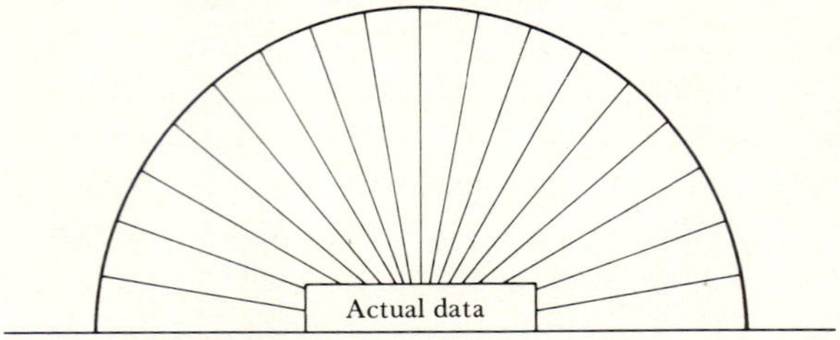

As the financial executive, or any executive for that matter, you could watch your projections become realities with the passage of time. You would be familiar with, at least, the probable results if your firm continued its present course of action. You would have at your fingertips the information you would need to give the directions to change the evolving results if it appeared desirable to do so. Likewise, you could predict with a high degree of confidence the composition of the year-end financial statements!

While we have not worked out the details for this complete analysis, we have established the basic framework for a capital and comprehensive budgeting program. The bibliography at the end of this chapter will serve as a guide for more detailed study.

Our capital budgeting efforts for the Jones Electronic Corporation were the result of an immediate need. No real effort was made to establish long-range goals and company objectives other than to "grow with Allied." When and if our immediate problems are solved, we should address ourselves to several basic considerations. We must define or redefine our business objectives. A second consideration, which is easier said than done, is to determine as far as possible our desired rate of growth. As we have seen and will see, further growth requires additional financing. The "desired rate of growth" may or may not be a practical rate of growth consistent with financing capabilities.

Growth with Allied and possibly other aeronautical and space contractors may to a large extent depend upon the contractor's ability to grow. However, "normal" growth may well depend upon our own research and product development, our market penetration potentials, and our ability to produce and sell an acceptable product at competitive prices. We will, therefore, be concerned with sales forecasts, production, warehousing, and marketing costs. A significant financial item that can be expected to increase, as indicated earlier, is working capital. All these factors, individually or collectively, depending upon our approach to the problem, will generate capital budgeting requirements.

Obviously, it would be more efficient if our planning could embrace all these considerations within a single program. However, as with all business organizations, our resources are limited. We must determine where these limited funds may be most effectively used. (Firm A's available funds may be $100,000 or less, and Firm B's available funds may be $10 million or more. However, the problem is the same—to find the most effective use of available funds.) This is the essence of efficient capital budgeting.

You have suggested to President Jones that our "long-range goals" be formalized as a plan for a given period of time—perhaps five to seven years. Each year, the plan can be extended an additional year so that, in effect, there will be a continuous five- to seven-year plan. These plans should involve every level of the business organization. Ideas may originate at any level (marketing, production, warehousing, or research and development). Sooner or later, all the ideas in the form of proposals must be subjected to a financial feasibility study.

For the most part, a completely detailed five- or seven-year plan not only will be impossible but likewise would be impractical. This is so because of possible technological changes in product requirements, changes in the general economic climate, changes in national defense activities, or a shift in international relations. As we organize our plans, we must remain as flexible as possible. Yet, as we learned earlier, decisions must be made and commitments must be entered into.

There are several approaches we can take to our capital budgeting problems. One alternative would be to use the *fixed* type of budget. By using this method, the amount of money the Jones Electronic Corporation is willing to invest or can invest for capital improvements for a given period of time is determined at the outset. Within this limit, the most promising project or projects are accepted. A second approach would be to project the capital investment needs without considering the availability of capital investment funds. Proposals would be ranked by means of one or a combination of the acceptable methods discussed earlier and would be selected or rejected according to our ability to raise the required financing. This type of capital budget has been termed the *financing* or *open-ended* budget. (We have, to some degree, adopted this latter approach in analyzing the Jones Electronic Corporation's present equipment needs. We are now faced with the problem of obtaining the required financing!)

We have not really been concerned with an "overall plan" at this point. Rather, we are taking a "one problem at a time" approach. In addition, we have not taken into consideration significant cost changes that could take place in other areas of our operation such as increased sales expense and additional warehousing or transportation costs, just to name a few.

However, you have discussed the entire matter with President Jones prior to taking the results to the executive committee. He understands that capital budgeting can be sophisticated indeed. A thorough analysis involves economics, accounting, taxation, statistics, mathematics, and certainly some computer capability plus a good foundation of common sense and judgment. Computer programs are available to deal with the many possible sensitivity and probability factors which we have briefly illustrated.

You will recall one basic assumption used throughout was that we had the funds to purchase the new machinery and equipment. This was a real assumption!

As you review the current balance sheet, it becomes obvious that our own cash position will not support any type of meaningful expansion. The acceptance of alternative 2 was one thing. Its financing appears to be quite another.

Jones Electronic Corporation
Balance Sheet
June 20, 1970

Current Assets			**Current Liabilities**	
Cash		$37,000	Liabilities	None
Accounts Receivable		25,000		
Inventories:				
Finished Goods		2,500		
Raw Materials		500		
Total Current Assets		$65,000	**Total Current Liabilities**	None
Fixed Assets			Long-term Liabilities	None
Equipment	$50,000		Stockholders' Equity	
Less			Capital stock no par	
Accumulated			(500,000 shares authorized,	
Depreciation	29,167	20,833	50,000 issued)	$85,833
Total Assets		$85,833	**Total Liabilities and Capital**	$85,833

President Jones has tossed the entire problem into your lap! Good luck! For now, I'm going to the golf course, again. I would be pleased to have you join me! (My handicap is still 20, or better (worse) than one stroke a hole.)

SUMMARY

This chapter introduces the basic capital budgeting process, which involves at least five phases. They are the:

1. Generation of investment proposals
2. Estimation of costs and benefits

3. Evaluation of the risks associated with the cash flows from individual proposals
4. Selection of the best group of investment proposals
5. Reevaluation of those proposals selected on the basis of their actual versus predicted performance

The financial success of the firm and the effectiveness of its capital budgeting effort are intimately related. Capital budgeting procedures result in the long-term commitment of large quantities of funds. The level and effectiveness of this commitment in turn determine both the level and the quality of the firm's earnings and, therefore, the value of its shares. For this reason, the direction of the firm's capital budgeting effort is one of the financial manager's most important tasks.

The Jones Company's capital budgeting effort has generated three alternative proposals for investment. In each case, costs and benefits are calculated. Selection standards are then formulated under four different methods. The selection methods explicitly described are:

1. Payback period
2. Average return
3. Rate of return
4. Net present value

Each method employs certain assumptions, and the decision maker must be conscious of them. If he fails to understand the implications of the selection method used, he may well find himself using a selection method whose assumptions are incompatible with the circumstances of the firm. For example, the rate of return system assumes that cash flows generated by an investment proposal will be reinvested at the rate of return being earned by the current proposal. Net present value selection methods assume that reinvestment of cash flows will earn the cost of funds rate. Obviously, in a given problem the two methods, although both theoretically sound, will not be equally appropriate.

The final area considered in the chapter is sensitivity analysis. Sensitivity analyses create still another dimension of capital budgeting. Initially, when we calculated costs and benefits, we did not admit the possibility of fluctuation in these elements of cash flows. Sensitivity analysis allows the decision maker to appreciate the potential consequences of changes in factor prices or selling prices.

Despite the fact that this has been an extended chapter, it has only scratched the surface of the capital budgeting process. In later courses in finance you will begin to appreciate the true scope of capital budgeting. For now, however, you have sufficient knowledge to handle the practical decisions with which you will be faced.

QUESTIONS FOR DISCUSSION

1. Define capital budgeting and relate the capital budgeting process to the goal of financial management.
2. Distinguish between independent and mutually exclusive investment proposals.
3. What similarity do you see between payback and the average-return system? What differences exist between the two?
4. Why do the above two selection devices fail to satisfy the requirements for sound capital budgeting techniques?
5. Define the internal rate of return selection system and the net present value selection system.
6. How do they differ and how are they interrelated in practice?
7. Define cash flows. How do cash flows differ from accounting profits?
8. Could the choice of one depreciation system over another affect capital budgeting decisions?
9. What is sensitivity analysis?
10. What type of information does sensitivity analysis furnish and how can it be used in a capital budgeting system?

PROBLEMS

1. If you could be guaranteed $1,000 today or $1,000 one year from today, which would you choose?
   a. By what amount would the payment a year from today have to exceed today's payment before you would be indifferent between the two?
   b. Your answer to (a) above will indicate your personal opportunity cost. What is it?
2. We have carried on our analysis by assuming that all investments involve single outlays. Investments can involve a series of outlays followed by a series of receipts. How would you handle the following investment?

   A firm can purchase a machine by paying $500 down and another $500 one year from today. The installation of the machine promises cash flows of $400 annually for a period of four years. The cost of funds employed by the firm is 10 percent. Required:
   a. What is the rate of return on this proposal?
   b. What is its net present value?
   c. Should the firm take advantage of this opportunity?
3. Your firm is considering the replacement of one of its machines. The machine cost $10,000 when new and has a current book value of $5,000. The company has been using straight-line depreciation based on a 20-year useful life with no salvage value.

   This machine could now be replaced with another which costs $5,000 and which will have an estimated salvage value of $1,000 at the end of its 10-year life. It is anticipated that the use of the new-machine will result in annual cost savings of $1,500. Depreciation will be on a straight-line basis for 10 years. Funds cost the firm 10 percent, and the tax rate is 50 percent.

a. Should the old asset be replaced?
b. Would your decision be the same if the savings attributable to the machine were to double and its life were to be halved?
c. Solve the problem again, taking into account these facts:
   (1) Removal costs for the old machine are $800.
   (2) Setup costs on the new machine amount to $600.
d. Using the same facts which were available in (a) above, assume that the new machine required an overhaul expense of $1,000 at the end of its fifth year of use. However will this fact affect your solution?

4. Suppose that you are presented with two investment opportunities. Each has a cost of $10,000. Each project has a 10-year life and will be depreciated on a straight-line basis assuming a zero salvage value. Taxes are at the rate of 50 percent. Funds cost the firm 10 percent.

PROJECT NO. 1

Cash Flows	Years
1,000	1
2,000	2
3,000	3
1,000	4
2,000	5
1,000	6
2,000	7
1,000	8
1,000	9
1,000	10

The flows associated with Project No. 1 are certain. Project No. 2 has the following cash flows; however, they are less certain.

PROJECT NO. 2

Cash Flows	Years
2,000	1
1,000	2
4,000	3
3,000	4
3,000	5
3,000	6
3,000	7
2,000	8
2,000	9
2,000	10

According to your best estimates there is a 30 percent chance that the cash flows listed for Project No. 2 will be realized. There is a 40 percent probability that the flows will be only three-fourths as large annually as those listed. Finally, there is a 30 percent probability that the actual cash flows will be one-half of the expected amounts.

a. Choose between Project No. 1 and Project No. 2.
b. Justify your choice.

REFERENCES

Alberts, William W.: Capital Investment by the Firm in Plant and Equipment, *Journal of Finance,* vol. XXI, pp. 178–201, May, 1966.

Baumol, William J., and Richard E. Quandt: Investment and Discount Rates under Capital Rationing: A Programming Approach, *The Economic Journal,* vol. LXXV, pp. 317–329, June, 1965.

Bierman, Harold, Jr., and Seymour Smidt: "The Capital Budgeting Decision," The Macmillan Company, New York, 1966.

Bodenhorn, Diran: On The Problem of Capital Budgeting, *Journal of Finance,* vol. XIV, pp. 473–492, December, 1959.

Cheng, Pao L., and John P. Shelton: A Contribution to the Theory of Capital Budgeting: The Multi-investment Case, *Journal of Finance,* vol. XIIX, pp. 622–636, December, 1963.

Cole, Terry D.: How to Obtain Probability Estimates in Capital Expenditure Evaluations: A Practical Approach, *Management Accounting,* July, 1970, p. 61.

Cord, Joel: A Method for Allocating Funds to Investment Projects When Returns Are Subject to Uncertainty, *Management Science,* vol. X, pp. 335–341, January, 1964.

Dean, Joel: "Capital Budgeting," Columbia University Press, New York, 1951.

Dougall, Herbert E.: Payback as an Aid in Capital Budgeting, *Controller,* vol. XXIX, pp. 67–72, February, 1961.

Edson, Harvey O.: Setting a Standard for Your Company's Return on Investment, *Controller,* vol. XXVI, pp. 411–415, September, 1958.

Elton, Edwin J.: Capital Rationing and External Discount Rates, *Journal of Finance,* vol. XXV, pp. 573–584, June, 1970.

Friend, Irwin, and Douglas Vickers: Re-evaluation of Alternative Portfolio—Selecttion Models, *Journal of Business,* vol. XLI, no. 2, pp. 174–179, April, 1968.

Grayson, C. Jackson, Jr.: "Decisions under Uncertainty, Drilling Decisions by Oil and Gas Operators," Division of Research, Harvard Business School, Boston, 1960.

———: Introduction of Uncertainty into Capital Budgeting Decisions, *N.A.A. Bulletin,* vol. XLIII, pp. 79–80, January, 1962.

Haynes, W. Warren, and Martin B. Solomon, Jr.: A Misplaced Emphasis in Capital Budgeting, *Quarterly Review of Economics and Business,* February, 1962.

Heebink, David V.: Postcompletion Audits of Capital Investment Decisions, *California Management Review,* vol. VI, pp. 47–52, spring, 1964.

Hertz, David B.: Risk Analysis In Capital Investment, *Harvard Business Review,* vol. 42, pp. 95–106, January-February, 1964.

Hespos, Richard F., and Paul A. Strassmann: Stochastic Decision Trees for the Analysis of Investment Decisions, *Management Science,* vol. II, pp. 244–259, August, 1965.

Hillier, Frederick S.: The Derivation of Probabilistic Information for the Evaluation of Risky Investments, *Management Science,* vol. IX, April, 1963.

——— and David V, Heebink: Evaluation of Risky Capital Investments, *California Management Review,* vol. VIII, pp. 71–80, winter, 1965.

Hirshleifer, Jack: On The Theory of Optimal Investment Decision, *Journal of Political Economy,* vol. LXVI, pp. 329–352, August, 1958.

———: Risk, the Discount Rate and Investment Decisions, *American Economic Review,* vol. LI, pp. 112–120, May, 1961.

———: Efficient Allocation of Capital in an Uncertain World, *American Economic Review,* vol. LIV, pp. 77–85, May, 1964.

Hunt, Pearson: "Financial Analysis in Capital Budgeting," Graduate School of Business Administration, Harvard University, Boston, 1964.

Jean, William H.: On Multiple Rates of Return, *Journal of Finance,* vol. XXIII, pp. 187–191, March, 1968.

Jeynes, Paul H.: The Significance of Reinvestment Rate, *Engineering Economist,* vol. II, pp. 1–9, Fall, 1965.

Joyce, Jon M., and Robert C. Vogel: The Uncertainty in Risk: Is Variance Unambiguous? *Journal of Finance,* vol. XXV, pp. 127–134, March, 1970.

Krainer, Robert E.: A Neglected Issue in Capital Rationing: The Asset Demand for Money, *Journal of Finance,* vol. XXI, pp. 731–736, December, 1966.

Latane, H. A.: Criteria for Choice among Risky Ventures, *Journal of Political Economy,* vol. LXVII, pp. 144–155, April, 1959.

Lerner, Eugene M.: Capital Budgeting and Financial Management, in Alexander A. Robichek (ed.), "Financial Research and Managerial Decisions," pp. 72–89, John Wiley & Sons, Inc., New York, 1967.

Levy, Haim: The Connection between Pre-tax and Post-tax Rates of Return, *Journal of Business,* vol. XLI, no. 4, pp. 477–483, October, 1968.

Lintner, John: The Evaluation of Risk Assets and the Selection of Risky Investments in Stock Portfolios and Capital Budget, *Review of Economics and Statistics,* vol. XLVII, pp. 13–37, February, 1965.

Lorie, James H., and Leonard J. Savage: Three Problems in Rationing Capital, *Journal of Business,* vol. XXVIII, October, 1955, reprinted in James Van Horne (ed.), "Foundations for Financial Management," pp. 295–309, Richard D. Irwin, Inc., Homewood, Ill., 1966.

Magee, J. F.: How to Use Decision Trees in Capital Investment, *Harvard Business Review,* vol. XLII, pp. 79–96, September-October, 1964.

Mansfield, Edwin, and Richard Brandenburg: The Allocation Characteristics and Outcome of the Firm's Research and Development Portfolio, *Journal of Business,* vol. XXXIX, no. 4, pp. 447–464, October, 1966.

Mao, James C. T.: The Internal Rate of Return as a Ranking Criterion, *Engineering Economist,* vol. II, pp. 1–13, winter, 1966.

———: Survey of Capital Budgeting, Theory and Practice, *Journal of Finance,* vol. XXV, pp. 349–60, May, 1970.

——— and John F. Helliwell: Investment Decision under Uncertainty, Theory and Practice, *Journal of Finance,* vol. XXIV, pp. 323–338, May, 1969.

Merrett, A. J., and Allen Sykes: "Capital Budgeting and Company Finance," Longmans, Green & Co., Ltd., London, 1966.

Moag, Joseph S., and Eugene M. Lerner: Capital Budgeting Decisions under Imperfect Market Conditions: A Systems Framework, *Journal of Finance,* vol. XXIV, pp. 613–621, September, 1969.

Myers, Stewart C.: Procedures for Capital Budgeting under Uncertainty, working paper, Sloan School of Management, Massachusetts Institute of Technology, Cambridge, Mass., 1967.

Naslund, Bertil: A Model of Capital Budgeting under Risk, *Journal of Business,* vol. XXXIX, no. 2, pp. 257–271, April, 1966.

——— and Andrew Whinston: A Model of Multi-period Investment under Uncertainty, *Management Science,* vol. IX, pp. 184–200, January, 1962.

Paine, Neil R.: Uncertainty and Capital Budgeting, *Accounting Review,* vol. XXXIX, pp. 330–332, April, 1964.

Pye, Gordon: Present Values for Imperfect Capital Markets, *Journal of Business,* vol. XXXIX, no. 1, part 1, pp. 45–51, January, 1966.

Quirin, G. David: "The Capital Expenditure Decision," Richard D. Irwin, Inc., Homewood, Ill., 1967.

Robichek, A., and James C. Van Horne: Abandonment Value and Capital Budgeting, *Journal of Finance,* vol. XXII, no. 4, pp. 577–590, December, 1967.

Robichek, Alexander A., and Stewart C. Myers: "Optimal Financing Decisions," chap. V, Prentice-Hall, Inc., Englewood Cliffs, N.J., 1965.

Sampson, Anthony A.: Measuring the Rate of Return on Capital, *Journal of Finance,* vol. XXIV, pp. 61–74, March, 1969.

Sarnat, Marshall, and Haim Levy: The Relationship of Rules of Thumb to the Internal Rate of Return: A Restatement and Generalization, *Journal of Finance,* vol. XXIV, no. 3, pp. 479–490, June, 1969.

Sau, Ranjit K.: The Optimal Rate of Investment in a Firm, *Journal of Finance,* vol. XXIV, pp. 1–12, March, 1969.

Schwab, Bernhard, and Peter Lusztig: A Comparative Analysis of the Net Present Value and the Benefit-Cost Ratio as Measures of the Economic Desirability of Investment, *Journal of Finance,* vol. XXIV, no. 3, pp. 507–516, June, 1969.

Solomon, Ezra: The Arithmetic of Capital-budgeting Decisions, *Journal of Business,* vol. XXIX, April, 1956.

Teichroew, Daniel, Alexander A. Robichek, and Michael Montalbano: An Analysis of Criteria for Investment and Financing Decisions under Certainty, *Management Science,* vol. XII, pp. 151–179, November, 1965.

Tuttle, Donald L., and Robert H. Litzenberger: Leverage Diversification and Capital Market Effects on a Risk-adjusted Capital Budgeting Framework, *Journal of Finance,* vol. XXIII, p. 427–443, June, 1968.

U.S. Congress, Subcommittee on Economy in Government of the Joint Economic Committee: "Economic Analysis of Public Investment Decisions, Interest Rate Policy and Discounting Analysis," U.S. Government Printing Office, 1968.

Van Horne, James: Capital Budgeting for the Liquid Company, *Financial Executive,* vol. XXXIV, pp. 50–52, 60, April, 1966.

———: Capital Budgeting Decisions Involving Combinations of Risky Investments, *Management Science,* vol. XIII, pp. 84–92, October, 1966.

Woods, Donald H.: Improving Estimates that Involve Uncertainty, *Harvard Business Review,* vol. XLV, pp. 91–98, July-August, 1966.

Chapter Six

INTERMEDIATE-TERM FINANCING

Up to this point in your experience with the Jones Corporation, you have been dealing generally with the controller function. You have become familiar with some data and techniques that provide guideposts as you test the effective utilization of the firm's funds. You have examined in some detail a few of the contributions the economist, the accountant, the mathematician, and the statistician can make toward the solution of financial management problems.

Your current problem forces you to assume the treasurer's function. Our goal is to provide the production capacity necessary for immediate and, we hope, future growth. This involves raising $332,100 in additional funds to finance our purchase of new equipment. As always, there are several alternatives that should be considered. We must first determine the possible sources of these funds. Next, we must weigh their respective costs and terms. Our decision in the final analysis will be based on practical rather than theoretical considerations; that is, we may or may not be in a position to draw investment funds from the most advantageous source.

SOURCE OF FUNDS

In a broad sense, there are only two sources of funds. These sources are internal and external. *Accountants, economists, and financial execu-*

tives have stated that internal funds are generated directly by retained earnings and indirectly by depreciation, depletion, or amortization. However, it is evident that internal funds, both direct and indirect, are generated by the sales of the company's products. Without sales, there cannot be a fund set aside to recover our investment via depreciation, depletion, or amortization. Without sales, there is no possibility of profit and thus no earnings which can be retained in the business. However, let's not get involved in this semantic discussion because we do know that if depreciation and depletion have been accumulated to replace capital investments, these funds are indeed available for further investment. The same argument follows for amortization and retained earnings.

There are two sources of external funds. These sources are debt and equity. In the case of debt, the corporation may be able to borrow the funds needed if someone is willing to lend. As an illustration of an equity source, President Jones could make an additional capital investment, or stock could be sold to other investors who would then become owners along with President Jones. In any of these cases, the funds would not be generated internally, but would be secured from sources external to the firm.

At the present stage of our development, our accumulation of internally generated funds via depreciation and retained earnings is woefully inadequate to finance the immediate acquisition of new machinery and equipment for $332,100. We must, therefore, look to external sources. President Jones has indicated that he does not want to dilute his ownership (that is, lose 100 percent control) by selling additional stock at this time, nor does he have the required amount of cash readily available to invest himself. This leaves debt financing as the only external source of funds.

The term "debt" includes a wide variety of borrowing procedures. Some of these are:

1. Short-term debt, payable within a year
2. Intermediate-term debt, payable within one to five or one to ten years
3. Long-term debt, payable over a period of more than 10 years[1]

We can promptly eliminate two of the three alternatives indicated above. Short-term debt usually requires repayment within a year. While our banker has indicated that for the most part short-term loans can be renewed annually and thus take on the characteristics of intermediate-term loans (payable in more than one year), there is the risk

[1] The distinction between a long-term, ten years, and an intermediate-term, five years, is an arbitrary but conventional one.

that general economic conditions and specific bank liquidity problems may force the bank to deny renewal. There exists then the constant threat that repayment will be demanded at a time when the Jones Corporation will be unable to meet the debt. This type of financing does not satisfy our immediate need. Further, the anticipated cash flows from alternative 2 is not adequate to repay $332,100 within a year.

Long-term debt is repaid over a period in excess of 10 years. We have estimated a 10-year life (or perhaps less) for the machinery we expect to purchase with the funds. We certainly do not want to, and probably could not, obtain funds beyond this period. The maturity of the loan most certainly would be limited to the economic life of the collateral, and the new machinery would be the only collateral available!

We must, therefore, examine in some detail intermediate-term loans. The sources of these loans include the following:

1. Commercial banks
2. Life insurance companies
3. The Small Business Administration
4. Consumer finance equipment companies
5. Manufacturers of equipment

Your first effort in the investigation of these possibilities was the commercial bank. The banker explained that banks make various types of loans. *In his opinion, the type of loan we would be most interested in would be the term loan.* Term loans are generally used to finance fixed assets. They are generally self-liquidating. That is, the cash flow generated by depreciation of the fixed asset and/or incremental income are used as a prime source of funds for repayment.

The ordinary term loan will have an original final due date. This sounds a bit ambiguous. How can something be original (implying more) and final at the same time? The banker explained that he used the term "original due date" because, in practice, term loans can often be renewed or extended beyond the original period. *The terms of the loan may require a lump-sum payment at maturity or specified periodic payments during the life of the loan designed to liquidate the loan by the maturity date.* Another alternative would provide for smaller periodic payments with a "balloon" payment (the entire large unpaid balance) at the maturity date. Thus, the terms of this type of loan can be and are tailored to meet individual requirements.

At first approximation, it would appear that the Jones organization would prefer periodic payments. As indicated, these payments could be arranged to coincide with the depreciation accumulation. However, let's think about this.

If the terms of the loan provided for interest at 7 percent and we could earn 10 to 15 percent with the same money employed in the firm, would we not prefer a lump sum or at least an annual payment? Can we apply our present-value and compound-interest concepts to this problem? We certainly can.

Interest rates to individual borrowers will depend upon the banker's judgment of the risk involved in making the loan and the market price of money. The interest rate finally agreed upon will reflect the borrower's bargaining power, his financial and credit strength, other terms of the loan, and the cash position of the bank. When the bank has large uncommitted cash reserves, one could expect more liberal terms. The bank is in the business of lending money. If the bank's cash reserve is low, higher interest rates and more stringent terms can be expected. A money and banking course will teach or has taught us about the effect of national monetary and fiscal policy on the cash position of individual banks.

When the bank has agreed to commit a portion of its reserves for the purpose of a loan and the borrower does not consummate the transaction immediately, a charge may be made by the bank. This charge is known as a commitment fee. This fee compensates the bank for the period of time during which the loan is not "taken down" but is made available to the borrower.

Commercial banks can only commit "excess" reserves to a 10-year period. However, from the commercial bank's point of view, a 10-year loan may be undesirable. Liquidity is a primary problem for a commercial bank. When checks or withdrawals are presented, payment must be made promptly. But periodic repayments of the principal of the loan may lessen somewhat the bank's liquidity problem.

With this basic information, you next arranged an appointment with an executive of a relatively large life insurance company. He explained that he would prefer a 10-year or even larger maturity date. This was so because of the nature of the insurance company's liabilities as compared with the liabilities of the commercial bank. Longer periods of time are generally involved before the life insurance company must pay the claims of the policyholders.

The insurance company executive explained that interest rates on his loans would in all probability be somewhat higher than bank rates, but not necessarily so. Longer-term loans involve other risks associated with changes in interest rates and the purchasing power of money. A higher interest rate now will be a hedge against these possibilities. We will have to face the fact that to obtain the loan, we will be competing with alternative investment opportunities available to the bank and/or the insurance company. In addition, a provision might be included in the loan agreement providing that if the loan should be paid in full prior to the maturity date, the borrower must pay a prepayment penalty.

At times this penalty can be equal to 1 percent of the remaining balance existing at the time repayment is made. This extra charge would be made to compensate the bank or the insurance company for the cost of reinvesting the funds in other markets or of making additional loans to recommit their funds.

It should be noted that it is possible to arrange a loan jointly with a bank and an insurance company. The bank could carry the loan for a relatively short maturity—one, five, or six years—and the insurance company could commit itself to pick up the loan at that time and carry the balance over a longer period of time.

Your next contact was with the Small Business Administration. This agency of the federal government has several functions. We are interested here in only their lending function. (They offer managerial assistance as well.) We learned that a small business is defined as one employing 250 or fewer persons (up to 1,000 in some cases), independently owned, and not dominating its field. (We seem to fit all these qualifications.) Retail and service businesses are classified as small if their total annual sales do not exceed $1 million. A wholesaler is classified as small if sales for this same period do not exceed $5 million. Ninety-five percent of all businesses fit either of these categories, including the Jones Electronic Corporation.

The SBA can make direct loans only when financing from conventional sources is not available on "reasonable" terms. On the other hand, the SBA may participate or join with a bank or other private lending institution in making a loan to a small business. In such a case, a participation agreement will be entered into between the SBA, the lending institution, and the small business. This agreement normally provides that the SBA will guarantee the payment of principal and interest of an agreed amount up to 90 percent of the total loan. This agreement usually provides that the SBA will purchase from the bank or lending institution that portion of the total loan included in the participation agreement after 90 days' default by the borrower. The SBA may also buy the guaranteed portion of the loan immediately upon the execution of the loan agreement. However, they may not do so if the loan can be arranged on a participating basis.

The maximum amount that can be guaranteed by the SBA on behalf of any one borrower and outstanding at one time is *$350,000.* Other more detailed limitations and conditions can be obtained from a reading of additional literature provided by the SBA at one of the many regional offices throughout the country.

Interest rates on an immediate purchase by the SBA are subject to a current limitation rate on that portion of the loan guaranteed by the SBA. The bank or lending institution can charge a higher rate of interest until such time as the SBA does, in fact, purchase their participating share. Most SBA participating loans require that repurchase can take place only after a 90-day default in the payment of principal and interest by the borrower.

The SBA information did indeed sound interesting, and we returned to our banker immediately to determine whether the bank would participate with the SBA in financing the acquisition of the equipment.

The banker explained that he would need a great deal more information and financial data concerning the Jones organization before he could make a definite commitment to participate in any SBA arrangement.

BANK FINANCING

If we were to seek bank financing directly, we would have to file a loan application that would include our financial statements for the past two years or more, the names and addresses of the officers of the organization, and complete data concerning the anticipated use of the requested funds. The banker indicated that he felt quite uneasy about the size of our current needs, some $332,100, as compared with our total equity of $83,333, although the reported earnings of $40,000 to date were quite satisfactory. These earnings, however, had to be reduced by the $16,000 President Jones had withdrawn for personal use prior to incorporation. However, that is still a return on our equity investment of almost 30 percent. The banker suggested that we file the loan application. A large factor in our favor would be the projected earnings for the coming year. *He explained that if the loan committee of the bank did approve of the loan, they would, no doubt, require specific agreements from us as a part of the loan contract. These agreements might include the following restrictions:*

1. The payment of dividends and other possible withdrawal of funds would be prohibited if to do so would reduce working capital and retained earnings below a predetermined minimum. The limitation is to provide the bank with a margin of safety with respect to its loan.
2. The sale or pledging of fixed and other assets would be prohibited without prior approval by the bank.
3. New and/or additional investments would require prior bank approval.
4. Additional borrowing or pledging of credit would be prohibited without prior approval by the bank.

The loan officer indicated further that while he was favorably impressed with the present management of the Jones organization, no doubt the loan committee would require periodic certified audited financial statements. In addition, it would be necessary to provide insurance protection possibly payable to the bank on the lives of key officers of the Jones organization in an amount equal to the loan balance. Moreover, if the loan were approved, the bank might also require under certain circumstances the right to name at least one of its officials to the board of directors of the Jones Corporation.

More significant, the loan agreement would, no doubt, require a chattel mortgage, or deed of trust, not only on the equipment to be purchased but perhaps also to include all after-acquired property. The net effect of the chattel mortgage, or deed of trust, would be to permit the bank to automatically repossess the mortgaged property in the event of default on the loan by the Jones organization. More often than not, the mortgage, or deed of trust, would contain an acceleration clause. This clause, in essence, would state that in the event a periodic installment or installments were not paid within a specified time after the due date, the entire unpaid balance would become due and payable immediately. This clause would permit the bank to act promptly to protect itself rather than being forced to bring a separate legal action as each installment went into default.

After this short introduction to intermediate-term financing, you returned to the office with mixed emotions and the loan application forms. In the final analysis, the Jones organization is a relatively small new enterprise with only a short history of proved ability. We are not bargaining from a position of strength. Looking at your own firm from the lender's point of view has been sobering indeed.

However, we mustn't hesitate to seek loanable funds from banking institutions. After all, they are in the money-lending business, and we are ready to pay for the use of this money. As indicated earlier, the interest rate we pay and the restrictions and limitations contained in the loan agreement will, in part, represent the judgment of the lender with respect to our ability to repay the amount borrowed. Assets and collateral that are pledged to ensure repayment are important only to minimize the lender's risk. The lending institution is not in the business of repossessing or foreclosing on collateral. Earnings and prospective earnings are far more important as evidence of the borrower's ability to repay. As the loan officer explained to you during your meeting, many loans, in fact most, are made as a result of the firm's or individual's reputation and proved record of repayment. Willingness to repay is one thing, but ability to repay is another.

Therefore, it would be foolhardy for the Jones Corporation to accept terms that were marginal as far as its ability to perform is concerned. The banker will assess the risk and express his judgment in terms of interest rate and other possible requirements, restrictions, and/or limitations. You must analyze the benefits and risks accruing to the Jones

Corporation. Loosely paraphrasing the economist's discussion of the marginal efficiency of capital, we can conclude that if the benefits outweigh the costs and, in addition, if repayment is feasible, a mutually beneficial agreement can be reached. With this thought in mind, you filed the loan application and forwarded it to the bank's loan committee.

The loan committee expressed an interest in the size of our business and in the general products produced. They were uneasy about the prospects for our product, electrical components for space and aeronautical hardware. (They would prefer a stable product, that is, a product that is not subject to cyclical or seasonal variations.) Obviously, there is some risk involved. The government contracts held by our prime customer, Allied Electronics, could be canceled and thus cause reduction in Jones Electronic's sales to Allied. However, the committee indicated that a three- to five-year maturity for the term loan (based on Allied's present contract) should give adequate protection to their bank. The fact that Jones Electronic is relatively small (net worth around $83,000 at this time) compared with the size of the loan application ($332,100) was not a major obstacle to a favorable recommendation by the bank's loan committee.

There had obviously been a thorough investigation of the Jones management team. The loan committee report included a high rating for the production capability and especially for the ability of President Jones. A comment was made concerning the relative inexperience and lack of depth in the financial management area. President Jones was requested to comment on this point. He did, as well as he could, but as a matter of fact, you are inexperienced and have no backup financial personnel. Apparently as a test of your ability, Jones Electronic was requested to present evidence to the bank's loan committee to support the need for the loan and to demonstrate its ability to repay.

President Jones accompanied you to the meeting with the loan committee. However, you made the main presentation. This presentation included a history of the development and growth of the Jones organization from the oversized garage to the present. You were pleased when the chairman of the loan committee expressed his interest and appreciation for the data you presented. (Your presentation included all the data and reports that had been presented to the Jones executive committee to date.) The chairman explained that such elaborate justification would not generally be required of a larger, more established business organization. Your reports answered questions concerning operating efficiency, balance sheet, and general financial condition as well as projected earnings. The committee indicated that the overall operating prospects appeared excellent and the ability to repay seemed assured. One comment was made about the lack of a cash-flow analysis, that is, a forecast of net cash flows and required outflows and inflows.

A more serious question was raised, however. This question concerned your lack of consideration of additional working capital requirements. In fact, one member of the committee commented that it would be more appropriate if the requested loan were increased from $332,100 to $400,000. The $400,000 was just an "off the top of the head" figure, for he meant for the excess to be used as additional working capital. One director suggested that amounts due from Allied during the term of the loan be assigned to the bank as additional security and that instead of monthly payments, the repayment of the loan be made in five equal installments. Annual payments would relieve the strain on working capital if the Jones organization could conveniently make up the difference between the billings to Allied and the amount of the annual payment once each year. There was some nodding of heads, but no further comment on this point. The committee indicated that a decision would be made forthwith.

In the meantime you made a limited investigation of commercial finance companies as a source of credit to finance the acquisition of the needed equipment. In general, the terms, restrictions, and maturity requirements were quite similar to those of the commercial bank. You did learn, however, that a considerable volume of commercial paper is purchased directly from manufacturers and/or distributors of manufacturing equipment. That is, the manufacturer or distributor would make a credit sale, after an adequate down payment, and then sell the note or other credit instrument to the commercial finance company at a discount. You also learned that the activities of these lending institutions are primarily in the financing of accounts receivable and direct consumer financing.

However, before we get too excited and also to reply to a question from the banker as to how we were going to repay the loan, we had better investigate the cost! Direct negotiations with the manufacturer indicated that we might be able to secure our needed equipment by buying the equipment on an installment contract. In this case, the manufacturer would extend the credit. For the purpose of building a framework for our decision, we will label this idea alternative 1. There are always alternatives!

Alternative 1—Manufacturer Financing

After extended discussions, the manufacturer has agreed to carry the financing necessary to purchase the equipment. However, a 10 percent credit charge will be made plus 8 percent interest on the unpaid balance. Payments are to be made at the end of each year after a down payment of 20 percent, and the equipment is to be secured by a chattel mortgage. We have the alternative of paying the balance of $292,248 in equal installments over a three-year period or in equal installments over a five-year period. If we pay off the loan prior to maturity, there will be a "payoff premium" of 1 percent on the unpaid balance at the date of payment in full.

In essence, we are saying:

Cash price	$332,100
Add 10% credit charge	33,210
	$365,310
Less 20% down payment	73,062
Balance due	$292,248

The manufacturer has indicated that under the five-year repayment plan, the annual payment would be $73,190, including 8 percent interest on the unpaid balance. Multiplying this annual payment by 5 and subtracting the original balance, we will have paid a total of $73,702 interest under this plan but, in effect, $36,851 since the interest is tax-deductible and the Jones Corporation is in the estimated 50 percent tax bracket.

If we use the three-year plan, our annual payments will be $113,406, which would include the 8 percent interest on the unpaid balance. Interest paid would be $47,970 ($23,985 after tax deduction).

Where in the world did the manufacturer get these figures?

Use of present-value concepts. As you will recall from our earlier discussion, the annual payments are quite easy to compute. Referring to our present worth of an annuity table (A-4), we see that the present value of an annuity of $1 at 8 percent interest for five periods is $3.993. How do we use this factor to determine our annual payments? We know that an annuity of $1 means five equal payments of $1. When we add 8 percent interest, we know that when the payment is made at the end of the first year, we really owe $1 + 8 percent interest for one year on that payment of $1. Therefore, the present value of $1.08 at 8 percent for one period is $1. When the second payment is made at the end of the second year, we owe $1 + 16 percent interest. When we repay the dollar the third, fourth, and fifth years, the interest on the dollar paid each year increases by 8 percent per year.

It has been much more convenient for us to use the present value of $1 rather than the present value of $1.08 because present-value tables are based on $1. When we arrive at the present value of $1, we can apply this figure to any number of dollars. To do the same with $1.08 would be awkward and time-consuming. Our present-value framework developed in Chapter 3 explained these concepts in detail.

You recall that we could go to Table A-2, which is the present value of $1, and calculate the present value of the payment plus interest due each year. Following the procedure developed earlier, we know that the present value of an annuity can be developed as follows:

Year	P.V. of $1.00 at 8%
1	$0.926
2	0.857
3	0.794
4	0.735
5	0.681
	$3.993

The present value of an annuity of $1 at 8% for five years is $3.993.

How does this help determine the annual payments?

To solve any problem, we must start with the data we have. We know that $292,248 is the present value of our total obligation, which we must pay plus interest at 8 percent of the unpaid balance. The terms of the mortgage will require that we pay five equal installments. We also know that $3.993 is the present value of five equal payments of $1, which includes 8 percent interest. Therefore, we can divide the present value of our anticipated obligation, $292,248, by the present value of $1, and determine the number of dollars that must be paid for each of the five annual installments, or:

$$\frac{\text{P.V. of total obligation at 8\%}}{\text{P.V. of \$1 at 8\%}} = \frac{\$292{,}248}{\$3.993} = \$73{,}190 \text{ (approx.) amount of each installment}$$

or stated another way:

$$\$292{,}248 = \$3.993 \times \$73{,}190$$

Let's prove this figure the hard way:

	Payment	8% Interest Accruing	Net Decrease in Principal	Balance of Principal
				$292,248
First	$73,190	$23,380	$49,810	242,438
Second	73,190	19,395	53,795	188,643
Third	73,190	15,091	58,099	130,544
Fourth	73,190	10,444	62,746	67,798*
Fifth	73,190	5,424	67,766*	0
		$73,734*		

* Allow for difference in last payment caused by rounding.

And:

$ 73,190	Annual payment
×5	Years
$365,950	Total payment
292,248	Amount of loan
$ 73,702	Interest

We can solve the problem for the three-year period in exactly the same manner.

But now a question. Why has the manufacturer added a 10 percent credit charge? In essence, we are buying his credit, or he is taking advantage of our lack of it! Admittedly, we are a relatively small, new firm with total capital of only $83,333. We may or may not get a direct loan from the bank. We are in a relatively weak financial position in relation to the amount of credit needed.

The 10 percent credit charge either could be additional income to the manufacturer or could be used to cover the charges the manufacturer would pay when he sells (discounts) your note to a bank or finance company. The finance company or bank would charge the manufacturer interest on the money advanced to him. In essence, you would pay interest twice. You would pay a flat 10 percent on the face amount of the contract plus 8 percent on the unpaid balance. This could be a stiff price to pay, but in some situations there may not be any other way!

Alternative 2—Add-on Interest

You received a call from the bank asking you to stop in. They wanted to discuss the term of the prospective loan and to learn more details about the Jones organization. They also wanted to explore President Jones' attitude toward assigning the Allied account receivable to the bank as additional collateral. Allied is an industrial giant. The bank's loan committee felt very comfortable with the possibility of the assignment. If the assignment were made, Allied would pay all funds due Jones directly to the bank to reduce the loan balance.

The banker sounded encouraging. However, we are still interested in cost. Extended discussions indicated that a 20 percent down payment would be required and the remainder could be secured with a chattel mortgage on the equipment and an assignment of the Allied receivables. The terms of the loan would require add-on interest at the annual rate of 6 percent of the total amount needed. In essence:

	Five Years	Three Years
Purchase price of equipment	$332,100	
Less 20% down payment	66,420	
Amount of loan available	$265,680	$265,680
Interest at 6% per year for 5 years (30%); 3 years (15%)*	$ 79,704	$ 47,822
Amount to be repaid in five equal annual installments†	$345,384	$313,502
Annual payment, five years (rounded)‡	$ 69,077	
Annual payment, three years‡		$104,501

* Assumes simple interest.

† $\frac{\$345{,}384}{5 \text{ years}} = \$69{,}077$ or $\frac{\$313{,}502}{3 \text{ years}} = \$104{,}501$

‡ Without considering the annual tax saving derived from the deduction of the interest.

The interest that is added to the principal amount in the first instance is the interest charge.

We are becoming somewhat knowledgeable. Why don't you consult other banks and see if you can improve these terms?

Alternative 3—Interest on Unpaid Balance

A second institution indicated that a mortgage loan, after a 25 percent down payment, plus interest at the rate of 8 percent on the unpaid balance, would be available. In essence:

Purchase price of equipment	$332,100
Less 25% down payment	83,025
Amount of mortgage loan	$249,075

The annual payment to include the 8 percent interest would be calculated as illustrated earlier.

Payment in five equal annual installments:

Present value of total payable / Present value of annuity of $1, five periods, 8%	$249,075 / 3.993 = $62,378 annual payment[1]	
Total to be paid over five years ($62,378 × 5)	$311,890	
Less principal amount of loan	249,075	
Interest to be paid over life of loan		$62,815[1]

Payment in three equal annual installments:

Present value of total payable / Present value of annuity of $1, three periods, 8%	$249,075 / 2.577 = $96,653 annual payment	
Total to be paid over three years ($96,653 × 3)	$289,959	
Less principal amount of loan	249,075	
Interest to be paid over life of loan		$40,884

Again, we must develop a framework to facilitate our decision. A summary of these alternative methods of financing the equipment acquisition appears as follows (without considering the tax saving derived from the interest deduction):

	Manufacturer Providing Credit	Bank Loan 20% Down Payment, 6%	Bank Loan 25% Down Payment, 8%
Down payment	$ 73,062	$ 66,420	$83,025
Annual payment, five years	73,190	69,077	62,378
Total interest, five years	73,702	79,704	62,815
Annual payment, three years	113,406	104,501	96,653
Total interest, three years	47,970	47,822	40,884

The analysis is fine. The alternatives are clearly defined except for the consideration of the tax saving derived from the deductibility of the interest payments. The tax factor is important in this decision. A basic problem remains which eliminates the need for calculating the tax factor in these alternative methods. The Jones organization does not have the cash to make the down payment!

[1] Without considering the annual tax saving derived from the deduction of the interest.

LEASING

There is yet another alternative that should be investigated as a method of acquiring the necessary equipment. The manufacturer has suggested that we might be able to lease the equipment on the following terms:

1. The period of the lease will be either five or ten years.
2. The lessor is to earn 10 percent gross return on the lease.
3. Rental payments are to be made at the end of each year.
4. The lessor will provide maintenance on the equipment at cost plus 10 percent.

This arrangement will have a particular advantage to the manufacturer. First, he will earn the profit on the "sale" of the equipment. That is to say, he will base the annual lease payments on the sales value of the equipment. Second, he may earn an additional 10 percent gross return on the lease itself. In addition, he has agreed to provide the maintenance on the equipment during the life of the lease. In fact, he insists on providing the maintenance as a means of assuring himself that the equipment will receive proper care. The maintenance contract, likewise, will contain a margin of profit for the manufacturer.

The next step in our investigation is to determine the lease costs to Jones. These calculations are, again, relatively simple.

Cost of equipment	\$332,100
Residual value	None
Life of lease is 10 years or 5 years	

The present value of 10 equal payments discounted at 10 percent (interest) must equal the "sales price" of the equipment. Therefore, referring to our present value of an annuity table (A-4), we find the discount factor to be 6.145 for the 10-year period.

Cost of equipment = present-value factor of annuity of \$1 at 10% × rental payment

or

\$332,100 = 6.145 × annual rental payment

or

$$\frac{\$332,100}{6.145} = \text{annual rental payment} = \$54,044 \text{ (rounded)}$$

Total rental payments for 10 years = \$540,440

Let's recalculate the rental payments on a five-year basis by substituting a five-period discount factor.

$$\frac{\$332{,}100}{3.791} = \$87{,}600 \text{ (rounded) annual rental for 5 years}$$

As we pause to reflect on the various alternatives available to secure the needed equipment, we should reexamine our problem. Our basic problem, of course, is to acquire the necessary fixed assets. Really, whether we borrow the funds to buy the equipment and acquire ownership or whether we borrow the equipment is quite immaterial from the point of view of producing our product. A leasing arrangement is simply borrowing equipment rather than funds to buy the equipment. The lease itself is then a fixed financial charge or annual payment obligation. In the one case, it is the repayment of the principal and the interest on the funds borrowed. In the other, it is the annual lease payments. Both the interest plus depreciation expense on the equipment and the rental payments are charges against income and are tax deductions.

However, there are several factors we should consider. One is the risk of obsolescence. If we purchase the equipment outright, we must bear this risk alone. In our earlier analysis, we estimated that the equipment would have a useful life of 10 years. Our lease arrangement could likewise have a 10-year life. We would not avoid the risk of obsolescence under this arrangement. However, there is the five-year lease and, perhaps, an option to buy the equipment at the end of that period at a substantially lower price.

Another significant calculation at this point is a consideration of the marginal tax rate. We will continue to assume that the maximum corporate tax rate is 50 percent.

Therefore, when we compare the annual rental under the 10-year lease with the annual rental under the 5-year lease, we know that the additional expense will in reality cost the Jones organization only 50 percent. This is so because, as we learned earlier, each additional $1 of expense will reduce our tax payment 50 cents.

A comparison of the 10-year lease and the 5-year lease, giving effect to these tax considerations, appears as follows:

Total rental, 10-year lease	$540,440
Total rental, 5-year lease	438,000
Difference in total rental	$102,440
Actual cost for the last 5 years before tax shield	$102,440
50% marginal tax bracket	50%
Additional cost for a 10-year lease	$ 51,220, or $5,122 per year

A question then arises: Is it worth the difference of $5,122 per year for the Jones Electronic Corporation to lease the equipment for 5 years instead of 10 years?

BUY VERSUS LEASE

Another consideration is the fact that the lease binds us to a 10 percent return to the manufacturer for a 5- or 10-year period. The most favorable bank or lending institution rate was only 8 percent. In addition, we could perhaps refinance the bank obligation if interest rates should drop and thus save interest charges, subject, perhaps, to a "payoff penalty."

It is significant, however, that the only requirement and/or restriction we have on our total operation under the lease arrangement is the payment of annual rental and the required maintenance contract with the manufacturer. As indicated earlier, the bank or lending institution may give considerable significance to the fact that our total net worth is only $83,333. To finance the acquisition of assets for $332,100 will require a down payment of $81,512 and a chattel mortgage on the balance of $250,588. The lending institution may consider the mortgage a substantial risk and may well require more restrictions on our operations, for example, a restriction on additional credit and/or some voice in management in order to protect their investment.

The down payment may be an insurmountable problem in itself without an additional capital investment by President Jones (he does not want to sell additional equity at this time). The down-payment problem may be more formidable than the repayment of the loan! The lease arrangement provides 100 percent financing. At this point in our development and growth, 100 percent financing is exactly what we need.

We must also consider the tax consequence of annual depreciation and interest on borrowed money versus the annual rental expense. This has not been done as yet.

At the next executive committee meeting, the committee received your report and tentatively decided that the lease was the best possible arrangement at this time. You were requested to consult with Jones' attorney and present recommendations at a subsequent meeting. President Jones himself would explore further the possibility of firming up the contract with Allied for the additional 20,000 units for the coming year.

The matter appeared to be wrapped up, primarily because the Jones Corporation did not have the down payment for purchase. However, you felt a little uneasy about the entire matter of buying versus leasing and especially about the financial and tax implications of depreciation plus interest charges as compared with the annual rental payments.

Upon returning to your office, you decided to reexamine the entire matter. You prepared the following work sheet:

COST OF BUYING VERSUS COST OF LEASING*

(1) Year	(2) Cash Outflow (Payments)	(3) Applied to Interest†	(4) Applied to Principal	(5) Balance Due	(6) Depreciation 10 Years	(7) Expense for Tax Purposes, (3) + (6)	(8) Tax Savings 50% Tax Rate	(9) Net Cost of Owning, (2) − (8)
Down payment	$83,025		$83,025	$249,075				$ 83,025
1	62,378	$19,926	42,452	206,623	$30,000	$49,926	$24,963	37,415
2	62,378	16,530	45,848	160,775	30,000	46,530	23,265	39,113
3	62,378	12,862	49,516	111,259	30,000	42,862	21,431	40,947
4	62,378	8,901	53,477	57,782	30,000	38,901	19,450	42,928
5	62,378	4,596	57,782	0	30,000	34,596	17,298	45,080
6					30,000	30,000	15,000	(15,000)
7					30,000	30,000	15,000	(15,000)
8					30,000	30,000	15,000	(15,000)
9					30,000	30,000	15,000	(15,000)
10					30,000	30,000	15,000	(15,000)
11	(32,100)‡							(32,100)
								$181,408

* You will note that maintenance expenses are not included. Such expenses are neglected since the lease alternative.
† Rounded.
‡ Salvage value at end of 10 years.

After the above work sheet was prepared, you sat long into the night examining and reevaluating your analysis. Clearly, something appeared to be wrong! The total cost of owning as indicated by column 9 was $181,408. The total cost of leasing as indicated by column 10 was $270,220. This is a difference of $88,812. Yet the present value of the cost of owning was an unfavorable $23,686! You checked your analysis step by step:

1. In column 2 you simply recorded the five equal annual payments calculated earlier. You then rechecked the amount of these payments ($62,378). It is correct.

2. In columns 3 and 4 you calculated the amount that would be applied to the interest and the principal each year. Checking these

(10) Lease Cost (10 years) after Tax 50%	(11) Advantage of Leasing, (10) − (9)	(12) 10% Present-value Factor	(13) Present Value of Advantage of Leasing (11) × (12)	(14)	(15) Growth Factor 10%	(16) Total Growth Dollars	(17)
	$83,025	1.000	$83,025	$83,025	2.594	$215,366	
$ 27,022	10,393	0.909	9,447	10,393	2.358	24,506	
27,022	12,091	0.826	9,987	12,091	2.144	25,923	
27,022	13,925	0.751	10,458	13,925	1.949	27,139	
27,022	15,906	0.683	10,864	15,906	1.772	28,185	
27,022	18,058	0.621	11,214	18,058	1.611	29,091	
27,022	(42,022)	0.564	(23,700)	(42,022)	1.464		(61,520)
27,022	(42,022)	0.513	(21,557)	(42,022)	1.331		(55,931)
27,022	(42,022)	0.467	(19,624)	(42,022)	1.210		(50,846)
27,022	(42,022)	0.424	(17,817)	(42,022)	1.100		(46,224)
27,022	(42,022)	0.386	(16,220)	(42,022)	1.000		(42,022)
	(32,100)	0.386	(12,391)	(32,100)	1.000		(32,100)
$270,220	($88,812)		($23,686)			$350,210	(288,643)
			Total present value of advantage of leasing				

SUMMARY:

Col. 16	$350,210	Col. 13	$23,686
Col. 17	− 288,643		× 2.594
	$ 61,567		$61,441

Difference of $126 caused by factor rounding.

it is felt that they would be much the same in amount and timing under either the purchase or

figures, you found them to be correct.

3. Column 5 is nothing more than the old balance due less the principal paid from the annual payment each year.
4. Depreciation was calculated on a straight-line basis for 10 years in column 6 (cost less salvage divided by 10 years).
5. Column 7 is the total deductible expense for tax purposes, interest plus depreciation.
6. Column 8 simply calculates the tax savings as a result of the deductions for depreciation and interest.
7. Column 9 is the net cost, which is the payment, column 2, less the tax savings.

8. Column 10 is the net cost of the lease each year, $54,044, less the 50 percent tax savings reduction.
9. Column 11 represents the advantage or disadvantage of owning the equipment each year. During the last five years, not only would we lose our depreciation deduction of $30,000 (or $15,000 net after tax effect), but we would still pay the annual rental. There appeared to be a total dollar advantage to owning in the amount of $88,812.
10. You assumed a cost of funds which means that you have estimated that you could reinvest the net savings and earn a 10 percent return consistently over the 10-year period. In column 12 you filled in the present-value factors for each of the 10 years.
11. You then arrived at a present value of the advantage of leasing of $23,686!

As we examine and reexamine our analysis, it appears that columns 9 to 11 show an advantage of owning in the amount of $88,812. Yet, column 13 shows that the present value of the advantage of leasing is $23,686! Is there something wrong with our calculations?

We can examine the indicated advantage to leasing from another point of view. You will notice that column 11 has been reproduced in column 14. Column 14 is then multiplied by 10 percent compound interest factors. The rationale for the procedure can be illustrated as follows:

> If the equipment is leased, it will not be necessary for the Jones Corporation to make the down payment of $83,025. The amount will then be available for other investment at the assumed rate of return of 10 percent. Column 15 contains the 10 percent compound interest factors. The $83,025 can be expected to grow to $215,366 over the 10-year period (column 16) and obviously can be expected to grow even further over succeeding years, because each year the annual advantage or the annual cash outflow differential will increase as indicated in column 16. However, after the fifth year, the $42,022 cash flow tax savings from depreciation plus annual lease cost will be lost for the next five years, as will the salvage value ($32,100) at the end of the 10-year period.

The summary of columns 15 and 16 indicates that there will be a net advantage to leasing in the amount of $61,567 over the 10-year period. Column 13 indicates that the present value of the advantage to leasing is $23,686. When this present value is projected over the 10-year period by using the 10-year, 10 percent compound interest factor of 2.594, the net savings amount to $61,441. This is a difference of $61,567 − $61,441 = $126.

Perhaps, as we burn the oil in the wee hours of the morning examining and reexamining our analysis, we can learn an extremely valuable lesson. We just cannot attack a problem neatly in one chapter and ignore significant elements of the total solution, simply because it might be easier to departmentalize our learning. Even more significantly, we may have learned that external debt financing may clearly involve internal financing implications as well.

It was just too late to continue. We left a note for President Jones to "hold everything" until we had had a chance to discuss the matter further. We'll try again tomorrow. There are no lights on the golf course.

When President Jones arrived the following morning, you presented him with our detailed analysis of the "cost of buying versus the cost of leasing." His eyes immediately went to the total figures on the bottom of the page:

Net cost of owning	$181,408
Net lease cost over 10 years	270,220
Disadvantages of leasing	$ 88,812

His first reaction was to buy the equipment and forget the last two columns. In fact, he asked you what they were and further wondered if you hadn't made a mistake on the title to column 13. That column is entitled "Present Value of Advantage of Leasing." The figures above indicate an apparent $88,812 disadvantage to leasing! We assured him that we had not made a mistake. This is the precise point of the entire analysis! While there would appear to be an $88,812 advantage to owning, the significant factor is that there is a definite advantage to leasing in our situation! Why?

President Jones is sharp, and he quickly pointed out why this is so. By making the down payment he would lose the opportunity to earn a 10 percent return on $83,025 each year for the next 10 years! The second year, likewise, his net payment of $37,415 would exceed the annual net lease cost of $27,022 by $10,393. Again, he would be losing the opportunity to invest the $10,393. The next four years, he would lose the opportunity to invest increasing amounts each year, $12,091, $13,925, $15,906, and $18,058.

The sixth, seventh, eighth, ninth, and tenth years, however, the balance would swing the other way. For these years, the lease cost would exceed the cost of owning. The Jones organization not only would pay a net lease cost of $27,022 each year, but would lose the annual tax saving from depreciation of $15,000. (We have already reduced the actual lease payments to reflect the tax effect.) Total loss would be $42,022 for each of the next five years. In addition, if we leased the equipment, there would be no salvage value at the end of the 10-year period.

This analysis is quite significant. If we have not explained our data clearly enough, go back and examine carefully the "cost of buying versus the cost of leasing." We have taken President Jones' estimate that there are available other opportunities to earn 10 percent per year. We have asked him to reexamine this assumption to be certain that it does reflect reality! He reminded us that we are presently projecting company returns that far exceed 10 percent. Further, he is certain that we could find many internal opportunities to use any excess funds such as plant improvement, research, and other areas that would contribute to further cost reduction and generate at least a 10 percent return on the funds. It is important to note that our present-value factor is determined by the return that could be earned in alternative opportunities.

The significance of column 13 is the total, $23,686. The net advantage to leasing, then, can be measured by an investment of $23,686 made today that would earn 10 percent compounded annually over a 10-year period. (Compound it daily, if you want, but annually will illustrate our point.)

Table A-1 indicates that $1 deposited at 10 percent compound interest for 10 years will grow to $2.594. In real dollars over the 10-year period, our net gain by leasing rather than buying is $61,477.80, if the advantage in the early years could be reinvested at 10 percent consistently over the 10-year period.

$\$23{,}700 \times \$2.594 = \$61{,}477.80$

When your analysis was presented to the Jones executive committee the following Monday, the general manager wondered why we were doing " . . . all of this, anyway? The equipment would be paid for from the cash flow generated by depreciation, and at least after 10 years we would own the equipment!" It was obvious he had missed the point. Do you see why we did " . . . all of this, anyway?"

Our basic problem here is the effective utilization of funds. Our reply to the general manager was simply that if we leased the equipment, the cash outflow for lease payments would cost us less in the long and short runs because the savings in the early years would be available for further investment and would clearly outweigh the disadvantage for the last five years, including the loss of the salvage value.

When President Jones saw that figure, he said, "Lease the equipment!" You were still not 100 percent convinced. There is still a significant basic assumption we have made. Remember, we used straight-line depreciation. Would the analysis have given a different result if we had used an accelerated-depreciation method?

Could we have made a similar type of analysis if we had been dealing with depletion (for example, 23½ percent oil depletion) and/or amortization (for example, leaseholds) instead of depreciation? Yes, we could have.

The day is over; that is, it is 3:30 p.m. and before we tackle our buy-lease problem again tonight, let's play nine holes of golf. We can solve problems at night, but we can't play golf—at least on our course. I'd like you to come along. I want the 50¢ back that you won last time!

SUMMARY

Chapter 5 was concerned with the selection of investment opportunities. Chapter 6, on the other hand, presents the problems of financing the investment proposal selected in Chapter 5. The funds which are required can have but two sources. They may be generated internally through operations or externally by credit extensions or security sales.

The Jones Corporation, like most rapidly growing firms, is unable to generate adequate investment funds internally. That is to say, funds furnished by depreciation flows and the retention of earnings are insufficient to meet the demands of the capital budget. We are then forced to consider external sources of financing. These external sources can be approached through the sale of securities or the use of less permanent debt instruments.

Because our securities, debt or equity, lack marketability, the Jones Corporation begins to explore the availability of loan financing. Commercial banks, life insurance firms, the Small Business Administration, finance companies, and, finally, equipment manufacturers are examined as potential sources of the required funds. In each case the loan is examined from the lender's and the borrower's point of view. Payment schedules and initial cash requirements are also noted. You are quick to realize that the calculation of payment schedules, etc., is nothing more than another exercise in the mathematics of finance with which you are already familiar.

Since we lack even the funds for an initial down payment, we are forced to consider yet another method of financing, leasing. Leasing provides the firm with the opportunity to secure and utilize an asset without incurring the initial costs and responsibilities of purchase. There exist many varieties of leasing plans. However, most contain as a common element a series of payments made by the lessee to the lessor. These payments are sufficient in level and duration to provide the lessor with a return of and a return on the capital he has committed to the leased asset. Thus, you can see that the annual lease payment contains two components: a return of principal and a payment for interest. When you prepared your work sheet which contrasted the cost of leasing versus that of buying, you noted that two significant figures were evolved and then compared. The after-tax cost of purchase and the after-tax cost of leasing were the critical figures. The annual differences between these costs were then discounted back to yield a present value of the advantage of leasing. This figure, you will recall, could have been either positive or negative, depending on the circumstances involved and the discount rate employed. As you continue your work in the field of finance, you will see many methods of leasing employed by different industries. You would do well to ignore blanket statements concerning the cost of leasing versus the cost of purchasing. Rules of thumb should not take the place of accurate cost calculations.

QUESTIONS FOR DISCUSSION

1. It has been stated that depreciation, depletion, amortization, and retained earnings are not a source of internally generated funds. Explain.
2. Distinguish between debt and equity.
3. Distinguish between intermediate- and long-term debt financing. What is a primary liquidity objective of each of these sources?
4. What are the sources of intermediate-term debt financing?
5. What data or information will generally be required by bank officials when Jones requests a bank loan? Why would these data be necessary?
6. Distinguish between simple interest, discount financing, and an add-on rate. What is the effective rate for each type of financing, assuming a loan of $1,000 for one year at 7 percent?
7. What relationship, if any, exists between present-value concepts and the determination of equal monthly or annual payments of an amount payable?
8. What is the justification for a "payoff" penalty?
9. What basic assumptions are involved in the buy-versus-lease analysis on pages 176 and 177?
10. What is the significance of each of these assumptions?
11. What effect would the buy-versus-lease analysis on pages 176 and 177 have on Jones' reported earnings per share?
12. Is it possible that the buy-versus-lease analysis on pages 176 and 177 would change significantly if the annual depreciation allowances doubled during the first several years with corresponding lower amounts in later years? Why?
13. Would the additional depreciation generate more funds? How?

PROBLEMS

1. J. Jones owes T. Smith $6,922 and has agreed to pay this amount in three equal annual installments, with the third installment to be adjusted for any odd amount. What will be the amount of each installment if Smith desires a rate of return on his loan of 10 percent?
2. On pages 176–177, the buy-versus-lease analysis assumes five annual installments. Change this assumption to eight installments. What then

would be your recommendation with respect to this particular buy-versus-lease decision?

3. T. Smith expects to earn $67,000 next year and has the option of leasing certain equipment over a five- or a ten-year period. The purchase price of the equipment is $500,000. The lessor wants an annual rental that will pay this amount plus 5 percent interest.
   a. What would be the annual rental over the five-year period?
   b. What would be the annual rental over the 10-year period?
   c. What is the significant difference between the two amounts?
   d. Which period would you recommend, and why?
4. You approach a banker, requesting a loan in the amount of $5,000. Several alternatives are presented to you. The banker will charge:
   a. An add-on interest of 5 percent for three years, payments being made monthly
   b. An add-on interest of 5 percent over five years, payments being made monthly
   c. A rate of 12 percent on the unpaid balance over two years, payments being made monthly
   d. A rate of 12 percent on the unpaid balance over two years, payments being made quarterly

   What are the equal payments under all four of the arrangements above?
   How much interest will be paid under each of the arrangements above?

REFERENCES

Agemian, Charles A.: Maintaining an Effective Bank Relationship, *Financial Executive*, vol. 32, pp. 24–28, January, 1964.

Arlt, C. T., Jr.: Member Bank Term Lending to Business, 1955–57, *Federal Reserve Bulletin,* vol. 45, pp. 353–368, April, 1959.

Baxter, Nevins D., and Harold T. Shapiro: Compensating Balance Requirements: The Results of a Survey, *Journal of Finance*, vol. XIX, pp. 483–496, September, 1964.

Bower, Richard S., Frank C. Herringer, and J. Peter Williamson: Lease Evaluation, *Accounting Review,* vol. XLI, no. 2, pp. 257–265, April, 1966.

Brigham, Eugene F.: The Impact of Bank Entry on Market Conditions in the Equipment Leasing Industry, *National Banking Review,* vol. II, pp. 11–26, September, 1964.

———: Equipment Lease Financing, *Bankers Magazine,* vol. 149, pp. 65–75, winter, 1966.

Budzeika, George: Term Lending by New York City Banks, *Essays in Money and Credit,* Federal Reserve Bank of New York, reprinted in James Van Horne (ed.), "Foundations for Financial Management," pp. 115–124, Richard D. Irwin, Inc., Homewood, Ill., 1966.

———: The Maturity of Loans at New York City Banks, *Monthly Review,* vol. XLIX, pp. 10–14, Federal Reserve Bank of New York, January, 1967.

Gibson, W. E.: Compensating Balance Requirements, *National Banking Review,* vol. 2, pp. 298–311, March, 1965.

Grant, Donald R.: Illusion in Lease Financing, *Harvard Business Review,* vol. XXXVII, pp. 121–142, March-April, 1959.

———: A Critical Look at Lease Financing, *Controller,* vol. XXIX, June, 1961.

Griesinger, Frank K.: Pros and Cons of Leasing Equipment, *Harvard Business Review,* vol. XXXIII, pp. 75–89, March-April, 1955.

Guttentag, J. M., and R. G. Davis: Compensating Balances, *Monthly Review,* vol. 43, pp. 205–210, Federal Reserve Bank of New York, November, 1961.

Hayes, Douglas A.: "Bank Lending Policies, Issues and Practices," chap. 6, Bureau of Business Research, University of Michigan, Ann Arbor, 1964.

Knutson, Peter H.: Leased Equipment and Divisional Return on Capital, *N.A.A. Bulletin,* vol. XLIV, pp. 15–20, November, 1962.

Laudadio, Leonard: Size of Bank, Size of Borrower, and the Rate of Interest, *Journal of Finance,* vol. XIIX, pp. 20–28, March, 1963.

Law, Warren A., and M. Colyer Crum: "Equipment Leasing and Commercial Banks," Association of Reserve City Bankers, Chicago, 1963.

Machinery and Allied Products Institute: Leasing of Industrial Equipment, Washington, 1965.

McLean, James H.: Economic and Accounting Aspects of Lease Financing, *Financial Executive,* vol. 31, pp. 18–23, December, 1963.

Moore, George S.: Term Loans and Interim Financing, in Benjamin Haggott Beckhart (ed.), "Business Loans of American Commercial Banks," pp. 208–282, The Ronald Press Company, New York, 1959.

Myers, John H.: "Reporting of Leases in Financial Statements," American Institute of Certified Public Accountants, New York, 1962.

Nelson, A. Thomas: Capitalized Leases: The Effect on Financial Ratios, *Journal of Accountancy,* vol. CXVI, pp. 49–58, July, 1963.

Shillinglaw, Gordon: Accounting for Leased Property by Capitalization, *N.A.A. Bulletin,* vol. XXXIX, pp. 31–45, June, 1958.

Stewart, William C.: How Business Picks Banks, *Burroughs Clearing House,* vol. XLIV, pp. 33–35, 80, January, 1960.

Thurlin, W. Bernard: Own or Lease? Underlying Financial Theory, *Financial Executive,* vol. 32, pp. 23–31, April, 1964.

Vancil, Richard F.: Lease or Borrow: Steps in Negotiation, *Harvard Business Review,* vol. 39, pp. 138–159, November-December, 1961.

———: Lease or Borrow, New Method Analysis, *Harvard Business Review,* vol. 39, September-October, 1961, reprinted in James Van Horne (ed.), "Foundations for Financial Management," pp. 125–136, Richard D. Irwin, Inc, Homewood, Ill., 1966.

——— and Robert N. Anthony: The Financial Community Looks at Leasing, *Harvard Business Review,* vol. 37, pp. 113–130, November-December, 1959.

Weston, J. Fred, and Rupert Craig: Understanding Lease Financing, *California Management Review,* vol. II, pp. 67–75, winter, 1960.

Wojnilower, Albert M.: "The Quality of Bank Loans," National Bureau of Economic Research, New York, 1962.

Zises, Alvin: Disclosure of Long-term Leases, *Journal of Accountancy,* vol. CXI pp. 37–47, February, 1961.

Chapter Seven

THE DEPRECIATION METHODS AND THE FLOW OF FUNDS

Our analysis of the advantages and disadvantages of buying versus leasing the needed equipment has made it perfectly clear to President Jones that additional study is needed before we arrive at any final decision. He first observed that you had used the straight-line method of depreciation in preparing your analysis of the cost of owning versus the cost of leasing the new equipment. He noticed that the cost of owning the equipment was adjusted downward because the depreciation expense would reduce the income tax to be paid. He asked you, "Would the cost of owning not be further reduced if one of the other generally accepted depreciation methods were used instead of the straight-line method?" He continued, "Would not the depreciation methods that provide considerably greater allowances during the early years provide more funds that could be invested to earn a return?"

The answer to both questions was yes, but perhaps not for any of the reasons President Jones may have been implying. All internal funds are generated by profit from operations after taxes. In arriving at these profits, certain expenses are included which do not require an outflow of cash. These expenses include depreciation, depletion, and amortization. As an example, assume that Jones Electronic reported a $100,000 profit *before taxes and depreciation* during a given year. This would indicate that Jones Electronic had generated additional funds in the amount of $100,000 during the year. If the profit was reduced by depreciation expense of $20,000 during the year, the reported profit before taxes would be reduced to $80,000. If we exclude tax considerations for the moment, would not Jones Electronic still have added a total of $100,000 in funds during the year? Does the fact that $80,000 of the $100,000 in funds had been reported as profit before taxes and that $20,000 of the $100,000 had been reported as an allowance for depreciation alter the fact that $100,000 in additional funds had been generated during the year from operations? The answer is clearly no.[1]

It is for this reason that accountants, when they prepare a statement of the firm's sources of funds, start with "profit after taxes" and add back the noncash expense items, including depreciation, depletion, and amortization, to arrive at the total of internally generated funds. In short, we can label our sources of funds as it is necessary for reporting purposes, but this does not alter the fact that internally generated funds are the end result of the business entity's operations—sales.

How, then, can different depreciation methods generate a higher or lower amount of funds? It seems that since all funds are generated by income from operations, whatever amount we allocate or label as depreciation would have no effect on the total amount of funds generated. This is correct as far as our analysis has gone. You will recall that we have excluded tax considerations thus far.

TAX IMPLICATIONS

When we consider the tax implications of depreciation, we can say that depreciation does generate funds to the extent of the income tax not paid as a result of the depreciation expense. We can recognize this fact readily when we return to our earlier example.

	Company A	Company B
Net income before depreciation and taxes	$100,000	$100,000
Less depreciation expense	0	20,000
Taxable income	$100,000	$ 80,000
Less income taxes (50%)	50,000	40,000
Net income as reported	$ 50,000	$ 40,000
Add funds labeled depreciation	0	20,000
Total funds provided	$ 50,000	$ 60,000

[1] In short, we have not written and will not write a check "payable to the order of" depreciation. It was, therefore, a noncash deduction from our gross figure and is still available to the firm.

Company A has no depreciation expense and thus must pay income tax at the assumed rate of 50 percent of $100,000 ($50,000). Funds provided by the operations of Company A thus amount to $50,000. Company B has depreciation expense of $20,000; thus, net profit reported is $40,000. Reported net income after taxes is, likewise, $40,000, and when the depreciation is added back, total funds provided are $60,000. Depreciation, then, provides $10,000 in additional funds because of the tax deduction and the subsequent tax saving.

Depreciation, then, is a noncash tax-deductible expense and serves to shield an equivalent portion of income from taxation. Therefore, the larger the depreciation expense, the larger the tax saving; thus, more funds will be provided.

Our next step in this analysis is to become familiar with the several generally accepted depreciation methods.

GENERALLY ACCEPTED DEPRECIATION METHODS

There are three basic depreciation methods, with variations, in general practice today. All three methods are approved by the Internal Revenue Service for tax reporting purposes. The accelerated methods are limited in use under the Internal Revenue Code. We are, however, free to use one method for tax reporting purposes and another for financial reporting. This statement is significant and will be examined later in this chapter. Presently, let's examine the alternative reporting methods. They are as follows:

1. Straight-line method
2. Service-life methods
   a. Service-hours method
   b. Productive-output method
3. Accelerated-depreciation methods
   a. Declining-balance method
   b. Sum-of-the-years-digits method

In order to illustrate and contrast the effects of the various depreciation computation methods, we will use the same numerical data and apply thereto each depreciation method noted above. (We also recognize that actually we are examining the second alternative plan dealing with the equipment acquisition.)

Original cost	$332,100
Estimated life	10 years
Salvage value	$32,100
Estimated service-hours	200,000 hours
Estimated total production	1,000,000 units

Straight-line Method

(We used this method in preparing our original buy-versus-lease analysis.) The straight-line method accumulates depreciation strictly in response to the passage of time. We are not concerned with productivity, efficiency, or the utilization rate of the equipment. The estimated salvage (or residual) value at the end of the useful life (10 years) is subtracted from the original cost.[1] The product is then divided by the number of years or months in the estimated useful life to arrive at the periodic depreciation charge.

Original cost	$332,100
Less estimated salvage value	32,100
Depreciation base	$300,000
$300,000 ÷ 10 = $30,000 per year	
$300,000 ÷ 120 = $2,500 per month	

End of Year	Annual Depreciation Expense	Accumulated Balance of Allowance for Depreciation	Book Value of Machine
			$332,100
1	$30,000	$ 30,000	302,100
2	30,000	60,000	272,100
3	30,000	90,000	242,100
4	30,000	120,000	212,100
5	30,000	150,000	182,100
6	30,000	180,000	152,100
7	30,000	210,000	122,100
8	30,000	240,000	92,100
9	30,000	270,000	62,100
10	30,000	300,000	32,100 (residual value)

Evaluation of the straight-line method. This is a simple way of calculating depreciation. The judgment factors involved are the estimated "useful" or "economic" life of the equipment in terms of years or months and the salvage value. The emphasis is on the words "useful" and "economic." This judgment is an uncertain one because of industry's continuing emphasis on automation and scientific improvements. As we make the equal charges for depreciation for each accounting period, we are not recognizing that most businesses operate on some sort of cycle with good and lean periods. Reported income may, therefore,

[1] For tax purposes, with respect to personal property, salvage value up to 10 percent of the basis of the property could be ignored in calculating straight-line depreciation. Thus the annual depreciation allowance could be $33,210 per year for tax purposes.

be somewhat distorted if the equipment is not, in fact, consumed in direct relation to the passage of time. In addition, straight-line depreciation does not recognize that machinery or equipment, more often than not, depreciates in dollar value more rapidly in the earlier years of its life than in later periods, simply because the equipment is "used" equipment after the first day of use.

If our goal is to report net earnings after taxes and earnings per share on the generally accepted accounting basis of matching revenues with the costs associated with producing that revenue, a serious miscalculation of the economic life (and the corresponding depreciation rate) can be significant indeed. If the economic life has been seriously underestimated, depreciation expense during the estimated life will be too high. Reported earnings per share will thus be underestimated. If uninformed investors are capitalizing the earnings by using the reported earnings per share as the base for judgment, the market price of the firm's stock may be expected to be lower than if a longer economic life and a lower depreciation expense had been used.

Clearly, this stock will be underpriced as a result of the capitalization of the incorrect earnings-per-share figure. For example:

Net income before taxes and depreciation: $100,000
Equipment cost: $300,000
Three estimates of economic life: 5 years, 10 years, and 15 years
No salvage value
Annual depreciation expense under straight-line method: $60,000, $30,000, and $20,000
Number of outstanding shares: 100,000
Tax rate: 50%

NET INCOME AND EARNINGS PER SHARE

	Five-year Life	Ten-year Life	Fifteen-year Life
Net income before taxes and depreciation	$100,000	$100,000	$100,000
Less depreciation expense	60,000	30,000	20,000
Net income before taxes	$ 40,000	$ 70,000	$ 80,000
Income tax (50%)	20,000	35,000	40,000
Net income after taxes	$ 20,000	$ 35,000	$ 40,000
Earnings per share	$ 0.20	$ 0.35	$ 0.40
Cash flow provided by depreciation—50% of depreciation expense	$ 30,000	$ 15,000	$ 10,000
Reported income, end of sixth year*	$ 0.50†	$ 0.35	$ 0.40
Reported income, end of eleventh year*	$ 0.50	$ 0.50	$ 0.40
Reported income, end of sixteenth year*	$ 0.50	$ 0.50	$ 0.50

* Assuming the same level of income for illustrative purposes.
† An additional 30 cents per share would be available. Income before taxes would increase by $20,000 (the former depreciation expense). Fifty percent of this amount would be taxed and fifty percent would be available to the stockholders ($30,000 ÷ 100,000 shares = 30 cents per share).

As always, there is a bit more to this analysis, and we will discuss it later in the chapter. Also, in our example the cost of the fixed asset is relatively high when compared with the net income before taxes and depreciation. This situation is not unusual. However, the observation must be made that if the asset to be depreciated is rather insignificant when compared with net income before taxes and depreciation, the impact on earnings per share of that asset's annual depreciation charge will be minimal, regardless of the economic life selected for depreciation purposes.

As soon as the equipment has been fully depreciated on the firm's books, and if the equipment is still producing, earnings per share will increase by some portion of the former depreciation charge. In passing, it should be noted that it will no doubt be in the best interest of the firm to purchase new or perhaps more modern equipment rather than continue to use equipment that has been fully depreciated. This is especially so when one realizes that at a 50 percent marginal tax rate the tax savings from the depreciation deductions will ultimately pay 50 percent of the original cost. If these yearly tax savings are reinvested annually, it is quite possible that the earnings on these funds will be able to pay for the original equipment from the tax savings. The key is the amount of the yearly tax savings and the rate of return earned from the investment of these savings.

Service-life Methods

Service-hours. The service-hours depreciation expense is directly related to the asset's actual service-hours contributed during the accounting period. A depreciation rate per service-hour is determined by dividing the asset depreciation base by the total estimated service-hours. This hourly rate is then multiplied by the number of service-hours contributed by the asset during the accounting period. Depreciation expense under this method will fluctuate from period to period in direct response to the asset's actual use.

Allocation of depreciation expense under this method is illustrated below:

$$\frac{\text{Cost less salvage}}{\text{Total estimated service-hours}} = \text{rate per hour}$$

$$\frac{\$332{,}100 - \$32{,}100}{200{,}000 \text{ hours}} = \$1.50$$

End of Year	Service-hours	Annual Depreciation Expense	Asset Book Value
			$332,100
1	20,000 × $1.50	$ 30,000	302,100
2	30,000 × $1.50	45,000	257,100
3	20,000 × $1.50	30,000	227.100
4	15,000 × $1.50	22,500	204,600
5	30,000 × $1.50	45,000	159,600
6	30,000 × $1.50	45,000	114,600
7	20,000 × $1.50	30,000	84,600
8	15,000 × $1.50	22,500	62,100
9	10,000 × $1.50	15,000	47,100
10	10,000 × $1.50	15,000	32,100
	200,000 hours	$300,000	

Productive output. Under this method, depreciation expense is related to units of output. Total depreciable cost is divided by the estimated total output of the machine over its useful life. A depreciation charge is thus calculated for each unit of output. Depreciation charges may again fluctuate from accounting period to accounting period in direct relation to unit output.

$$\frac{\text{Cost less salvage value}}{\text{Estimated total output}} = \text{depreciation expense per unit}$$

$$\frac{\$332{,}100 - \$32{,}100}{1{,}000{,}000 \text{ units}} = \$0.30 \text{ depreciation charge per unit}$$

End of Year	Unit Output	Annual Depreciation Expense	Asset Book Value
			$332,100
1	90,000 × $0.30	$ 27,000	305,100
2	120,000 × $0.30	36,000	269,100
3	120,000 × $0.30	36,000	233,100
4	80,000 × $0.30	24,000	209,100
5	90,000 × $0.30	27,000	182,100
6	100,000 × $0.30	30,000	152,100
7	100,000 × $0.30	30,000	122,100
8	80,000 × $0.30	24,000	98,100
9	120,000 × $0.30	36,000	62,100
10	100,000 × $0.30	30,000	32,100
	1,000,000 units	$300,000	

Evaluation of service-life methods. Under these methods, depreciation is a fluctuating charge. Higher rates of depreciation will be charged during periods of higher income, and lower depreciation will be charged during periods of lower income. Uncertainty is involved in determining the service life of the asset. However, when the service life of an asset can be reasonably estimated, these methods can produce highly satisfactory results. Net income after taxes and earnings per share should more clearly reflect actual operations with respect to the influence of depreciation expense.

Accelerated Methods

Declining balance. Under this method the depreciation rate for each year is determined by multiplying a fixed annual rate by the book balance of the asset at the beginning of the year. The salvage value is ignored for the purpose of determining the annual depreciation rate. The book value of the asset (original cost less accumulated depreciation) is reduced until the book value itself is equal to the salvage value. At this point, no additional depreciation is taken.

By using the declining-balance method with a 10-year life as the factor, it would take considerably more than a 10-year period of time for the asset to be written off. But if we were to write off the asset over a 10-year life, we would determine the fixed annual rate as follows:

$$\text{Rate} = 1 - \sqrt[10]{\frac{\text{salvage value}}{\text{original cost}}}$$

which is saying that the rate is equal to 1 minus the tenth root (because in our case, a 10-year useful life is estimated) of the ratio of the salvage value to the initial cost. By substituting the Jones data (machinery and equipment costing $332,100 with a 10-year life), the equation appears as follows:

$$1 - \sqrt[10]{\frac{\$32{,}100}{\$332{,}100}} = 1 - \sqrt[10]{0.0966}$$

Checking the logarithm tables for the log of 0.0966, we find the mantissa 0.98498. You may remember from a study of logarithms that the characteristic of 0.09 is −2. Transposing −2.98498, or 10 minus 2.98498, we get 8.98498. Because we are dealing with a 10-year life, we now need one-tenth of 8.98498, or 0.898498. Checking our logarithm tables again for the antilogarithm of 0.898498, we get approximately 0.79104, or 79.104 percent.

This means that the depreciable balance each succeeding year must be 79.104 percent of the year preceding it. By using this method, at the end of 10 years the balance will be approximately \$32,100, the salvage value. The reduction, then, is 20.896 percent per year (100 percent −79.104 percent = 20.896 percent). This percentage (20.896 of the normal rate) is our annual depreciation factor to be applied to the declining balance over a period of 10 years.

We can illustrate this procedure as follows:

End of Year	Annual Depreciation Expense	Remaining Book Value
		\$332,100.00
1	20.896% × \$332,100.00 = \$69,395.62	262,704.38
2	20.896 × 262,704.38 = 54,894.71	207,809.67
3	20.896 × 207,809.76 = 43,423.91	164,385.76
4	20.896 × 164,385.76 = 34,350.05	130,035.71
5	20.896 × 130,035.71 = 27,172.26	102,863.45
6	20.896 × 102,863.45 = 21,494.35	81,369.10
7	20.896 × 81,369.10 = 17,002.89	64,366.21
8	20.896 × 64,366.21 = 13,449.96	50,916.25
9	20.896 × 50,916.25 = 10,639.46	40,276.79
10	20.896 × 40,276.79 = 8,416.24	31,860.55*

* Difference between the salvage value of \$32,100 and this amount (\$239.45) is caused by rounding out the 20.896%.

The Internal Revenue Service has approved the declining-balance method of depreciation. However, the tax rules state that we can use twice the normal straight-line rate for new tangible personal property with a life of three years or more and for new residential rental realty. Used residential rental property having a useful life of 20 years or more may be depreciated under a 125 percent declining-balance method. All other new property, such as new commercial property, will be limited to the 150 percent declining-balance method, and other used real property will be limited to straight-line depreciation. One and one-half the normal straight-line rate can be used also with respect to used tangible personal property. The tax rule requiring not more than double the straight-line rate for tax purposes would indicate that the Jones Corporation could use only a maximum depreciation rate of 20 percent per year (10-year life) on the new equipment, while the rate above indicates a 20.89 percent rate. In our case, the 20 percent limitation would force a longer life for the asset than originally anticipated. However, the Internal Revenue Service permits a switch from the declining-balance method to the straight-line method without obtaining prior consent from the Internal Revenue Service. The straight-line depreciation is based on the machinery's unrecovered cost, less salvage value and estimated life from the date of the switch. In this way, the property is depreciated to salvage value within the 10-year period. In the example that follows, the conversion to straight line was made at the end of the seventh year.

End of Year	Percentage Calculation	Annual Depreciation Expense	Remaining Book Value
			$332,100.00
1	20 % × $332,100	$66,420.00	265,680.00
2	20 × 265,680	53,136.00	212,544.00
3	20 × 212,544	42,508.80	170,035.20
4	20 × 170,035.20	34,007.04	136,028.16
5	20 × 136,028.16	27,205.63	108,822.53
6	20 × 108,822.53	21,764.51	87,058.02
7	20 × 87,058.02	17,411.60	69,646.42
8	$33\frac{1}{3}$ × 37,546.42	12,515.47	57,130.95
9	$33\frac{1}{3}$ × 37,546.42	12,515.47	44,615.48
10	$33\frac{1}{3}$ × 37,546.42	12,515.47	32,100.01

End of seventh year:	
Remaining life	Three years
Book value	$69,646.42
Estimated salvage value	32,100.00
Depreciable base	$37,546.42
Annual depreciation for next three years	$12,515.47

Sum of the years digits. This method likewise provides decreasing depreciation charges each year. Fractions are developed in terms of the useful life of the asset and are used in inverse order. By taking the 10-year life of our asset, the fractions would appear as follows:

Years of Useful Life	Fraction to Be Used
1	10/55
2	9/55
3	8/55
4	7/55
5	6/55
6	5/55
7	4/55
8	3/55
9	2/55
10	1/55
55	55/55

End of Year	Annual Depreciation Expense	Remaining Book Value
		$332,100.00
1	10/55 × $300,000 = $ 54,545.45	277,554.55
2	9/55 × 300,000 = 49,090.91	228,463.64
3	8/55 × 300,000 = 43,636.36	184,827.28
4	7/55 × 300,000 = 38,181.82	146,645.45
5	6/55 × 300,000 = 32,727.27	113,918.19
6	5/55 × 300,000 = 27,272.74	86,645.45
7	4/55 × 300.000 = 21,818.18	64,827.27
8	3/55 × 300,000 = 16,363.64	48,463.63
9	2/55 × 300,000 = 10,909.09	37,554.54
10	1/55 × 300,000 = 5,454.54	32,100.00
	$300,000.00	

Generally, the tax rules with respect to the use of the sum-of-the-years-digits method are the same as those dealing with the declining-balance method.

Evaluation of accelerated-depreciation methods. *Methods of depreciation where the amount of the depreciation is not uniform over the life of the asset can be justified in those situations where the contribution from the asset declines as the asset grows older.* In determining a depreciation method there is an exercise of judgment of the estimated "useful" or "economic" life of the equipment and the rate of decline in usefulness. Possible inadequacy and obsolescence resulting in early retirement of the asset should also be recognized in the calculation. Quite often the accelerated method is used for income tax reporting while another method is used for financial statement purposes. Earlier we examined briefly the effect that a change in the estimated economic life can have on net earnings after taxes and earnings per share. *We will now see the impact of the several depreciation methods upon earnings per share.*

THE TAX SHIELD AS A SOURCE OF FUNDS WITH EMPHASIS ON EARNINGS PER SHARE

Straight-line Method

We can think of the funds provided by the tax savings when we use the straight-line method as an ordinary annuity of $15,000 per year for 10 years ($30,000 depreciation allowance less the 50 percent tax savings thereon). As previously indicated, *a significant function* of successful financial management is to keep these funds invested to produce the highest rate of return. The total sum provided by the depreciation flows at the end of the 10-year period if we could constantly reinvest the tax savings at 10 percent per year[1] would be calculated as follows:

STRAIGHT-LINE METHOD

Year	Annual Depreciation Allowance	Tax Savings (50%)	×	10% Compound Interest Factor	=	Total Funds Generated
1	$30,000	$15,000	×	2.358	=	$ 35,370
2	30,000	15,000	×	2.144	=	32,160
3	30,000	15,000	×	1.949	=	29,235
4	30,000	15,000	×	1.772	=	26,580
5	30,000	15,000	×	1.611	=	24,165
6	30,000	15,000	×	1.464	=	21,960
7	30,000	15,000	×	1.331	=	19,965
8	30,000	15,000	×	1.210	=	18,150
9	30,000	15,000	×	1.100	=	16,500
10	30,000	15,000	×	1.000	=	15,000
						$239,085

Service-life Methods

There is little point in calculating the sum made available by the service-life methods at the end of the 10-year period if the yearly depreciation allowance under this method was invested at 10 percent. Clearly, if more than the average of 200,000 service-hours or 1 million units output were contributed by the asset in early years, the sum accumulated would exceed the accumulated sum at the end of 10 years under the straight-line method.[2]

Accelerated-depreciation Methods

Our analysis indicates quite clearly that the declining-balance method of depreciation will generate the larger amount of funds, both in the short run and in the long run. This is an important consideration, especially when we remember that we can use one depreciation method for tax purposes and another for accounting purposes. As a source of

[1] The 10 percent rate is obtained by assuming that the depreciation flow would be reinvested in the Jones Corporation operations, which will net, conservatively, an average of 20 percent per year less an assumed tax of 50 percent on the earnings.

[2] This result follows from the fact that the larger flows received earlier in the 10-year period under these methods are reinvested for a greater number of periods.

DECLINING BALANCE—TWICE THE NORMAL RATE AND CONVERSION TO STRAIGHT LINE AT THE END OF THE SEVENTH YEAR

Year	Annual Depreciation Allowance	Tax Savings (50%)	×	10% Compound Interest Factor	=	Total Funds Generated
1	$ 66,420.00	$ 33,210.00	×	2.358	=	$ 78,309
2	53,136.00	26,568.00	×	2.144	=	56,962
3	42,508.80	21,254.40	×	1.949	=	41,425
4	34,007.04	17,003.52	×	1.772	=	30,130
5	27,205.63	13,602.82	×	1.611	=	21,914
6	21,764.11	10,882.05	×	1.464	=	15,931
7	17,411.68	8,705.84	×	1.331	=	11,587
8	12,515.58	6,257.79	×	1.210	=	7,572
9	12,515.58	6,257.79	×	1.100	=	6,884
10	12,515.58	6,257.79	×	1.000	=	6,258
	$300,000.00	$150,000.00				$276,972

DECLINING BALANCE—ONE AND ONE-HALF THE NORMAL RATE AND CONVERSION TO STRAIGHT LINE AT THE END OF THE FIFTH YEAR

Year	Annual Depreciation Allowance	Tax Savings (50%)	×	10% Compound Interest Factor	=	Total Funds Generated
1	$ 49,815.00	$ 24,907.50	×	2.358	=	$ 58,732
2	42,342.75	21,171.38	×	2.144	=	45,391
3	35,991.34	17,995.67	×	1.949	=	35,074
4	30,592.64	15,296.32	×	1.772	=	27,105
5	26,003.74	13,001.87	×	1.611	=	20,946
6	23,050.90	11,525.46	×	1.464	=	16,873
7	23,050.90	11,525.45	×	1.331	=	15,340
8	23,050.91	11,525.45	×	1.210	=	13,946
9	23,050.91	11,525.45	×	1.100	=	12,678
10	23,050.91	11,525.45	×	1.000	=	11,525
	$300,000.00	$150,000.00				$257,610

internal funds, then, why could we not always use the accelerated methods? The answer is simply that perhaps we will, at least for tax purposes.

However, we must remember that the accelerated-depreciation expense deductions do reduce reported income in the early years when the accelerated-depreciation methods are used as the basis for the report-

SUM OF THE DIGITS

Year	Annual Depreciation Allowance	Tax Savings (50%)	×	10% Compound Interest Factor	=	Total Funds Generated
1	$54,545.45	$27,272.73	×	2.358	=	$ 64,309
2	49,090.91	24,545.45	×	2.144	=	52,625
3	43,636.36	21,818.18	×	1.949	=	42,524
4	38,181.82	19,090.91	×	1.772	=	33,829
5	32,727.27	16,363.64	×	1.611	=	26,362
6	27,272.74	13,636.37	×	1.464	=	19,964
7	21,818.18	10,909.09	×	1.331	=	14,520
8	16,363.64	8,181.82	×	1.210	=	9,900
9	10,909.09	5,454.55	×	1.100	=	6,000
10	5,454.54	2,727.27	×	1.000	=	2,727
						$272,760

SUMMARY

Depreciation Method	Tax Savings from Depreciation First Year	Total Funds Generated from Investment of First Year's Tax Savings at 10%	Total Funds Generated from Investment of Tax Savings over 10-year Period at 10%
Straight line	$15,000	$35,370	$239,085
200% Declining balance	33,210	78,309	276,972
Sum of the digits	27,272	64,309	272,760

ing of income to shareholders. Consequently, we may be less enthusiastic about using these methods for reporting to stockholders. Shareholders and their advisers place a great deal of emphasis on the figure of earnings per share. Changes in that figure and anticipations with respect to it have a great influence on the short-run market value of the firm's shares. At first glance it would appear that the figure earnings per share is fairly straightforward and does not lend itself to easy manipulation. As you have just seen, this view is obviously incorrect!

THE TAX SHIELD APPLIED

To bring this idea closer to home, the effect of the several depreciation methods on the corporate earnings per share can be illustrated as shown below. An economic life of 10 years has been adopted for the equipment, so there will be no adjustment on that score. We are dealing only with the depreciation method, not the estimated economic life. We will compare the earnings per share when the straight-line method of depreciation is used with the earnings per share when the 200 percent declining-balance method is used (assuming that the methods employed are the same for book and tax purposes). In the first year, the earnings per share under each of the methods are as follows:

Straight-line method:	
Net profit after taxes, first year, as estimated in Chapter 5	$179,374
Earnings per share (50,000 shares)	$ 3.587
200% Declining-balance method:	
Net profit before taxes (50%), as estimated in Chapter 5	$358,748
Add straight-line depreciation to restate net income before taxes and depreciation	30,000
Net income before taxes and depreciation	$388,748
Less 200% declining-balance depreciation	66,420
Net income before taxes	$322,328
Less income tax 50%	161,164
Net income after taxes	$161,164
Earnings per share (50,000 shares)	$ 3.223

The differences in reported earnings per share caused by applying different depreciation methods after taxes over the 10-year life appear as follows:

Taxes per straight line	$179,374
Taxes per double declining balance	161,164
Tax savings first year via double declining balance	$ 18,210

or, expressed another way:

Depreciation expense first year—double declining balance	$66,420
Depreciation expense first year—straight line	30,000
	$36,420
Tax savings at 50%	$18,210

Therefore, we can take the differential depreciation expense each year (straight line versus double declining balance), apply the 50 percent tax rate, and divide the result by the number of outstanding shares (50,000). This procedure will result in the tax savings per share ($18,210/50,000 shares = 36.42 cents). It may be noted that when the double declining-balance method of depreciation is used instead of the straight-line method, two things are happening. First, during the early years, the higher depreciation expense reported lowers the reported net income before taxes; second, the tax saving resulting from the accelerated method lowers the tax liability and mitigates against the earnings-per-share reduction. As illustrated above, the additional depreciation expense, per se ($66,420 versus $30,000), immediately causes a decline in reported earnings per share of 36.42 cents.

$$\frac{\text{Additional expense } \$36{,}420}{\text{Shares outstanding } 50{,}000} = 72.84 \text{ cents per share}$$

However, the tax saving per share will be 36.42 cents ($18,210/50,000 shares = 36.42 cents). The net effect of the double declining-balance depreciation method when compared with the straight-line method will likewise be 36.42 cents because we are using a 50 percent tax rate.

Loss in EPS	72.84¢	EPS (straight line)	= $3.587
Less tax savings	36.42	EPS (declining balance) =	3.223
Net loss first year	36.42¢		.364

A comparison of the annual depreciation charges indicates the following:

Year	(1) Straight Line	(2) Double Declining Balance	(3) Increase (Decrease) in Expense	(4) Increase (Decrease) in EPS*	(5) Increase (Decrease) in EPS after Tax Savings
1	$30,000	$66,420	$36,420	(72.84)¢	(36.420)¢
2	30,000	53,136	23,136	(46.27)	(23.135)
3	30,000	42,508	12,508	(25.02)	(12.51)
4	30,000	34,007	4,007	(8.01)	(4.00)
5	30,000	27,205	(2,795)	5.59	2.80
6	30,000	21,764	(8,236)	16.47	8.23
7	30,000	17,412	(12,588)	25.18	12.59
8	30,000	12,515	(17,485)	34.97	17.48
9	30,000	12,515	(17,485)	34.97	17.48
10	30,000	12,515	(17,485)	34.97	17.48

* 50,000 shares outstanding.

The significant column is 5. This column indicates the annual change in earnings per share caused by using the double declining-balance method of depreciation.

The accountant would then report the earnings per share for the 10-year period as follows:

Year	(1) Straight Line Earnings per Share	(2) Increase (Decrease) Caused by Double Declining Balance	(3) Double Declining Balance Earnings per Share
1	$3.5874	(36.420)¢	$3.2232
2	3.5874	(23.135)	3.3561
3	3.5874	(12.510)	3.4623
4	3.5874	(4.000)	3.5474
5	3.5874	2.80	3.6154
6	3.5874	8.23	3.6697
7	3.5874	12.59	3.7133
8	3.5874	17.48	3.7622
9	3.5874	17.48	3.7622
10	3.5874	17.48	3.7622

It is clear that reported earnings per share for the first four years would be lower via the double declining balance depreciation method. Now, examine the reported earnings per share if the straight-line method is used for book purposes and the declining-balance method is used for calculating the annual tax liability.

Year	Reported After-tax Book Earnings per Share Using Straight Line	Add Tax Differential When Actual Taxes Paid on Double Declining-balance Basis	Reported Earnings per Share after Taxes on Double Declining-balance Basis
1	$3.5874	36.420¢	$3.9516
2	3.5874	23.135	3.8187
3	3.5874	12.510	3.7125
4	3.5874	4.000	3.6274
5	3.5874	(2.80)	3.5594
6	3.5874	(8.23)	3.5051
7	3.5874	(12.59)	3.4615
8	3.5874	(17.48)	3.4126
9	3.5874	(17.48)	3.4126
10	3.5874	(17.48)	3.4126

Again, the first four years are significant. It is clear that we can arrive at different earnings per share by using different methods or combinations of methods of depreciation for reporting purposes.

President Jones indicated that if there were no compelling reason that we should not do so, it appeared to him that it made sense for Jones Electronic to use the declining-balance method of depreciation for tax purposes and the straight-line method for book purposes. (See earnings-per-share calculation earlier.)

THE EFFECT OF DEPRECIATION METHOD ON THE BUY-VERSUS-LEASE DECISION

President Jones then inquired about any significance the declining-balance method of depreciation with the larger early years' tax savings would

9-10.

(1) Year	(2) Cash Outflow (Payments)	(3) Applied to Interest*	(4) Applied to Principal	(5) Balance Due	(6) Depreciation (Declining Balance) 10 Years	(7) (3) + (6) Total Expense for Tax Purposes	(8) Tax Savings 50% Tax Rate	(9) Net Cost of Owning (2) — (8)
Down payment	$83,025		$83,025	$249,075				$ 83,025.00
1	62,378	$19,926	42,452	206,623	$66,420.00	$86,346.00	$43,173.00	19,205.00
2	62,378	16,530	45,848	160,775	53,136.00	69,666.00	34,833.00	27,545.00
3	62,378	12,862	49,516	111,259	42,508.80	55,370.80	27,685.40	34,692.60
4	62,378	8,901	53,477	57,782	34,007.04	42,908.04	21,454.02	40,923.98
5	62,378	4,596	57,782	0	27,205.63	31,801.63	15,900.82	46,477.18
6					21,765.11	21,765.11	10,882.56	(10,882.56)
7					17,412.08	17,412.08	8,706.04	(8,706.04)
8					12,516.11	12,516.11	6,258.06	(6,258.06)
9					12,516.11	12,516.11	6,258.06	(6,258.06)
10					12,516.11	12,516.11	6,258.06	(6,258.06)
11	(32,100)†							(32,100.00)
								$181,405.98

* Rounded.
† Salvage value at end of 10 years.

make in our buy-versus-lease analysis made earlier. You then prepared the analysis on the following pages, using the declining-balance depreciation method. You will recall our original analysis was made on the basis of straight-line depreciation.

This second analysis narrows the present value of the advantage of leasing from $23,686 to $9,093. What is the significance of this advantage? The answer to this question is directly related to the effect leasing has on earnings per share as compared with owning when the declining-balance method of depreciation is adopted. The answer involves exactly the same type of analysis that we completed when we compared straight-line depreciation with the declining-balance method on page 199. Perhaps we can short-cut some of the details here if you thoroughly understand the former analysis. If you do not understand the shortcuts—get going back—now! We will again assume a 10 percent annual earning rate after taxes.

A-2

(10) Lease Cost after Tax 50%	(11) Cash Flow Advantage to Leasing (10) − (9)	(12) Present-value Factor	(13) Present Value of Advantage of Leasing (11) × (12)	(14)	(15) Growth Factor 10%	(16) Total Earnings on Excess Lease Dollars	(17) Total Earnings on Excess Purchase Dollars
	$83,025.00	1.000	$83,025	$83,025.00	2.594	$215,336	
$ 27,022	(7,817.00)	0.909	(7,106)	(7,817.00)	2.358		$(18,432)
27,022	523.00	0.826	432	523.00	2.144	1,121	
27,022	7,670.60	0.751	5,761	7,670.60	1.949	14,950	
27,022	13,901.98	0.683	9,495	13,901.98	1.772	24,634	
27,022	19,455.18	0.621	12,082	19,455.18	1.611	31,342	
27,022	(37,904.56)	0.564	(21,378)	(37,904.56)	1.464		(55,492)
27,022	(35,728.04)	0.513	(18,328)	(35,728.04)	1.331		(47,554)
27,022	(33,280.06)	0.467	(15,542)	(33,280.06)	1.210		(40,269)
27,022	(33,280.06)	0.424	(14,111)	(33,280.06)	1.100		(36,608)
27,022	(33,280.06)	0.386	(12,846)	(33,280.06)	1.000		(33,280)
	(32,100.00)	0.386	(12,391)	(32,100.00)	1.000		(32,100)
$270,220	($88,814.02)		$ 9,093			$287,413	($263,735)
			Total present value of advantage of leasing				

SUMMARY:

Col. 16	$287,413	Col. 13	$9,093
Col. 17	− 263,735		×2,594
	$ 23,678		$23,587

Difference of $111 caused by factor rounding.

Analysis of Effect on EPS of the Jones Buy-versus-Lease Decision

Income per year provided by the investment of funds in column 11 of the buying-versus-leasing analysis on page 203, assuming a 10 percent annual return compounded, can be seen below:

		Annual Income Available from Growth in Excess Funds									
End of Year		**1**	**2**	**3**	**4**	**5**	**6**	**7**	**8**	**9**	**10**
Excess Annual Funds Provided by Decision to Lease	1	$8,302	$9,132	$10,046	$11,050	$12,155	$13,371	$14,708	$16,179	$17,797	$19,576
	2		(781)	(860)	(945)	(1,040)	(1,144)	(1,258)	(1,384)	(1,523)	(1,675)
	3			52	57	63	69	76	84	92	101
	4				767	843	928	1,020	1,122	1,235	1,352
	5					1,390	1,529	1,682	1,850	2,035	2,238
	6						1,945	2,140	2,354	2,589	2,848
	7							(3,790)	(4,586)	(5,044)	(5,549)
	8								(3,573)	(3,950)	(4,345)
	9									(3,328)	(3,660)
											(3,660)
	10 Salvage										(3,210)
	Additional income to EPS	$8,302	$8,351	$ 9,238	$10,929	$13,411	$16,698	$14,578	$12,046	$ 9,903	$ 7,336
	Addition to EPS by leasing rather than buying	16.64¢	16.70¢	18.48¢	21.8¢	26.8¢	33.4¢	29.1¢	24¢	19.8¢	14.7¢

The entire first year and for nine additional years, $83,025 could have been invested to earn a 10 percent return. Thus, the annual return on this amount plus the additional cash generated each year would be available as an investment. As an example, the annual earnings for the ten-year period from this sum are shown on line 1 of the summary above. However, we know that this sum would continue to earn a return indefinitely, or as long as we could keep it invested! Line 2 shows the loss of income for 9 years.

You will note from our buy-versus-lease analysis that the cash outflow if we lease would exceed the cash outflow if we buy by $7,817 for the second year. The earnings on this sum will be lost for the next nine years (in reality the earnings will be lost indefinitely also). These earnings are shown here as a subtraction on line 3 under years 2 through 10. From the third to the sixth year the cash outflow associated with leasing will be less than the cash outflow by buying. The anticipated earnings for these years are again positive. Beginning with the seventh year, the cash flow will again become negative and is so shown.

The real significance of the buy-versus-lease analysis, as indicated earlier, is the effect on earnings per share. The addition to earnings per share caused by the decision to lease can be summarized as follows:

First year	16.64¢	Sixth year	33.40¢
Second year	16.70	Seventh year	29.10
Third year	18.20	Eighth year	24.00
Fourth year	21.80	Ninth year	19.80
Fifth year	26.80	Tenth year	14.70

If you follow the trend of the increase in earnings per share, you might jump to the conclusion that the addition to EPS is decreasing and will probably continue to do so the eleventh year and thereafter. Don't you do it, because when we carry the analysis to the eleventh year, after the equipment would have been fully depreciated, the excess cash made available by the original lease decision will continue to compound earnings, and these earnings will continue to grow if these funds continue to be invested indefinitely!

Excess Cash from Year	Original Amount	Earnings Eleventh Year
Down payment	$83,025.00	$21,534
2	523.00	111
3	7,670.60	1,493
4	13,901.98	2,462
5	19,455.18	3,133
Total earnings eleventh year		$28,733
Addition to EPS eleventh year		57.4¢

Of course, all these lease-buy earnings are predicted upon the ability of the financial vice-president to continue to earn a return of 10 percent per year on all funds available from this particular source. This is a serious responsibility. However, the results are quite clear, if you and the firm are successful. One further thing is also quite clear. If you buy the equipment, you will not have this opportunity! Even if the earnings percentage is not constant at 10 percent as anticipated throughout the 10-year period, any earnings on these marginal funds are an addition to earnings per share. Also, the opportunity may come along whereby these funds can be diverted to other corporate use and perhaps earn an even larger return. However, this discussion could get out of hand and it's late. The phone rang (at 2 a.m.). President Jones had been returning from the airport and saw the lights on in your office. He inquired about your progress and suggested that you leave your analysis on the desk and not come in tomorrow (Monday) until about 3 p.m.! You quickly agreed and told him that if he needed you he could call the Country Club. He agreed, and I'll see you on the first tee!

SUMMARY

This chapter introduces you to the various methods of depreciation and investigates their impact on the flow of funds available to the financial manager. Accountants are quick to tell us that depreciation allowances are not sources of funds. This is quite true, but while such allowances are not sources of funds, they act as if they were. It is, therefore, important to understand that sales are the primary source of funds, and depreciation allowances, as noncash deductions from our sales figure, must be added back to our reported profit after tax in order to fully reflect funds generated from operations.

The Internal Revenue Code currently approves three basic types of depreciation methods. They are:

1. Straight-line method
2. Service-life methods
    a. Service-hours method
    b. Productive-output method
3. Accelerated-depreciation methods
    a. Declining-balance method
    b. Sum-of-the-years-digits method

We have already used the straight-line method in our capital budgeting procedure. Under this method an asset is depreciated at a constant annual rate over its economic life. Service-life methods, on the other hand, relate annual depreciation charges to hours of asset use or volume of production. Thus, they normally result in a fluctuating level of depreciation writeoffs over the asset's life.

Accelerated-depreciation methods, while recognizing a useful life for each asset, result in larger writeoffs in the early years and lower writeoffs in the later years of the asset's economic life.

Several conclusions relating to reported earnings and the use of the several depreciation methods may be drawn.

1. All methods provide the same total depreciation over the life of the asset.
2. All methods provide the same tax savings over the life of the asset.
3. Accelerated methods have the effect of changing the timing of tax savings and depreciation flows.
4. The use of accelerated methods rather than straight-line methods of depreciation does not change real earnings. The use of accelerated depreciation reduces earnings per share but matches that reduction with an increased tax savings. In consequence, the total flow of funds over the life of the asset is unchanged when accelerated rather than straight-line depreciation is used.

There is, however, one special situation in which our choice of depreciation methods can have a significant impact on reported earnings. If we elect to report to IRS on an accelerated basis and to our shareholders on a straight-line basis, our reported earnings reflect both lower tax payments and lower depreciation charges. The financial manager, however, must understand that the flow of funds remains the same.

The final topic covered in the chapter involved a recalculation of our lease-versus-buy decision from Chapter 6. The use of an accelerated-depreciation method had the effect of changing the timing of our expenses for tax purposes. The decrease in our net cost of owning (column 9) in the early years had the effect of reducing the net advantage to leasing which had originally been calculated by using a straight-line depreciation method.

QUESTIONS FOR DISCUSSION

1. What are the basic assumptions underlying straight-line depreciation?
2. How is straight-line depreciation calculated? Give an example.
3. What are the basic assumptions underlying the service-life methods of depreciation?
4. How are the service-life methods calculated? Give an example.
5. What are the basic assumptions underlying the accelerated-depreciation methods?
6. Compare and contrast the sum-of-the-digits method with the declining-balance method.
7. What effect will each of the above depreciation methods have on a firm's earnings per share? Why?

8. What effect, if any, does the substitution of the declining-balance method of depreciation for straight-line depreciation have on the lease-versus-buy analysis made in Chapter 6?

PROBLEMS

1. XYZ Company, with total capital stock in the amount of $50,000, $100 par, common stock, has three competing proposals that have been suggested for the purchase of a new milling machine. The relevant data are shown below:

Item	A	B	C
Machine cost	$7,000	$14,000	$10,000
Incremental cash benefits (before taxes)	2,500	4,500	4,000
Salvage value	0	1,000	0
Setup cost	500	1,000	0 (Pd. by mgr.)
Estimated life	3 years	7 years	5 years

   a. Use the double declining-balance method of depreciation and assume a tax rate of 50 percent:
      (1) Rank in order of rapidity of payback.
      (2) Rank in order of average annual rate of return on average annual investment.
      (3) Rank in order of rate of return.
      (4) Which proposal do you, as financial manager, recommend? Why?
   b. Use the straight-line method and revise your answer to part a.
2. Assume a cost of capital of 12 percent. Further assume that XYZ Company has infinite investment opportunities that will yield 12 percent. What are the earnings per share in Problem 1, above, under each of the alternatives in parts a and b?
3. Gentry, Inc., is presently earning $67,000 annually after taxes and decides to buy an asset at a cost of $300,000. This asset will generate earnings before depreciation and taxes of $120,000 per year. This machine will have an estimated life of 10 years and no salvage value. Gentry has no other assets.
   a. Compute the depreciation, assuming:
      (1) Straight-line method
      (2) Sum-of-the-years-digits method
      (3) Double declining-balance method
   b. Compute the earnings per share under each alternative of part a, above, if there are 200 shares outstanding, assuming that a 10 percent return is average and probable.
4. Change the assumption of a double declining-balance depreciation method used in the buy-versus-lease analysis on pages 202 and 203 to the sum-of-the-years-digits method, and compute the difference in earnings per share contributed by the difference in the actual annual cost.

REFERENCES

Anthony, Robert N.: "Management Accounting," 4th ed., chap. 6, Richard D. Irwin, Inc., Homewood, Ill., 1970.

Brigham, Eugene F.: The Effects of Alternative Depreciation Policies on Reported Earnings, *The Accounting Review,* vol. 43, pp. 46–61, 1968.

Miller, Robert D.: A Short-cut Method to Calculate Declining Balance Depreciation, *Management Accounting,* July, 1970, p. 68.

Niswonger, C. Rollin, and Philip E. Fess: "Accounting Principles," 10th ed., chap. 10, South-Western Publishing Company, Incorporated, Cincinnati, 1969.

Pyle, William W., and John Arch White: "Fundamental Accounting Principles," 5th ed., chap. 12, Richard D. Irwin, Inc., Homewood, Ill., 1969.

Summers, Edward L.: Observations of Effect of Using Alternative Reporting Practices, *The American Accounting Association,* vol. XLIII, no. 1, January, 1968.

Weston, J. Fred, and Eugene F. Brigham: "Managerial Finance," 3d ed., chap. 2 appendix, Holt, Rinehart and Winston, Inc., New York, 1969.

Chapter Eight

THE INTERNAL CONTROL AND MANAGEMENT OF CASH

It is not our purpose to burden the financial executive with the details involved in the internal control of cash and other assets quickly convertible into cash. However, because cash is immediately transferable, easy to handle, and lacks owner identification, we must be aware in a general way of the problems involved in controlling cash from the time it is received until it is disbursed. In addition to the control of cash, and perhaps more closely identified with the financial executive's function, is the management of cash. In essence, this latter problem involves, initially, the providing of sufficient cash to meet the Jones organization's financial obligations when they fall due and, secondly, the maintenance of a sufficient cash flow to enable the Jones organization to take advantage of growth and investment opportunities.

The first function is commonly called the liquidity responsibility; the second, the profitability activity. The relation between the two, although not readily apparent, is of tremendous importance.

THE LIQUIDITY RESPONSIBILITY

The business firm employs numerous resources. One of these is cash. When the enterprise is first begun, cash is generated from the sale of equity interests (for example, stock). Cash changes radically when it is consumed. Buildings and machinery are procured, raw materials are purchased, and inventories are produced. When this has been done, a portion of the cash resource is usually retained in its original and highly liquid form. The vast majority of cash, however, has been transformed into tangible operating assets from which sales and profits may be generated in the future.

If the above process has been effectively administered, the enterprise will have sufficient cash available to meet creditors' demands as they fall due, and assets have been purchased in sufficient quantity to permit the generation of a level of sales which will create profits for the owners of the firm. This Solomon-like allocation of cash resources represents a true test of the financial manager's skill.

Let us briefly consider the firm's liquidity requirement. We have pointed out that all assets emerge from cash. In like manner, all assets return to their original cash form as the business cycle is completed. At one end of the spectrum we can envision the situation wherein the enterprise fails to perform effectively and is liquidated. In this event, the amount of cash which returns to its original form is usually negligible. In more normal circumstances, the cash-to-cash cycle depends on profits, which, in turn, depend on sales. As the firm sells products, cash funds which were invested in raw materials and inventories return to their cash form when the accounts receivable are collected.

If sales, price level, wage rates, and purchasing power of the dollar and manufacturing and selling costs were predictable with certainty, then the amount of cash which the firm would be required to maintain could be determined with certainty. Unfortunately, in many business situations these factors affecting the cash-to-cash cycle are not predictable. Consequently, the firm normally must hedge against unforeseen developments by carrying a cash balance in excess of absolute requirements.

Some of the normally more important factors which affect the cash-to-cash cycle are:

1. *The stability of sales.* If sales patterns are highly predictable, cash inflows and cash outflows can be relatively accurately determined. The firm can plan to carry an adequate cash balance to cover cash outflows when it is known that cash outflows will exceed inflows. Take the case of a firm which manufacturers snow skis. Production may occur on a year-round basis. However, sales and collections on sales may be bunched at one point within the year. Adequate cash must be carried during the production phase to pay wages, to buy raw materials, and to cover other costs until cash collections are made. If the sales pattern is well established, production requirements will be known or can be estimated with some reasonable degree of confidence. As a result, any excess cash can be invested

in other assets. Any return is better than the amount that would be earned if the funds were lying idle in a checking account! However, as we will see, there are investments that can be made that are highly liquid, that is, that can be turned into cash quickly without any or with very little risk of loss. These highly liquid investments will normally earn a considerably lower rate of return. In short, if our cash needs can be reasonably predicted, the low return which we earn on excess cash balances, carried as a liquidity hedge, can be improved by investing in more profitable assets.

In the case of the rapidly growing firm with unpredictable sales levels and patterns, it is obvious that a somewhat higher cash balance or lower-yield, highly liquid investments must be carried as a liquidity hedge.

2. *Price-level changes.* Again, it is apparent that our ability to predict cash outflows depends in large measure on our ability to foresee price-level changes with respect to the wages we must pay our employees, prices we must pay to our suppliers for raw materials, and other costs. The bottler of Coca-Cola knows that the price he must pay to the Coca-Cola Company for his syrup is contractually related to the price of sugar. If changes in the price of this commodity are predictable with accuracy, the bottler can feel more confident carrying a smaller cash balance to allow for price changes than if the cost of sugar were highly variable.
3. *Other factors.* Predicting cash inflows and outflows over a given period can be complicated by taxes, or rather our assumptions about the tax level over the forecasting period. If we are completely confident that tax rates will remain unchanged, then our cash balance for liquidity purposes will contain no hedge factor for tax changes.

You will perhaps recall a recent governmental action which affected the cash flows of many firms. In the fall of 1969, the federal government required all soft-drink bottlers to withdraw from the market beverages sweetened with cyclamates. Those beverages could be replaced with beverages sweetened with saccharin. The bottler may have made a decision that the new beverage required an extensive advertising campaign. This campaign required immediate cash outflows. In a like manner, internal decisions related to wage contracts, credit, and purchase policies all affect cash inflows and outflows with respect to their timing and amount. The cash position of the firm must be adequate to meet changes in policies without causing a liquidity crisis.

In summary, the cash balance which the firm ultimately elects to carry is important. If that balance is larger than necessary, the firm is employing the cash resource in a less-than-optimal manner. In consequence, the returns which are earned for the owners are somewhat lower and the value of their equity is correspondingly reduced. If, on the other hand, the firm carries a cash balance which is too small, there exists the possibility that the firm will be unable to meet its cash obligations. It will be forced to run to its banker "hat in hand" and request an immediate loan to stave off the crisis. The results of these actions are less than desirable from the point of view of the owners of the firm. Initially, our demonstrated lack of ability to forecast our financial requirements reduces our banker's confidence in the management and may occasion a higher rate of interest on the loan he grants. Ultimately, this lack of confidence may extend to the investment community and result in the application of higher capitalization rates on the firm's securities, that is, lower stock values. In this case, the market value of the firm's stock may well be reduced, not because sales and profits are inadequate but rather because of some problem in the financial management. The problem may be simply that the firm was undercapitalized, that is, did not begin business with a strong enough capital base; or perhaps the problem is poor forecasting or just plain "bad luck." Regardless of the reason, maintaining the "proper" liquidity level is a serious responsibility of the financial executive.

THE PROFITABILITY OF CASH

Not only must the financial executive deal with the problem of liquidity; he must also come to grips with problems relating to profitability. Clearly, the two problems are related. The financial executive must work within the existing capital structure of his firm and must allocate his resources, cash included, to their most productive uses. Inadequate cash may force decisions that limit profitability. Limited profitability can further aggravate the inadequate cash problem. As an example, his decision concerning the level of the firm's cash balance can affect the firm's ability to purchase machinery and equipment that would increase sales and earnings. Thus, his decision with respect to liquidity affects the earning power or profitability of the enterprise. Perhaps it is unnecessary—you probably "got the point"—but if you like, we can restate the "point" in a more sophisticated manner.

Fundamentally, high earning power is an outgrowth of the firm's ability to show a substantial margin of profit on each dollar of sales and a high level of sales for each dollar of assets. The margin of profit on each sales dollar is determined by the relationship which exists between the net income of the firm and its total sales. Thus, margin is equal to

$$\text{Margin} = \frac{\text{net income}}{\text{sales}}$$

Equally important is the relationship between sales and assets, commonly called turnover:

$$\text{Turnover} = \frac{\text{sales}}{\text{assets}}$$

(Would you rather invest $1 million or $500,000 in assets to generate $100,000 in sales? Clearly, if you had to invest only $500,000, the balance of $500,000 would be in a more liquid form and could earn a return elsewhere!) Earning power is the product of *margin* times *turnover:*

$$\text{Margin} \times \text{turnover} = \text{earning power}$$

$$\frac{\text{Net income}}{\text{Sales}} \times \frac{\text{sales}}{\text{assets}} = \frac{\text{net income}}{\text{assets}}$$

What we are really saying, then, is that the profitability of the firm will depend on the margin of profit per dollar of sales and the number of sales per dollar of assets employed. The financial executive will then realize his profitability objective within an existing capital structure when he maximizes both margin and turnover.

Therefore, the decision which the financial manager reaches with respect to liquidity will affect the potential earning power of the firm. For example, a decision to carry a large cash balance in order to maintain a highly liquid position will directly affect turnover and indirectly reduce margin. A large cash position will increase the size of our asset base, but will not increase our sales level. With respect to our turnover, we have then increased the denominator, assets, and failed to increase the numerator, sales. The result is, of course, reduced turnover or fewer sales per dollar of invested assets, which, in turn, reduces the firm's earning power. If additional shares of stock had to be sold to provide the larger asset base which resulted in the same overall sales and profit, earnings per share would be reduced, and earnings per share is the "name of the game"!

If the excess cash is borrowed from banks or other financial institutions, the interest which we pay will add to our costs and, therefore, reduce net profit and earnings per share. If the firm's own funds are used in this same manner, the result is still the same—lower earnings per share.

Some analysts like to express the above observations in terms of percentages. We can quickly put some numbers to work in our earning-power equation and arrive at earning power expressed as a percentage. Take a firm with an asset base of 10 million, a sales level of 20 million, and net income of 1 million. In order to calculate its earning power expressed as a percentage, we simply substitute the above figures into the equation

$$\text{Margin} \times \text{turnover} = \text{earning power}$$

$$\frac{\text{Net income}}{\text{Sales}} \times \frac{\text{sales}}{\text{assets}} = \text{earning power}$$

$$\frac{1{,}000{,}000}{20{,}000{,}000} \times \frac{20{,}000{,}000}{10{,}000{,}000} = 5\% \times 2 = 10\%$$

If an excessive liquidity position had been maintained—let us say in the amount of $1 million—what impact would its correction have on earning power expressed as a percentage?

$$\frac{1{,}000{,}000}{20{,}000{,}000} \times \frac{20{,}000{,}000}{9{,}000{,}000} = 5\% \times 2.2 = 11\%$$

If the maintenance of this cash balance in the example above had required borrowing at 7 percent, its reduction would have resulted in an increase of income from $1,000,000 to $1,070,000, caused by reduction in interest expense of $70,000 and an increase in margin from 11 to 11.7 percent (neglecting the tax effect):

$$\frac{1{,}070{,}000}{20{,}000{,}000} \times \frac{20{,}000{,}000}{9{,}000{,}000} = 5.35\% \times 2.2 = 11.7\%$$

We can see that an excessive commitment of cash has a dual effect. It increases costs when the funds are borrowed, thus reducing profit margins per dollar of sales and net income. In addition, an excess commitment of cost likewise increases the size of our asset base, thus causing a decline in turnover or sales per dollar of invested assets. However, express it as you will, the significant result is a lower earning per share.

In summary, then, it is very clear that proper cash management or the lack of proper cash management is a significant factor that will affect company policies and may well dictate and/or force short-run decisions that have serious long-run implications, for example, credit standing, bankruptcy, availability of future funds on reasonable terms, earnings, dividend policy, overall capital cost, and earnings per share.

INTERNAL CONTROL OF CASH

Perhaps a recent experience of the Jones organization will illustrate the significance of the internal control of cash.

President Jones came to your office and expressed his concern about the cash balances that have been reported to him from time to time and requested that you look into the matter at your convenience. The next morning you requested the cashier to bring to your office the bank reconciliation he had prepared a few days earlier to reflect the cash position of the firm for the past month.

The statement he prepared follows:

Jones Electronic Corporation
Bank Reconciliation
as of May 31, 1970

Balance per books		$17,969.48
Add outstanding checks:		
#6314	$182.25	
#6321	207.96	
#6332	342.21	732.42
		$18,701.90
Less cash on hand		7,321.87
Estimated balance per bank		$11,380.03
Less unrecorded credit given by bank		310.00
Actual cash balance		$11,070.03

The statement itself did not appear to be in the proper form according to your best recollection of your elementary and intermediate accounting courses. You called a CPA friend of yours and invited him to lunch. You explained your problem and indicated that you didn't want to stir up a hornet's nest, but would appreciate it if he would stop by the office some evening and help you examine the statement you had just reviewed.

Your CPA requested that you secure the bank reconciliation prepared for the prior month as a point of departure for a current investigation. Together, you worked some three hours, and at the end of that time, the picture was complete. It was quite clear that the internal control of cash had been entirely inadequate. There was evidence that a minimum of $4,300 was unaccounted for during the past months.

While we are not interested in acquiring proficiency at bank reconciliations, observing the methods used to find the evidence of the unaccounted-for funds and the recommendations that were made to correct the deficiencies is significant to the broad financial function. You started with the prior month's statement, which appeared as follows after it was put in proper form by the CPA.

Jones Electronic Corporation
Bank Reconciliation
as of May 31, 1970

Balance per bank			$22,612.93
Add deposit in transit			1,722.67
			$24,335.60
Less outstanding checks:			
#4167	$197.28		
#4168	214.95		
#4169	118.27	$530.50	
Deposited check, N.S.F., returned by bank—unrecorded, deposited again following month		123.90	654.40
Balance per books			$23,681.20

First, an adding-machine tape was prepared to include all deposits recorded by the bank during the month. A second tape was prepared to include all desposits recorded on the company records.

Deposits per bank: Date	Amount
6/3	$ 7,631.87
6/10	18,208.96✓
6/12	310.00
6/17	9,124.22✓
6/24	13,330.45✓
Total	$48,605.50

Deposits per books: Date	Amount
6/5	$18,208.96✓
6/7	9,124.22✓
6/13	13,330.54✓
6/20	1,722.67
Total	$42,386.30

The difference between the total deposits recorded by the bank and the total deposits recorded on the books is $6,219.20.

Deposit recorded on books last month, 5/27, but recorded by bank this month, 6/3	$7,631.87[1]
Add bank collection on note receivable recorded by bank, 6/12, unrecorded on books	310.00[2]
	$7,941.87
Less deposit recorded on books, 6/20, but not deposited	1,722.67[3]
Difference	$6,219.20

[1] Verified amount but was held in cash drawer over the long holiday weekend. Noted long delays in all deposits and requested that in the future deposits be made promptly.

[2] Recorded on books immediately as cash income.

[3] Verified amount and made deposit immediately.

The deposits recorded by the bank were thus reconciled and, except for the omission of the $310 noted earlier and the delays in making deposits, the cash deposits were verified satisfactorily. We have not, at this point, made an examination to determine whether or not all cash received was recorded on the books of the company. All we are saying now is that all cash that has been recorded on the books for this period of time has been deposited.

The withdrawals and disbursements were, likewise, taped per the bank and per the books.

Withdrawals per bank	$47,776.63
Withdrawals per books	48,509.05
Difference in withdrawals	$ 732.42

You recognized immediately that the difference of $732.42 represented the checks that had been recorded on the books but had not been presented to the bank for payment. This appeared proper enough. The withdrawals per books should exceed the withdrawals per bank by this amount. You were satisfied.

However, the CPA asked a penetrating question: "What happened to the outstanding checks listed the previous month in the amount of $530.50?" If checks #4167, #4168, and #4169 had cleared the bank, the withdrawals per bank would have included these checks amounting to $530.50. The withdrawals per books would have exceeded the withdrawals per bank by only $101.92! ($732.42 – $530.50 = $201.92.)

At this point, we didn't know the answer to the missing checks, but we certainly knew the question. The red flag had been raised. These checks were not listed as outstanding on the last reconciliation, and we suspected that they were not presented for payment during the month. To test our suspicions, we examined all the returned checks for the month involved. The missing checks were not there. We could tell by the check numbers that the checks had been written, or purportedly had been written, several months ago.

The following morning when the cashier was questioned, he admitted that four months ago, a sale amounting to $530.50 had been recorded. When payment was made, however, he pocketed the money. He planned to return the money, but to balance the cash "temporarily" he recorded three disbursements that were never made, using checks #4167, #4168, and #4169. He further admitted having followed the same procedure on previous occasions. No one had checked his work. A complete audit followed by the CPA, and the total shortage was determined to be a minimum of $4,300. Restitution was made and a resignation soon followed. President Jones did not want to prosecute. This may have been a mistake.

The real significance of this experience is that the CPA made some sound recommendations about the internal control of cash. These were very interesting and were followed to the letter by the Jones Corporation in the ensuing months.

The first recommendation was related to the internal control of cash. The minimum requirement for the proper internal control of cash calls for the separation of the recording function and the custodial function. The person who receives and is responsible for depositing the cash funds should not be responsible for keeping the records of cash receipts and disbursements. In short, it takes two to tango! Daily deposits should be made of all cash received. Disbursements should be made only after receipt of supporting data justifying and/or authorizing the expenditure. Disbursements should be made by check except for petty cash items. An internal audit to review company transactions should be made at irregular intervals. Bank accounts should be reconciled with the book entries for deposits and withdrawals on a regular basis. This reconciliation is generally made once each month.

While we were reviewing the general principles of good internal control of cash, the CPA also outlined briefly other ways in which misappropriation can occur.

1. Unrecorded cash sales.
2. Unrecorded credit sales with misappropriation of the cash when payment is made.
3. Entries recorded as "sales returns and allowances" when cash is received in payment of customers' accounts.
4. Personal expense charged as business expense and paid.
5. Unsupported and fictitious charges paid and funds misappropriated.

In order to emphasize the importance of the separation of the duties of handling the cash and maintaining the records, our CPA illustrated "check kiting" and "lapping." "Check kiting" is an effort to show cash in bank balances at the end of the month or other accounting period that are higher than they actually are. For example, it may take several days for a check written on Bank A and deposited in Bank B to be recorded as a deposit by B and be returned to Bank A to be recorded as a withdrawal. Thus, it would be possible to prepare a check drawn on Bank A and deposit it in the company's account in Bank B on the last day or near the last day of the month or accounting period and have the deposit shown by B for the month. Bank A, however, would not show the withdrawal until the following month. Cash in the bank could then be verified on the last day of the month at a higher figure that would include B's record of the deposit referred to above. This is kiting.

"Lapping" occurs when a payment is received on X's account and the money is pocketed. Then, when Y pays, X's account is credited. When Z pays, Y's account is credited. This lapping procedure may continue without attracting too much attention as long as the payment intervals are frequent. Clearly, then, the responsibility for handling cash and the responsibility for recording the receipts and disbursements of cash must be separated and must be specifically defined and scrupulously carried out.

"Window dressing" is another way of improving the cash position at the end of an accounting period. Cash receipts records are simply held open a few days or so following the end of the month or year, and cash received during this period is recorded as having been received earlier. This results in the appearance of larger cash balances at the end of the accounting period. Proper internal or external audit procedures would eliminate, or at least bring to light, all the shenanigans described above.

MANAGEMENT OF SHORT-TERM INVESTMENTS

You felt quite satisfied with yourself and especially with the Jones liquidity problem. You could see dancing before your eyes the prospects of something in the neighborhood of $170,000 in profit after taxes at the end of the first full year's operations using the new equipment. Jones Electronic Corporation would be on top of the world. You knew that your first project would be to prepare or have prepared a short-term cash forecast. This forecast would estimate the cash inflow and cash outflow requirements for the immediate three-, six-, or twelve-month period. Two distinctly different types of funds would then be set up. The first we can term the *cash fund* or the *liquidity fund.* The purpose of this fund would be to provide the cash needed for predictable transactions during the forecast period. The second fund we will term the *operating fund.* The *operating* or *fixed asset* fund would include those assets from which the Jones organization expects to earn the major portion of total income. For the Jones organization, this would include the plant, equipment, inventories, research activities, and the marketing organization.

As you have learned, the balance of actual cash held in the cash or liquidity fund for business transactions will ordinarily be held to a minimum. Any temporary excess of cash will be earmarked for short-term investments. Any excess of cash in this fund that appears to be a permanent excess will be transferred to the operating fund for more permanent investment. Our problem now is the management of the temporary investments occasioned by idle cash balances.

The basic criterion we must use in the investment of temporary excess cash is, of course, liquidity. Liquidity concerns itself with marketability and an interest-rate risk. We should be certain, in the first instance, either that there is an established market for the security purchased or that a repurchase agreement is made with the seller at the time we buy the security. An established market implies that there is sufficient volume of the particular security being bought or sold on a continuing basis that a sale by Jones will not materially affect the price. High marketability assures us that a minimum risk of loss of principal is likely to result from the future sale of the securities in question.

The interest-rate risk refers to the potential loss of principal and/or earnings which would result from an increase in the rate of interest being paid for the type of security purchased by Jones as a temporary investment (or a long-term investment, for that matter). In Chapter 12, we will clearly illustrate that after a security has been purchased for a given price to yield a given rate of interest, any change in the rate of interest will result in a change in the selling price of the security. Perhaps a brief example now will be sufficient to illustrate this point.

If you paid $1,000 for a bond which carried an agreed interest rate of 4 percent and the market rate of interest for bonds of this same type increased to 5 percent, clearly, you would not expect a subsequent buyer to pay $1,000 for your bond. The bond would have to be sold at a discount, that is, at a price less than $1,000, to compensate for the increase in the market rate of interest. There could, therefore, be a loss of principal, accruing to the seller and caused solely by a change in the market rate of interest. This contingency is called interest-rate risk. There is considerably less risk in short-run interest-rate changes than there would be over a longer period of time.

The degree of risk that you are willing to take may be, to a large degree, determined by the ultimate use which you plan to make of the funds. For example, a portion of the funds may be set aside for seasonal or anticipated upswings in the Jones business activity; or we may be husbanding funds for future dividend or tax payments, for capital expansion, or to pay off debt as it becomes due. As we will see, the various short-term securities have somewhat different characteristics. With these basic concepts of marketability and interest-rate risk in mind, you began your investigation of a multiplicity of money-market instruments through which idle funds may be invested on a temporary basis. As always, there are alternatives. The results of your investigation may be summarized as follows:

United States Government Marketable Debt

The largest available investment opportunity is in marketable securities issued by the U.S. Treasury. These securities include treasury bills, treasury certificates, treasury notes, and bonds. The significant difference between these various treasury obligations is the length of maturity. Treasury issues can normally be converted into cash within 24 hours. United States Treasury bills maturing in three and six months are auctioned weekly and are sold at discounts from par value. The full return on such bills is realized by holding them until maturity. The Treasury also offers issues that mature in up to one year on the same discounted basis; these are sold via special auctions. There is an active resale market for all these securities. Therefore, these issues offer excellent liquidity and safety. (They are high in marketability, but are subject to a certain level of interest-rate risk.) The denominations offered range from $1,000 to $1 million.

Prime Sales Finance Paper

This type of investment involves unsecured promissory notes of sales finance companies sold directly to the investor or through the investor's bank or agent. The maturity period runs from 3 to 270 days with denominations ranging from $1,000 to $5 million with a $5,000 minimum trading limit. There is no regularly established resale market. This type of paper is usually sold to "bearer" on a discount basis. An advantage of this type of short-term investment is that the investor may select both the date of issue and the date of maturity so that the funds will become available to coincide with specific commitments such as tax payments or scheduled debt repayments affecting the buyer.

Dealer Paper—Industrial

These are promissory notes of leading industrial firms sold through dealers with a maturity of 60 to 180 days in most instances. The denominations of these notes range from $5,000 to $5 million, and they are sold on a discounted basis. There is no regularly established resale market for this so-called commercial paper.

Bankers' Acceptances

A bankers' acceptance or bill of exchange is an unqualified order in writing requiring the institution to whom it is addressed to pay on demand a definite amount of money at a particular time. By accepting the draft, the bank substitutes its credit for the credit of the person or institution making the order. The term "acceptance" is applied to this type of instrument because of the fact that in the normal course of business, banks do accept this liability in return for a fee (interest paid by the maker.)

For example, if the Jones organization desired to purchase goods from abroad, President Jones could request his bank to issue a commercial letter of credit in favor of the request exporter. This letter allows the exporter to draw a draft on the American bank and implies or states that Jones' bank will accept a draft within the credit limits specified. The exporter could then discount the draft at his local bank and receive the proceeds. The draft is then forwarded to the Jones bank for acceptance. When the Jones bank accepts the draft, the Jones bank becomes the primary obligor to the exporter. The Jones organization is then in turn obligated to repay its local bank. The local bank is thus substituting its credit for the credit of Jones.

Bankers' acceptances have become a very important part of the short-term investment market, offering usually higher rates of return than U.S. Treasury bills and yet providing both safety and liquidity. They are sold on a discounted basis on a 360-day year in denominations of $25,000 to $1 million with maturities up to six months.

Dealer Paper—Finance

These are promissory notes of finance companies sold through commercial paper dealers in denominations of $5,000 to $5 million. This paper is sold on a discounted or interest-bearing basis on a 360-day year to mature in 30 to 270 days. There is no resale market as such, but repurchase or buy-back arrangements can usually be made through a dealer at adjusted rates of interest. This adjusted rate will be the difference between the short-term and the long-term rate (for example, the 30- or 60-day rate versus a 90- or 180-day rate). Many companies also guarantee "rate protection" for three business days. That is, if the interest rate for the period of time specified on the paper itself increases within three business days, the seller will pay the higher rate of interest.

Negotiable Certificates of Deposit

The certificate of deposit, commonly known as the CD, is a relatively new type of short-term investment. In simplest terms, a CD is a negotiable receipt for a time deposit indicating the rate of interest the deposit will earn and for what period of time. There is a good resale or secondary market for these certificates. The maximum rates authorized by the Board of Governors of the Federal Reserve System are subject to change. Presently, the maximum rates of interest that can be paid by member banks for this type of deposit are as follows:

Period of Deposit	Maximum Annual Rate
30–59 days	$5\frac{1}{2}\%$
60–89 days	$5\frac{3}{4}\%$
90–179 days	6 %
180 days or more	$6\frac{1}{4}\%$

SOURCE: Board of Governors of the Federal Reserve System, effective April 19, 1968, supplement to Regulation Q.

The CDs issued by the major banks located in the larger money centers, such as Chicago and New York, have a well-developed resale market. The CDs are sold at discounts to reflect the current yield in the money markets on a 360-day-year basis. These securities are usually issued in denominations of more than $100,000, and the majority are issued in the amount of $1 million.

Short-term Tax-exempt Bills

A significant feature of this type of security is that all earnings are tax-free with respect to interest payments as far as federal income taxation is concerned. Usually, these notes and bonds will have a fixed interest rate stated on the face of the instrument. However, when the bonds sell on a discounted basis, the difference between the amount paid for the security and the face value of the security is also tax-free, as indicated above.

These nontaxable securities can be classified into three broad categories:

1. Temporary and preliminary notes of local public agencies
2. Temporary securities issued by states and municipalities
3. Short-term serial bond issues of states, municipalities, or federal housing authorities

The temporary and preliminary notes of local public agencies are usually issued under the authority of the Housing Assistance Administration and the Renewal Assistance Administration. These obligations carry as security "the full faith and credit of the United States," and the federal government is pledged to the payment of all amounts agreed to be paid by the Authority. State and municipal securities carry the "full faith and credit" of the issuing political subdivision.

These obligations are sold in denominations of $1,000 to $1 million with maturities ranging from three months up to a year. There is an active resale market in the larger money centers for such instruments.

Repurchase Agreements

The repurchase agreement, or "repo" agreement, is simply a sale of short-term securities (generally by a dealer) and their repurchase at a specified time. Normally, government obligations are involved. The investor may select the date of repurchase ranging from one day to several weeks at an agreed rate of interest. The investor is thus protected against fluctuations in the money market during the specified period. Government bond dealers use the "repos" to finance their inventory during periods of extremely tight money conditions.

It is obvious that there are available a variety of opportunities for short-term investment of temporarily idle cash balances. Our next problem would be to determine probable liquidity needs and to establish an overall investment or portfolio plan for funds not immediately required for operating payments. In general, we could view the investment of temporary cash balances in relation to the ultimate purpose for which the funds will be used. For example, funds might be accumulated for:

1. *Regular and unexpected operational needs.* This type of investment must emphasize flexibility and limited price change risk. United States Treasury Tax Exemption Securities guaranteed by the federal government, certificates of deposit from prime banks, and certain commercial paper offer the best opportunities consistent with these needs.
2. *Dividends, tax payments, debt retirement, or other specific payments.* The problem here is to select the type of security that will carry the option of specifying the appropriate maturity date to coincide with the date of the need for the funds. Certificates of deposit, repurchase agreements, and commercial paper offer this advantage. Other securities can likewise be used if there is an adequate and dependable resale market, although sale before maturity generally would involve the sacrifice of some earnings and possibly small principal losses.
3. *Longer-term commitments and future capital expansion.* Longer-term United States government and tax-exempt securities generally offer higher earnings yields after taxes. Again, however, the risk involved is the possibility of being forced to liquidate prior to maturity at a possible loss. The longer the term of the security, the more risk we will take with reference to fluctuations in the money market, that is, the example of the reaction of bond prices to changing interest rates.

The temporary investment of cash does involve alternative possibilities. The Jones organization will be delighted to face this problem! The day went by and you went home a bit early. I called at 2:30 p.m. and was advised by your secretary that you were on an "inspection trip." Boy! Is she well trained! However, I made a second phone call. The Club pro advised that you had just left the first tee—alone and playing three balls. You were obviously getting in a little practice on the Duffer—for our match Saturday morning!

(You bounced into the office the next morning like a yo-yo. All I can say is enjoy it—I'm about to pull the string! You didn't need the practice, I did.)

CASH-FLOW ANALYSIS

You began to gather the information necessary to make your cash-flow analysis for the coming year. You must estimate the required monthly cash outflows and the monthly cash inflows. You pulled out your Projected Statement of Profit and Loss. It appears below:

Jones Electronic Corporation
Projected Statement of Profit and Loss
For the Year October 1, 1971, to September 30, 1972

Sales:		
Jones, 115,000 units at $6	$690,000	
Allied, 40,000 units at $5	200,000	
		$890,000
Cost of Goods Sold:		
155,000 units at $3.50 + 12.4¢ = $3.624		561,720
Gross Profit		$328,280
Less:		
General and Administrative Expenses (Including Jones' Salary, $102,000)		147,846
Net Profit Before Taxes		$180,434
Income Tax—22% × $25,000 =	5,500	
48% × $155,434 =	74,608	80,108
		$100,326

Upon completion of the projected or *pro forma* income statement, you checked each figure in order to determine its source and its accuracy.

1. *Sales.* The sales figure has been generated on the basis of a forecast. The forecast assumes that Jones Electronic will deliver 40,000 units to Allied and increase its sales to other customers

by 15,000 units. Total sales in units are then expected to be 155,000 units. The dollar sales figure is simply a translation of unit sales into dollars. Thus, 115,000 units at a $6 selling price will generate revenues of $690,000. The 40,000 units sold to Allied at $5 per unit will bring in an additional $200,000. Total sales are then expected to be $890,000.

2. *Cost of goods sold.* The cost of sales figure was derived from our flexible budget. The costs are broken down into $3.50 per unit variable cost and 12.4 cents per unit of other allocated fixed cost at the 155,000-unit production level. Since our ability to predict these costs is partially dependent on the interaction of several variables (material and labor cost plus volume of sales and production cost) over which we have no control, the accuracy of this figure is in some doubt. However, it does represent our best judgment on the basis of extensive sensitivity analysis like that undertaken in Chapter 5.
3. *General and administrative expenses.* These expenses are predictable with some accuracy, since they are largely fixed in nature over the short run. The increased salary which will be earned by President Jones is also a fixed commitment, at least during the planning stage. (By the way, in view of the projected profits, you just agreed with President Jones that he could increase his salary from $40,000 to $102,000 annually.)
4. *Income tax.* The tax figure which we have generated depends on two variables. The tax rates may be assumed constant over the planning period. However, the figure net profit before tax, to which these rates are applied, will be accurate only to the extent that our predictions relating to sales and costs have been accurate.

With this in mind, you turned to the projection of your balance sheet. You are aware that the balance sheet is simply a picture of the firm's asset and claim structure at one point in time. Our *pro forma* balance sheet will present such a picture as of a date one year from now, assuming that operations have proceeded as we predicted when we drew up the projected income statement.

Let us again review each figure in the statement in order to assure ourselves of its source and probable level of accuracy.

1. *Cash.* The figure which appears in the projected balance sheet will be the sum of the cash with which we began the accounting period and the net cash which was generated during the period. We began the year with $37,000 in cash and during the year generated net cash of $48,902, including $10,000 received from the sale of the old equipment, or our projected cash balance of $85,902. (The

Jones Electronic Corporation
Projected Balance Sheet
For the Year October 1, 1971, to September 30, 1972

ASSETS			
Current Assets			
Cash			$ 85,902
Accounts Receivable			82,800
Inventories			
Raw Material		$ 500	
Finished Goods		6,124	6,624
Fixed Assets			None
Total Assets			$175,326
LIABILITIES AND CAPITAL			
Current Liabilities			None
Common Stock		$85,833	
Retained Earnings, 10/1/70	None		
Add Profit after Taxes	$100,326		
Less Loss on Sale of Equipment	10,833		
Total Retained Earnings		89,493	
Total Liabilities and Capital			$175,326

cash figure will be calculated as part of our cash budget which follows.)

2. *Accounts receivable.* The balance which is projected in this account will represent the sum of those sales which remain uncollected at the end of the accounting period. The figure will be dependent on the firm's collection pattern. The Jones Corporation has discovered that collections on sales seem to follow a distinct pattern. On the basis of prior experience, we know that 10 percent of the sales made in any one month will be collected in that same month, while 60 percent will be collected the next month and 30 percent the month following that. We know that in the final three months of the period our sales will be $69,000 per month. (See sales forecast, page 232.) Given these monthly sales and our collection pattern, we would have $82,800 uncollected accounts receivable. This figure is calculated as follows:

Sales		% of Sales Remaining Uncollected	
$69,000	September	0.90	$62,100
69,000	August	0.30	20,700
			$82,800

3. *Raw material and finished goods.* The balance which we project in this account comes directly from our production budget. The accuracy of the projection is, of course, in turn determined by the accuracy of our sales forecast.
4. *Fixed assets.* The projected zero balance in this account is caused by the fact that we lease our productive equipment and sell our existing and now inadequate assets. Since both of these actions have been taken, our fixed asset account is accurately projected.
5. *Current liabilities.* We have projected a zero balance in this account. The basis of the projection is the fact that the Jones Corporation pays for all purchases during the month in which they are made. Consequently, at the end of September, 1971, all purchase obligations will have been met.
6. *Common stock.* The figure of $85,833 represents the value of the original ownership interest. Since no additional shares are expected to be sold during the fiscal year, we can be confident that the balance in this account will remain unchanged.
7. *Retained earnings.* The projected balance of $89,495 is dependent on the accuracy of several of our other predictions for the upcoming fiscal year. The after-tax profit which will be earned if we have accurately estimated sales and costs is $100,326. This figure comes from our income statement; as the earnings will be retained in the business, they are transferred to the retained earnings account. The retained earnings account will thus reflect our profit for the period less any book losses which have occurred. The loss on the sale of our old equipment ($10,833) is such a book loss and, consequently, is netted out against our retained profits for the period.

Your review of the method by which the projected income statement and balance sheet have been prepared satisfies you that no glaring errors have been made.

These two statements, the projected income statement and the projected balance sheet, alone do not give very much information about our liquidity position except to project a cash balance of $85,904 at the end of the year. This certainly is an indication that our cash position at the end of the year would appear to be greatly improved. As you recall, our present cash balance is $37,000. A cash-flow analysis prepared on a monthly basis will give us a more detailed indication of our estimated liquidity position and may better pinpoint problem areas if they exist.

The Jones organization had never prepared a cash-flow analysis. Experience with our cash sales and accounts receivable collection, however, indicates that 10 percent of our sales are either cash sales or payments received on invoices billed during the month of the sale.

Another 60 percent are received the following month, and the balance of 30 percent is received the second month following the month of the sale. Allied forwards payments during the first month following delivery, and these payments are included in the estimated 60 percent. Planned production is 13,000 units per month. Anticipated cash outflow each month would be as follows. Note that the outflow is constant since production is stable. We can follow a stable production schedule by virtue of our ability to handle monthly sales variations with adjustments to our inventory position.

Production costs, 13,000 units at $3.624	$47,112
Add administrative and general expenses	12,000
Estimated cash outflow	$59,112

The next step in our analysis will be to prepare a sales forecast and to translate the sales forecast into a cash receipts budget. The sales forecast must be prepared with care because our entire cash-flow analysis is based upon these figures. Note carefully also the basic assumptions we are using concerning the collection of our accounts receivable. The sales forecast and the related cash receipts budget appear as follows:

SALES FORECAST
First and Second Quarters

	Oct.	Nov.	Dec.	Jan.	Feb.	Mar.
Est. sales (units)	9,000	9,000	14,000	13,000	16,000	16,000
Jones at $6	$36,000	$36,000	$42,000	$60,000	$78,000	$78,000
Allied at $5	15,000	15,000	35,000	15,000	15,000	15,000
Total estimated sales	$51,000	$51,000	$77,000	$75,000	$93,000	$93,000

CASH RECEIPTS BUDGET
First and Second Quarters

Cash Sales and Collections:	Oct.	Nov.	Dec.	Jan.	Feb.	Mar.
A/R bal.*	$20,000	$ 5,000				
Month of sale 10%	5,100	5,100	$ 7,700	$ 7,500	$ 9,300	$ 9,300
Second month 60%		30,600	30,600	46,200	45,000	55,800
Third month 30%			15,300	15,300	23,100	22,500
Est. cash inflow	$25,100	$40,700	$53,600	$69,000	$77,400	$87,600

* See balance sheet, page 229.

SALES FORECAST
Third and Fourth Quarters

	Apr.	May	June	July	Aug.	Sept.
Est. sales (units)	16,000	14,000	12,000	12,000	12,000	12,000
Jones at $6	$78,000	$66,000	$54,000	$54,000	$54,000	$54,000
Allied at $5	15,000	15,000	15,000	15,000	15,000	15,000
Total estimated sales	$93,000	$81,000	$69,000	$69,000	$69,000	$69,000

CASH RECEIPTS BUDGET
Third and Fourth Quarters

Cash Sales and Collections:	Apr.	May	June	July	Aug.	Sept.	Bal. A/R 9/30/71
Month of sale 10%	$ 9,300	$ 8,100	$ 6,900	$ 6,900	$ 6,900	$ 6,900	$62,100
Second month 60%	55,800	55,800	48,600	41,400	41,400	41,400	
Third month 30%	27,900	27,900	27,900	24,300	20,700	20,700	20,700
Est. cash inflow	$93,000	$91,800	$83,400	$72,600	$69,000	$69,000	$82,800

Thus far, we have projected our cash receipts based upon the assumption that the Jones Corporation will receive cash in an amount equal to 10 percent of a given month's sales during the month of the sales, 60 percent during the following month, and 30 percent the second month following the sale. Significantly, we note our accounts receivable will increase from $25,000 to $82,800. As we must do with all our analyses, we must compare reality (the actual cash inflow) with the assumptions made in the analysis. If there is any major departure from our projected estimates, we must take appropriate action. Our analysis will serve, then, as an excellent bench mark, a point of departure, for future managerial decisions.

A cash-flow summary appears at the top of page 233.

As we compare our projected profit and loss statement with the cash-flow analysis, the significance of our concern with profitability versus liquidity is quite apparent. The profit and loss statement forecasts a profit of $100,326 after a deduction for President Jones' salary of $102,000. This presents a bright picture indeed!

However, as we review the cash-flow analysis, we can clearly see that at the end of the first quarter, our cash payments will exceed our cash income by a net total of $78,924! Therefore, if we do not have a cash balance of at least this amount when we enter the period, we will be unable to finance our projected production for the period. It

CASH–FLOW SUMMARY

	Cash Receipts	Cash Payments	Cumulative Cash Bal.		Cash Receipts	Cash Payments	Cumulative Cash Bal.
Oct.	$25,100	$59,112	$(34,012)	Apr.	$93,000	$59,112	$(9,360
Nov.	40,700	59,112	(52,424)	May	91,800	59,112	23,328
Dec.	53,600	59,112	(57,936)	June	83,400	59,112	47,616
Quarterly tax payment		20,988	(78,924)	Quarterly tax payment		20,988	26,628
Jan.	69,000	59,112	(69,036)	July	72,600	59,112	40,116
Feb.	77,400	59,112	(50,748)	Aug.	69,000	59,112	50,004
Mar.	87,600	59,112	(22,260)	Sept.	69,000	59,112	59,892
Quarterly tax payment		20,988	(43,248)	Quarterly tax payment		20,990	$38,902

Units produced	156,000		Total receipts	$832,200
Units sold	155,000		Total disbursements	793,298
			Increase in cash	$ 38,902
Units added to finished goods inventory	1,000			
	× 3.624			
Inventory Sept. 30, 1972	$3,624	(addition to inventory during year)		

will be eight months until our total cash inflow will catch up with our total cash outflows. Unless we can solve this liquidity problem, the Jones organization may not be in operation at the end of the year to realize the projected profitability. The Jones Corporation's liquidity problem, then, is concerned with the ability to pay business obligations as they become due and also the ability to raise the required amount of cash when and if needed.

You checked your calculations carefully, but the significance was clear. The honeymoon involving our success with the Allied sales, the details of the equipment acquisition, and the tremendous increase in our knowledge of the Jones organization was over, and especially our dreams of investing the temporary cash! It is true that you had matured in your job and you were just beginning to feel the joy of knowing that you were making a major contribution to the success of the Jones organization. President Jones has been, likewise, elated at the prospects for the coming year. Now, his feet must also return to the ground. It was, and is, a bitter pill, but you must discuss with him the need for immediate short-term financing. This discussion may well involve a reduction or deferment of his anticipated salary increase. You will recall, you agreed with him that his salary could be increased from $40,000 annually to $102,000 based upon the projected profit analysis.

His reaction, after you reviewed the expected cash position, was simply that he had been anticipating the results of your cash-flow study. He remarked that he had lived with Jones Electronic from the days it started in his garage. He has experienced the fact that the more a business grows and the larger a business becomes, the tighter the cash position becomes, and the more financing one needs. He indicated that he was confident you would find a way to weather the storm, with the emphasis on the you!

STATEMENT OF SOURCE AND APPLICATION OF FUNDS

You had just returned to your office and had just begun to think about your liquidity problem when President Jones came in and said, "By the way, what in the world will happen to our projected profits? Can't we raise part of our cash requirements from our profits?"

When he asked this question, it was obvious that he didn't fully understand our analysis. Do you? It was at this point that we decided to ask our accountant to prepare a statement of the source and application of funds. He first prepared the following worksheet.

Work Sheet for the Projected
Statement of the Sources and Application of Funds
For the Year Ending 9/30/71

Current Assets		**10/1/70**		**9/30/71**	**Source of Funds**	**Use of Funds**
Cash		$37,000		$ 85,902		$ 48,902
Accounts Receivable		25,000		82,800		57,800
Inventories						
Raw Material		500		500		
Finished Goods		2,500		6,124		3,624
Total Current Assets		$65,000		$175,326		
Fixed Assets						
Equipment	$50,000					
Less Accumulated Depreciation	29,167					
Total Fixed Assets		20,833		None	$ 20,833	
Total Assets		$85,833		$175,326		
Current Liabilities		None		None		
Long-term Liabilities		None		None		
Common Stock		$85,833		$ 85,833		
Retained Earnings 10/1/70		None		None		
Add Projected Profit from Operations after Taxes			$100,326			
Less Loss on Sale of Equipment			10,833	89,493	89,493	
		$85,833		$175,326	$110,326	$110,326

We decided to prepare an explanation for each item:

1. *Cash*

10/1/70 balance	$37,000
Add proceeds from sale of equipment	10,000
Estimated cash inflow	38,902
	$85,902

2. *Accounts receivable and inventories.* Funds were used to increase both of these current assets.
3. *Fixed assets.* Equipment with a book value of $20,833 was sold for $10,000. We have included the loss as a "use" or a reduction in the capital accounts.
4. *Profit from operations.* The profit from operations was $100,326 after taxes. This is a source of funds.
5. *Sale of equipment.* When the sale of the equipment was shown as a source of funds, the "use" was to increase cash by $10,000, the sales price, and to lower capital by the loss, $10,833.

If we examine the "use of funds" column, it is clear why the total profit will not contribute toward the needed cash. The profit is tied up in the addition to the cash account in the amount of $48,902 and in accounts receivable and finished goods inventory in the amounts of $57,800 and $3,624, respectively.

Cash	$ 48,902
Less $10,000 received from sale of equipment	10,000
	38,902
Accounts receivable	57,800
Finished goods inventory	3,624
Profit projected	$100,326

What is the importance of all this analysis? One significant aspect is the fact that not only do we know where our projected profit will be used, but it is also quite clear that at the end of the first quarter, we will need $78,924 in additional funds in order to meet our obligations and to make our first quarterly income tax payment. We could almost repay this sum by the end of the eighth month (April), and our cash flow would clearly permit us to repay this sum by the end of May, barring unforeseen cash requirements. Therefore, we need short-term financing to cover a period of eight months to a year.

Basically, we would have no problem if all sales were cash sales; however, this is not the case. The firm's sales are simply not primarily cash sales. A review of our *sales* forecast and estimated cash outflow for the first four months indicates that a favorable balance of payments would exist if we could somehow speed up our cash collections.

	Projected Sales	Projected Cash Payments	Cumulative Balance
October	$51,000	$59,112	$ (8,112)
November	51,000	59,112	(16,224)
December	77,000	59,112	1,664
January	75,000	59,112	17,552
Tax payment		20,988	(3,436)

An examination of our current liabilities indicates that there is little doubt we could borrow the $3,436 to $5,000 we would need to cover our first-quarter tax payment (due January 15). An answer to this problem might be to formulate policies which encourage the prompt payment of our invoices as they are rendered. Of course, this answer assumes that our invoices are rendered promptly.

CREDIT AND BILLING PROCEDURES

A review of our credit and billing procedures did disclose an opportunity to obtain payment from our customers a little more promptly. The Jones invoices were presently being mailed on the twenty-sixth of each month without regard to the date of the sale. The delayed billing clearly eliminated any possibility of receiving cash from accounts receivable during the month of the sale. Quite often billing did not take place until the first or even the second week of the following month! It is quite clear that the Jones organization can solve this aspect of the problem by more prompt attention to billing procedures. In fact, you decided to have all invoices prepared for delivery at the same time the product was delivered. A larger organization could perhaps not be so prompt, but the Jones' sales involve a relatively small number of customers each month; consequently, an accelerated billing procedure is feasible.

Closer contact and good personal relations with those persons in our customers' offices who are in charge of approving invoices for payment may allow for some improvement in our cash-flow problems. In addition, it was noted earlier that considerable delay in processing and depositing checks made our collection policy appear to be somewhat slower than it really was. As has been discovered, deposits were sometimes made one or two weeks after the receipt of payment. In addition, you decided that on those deliveries when the driver collected the amounts due he would mail them promptly to your assistant's office in a preaddressed envelope, via airmail if necessary. It is estimated that this procedure would save seven to ten days over the old policy whereby the driver retained the checks until his deliveries had been completed (sometimes as much as a week or 10 days). The driver would then turn all receipts in to the warehouse to be forwarded to the accounting office after proper records had been made.

Lockbox System

For one particular sales region quite some distance from the home office a "lockbox" system could be established. This involves simply the renting of a post-office box in the locality and requesting the customers in that area to mail their remittances to that particular post-office box. Arrangements could then be made authorizing a local bank to open the post-office box daily and to deposit the funds received to the Jones account. Under such a system there would be several advantages to the Jones Corporation. Our staff would be relieved of the cost of receiving, recording, and the preparation of the checks for deposit. These functions would be performed by the bank. Daily or semiweekly phone calls to the bank could be made to secure a list of payments received and the total cash available. The bank would receive a fee for this service, or the Jones Corporation might be requested to keep a minimum balance to compensate the bank for this service.

Float Time

The decentralization of cash collection has an advantage if prompt payment to creditors in these locations is desirable. Prompt payment can be made from the funds deposited in the local bank. However, there is a disadvantage. This disadvantage is the elimination of "float" time. Float refers to the length of time necessary for a check to make its way from the issuing company to the payee, back through the clearing process until the check is finally charged against the issuing account.

We have examined earlier both the present-value-of-a-dollar concept and the matter of accrued interest. Large companies may have considerable sums of money in the float process. Calculating the time necessary for these funds to clear the banking process may mean that the funds necessary to pay the checks could be invested several extra days or, perhaps, even a week. When large sums of money are involved, these additional earnings could be significant. (Example: $1 million × 3/360 × 6 percent = $500 every three days.)

Another way of using float time, although the term is incorrectly used in this connection, is to request our creditors to forward a draft for the amount due to them to our bank for payment. Our bank would then notify us upon the receipt of the draft, and funds could be released from an interest-bearing account at the last possible moment to pay the draft. We would thus earn as much income from our funds as possible.

In short, we may minimize our required cash balances by maximizing our turnover and retention of funds. These efforts should contribute some relief in our cash problems forecasted for the coming 90 to 120 days. The least these efforts can do is to keep our cash problem from going from the problem category to disaster because of a lack of attention.

All these ideas and more can be investigated in due time. However, the general manager has suggested that perhaps cash discounts could be offered to encourage prompt payment. You have had no experience with offering cash discounts. Therefore, you must examine this suggestion quite carefully. Jones could offer a cash discount in order to induce the payment of our accounts receivable within a specified time period.

Effect of Cash Discounts

The customary terms of discount have been expressed as follows:

Credit Terms	Cost of Credit to Purchaser if Cash Discount Not Taken, or Cost to Seller if It Is (on an Annual Basis)
1/10 n 20	36.36%
1/10 n 30	18.18
2/10 n 20	73.44
2/10 n 30	36.72

By the symbols 1/10 n 20, for example, we mean that if the purchaser pays his invoice within 10 days from the invoice date he may remit to us the invoice price less 1 percent. The "n" stands for net, which means the entire amount of the invoice is due within 20 days from the date of the invoice. A discount policy may include any combination of terms. As an example, we might set discount terms 2/10 net 30 AG. This could mean that the 10-day period starts to run upon the arrival of goods. We could use EOM, or end of month, as the time when the discount period begins to run. We could say 10th prox. (means the next month). This discount period would end on the tenth of the following month.

The following equation has been used for calculating the cost of offering cash discounts:

$$\text{Cost} = \frac{\text{discount \%}}{100\% - \text{discount \%}} \times \frac{360}{\text{final due date} - \text{discount period}}$$

What we are really doing when we use this formula is as follows:

The Jones Corporation is thinking in terms of 2 percent 10 days (EOM), net 30 days. Substituting our figures into the first part of the formula gives the following results:

$$\frac{0.02}{1.00 - 0.02} = \frac{0.02}{0.98} \text{ or } 0.0204$$

This is telling us that it would cost us 2.04 percent of the amount we would actually receive after the discount has been taken if we receive the cash 10 days after the end of the month of the sale.

We would then, according to the formula, multiply 2.04 percent by 18:

$$\frac{360 \text{ days}}{20 \text{ days}} = 18 \times 2.04 = 36.36\%$$

the theory being that the 20 days would occur 18 times during the year. The product purports to indicate an annual interest rate of 36.36 percent.

If you feel uneasy about the conclusions for the Jones organization, we join you from a practical point of view, unless invoices are sent out daily, and in some businesses they are (for example, utility bills). In the first instance, the 20-day period does not occur 18 times per year, but only 12 (once each month). Thus, the maximum calculation would be 0.0204 × 12 months, or 24.48 percent per year, but 24.48 percent of what? The answer is 24.48 percent of one month's accounts receivable, or $24,480 per year based on our hypothetical example below:

Monthly Accounts Receivable		**Discounts Taken**		
January	$100,000	$ 2,040	=	2.04%
February	100,000	2,040	=	2.04
March	100,000	2,040	=	2.04
	$300,000	$ 6,120 per quarter		6.12% per quarter
		×4		×4
		$24,480		24.48%

The best that can be said is simply that if we need the funds 20 days earlier than we would receive them normally and if it is possible to borrow the amount needed at any rate of interest less than 0.0204 per month to finance our operations for the extra 20 days, we should do so. Two and four hundredths percent can be a high price to pay for receiving our cash 20 days ahead of schedule!

In addition, if discounts were not given on cash sales, it would be wiser and cheaper for the cash customer to charge his sales! As an example, if Allied's purchase of 3,000 units for a given month were cash sales, we would receive $15,000 ($5 per unit price). However, if Allied pays within the discount period the following month, we would receive only $14,700 (15,000 × 0.02 = $300 discount)! We would be encouraging our cash customers to delay payment and losing the 2 percent discount for customers who would have paid anyway! At the conclusion of the above presentation President Jones advised that the discussion of cash discounts was over!

However, the problem of the first-quarter cash crisis remains unresolved. We do not know the answers at this point, but we certainly recognize the problems! Let's go to the golf course. Tomorrow is another day and no doubt will bring another problem. You couldn't make it! I went out for a little practice and gave instructions at the club house—that no one had seen me that afternoon.

While we could and did implement the earlier suggestions to speed up cash collections (for example, prompt billing, lockbox arrangement), we were not certain that these measures would be adequate to overcome the first quarter's negative cash flow of $78,924. We had to be certain. We had to be certain that we could raise the needed financing if these methods were unsuccessful. Things just didn't appear to be too bright. (Furthermore, I shot 102 for 18 holes—that's six strokes better than my handicap.)

But, wait a minute. There is more than one type of financing! Perhaps we can finance part of our needs through the use of credit with our suppliers. A 90- to 180-day credit arrangement with our suppliers would reduce our anticipated first-quarter cash deficit. The 39,000 units of production included a materials cost of $1 each. This will total $39,000. That's a start! President Jones could volunteer to defer payment on his salary for six months. That's another $8,500 per month. Over the three-month critical period, the salary alone would reduce the cash outlay $25,500. We are only $14,424 short of our 90-day or first-quarter requirements.

Total first-quarter cash deficit		$78,924
90- to 180-day credit extension	$39,000	
Deferred salary to Jones	25,500	64,500
Remaining cash first-quarter deficit		$14,424

Things really aren't as bad as they might seem. In our concern over the cash-flow analysis we have completely overlooked our present cash balance of $37,000 plus the $10,000 received from the sale of our old equipment! So, if we can arrange the credit with the suppliers and if President Jones will defer his compensation, the $47,000 on hand will give us a cash balance of $32,576 as a "cushion" against uncertainty and risk. It may even be possible for President Jones to receive some compensation during these first three months. President Jones agreed that we needed some "cushion."

The credit with the suppliers was arranged and President Jones agreed to defer his salary until later in the year. In addition, President Jones indicated that he could personally raise any additional funds if necessary. In addition, he was confident that short-term bank credit could be arranged for any amount below $15,000. Why he picked $15,000 you do not know. However, it was decided to forge ahead. We have learned a tremendous lesson. There is quite a difference between profitability and liquidity.

It is quite clear that liquidity is a most serious problem, and the Jones organization must face it squarely. We must review our billing and shipping procedures to ensure that they are both prompt and accurate. Inaccurate billings or inexact shipments may cause our customers to delay payment until discrepancies are cleared to their satisfaction. Electronic data processing and computer technology can accelerate these procedures and eliminate significant human error and, thus, perhaps maximize the speed of the cash flow. However, we would have to balance the costs of such procedures against the benefits we would derive from the employment.

You were beginning to feel some better. In fact, you inquired about golf that afternoon—about 4:30 p.m. However, the cold water was turned on. The general manager advised you that you are not out of the woods yet. Remember, all that you have done thus far has been to present a forecast. All managerial decisions dealing with the future are surrounded with uncertainty and clouded with risk. You have made some basic assumptions in arriving at your mathematical precision. You have assumed that the receipt of payments from the accounts receivable will follow the historical pattern of 10 percent during the month of the sale, 60 percent the following month, and 30 percent the second following month. Any change in this schedule will change your problem. We are well aware of this fact, and we will watch the results, if any, of our efforts to speed up collections and face the problems as we come to them. The 10-60-30 percent pattern of receivable collections may improve. A careful review of our credit policies indicates that the pattern is unlikely to get worse. At least we have a reasonable and what appears to be feasible framework within which to operate.

It is quite clear that the next time we consider capital budgeting, we will also include the need for additional working capital as we plan for increased profitability. There is little doubt that our commitment to the profitability of the new equipment helped in no small measure to aggravate, if not cause, our liquidity crisis. However, growth requires funds, and if we grow we will no doubt have more liquidity problems. At least, we can face the problem with knowledge (and experience), and knowledge is strength.

The next morning came too soon. I'm just tired! I want to end this chapter right here. However, you said, "Go ahead and tell 'em." All right, I shot my 102 yesterday and you shot 98 and beat the Duffer again. All I can say is, "Sit tight, I'll find another string!"

SUMMARY

The control and management of the cash resource is one of the financial manager's major responsibilities. This activity is a part of the larger activity of current-asset management. Initially, the chapter introduces you to the concept of the cash-to-cash cycle. This circular flow of cash through the current accounts is regulated in large measure by internal decisions made by the firm in areas such as inventory control and accounts receivable management. Certain external factors, however, can change the character of this flow and the timing of flows within the cash-to-cash cycle. Chief among these external factors are:

1. Changes in sales levels
2. Changes in price levels
3. Changes in other factors such as tax rates or tax-collection schedules

The financial manager would not be as concerned with maintaining as low a cash balance as is consistent with operational demands if large cash balances could be maintained without cost. You now recognize that excessive liquidity positions are maintained only at the cost of reduced profitability and earning power. In short, then, the financial manager must make those decisions which both safeguard the cash asset and ensure that sufficient cash is available to meet obligations as they fall due.

The control of cash is in reality a security function. The experiences of the Jones Corporation demonstrated its need for a more sophisticated system of internal control to combat the most common forms of misappropriation. Misappropriation of corporate funds usually involves at least one of the following techniques:

1. Unrecorded cash sales
2. Unrecorded credit sales with subsequent misappropriations when cash payment is made

3. Entries recorded as "sales returns and allowances" when cash has actually been received in payment for such goods
4. Personal expenses charged as business expenses and then paid by the firm
5. Unsupported or fictitious charges paid and funds misappropriated.

The Jones Company, like many other small and growing firms, fell victim to employee misappropriations largely because it had failed to separate the cash-handling and record-keeping activities. This separation is basic to any system of cash control.

In addition to controlling cash and providing a sufficient level of cash for normal operations, the financial manager must also from time to time accumulate cash for special purposes. Accumulations of cash over and above actual operational requirements may be made to meet:

1. Unexpected operational needs
2. Dividend, debt, or tax payments
3. Needs of future expansion

When cash balances are maintained in order to meet any of the above needs, the financial manager is normally faced with a short-term investment problem. You should be familiar with the instruments of short-term investment discussed in the chapter. The actual instruments which are selected and form the asset account, marketable securities, will depend on the yield of the securities and the purpose for which the accumulation is being made. In many firms the management of these accumulated funds is a continuing and important activity which demands special training of the financial executive or the retention by the firm of outside consultants.

The operating cash budget which you finally prepared for the Jones Company is a basic tool of financial management. You will note that the budget itself does not make decisions; rather, it reflects decisions. For example, our decision to pay our accounts payable promptly results in a cash drain because we are collecting our accounts receivable more slowly. Using our cash budget, we can demonstrate the effects of policy changes on cash flows. Thus, if we were to reduce our credit period and collect accounts receivable more quickly while at the same time meeting our accounts payable obligations more slowly, the profile of our cash flows would change appreciably. The importance of the cash budget as a planning device is difficult to overemphasize. The preparation of the cash budget forces the financial manager into a complete reappraisal of policies which affect cash flows. In addition, it enables the firm to anticipate and prepare for cash problems well into the future. Firms like the Jones Corporation can and do confuse profits with cash, and many have "gone broke" making a profit.

QUESTIONS FOR DISCUSSION

1. What is the liquidity function of the firm?
2. Compare and contrast liquidity and profitability.
3. What is the cash cycle, and what factors affect this cycle?
4. What are margin and turnover, and what effect do these factors have on earning power?
5. What is the purpose of a bank reconciliation?
6. What effect do outstanding checks and deposits in transit have in reconciling the bank balance per books with the cash balance per bank?
7. What steps, in your judgment, could be taken to eliminate or lessen the possibility of the types of cash misappropriations outlined on page 219?
8. Distinguish between "kiting" and "lapping."
9. What is the basic criterion for the temporary investment of cash, and what are some of the sources of such investment?
10. Why or how do the sources from Question 9 meet the criterion?
11. What is the interest-rate risk, and what is its significance?
12. What data are necessary in order to prepare a projected-cash-flow analysis?
13. What financial-statement information is made available by the projected-cash-flow analysis?
14. What is the significance of the cash-flow analysis prepared for Jones Electronic Corporation in this chapter?
15. What change in the basic data used could significantly change the results obtained?
16. What is the function of the "Statement of the Sources and Application of Funds"?
17. Are there basic assumptions involved in the preparation of this statement (Question 16)?
18. What is the answer to President Jones' question on page 234 about what happened to all the profits?
19. What is the relationship between billing policies and liquidity? Give examples.
20. Why did President Jones reject a cash-discount policy?
21. How did the Jones organization solve the first-quarter cash problem?
22. What relationship, if any, would liquidity problems have with capital budgeting considerations?

PROBLEMS

1. Two firms each have earning power of 20 percent. Firm A has a margin of 5 percent, while Firm B's margin is 10 percent. What are their respective turnover ratios?
2. Take the projected balance sheet and income statement of the Jones Corporation and determine its margin, turnover, and earning power.
3. Using the financial statements of Jones Corporation presented in the chapter, generate a graphic presentation of the firm's earning power.

4. You are the financial manager for a large chemical firm whose offices are located in New York City. Approximately $50 million in sales is done on the west coast. A Los Angeles bank will create a lockbox system, which will reduce float from nine to three days. In return, the bank will require that we maintain a balance with them of $200,000. In addition, they will charge an annual fee of $2,000.
   a. What amount of cash would be freed by the acceptance of the bank's offer?
   b. Would you accept the offer?
5. You are a financial manager in the enviable position of having $1 million in cash for which you have no need until six months from now.
   a. List the possible financial instruments which are available for the investment of these funds.
   b. Consult a current wall Street Journal and select the instrument which offers the highest return currently.
   c. What are the important considerations in the investment of excess balances of this type?
6. White Fang Happy Mouser Cat Food, Inc., desires to project a *pro forma* income statement. The financial manager has the following information:

   Last year's sales were $10 million, and this year a 15 percent increase is anticipated.
   Cost of goods sold has been about 65 percent of sales, and this relationship is expected to continue.
   Selling and general administrative expense has been running about 10 percent of sales.

   In addition to these facts, the financial manager also knows that an $80,000 sinking-fund payment must be made and $300,000 of new equipment purchased.
   a. Write up a projected income statement for White Fang on the basis of the information given above.
   b. How will this projected income statement affect a projected balance sheet composed at the same time?
7. On January 1 you are instructed by your employer to create a monthly cash forecast for the coming year. You have the following data:

   Your cash balance at the beginning of the year is $50,000.
   Both sales and production follow a stable pattern.

   Annual sales are $20 million.
   Prior experience has demonstrated that our sales follow a monthly pattern of:

January, 10% of annual sales	July, 6% of annual sales
February, 5% of annual sales	August, 10% of annual sales
March, 5% of annual sales	September, 10% of annual sales
April, 15% of annual sales	October, 5% of annual sales
May, 7% of annual sales	November, 5% of annual sales
June, 7% of annual sales	December, 15% of annual sales

Collections on sales take the following pattern: 20 percent of sales are collected in the same month the sale is made, 60 percent in the month following, and 20 percent in the month following that.

Our current accounts receivable figure is $2,600,000.

Our cost of goods sold is 70 percent of sales. Purchases are made in the month preceding the anticipated sales and paid for in the same month in which the sales are made. Our current accounts payable figure is $1,400,000.

Selling and general administrative expense is 10 percent of sales and is applied evenly over the 12 months.

Tax payments will be made quarterly.

Finally, a sinking-fund payment of $500,000 must be made in July, and a new machine costing $80,000 must be paid for in August.

a. Construct the required cash forecast and income statement.

b. What financing, if any, will be required?

8. Out-of-Style, women's wear manufacturer, is contemplating a liquidity crisis. Their sales for the next six months are as follows:

January,	$20,000	April,	$50,000
February,	$30,000	May,	$60,000
March,	$40,000	June,	$60,000

Prepare a cash budget, using the following data:

Ten percent of each month's sales are cash sales involving a 2 percent discount.

Sixty percent of a month's sales are collected during the month of the sale.

Thirty percent are collected in the following month, and 10 percent in the second month following the sale.

Collections during January from prior sales are anticipated to be $3,000.

Monthly cash operating expenses are 50 percent of sales.

The cash balance on January 1 is $5,000.

The desired cash balance as of August 1 is $10,000.

Short-term bank credit is available at 1 percent per month with interest paid monthly. Money is borrowed only on the first day of a calendar month, and repayment is made on the last day of a calendar month.

REFERENCES

Anderson, Clay J.: Managing the Corporate "Money" Position, *Business Review,* Philadelphia, Federal Reserve Bank of Philadelphia, March, 1961, pp. 3–10.

Anton, Hector R.: "Accounting for the Flow of Funds," Houghton Mifflin Company, Boston, 1962.

Archer Stephen H.: A Model for the Determination of Firm Cash Balances, *Journal of Financial and Quantitative Analysis,* vol. 1, pp. 1–11, March, 1966.

Baumol, William J.: The Transactions Demand for Cash: An Inventory Theoretic Approach, *Quarterly Journal of Economics,* vol. LXV, pp. 545–556, November, 1952.

Baxter, Nevins D.: "The Commercial Paper Market," Princeton University Press, Princeton, N.J., 1964.

———: Marketability, Default Risk, and Yields on Money Market Instruments, *Journal of Financial and Quantitative Analysis,* vol. IV, pp. 75–86, March, 1968.

Beckman, T. N., and R. S. Foster: "Credit and Collections," 8th ed., McGraw-Hill Book Company, New York, 1969.

Benishay, Haskel: Managerial Controls of Accounts Receivable: A Deterministic Approach, *Journal of Accounting Research,* vol. III, pp. 114–133, spring, 1965.

———: A Stochastic Model of Credit Sales Debt, *Journal of the American Statistical Association,* vol. LXI, pp. 1010–1028, December, 1966.

Bierman, Harold Jr.: Measuring Financial Liquidity, *Accounting Review,* vol. XXXV, October, 1960, reprinted in James Van Horne (ed.), "Foundations For Financial Management," pp. 3–10, Richard D. Irwin, Inc., Homewood Ill., 1966.

——— and Alan K. McAdams: "Management Decisions for Cash and Marketable Securities," Graduate School of Business, Cornell University, Ithaca, New York, 1962.

Cyert, R. M., H. J. Davidson, and G. L. Thompson: Estimation of the Allowance for Doubtful Accounts by Markov Chains, *Management Science,* vol. VIII, pp. 287–303, April, 1962.

——— and G. L. Thompson: Selecting a Portfolio of Credit Risks by Markov Chains, *Journal of Business,* vol. XLI, no. 1, pp. 39–46, January, 1968.

Davidson, Signey, George H. Sorter, and Hemu Kalle: Measuring the Defensive Position of a Firm, *Financial Analysts Journal,* vol. 20, pp. 23–39, January-February, 1964.

Federal Reserve Bank of Richmond: Prime Commercial Paper, *Monthly Review,* July, 1964, pp. 8–10, Richmond, Va.

Gross, Herschel I.: The Term Structure of Interest Rates, *Journal of Finance,* vol. XXII, pp. 611–622, December, 1967.

Helfert, Erich H.: "Techniques of Financial Analysis," rev. ed., chap. 1, Richard D. Irwin, Inc., Homewood, Ill., 1967.

Hendershott, Patric H.: The Structure of International Interest Rates, the U.S. Treasury Bill Rate and the Eurodollar Deposit Rate, *Journal of Finance,* vol. XXII, pp. 455–465, September, 1967.

Horn, Frederick E.: Managing Cash, *Journal of Accountancy,* vol. CXVII, April, 1964; reprinted in "Foundations for Financial Management," James Van Horne (ed.), pp. 25–35, Richard D. Irwin, Inc., Homewood, Ill., 1966.

Horngren, Charles T.: The Funds Statement and Its Use by Analysts, *Journal of Accountancy,* vol. XCIX, pp. 55–59, January, 1956.

Hunt, Alfred L.: Credit Management in the Electronic Accounting Era, *Controller,* vol. XXVIII, pp. 374–375, 384, August, 1960.

Jacobs, Donald P.: The Marketable Security Portfolios of Nonfinancial Corporations: Investment Practices and Trends, *Journal of Finance,* vol. XV, September, 1960; reprinted in James Van Horne (ed.), "Foundations for Financial Management," pp. 36–48, Richard D. Irwin, Inc., Homewood, Ill., 1966.

Jaedicke, Robert K., and Robert T. Sprouse :"Accounting Flows, Income, Funds, and Cash," chaps. 5 and 6, Prentice-Hall, Inc., Englewood Cliffs, N.J., 1965.

Johnson, Robert W.: "Financial Management," 3d ed., chap. 3, Allyn and Bacon, Inc., Boston, 1966.

———: More Scope for Credit Managers, *Harvard Business Review,* vol. XXXIX, November-December, 1961; reprinted in James Van Horne (ed.), "Foundations for Financial Management," pp. 49–69, Richard D. Irwin, Inc., Homewood, Ill., 1966.

Kessel, Reuben A.: "Cyclical Behavior of the Term Structure of Interest Rates," National Bureau of Economic Research, Inc., New York, 1965.

Kuehn, Hayden: What a Credit Rating Signifies, *Banking,* vols. LIII and LIV, pp. 80–82, 138, 79–82, December, 1960, and January, 1961.

Leone, Edmund: Techniques for Improving Cash Turnover, *Financial Executive,* vol. XXXII, pp. 38–42, January, 1964.

Miller, Merton H., and Daniel Orr: A Model of the Demand for Money by Firms, *Quarterly Journal of Economics,* vol. LXXX, pp. 413–435, August, 1966.

"Money Market Instruments," 3d ed., Federal Reserve Bank of Cleveland, 1970.

"Money Market Instruments: The Risk and the Return," Morgan Guaranty Trust Company, New York, 1964.

Reed, A. E.: Corporate Cash Management, *Financial Executive,* vol. XXXI, pp. 13–19, October, 1963.

Reinhardt, Hedwig: Economics of Mercantile Credit: A Study in Methodology, *Review of Economics and Statistics,* vol. XXXIX, pp. 436–467, November, 1957.

Robbins, Sidney: Getting More Mileage out of Cash, *N.A.A. Bulletin,* vol. XLII, pp. 65–74, September, 1960.

Robinson, Roland I.: "Money and Capital Markets," McGraw-Hill Book Company, New York, 1964.

Ross-Skinner, Jean: The Profitable Art of Handling Corporation Cash, *Dun's Review,* May, 1962, pp. 38–41, 109–111.

Seiden, Martin H.: "The Quality of Trade Credit," Occasional Paper 87, National Bureau of Economic Research, Inc., New York, 1964.

Selden, Richard T.: "Trends and Cycles in the Commercial Paper Market," National Bureau of Economic Research, Inc., New York, 1963.

Sisson, Roger L., and Normal L. Statland: The Future of Computers in Credit Management, *Credit and Financial Management,* vol. LXVII, pp. 13–15, 40, 44, May, 1965.

Sorter, George H., and George E. Benston: Appraising the Defensive Position of a Firm: The Internal Measure, *Accounting Review,* vol. XXXV, pp. 633–640, October, 1960.

Tobin, James: The Interest Elasticity of Transactions Demand for Cash, *Review of Economics and Statistics,* vol. XXXVII, pp. 241–247, August, 1956.

Trumbull, Wendell P.: Developing the Funds Statement as the Third Major Financial Statement, *N.A.A. Bulletin,* vol. XLV, pp. 21–31, April, 1963.

Vatter, William J.: Fund Flows and Fund Statements, *Journal of Business,* vol. XXVI, pp. 15–25, January, 1953.

Vogel, Robert C., and G. S. Maddala: Cross-section Estimates of Liquid Asset Demand by Manufacturing Corporations, *Journal of Finance,* vol. XXII, pp. 557–575, December, 1967.

Weston, J. Fred: Forecasting Financial Requirements, *Accounting Review,* vol. XXXIII, pp. 427–440, July, 1958.

Weston, J. Fred, and Eugene F. Brigham: "Essentials of Managerial Finance," chap. 5, Holt, Rinehart and Winston, Inc., New York, 1968.

Whalen, Edward L.: A Cross-section Study of Business Demand for Cash, *Journal of Finance,* vol. XX, no. 3, pp. 423–443, September, 1965.

———: An Extension of the Baumol-Tobin Approach to the Transactions Demand for Cash, *Journal of Finance,* vol. XXIII, pp. 113–134, March 1968.

Chapter Nine

MANAGEMENT OF ACCOUNTS RECEIVABLE AND INVENTORIES

At the next meeting of the executive committee everyone seemed to be relieved that the cash crisis had been faced squarely and that the problem areas had been identified. The focal point of our analysis of the projected cash flow was, of course, accounts receivable. The sales manager expressed some concern about a possible change or a tightening of our credit policies. This was a natural concern inasmuch as his income as well as the income of the entire sales force is primarily based on a percentage of sales. He expressed an opinion that any significant tightening of our credit policies would cause a drastic change in total sales. In fact, he stated that he was about to present the results of a study he had just completed but was hesitating to do so. The study involved the extension of additional credit to generate additional sales.

He confessed that when the study was prepared he was really not aware of the problems that liquidity or lack of liquidity could cause. He added that he has received quite an education while sitting as a member of the executive committee. He now clearly realizes that additional credit may generate additional profits but could likewise aggravate liquidity problems. It was the old profitability-versus-liquidity problem again!

You advised that while his latter analysis was quite correct, he should not hesitate to present his study. Once the facts and projections had been placed on the table, the merits of a proposal could be evaluated within the broad framework of the corporation's resources and capabilities. In addition, our current liquidity position should improve within the next eight months to a year. You asked, however, that the sales manager withhold his proposal while the executive committee discussed credit policy in general. He agreed.

ACCOUNTS RECEIVABLE POLICY

You explained that the Jones Electronic Corporation really had no firm policy regarding the management of its accounts receivable. The corporation had just been drifting in this respect. In addition, you stated that you were uneasy about establishing a policy of ironclad rules. (One of our very best customers remits his payment to our offices only four times a year.) Any policy evolved must contain some flexibility. Our goal for such a policy will be to provide an optimal liquidity-profitability balance within the firm.

The receivables policy which we will ultimately adopt will provide a basic framework within which two significant questions may be resolved:

1. Under what conditions will we grant credit?
2. To whom shall we offer those credit terms?

The granting of credit involves certain costs, the most obvious of which is the loss that may occur when customers fail to pay for merchandise received. An investment in accounts receivable as a result of granting credit is similar to an investment in any other asset. A significant cost associated with an accounts receivable investment is the loss of the return which the invested funds could have earned when employed elsewhere.[1]

Increased sales generated by more liberal credit could involve a change in our production schedule and a confrontation with all the problems discussed in detail in an earlier chapter, for example, a possible change in the "cost per unit," which would affect all sales!

In short, then, the firm's accounts receivable policy represents, like our other decisions, a balancing of marginal costs versus marginal returns. Our decision concerning the marginal cost of our credit policy

[1] The source of this material is an expanded discussion of receivables and credit policy by William Beranek, "Analysis for Financial Decisions," pp. 272–308, 320–335, Richard D. Irwin, Inc., Homewood, Illinois, 1963.

as compared with the marginal revenue will be reflected in the terms and the conditions under which credit is granted. These terms, which largely determine the level of our investment in accounts receivable, are: (1) the credit period, (2) the total amount of credit granted to a single customer or class of customers, and (3) the cash discount allowed, if any. In addition to these factors, we must also add the level of expenditures which we are willing to incur in an attempt to collect accounts receivable when past due. Let us investigate the relationship which exists between each of the credit terms and the level of receivables evidenced by the firm.

The *credit period* is generally defined to be the total number of days or months a bill may normally be outstanding without becoming past due. This figure will vary from industry to industry. For example, a toy manufacturer's yearly production is geared to two seasonal peaks—the summer months and Christmas time. The manufacturer may have a simple choice to make that will affect the credit period. Will he be better off paying the warehouse and storage expense for the intervening months, or would it be less expensive to encourage the retailer to buy and accept delivery several months ahead of peak demand? The latter approach may make it necessary to extend the credit period from March or April to late September or October for the summer demand and from September or October to January or February for the Christmas peak. The extended credit terms would serve to significantly lower warehousing costs since these costs would be transferred to the customer. The extended credit period would have no effect on the investment costs of the inventory—loss of return on investment would be the same whether the inventory is stocked in the producer's warehouse or in the customer's warehouse. Furthermore, competitors may force both the producer and the retailer to live with an extended credit period.

The Jones Corporation has been extremely fortunate in that Allied remits each month. Other defense contractors may not be able to pay until remittances are received from the government or other prime contractors. It is quite clear that the ability to extend credit terms without impairing proper liquidity could easily affect profitability if our customers could not buy without extended credit. In fact, as you recall, extended credit from our raw-material supplier was a major factor in helping the Jones Corporation with its own liquidity problem! Had our present suppliers been unwilling to extend the needed credit, we might have been forced to look elsewhere for the raw material on terms we could afford to live with.

It is quite clear, as stated earlier, that in establishing the credit period we must be flexible and yet we must recognize that any increase in credit terms represents an investment that must earn a return at least equivalent to what could be earned by alternative investment opportunities. Underlying the entire matter is the marginal cost–marginal revenue concept.

To Whom Should Credit Be Offered and How Much Should Be Offered to a Single Customer

As we have seen, the decision to extend credit per se and the terms which generally apply to such credit once issued are normally governed by the policies of the industry. However, the decision to grant normal credit terms to any one customer is largely within the discretion of the firm. With respect to the decision to lengthen the credit terms, the credit manager will usually evaluate the potential customer with special reference to "the five C's of credit":

1. Character
2. Capacity
3. Capital
4. Collateral
5. Conditions

Character. The credit relationship depends primarily on the good faith of the participating parties. Character rating for credit purposes, then, is really little more than an assessment of the customer's desire and willingness to meet his obligations as indicated by past performances.

Capacity. A potential customer's capacity to repay a debt depends on his ability to meet a particular debt. His ability depends on his capital.

Capital. This measure of credit worthiness attempts to determine total ability to meet all obligations. Financial ratios and analysis of balance sheet accounts may be helpful in this measurement.

Collateral. This particular measure of credit worthiness is less important perhaps than any of those already discussed. The measure itself deals with the relationship between debt to be incurred and particular assets which would be pledged as security for the debt. Collateral is not, however, basic to the establishment of credit. Credit managers have little desire to foreclose on assets. They are primarily concerned with timely repayments, which in turn are dependent on the business success of the debtor.

Conditions. The term "conditions" refers to the economic posture of the industry and the economy. Certain customers will be better able to meet their obligations in recession periods than others. In times of prosperity the credit manager may safely grant credit to certain customers who were previously denied normal credit.

It is apparent that if the potential customer is to be rated with reference to the five C's of credit, a great deal of information must be compiled. This information is available to the credit manager from both internal and external sources.

Sources of Credit Information

In regard to the continued extension of credit to existing customers, the credit manager has a great deal of information internally available. He knows, for example, the past credit performance of the customer, his prior level of purchases and past history of meeting such debts on time. He may also receive from his own firm's salesmen their assessment of the customer's current financial condition and operating success. His own records may well reveal some change in the customer's payment capabilities. For example, a customer of long standing who has consistently taken advantage of cash discounts may no longer be doing so. This information is meaningful. Suppose that selling terms are 2/10 net 30. If a customer no longer pays by the tenth of the month, he is in effect paying 2 percent interest for the 20-day reprieve. On an annual basis the effective cost of such a policy to the customer is 24 percent. His failure to take advantage of the cash discount means that he is borrowing from the supplier at 24 percent yearly interest rate. Surely a firm in sound financial condition could pay its debts within the discount period and thereby reduce its cost of credit.

Last, but by no means least important, is personal contact between the credit manager and the customer. A simple telephone call could well clear up any doubts which remained in the credit manager's mind. Too often we forget that behind all corporate facades lurk human beings who are basically ethical and honest men. Our personal contact with them and our assessment of them are focal to the determination of a successful credit relationship.

Since credit relationships facilitate commerce, national organizations have been developed solely to furnish credit information. Perhaps the largest and best known of these is Dun and Bradstreet, Inc. Table 9-1, a facsimile of a Dun and Bradstreet report, provides information regarding Dun and Bradstreet's ratings of financial strength. Table 9-2 is an example of a special report by the credit-rating agency on a single firm. This latter report would be received by a credit manager on request.

It can be easily seen that such information is invaluable to the credit manager in his evaluation of credit risks.

The financial data published by Dun and Bradstreet appears six times annually, as the Dun and Bradstreet Reference Book. Firms rated by the organization are listed by locality. In addition, their financial

TABLE 9-1

Estimated Financial Strength				Composite Credit Appraisal			
				High	Good	Fair	Limited
Aa	Over	$1,000,000		A1	1	1½	2
A+	Over	750,000		A1	1	1½	2
A	$500,000 to	750,000		A1	1	1½	2
B+	300,000 to	500,000		1	1½	2	2½
B	200,000 to	300,000		1	1½	2	2½
C+	125,000 to	200,000		1	1½	2	2½
C	75,000 to	125,000		1½	2	2½	3
D+	50,000 to	75,000		1½	2	2½	3
D	35,000 to	50,000		1½	2	2½	3
E	20,000 to	35,000		2	2½	3	3½
F	10,000 to	20,000		2½	3	3½	4
G	5,000 to	10,000		3	3½	4	4½
H	3,000 to	5,000		3	3½	4	4½
J }	Up to	3,000	J.....	3	3½	4	4½
K }	Up to	3,000	K.....	3	3½	4	4½
L }	Up to	3,000	L.....	3½	4	4½	5

K & L are being phased out

Classification for Both Estimated Financial Strength and Credit Appraisal

Financial Strength Bracket		Explanation
1	$125,000 and Over	When only the numeral (1, 2, 3, or 4) appears, it is an indication that the estimated financial strength, while not definitely classified, is presumed to be within the range of the ($) figures in the corresponding bracket and that a condition is believed to exist which warrants credit in keeping with that assumption.
2	20,000 to 125,000	
3 } 4 }	Up to 20,000	

4 is being phased out

"Inv." shown in place of a rating indicates that the report was under investigation at the time of going to press. It has no other significance.

Not Classified or Absence of Rating
The absence of a rating, expressed by two hyphens (--), is not to be construed as unfavorable, but signifies circumstances difficult to classify within condensed rating symbols. It suggests the advisability of obtaining a special report for additional information.

Absence of a Listing
The absence of a listing is not to be construed as meaning a concern is non-existent, has discontinued business, nor does it have any other meaning. The letters "NQ" on any written report mean "not listed in the Reference Book."

Year Business Started
The numeral shown is the last digit of the year date when the business was established or came under present control or management. Thus, 8 means 1958; 9 means 1959. No dates go past ten years. Thus, the feature is not used in connection with branch listings.

TABLE 9-2

Dun & Bradstreet Report **RATING**

SIC	D-U-N-S	Date of Report	Started	Rating
34 61	803-4520	CD 13 APR 21 19— N		
	FABRICATORS, INC.	ALUMINUM STAMPINGS	1957	D 1
	53 S MAIN ST			
	PENSACOLA FLA 32501			
	TEL 904 477-5432		SUMMARY	
	HIRAM SPRAGUE	OWNER	PAYMENTS	DISC PPT
			SALES	$177,250
			WORTH	$ 42,961
			EMPLOYS	8
			RECORD	CLEAR
			CONDITION	SOUND
			TREND	UP

Payments	HC	Owe	P Due Terms	Apr 1 19—	Sold
	3000	1500	1 10 30	Disc	Over 3 yrs
	2500	1000	1 10 30	Disc	Over 3 yrs
	2000	500	2 20 30	Disc	Old account
	1000		30	Ppt	Over 3 yrs
	500		30	Ppt	Over 3 yrs

Finance On Apr. 21 19— H. Sprague, Owner, submitted statement Dec. 31 19—

Cash	$ 4,870	Accts Pay	$ 6,121
Accts Rec	15,472	Notes Pay (Curr)	2,400
Mdse	14,619	Accruals	3,583
Current	34,961	Current	12,104
Fixed Assets	22,840	Notes Pay (Def)	5,000
Other Assets	2,264	NET WORTH	42,961
Total Assets	60,065	Total	60,065

19— sales $177,250; gross profit $47,821; net profit $4,204. Fire Insurance mdse $15,000; fixed assets $20,000. Annual rent $3,000. Signed Apr. 21 19—

Sales and profits increased last year due to increased sub-contract work and this trend is reported continuing. New equipment was purchased last Sept for $8,000 financed by a bank loan secured by a lien on the equipment payable $200 per month. With increased capacity, the business has been able to handle a larger volume. Sprague stated that for the first two months of this year volume was $32,075 and operations continue profitable.

Banking Medium to high four-figure balances are maintained locally. An equipment loan is outstanding and being retired as agreed.

History Incorporated June, 1957, by the owner Hiram Sprague. Sprague born 1927, named 1947 graduate of Virginia Polytechnique Institute, 1950. Employed by Alco Aluminum in various capacities until 1957. Started this business in 1957.

Operation Manufactures light aluminum stampings for industrial concerns and also does some work on a sub-contract basis for aircraft manufacturers. Terms net 30. 12 accounts. Five production, two office employees, and one salesman. LOCATION: Rents one-story cinder block building with 5,000 square feet located in industrial section in normal condition. Housekeeping is good.

4-21 (803 77) PRA

PLEASE NOTE WHETHER NAME, BUSINESS AND STREET ADDRESS CORRESPOND WITH YOUR INQUIRY. This report is furnished by DUN & BRADSTREET, Inc., in STRICT CONFIDENCE of your request under your subscription agreement for your exclusive use as a basis for credit, insurance, marketing and other business decisions and for no other purpose. DUN & BRADSTREET, Inc. does not guarantee the correctness of this report and shall not be liable for any loss or injury caused by the neglect or other act or failure to act on the part of said company and/or its agents in procuring, collecting or communicating any information. 9R2-2(12-65) strength and credit worthiness are assessed. More detailed reports, like Table 9-2, are published and sold upon request. The detailed report includes a current balance sheet and payment record. The payment record represents the response of five of the firm's suppliers to questions relating to the amount of the highest credit supplied and the payment history of that amount. DISC and PPT refer to the firm's taking discounts when available or its record of prompt payment when discounts were not available. The remainder of the report, Table 9-2, is self-explanatory.

Some industries provide, through trade associations, their own credit information and even collection service for members. For example, the Toy Manufacturers of the U.S.A. compile a list of the industries' customers and the credit experience of these firms in dealing with members of the toy industry. Similar groups offer such sources in other industries.

Credit Extension

Information upon which sound credit decisions may be made is available. However, it is not compiled and analyzed without cost. In some situations the cost of obtaining and studying this information exceeds the profit which may result from the credit sale under consideration. In such cases the prospects for a continuing credit sales relationship should be considered before deciding against extending credit terms. A credit manager who prides himself on credit relationships devoid of bad debts may be guilty of the type of information overkill alluded to above, or he may simply have credit standards which are too conservative. Often, some small exposure to bad-debt risk may result in significant sales increases. For example, available credit information may allow the credit manager to place existing and potential customers in various risk categories. Once this has been done, the relationship between risk and profit may be determined and credit policies adjusted to reflect a level of risk acceptance which promises a rate of return on the funds employed which is at least as high as the return those funds would earn elsewhere. The problem of profitable risk-taking may be approached in the following manner:

Step 1. Using information generated internally and externally, we are able to place our customers, existing and potential, into several risk categories.

Step 2. Consider for each category the profitability consequences of sales made to customers in this category.

For example, let us devote our attention to a category of marginal customers for whom we calculate a 15 percent risk of nonpayment.

Would sales to such marginal customers offer a rate of return which was satisfactory in view of the resources employed? Several questions must be answered before this determination can be made.

1. How much will sales increase if such a category of customer is accepted?
2. What added expenses must be met respecting these added sales?
3. What income will be generated by these sales, net after the expenses attributable to these sales?

Example:

Incremental sales	\$3,000
Resultant bad debts (15%)	450
Incremental gross revenue	\$2,550
Cost of goods sold (50%)	1,500
	\$1,050
Additional collection expenses	500
Net income on sales	\$ 550

The net result, then, of the extension of credit to this group of customers has been a cost increase of \$2,000, an increase in net sales of \$2,550, and an increase in net income before tax of \$550. The focal question which must be considered relates to the rate of return offered by our commitment to make such sales. In short, what investment have we made and what return have we secured? Our investment will depend on the turnover of these new accounts and can be calculated as follows:

Accounts receivable turnover in this group of accounts is three times annually	
Average receivables outstanding	$\frac{\$3,000}{3} = \$1,000$
Average receivables outstanding at cost	$0.50(\$1,000) = \$500$
Average annual investment in this category of accounts	\$500
Annual income from these accounts	\$550

Given an investment of \$500 in these accounts and a return of \$550, we calculate the rate of return on this investment to be 10 percent. Our final decision with respect to servicing accounts in this risk category would be dependent on the acceptability of the anticipated return of 10 percent.

We have covered a great deal of ground while building a framework for a discussion relating to our own policy regarding accounts receivable management. Much of what you have done will not be immediately useful. Jones Electronic is currently a subcontractor in the aerospace industry. As such, our customers are large and well-established prime contractors such as General Electric and McDonald Douglas. Because of this fact, our accounts receivable are subject to little or no bad-debt risk. However, we have come to realize that our investment in a level of accounts receivable is not without cost and should produce a return commensurate with the commitment of resources demanded. The level of our investment in accounts receivable can be affected by the decisions we make with respect to the credit period, cash discount, and total credit extended to a single customer.

Collection expenditures. These expenses arise in conjunction with our efforts to collect the amounts due and represented by our accounts receivable. In most cases the firm is unwilling to spend an amount, in collecting an account, which exceeds the amount of the account itself. Aggressive policies with respect to the collection of accounts receivable may result in a higher rate or level of collections, but a lower margin of profit on the accounts collected. (Perhaps the most aggressive policy of collection is evidenced by the IRS, who will spend more to collect a delinquent account than the account is worth. However, the point of this policy is that such collections encourage other potential delinquents to pay in full and on time. The overall effect is then not illogical.) The costs of our collections consist of the increased expenditures related to correspondence, legal enforcement of claims, and loss of customers who gravitate to our competitors who have more liberal policies respecting delinquent accounts. Changes in our collection policy may increase our cost and in some cases may result in a reduction in profits.

Up to this point in the Jones Corporation's experience it has had very little trouble with uncollectable accounts. In fact, there have been no bad debts. However, it cannot be expected that this happy situation will continue to exist as we expand our normal sales volume. It was this exact point, expanded sales volume and credit risk, that the sales manager wanted to discuss within the framework of his proposal.

President Jones inquired about this proposal. The sales manager was a bit hesitant but was encouraged to present his ideas. He stated that his office had received offers to purchase Jones' components from several firms that were manufacturing for the retail field. Two of the firms making the inquiry were relatively small and apparently were operating on somewhat of a shoestring. They had heard of Jones' reputation for quality and had inquired about our products. The sales manager then instructed his sales force to expand their efforts and to call upon several of these smaller companies each week and report to him the type of reception they had received and their impressions of the sales potential offered by these smaller firms. The reports were unanimous and good. The Jones Electronic Corporation, with an additional investment of only $8,400 for a "finishing" machine, could supply this market.

He had prepared an estimate of prospective revenue and expense as follows:

Machinery cost: $8,400, 10-year life and no salvage value
Selling price: $6.25 per unit
Estimated sales per *month:* 5,000 units
Additional selling and general expense at the level of production, 15%
Probable credit loss: 10%
Collection costs: $400 per month

Total revenue (5,000 units)		$31,250
Cost of goods sold:		
Variable costs—5,000 units at $3.50	$17,500	
Fixed costs (including depreciation)	2,100	19,600
Gross profit		$11,650
Less selling and general expenses (15% of sales)		4,687
		$ 6,963
Less collection costs	$ 400	
10% credit losses	3,125	3,525
Net profit before taxes		$ 3,438
Income tax (50%)		1,719
Net income after taxes per month		$ 1,719

Annual income ($1,719 × 12) = $20,628
Addition to earnings per share (50,000 shares) = 41.25¢

The sales manager had calculated that on an investment of $8,400 a 41.25 cent yearly increase in earnings per share would result. However, he did not give effect to the loss of yearly income that the investment of $8,400 would have generated had it not been invested in the machinery. Had this been done, the yearly increase in earnings per share would be slightly reduced.

President Jones advised the sales manager to continue his study and to expand his survey to test the entire area of one of our regional markets. In addition, he requested a statement of proposed credit policy for each customer based upon the following criteria.

The level of credit which is to be offered to a single customer will vary, depending upon our own ability to withstand a single large loss, our experience or probably lack of experience with the customer, the size of his orders, and the general credit standing of the customer. President Jones further stated that he had a particularly strong interest in the smaller customer who appeared to have the potential to grow. He stated that he remembers clearly his early "garage days" when a little credit here and a little credit there was all that pulled him through. He stated that he didn't want to be foolish, but 90 to 120 days would not bother him at all as long as the total of such credit did not reach significant proportions. In short, he wanted each little customer to be rated as to potential to grow into a big customer. (Jones is still buying from the firm who not only rendered credit when needed but also provided technical "know-how" at critical times when he was still learning. He thinks that it is good business to adopt a genuine "big-brother" attitude within practical limits.) In addition, he instructed that the name of every firm, together with the names of the executive officers, be reported to his office. It was clear that he was thinking in terms of future acquisitions and growth.

This discussion on accounts receivable and credit policy took most of the morning. President Jones invited the entire committee to lunch at the country club. In fact, in order to save time he leaned over to the phone and placed the orders so they would be ready. See you later, I'm going to the plant cafeteria—he didn't invite me . . . .

CONTROL OF INVENTORIES

You returned from lunch and together with the entire executive committee felt that a great deal of ground had been covered and a considerable amount of communication had taken place between the keymen of the Jones organization. Your satisfaction and contentment were short-lived.

First, it was the production manager! He had expressed concern to you on several occasions about the limited size of the raw material inventory. A review of the latest balance sheet indicated that only 500 units are kept on hand as a safety stock. Discussion with the production manager indicated that while the books do indicate 500 units, there must be at least 1,000 units in the warehouse, the excess having been built up over a period of time. (A physical count revealed 978 units.) Weekly deliveries are received from ADCO, our chief supplier. However, production is scheduled for 13,000 units per month, or about 600 units per day. The safety stock does appear to be very marginal. The production manager requested that the raw-material inventory be increased to 26,000 units, or a two-month supply.

Then came the sales manager again. He expressed the same concern with regard to the level of finished goods inventory. His actual inventory is approximately 2,000 units, and he was suggesting that it be increased to 26,000 units, or roughly two months' average supply. The added investment involved in meeting these two requests at present prices is shown below:

Raw material, 25,022 units at $1	$ 25,022
Finished goods, 24,000 units at $3.50 (variable cost)	84,000[1]
Total additional investment in inventories	$109,022

[1] We are assuming that the increase in finished goods inventory will not entail an increase in fixed costs.

We just weren't up to attacking another major funding problem so soon after the last one involving liquidity. However, it is quite clear that inventories can be a significant factor in any discussion of liquidity. Things have been rather bumpy for you the last couple of days as you faced issue after issue. However, you might as well face this issue also.

We know that inventories can and at times do represent a large proportion of current assets, and they account for a large percentage of the total accounts payable. Inventories thus involve funds. Any funds tied up in *excess* raw material, goods in process inventory, or finished goods inventory can only complicate our current liquidity problems. These funds, if we had them, could be, and should be, employed elsewhere, earning a return and adding to earnings per share. On the other hand, inadequate raw material inventories can cause expensive production delays which will increase unit cost and may result in inadequate finished goods inventories. Inadequate finished goods inventories, or "stock-outs," may create customer dissatisfaction, and could motivate the customer to develop a secondary source of supply from one of our competitors. At times, excess finished goods inventory may be unavoidable, but these excesses should be, if possible, kept at a minimum. We must, therefore, strike a balance between the cost of excess inventory and the costs, tangible and intangible, associated with inadequate inventory levels.

In addition, any level of inventory may involve certain risks and uncertainties over which we may have no direct control. These can be summarized as follows:

1. *Price-level changes—up or down.* A continuing alertness and a faithful study of the national and/or regional economy may provide data and insights that will influence our inventory practices. We have seen from our examination of the microeconomic framework that, as our suppliers move toward the full utilization of their plant, price increases are very likely. The marginal cost curve will sweep rapidly upward. We have experienced this problem! This very factor was the primary reason we were forced to install new and more efficient production machinery. We know that governmental action or inaction in response to inflationary or deflationary trends will affect price levels. We must be alert. We must understand. We must plan to take advantage of price movements and not be forced to react after the movements have taken place.

   Generally speaking, raw material price increases can, to some degree, be anticipated. In many instances, the sales representatives of our suppliers will pass along this information. Industry trade association publications and/or meetings may give some indication of price direction. Labor contracts and negotiations in related industries or in the economy as a whole may indicate either a trend or a reason to expect imminent changes in price. If raw material inventories are a significant factor in production costs, it may be wise to have a representative attend the applicable trade association meeting and/or maintain a close liaison with suppliers' representatives.

Clearly, during inflationary periods, it may be wise and ultimately less costly to increase our raw material purchases and endure a corresponding increase in raw material inventory levels. During deflationary periods, perhaps, raw material purchases should be kept at a minimum. Inflationary and deflationary trends may or may not be easily discernible. However, again, we must be alert. We must be knowledgeable. In the final analysis, however, we are still weighing the costs of buying and maintaining inventories versus the costs of not having inventory available when required.

2. *Obsolescence.* Style or technological requirements may affect our inventory policies. Styles and/or technologies that are prone to change rapidly would suggest a minimum of inventory. (The retailer in women's clothing must be alert for such changes, as they will significantly affect the value and selling price of the stock on hand. Industrial inventories, while subject to risk of obsolescence, are generally far more stable than retail inventories.)
3. *External influences.* Strikes or labor unrest in our own industry or in related and even unrelated segments of our economy not only may affect the availability and price of raw materials but also, as indicated, may influence the size of both the raw material and the finished goods inventory we wish to carry.

INVENTORIES AND COSTS

In addition to the risks and uncertainties, over which we have no control, there are some cost factors over which we do have some control. We control these costs by controlling the size and composition of our raw material and finished goods inventories. We are talking about those costs associated with the investment in inventories and the necessary housing and handling of the inventories. They include depreciation, rental expense, taxes, utility expense, janitorial labor, security, insurance, and record and bookkeeping requirements.

Unfortunately, sales and inventory requirements do not remain static or constant. It is quite obvious that it takes the wisdom of Solomon, the patience of Job, and the vigilance and attention of a good patriot to maintain proper and adequate inventory levels.

One member of the executive committee inquired about the use of a quantitative technique to determine the most economic quantity to order at any one time. He indicated that this formula had appeared quite often in the financial literature. You explained briefly that, in general, the assumptions are too rigid, as the model is typically presented, for application to raw material and finished goods inventory problems.

Economic Order Quantity

We will test this last observation by examining the economic order quantity (EOQ) model as it is typically presented with reference to our raw material inventory. In essence, what we are doing when we use this model is measuring the cost of "carrying" the raw material inventory against the cost of ordering the inventory. It is very significant to note that we are dealing only with variable costs, that is, those costs which will change as inventory levels change.

Obviously, if there were no costs associated with carrying our inventory, we would simply order 155,000 units at one time. In this way our supply would be assured. However, in some cases the costs of carrying inventory can be as high as 25 percent of the value of the units held. If that were the case, our carrying cost would be as much as $38,750. Our net profit and earnings per share would decline, as would inventory turnover and thus earning power. The alternative, of course, is to let our suppliers bear the cost of carrying our inventories by ordering goods only as needed. This course of action, however, is usually not feasible since we cannot be 100 percent confident of the suppliers' ability to deliver. Our best policy will, as you have already guessed, lie somewhere between these extremes. Further, it will be a policy which balances the costs of carrying inventories against the costs associated with running out of either raw materials or finished goods.

The economic order quantity model attempts to balance costs and benefits with respect to the number of times we order raw materials during a given period. Again, we repeat, the Jones organization will not be able to use this model because of the rigid assumptions necessary to make it function properly. Let's examine two versions of this inventory model and then you can arrive at your own conclusions. We will start with the basic assumptions as they are usually presented. We will then test these assumptions after we analyze the model.

Variable inventory carrying costs	10% of inventory value (assumed)
Variable purchasing cost per order	$10.00
Price per unit	$1.00
Requirement for the year	155,000 units

From these data we can construct the following table:

CALCULATIONS FOR ECONOMIC ORDER QUANTITY
(Alternative 1)

A. Number of orders	40	28	24	12	6	3	1
B. Order size	3,875	5,535	6,458	12,917	25,833	51,667	155,000
C. Average inventory B ÷ 2 ($1 per unit)	1,938	2,768	3,229	6,459	12,917	25,833	77,500
D. Total carrying costs = 10%	$193.80	$276.80	$322.90	$645.90	$1,291.70	$2,583.33	$7,750
		↕					
E. Total ordering costs, A × $10 per order	$400.00	$280.00	$240.00	$120.00	$ 60.00	$ 30.00	$ 10
F. Total cost purchasing + ordering (D + E)	$593.80	$556.80	$562.90	$765.90	$1,351.70	$2,613.33	$7,760

Can you see what is really happening as we constructed the table above? As the size of the order increases in dollar value, the 10 percent carrying charge increases in the *same proportion.* On the other hand, the flat charge of $10 per order increases only at the constant rate of $10 per order. As you examine the numbers in the blocks of lines D and E, you will see that the economic order quantity is determined at the point illustrated by the arrow, where the total ordering cost is approximately equal to the total carrying cost. We could generalize ad infinitum, but the essence of our examination is the comparison of the "cost of ordering" with the "inventory carrying cost." This model indicates that the optimum number of orders will be determined at that point where the "total carrying costs" and the "total ordering costs" are approximately equal. When the cost of placing the orders exceeds the cost of carrying the inventory, we will place fewer orders and carry larger inventory balances (if we follow this approach).

This analysis, based on the given data, indicates that we should place 28 orders for approximately 5,535 units per order, or slightly more than two orders each month.

Before examining a second alternative presentation of the EOQ concept, are we clear about what "inventory carrying costs" are? These costs, as used in this analysis, are those *variable costs* associated with warehousing and having the stock available when needed. In addition to the obvious charges for insurance, taxes, and special heat or refrigeration expense, a more significant carrying cost is the opportunity cost of the investment in the inventory itself. We were referring to the point earlier when we stated that "any funds tied up in excess inventory should be invested elsewhere and earning a return." Likewise, the return that could be earned with any funds tied up in necessary inventory is one cost we must pay for "carrying" the inventory!

(Parenthetically, the twice-a-month ordering policy may turn out to be a good one. But, as we will see, if it is a good policy, it is not good because the EOQ formula said so. "Bias, Bias, Bias!" We just pulled the numbers used as carrying costs and the ordering costs out of the air for the illustration! We will examine these items in more detail.)

First, let's examine a second alternative presentation of the same ideas using the same data. EOQ in this case would appear as follows:

ECONOMIC ORDER QUANTITY (ALTERNATIVE 2)

$$\sqrt{\frac{2 \times \text{Annual inventory requirements} \times \text{purchasing cost per order}}{\text{Cost per unit} \times \text{inventory carrying costs}}}$$

which means

$$\sqrt{\frac{2 \times \text{Annual inventory requirements} \times \text{purchasing cost per order}}{\text{Inventory carrying expressed as a \% of inventory unit cost}}}$$

or

$$\sqrt{\frac{2 \times 155{,}000 \text{ Units} \times \$10.00}{\$1.00 \times 0.10}} = 5{,}567.7 \text{ units per order}$$

$$\frac{155{,}000 \text{ Units}}{5{,}567.7 \text{ Units}} = 27.8 \text{ orders}$$

Using this version of the EOQ model, we arrive at approximately the same answer as before, 27.8 orders. We would place 28 orders per year. However, we have not built into our calculations possible quantity purchase discounts or freight-in differentials caused by larger individual order sizes! By overlooking this deficiency in our model (which could be corrected), it is clear that the basic point of consideration is, again, the "variable cost of placing the order" versus the "variable cost of carrying the inventory." We must examine these cost items carefully. We must not assume that all inventory carrying costs and all purchasing costs are variable. Would the model answer change if the *carrying costs* were 1 percent instead of 10 percent? Would your EOQ change if your ordering costs were $1.00 per order instead of $10? The answer to both questions is yes. As we have seen, the essence of the EOQ calculation is the relationship between the variable inventory carrying cost and the variable cost of placing the order.

The problem with the model is that for all practical purposes ordering costs are generally fixed. As an example, normally the salaries paid to the purchasing agent, his secretary, and/or helpers are established on a monthly or weekly basis. These costs then are fixed and will not vary until additional help is needed. Once new help is acquired, costs are again fixed. The same can be said of office equipment and space rented. These costs will not change in total if the office places 1 order or 100 orders each day. Cost per order change, but clearly these costs are not variable! This is not to say that there can be variable ordering costs. Variable costs may include postage, long-distance phone calls, and stationery requirements.

The variable costs of "placing an order" in practice would appear to be very insignificant when compared with possible variable "inventory carrying costs," which include (1) implicit and/or explicit interest paid on the value of the inventory; (2) any special utility requirements; (3) incremental taxes and insurance on the inventory; and (4) the inventory loss caused by deterioration, shrinkage, or pilferage.

If this is so, that is, if the actual variable costs of placing an order are relatively insignificant when compared with the variable inventory carrying charges, and thus for all practical purposes are fixed, then we have no equation (2 × annual inventory requirement × zero is zero!). If any number in a mathematical model is multiplied by zero, the answer is zero and the model's usefulness is over! (As stated earlier, in our judgment, the typical EOQ model, as presented in the financial literature, contains implicit and explicit assumptions with respect to the level of variable ordering costs that are unrealistic and too rigid to be useful in most situations.)

The economic order quantity (EOQ) formulas have been available for more than 50 years. However, an excellent study of various alternative uses of these formulas conducted by the National Association of Accountants reports that " . . . it must be concluded that the actual use of these techniques is less frequent than the literature on this subject might lead one to believe."[1] The Research Report contains the results of a field study, including a summary of the actual practices of 39 business organizations that had demonstrated an interest in modern methods of inventory management. Thirteen of these business organizations were applying the EOQ concepts, and two of these " . . . were doing this so informally that their inclusion . . . is perhaps unwarranted. . . . Ten of these companies were applying statistical concepts in setting reorder points, but three of these had very informal systems."[2]

Perhaps we have belabored the point, but it merits emphatic treatment. We must examine the implicit or explicit assumptions involved carefully, as more and more mathematical models are offered for the solution of complex business problems.

An examination of the ordering costs for the Jones Electronic Corporation indicates that for all practical purposes, the ordering costs are fixed. If this is so, then the EOQ model will not make a contribution

[1] Techniques in Inventory Management, *N.A.A. Research Report* 40, p. 2, New York, 1964.

[2] *Ibid.*

toward our raw material inventory problem. Therefore, our main concern with our raw material inventory is the carrying cost versus the price we will pay if our main supplier, ADCO Corporation, is unable to deliver our monthly requirements and as a result we incur the expense of a production shutdown. We have inquired about our main supplier's (ADCO) inventory policy and have found that ADCO maintains a three-month supply on hand. We have received assurance that weekly deliveries to our plant will be made. We have further been assured that if any change is made in ADCO's three-month policy, we will be promptly notified. If ADCO can maintain the weekly deliveries, we will have transferred most, if not at all, of the inventory carrying charges to them! ADCO's finished goods inventory is the source of our raw material inventory. ADCO's policy with respect to the level of its finished goods inventory will be one of the factors which will ultimately determine our own raw material inventory level. Further inquiries determine that ADCO has never suffered a production shutdown as a result of labor difficulties. In addition, ADCO has recently negotiated a three-year contract with its unionized employees. Therefore, in view of ADCO's three-month supply of inventory, a policy which required Jones Corporation to maintain a two-month raw material inventory would furnish us with an assured five-month supply of raw materials. As a first approximation, a five-month supply is excessive.

Consequently, at the next meeting of our executive committee we will suggest with mixed emotions that our commitment to inventory be gradually increased to 13,000 units. This increased level of raw material inventory will satisfy our production manager's desire for an assured supply and will also provide Jones Electronic with additional leeway should any unforeseen difficulties arise.

INVENTORY TURNOVER RATIOS

The matter of inventory turnover ratios came up during the discussion of inventory policy and the determination of the proper level of inventories the Jones organization should maintain. You explained that the inventory ratios were not designed to determine inventory policy and are only of limited help in measuring the effectiveness of established inventory policy. You first defined what you meant by inventory turnover.

Inventory turnover is the ratio of the inventory withdrawn to the average inventory on hand during the period. As an example, the following inventory turnover concepts are often presented:

1. $\text{Raw material turnover} = \dfrac{\text{cost of material used}}{\text{av. raw material inventory}}$

2. $\text{Work in process turnover} = \dfrac{\text{cost of goods manufactured}}{\text{av. inventory of work in process}}$

3. $\text{Finished goods turnover} = \dfrac{\text{cost of goods sold}}{\text{av. finished goods inventory}}$

Ratio 1 above will tell us how many times we have used our inventory in production during the period. As an example, if our average raw material inventory is valued at $500 and the total material used during the period is $5,000, it is obvious that we turned over our raw material inventory 10 times during the period. This would appear to be a much more efficient use of funds than if we maintained an average raw material inventory of $2,500 and total material used during the period was $5,000. This is a turnover of only two times. Similar observations could be made from an analysis of ratios 2 and 3.

We can get into difficulty, however, if we draw conclusions from these ratios without first analyzing the makeup of the figures used in the computation. As an example, the dollar value per unit of inventory can be misleading. If the manufacturing costs or the cost of merchandise purchased for resale were increasing and if we were using the Lifo method of inventory valuation (that is, the last units are the first to be withdrawn), then the inventory would reflect a lower unit cost and the cost of goods sold would reflect the higher unit cost. The Lifo method of valuing inventory (to be examined later) would build into our ratios unrealistic "turnovers." To illustrate:

1,000 units of material used:

1. $\text{Before price change} = \dfrac{\text{cost of material used}}{\text{av. raw material inventory}} = \dfrac{\$10{,}000}{\$500} = 20 \text{ times}$

1,000 units used purchased at increased prices.

2. $\text{After price advance} = \dfrac{\text{cost of material used}}{\text{av. raw material inventory}} = \dfrac{\$12{,}000}{\$500} = 24 \text{ times}$

If we were unaware of the merchandise cost increase and/or if we did not know that the Lifo method of inventory was being used, we might be inclined to compliment management, or that part of management dealing with inventories, for what appears to be a more efficient use of funds based on the increase in inventory turnover! Similar observations could be made about all other inventory turnover ratios. A knowledge of price-level changes and inventory valuation methods is a prerequisite for effective use of inventory turnover ratios as a financial management tool.

Perhaps it would be more meaningful if the turnover ratios, that is, the cost of goods sold and the average inventory in our example, were expressed in terms of units instead of dollars. There would then be no artificial "turnovers" caused by a change in dollar costs. However, few economic conclusions are possible even if the unit method of calculating inventory turnover is used. For example, assume we stock one unit of inventory on the shelf and only replace this unit when it is sold. Two hundred units are sold during the accounting period. The "turnover" ratio is 200 times. Sounds wonderful! However, subsequent examination reveals we could have sold 500 units had we carried adequate inventory.

This is not to say that we should abandon all use of inventory turnover ratios. Rather, we will be very careful about voicing the significance of the ratios until we "know" what they mean. We must be careful about comparing the ratios of one company with the ratios of another company without adequate knowledge about each company as to types of market, size of market, warehousing policy, sales policy, and especially inventory valuation method (for example, Lifo Fifo, weighted average, moving average), possible significant changes in prices, method of operation, and the like. Inventory ratio analysis may be valuable in signaling a problem, such as the need for attention to inventory policies, but very seldom, if ever, will these ratios present an answer to the problem itself. (We could and will make similar observations about other ratios that are presented in financial and accounting literature, for example, inventory to working capital or inventory to net assets.)

These turnover ratios will not be significantly helpful in setting policy for any given business organization but might be of limited value in testing the effectiveness of inventory policy once determined. A given 2-to-1 ratio or a ratio of 6 to 1 might be excellent today and very poor tomorrow! This is so because of the constant changes of sales, prices, general economic climate, and other day-to-day factors. Moreover, all the above factors (sales, prices, and general economic condition) might be fluctuating in different directions!

Although inventory levels are important, often the composition of inventory carried is more significant. The Jones Corporation is a single-product firm. Thus, the problem of composition is not vital. However, if we sold several different products, the composition of inventory would be of real consequence. For example, a used-car dealer must be concerned about the level of his inventory, and if he is to improve its turnover he must know which models are moving quickly and which are not moving. Those models which are not selling will add to the level of inventory but not to sales. Consequently, they reduce inventory turnover. Once the composition of the inventory is related to models that have been and are selling, effective action can be taken to reduce the inventory of those models which have been slow to sell.

The afternoon wore on, and about 4:45 p.m., President Jones remarked that he had heard considerable discussion about factors that did not affect or aid in inventory-level determinations. However, he observed, he did not learn much of immediate value to the Jones enterprise. You indicated that you were coming to that. He asked how long it would take! You replied about two hours. With that everyone went to dinner. You were promised 45 minutes after dinner, and the meeting was scheduled to resume at 6:15 p.m.

RECONCILIATION OF INVENTORY POLICY WITH SALES AND PRODUCTION BUDGETS

When the meeting resumed, you turned to the major question of what size finished goods inventory the Jones organization should carry on hand. The first consideration is "what 'safety stock' is needed to cover unexpected sales increases or production interruptions."

The sales manager was requested to estimate the total sales for the year (1971–1972) for the Jones Electronic Corporation on a monthly basis. He presented the following analysis, including the Allied requirement of 3,000 units per month except December, when Allied will require 7,000 units.

	Units		Units		Units
October	9,000	February	16,000	June	12,000
November	9,000	March	16,000	July	12,000
December	14,000	April	16,000	August	12,000
January	13,000	May	14,000	September	12,000
		Total sales	155,000 units		

When plotted, these figures appear as shown in Figure 9-1.

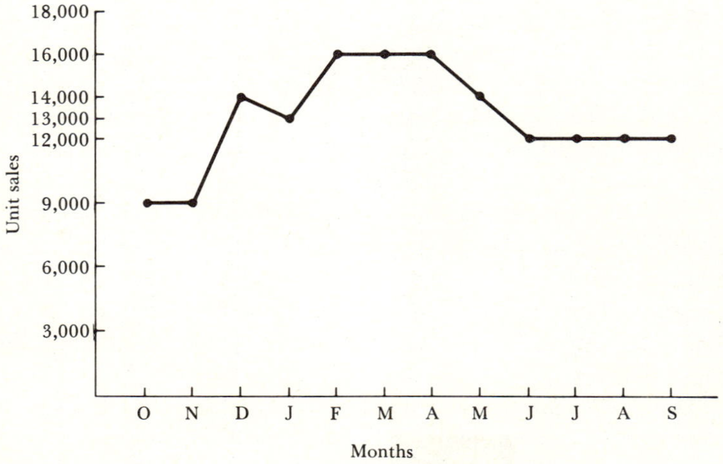

Figure 9-1 Graph of sales forecast.

It is quite clear that the accuracy of the monthly sales forecast is critical because our production and inventory plans will be closely related to and predicated upon these estimates. But, then, is not the same true for fixed cost and profit projections? Wasn't the fixed cost per unit that we have projected based upon a given rate of production? Our financing plans are likewise based upon these estimates. Funds must be provided for raw material purchases, payrolls, and other variable operating expenses that are related to the quantity of production. Idle funds not earning a normal return are a luxury, detrimental to our profitability, but the lack of funds when needed can be a disaster! (Shades of our liquidity problem!) However, we cannot answer all the problems in one paragraph. We have observed again and again that a big problem is nothing more than a series of little problems.

Let's begin by testing a production schedule based on data we know:

1. Our flexible budget indicates that our anticipated average total variable cost per unit will be $3.50 at an annual production rate of 155,000 units, or approximately 13,000 units per month. As we know from our flexible budget and cost curves, any rate of production less than this amount will cause the fixed and variable cost per unit to increase, and any rate of production in excess of 13,000 per month will cause average fixed cost per unit to decrease while average variable cost per unit increases.
2. While inventory must be adequate at all times to meet sales demands, it should not be excessive.

PRODUCTION, SALES, AND INVENTORY PROJECTION

	Anticipated Sales, Units	Desired Production Level	Monthly Excess or Deficiency	Finished Goods Inventory on Hand Beginning of Each Month, Units
Bal. on hand				1,000
October	9,000	13,000	+4,000	5,000
November	9,000	13,000	+4,000	9,000
December	14,000	13,000	−1,000	8,000
January	13,000	13,000	—0—	8,000
February	16,000	13,000	−3,000	5,000
March	16,000	13,000	−3,000	2,000
April	16,000	13,000	−3,000	(1,000)
May	14,000	13,000	−1,000	(2,000)
June	12,000	13,000	+1,000	(1,000)
July	12,000	13,000	+1,000	
August	12,000	13,000	+1,000	1,000
September	12,000	13,000	+1,000	2,000
Bal. October	155,000	156,000		

> From a profitability point of view it would be most desirable to maintain production at the 13,000-unit monthly level. Let's relate this level of production to our projected sales.

On the basis of the above projection, we will be "out of stock" three months of the coming year—April, May, and June—even though we will add 1,000 units to finished goods inventory by the end of the year. (If we produce 13,000 units each month, total production will be 156,000 units. Sales forecasts indicate that 155,000 units will be sold.) It is clear that the present inventory of 1,000 units will be totally inadequate. In addition, we will have no protection against possible sales increases or unavoidable production slowdowns. We must therefore reexamine our "safety stock" (inventory). On the other hand, if projected profit margins are to be met, we must basically follow the 13,000-unit monthly production schedule. This latter point we know for certain.

It is quite clear that in our situation, as with most manufacturing operations, the size of finished goods inventories and the cost of production are inescapably interrelated. The production schedule we have prepared gives consideration only to production costs. We must now consider the alternatives. We must balance the change in production costs (should we revise the production schedule) against the price we will pay if we are unable to fulfill sales commitments because the available finished goods inventory is exhausted. If in our judgment the increase in production costs (as we move from the 13,000-unit monthly production schedule to meet sales requirements) is less than the price we will pay because of unfilled orders, loss of customer goodwill, or loss of competitive advantage, then we will abandon our monthly 13,000-unit level. On the other hand, if our judgment indicates that production can be increased *one month* to build an adequate safety stock without a substantial increase in production cost, we will by all means do so without changing our entire production policy based on 13,000 units monthly. After the buildup of inventory levels, we can then return to the 13,000-unit monthly production schedule.

In short, effective finished goods inventory management as far as the Jones organization and other similarly situated manufacturing organizations are concerned will depend on a fairly constant production schedule. It is clear that if we are to achieve all the manufacturing economies of scale, production must proceed at a rate that is as constant as possible. Our cost curves and/or flexible budget indicated that this level of production is 13,000 units per month. If our actual sales pattern is lower than our sales forecast and we anticipate that the sales decrease is only temporary, we have a second decision to make. That decision is, simply, Will the per-unit cost of carrying the unused finished goods be less than the increased cost to manufacture each unit as we cut back production from time to time and move back along our cost curves?

The conversation continued for 10 or 15 minutes. Finally, the executive committee, after carefully reviewing the factors indicated above, decided that permanent finished goods inventory level should be 9,000 units. You were requested to consult with the production manager and reexamine your flexible budget and/or cost curves. You would then be in a better position to decide whether the increase in safety stock could be accomplished by increasing production 2,000 units each month until the 9,000-unit level is reached or whether it would be more feasible and economical to wait and see if sales meet the projected levels and produce the extra 9,000 units during February or March.

We hope that we may be able to stay within the 13,000-unit monthly production limit until February or March and still be within the constraints of the liquidity analysis made in the last chapter. We can almost not afford a substantial increase in sales until March or April.

In summary, good inventory management (that is, having a sufficient inventory on hand to meet all contingencies at a minimum of cost) involves the consideration of these four important factors:

1. Production costs
2. Sales forecast
3. Lead time and safety stock
4. Costs associated with having or not having the inventory available when needed (so called stock-out costs)

Production Costs

This first factor is a serious matter to a manufacturing organization. Production costs include (1) direct material and direct labor entered into and consumed in connection with the product manufactured and (2) indirect expense necessary for and incident to the production of the particular article. If a new machine is added to a production operation or if there is a changeover of machines, production costs will include cost of machine setup and overtime compensation to make up for loss of time during an equipment changeover (if more than one product is involved).

Sales Forecast and Sales Pattern

The sales forecast or sales pattern is a basic consideration. This consideration may include style changes, innovation, and obsolescence. The

Jones organization may have been fortunate in being able to schedule production at 13,000 units per month with an increase only in the month of March and an overall annual increase in finished goods inventory of only 1,000 units. Production costs can be maintained at a minimum. It appears that after the March adjustment, inventory levels will be adequate. We must either delay further sales increases or face an even more serious liquidity problem than anticipated earlier. This is an excellent example of liquidity or the lack of liquidity affecting profitability.

Lead Time and Safety Stock

Lead time and safety stock are related. Lead time refers to the time elapsing between placing the order with the plant and receiving the finished product for sale. In the case of raw material it is the time elapsing between placing the order with the supplier and receiving the material at our plant site. Transportation may be a significant factor. The longer the lead time, the more essential becomes the timely placement of orders. The purpose of safety stock is to compensate for conceivable lead-time delays and/or to cover an unexpected increase in the demand for the product.

Stock-out Costs

The costs associated with having or not having the inventory available when needed refer to the inventory carrying cost and customer dissatisfaction. This requires very careful judgment and must take into consideration the particular customer or type of customer, the price of the inventory item, the demand for the particular item, and the lead time necessary for its delivery. Proper inventory policy under a given set of conditions will involve a delicate balance between all four of the factors indicated.

(1)	(2)	(3)	(4)
Change In Production Costs	Lead Time	Variable Inventory Carrying Costs	Customer Goodwill

In our judgment, customer goodwill, in the long run, is the paramount consideration. The cost of recapturing a good customer may be far more than the cost of carrying adequate inventory. After adequate inventory size has been determined to satisfy this latter demand, further possible adjustments in the size of the inventory will be determined by balancing the change in production cost per unit and lead time on one hand and the variable inventory carrying costs on the other.

The first three factors we can quantify and put in a mathematical formula with production cost figures taken from our flexible budget. If these calculations are complicated, the computer can be programmed to print out cost comparisons within a minute. The fourth factor, customer goodwill, as indicated, must be based on informed managerial judgment.

Inventories have been called the "graveyard of American business." This is not to say that inventories are the cause of death. The cause of the death is poor inventory management. A significant result of poor management is a "locked-in" inventory position (small turnover) with perhaps a forced liquidation sale at a substantial loss.

INTERNAL CONTROL OF INVENTORIES

Inventory is like cash. Therefore, adequate procedures are necessary to safeguard the inventory. An important technique for inventory control is the maintenance of proper records and division of responsibility for handling the flow-through of the inventory items from the receipt to withdrawal. Effective internal control of inventory will involve the following:

1. There should be a separation of the receiving, shipping, storing, and accounting duties.
2. Responsibility should be clearly fixed with respect to the custody and the proper maintenance of records.
3. Authorization should be required prior to all inventory movements.
4. If the occasion warrants, employees directly concerned with the inventories should be bonded.
5. When perpetual inventory records are maintained, periodic checks should be made by physical count. The inventory may be so large that an entire physical count is not practical. Under these circumstances, various parts of the perpetual inventory records should be tested by physical count periodically on a sampling basis until the entire inventory has been confirmed.
6. Adequate protection via properly secured storerooms, fences, and/or guards must be provided.
7. Adequate insurance coverage must be maintained.

In order to determine the number of units on hand and to provide a test for our control measures, inventories may be physically counted, measured, or weighed at the end of the accounting period. This procedure is not always easy or even practical for some items. On the other hand, perpetual inventory records may be maintained and supplemented by periodic physical counts to test the accuracy of the inventory records. Perpetual inventory records involve the careful recording of each receipt and each withdrawal of each inventory item. Data-processing equipment is widely used as an aid in maintaining these records. As goods are received, the necessary information is transferred to data-processing punch cards or tape and fed into the memory bank of a computer. A data-processing card is often attached to each item of inventory. As the inventory is withdrawn from storage, the card is detached and again fed into the memory bank of the computer. If this procedure is followed carefully, the push of a button will print out instantaneously the number of units of the particular type of inventory on hand.

VALUATION OF INVENTORIES

The next problem we must face is the valuation of inventories. This problem may at first glance appear to be quite an easy matter. Usually, we value the inventory at the lower of the prices we paid or current market value. However, this simple procedure can create problems. As an example, let's assume that you are the owner of a hardware store. One morning a customer comes in to buy several bales of wire. You check your inventory and ascertain that you have the wire available. You then go to the file to find your invoice to see how much you paid for the wire so you can arrive at the selling price. You find that you paid $50 for the wire, and you tell the customer the price is $75. He pays you and takes the wire. That very afternoon, the wholesale hardware salesman stops by to get your order. You replace the wire, but you find the cost to you has increased to $100. A pertinent question is, "Did you have a $25 profit on the sale or did you lose $25?"

Now, let's change the assumption and say that you had purchased the exact quantity of wire that your customer purchased on two different occasions. The first purchase cost you $50 and the second purchase cost you $75. Which wire did you sell? Would you average the cost at $62.50 for each lot? If you decide you sold the first lot, you would be valuing your inventory on a first-in-first-out basis. The transaction would be reflected on your income statement and balance sheet as follows:

On Income Statement		**On Balance Sheet**	
Sales	$75	Inventory	$75
Cost of sales	50		
Gross profit	$25		$75

On the other hand, if you decide you sold the last lot first, you would be valuing your inventory on a last-in-last-out basis, and your financial statements would appear as follows:

Income Statement		Balance Sheet	
Sales	$75	Inventory	$50
Cost of sales	75		
Gross profit	$ 0		$50

If you used a simple average, your financial statements would appear as follows:

Income Statement		Balance Sheet	
Sales	$75.00	Inventory	$62.50
Cost of sales	62.50		
Gross profit	$12.50		$62.50

These small numbers may not appear to be very significant. On the other hand, if we add 000,000 behind the numbers, the different methods of inventory valuation may be quite significant in the financial planning process. It is not our purpose to involve you with the expertise of the accountant. However, we must recognize that there are various methods of valuing inventory and that each method will lead to operating reports that are quite different.

SIGNIFICANCE OF VALUATION METHODS

The quantity and valuation of each inventory item on hand at the end of the accounting period is a significant factor as an asset on the balance sheet or as a part of the cost of goods reflected on the income statement. [As an example, if the inventory at the end of the accounting period is understated, this asset on the balance sheet will be understated, the cost of goods sold for the period will be overstated, and profit for the period will be understated.] Thus inaccurate reporting will result in increased cost for the period, decreased profit, and a lower current-asset ratio (ratio of current assets, which include inventory, to current liabilities). We will get the same results if the inventory is misused, spoiled, or perhaps stolen.

The ending inventory of one accounting period is the beginning inventory of the next period. The error illustrated above will be compounded in the following period when the cost of goods sold will be understated and profit will be overstated. Continued errors of this nature will make our statements meaningless. It is apparent that proper inventory determinations are vital for accurate and meaningful financial statements.

For income tax purposes, once an election is made to carry inventories on the basis of a particular valuation method, for example, Fifo or Lifo or otherwise, this election is binding and a change cannot take place without permission from the Internal Revenue Service. However, for company planning purposes as well as statement preparations, a change in inventory valuation methods may be prudent; remember your experience in selling the wire. During periods of anticipated price rises when costs of material and/or labor are increasing, thereby causing an increase in unit costs, it may be realistic to base your inventory valuations and indirectly your selling price on the last-in-first-out method. When declining prices are anticipated, the first-in-first-out method may be more realistic to avoid inventory losses. The effect of a change in valuation methods on earnings must be shown on the financial statements.

Our executive committee meeting was about to break up when a second member inquired about "hedging." We again explained that our particular raw material and finished product are not subject to violent price changes which would justify entering into hedging transactions. Generally, a producer, merchandiser, manufacturer, processor, or exporter dealing with what are known as "commodities" enters into hedging transactions. The term "commodities" includes, among others, wheat, corn, oats, rye, cotton, etc. By hedging, one is able to minimize the effect of price changes as he plans future production and sales. As an example, let's follow a grain trader as he plans his protection against a price decline affecting the 5,000 bushels of soybean inventory he now has on hand. The present sales price is $2 per bushel. His cost is $1.50 per bushel. However, our operator would like to defer his income a few months for tax considerations or to take advantage of a future price increase. Still, it is possible that prices will fall. If so, he will lose not only the differences in price but also his inventory carrying charges and shrinkage.

The farm news indicates that the "future price" of soybeans for next July delivery is $2.29 per bushel. This is the price that traders think soybeans can be sold for next July. Our operator calculates his storage cost and on October 1 requests a broker to sell his 5,000 bushels on the July "future market." Our operator has really entered into a contract to sell and the purchaser has agreed to buy the 5,000 bushels of soybeans for delivery in July at the anticipated July price. Some, but not all, of the risk of holding the inventory has been eliminated. Should the price of soybeans fall in July to $1.85 from the present price of $2, our operator is assured of his sale at $2.29. If the price of soybeans increases in July to $2.35, our operator has lost the opportunity to earn the additional 6 cents per bushel.

Commodity dealers are not the only ones who engage in hedging transactions. Transactions to protect against sudden price changes are used also by investors in securities—selling securities short and purchasing puts and calls. Also, domestic corporations doing business abroad hedge against devaluation of the currency of the country in which they do business by dealing in the foreign currency prior to devaluation. Nothing further need be said on this topic, as it is more appropriate for a course of study in investments. All we have done is to throw out a few bits of information so that you can at least recognize the problem should it arise in the future.

It has been a long day and it's still raining. There goes my golf handicap up two more strokes from lack of practice. But, let's look at the brighter side. I just saved five dollars. I generally lose four balls each round in the lakes or in the woods at $1.25 each!

SUMMARY

Chapter 9 continues our investigation in the area of current-asset management. You realize by now that decisions respecting both accounts receivable management and inventory management are, in reality, investment decisions. The funds the firm commits in these areas should produce acceptable returns. The policies which are evolved should not be developed in isolation, but rather should be formulated with full recognition of the interdependence of the current asset accounts and their relationship to sales levels and ultimate profitability.

Accounts receivable management requires the development of credit policies. For all intents and purposes the credit period and terms of credit are largely determined by the industry. The individual firm may have little or no latitude in this area. However, the individual firm is in complete command of the extension of those credit terms. That is to say, the firm is free to select the customers to whom it will extend the normal terms of trade. It is in this latter activity that crucial policy and procedure must be developed. For example, if the firm formulates a policy of extending credit whenever there is a reasonable assurance that payment will be made, there is underlying this policy the belief that customers want to pay their bills. If this belief is well founded, the firm will be required to establish procedures which measure a customer's ability to meet his obligations. Once this has been done, the firm can extend credit to those customers who possess this reasonable ability to pay their bills. In some firms a sophisticated credit matrix and a computer model may be used in an attempt to measure a customer's ability to pay and the level of risk on nonpayment.

Control of inventories also requires the development of policy and procedure. Inventory policy, however, is largely derived from and dependent on internal sales programs and external market characteristics. For example, an aggressive sales effort involving new products and stressing their immediate availability to potential customers will require substantial incremental investments in inventories. These investments, however, must, like other commitments, meet specific profitability criteria. In like manner, inventory policies may, at the margin, reflect management's anticipations of price changes, risks of short-term obsolescence, assessments of potential labor strikes against suppliers, etc.

In short, the firm will usually formulate a basic inventory policy. Procedures to implement this policy will also be developed. In conjunction with these basic policies and procedures, special situation programs will also be established. These special situation programs will then be implemented when the underlying assumptions relating to the firm's basic policies become temporarily inappropriate.

QUESTIONS FOR DISCUSSION

1. What are the basic questions an established credit policy should, in general, answer?
2. What costs are involved in the consideration of credit policy?
3. How does credit policy relate to the microeconomic framework developed in Chapter 3?
4. How does credit policy relate to the material studied in Chapter 4?
5. What are the sources of credit information?
6. How does inventory policy relate to the material in:
   a. Chapter 3
   b. Chapter 4
   c. Chapter 5
   d. Chapter 8
7. What risks must be considered in the establishment of inventory policy?
8. What information do economic order quantity (EOQ) formulas purport to present?
9. What basic assumptions are necessary to make the EOQ results meaningful?
10. What factors do the EOQ formulas attempt to equate?
11. Given no liquidity problem, what are the factors that must be considered in the establishment of inventory policy?
12. What do the inventory ratios purport to present?
13. What assumptions are necessary in order for the inventory ratios to be meaningful?
14. What is the significance of the statement "perhaps it would be more meaningful to express the inventory ratios in terms of units rather than dollars"?

15. What is the significance of the production schedule with reference to inventory policy?
16. Relate the factors involved in inventory policy with reference to the overall planning function.
17. What is meant by the statement "Inventories are the graveyard of American business"?
18. What factors are involved in the internal control of inventories?
19. What is the significance of the valuation of inventories to the:
    a. Reported earnings per share
    b. Balance sheet

PROBLEMS

1. You are contemplating an increase in finished goods inventory levels. Cost and financial statement analysis indicates that you are currently earning a profit with fixed costs per unit of $15 based on 100,000 units of production and that variable cost will increase an average of $1 per unit as production increases to the 150,000-unit production level. Current variable production cost is $10 per unit.

   It would be desirable to increase the finished goods inventory by 18,000 units. Carrying costs are $2 per unit per month, one half of this amount being fixed and the other half variable. No change in carrying-cost rate is contemplated.

   a. What will be the additional cost of providing the increase in inventory?
   b. What is the present value of this increased investment in inventories? Assume a 14 percent opportunity cost for the funds involved.

2. Given:

Price per unit	$1.00
Annual sales	$200,000
Inventory carrying costs	
Fixed	$32,000
Variable	10% of inventory value
Ordering cost:	
Fixed	$13,000
Variable	$15 per order (broker's fee)

   a. Calculate the optimum size of each order—assuming all other things equal.
   b. Assume the same as in part a, except that the variable ordering costs are infinitesimally small— 2 cents per order.

3. Calculate (a) the raw material turnover, (b) the work in process turnover, and (c) the finished goods turnover, given the following data:

   Raw material on hand, 1/1/71—17,000 units at a cost of $5 per unit.

Work in process inventory, 1/1/71—18,000 units at $9 per unit.
Finished goods inventory, 1/1/71—13,000 units at $12 per unit.
Raw material on hand, 12/31/71—17,000 units at a cost of $5 per unit.
Work in process inventory 12/31/71—20,000 units at a cost of $9.50 per unit.
Finished goods inventory, 12/31/71—16,000 units at a cost of $12.75 per unit.
Cost of goods manufactured and sent to warehouse:

Material	$22,000
Labor	14,000
Overhead	7,000
Total	$43,000

4. Your cost curves and/or flexible budget indicates that a desirable level of production would be 20,000 units per month. Your sales forecast for the next year, in units, appears as follows:

January	21,000	July	16,000
February	22,000	August	14,000
March	26,000	September	18,000
April	25,000	October	19,000
May	20,000	November	21,000
June	18,000	December	21,000

You are presently earning a profit, and variable production cost is $3 per unit; fixed production cost is $72,000 per month. Fixed inventory carrying cost is $3,500 per month, and variable carrying cost is $2 per unit per month. Your current inventory totals 5,000 units, and variable production costs will increase $2 per unit for each 5,000-unit increase in production.

Prepare an analysis of monthly production requirements that will result in the optimum inventory balances.

REFERENCES

Addison, Edward T.: Factoring: A Case History, *Financial Executive,* vol. 31, pp. 32–33, November, 1963.

Beranek, William: Financial Implications of Lot-size Inventory Models, *Management Science,* vol. 13, pp. 401–408, April, 1967.

Buchan, Joseph, and Ernest Koenigsberg: "Scientific Inventory Management," Prentice-Hall, Inc., Englewood Cliffs, N.J., 1963.

Eiteman, Wilford J., and James N. Holtz: Working Capital Management, in Karl A. Boedecker (ed.), "Essays on Business Finance," 4th ed., Masterco Press, Ann Arbor, Mich., 1963.

Hadley, G., and T. M. Whitin: "Analysis of Inventory Systems," Prentice-Hall, Inc., Englewood Cliffs, N.J., 1963.

Levy, Ferdinand K.: An Application of Heuristic Problem Solving to Accounts Receivable Management, *Management Science,* vol. 12, pp. 236–244, February, 1966.

Lock Box Credit and Financial Management, vol. 69, pp. 16–21, June, 1967. Banking: Key to Faster Collections,

Magee, John F.: Guides to Inventory Policy, *Harvard Business Review,* vols. I to III, pp. 34, 49–60, January-February, 1956; pp. 49–60, March-April, 1956; pp. 103–116, 57–70, May-June, 1956.

Meltzer, Allan H.: Mercantile Credit, Monetary Policy, and Size of Firms, *Review of Economics and Statistics,* vol. XLII, pp. 429–437, November, 1960.

Moore, Carroll G: Factoring: A Unique and Important Form of Financing and Service, *Business Lawyer,* vol. XIV, pp. 703–727, April, 1959.

Snyder, Arthur: Principles of Inventory Management, *Financial Executive,* vol. 32, April, 1964; reprinted in James Van Horne (ed.), "Foundations for Financial Management," Richard D. Irwin, Inc., Homewood, Ill., pp. 70–80, 1966.

Soldofsky, Robert M.: A Model for Accounts Receivable Management, *N.A.A. Bulletin,* January, 1966, pp. 55–58.

Starr, Martin K., and David W. Miller: "Inventory Control: Theory and Practice," Prentice-Hall, Inc., Englewood Cliffs, N.J., 1962.

Vienott, Arthur F., Jr.: The Status of Mathematical Inventory Theory, *Management Science,* vol. XII, pp. 745–777, July, 1966.

Chapter Ten

THE FINANCIAL EXECUTIVE AND THE ECONOMIC ENVIRONMENT

President Jones walked into your office and expressed his appreciation for the significant contribution you have made to the firm. He was especially pleased with the manner in which you have "taken charge" and have analyzed potential problem areas that previously he had not even considered. He went on to say that no doubt it would have been helpful to you if everyone in and out of the organization had understood that your inquiries and questions had the approval of the president of the organization. He then casually announced that he would propose to the executive committee the creation of the position of financial vice-president. Unless there was some reason that this position should not be created, and unless you would not accept this position, you could plan to assume this office the first of the following month. With tongue in cheek he added that unless you came up with another cash crisis, you could expect an increase in compensation of 100 percent to $24,000 per annum.

After President Jones left your office, your day continued as usual—busy. However, later that evening, as you attempted to relax in your favorite chair, the full impact of the day's events hit you. President Jones had restated his personal position, just as he had done your very first day. He just wants to return to his lab and the plant and be the "genius." The rest of the firm's responsibilities are yours! You have been authorized to acquire whatever additional personnel you need, but the firm's future is clearly "your baby"! You were pleased.

Your promotion to the position of financial vice-president was a tribute to your success at one level in the organization. However, your prior accomplishments are no guarantee of future achievements. In fact, it has been said that many individuals are promoted, perhaps again and again, until they reach the level of their incompetency! It is true that success breeds success, but you must continue to study and grow so that you do not find yourself incompetent as you assume new responsibilities.

In the past, your responsibilities have been primarily internal in nature. You solved problems and coped with crises as they appeared. Your frame of reference and the scope of your responsibilities must now be broadened significantly. You will soon recognize that your firm is but a small unit in a larger and more complex system of production and consumption. You must understand and anticipate changes in the general economic environment within which the Jones firm must live. If the general economic forces are ignored or misinterpreted, you may well discover that your goals are unattainable. In short, you will be as busy forecasting future events in order to prevent crises as you have been busy putting out the day-to-day fires. In a moment, you will be involved in a little of both.

The next day, the phone rang twice. First it was the sales manager, and the second time it was your assistant. Both were requesting a meeting with you. The sales manager was the first to arrive, and he was soon followed by your assistant with a folder full of work sheets and statements.

There appeared to be two problems: (1) the flexible budget and cost reports indicated that Jones was losing money on the last 20,000 units sold to Allied at $5 each and the last 15,000 units sold through normal channels at $6, and (2) cash collections were not coming in as fast as has been projected when you developed the cash-flow analysis earlier. Both of these problems are serious. Your assistant was taking the position that sales should be reduced. The sales manager was objecting to the reduced sales volume, which means lower sales commissions earned by his staff, not to mention his own paycheck.

Your assistant seemed to think that there was an obvious conflict of interest, vis-à-vis commissions earned versus overall profit to the firm. The sales manager took the position that there had to be another answer. You assured both men that the firm was certainly vitally interested in retaining a stable, aggressive sales force and was equally interested in maintaining a profitable level of operations. Both men were waiting for your plan of action. Candidly, you didn't have one at that moment. Subtle and not-so-subtle implications are involved in such broad policy matters. You so stated and advised both men that you would give the matter your early attention and that the three of you would discuss the matter further—soon.

ECONOMIC ENVIRONMENT

In thinking the situation through, you knew that any solution to the sales problem would clearly involve the cash-flow deficiency as well—A sale has not been completed until the funds have been collected. In your judgment, the most important single factor contributing to the success of the Jones firm was demand for the Jones production and, of even more importance, effective demand for the Jones production, which means that the customer has the funds available to purchase the product. Would this not lead to a significant interest in not only the amount of purchasing power available in the economy but, more specifically, the purchasing power available to your present and potential customers? Intuitively, you knew this to be so. However, there are some subtle and not-so-subtle implications involved in speaking of purchasing power. As an example, how do you think an economy with the following characteristic would operate?

1. One producer.
2. No credit.
3. No savings.
4. The producer rents the land, buys the material, hires the labor, pays each of these factors of production $1, and produces four units of his product.

In order to produce a profit, he sets a price of $1 per unit. With the assumption of "no savings" three units could be sold. The accountant would present an accounting statement that would include the following:

Sales (three units)	$3.00
Cost of sales ($\frac{3}{4}$ of $3.00)	2.25
Profit	$0.75

Notwithstanding the accounting statement, the producer has had no profit. Clearly the fourth unit cannot be sold because the available purchasing power has been exhausted, and the economic cycle will stop. The producer's profit is the unsold unit in his warehouse. This brings up a question: Is there anything built into this economic system that will automatically cause the system to start upward again? (The standard answer, you remember, as given in elementary economics textbooks, to the problem of the unsold inventory is simply that "the producer will spend his profit and thus furnish the purchasing power to purchase the fourth unit." However, this he cannot do in your little economy! The producer will have no "profit" to spend until he sells the fourth unit.)

In seeking the answer to the question, you observed that the assumptions are very tight and unrealistic. Therefore, relax the assumption of "no credit." The producer can then sell the fourth unit by the extension of credit. However, he will still have no spendable profit until the account receivable is collected. If he again manufactures four units and releases $3 in purchasing power to the marketplace, the same problem will arise. In addition, if he collects the $1 due from the prior sale, he will again be unable to sell all four units without extending $2 in credit. Credit sales must then expand or the cycle will stop as before. Relax the assumption of no savings and permit the spending of previous savings. The cycle will continue until savings have been used up, and then production will again cease.

Relax the assumption of only one producer. Start again with three manufacturers producing, perhaps, different products. (It is really immaterial whether the number of producers is three, thirty, three thousand, or an infinite number; the same analysis will apply as in this hypothetical situation.) The three producers produce four units each, and each pays rent, wages, and interest in the amount of $3. There is now a total of $9 in purchasing power on the market, and the goods available from all three are priced at a total of $12. Has the picture changed very much? In one respect it has. While it is quite true that not all producers will sell all their production during the *first complete turn* of the cycle, the successful producer can now spend his profit! There will be an obvious *time lag*. That is, the unsuccessful producer must wait perhaps until the second turn of the cycle to sell his product. What if the successful producer does not spend all of his profit? *This time lag is significant*! You couldn't put your finger on it immediately, but you did pause to reflect on the matter.

It appeared to you that the critical and significant aspect of the time lag is that if any producer withdraws purchasing power from the market (for whatever reason) in the form of savings that are not available as purchasing power, the cycle will start to slow down. The producer relying upon the "time-lag sales" will not sell his product. Producers experiencing the slowdown could be expected to cut back production even further, and the spiral will start downward. You began to see the light and things began to come into focus.

Your thoughts returned to the earlier question, Is there something built into our economic system that will automatically start the cycle upward if and when it starts a downward path? Unfortunately, the answer is no. It is clear that when purchasing power is removed from the marketplace, for whatever reason, the economic cycle will turn downward.

You did seem a bit depressed about this lack of an internal force that would automatically start an upward movement of the economy. You noted, as you had recognized earlier, that additional credit would solve an immediate problem; and if an expansion of credit were continued at an increasing rate, the whole problem of a downward trend in the economy could perhaps be avoided. You cited the continuous increase in the volume of credit as the United States economy has grown and expanded since the 1940s and World War II. However, you still felt uneasy. You knew that sooner or later credit must be repaid. You were back to the original $4–$3 problem again. You were likewise concerned about the slowdown in the collection of the Jones receivables. A thought struck you—"Does Jones sell to lead or lag industries?" This will be a significant analysis as you chart your future course of action from time to time.

The analysis will be especially significant as you attempt to relate the effect of governmental and other institutional decisions that affect the supply of money and/or purchasing power (that is, possible restrictions relating to the amount of credit or to the terms of credit.) It is becoming obvious that these kinds of questions will be, and in fact are now, significant factors that will affect the degree of success you will attain.

Then you were reminded of another approach to the problem. A German economist, Joseph Schumpeter, originally offered an idea in the early 1900s. Schumpeter's contribution was the idea that new investment in the form of additional plant or plant capacity would or could fill the gap between purchasing power created and the price of goods offered for sale. He wasn't talking about "investment" in the form of the purchase of stocks and bonds and other securities. This type of investment would not create purchasing power unless the recipient used the funds received to build new plants, or to expand an existing plant. Savings shuffled from one individual or group to another will not solve the problem.

If this approach is used to fill the "gap," in order for it to be effective, the new "investment" must be used to purchase building materials, labor, and other services that could add immediate purchasing power to the market. However, once the new plant was completed and its production became available to the market, the problem would no longer be $4–$3, but some larger number depending on the size of the new plant. Additional and larger new investments would then be needed to again take up or fill the larger gap thereby created. Assume a third, a fourth, a fifth, and a sixth new investment; the picture could appear as follows:

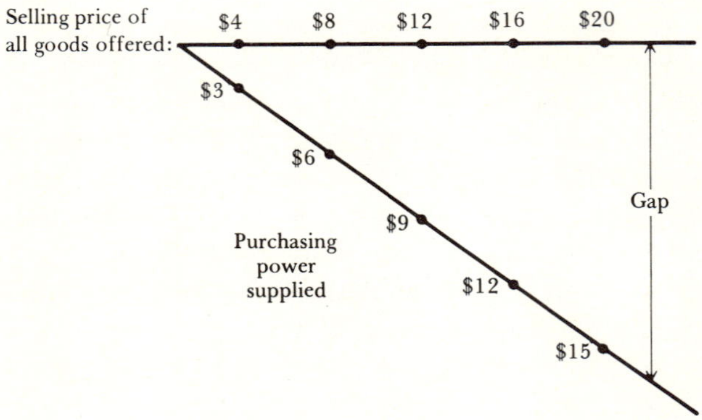

On the surface, it would appear that the problem is without solution and without end. You are probably right! There probably is no permanent solution in sight, and the economy will ever ebb and flow or, more seriously, move forward rapidly, from which point it could then decline just as fast. The ebb and flow you can probably live with. However, a rapid increase or decrease in economic activity can cause rapid increases or decreases in price levels and interest rates, among other things.

You will therefore be quite interested in statistics reflecting new or contemplated investment by government or the private sector of the economy. You will be more interested in correlating the size of the investment and the ability of the economy to absorb the immediate purchasing power provided as well as the goods and services available once the construction has been completed.

As an example, assume the economy has a $16 to $12 gap, as illustrated above. This situation would indicate that $4 in new investment was needed immediately. And assume that new investment was forthcoming. However, assume that the new investment provides $8 instead of the $4 needed to fill the gap. Excess purchasing power in the amount of $4 would be created to purchase the available goods and services without a corresponding increase in production. Consider what you would do if the Jones Corporation found itself facing this type of economic condition. You might react by increasing prices and/or by increasing production to take advantage of the obvious demand for Jones products. But before you made the decision to increase production, you would have to refer to the reaction on the cost curves and flexible budget (Chapters 3 to 5 again). As long as price would support the increase in marginal cost as production increased, you could safely increase production with the existing plant. Increased production by your plant and others would create additional purchasing power and would likewise produce more goods for sale. If all plants and producers could do likewise, the difference in purchasing power created and the sales price of the goods created would help eliminate the excess purchasing power created by the new investment. That last sentence involves two big assumptions. The first assumption is that no new plants or "investments," as we have been using the term, will be made during the same period to compound the problem. The second assumption is that no purchasing power will be withdrawn from the market as sterile savings. (Sterile savings alone would help the inflation problem—but now we're balancing eggs.)

However, when the new plant that started this problem in the first instance by creating purchasing power in the amount of $8 instead of the $4 needed comes "on the line," that is, produces goods for sale in the marketplace, we are right back to the "gap" problem—bigger than ever.

It is clear to you that increasing Jones plant capacity is a more serious undertaking than we seemed to think as we plunged ahead with Chapters 5 and 6. It is clear to you that the economy must ebb and flow or plunge ahead and retract. This is clear because in a free economy the individual and/or combined judgment of those making investment decisions could not be expected to provide the new purchasing power exactly when needed and exactly in the proper amount. Too much "new investment" will cause dislocations, as will too little new investment. In a completely self-regulatory economy, that is, one with no governmental activity to encourage or discourage new investment, dislocations appear inevitable.

In addition, some inflation is to be expected as the economy moves toward full employment. You recalled again what happens to the marginal cost curve in a "typical" manufacturing operation as production moves toward full capacity. The diseconomies of scale set in, bringing premium overtime pay for labor and increased maintenance cost beyond normal standards as well as other higher overhead and nonproductive costs. To permit this higher level of production, prices must increase. In the earlier analysis "demand" was pulling the price level up, and now costs would be pushing prices in the same direction! (More sophisticated examples could be used to illustrate a combination of both cost-push and demand-pull price increases or inflationary trends. However, it is quite clear that as the economy moves toward full employment, some inflation and thus higher prices can be expected, and it will become equally clear later that the reverse may not happen; that is, prices may not fall in a deflationary period.)

We will defer the analysis of this latter statement. First we must observe that individual businessmen will differ in their own self-interest about the desirability of inflation versus deflation. The question the individual businessman must ask is whether or not the price that must be paid for full employment is worth the benefits. A single businessman in his own self-interest will change his position on this question, perhaps several times, as his business affairs change. As an example, a businessman with a fixed obligation of, say, $150,000—perhaps a bank loan—would welcome slightly inflated prices for the same quality of goods sold. Why? If he could hold the level of increased costs below the increased change in price, he could repay the loan more quickly with the same volume of sales. To clearly and quickly illustrate the point, let us assume that the selling price of a product manufactured by our businessman was $1, with a profit of 50 cents that could be applied to reduce the loan. If the price increased to $1.35, with a resulting profit of 85 cents per unit, obviously the loan could be repaid more quickly.

If, on the other hand, the businessman had no fixed debt and instead had investments that paid a fixed rate of return, his self-interest would require him to resist inflationary tendencies. The answer to both problems is for the businessman to be knowledgeable and to conduct his business affairs in such a manner as to take advantage of any swing in the economy, either up or down. In addition, we do know that the government does get involved in economic matters. Therefore, the question What can and does government do in the attempt to control inflation or to stimulate a lagging economy? must be examined.

We are not purporting to judge whether or not governmental activity has been or is proper or improper, timely or ill timed. Rather, we are simply noting that government, in the recent past, has made efforts to both encourage and discourage private investment and will probably do so again. As an example, changes have been made in the income tax regulations that have provided:

1. An investment credit. When a new investment is made, a percentage of the new investment is allowed as a credit against income taxes actually due and payable to the government. In effect, this reduction represents a cash tax savings that can be viewed as a reduction in the purchase price or an increase in the return provided by the new investment or both.
2. Accelerated depreciation rates which, likewise, reduce taxes due during the early life of the investment. Cash is thus retained in the business entity when it may, perhaps, be needed most.
3. Tax cuts for all taxpayers which should stimulate purchasing power and indirectly induce investment.

Interestingly, all these measures have been reversed during periods when governmental officials and agencies have determined that the economy was "overheating" or growing too fast, that is, producing $8 when only

$4 was needed. Likewise, efforts have been made to discourage private investment by:

1. Increasing interest rates to make borrowing more expensive
2. Increasing national bank reserve requirements to dry up loanable funds
3. Tightening credit restrictions to discourage or make more difficult the expansion of credit

In addition to the above measures, government does provide purchasing power to the marketplace by public works, that is, the building of roads, parks, lakes, dams, education facilities, and other public projects.

It must be recognized also that these and other efforts by the government may not affect all business in the same manner. Larger business entities usually have multiple bank connections and usually represent a better risk. Therefore, a large percentage of available funds could be channeled to the larger enterprises. Smaller business entities, however, could be quickly and directly affected by government policy. As indicated earlier, each financial manager must analyze carefully not only his firm's position but also the possible position of the firm's customers. Thus, production schedules and credit policies may well be directly related.

It is clear that government and politics can and do play an important part in the operation of our economy. It is equally clear that activity by government plays an important role in the economic framework within which the financial executive must operate. We do not have to agree to explicit policies and/or determinations, but we must understand. Knowledge is strength. Also, it must be recognized that predicting governmental policy with respect to economic activity is not easily accomplished. Economic theory is one thing; practical politics is quite another! However, predict and forecast you must. Unfortunately, forecasting is an art and not a science. Forecasting involves informed instinct and intuition, if you will. Accurate predictions are not always possible since the assumptions which the forecaster is forced to make can seldom be made with a high level of confidence. Even if general assumptions with respect to such things as war and peace, governmental policies, and consumer tastes and desires could be accurately predicted, forecasting would still prove difficult. The economy is like a living organism, in that it evolves, adjusts, and reorients itself continually. Thus, you cannot simply assume that familiar relationships will continue to produce the same historical results. You must be familiar and astute with respect to the basic political philosophy of the governmental unit in office, and again, and as stated earlier, whether you agree or disagree is really immaterial. (We could continue on and on. However, we must return to your problem.)

The original problem was twofold. First, Jones was losing money on the last 15,000 units of normal sales as well as the last 20,000 units sold to Allied. Secondly, cash collections were not as prompt as our earlier experience had predicted. However, on the latter point, no real cash crisis was indicated for the near future. The outlook seemed somewhat brighter because governmental monetary policy, which had been fostering higher interest rates and corresponding smaller supplies of money, appeared to be relaxing considerably. We decided on this latter point to sit tight a bit longer. We have enjoyed a fine relationship with our customers and in fact could afford the longer payment period. However, constant vigilance would be exercised with more personal contact by the sales representative.

You remembered very vividly what personal contact could accomplish! During your early experience with Jones, a representative of one of Jones' creditors called to inquire about payment. You spent every bit of an hour with him explaining why Jones couldn't pay at that time. You gave him every rational reason possible. At the end of the 60 minutes, he looked at you. After a 60-second pause that seemed like an hour, he simply said very calmly, "Tom, when do I get my money?" You got up, took him to the bank, and arranged for the $3,200 loan. There was no fuss, no muss, no loud words—just a request: "When do I get my money?" A couple of hours later both of you were having dinner together, and soon he was on the plane home. His manner and attitude had won your respect and a little of your credit reserve.

The price-level problem was another matter. The first step toward solving this problem will be to analyze the type of economic market or markets in which Jones is selling. It's late for that now and I must go. I have an early foursome tomorrow!

MARKET STRUCTURE AND PRICES

The next morning you started in earnest to examine this important question. In essence, the problem requires that you determine, if possible, what sort of and how much economic power, if any, Jones has in the economic market or markets within which it sells its product. If Jones Electronic indeed has some economic power, it can increase its selling prices and perhaps retain the same sales and/or income level. The answer to the question of whether Jones has economic power will depend upon the availability to our customers of "good substitute products" from other manufacturers. As an example, if we were dealing with a standardized product, and if there were many manufacturers who were selling exactly the same product that Jones manufactures, these competing firms could limit our ability to control price. If new firms could easily enter the market because the financial and technical requirements were not prohibitive for making the product, we would be in a difficult position to raise prices. We could reasonably assume that these competitors or potential competitors would seek out our customers and the competition would prevent sales prices from increasing. If all these factors were present, economists would say that we would be selling in a perfectly competitive economic market.

Monopolistic Competition

Fortunately, however, the Jones organization does not deal in a standardized product. In fact, in our economy today, it is difficult to find many industries that truly do deal with a standardized product. There are a few, such as basic coal, aluminum, and pig iron. (Agricultural products are usually cited as standardized products. However, in many instances even these products are differentiated by labels, slogans, and trademarks.) We would be hard pressed to find many standardized products of the type envisioned in a perfectly competitive economic market. Almost every producer takes pride in the fact that his product is different and is the "best." Economists would term an economic market which is characterized by many sellers, product differentiation, and ease of entry as *monopolistic competition.* The term "monopolistic" is used because to the extent that a producer can convince the consumer that his product is "best," the producer has a monopolistic relationship with that customer. As an example, if you thought Lone Valley cheddar cheese was the best cheddar cheese on the market, the producer could perhaps increase his price 1, 2, 5, 10, or 25 cents per pound and continue to retain your business. However, for most customers there would be a limit to the increase because of the availability of good substitute products; thus the term "monopolistic competition." The Jones Electronic Corporation has made every effort to differentiate its product. If it is to exercise any control over its selling price, the corporation must continue to demonstrate that its product and/or service is different from and better than other products in the industry. There are various methods used to create buyers' preference. Generally, these methods are designed to indicate that "our product is the best." Advertising is essential. However, what is "best" is a subjective determination. Each of us may have his own idea about what is "best." Our own judgment will, no doubt, change from time to time. As an example, we may not wish to purchase extremely durable clothing for our children. Children grow rapidly. We may not wish to pay the higher price for a coat with a five-year guarantee unless the coat can be handed down to other members of the family. The "best" napkin may be a lacy linen one. For many purposes, however, a paper napkin can be more useful.

What is "best" may be a simple psychological reaction. The local drugstore may offer two or more different brands of aspirin that have been tested and certified to contain equal drug content. Brand A may give you complete satisfaction. Other customers may insist upon Brand B. Whether or not the actual choice is based upon valid or invalid reasons makes no real difference to the seller. The intended result is the same—larger volume, higher prices, or both.

There are other factors responsible for a buyer's preference for one product or one producer rather than another product or producer.

1. *Location.* We may prefer to buy from a particular store or producer because of the convenience of location. Convenient parking or drive-in facilities may also be available. Perhaps it is just a matter of the distance to another store. The prestige value of the particular location may also be a factor. The products may or may not be superior. In fact, they may well be inferior. The important consideration could be the prestige location and the label that indicates that the article was purchased there.
2. *Extra services.* A particular store may offer a dining room with fashion models strolling among the tables, a credit department, or baby-sitting service. Those extra services may or may not be worth paying for. To those without children, baby-sitting is not attractive. Perhaps we would prefer to eat elsewhere or we may not be interested in credit charges. On the other hand, these conveniences may be important to some buyers. Consequently, the establishment which offers such services becomes unique and achieves some real ability to charge higher prices.
3. *Atmosphere.* A particular store may provide soft or loud music throughout the shopping area. Attractive seasonal displays may add to or detract from comfort and pleasure. Cleanliness or the lack of cleanliness may influence preference for one store or another.
4. *Personality.* The personality and attitude of the sales personnel may be the basis for differentiation. As we all know, some salespeople are very pleasant and make an extra effort to please, while others can be quite rude.
5. *Premiums and gifts.* Some of us may be influenced in our preference of shopping areas or products by the premiums and gifts that are offered. Others may consider the premiums and gifts a nuisance and would avoid stores which offered them unless these same stores offered reduced prices on the merchandise required.

Oligopoly

We have not yet completely identified the type of economic market that describes the Jones Electronic Corporation's situation. There simply are not many producers that compete with the Jones Electronic Corporation. Patents and trademarks, as well as the technical "know-how," limit significantly the number of Jones' competitors. It is just not easy for new firms to enter the Jones market. In fact, there are only a "few" firms in the entire industry. This fact is significant. It is the basis for what economists call an *oligopolistic market.*

It is difficult to state explicitly what is meant by a "few sellers" or a "few producers." We cannot really define these terms with respect to oligopoly or an oligopolistic industry except to say there are a limited number of producers. We can add that we are describing a situation where each producer produces and/or sells a substantial part of the total industry production. Any one firm in the industry can influence the price of the product by a change in output.

Let us consider an example. If any of our "big four" automobile manufacturers were to flood the marketplace with a particular model, it is quite likely that prices would be forced down during and most assuredly at the end of the model year. This price reduction would seriously affect the selling price of competitive firms. The same could be said of the rubber, aluminum, basic steel, glass and cement industries.

How many, then, represent a "few"? The answer will vary with the industry. How many firms manufacture automobiles in this country—four or five? How many firms produce aluminum—three? How many basic steel producers are there—the big eight and the little eight? The significant point is that any one producer in an oligopolistic industry can drastically affect price by a change in the quantity of his production. This is in contrast to firms operating under perfect competition and monopolistic competition conditions because there are many sellers and good substitute products; only the most successful firms can manipulate selling price, and then only within a limited range.

Types of oligopoly. Oligopoly emphasizes a "few" sellers, and there may or may not be good substitute products. There are two types of oligopoly—pure and differentiated. The term "pure oligopoly" describes those firms that do manufacture a relatively standardized product such as pig iron, basic aluminum, plate glass, or cement. The differentiated oligopoly makes substantial efforts, through original design, planned obsolescence, and annual model changes, to differentiate one product from another. Product differentiation is clearly evident in the automobile, tobacco, rubber, and electrical appliance industries. (The analysis of product differentiation that we made when we examined monopolistic competition is clearly applicable to product differentiation under oligopoly and will not be repeated here.)

The key to the analysis of oligopoly lies in the fact that price cuts by one producer could lead to swift retaliation by other producers. The standard or normal pricing policy in oligopolistic industries is to maintain relatively high, stable prices.

The oligopolistic market appears to describe the Jones Electronic situation except in some very small local markets, where competition can be quite keen. Clearly, there are only a few main producers. Because of Jones' technical know-how, it is not easy for new firms to enter the market. However, although it is unlikely in the immediate future, it is possible that a better design for the product together with the right combination of know-how and capital could provide more major competition. On the other hand, in some geographical areas and with some customers, notably Allied, the Jones Electronic Corporation does have a near-monopoly situation.

Monopoly

A *monopolistic* market implies the existence of only one producer who in fact is the entire industry for a particular product or products. This type of market further assumes that entry into the market is extremely difficult. The Jones Electronic Corporation does not have a clear, absolute monopoly with Allied. Allied has a subsidiary corporation called Allied Development Corporation, or ADCO. ADCO, in fact, supplies the Jones Corporation with raw material and was originally set up to manufacture and supply the parent corporation with the parts and supplies that the Jones Corporation is presently supplying to Allied. ADCO, for some reason, could not and cannot compete with Jones. At this point in time, at least, ADCO simply supplies the raw material necessary for the Jones and other manufacturers' production processes. However, the very existence of ADCO places a restraint on Jones' ability to raise selling prices to Allied. At some point, it would become worthwhile for ADCO to manufacture the product that Jones is presently producing, and for its parent, Allied, to purchase from its subsidiary rather than from Jones.

PRICING

We can now return to our pricing problem. To do so, we must deal with the elasticity of the Jones demand curve. As we have seen, Jones does sell primarily but not completely in an oligopolistic economic market.

In those markets where Jones does not have an oligopolistic control, the answer may be simply that Jones has not made adequate effort to differentiate the Jones product. Therefore, Jones is probably limited to the price charged by local competition. (On the other hand, it is quite possible that the local competition feels that the price they can charge is limited by the Jones pricing policies!) We will proceed on the basis of the first assumption, namely, that the Jones price is limited by the price established by local competition.

Once these basic principles are recognized, the Jones firm has several alternatives in this particular market:

1. Maintain the established price and limit sales to the present level
2. Make a stronger effort to differentiate the Jones product
3. Abandon the market altogether

President Jones indicated that he did not intend to abandon these smaller markets and suggested that you provide him with a somewhat more detailed analysis of the second alternative above, namely, the possible effects of a stronger effort to differentiate our product. The answer to this question involves the marginal revenue that could be expected, balanced against the additional cost involved. It is quite possible that no additional manufacturing costs are involved. It may be simply a matter of additional sales effort!

The Price-Volume Relationship

You were now ready to reexamine the problem of possible changes in volume caused by a change in selling price. It is possible that quantity sold will remain constant at 130,000 units when the price is increased from \$6 to \$6.40 or to \$7.20. There is also the possibility, though an unlikely situation, that volume will remain at 130,000 units if all prices are reduced to \$5. In such a case, we would be dealing with a perfectly inelastic demand curve within the price range of \$5 to \$7.20. The situation is illustrated in Figure 10-1 by the straight line from *X*3 to *X*7.

A question then presents itself. Could we continue to increase or decrease price indefinitely with total volume remaining constant at 130,000 units? Realistically, if the price increased beyond some point, some substitute product would be used or developed or the end product would be redesigned (pure rubber versus synthetic rubber, nylon versus silk) and the volume sold by Jones would decrease (*X*5). Likewise, if the price per unit were dropped to some level below \$5, increased volume could be expected (*X*9).

(The slope of the firm's demand curve, or elasticity of the demand curve, is a measure of the success the nonmonopolistic seller has attained in establishing a preference for his product. The more inelastic the demand curve, the more successful the firm has been in establishing buyer's preference for its product.)

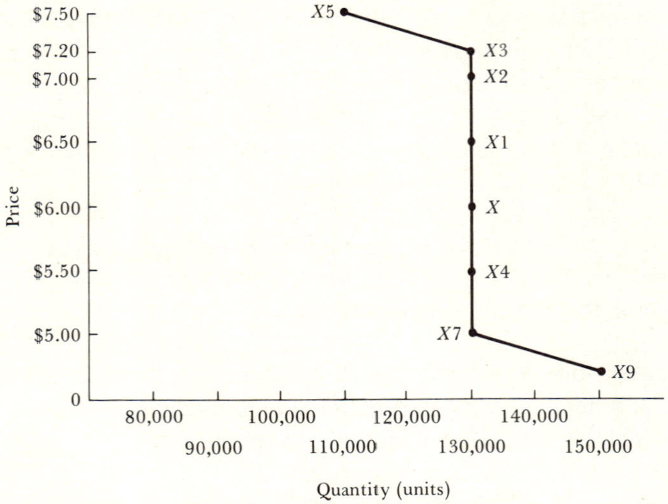

Figure 10-1 Normal sales; inelastic demand curve.

Thus, the picture we have drawn above indicates that we will sell exactly the same quantity of goods when the price varies from $5 to $7.20. If the price falls below $5 (toward *X*9), Jones may bring new customers into its market for the present product and possibly create new uses for the product which will attract new customers. Given this increase in volume, it is possible that we could supply lower-priced output at a profit. (Retailers would say they can now reach lower income levels.) When the price increases beyond $7.20 toward *X*5, we may eliminate some of our present customers either because they are purchasing elsewhere identical products at lower prices or because they are using cheaper substitutes. (Textbooks usually cite drugs to a drug addict or alcohol to an alcoholic as examples of products with a perfectly inelastic demand curve, *X*3 to *X*7. War material in time of war would certainly represent a class of products where price is immaterial since the need is great. However, any product which we think is badly needed and for which there is no close substitute will in the short run have an inelastic demand curve.)

In summary, we must know something about the elasticity of the Jones demand curve before we can at least start to analyze the problems involved in formulating any change in the selling price of Jones products. Some of the problems are subtle, while others are apparent. For example, we know from our earlier study of Chapter 3 that a firm will maximize profits when the quantity of units sold is at the point where marginal cost is equal to marginal revenue. You will recall that marginal cost is the addition to total cost caused by the production and/or sale of "one more unit." Likewise, marginal revenue is the addition to total revenue caused by the sale of "one more unit." This is the subtle import; and in the longer run this is the real significance of the elasticity of the demand curve. Jones is not in the business of increasing sales simply for the sake of increased sales—the name of the game is "increasing profits." This is what satisfies shareholders and keeps management in power.

Marginal and Average Revenue

Marginal revenue (average marginal revenue between two levels of production) is not hard to calculate once a given price has been determined. For example, at the $6 price you know that marginal revenue, or the addition to total revenue caused by the sale of "one more unit," is $6! The company cost curves and the flexible budget would clearly indicate the maximum limits of production and sales. However, while we are still in the planning and analyzing process, we should examine this marginal concept a little closer. You have prepared the price-quantity schedule illustrated below.

JONES ELECTRONIC CORPORATION
NORMAL SALES
PRICE-QUANTITY SCHEDULE

Price	Quantity, Units	Total Revenue	Average Marginal Revenue (Average Addition to Total Revenue Caused by Sale of One More Unit)
$7.20	80,000	$576,000	
			$ 74,000 = 20,000 units × $3.70
6.50	100,000	650,000	
			$ 130,000 = 30,000 units × $4.33
6.00	130,000	780,000	
			$ 70,000 = 40,000 units × $1.75
5.00	170,000	850,000	
			$—17,000 = 5,000 units × $—3.40
4.00	175,000	833,000	

When this schedule is plotted on a graph, it appears as shown in Figure 10-2.

As we reexamine the price-quantity schedule presented above, it is significant to keep in mind that "all managerial decisions are marginal." We are always concerned with the effects of "one more of this or one more of that" (a branch sales office, a new production unit, the sale of one more unit of production). With respect to the problem at hand, we anticipate that two things will happen when we increase our selling

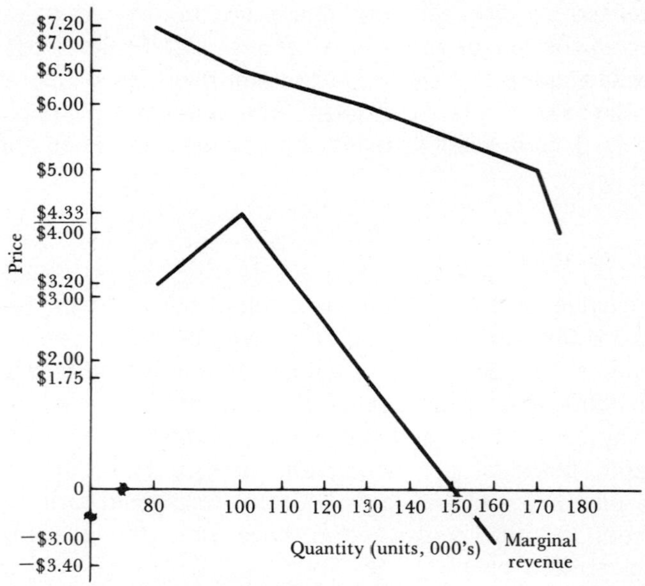

Figure 10-2 Jones Electronic Corporation normal sales price-quantity schedule.

price from \$6 to \$6.50 per unit with the corresponding decrease in anticipated sales.

1. Revenue increase = 100,000 units × 50¢ = \$ 50,000
2. Revenue loss = 30,000 units × \$6 = −180,000

Net change in total revenue (decrease) = \$−130,000

Average revenue lost per unit for 30,000 units = $\dfrac{-\$130{,}000}{30{,}000 \text{ units}} = -\$4.33$

By looking at the same schedule from another point of view, it is clear that if we were selling 80,000 units at \$7.20 per unit and were contemplating selling 100,000 units at \$6.50 per unit, two things would happen again. We would lose 70 cents per unit on each of the 80,000 presently sold (\$56,000), but gross revenue would increase \$6.50 for each of the anticipated additional 20,000 units (\$130,000). Total marginal income would be \$74,000 or \$3.70 per unit. As you know, marginal revenue is only one factor in the analysis of the effects of a price change. The marginal cost, or the change in the total cost caused by producing or not producing, is the other factor we must consider.

Economists would properly say that the Jones organization could continue to manufacture and sell their product as long as marginal revenue is equal to or greater than marginal cost. As indicated earlier, profits would be maximized at that level of sales where marginal revenue is equal to marginal cost. However, economists would be quick to point out that the estimate of anticipated changes in volume that will result when price is changed is just that—an estimate. Very few, if any, businessmen know the elasticity of their demand curve as definitely as we have set it forth in the estimates above. More often than not, the great majority of businessmen do not know or have the least idea about their elasticity factor. Does this mean that all our analysis has been nothing more than an academic exercise? The answer is, certainly not!

You can calculate as illustrated below the exact number of unit sales Jones can lose and still earn the same total profit if prices are increased from $6 to $6.50 per unit:

Present selling price	$6.00	New selling price	$6.50
Average total cost	3.10		3.10
Contribution per unit	$2.90		$3.40

New contribution = $3.40; old contribution = $2.90.

New contribution is 117.241 percent of old contribution: $\frac{\$3.40}{\$2.90} = 117.241\%$

Present normal sales $= \frac{130{,}000}{117.241\%} = 110{,}882$ units

130,000 units
−110,882
19,118 units

As a first approximation it would appear that the Jones organization can stand a decrease in total volume of some 19,118 units and still earn the same gross profit that was earned before the price increase. However, in this particular case there is more to the analysis than that fact. In addition, Jones will eliminate the loss being sustained on the last 15,000 units being currently sold at the $6 price. This will cause an increase in gross profit as the loss is eliminated. (You did not consult the cost curves or flexible budget to determine the per-unit loss on the last 15,000 units sold at $6, nor did I call it to your attention. Without doing so now, in order to avoid further detail at this point, take my word for it, the loss was 20 cents per unit, or a total of $3,000. This $3,000 would really be additional profit.)

As indicated above, the essence of the calculation is that if you set aside the present $3,000 loss and if the price for "normal" sales is increased from $6 to $6.50, we must sell 110,882 units instead of the current 130,000 units in order to realize the same gross revenue, providing average total cost per unit will remain at approximately $3.10.

Units		**Contribution**		**Gross Profit**
110,882	×	$3.40	=	$376,998
130,000	×	$2.90	=	$377,000

These calculations provide a minimum parameter. Should Jones' sales volume decrease, as a result of a price increase, by more than 19,118 units, there will be a loss of $2.90 per unit! On the other hand, every sales unit Jones can retain above the minimum figure of 110,882 units will contribute $3.40 toward increased profits. Neither the economist, the accountant, nor the statistician can answer the elasticity question with an absolute degree of certainty. However, we are establishing basic parameters. The minimum parameter is the fact that sales volume must not fall below 110,882 units!

The maximum parameter, or the maximum that Jones can sell at the new price of $6.50 per unit, will depend entirely upon the marginal cost movement as production and sales increase, if they do! We can increase sales to the point but only to the point where marginal cost is equal to marginal revenue.

We have made some progress in understanding our problem, but we haven't supplied a concrete answer. We have established minimum and maximum parameters. The marketing department, sales manager, or whatever or whoever, must make this basic decision. You cannot do so. However, you do have basic data upon which to base the final decision. However, that is enough for today. I'm going home—I have a turf inspection date!

ADMINISTERED PRICES

As you sat around discussing the pricing problem with colleagues in the coffee shop the following day, the matter of administered prices was brought up. A question was raised concerning the Jones Electronic Corporation's ability to administer their selling prices. A second inquiry promptly came: "What in the world are you talking about? What is an 'administered price'?" You began by explaining that administered prices involve what is known as "target pricing" or a "target return on investment or sales." A target price is calculated to provide either a predetermined percentage return on capital invested or a predetermined percentage of the sales value as profit. You explained that while the theory and concept in the abstract are relatively simple, the detailed calculations and judgment factors can be quite complicated and complex. To implement the system, each Jones marketing area, division, and region must first prepare a forecast of the probable demand for the product for some period of time in the future, usually annual. This forecast is then translated into a percentage of total plant capacity necessary to produce the volume required. The flexible budget is then used to arrive at the fixed and variable cost at the required level of production. The desired return on investment is then determined. As an illustration, you used the reverse side of several coffee shop place mats. Your illustration was as follows:

Given:	1. Practical plant capacity	1,000 units
	2. Total plant investment	$10,000
	3. Variable cost per unit	$5
	4. Total fixed cost	$1,000
	5. Production per forecast	40% or 30% (of plant capacity)
	6. Desired return on investment	8%
	7. No consideration of tax matters	

Administered price determination

Production per forecast:	40% 400 Units	30% 300 Units
Fixed cost per unit ($1,000 ÷ 400 and 300)	$2.50	$ 3.33
Variable cost per unit	5.00	5.00
8% return on investment, or $800		
$\frac{\$800}{400} = \$2 \quad \frac{\$800}{300} = \$2.67$	2.00	2.67
Selling price as "administered"	$9.50	$11.00

It is quite significant and quite clear that if the selling price is determined on the basis of the sale of 400 units, the "profit" on the 401st unit and all additional units produced will increase substantially. Why is this so? Because total fixed cost and required return on investment have been recovered with the sale of the first 400 units. The differential or marginal cost of the 401st unit will be only variable cost. "Profits" will increase by the amount originally allocated to fixed cost per unit plus the required return on investment per unit. In our example at 40 percent capacity the selling price was $9.50. The additional cost for "one more unit" of the 401st unit is the $5.00 variable cost. Economic profit on the 401st unit then is $4.50, or 47.36 percent of the selling price. All sales beyond the 400-unit level will result in additional profit at the rate of 47.36 percent of selling price. [A major feature of this pricing technique is the fact that as volume decreases, prices increase! Does this fact appear to have any significance in explaining increasing prices (for example, inflation) in a depressed market situation as illustrated by the United States economy in 1969/1970? This is not an economics course, or we would discuss the effectiveness of monetary and fiscal policy as an anti-inflation tool! You as a financial vice-president cannot ignore these factors—discuss it with your economics professor.]

A remark was made that if the Jones organization adopted this pricing method, there would be an almost guaranteed profit! You replied that this was not quite so because of the old bugaboo—the elasticity of the demand for Jones' production. On yet another place mat you drew an illustration of the possible demand curve facing the Jones organization (see Figure 10-3).

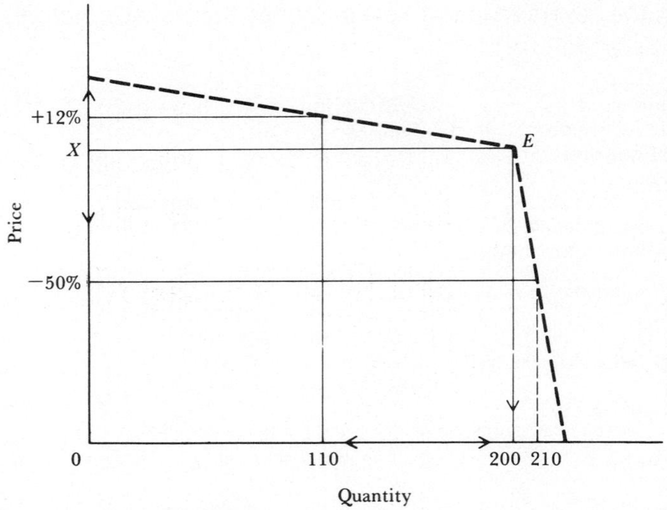

Figure 10-3 Typical oligopolistic demand curve.

Point *E* on the illustration represents two things. First, it indicates the price *X* that the firm is presently charging. Second, it shows that the firm is producing 200 units. As we have drawn the picture, a $12\frac{1}{2}$ percent increase in Jones' price could result in a loss of 45 percent of the firm's total market if other producers do not follow the price increase and if Jones' customers switch suppliers because of the price increase. Also, the illustration shows that the firm will increase sales only some 5 percent if it reduces prices 50 percent and the other producers of good substitute products retaliate and also lower prices. The 5 percent increase perhaps represents additional sales to lower-income consumers who come into the market for the first time or, perhaps, present consumers who will purchase an additional unit (for example, a family would purchase a second small low-priced car to eliminate their teen-agers' demands on the family car).

The above illustration explains exactly the Jones dilemma. Would our competitors follow our lead and also raise their prices? In the event our competitors did not, have we established a strong enough product differentiation and buyers' preference to retain the volume necessary to meet the minimum parameter established earlier; that is, would sales drop more than the units calculated earlier that you could lose and still earn the same dollar profit as earned prior to the price increase?

MARKET SUMMARY

The coffee break turned out to be considerably longer than you had anticipated. However, it provided a good forum for an informal discussion of problems with your colleagues. Returning to your office, you continued to reflect upon the significance of the various types of economic markets and the relationship of these markets to the probable or possible elasticity characteristics of the Jones demand curve. The entire picture is considerably clearer than it was some pages ago. You have summarized the characteristics of the Jones firm and the market within which it is selling as follows:

1. The Jones Corporation is clearly establishing a buyer's preference for its product. The reason for this is twofold. First, we have established a reputation for quality. The percentage of "rejects" or components not meeting exacting specifications is extremely low. This saves our customers both time and money. Second, by careful planning and by a conscious effort we render what one customer has described as "superb service." (As an example, service is provided 24 hours per day, 365 days per year. Members of our seven-man shipping department "have the duty" on a rotating basis every night and all day Saturdays, Sundays, and holidays. By this we mean the "duty man" has a portable radio receiving set that can be taken to his home, in his car, or to the golf course. The company has a telephone answering service for off-duty hours. The operator can call over the radio and notify the "duty man" that he has a call. President Jones himself insists upon taking a turn, and on more than one occasion he has returned to the warehouse on Saturday afternoon to supply a customer with a badly needed component which if not available would have shut down the customer's production for several days.)
2. There are only a "few" competitors. We have applied for patent rights to a new process that will assure very few competitors, if any, if the final product is as good as research indicates.

We are clearly in an oligopolistic market. President Jones indicated that there are not more than four national firms that are presently furnishing competition.

It was decided to call a general sales meeting to discuss the matter of increased selling prices. President Jones has already discussed the matter with Allied, and they have agreed that a 15 to 20 percent increase in the price Allied pays Jones would be acceptable if we would establish a research center. President Jones had been planning to do this very thing for some time. This was not a major obstacle, and it was a favorable beginning. Normal sales may be another matter. The meeting was recessed for two weeks to give each salesman time to call personally upon the larger accounts and to sound out customer reaction to the new price schedule. The sales manager was requested to summarize the customer reaction and report back to your office.

After several agonizing months, prices were increased 20 percent to Allied and 20 percent on "normal" sales. In general, the reaction from the Jones customers was "reluctant but agreeable." Fortunately, our competitors did likewise. The firm that started in the garage was now leading the industry! (At least temporarily.) This was quite a boost for company prestige. Some of you were beginning to feel that in the industry, perhaps, you were number one!

Even the golf score improved. Except for a 35-foot putt on the eighteenth green, I would have beaten a rival of long standing (you were lucky) for the first time in months. That putt tied the score at 95 each. (Editor's note—"some duffers!")

QUESTIONS FOR DISCUSSION

1. What is the significance of the "elasticity of the demand curve"?
2. What are the characteristics of the following economic markets:
   a. Perfect competition
   b. Monopolistic competition
   c. Oligopoly
   d. Monopoly
3. In general, in which of the above economic markets does the Jones Electronic Corporation sell?
4. What is the significance of the answer to Question 3 above?
5. What is meant by "marginal revenue"?
6. What is the significance of the answer to Question 5 above?
7. Why would profits be maximized when marginal cost equals marginal revenue?
8. What parameters did the Jones organization establish with respect to the pricing decision? How?
9. What is an administered price?
10. How are administered prices determined?
11. What is the significance of an administered price?
12. What is a "price leader," and in what type of economic market is it possible for him, or it, to operate?

PROBLEMS

1. A. Jones owns and operates 11 dry-cleaning pickup stores that feed a central plant. The central plant does all the cleaning and finishing and delivers the finished product to the stores for distribution to the customers. The plant is operating at about 70 percent of capacity. A standard price of $1 per man's suit or lady's dress and 50 cents per man's trousers or lady's skirt or sweater is currently being charged at all stores. Jones has the feeling that several of the locations may have different demand

elasticity characteristics. He began to experiment with his prices at one location with the following results: As price was increased beyond the $1.35 price, he also upgraded the appearance of the store as well as his packaging material.

Price		Average Volume per Week
January	$1.00	325 units
February	1.10	325 units
March	1.25	360 units
April	1.35	370 units
May	1.50	500 units
June	1.75	510 units
July	2.00	300 units

What were the average revenue and the marginal revenue for each of the seven months?

2. Recognizing the obvious success of his elasticity test of the first store, he tried the same price schedules in a second store with the following results:

Price		Average Volume per Week
August	$1.00	200 units
September	1.10	190 units
October	1.25	150 units
November	0.90	225 units
December	0.80	550 units
January	0.80	540 units

What were the average revenue and the marginal revenue for each of the seven months?

3. Having had the two different experiences with exactly the same product at the two different locations, Jones decided to plan a little more before he made the third attempt to test the elasticity of the demand curve at a third location. His records revealed the following:

Price, $1.00 Weekly volume, 300 units

He posed this question to you. How many units must I sell at a price of $1.20 to have the same total revenue that I now have from this store?

4. At a fourth location Jones made plans to increase his price from $1 to $1.15. However, his only competitor, who was currently charging 85 cents per unit, refused to increase his price; Jones, after requesting the competitor again and again to raise his price 15 cents per unit to $1 per unit and to maintain his price differential, decided to cut his prices 50 percent in an attempt to force the competitor to increase prices to $1 per unit. Jones figured his costs were 90 percent fixed and the variable cost was equal to 10 percent based on the $1 price. His current

volume at this store was 400 units weekly. His plant capacity would tolerate only an additional 700 units weekly. Several questions occurred to him, however.

a. How many additional units must he sell to break even on the price war, that is, maintain the same profit?
b. What would be the maximum profit he could expect, if any, if the plant reached 100 percent of capacity because of increased volume at the price-war price?

5. Jones' volume did reach capacity as a result of the price war in Problem 4 above. In the process, he thought he had learned a valuable lesson. He decided to increase the 80-cent price referred to in Problem 2 to $1 and to settle on the $1.75 price in Problem 1.

Given the pertinent data in Problems 1 and 2 above, could his plan to occasionally use a half-price sale at the store with the $1.75 price as an advertising gimmick result in the same or more overall profit? How? Why or why not?

REFERENCES

Chamberlin, E. H.: "The Theory of Monopolistic Competition," 8th ed., Harvard University Press, Cambridge, Mass., 1962.

DeLeeuw, F., and E. M. Gramlich: The Federal Reserve–MIT Econometric Model, *Federal Reserve Bulletin,* January, 1968, pp. 11–40.

Eisner, Robert: Factors Affecting the Level of Interest Rates, in "Savings and Residential Financing," pp. 28–40, U.S. Savings and Loan League, Chicago, 1968.

Federal Home Loan Bank Board Staff: Cycles in Mortgage Credit Availability and the 1966 Experience, *A Study of Mortgage Credit,* pp. 19–40, Subcommittee on Housing and Urban Affairs, Committee on Banking and Currency, United States Senate, May 22, 1967, Washington; reprinted in W. L. Smith, and R. L. Tergen (eds.), "Readings in Money, National Income, and Stabilization Policy," rev. ed., pp. 433–448, Richard D. Irwin, Inc., Homewood, Ill., 1970.

Freund, William C., and Edward D. Zinbarg: Application of Flow of Funds to Interest-rate Forecasting, *Journal of Finance,* vol. XVIII, pp. 231–248, May, 1963.

Friedman, Milton: Factors Affecting the Level of Interest Rates, in "Savings and Residential Financing," pp. 10–27, U.S. Savings and Loan League, Chicago, 1968.

Friend, Irwin (director): "Study of the Savings and Loan Industry," submitted to the Federal Home Loan Bank Board, vols. I to IV, U.S. Government Printing Office, 1969.

Kaplan, A. D. H., J. B. Dirlam, and R. F. Lanzilloti: "Pricing in Big Business," The Brookings Institution, Washington, 1958.

Kuhlman, John M., and Gordon S. Skinner: "The Economic System," rev. ed., chap. 7, Richard D. Irwin, Inc., Homewood, Ill., 1964.

Leftwich, Richard H.: "An Introduction to Economic Thinking," chap. 11, Holt, Rinehart and Winston, Inc., New York, 1969.

Lewis, John P.: Short-term General Business Conditions Forecasting: Some Comments on Method, *Journal of Business,* vol. XXXII, pp. 343–356, October, 1962.

Liv, T. C.: An Exploratory Quarterly Econometric Model of Effective Demand in the Postwar U.S. Economy, *Econometric,* July, 1963, pp. 301–348.

Lloyd, Cliff: "Microeconomic Analysis," chap. 7, Richard D. Irwin, Inc., Homewood, Ill., 1967.

Machlup, Fritz: "The Political Economy of Monopoly," chap. 5, The Johns Hopkins Press, Baltimore, 1952.

Maisel, S. J.: A Theory of Fluctuations in Residential Construction Starts, *American Econometric Review,* June, 1963, pp. 359–383.

———: Nonbusiness Construction, in J. S. Duesenberry, G. Fromm, L. R. Klein, and E. Kuh (eds.), "The Brookings Quarterly Econometric Model of the United States," pp. 179–203, Rand McNally & Company, Chicago, and North-Holland Publishing Company, Amsterdam, 1965.

———: The Effects of Monetary Policy on Expenditures in Specific Sectors of the Economy, *Journal of Political Economy,* part II, July-August, 1968, pp. 796–814.

Massel, Mark S.: "Competition and Monopoly," The Brookings Institution, Washington, 1962.

Mayer, Thomas: Trade Credit and the Discriminatory Effects of Monetary Policy, *National Banking Review,* vol. III, pp. 543–545, June 1966.

Muth, R. F.: The Demand for Nonfarm Housing, in A. C. Harberger (ed.), "The Demand for Durable Goods," pp. 29–96, The University of Chicago Press, Chicago, 1960.

Silber, William L., and Murray E. Polakoff: The Differential Effects of Tight Money: An Econometric Study, *Journal of Finance,* vol. XXV, pp. 83–97, March, 1970.

Sparks, G. R.: A Model of the Mortgage Market and Residential Construction Activity, *1967 Proceedings of the Business and Economic Statistics Section,* pp. 77–83, American Statistical Association, Washington, 1968.

Stigler, G. J.: The Kinky Oligopoly Demand Curve and Rigid Prices, *The Journal of Political Economy,* vol. LV, 1947.

Stocking, George W., and Myron W. Watkins: "Monopoly and Free Enterprise," The Twentieth Century Fund, New York, 1951. Reprinted Greenwood Press, New York. 1968.

Sylos-Labini, Paolo: "Oligopoly and Technical Progress," part 1, rev. ed., Harvard University Press, Cambridge, Mass., 1969.

Tussing, A. Dale: Can Monetary Policy Influence the Availability of Credit? *Journal of Finance,* vol. XXI, pp. 1–13, March, 1966.

Winger, Alan R.: Regional Growth Disparities and the Mortgage Market, *Journal of Finance,* vol. XXIV, pp. 659–662, September, 1969.

Chapter Eleven

FINANCIAL STATEMENT ANALYSIS

At the next meeting of the Jones Electronic executive committee, President Jones congratulated the entire management team for the excellent guidance and the tremendous success of the past $2\frac{1}{2}$ years. Operating statements were reviewed. It was almost a jovial party. Everyone was patting each other on the back. The Jones Electronic Corporation had arrived, there was no doubt about that. As the meeting was breaking up, President Jones asked you to stop in his office in the morning at your convenience.

As you were reviewing your outgoing correspondence the following morning, President Jones walked into your office. He requested that you speed up your efforts to acquire the additional staff in order to free yourself from the details that have occupied most of your time. He indicated that he would like you to accept 5,000 shares of his personally owned Jones common stock as a bonus (this has the effect of Jones' contributing his 5,000 shares to the company and the company's issuing the stock to you as compensation for services rendered); also, at the next full meeting of the board of directors, he would offer a resolution giving you the option of purchasing 20,000 additional shares from the corporation at its present book value with restrictions as to its disposability. For the most part, this simply means that if you want to sell the stock, the Jones Corporation has the first option to buy. There is at the present no market value for the Jones stock, but you know that with the earnings record, both past and projected, the book value of the stock would be considerably lower than what investors would be willing to pay. However, we will examine the implications of this situation later.

Both the shares issued to you as a bonus and the option to purchase additional shares below fair market value represent a recognition by President Jones of your past performance and the introduction by him of added incentives to prompt you to continue your efforts. As things stand now, your financial future is intimately associated with the success of the firm. You recall that in the past, the goal of your activities was to maximize the value of the firm as represented by the value of its common stock. This goal is an even more personal one now. President Jones is, you conclude, not only a capable engineer but also a capable, industrious psychologist.

As President Jones was leaving the office, he dropped a real bombshell. Allied, a Swiss corporation (Switzerland is a low foreign income tax country) and our best customer, owns a 60 percent interest in the firm that is supplying our raw material, Allied Development Corporation, commonly known as ADCO. ADCO is a relatively small integrated company that was developed by Allied to manufacture and supply the parent company with the very products we are selling to Allied. The remaining 40 percent interest in ADCO is owned by four of the officers of Allied. For some reason, ADCO was never able to fulfill its role in Allied's overall plans. In fact, it was the inability of ADCO to supply Allied's requirements that forced Allied to turn to the J. T. Jones organization, now the Jones Electronic Corporation, for its raw material.

President Jones stated that he had spent most of yesterday afternoon at lunch with the president of Allied. At this time he was "advised" that a high-level decision had been made by Allied either to (1) buy out the Jones Electronic Corporation, (2) arrange a merger with the Jones Corporation, or (3) arrange a sale of the entire ADCO operation to the Jones Corporation. President Jones indicated that he was not interested in selling or merging at this time, but would consider purchasing ADCO. He requested you to look into the proposition. The asking price is $5 million. Until now you thought you had financing problems. As a famous Broadway performer once said, "You ain't seen nothin' yet."

As always, there will probably be several avenues we can explore that will result in several alternative courses of action. Again, we must build a framework within which to work.

A FRAMEWORK FOR ACQUISITIONS

In the past you have fruitfully approached the solution of your operating and financial problems by creating a basic framework within which your ultimate decision was finally reached. The same methodology is also appropriate in this situation. Like the successful quarterback, you go with what has been good to you in the past.

Since you first began your career with Jones Electronic, you have faced those problems which affect most growing enterprises. Your decisions have always emphasized the proper balancing of a desire for increased growth and a responsibility to realize this goal in a manner consistent with the preservation and enhancement of profits. You have been quick to recognize that truly desirable growth must be the product of careful planning and control.

Effective planning for organizational growth must, necessarily, consider and evaluate a large number of alternative procedures and strategies. The first, and in some cases most important, consideration deals with our own conception of our industry and product mix. How broad should our operations be and what markets should we serve? If we narrowly define our goals and our industry, we have simultaneously restricted our potential for growth. For example, if the Xerox Corporation viewed itself as simply a manufacturer of office duplicating equipment, its potential growth, even assuming a complete dominance of this sector of the office equipment industry by Xerox, would be limited. This limitation would also have a significant impact on earnings per share and the current high price of the firm's common stock. How does Xerox view itself and its product mix? The philosophy of the firm is that its business is to help people better understand each other. Its industry is not simply office equipment; rather, it is graphic communications. Given this conception of self and industry, it is easy to see that growth potential is limited only by the resourcefulness of the organization.

In general, then, corporate growth is a function of the discovery of opportunities and the existence of the capability and talent required to exploit those opportunities. This final phrase is important. No corporation can be all things to all people, and more than one financial disaster has resulted from such attempts. While the discovery of opportunities for growth should and does receive emphasis, we must also assess the organization's strengths and weaknesses, which will largely determine the firm's success or failure in taking advantage of newly discovered opportunities.

The decision we must make with respect to ADCO calls for a determination of our corporate goals and a delineation of our own concept of what industry or industries we should serve and the manner in which we ultimately hope to serve them. If the acquisition of ADCO is compatible with these conceptions and goals, we may fruitfully consider the terms under which such an acquisition could be made. If, on the other hand, this initial filtering or screening device reveals the acquisition to be potentially contradictory in nature to our ultimate goals, negotiations should cease.

At our behest, President Jones called a meeting of the executive committee to discuss these issues. At the beginning of the meeting, each member of the policy committee gave his views with respect to his image of the firm and what he felt are its ultimate goals. The discussion was revealing. An outsider would scarcely believe that these executives work for the same firm. At one end of the spectrum our production manager believed the firm was now and would in the future be simply a component supplier and small subcontractor within a sector of the aerospace industry. He further believed that the potential size of this market is controlled almost exclusively by federal commitments to the manned space program. When this view was expounded, our sales manager appeared shocked. He indicated that such a view, although consistent with our present product mix, was certainly contrary to our ongoing research in product development for the consumer electronics industry. It was his view that the firm's position as an aerospace subcontractor was only the most efficient means by which the size, experience, and resources required for subsequent participation in the area of consumer electronics could be generated.

From the point of view of the production manager, the utilization of our resources to purchase ADCO would be quite consistent with our position as a subcontractor in the aerospace industry. ADCO would provide the added plant capacity. On the other hand, such a utilization from the point of view of our sales manager would be unwise, in that it would further delay our entry into the consumer electronics field because, in his judgment, all our resources could be tied up for a considerable period of time.

The views which were expressed revealed the fact that certain communications problems existed. We might not all be headed in the same direction. President Jones was quick to grasp this fact. He indicated that he had always had, in his own mind, a concept of what our corporate goals should be. "I thought that each of you shared this common outlook, and so I never made a point of articulating my ideas." He then began to discuss, for the benefit of the entire committee, his own concept of corporate development. Everyone listened carefully. President Jones does own 95 percent of the firm's stock, and, at this point at least, his ideas are the firm's ideas. But he's always willing to listen and has changed his mind before. However, you could have heard a pin drop as he continued. In his view, the firm must develop along a broad base which emphasizes the firm's strong points, which are:

1. A high level of expertise in applied electronics research with a specific orientation toward communication systems and telemetry devices.

2. An extemely efficient production staff and plant which allow the firm to realize profits in areas which have proved unprofitable for major contractors. The example of ADCO's failure is proof of this factor.
3. A young but sophisticated management team which provides the organization with the high level of flexibility necessary for goal achievement.

On the other hand, the president recognizes that we have certain weaknesses:

1. We have not yet developed a sound product distribution system and have relied largely on contractual sales to a limited number of prime contractors.
2. We have no real strength in the area of consumer sales and marketing.

He continued by stating that any plans for growth, if they are to be successful, will have to emphasize building on our strengths rather than our weaknesses. Growth, he feels, will be a function of increased research and continued emphasis on our production capabilities. The two are related. The current Jones productive efficiency is providing funds, a part of which is being devoted to research. This research, it is hoped, will create additional and more profitable employment of our productive facilities. He would like to continue in this direction with open-ended horizons. In essence, "come up with an idea that has been carefully researched, convince the executive committee, and Jones Electronic Corporation will forge ahead with it as fast as resources [and he smiled as he said this] and liquidity will permit."

By the time the meeting adjourned, general agreement had been reached with regard to corporate goals. It had been determined that Jones Electronic serves the communication industry in the capacity of a sophisticated subcontractor of highly technical components. In the future, it is hoped that internal research will allow the firm to produce and market integrated communication systems to customers in many industries.

A major step has been taken to put our proposed purchase of ADCO into perspective. An overall coporate policy with respect to growth has been conceived and, more important, successfully communicated. An assessment of the organization's major strengths and weaknesses has also been made. What more remains to be done before we can begin our specific consideration of the Allied proposal? President Jones really answered this question: "Research it and convince the executive committee."

The takeover of ADCO will be largely a financial operation. It is an operation of considerably larger scope than we have ever undertaken. However, we are not unfamiliar with decisions involving choices between alternatives. After all, we have had sufficient exposure to this kind of decision making throughout our capital budgeting process. Can we not transfer much of what we learned in capital budgeting and apply that knowledge in the area of acquisitions? The answer is yes, we can. An acquisition is an investment. It involves an expenditure of funds or corporate credit in order to secure an asset which offers a level of returns over time. In a larger firm an acquisition could well be one of the many proposals considered by the capital budgeting committee of the firm. You are the capital budgeting committee for the Jones Corporation! We are in this case making a choice between doing something and doing nothing. If the acquisition proves to be acceptable, it will mean that the firm is better off with ADCO than without it. How much better off will depend on the terms under which ADCO is acquired and the operating results which it achieves in future periods.

In substance, the foregoing raises the basic question whether the acquisition of ADCO would be financially advantageous to the stockholders of the Jones Corporation. In short, would the acquisition increase the earnings per share? True, the acquisition will, no doubt, cause additional complex problems which will require additional efforts from the Jones management team. However, this is the penalty business establishments have to pay for growth in a complex competitive economy. The alternative is status quo, which means retrogression. Retrogression means eventual extinguishment in the economic arena.

We are familiar with our own operations, but we know little of ADCO's. Let us examine its balance sheet and income statement and see what information we can generate from these sources.

ANALYSIS OF FINANCIAL STATEMENTS

ADCO
Statement of Profit and Loss
For Year Ended October 31, 1970

Sales		$10,350,000
Cost of Goods Sold		10,338,000
Gross Profit		$ 12,000
General and Administrative Expense	$207,000	
Interest Expense	105,000	312,000
Net Loss		$ (300,000)

ADCO
Balance Sheet
As of October 1, 1970

Assets		**Liabilities**	
Cash	$ 362,000	Accounts Payable	$ 102,100
Marketable Securities	560,000*	Notes Payable	600,000
Accounts Receivable	76,000		
Inventory	125,000		
Patents	100		
Total Current Assets	$1,123,100	Total Current Liabilities	$ 702,100
Plant and Equipment Net	4,179,000	Mortgage Payable (6%)	1,600,000
		Total Liabilities	$2,302,100
		Capital	
		Common Stock	3,000,000
		Retained Earnings	None
Total Assets	$5,302,100	Total Liabilities and Capital	$5,302,100

* Includes $432,100 temporary investments which are immediately available or will be immediately available soon for the payment of current liabilities.

Ratio Analysis

Even casual and superficial glance at the above statements would indicate that something was radically wrong. Selling price too low? Costs too high? Interest-bearing debt too high? Perhaps so, and again maybe not any of these. Let's explore the situation further. You perhaps recall that during your school days certain ratios were used to analyze financial statements. Four types of ratios were usually prepared for analysis. There were (1) liquidity ratios, (2) leverage ratios, (3) activity ratios, and (4) profitability ratios. The accounting clerk prepared the following:

Liquidity ratios. The following financial ratios are designed to measure the firm's ability to meet its short-term liabilities or obligations. In addition, certain industry ratios are provided so that data generated with respect to ADCO may be compared with like data available for the entire industry.[1]

[1] Typical sources of such data are "Key Business Ratios in 125 Lines," Dun and Bradstreet, New York, and "Statement Studies," Robert Morris and Associates.

		Formula		ADCO Data	Industry Data
1.	Current ratio	$= \frac{\text{current assets}}{\text{current liabilities}}$	$= \frac{\$1{,}123{,}100}{\$\ 702{,}100}$	= 1.6 times	2 times
2.	Quick or acid-test ratio	$= \frac{\text{cash and liquid assets such as receivables less inventory}}{\text{current liabilities}}$	$= \frac{\$\ 998{,}100}{\$\ 702{,}100}$	= 1.42 times	1.5 times
3.	Inventory to working capital ratio	$= \frac{\text{inventories}}{\text{current assets (minus) current liabilities}}$	$= \frac{\$\ 125{,}000}{\$\ 421{,}000}$	= 29.69%	35%

What is the significance of these ratios? The best that can be said now is simply that there are 1.6 times as many current assets as there are current liabilities. Short-term creditors and management could expect a 60 percent cushion based on the current ratio and a 42 percent cushion based on the acid-test ratio to allow for possible loss in current-asset valuation. A rule of thumb often applied is that the current ratio should be 2 to 1. It would appear that the ADCO current ratio as compared with this rule of thumb is low. If we were to accept this standard (2 to 1), we might be able to anticipate a future cash strain or the need for additional short-term or even long-term financing. (Liquidity again!) The third liquidity ratio, inventory to working capital, indicates that 29.69 percent of the excess of current assets over current liabilities is inventory which may or may not bring the price we paid for it at a quick sale to pay creditors. This is why the acid-test ratio is 1.42 times and the current ratio is 1.6 times!

However, for our immediate decision—to buy or not to buy ADCO—these ratios do not reveal very much. They are not supposed to do so.

The next set of ratios the clerk had prepared were the leverage ratios:

Leverage ratios

		Formula		ADCO Data	Industry Data
1.	Debt to total assets	$= \frac{\text{total debt}}{\text{total assets}}$	$= \frac{\$2{,}302{,}100}{\$5{,}302{,}100}$	= 43.4%	50%
2.	Times interest earned	$= \frac{\text{profit before taxes plus interest charges}}{\text{interest charges}}$	$= \frac{\text{—0—}}{\$\ \ 96{,}000}$	= None	5 times

			ADCO Data	Industry Data
3. Fixed-charge coverage	=	net profit before fixed charges / interest + rent + sinking fund + taxes related to sinking fund	= None	4 times
4. Current liabilities to net worth	=	current liabilities / net worth	$= \frac{\$\ 702{,}100}{\$3{,}000{,}000} = 23.4\%$	30%
5. Fixed assets to net worth	=	fixed assets / net worth	$= \frac{\$4{,}179{,}000}{\$3{,}000{,}000} = 139\%$	150%

These ratios show that we are "trading on the equity" (using borrowed money) to the extent of 43.4 percent of our total assets. One significance of this debt financing is indicated by the second and third ratios in this series. ADCO is operating at a loss, but for a profit-earning organization the "times-interest earned" and the "fixed-charge coverage" can be extremely important. The ability to attract additional financing is largely determined by the ability to pay the interest charges from earnings. In addition, the ability to avoid bankruptcy or other financial crises can be estimated by these same ratios.

The fourth and fifth ratios on this series, current liabilities to net worth and fixed assets to net worth, clearly indicate another problem. ADCO may have entirely too much and too sophisticated equipment to support the present sales level. Equipment wise, it may be the Cadillac of the industry. There is little point in stating that a Cadillac is a good car. The point is, do you need it and can you afford to drive it at the present sales level? Clearly, ADCO did not reach its anticipated potential. The fixed assets are 139 percent of equity. Fixed interest charges (every year or payment period this will be a current liability) amount to \$96,000, and depreciation on fixed assets (estimated at $6\frac{2}{3}$ percent, 15-year life, on present balance of \$14,179,000) would amount to \$278,321 each year. Therefore, profit before fixed charges and depreciation must equal \$374,321. The loss suffered this past year was \$300,000, and this indicates that ADCO did not earn the depreciation expense by \$74,321 after the interest was paid! At this point, another financial crisis could be indicated.

We will now turn to so-called activity ratios. These ratios are designed to show how effectively the business is utilizing the assets available.

Activity ratios

				ADCO Data	Industry Data
1. Cash velocity	=	$\frac{\text{cost of goods sold}}{\text{beginning cash and equivalents}}$	$= \frac{\$10{,}338{,}000}{\$\ 2{,}700{,}000}$	= 3.83 times	2 times
2. Inventory turnover	=	$\frac{\text{cost of goods sold}}{\text{inventory}}$	$= \frac{\$10{,}338{,}000}{\$\ \ 125{,}000}$	= 82.8 times	Not available
3. Fixed asset turnover	=	$\frac{\text{cost of goods sold}}{\text{fixed assets}}$	$= \frac{\$10{,}338{,}000}{\$\ 4{,}179{,}000}$	= 2.47 times	3 times
4. Average collection period	=	$\frac{\text{average receivables}}{\text{sales per day}}$	$= \frac{\$\ \ 80{,}000}{\frac{\$10{,}350{,}000}{365}}$	= 28.2 days	30 days
5 Total asset turnover	=	$\frac{\text{sales}}{\text{total assets}}$	$= \frac{\$10{,}350{,}000}{\$\ 5{,}302{,}100}$	= 1.9 times	2.1 times

Some of the figures we needed for these ratios were not included on the statements received from Allied. However, after a quick call to the financial executive, they were made available. You couldn't help noticing a couple of the items reported on the phone. The beginning cash and cash equivalents is one example. At the beginning of the year these items totaled $2,700,000, and at the end of the year they had been reduced to $998,100. The inventory figures likewise caused you some concern. ADCO had indicated to us much earlier that they maintained a three-month supply on hand when, in fact, inventory turned over more than once a week, 82 times. (The explanation was that the processing time is about 40 minutes, and Allied feeds the basic material to ADCO and Allied does maintain more than a three-month supply in inventory.) Your conversation also revealed that ADCO could buy the raw copper and alloys needed and avoid the markup by Allied, but the present procedure had been a long-standing arrangement.

It is clear that the fixed-asset turnover was very slow, but you also knew that ADCO was using very little of their finishing equipment. The Jones Corporation is rapidly taking their customers. ADCO primarily processes only the raw material into a semifinished product that becomes the raw material for Jones and other firms. The collection period is typical and much better than most firms in the industry. It is obvious that ADCO requires an increase in volume and especially needs to make the relatively idle equipment earn a return.

The profitability ratios are self-explanatory, and express earning power in various ways. These can be valuable in comparing operations from period to period. Since there is practically no gross profit and certainly no net profit before or after taxes, these ratios did not occupy our attention for very long. However, the first one, gross operating margin, did attract our attention. A critical point is the high percentage the cost of sales is of gross sales. (We are about to learn another very important lesson.)

Profitability ratios

		ADCO Data	Industry Data
1. Gross operating margin	$= \frac{\text{gross operating profit}}{\text{sales}} = \frac{\$\ \ 12{,}000}{\$10{,}350{,}000}$	= 0.0012%	70%
2. Net operating margin	$= \frac{\text{net operating profit}}{\text{sales}}$	= None	10%
3. Sales margin	$= \frac{\text{net profit after taxes}}{\text{sales}}$	= None	5%
4. Productivity of assets	$= \frac{\text{gross income less taxes}}{\text{total assets}}$	= None	20%
5. Return of net worth	$= \frac{\text{net profit after taxes}}{\text{net worth}}$	= None	15%
6. Price-earnings ratio	$= \frac{\text{market price per share}}{\text{earnings per share}}$	= No market price per share and no earnings	Not available
7. Dividend yield	$= \frac{\text{dividend per share}}{\text{market price per share}}$	= (60% of the stock is owned by Allied and 40% by the principal officers of Allied. The stock had been given to the officers by the Allied board of directors as a bonus 6 years ago.) No dividends	Not available

8. Payout = $\frac{\text{Dividend}}{\text{earnings}}$

On the basis of our limited analysis, and assuming for the moment the validity of the accounting information presented, we can summarize ADCO's position in the following manner: ADCO can currently meet all its short-term obligations as they mature. The current ratio indicates that for each $1 demanded by short-term creditors, the firm will be able to furnish $1.60. The implied assumption with respect to this analysis is that current assets will complete their cash-to-cash cycle within a one-year period.

Our quick ratio refines this assumption somewhat by indicating that even in the worst of circumstances highly liquid assets ("quick assets"—cash, temporary investments in marketable securities, and receivables) demonstrate an ability to cover short-term claims 1.42 times. In short, this quick ratio assumes a zero value for ADCO's inventory. Finally, our inventory-to-working-capital ratio shows the percentage relationship between working capital and our least liquid current asset, inventory.

ADCO's debt position as compared with the industry's debt position has been revealed by our leverage ratios. The firm carries less debt and yet fails to service it (earn enough income) to provide security for creditors. ADCO has a higher proportion of ownership investment with respect to total assets, fixed assets, and current debt than does the industry. Ordinarily, this relationship would provide the basis for increased financing through debt. However, given the firm's poor record with respect to debt service, we can conclude that any additional financing in the form of debt would be unavailable on acceptable terms. ADCO has been unable to achieve the positive and desirable effect of using the debt to realize a return which would increase the firm's overall return on equity. To wit, the firm has not realized a rate of return on its investment which exceeds the rate of payment to its creditors. Had the firm been able to do so, the excess in return over the payments to creditors would have been available for the common shareholders. Thus, if ADCO could have earned 10 percent or any return on the borrowed funds higher than the interest rate, the excess would have been available as earnings.

The activity ratios, which we calculated, demonstrated that ADCO was unable to generate a sales level consistent with its asset size as other firms in the industry have done. Accounts receivable were collected in less time by ADCO than by its competitors. Finally, ADCO's fixed-asset base did not turn out as high a level of sales per dollar invested as did other firms in the industry. This situation probably results from the fact that ADCO maintains some assets which are inappropriate to its current sales mix, namely, the finishing machines. These assets simply are not being used.

Our calculation of profitability ratios has been an exercise in futility since no profit has been earned. However, our industry data do indicate that profit potentials exist within the industry. Hence the question, Why has ADCO failed to generate any profits?

What have we really learned about ADCO? On the surface, it would appear that we had generated a good deal of information. However, its usefulness for our purposes is somewhat limited.

Value of internal data. The data which were generated with respect to ADCO's liquidity, leverage, activity, and profitability were based entirely on the presumed accuracy of the accounts studied. The figures in the balance sheet and income statement were uncertified, and so we have only the honesty and integrity of ADCO to depend on. If we purchase the firm, we will be buying these accounts, and their real values may be quite different from those reported. Your prior experience with inventory accounting should have made you highly suspicious of book values as stated by accountants. The work we have done to date has provided us with a little background. However, on the basis of this background, major questions may be asked and investigations may be launched.

Industry data usefulness. As a part of our financial-statement analysis we compared certain ADCO ratios with the industry ratios (a composition of ratios of many diverse companies within the industry). How valuable is this information and how valid are the conclusions drawn from these ratio relationships? One significant thing we must remember is that industry ratios for the most part are averages of varied types of firms, some having higher ratios and others having lower ratios. But if we are dealing with an industry where all firms are of comparable size, selling a homogeneous product and using the same accounting methods, we may find the ratio comparisons to be extremely valid and very useful. The usefulness of industry data will be quite limited where the industry comprises companies of different sizes and who sell a varied product mix. An example of this situation can be found in the office equipment industry. This industry's data include Swingline, Inc., with sales of approximately $70 million, which manufactures staplers and fastening devices for industrial and home use, and International Business Machines, with sales of over $5 billion, which produces a large number of different products ranging from typewriters to computers. If we were to compare industry ratios with Swingline's ratios, we would be hard pressed to show any meaningful relationships. Any comparisons made on the basis of these data would be invalid.

ADDITIONAL ANALYSIS

We were given some food for thought when we discovered, after the phone call to Allied, the large difference between the cash balance at the beginning of the year and the cash balance at the end of the year ($2,700,000 versus $962,000). Why the large decrease? Cash collections and cash inflow appear to have been excellent. Sales totaled $10,350,000, and the accounts receivable balance is only $76,000, or about 0.73 of 1 percent. The real key was provided when we learned from Allied's management that the cause of the reduction in the cash balance was a $1,500,000 cash distribution paid by ADCO to its stockholders during the last month of the fiscal year. Allied indicated that the asking price for 100 percent of the ADCO stock would have been $6,500,000 if the cash had remained in the ADCO assets. (Present asking price is $5 million.)

The reason for the cash distribution is clear when we recall from Chapter 2 the effective tax rate on capital gains, the low effective income tax rate on dividends received by one domestic corporation from another domestic corporation, and that distributions from corporations not out of current earnings or accumulated earnings could be a return of capital and not taxable to the recipient. Do you recall? (If you do not, go back now and review this entire chapter. Tax implications will be very significant as we continue our analysis. How can any financial executive consider almost any financial transaction without considering tax implications?) The tax treatment of dividends is very significant at this point and will go a long way toward explaining the difference in the cash positions of ADCO.

Allied's financial executive explained that earlier in the year Allied had enjoyed a capital gain of $2 million. It took some real digging, but we discovered in a long chat with the president of Apex Electronics Corporation, a competitor, that Allied, for the past two years, had been quietly buying the stock of Apex Electronics Corporation, with the intention of acquiring working control of the corporation. The stock at that time was depressed in price. That is, it was underpriced. The management of the target corporation, Apex, finally realized what was happening and made every effort to acquire and to influence others who were friendly toward the present management to acquire the stock. The continuous steady activity in the stock and rumors of a take-over by Allied caused the stock to rise in price to a point where Allied no longer felt that the acquisition would be a good investment. Allied finally sold their stock this year and as a result realized the $2 million long-term capital gain.

We learned earlier via our tax framework that corporate net long-term capital gains (in excess of short-term losses) are taxed at the maximum rate of 28.7 percent of the gain (for taxable year beginning in 1970 and ending before January, 1971). The capital gains tax would thus be $574,000 on the Apex transaction, assuming no other capital gains or losses for the year. Allied's adjusted basis for its investment in ADCO is $5 million. As will be seen, if ADCO were sold for $5 million, Allied, who has a 60 percent interest in ADCO, would receive $3 million and realize a long-term capital loss of $2 million. Thus Allied could then apply the capital loss it will occur on the sale of ADCO to offset taxable gain on Apex and avoid paying the tax of $574,000.

There are several additional steps we must go through to fully understand all the implications. We will do this shortly.

Analysis of Retained Earnings

We ask for and receive an analysis of the ADCO retained earnings account since the date of ADCO's incorporation. This analysis appears as follows:

ANALYSIS OF ADCO'S RETAINED EARNINGS ACCOUNT

Year	Net Profit (Loss) for Period after Taxes	Balance
1960		—0—
1961	$ 875,000	$ 875,000
1962	2,600,000	3,475,000
1963	500,000	3,975,000
1964	50,000	4,025,000
1965	(50,000)	3,975,000
1966	(50,000)	3,925,000
1967	(250,000)	3,675,000
1968	(1,300,000)	2,375,000
1969	(1,575,000)	800,000
1970 (Estimated)	(300,000)	500,000*

* Balance shown is prior to cash distribution of $1,500,000.

Therefore, it is clear that $500,000 of the $1,500,000 distribution is to ADCO stockholders and is from earnings taxable as a dividend. This $500,000 dividend will be taxable 60 percent to Allied and 40 percent to Allied's principal officers. The balance of $1 million is a return of capital to the stockholders and will be used to reduce the stockholders' investment in ADCO. Allied's share of the $1 million, $600,000, will reduce its cost basis in ADCO to $5 million.

Cash distribution	$1,500,000
Less balance in ADCO retained earnings	500,000
Return of capital to stockholders	$1,000,000
Allied's share of the return of capital	$ 600,000
Allied's share of the dividend portion of the distribution (60% of $500,000)	$ 300,000

We'll first deal with Allied's share of the $500,000 from retained earnings, which will be taxed as a dividend—which it is!

Thus, of the $300,000 cash dividend received by Allied from ADCO's retained earnings (60 percent of $500,000), only $45,000 is taxed at 50 percent (the assumed marginal rate), so that the effective rate of tax on the $300,000 dividend is 7.5 percent ($22,500). Why the 7.5 percent? Because 85 percent of the dividends received by Allied from ADCO's retained earnings are tax-free (if you do not know why, go back now—you must learn to recognize this situation). This leaves only 15 percent (15 percent of $300,000 = $45,000), which is added to regular income and is taxed at the assumed marginal rate of 50 percent (50 percent × 15 percent = 7.5 percent, the effective rate of tax, or 15 percent of $300,000 = $45,000 × 50 percent = $22,500). It is apparent, therefore, that the $300,000 dividend distribution out of retained earnings resulted in a tax savings to Allied of $63,000 (the difference between 28.7 percent capital gain rate and the 7.5 percent effective rate on the dividend—21.2 percent of $300,000, or $63,600). Incidentally, this analysis goes a long way in explaining ADCO's liquidity ratios.

The next step is to recognize that the return of capital to Allied (60 percent of $1 million) reduces Allied's investment in ADCO from $5,600,000 to $5,000,000. That number, $5,000,000, is certainly familiar—it is Allied's asking price for ADCO!

Allied's investment in ADCO	$5,600,000
Less return of capital	600,000
Remaining investment in ADCO	$5,000,000

Allied would receive only 60 percent of the $5 million asking price. The significant point to notice next is the long-term capital loss Allied would suffer after the cash distribution of $1,500,000 as compared with the loss Allied would suffer if the $1,500,000 were not distributed and if ADCO were sold for $6,500,000.

	Selling Price if Cash Distribution Had Not Been Made	**Selling Price after Cash Distribution**
Selling price for 100% of ADCO	$6,500,000	$5,000,000
Allied's 60% share	$3,900,000	$3,000,000
Allied's investment in ADCO after cash return of capital	5,600,000	5,000,000
Allied's long-term capital loss	($1,700,000)	($2,000,000)

The significance of the cash distribution can be emphasized again when we note that if the cash distribution had not been made, Allied would have had to pay a capital gains tax of $86,100. After the cash distribution the capital gains tax is zero.

	Selling Price if Cash Distribution Had Not Been Made	Selling Price after Cash Distribution
Long-term capital gain from sale of Apex	$2,000,000	$2,000,000
Long-term capital loss from sale of ADCO	1,700,000	2,000,000
Balance taxed at 28.7%	$ 300,000	None
Amount of capital gains tax to be paid in cash	$ 86,100	

The cash distribution will result in a taxable dividend to Allied of $45,000 (taxable dividend $300,000, 85 percent of which is allowed as a tax deduction). The tax on $45,000 at the assumed marginal rate of 50 percent will be $22,500. The difference between this tax and the capital gains tax of $86,100 that Allied would have had to pay had the cash distribution not been made is the tax saving of $63,600 brought about by the cash distribution.

This is a significant reason that Allied would like to sell their interest in ADCO this year. Could the loss be carried back if the ADCO sale were made next year? (It's in Chapter 2.) These factors, and especially the long-term capital gains tax savings, may give us a little leverage as we talk price with Allied!

Reviewing the analysis of ADCO's retained earnings account, it should be noted at this point that ADCO has an unused operating loss carryforward of $3,375,000. We shall discuss this aspect later.

With the tax problems out of the way, the Allied executives then took up ADCO's question of plant efficiency.

The losses attributed to an increase in the cost of goods sold were of extreme interest, to say the least. We do know, of course, that any plant limping along at a very low percentage of capacity will have higher per-unit costs. (We're back to cost curves and flexible budgets again!)

While the Allied financial executive explained the Allied-ADCO relationship, we were gaining valuable information which proved beneficial to us later. Incidentally, the discussions with the Allied executive turned out to be a week-long conference.

You learned that Allied considered ADCO more or less an operating division. Raw material for the ADCO operation, as well as other supplies and services, was "sold" to ADCO by Allied at "transfer prices." "Transfer prices" include not only the cost of the goods and services but also a margin of profit. In general, Allied operates their plants on the basis of cost-profit centers. The significance of this fact will be clear in a minute.

If we move on down the ADCO balance sheet, it is obvious that the inventory figure is unrealistically low. It had been explained earlier, however, that Allied really carried the inventory, and we were not too concerned about this point. However, in discussing the inventory matter, we moved over to the cost of goods sold figure and the very low margin of gross profit ($12,000 on sales of $10,350,000). We asked for and received a breakdown of the cost of goods sold figure, $10,338,000. This figure was the exact charge made by Allied when the material was shipped to ADCO for processing. We soon disovered the major problem.

Allied purchases the basic raw material. The raw material is put into process in one department (or division). The product moves from one department (or division) to another for further processing until the product is finished and ready for sale. Each of the departments is considered a separate cost-profit center. Each cost-profit center is charged with a percentage of the company-wide overhead expense and the company-wide general and administrative expense. To these general charges each profit center will add its costs plus a predetermined percentage of profit. As the products are transferred from one cost-profit center to another, the total charges accumulated in one cost-profit center become the "transfer price" to the next cost-profit center. Therefore, it is apparent that the present ADCO "cost of goods sold" is loaded with general company overhead and profit in addition to actual costs! This is quite significant! The Jones organization will sooner or later be forced to decentralize. You have promised yourself to look into the implications of transfer prices in more detail when you have the time. For the time being, however, ADCO's losses for the past six years may be more understandable. We will need a detailed study later. (We are skirting the area of joint costs.)

Accountants are self-critical about the various ways of charging joint costs to various operating divisions and the various percentages of profits to be earned by the different divisions, but no satisfactory solution has been found to the problem. How to allocate joint costs effectively among divisions and what is a proper percentage of profit that each department earns are questions of pure judgment, and judgments are subject to differences of opinion. Marketing men speak about the "value added" in the various operating departments as the product moves to completion. These arguments, however, will not directly concern us. On the other hand, the "transfer-price" concept is extremely important to us. We clearly recognize that the cost of goods sold without the transfer-price concept will be very significantly reduced if Jones processes the raw materials.

The Jones top-level management salaries and the general and administrative expenses are about one-fourth the size of Allied's and for all practical purposes are fixed. If we are able to absorb the ADCO operation without significant addition to these costs (remember in the beginning of this chapter we were increasing our own staff), the cost per unit (total cost expressed on a per-unit basis) for all the present Jones production as well as the ADCO production will probably be considerably reduced. Profits derived from the present Jones production would be increased by reason of lower raw-material costs. (And probably still lower manufacturing costs when we use ADCO's fully automated equipment. Sounds as though we have already purchased ADCO! Things are looking better.)

Allied has made available to you ADCO's detailed cost records. It was quite time-consuming, but you have had a flexible budget and cost curves prepared for the ADCO operation. A careful review of the data indicates that ADCO is operating on the descending slope of the cost curves and that additional volume will cause average total cost to be reduced still further.

The net effect of our examination of ADCO's cost data would be a planned cost reduction of 36 to 38 percent. Without further detailed analysis, this saving alone would result in a minimum cost reduction of $362,864. In addition, ADCO produces several different products. This product mix has never been carefully analyzed in the effort to improve overall sales volume. A quick examination reveals that if some of these sales were cut back to an economically sound level (where marginal cost equals marginal revenue), profits could be increased to the point where, even at the present level of production (including the elimination of the transfer prices), there would be a 10 percent return on $5 million after interest cost and taxes. A second alternative would be to examine the demand for these marginal products. If the demand continued strong, it is possible that the elasticity of the ADCO demand curve would support an increase in unit selling price. Marginal revenue would then be increased and perhaps the present sales volume could be sold at a profit.

An executive committee member inquired about the usefulness of an independent appraisal of the value of the ADCO assets. You explained that for reasons you would advance later, the appraisal really wasn't that important, barring possible asset obsolescence. However, if he would like to have one, you would arrange for it.

Significance of Asset Appraisals

We received permission to inspect the plant and equipment. An engineering consulting firm was retained to appraise the value of the plant and equipment and was requested to give proper consideration to obsolescence and recent technological developments. We know the equipment can do the job.

The plant and equipment have been appraised by our consulting engineers at a replacement cost of $5,500,000 (cost of reproducing the property new on the basis of current prices), and were estimated to be 25 percent depreciated. This means the plant and equipment have a fair market value of $4,125,000 ($5,500,000 – 25 percent). The same engineers place a conservative market value of $1,500,000 on the patent. The original patent has 10 years to run, and amortization would be $150,000 per year (tax savings $75,000 annually for 10 years). ADCO has amortized the patent over five years because of the fear of obsolescence. However, the original design for which the patent was issued has stood the test of time and is still quite valuable.

Their appraisal is as follows:

APPRAISAL—FAIR MARKET VALUE—ADCO

Assets		Liabilities	
Cash	$ 362,000	Accounts payable	$ 102,000
Marketable securities	560,000	Notes payable	600,000
Accounts receivable	76,000	Mortgage payable	1,600,000
Inventory	125,000	Total liabilities	$2,302,000
Patents	1,500,000	Total assets	6,748,000
Plant and equipment	4,125,000	Estimated appraisal	
Total assets	$6,748,000	value	$4,446,000

At the next executive committee meeting it was suggested that the revaluation indicated that Jones could pay $4,446,000 for ADCO (assets $6,748,000 less liabilities $2,302,000 = $4,446,000). However, you quickly pointed out that the ADCO plant and equipment are worth only as much as we could obtain for them on the secondhand equipment market unless we anticipate that it will generate a stream of future income. One member then remarked that perhaps we could capitalize past earnings and arrive at a valuation for the ADCO stock. The answer to that question is absolutely no, if he really meant to capitalize past earnings. Why are past earnings now irrelevant?

PRESENT VALUE AND PURCHASE PRICE

We would not be purchasing past earnings. If he meant to use past earnings as a basis for estimating future earnings, perhaps. However,

Advantage to the 40 percent individual stockholders:

1. A possible $2 million long-term capital gain windfall to be taxed to each shareholder on his share of the gain at a maximum rate of 25 percent of the first $50,000 and 29.5 percent on the excess over $50,000 (for 1970; 32.5 percent for 1971 and thereafter). For 1970, there will also be a surcharge of 2.5 percent on the capital gains tax so computed.

Advantage to Jones:

1. Increased earnings per share of Jones Corporation stock.
2. Possible carry-forward loss to be applied to future profits in the amount of $3,375,000 resulting in a total possible tax savings of $1,687,500 at an assumed marginal tax rate of 50 percent.
3. If we are unable to secure a favorable loss carry-forward ruling, we will still secure about a $100,000 yearly tax saving by liquidating ADCO within two years from the date of acquisition either into Jones Corporation or into a newly created subsidiary of Jones Corporation.[1]
4. Cost curves and/or a flexible budget must be prepared. However, our experience with increased capacity indicates an excellent possibility that average total cost per unit will decrease with the increase in capacity and a corresponding increase in profit per unit for all units produced. This is quite significant!
5. ADCO was the prime supplier within an oligopolistic industry with at least a regional monopoly as a raw-material supplier, not only to Jones but also to Jones' competitors. We would succeed to the position.

There appears to be ample reason that the sale should be completed both by Allied and by the individual stockholders of ADCO and the Jones Corporation. However, President Jones is concerned about the future sales to Allied. Jones Electronic Corporation would be putting a lot of

[1] This estimated yearly tax saving of $100,000 comes about because certain provisions of the Internal Revenue Code allow a corporation who acquires 80 percent or more of the stock of another corporation to liquidate the latter corporation, tax free, either into the acquiring corporation or into its subsidiary. If such liquidation takes place within two years after the controlling stock acquisition, the purchase price of the stock could be allocated over the assets acquired from the liquidation. As a result, the acquiring corporation will obtain a higher annual depreciation deduction should the purchase price of the stock allocated to depreciable assets result in a higher basis for depreciation. In the case under discussion, a purchase price of $5 million for 100 percent of the stock of ADCO plus the assumption of total liabilities of $2,302,000, a total of $7,302,000, would constitute a payment of $6,748,000 for the tangible assets (the appraised value as shown on page 334) and a payment of $554,000 for goodwill, which is not depreciable. The price paid for the tangible assets would be allocated over the various assets, resulting in a higher depreciable basis for the patents. We estimate that this would result in a higher yearly depreciation of $100,000.

eggs in one basket. Should Allied discontinue their purchases from Jones, Jones could be in a very difficult, if not tragic, position. Furthermore, President Jones remembers very well that at the very time our sales to Allied were increasing, Allied was in the process of buying up the Apex stock. Presumably, purchases from Jones would be curtailed if the purchase had been successful. A very serious matter, indeed.

You have been requested to examine and reexamine your data very carefully. With that you went home. I had left earlier. You're earning the $2,000 per month—not me. I'm not even on the payroll! You couldn't rest. Your conscious and subconscious were racing. At times they seemed to be going in opposite directions. You called me and we played nine holes. I'm five bucks richer, but you did come up with an idea or two. "Had" to be the subconscious because on a couple of shots you appeared to be unconscious!

SUMMARY

In this chapter the Jones Electronic Corporation is faced with a somewhat different type of decision. You began your analyses by building an incomplete framework for acquisition. We say incomplete because you will in a subsequent chapter formulate a theoretically more rigorous framework. In planning for the purchase of ADCO, you did, by means of your framework, force the corporation to delineate its goals and assess its strengths and weaknesses. This activity was an important one.

You next examined ADCO's financial statements. You began by using four standard types of ratios:

1. Liquidity ratios
2. Leverage ratios
3. Activity ratios
4. Profitability ratios

Liquidity ratios attempt to assess the firm's immediate solvency. Leverage ratios compare the relationship between owners and creditors in our claim structure and also measure our ability to service the claims of creditors. Activity ratios attempt to measure the effectiveness of asset utilization. For example, fixed-asset turnover rates show how effectively we use this class of assets to generate sales. Profitability ratios assess our overall managerial efficiency in using all assets to generate profits. You were wise to look behind the ratios and understand their inherent limitations. Your examination of ADCO's cost structure, etc., revealed that what the financial ratios fail to show may be as important as what they do reveal.

You then moved on to an examination of the proposed purchase price of $5 million. This also proved to be most instructive in that the price was a function of:

1. Asset values
2. Anticipated income streams
3. Tax factors

Let's review each area. Our first attempt to justify the asking price for ADCO was based upon the valuation of ADCO's assets. We arrived at a figure of $4,446,000. We were quick to realize that this approach was less than fruitful since we desired not so much the ownership of the assets, but rather the income streams they could produce. We then valued these streams under several assumptions and generated a number of potential purchase prices. Finally, tax implications were introduced in order to formulate the possible tax consequences of the purchase on both Allied and Jones.

You should note that you have not yet made a decision but have only begun to put the proposed purchase price into perspective.

QUESTIONS FOR DISCUSSION

1. What are the liquidity ratios, and what do they purport to indicate?
2. What are the leverage ratios, and what do they purport to indicate?
3. What are the activity ratios, and what do they purport to indicate?
4. What are the profitability ratios, and what do they purport to indicate?
5. What basic assumptions are involved in the use of the above ratios for analysis purposes?
6. What problems are involved as one attempts to use the financial ratios of other firms and industry averages as criteria for evaluating a firm's position?
7. What is, or was, the significance of the cash dividend paid by ADCO to its stockholders?
8. What is the significance of the analysis of ADCO's retained earnings account on page 329?
9. Distinguish between the treatment of the cash distribution by ADCO to Allied and the distribution to other stockholders.
10. What are "transfer prices"?
11. What effect did Allied's transfer prices have on the analysis of ADCO's financial statements?
12. What is the significance of the "appraised value" of the ADCO assets as compared with the book value, with respect to our analysis of the ADCO financial statements?
13. What effect would the appraised value of the assets have on the price Jones may be willing to pay for the ADCO stock?
14. What are the basic criteria Jones is contemplating as a basis for the minimum and maximum price Jones would pay for the ADCO stock?

15. What basic assumptions are involved in this evaluation?
16. Why should Allied sell the ADCO stock to Jones?
17. Why should Jones give serious consideration to the purchase of ADCO's stock? What risks are involved?

PROBLEMS

1. Comparative data for Brock-Wood, Inc., for the three-year period 1969–1971 are presented below:

INCOME STATEMENT DATA
(000's omitted)

	1969	1970	1971
Net Sales	$700	$1,000	$1,200
Cost of Goods Sold	400	600	700
Gross Profit on Sales	$300	$ 400	$ 500
Selling, General, and Other Expense	240	280	300
Net Operating Income	$ 60	$ 120	$ 200
Income Tax	30	60	100
Net Income After Taxes	$ 30	$ 60	$ 100
Dividends Paid	15	30	40
To Retained Earnings	$ 15	$ 30	$ 60

BALANCE SHEET DATA
(000's omitted)

	1969	1970	1971
Assets			
Cash	$ 50	$ 35	$ 55
Accounts Receivable	245	320	400
Inventory	320	380	420
Prepaid Expenses	20	10	30
Plant and Equipment	650	600	680
Patents and Goodwill	100	100	100
Other Assets	5	5	15
	$1,390	$1,450	$1,700
Liabilities and Stockholders' Equity			
Accounts Payable	$ 105	$ 115	$ 140
Wages and Dividends Payable	15	25	45
Income Tax Payable	30	60	100
Miscellaneous Current Liabilities	10	15	10
5% Bonds Payable	300	300	300
Unearned Income	15	15	10
6% Preferred Stock	200	200	200
No-par Common Stock ($10 Stated Value)	400	400	500
Paid-in Capital	200	200	260
Retained Earnings	115	120	135
	$1,390	$1,450	$1,700

From the foregoing, calculate the following:

Ratio	Brock-Wood	Norm
$\frac{\text{Current assets}}{\text{Current liabilities}}$	________	2.5 times
$\frac{\text{Inventories}}{\text{Net working capital}}$	________	62.0%
$\frac{\text{Sales}}{\text{Inventories}}$	________	9.9 times
$\frac{\text{Sales}}{\text{Net worth}}$	________	3.0 times
$\frac{\text{Sales}}{\text{Total assets}}$	________	1.3* times
$\frac{\text{Current debt}}{\text{Net worth}}$	________	32.1%
$\frac{\text{Total debt}}{\text{Net worth}}$	________	65.0%
$\frac{\text{Fixed assets}}{\text{Net worth}}$	________	43.5%
$\frac{\text{Net profit}}{\text{Sales}}$	________	3.3%
$\frac{\text{Net profit}}{\text{Total assets}}$	________	3.8%
$\frac{\text{Net profit}}{\text{Net worth}}$	________	10.7%

* Assumed.

2. The balance sheets for the Gray Company included the following accounts at the end of the year:

	1969 (000's)	1970
4% Bonds Payable	$ 500	$ 500
6% Preferred Stock, $100 par	500	500
Common Stock, $25 par	1,000	1,000
Additional Pair-in Capital	50	50
Retained Earnings	250	250

100×.06.

Net income after taxes was $70,000 in 1969 and $95,000 in 1970. Calculate the following for each year:

a. Number of times bond interest was earned
b. Number of times preferred interest was earned
c. Rate of earnings on total stockholders' equity at the end of each year
d. Earnings per share on common stock

3. Statements for the Eagle Company show the following balances:

	1969	1970	1971
Net Sales	$345	$390	$480
Average Accounts Receivable (net)	30	40	60

Assume a 300-day business year with 25 percent cash sales and the balance credit sales. Calculate any measurements that may be significant. Sales are made on a 2/30 net 60 basis.

4. Statements for the Ace Company show the following balances:

	1969	1970	1971
Sales	$80	$ 95	$105
Cost of Goods Sold			
Beginning Inventory	15	20	35
Purchases	70	80	105
	$85	$100	$140
Ending Inventory	30	35	65
	$55	$ 65	$ 75
Gross Profit on Sales	$25	$ 30	$ 30

Calculate any measurements that might be significant in analyzing the inventory position of the firm.

REFERENCES

Foulke, Roy A.: "Practical Financial Statement Analysis," 6th ed., McGraw-Hill Book Company, New York, 1968.

Ghandhi, J. K. S.: On the Measurement of Leverage, *Journal of Finance,* vol. XXI, pp. 715–726, December, 1966.

Graham, Benjamin, and George McGobrick: "The Interpretation of Financial Statements," rev. ed., Harper & Row, Publishers, Incorporated, New York, 1964.

Helfert, Erich A.: "Techniques of Financial Analysis," rev. ed., chap. 3, Richard D. Irwin, Inc., Homewood, Ill., 1967.

Horrigan, James O.: Some Empirical Bases of Financial Ratio Analysis, *Accounting Review,* vol. XXXX, July, 1965.

McCloud, B. G., Jr.: Pitfalls in Statement Analysis, *Bulletin of the Robert Morris Associates,* vol. 39, pp. 143–148, January, 1957.

Meyer, John M.: "Financial Statement Analysis," 3d ed., Prentice-Hall, Inc., Englewood Cliffs, N.J., 1961.

Sanzo, R.: "Ratio Analysis for Small Business," Small Business Management Series, no. 20, U.S. Government Printing Office, 1957.

Chapter Twelve
THE COST OF CAPITAL

After a series of conferences with Allied's executive officers, President Jones recommended to the Jones executive committee that steps be taken to acquire the ADCO operation. He further indicated that in his opinion, ADCO could be purchased for about $1 million less than the $5 million asking price. You were instructed to look into the matter and report back to the executive committee at an early date. We must obviously raise the $4 million from external sources. We can raise the needed funds by increasing equity (by selling stock) and/or we may be able to raise the needed funds by the use of debt (direct borrowing or some other credit arrangement).

President Jones expressed a concern about the rate of interest we might be required to pay if the $4 million were to be financed via debt. He explained that he had often heard that the interest rate was the result of the interplay of the supply of and the demand for money, and that this was a rather vague concept to him. We explained that, for the most part, the rate of interest is a function of the supply of and the demand for loanable funds rather than money in general. There is a distinct difference between the supply of money and the supply of loanable funds. "Loanable funds" is that portion of the total money supply which is available at any given time for the purchase of debt instruments or debt securities. We assured him, however, that the interest rate Jones would be required to pay would be a relatively insignificant factor in our decision to market bonds or other forms of long-term debt to finance the purchase of ADCO. Moreover, we continued, the interest rate paid to those who would have loanable funds available from their savings would play a very small part in the supply of funds available on the market. (It should be noted that in the first statement we were referring to the relatively small change in the product cost per unit that would result when the interest rate moved from $6\frac{1}{2}$ to 9 percent, while in the second statement we were in effect saying that the motives that savers have for saving generally do not include the interest rate they will earn therefrom.)

President Jones countered with just two powerful words—"Show me!" We explained to the president that we have no intention of getting involved in the scholarly theories of interest at this time. It wasn't really necessary. However, it would serve a useful purpose if we became familiar with the classical explanation of interest. In short, his knowledge or lack of knowledge with respect to these concepts was probably at the root of his uneasiness.

CLASSICAL THEORY OF INTEREST

The classical theory of interest can be summarized in Figure 12-1.

The classical analysis stated that the supply of and the demand for investment funds was elastic with respect to the rate of interest. Interest was defined as a payment for abstinence—for the investor's abstaining from using his purchasing power now in favor of renting the same to the borrower. This interest payment was termed an *agio.* Therefore, the higher the agio the more funds that would be made available. No agio—no savings—no supply of funds.

In order to test this classical assumption, we must first deal with the supply of funds and, more especially, with the people and institutions

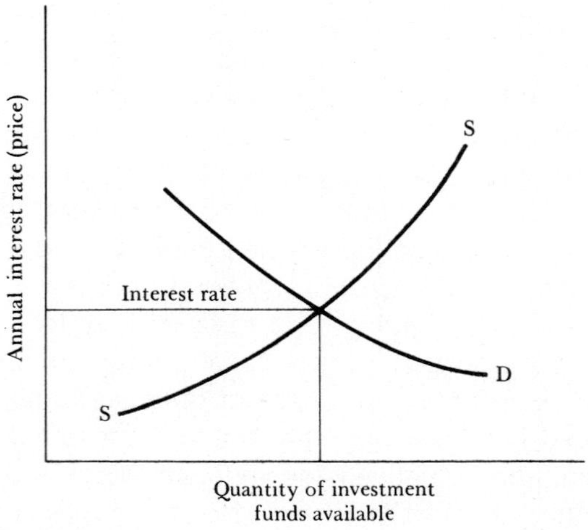

Figure 12-1

that save; even more important, we must inquire into why and how the decision to save is made. If the interest rate, per se, has nothing to do with this decision (the decision to save), the supply of investment funds from these sources is inelastic with respect to interest rather than elastic as the classicists assumed. Let's test these observations.

In general, there are four sources of investment funds:

1. Personal savings
2. Corporate savings
3. Government savings (provided by taxes)
4. Newly created bank credit

Let's examine these sources in order.

The first question is why people save, and this is closely related to how they save. Individuals save:

1. To provide protection or deferred income by buying insurance policies.
2. For rainy days or emergencies.
3. To provide funds for business opportunities.
4. In anticipation of general price declines.
5. To provide funds for ordinary household or business transactions.
6. (You could probably list many more.)

The point is that the rate of interest is immaterial with respect to the types of saving considered above.

John Maynard Keynes has more specifically designated these motivations. When he set forth his reasons that individuals and firms demand funds, Keynes emphasized the demand side, as you perhaps recall, and we are saying that these are the exact reasons that individuals save! Keynes' four motives were as follows:

1. Precautionary motive
2. Transactions motive
3. Financial motive
4. Speculation motive

(You can see that the motivation provided by the level of interest rates with respect to such saving is minimal.)

We must next deal with the sources of corporate savings and the nature of the corporate decision to save. We are really dealing primarily with internally generated corporate funds. These sources are:

1. Depreciation accumulations
2. Retained earnings or undistributed profits
3. Special-purpose funds (for example, a bond sinking fund)

The significant question is why corporations accumulate funds. As we know, in the overwhelming majority of cases professional management, rather than the owners of the corporate shares, directs and controls the corporate decision. Our question, then, is what motivates professional management to accumulate funds and, more specifically, does the rate of interest provide that motivation? Corporate funds are accumulated to provide for the following needs:

1. To retain as much "plow-back" as necessary to provide for growth and progress
2. To provide management compensation and benefits
3. To provide a stable dividend policy that will adequately compensate investors for the funds they have made available and to maintain the value of the firm as reflected by the long-run market price of the outstanding stock

If depreciation policies are adequate (that is, the rate of depreciation exceeds the actual decline in the economic value; that is, replacement prices are falling), there are built-in savings that can be reinvested to earn a return. As we have seen, accelerated depreciation methods provide the same result. The essential point again is that in general the rate of interest plays no part in determining the supply of funds from this source. However, during periods when the interest rate being charged on loanable funds is considerably higher than is, or has been, customary, corporate management may deem it advisable to "pass" or omit a normal dividend in order to use these same funds internally. (During the recent periods of "high interest rate" this latter policy has been the exception rather than the rule.)

In short, what we have been saying is that there is a supply of funds available at almost any rate of interest within reasonable levels. During the 1930s, savings deposits held by banks were earning no interest or as little as $\frac{1}{2}$ or 1 percent per annum! Savings clearly were not being accumulated to earn interest. Rather, these funds were being accumulated, slowly to be sure during this depression period, for the reasons cited earlier. It is certainly correct to state that available funds will shift between institutions as the interest rate paid on savings varies from institution to institution. However, this shifting of funds represents the decision about where to save rather than the basic decision of whether or not to save at all. In addition, the decision involving the question of how to save may vary as opportunities present themselves, for example, savings and loan accounts, government bonds, and private stocks, and bonds. We will have some elaboration on this point later in the chapter.

What is involved in the governmental decision to save (at the national level)? The decision to save manifests itself in the decision to tax, which will ultimately reduce corporate and individual consumption (or savings). Involved in the taxing decision are the following:

1. Political structure, which implies confidence that the public will recognize and endorse proper taxing policy in the long run
2. The level of employment and/or prices (as they depict the productive posture of the economy)

The point again is that the interest rate, per se, is immaterial to the basic rationale for these decisions.

Newly created bank criteria is a significant source of the supply of funds. The primary criteria involved in the decision by banks to extend credit and thus increase the supply of funds are twofold:

1. The banks' reserve position
2. The demand for loans

Central bank action or reaction can force changes in the available supply of newly created bank credit. Our inquiry here is into the nature of the factors that influence this decision. In general, there are two basic factors:

1. The current level of prices
2. The current level of business activity

These factors or the Federal Reserve Board's judgment with respect to these factors will cause changes in the following policies which will affect interest rates, but the changes are not **caused** by interest rates. The interest rate is a tool and not a reason for:

1. Changes in bank reserve requirements
2. Sale or purchase of government securities in the open market
3. A change in the discount rate

SIGNIFICANCE OF INTEREST RATE ON THE SOURCE OF FUNDS

During the Nixon administration, governmental policy reflected the belief that the United States economy was experiencing an inflationary trend that was far too rapid for a healthy economy. Accordingly, the Fed (Federal Reserve Board) made several moves that were designed to check the availability of loanable funds. A significant move was to increase the rate of discount (the interest rate) the central bank charged for funds borrowed by member banks. Member banks followed suit by increasing the interest rate charged to customers who would borrow bank funds. These increased interest rates rippled through the economy and in general restricted the loanable funds available from newly created bank credit. The tightening of this source of credit caused an increase in the demand for funds from private sources. An increase in interest rates in this sector soon followed. However, you will note we are now talking about the demand for and the limitations of bank financing as a source of funds. It is interesting to note that during this same period the nation's largest corporations promptly, without much difficulty, sold entire issues of bonds valued at many millions of dollars to the private sector.

The interest rate was used as a tool to limit the supply of available loanable funds from banking institutions. Governmental activity in this area likewise had a significant influence on the decision of where to save. That is, as interest rates were forced upward, the loanable funds available in the private sector moved to the source of the higher rate. While we do not want to get into an empirical study, there is no obvious evidence that the amount of loanable funds available increased in response to the higher interest rates; rather, it was a sideward movement of the available funds.

President Jones was satisfied with our judgment concerning the factors responsible for the general supply of investment funds. As a starting point, we could agree that the market rate of interest was directly related to government monetary and fiscal policy. He added also that when one savings institution or other interest-paying institution offered a higher rate of interest than its competitor, a decision might be made by individuals or corporations as to where to save; but how much is saved would still be guided by the motives generally unrelated to the interest level. Where to save and how much to save are two different questions. Of course, if the rate of interest increased to a point where one could invest safely and receive a 20 or 25 percent return, the rela-

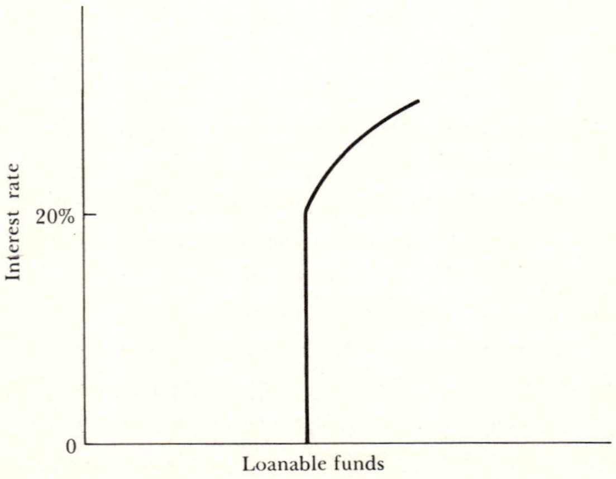

Figure 12-2

tionship between the decision to save and the interest rate could be changed substantially.

After a short period of reflection, President Jones inquired about our statement that "the rate of interest would not be a primary factor in our decision to borrow the funds or not to borrow the funds" (again within a practical range). He was really talking about the demand for funds. The rate of interest may not be a serious factor in the demand for business investment funds for at least two reasons. First, an extra 1 percent in interest before taxes is one-half of 1 percent after taxes (assuming a marginal tax rate of 50 percent). Second, the interest expense divided by total annual output would add significantly little to our cost per unit.

As an example, an increase in the interest rate from 5 to 6 percent on a $4 million bond issue would increase net interest expense $20,000 per year ($\frac{1}{2}$ percent × $4 million). Twenty thousand dollars divided by a minimum anticipated total annual production with the new plant of 400,000 units would add only $0.05 to the cost of each unit. On the other hand, the $4 million investment in the new plant will reduce average total cost per unit from $3.50 to $2.10. Total additional profit would be $1.40 per unit less interest cost per unit. For our purposes, then, we will treat the rate of interest as we would any other cost factor. President Jones indicated, and it was obvious from his optimistic attitude, that a considerable amount of his apprehension had been relieved. However, he did inquire, "What, then, will determine the rate of interest which we would have to pay?"

We quickly answered, "The supply and demand for loanable funds!" What we really meant was the supply and demand for the type of security that we would offer. Investment funds are available. It would be a matter of attracting these funds with our securities offering. This could mean inducing the investor to transfer his funds from one type of market to another (for example, from the short-term market to the long-term market or from common stocks to straight bonds or convertibles). If investment funds are in fact available, what factors will determine our success in attracting a portion of these funds into our own particular firm? This question is perhaps best answered by an examination of the ultimate source of these funds—the investor. The term "investor" represents a heterogeneous grouping of individuals and institutions which furnish capital to both private and public enterprise. Included in this group we would find individuals, pension funds, mutual funds, and investing institutions of many other types. A complete description of investors would constitute a monumental undertaking; however, a description of their collective goals can be more easily handled. Once we know their investment goals, we can more easily understand the process through which they commit their funds to various enterprises, our own included.

Investors, be they individuals or institutions, are fundamentally rational. Some prefer large monetary returns to small monetary returns. In order to secure a particular level of returns, they will accept a level of risk which is commensurate with the expected return. The structure and function of the investment portfolio will determine the level and type of risks which can be profitably endured. For example, a fire and casualty insurance firm is subjected to large and unpredictable claims which must be met immediately. Such a firm must, consequently, emphasize the liquidity of its investment mix. This emphasis normally results in some sacrifice of return. A life insurance firm, on the other hand, using standard mortality tables, can predict the level of cash claims which will be made against it. A life insurance firm can then be less concerned with a substantial liquidity position and emphasize longer-term, higher-return securities in its portfolio.

Initially, when you discussed the interest rate with President Jones, you indicated that in your opinion the interest rate had little effect on the *aggregate* supply of funds available for investment. However, the prospective return in the form of interest on bonds or yields on stocks does have a great effect upon the *allocation* of this total investment among the various firms competing for the funds available. Thus, the ability of Jones Electronic to secure investment funds will be determined on the basis of:

1. The prospective returns which the securities offer
2. The level and kinds of risks associated with the expected returns

If Jones Electronic were to successfully offer new stock, the return on this security in the form of dividends and capital appreciation must be as high as or higher than such returns offered by the securities of other firms in the same risk category. In short, the firm will be successful in attracting capital investment when it meets the opportunity costs of prospective investors.

However, no stock offering or debt security can hope to be all things to all people. People are different. Just as people differ in their tastes and preferences for all types of consumer goods, so do people differ in the level of risk they are willing to take at any particular point in time. As an example, there are those people who will only accept a very minimum risk. Others will accept, and in fact enjoy, a high degree of risk. An individual attempting to put together a balanced portfolio of investments may have already secured an adequate supply of higher than average risk securities and may be at a particular point in time in the market for only low risk opportunities, or vice versa. On the other hand, the same investor may be in the market for high risk values.

Before pursuing this matter further, what are the risk factors? There are four such.

Purchasing-power Risk

Purchasing-power risk is generally referred to in terms of the uncertain future purchasing power of income derived from investments. This risk is most easily explained with reference to fixed-income securities. However, the principle is also illustrated by the failure of returns on many equity securities to keep pace with increases in the cost of living. Let us suppose that an investor purchases a 20-year, 5-percent, $1,000 bond. Over the lifetime of the commitment, the investor will receive 20 payments of $50 each, and at the end of the 20-year period his initial $1,000 will be refunded. If this bond has been issued by the United States Treasury, the investor can be assured that he will suffer no losses with respect to interest or principal. Does it then follow that he incurs no risks whatever? The answer, of course, is that he does in fact run a sometimes substantial risk of a loss in purchasing power. He is, in effect, locked into a position wherein he receives an assured constant number of dollars, but these dollars are of uncertain value. To illustrate this point, consider the following extreme situation. The $1,000 used to purchase the 20-year bond referred to above has a current value of $1,000. If, during the 20-year life of the instrument, price levels double or dollars become worth half as much, the value of the $1,000 when returned 20 years from now is only $500.

In consequence, when investors anticipate that the economy is embarking on an inflationary trend, they will be unwilling to risk a loss in purchasing power unless they are compensated by means of extremely high coupon rates on fixed-return securities. In 1969 and 1970, such inflationary tendencies were very evident, and so too was the resistance of investors to fixed-return securities. In recognition of these factors, new issues of corporate bonds of the highest quality offered interest yields in excess of 9 and 10 percent, compared to 4 to 6 percent 10 years ago.

The purchasing-power risk is then a very real hazard from which rational investors seek protection. That protection may take the form of a shift of funds to common stocks whose variable returns should keep pace with rising price levels or a demand for higher interest rates on fixed-return securities. In either situation, available investment funds will be allocated to the securities of those firms which the investor thinks can provide adequate protection against the purchasing-power risk.

Interest-rate Risk

Yet another risk with which investors must cope is interest-rate risk. This concept can be most fruitfully defined by using as an example a fixed-return security which is safe from any threat of default by the issuer. We will use a United States government bond. If an investor purchases such a bond, he agrees contractually, let us say, to accept a specified return, such as 4 percent over a specified period of 10 years duration. The yield on this instrument purchased at par is definitionally 4 percent. After the investor has held the bond for one year, there occurs a general increase in interest rates for such instruments. At that time interest rates have risen to $4\frac{1}{2}$ percent. Has the value of the original investment been affected by this increase in interest rates? Let's give it some thought. You paid $1,000 for your bond one year ago. Would another investor be willing to purchase it from you now for $1,000? Obviously not, if he can buy a similar instrument which offers a $4\frac{1}{2}$ percent yield. Your bond is then unsalable at $1,000. This does not, however, mean there is no market for your security. There are other investors who would be willing to purchase your 4 percent bond at some price less than $1,000. In short, you will find a ready market only if you offer the bond at a price less than $1,000 which results in a $4\frac{1}{2}$ percent yield to the prospective buyer. Standard bond yield tables are available to solve the pricing problem. They would show that at a price of $96\frac{5}{16}$ rather than 100, your bond would yield $4\frac{1}{2}$ percent. The resultant sale would involve a loss of $37 to you as an investor.

The risk that such sales and losses will be realized by investors in fixed-return securities is commonly known as interest-rate risk. It is obvious that a general decline in interest rates would cause the bond described above to increase rather than decrease in value. Consequently, when investors are generally assuming that interest rates will fall, they are normally willing to pay premiums for new securities, especially those of long maturities. These uncertainties with respect to securities values require compensation.

Financial Risk

Basically, the two types of investment risks, which have been described above are risks which are incurred by purchasers of bonds and preferred stocks. Financial risk, on the other hand, must be endured by almost all investors except those who purchase government securities.[1] Securities are claims on the earning power and assets of the issuers. Financial risk relates to the uncertainty that the issuer will be able to meet these claims. The claims of bonds to interest and eventual repayment are clear. The claims of common stockholders are less easily defined, but may be viewed as anticipated dividends and the eventual income resulting from resale of the shares held. In either case, there exists the risk that

[1] Since the federal government can both tax and print currency, investors who hold its obligations are secure.

the anticipated payments will not be received because of the legal or economic failure of the issuer.

The financial risk associated with any one issuer will be a function of its industry and capital structure. It is evident that certain industries are inherently more risky than others. Those which supply consumers with necessities are unlikely to find their markets disappearing as readily as those which furnish consumers with optimal or luxury items. On this basis alone, an electric utility firm would be required to furnish a much lower level of compensation for financial risk to its investors than would a manufacturer of high-style women's sportswear. These two firms present entirely different risk profiles. You may ask then why any investor would purchase the securities of the sportswear manufacturer in preference to the public utility. You have only to recall that we began our entire discussion by showing that some investors prefer large returns to small returns and are willing to endure risk when the level of returns is an adequate compensation for the risks undertaken. The securities of the sportswear manufacturers are attractive because they promise higher returns as compensation for the increased risk.

In addition to basic business risks which are related to the issuer's industry, other risks can and do result from the financial structure which has been evolved by the firm.

As we have previously determined, the right-hand side of the firm's balance sheet sets forth the claims of all who are involved in the business. Our suppliers are represented by accounts payable, the government by accrued taxes, etc. Long-term claimants such as bondholders and owners are represented by the accounts of bonds payable and owners' equity (capital stock), respectively. Within certain limits, the corporation is free to structure these claims in any manner which the directors and management feel to be optimal. If the firm chooses to include in its capital structure a high percentage of legal debt, that is, debt which if unsettled leads to bankruptcy, the corporation has added financial risk to the basic business risk which is present in all enterprises. Investors in corporate securities prefer less risk to greater risk and, consequently, will demand higher returns from the firm which chooses to burden itself with a high level of legal debt. While a discussion of optimal financial structure is considered in the following chapter, it must be noted here that the manner in which assets are financed greatly affects the value and, consequently, the price of the firm's securities, which are the claims on the anticipated returns of those very assets.

With respect to financial risk, then, investors demand compensation which is consistent with the level of risk involved. Corporate financial managers, if they are to attract investment funds, must pay this price.

Market Risk

The fourth and final investment risk which requires some discussion is market risk. Market risk takes the form of a decline in the investment value of a security which is not occasioned by a change in the business prospects of the issuer. For example, buyers of electric utility stocks in late 1961 paid prices which were as high as 23 times current earnings. Soon thereafter, the prices of these stocks retreated rapidly as the general level of the stock market declined. Thus, a stock which was earning $2 per share and selling for $46 declined in value to $22, or 11 times the earnings in 1962. Investors suffered losses in these stocks despite the fact that the earnings and the prospects of the issuers had not been greatly changed. The price changes which had occurred resulted from the fact that general market levels of all stocks had been greatly inflated and consequently declined rapidly during the 1962 market reappraisal. Just as there is an opportunity to suffer losses when the stock market turns down, there exists a like opportunity to realize gains when a change in the pessimistic anticipations of investors causes stock prices to rise from their current low levels.

Figure 12-3 indicates that since 1950, stock prices have risen on a generally upward trend, but there have been significant variations from this trend. Thus, even in a generally rising market, it is conceivable that losses will be realized when securities are purchased at high points and sold at the following low point of the cycle. If the investor's tenure of ownership or ability to hold the security once purchased is high, losses may then be avoided by holding the security through the declining market phase rather than selling it. Not all investors, however, have this ability,

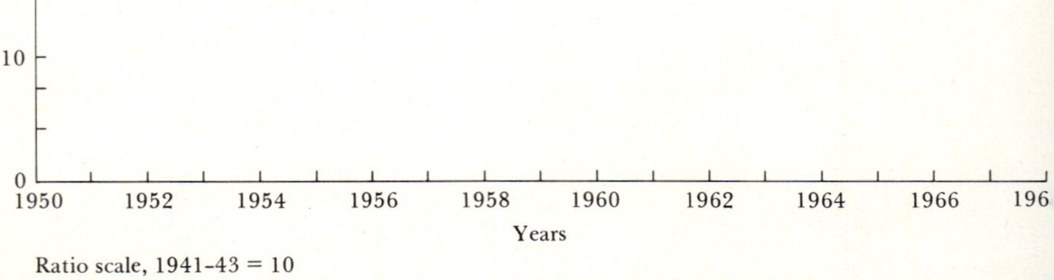

Figure 12-3 Stock prices, Standard and Poor's Corporation, 500 common stocks.

and they must therefore endure the risks associated with potential sales in declining markets.

Significance of Investment Risks to Cost of Capital

The investor, as we have seen, requires compensation for risks before he commits his investment funds to any one firm. He will, as we have seen, be willing to assume a high level of risk only in response to the anticipation of a high level of return.

The terms or costs which are involved in attracting available investment funds into the enterprise are then related to the risks which are associated with investment in that enterprise. Consequently, one of the tasks of the financial manager will be to reduce the uncertainties or risks associated with investment in the firm's securities. In so doing he will assure the business of adequate financing on reasonable terms. What can he do in this regard?

1. He can diversify in order to reduce the level of business risk which would be inherent in a firm whose total sales are dependent on a single industry.
2. He can ensure that capital allocations to new investment opportunities are thoroughly investigated during the capital budgeting procedure. In this way, hazards associated with new investment can be anticipated and successfully met.
3. He can ensure that the financial structure of the firm is compatible with the firm's ability to service all claims. In this way the threat of bankruptcy is reduced.
4. He can communicate to the investing public through investment advisory services. If such communication is maintained with a high level of credibility, investors will be well informed with regard to the firm's intermediate and long-run prospects. In this manner some uncertainty can be eliminated or controlled.

There are, of course, numerous other actions which he can take to affect the terms on which he can secure investment capital. His own ingenuity is paramount in this respect. President Jones has been justifiably concerned with the firm's ability to attract new capital. He has been concerned with the cost and terms under which investors will be willing to supply the firm with additional funds. These problems are ongoing ones for Jones Electronic, especially at this time when the proposed acquisition of ADCO requires definite action. Your decision will be made on the basis of ADCO's inherent potential for profitable operations and the cost of obtaining the required financing from the investment community. Let us turn to a consideration of the cost of capital.

COST OF CAPITAL

The term "cost of capital" as generally used in the study of financial management is a broad concept and is not subject to a single definition. This is so because, in general, we use the term with reference to three distinctly different groups. More important, these three groups often have three distinctly different interests, aims, or goals. It is, therefore, convenient to define the term "cost of capital" within a framework that will recognize these differences. This we will do. We will have, in fact, three definitions. "Cost of capital" will be related to (1) the firm itself as represented by professional management, (2) the new equity investor, and (3) the purchaser of debt securities.

The Firm as Represented by Professional Management

The ultimate normal goal of professional management is to maximize the market value of the equity investor's investment. This maximization will normally manifest itself via increasing long-run earnings per share, which in turn will ultimately result in a continuous long-run increase in the market value of the firm's stock. The minimum goal professional management must meet is to produce a level of earnings per share that will not dilute the current value of the present stockholder's equity. As a first approximation and in a general way, we will define this minimum goal as the cost of capital for the firm.

The phrase "current value" as applied to a given firm is in turn difficult to define. From the financial executive's point of view, the word "value" itself implies some standard that cannot be explained in a word. It is obvious that machinery is machinery, equipment is equipment, and assets are assets. However, when these factors are brought together with the personality, ability, and knowledge of management, the combination forms an entity that in itself has a personality and presents a public image. When this personality and/or image is placed within a framework that includes earnings, dividends, growth prospects, and public participation, the firm as an entity then has *intrinsic* financial *value.* This value will, of course, not remain static, but will vary from time to time as the component factors change. Professional management's concern is the rate of the firm's growth (or decline) as compared with other firms in the industry and/or the economy in general. In the long run, with emphasis on the word "long," the value of the firm will in general be expressed by the market price at which rational and informed investors are willing to buy and sell the firm's stock. In the short run, irrational and/or psychological factors can and do cause the market value of the firm's stock to fluctuate around its intrinsic value. In fact, it is this discrepancy between the market value in the short run and the intrinsic value over a longer period that gives rise to many extraordinary capital gain opportunities for equity investors.

The New Equity Investor

The second interested group is composed of the new equity investor and his advisors. There are several types of equity investors. The first type can be labeled the conservative investor. This type of investor is primarily interested in the safety and security of the principal of his investment and will, therefore, not generally accept high levels of risk even in return for a prospectively high rate of return (earnings per share and/or dividends per share). At the other extreme is the speculator. This type of investor will take a higher risk and expects a correspondingly higher rate of return. Between these two extremes there are the many equity investors who will take various degrees of risk and expect various levels of return with respect to the risk on their investments.

Once an equity investor identifies or defines the degree of total risk he is willing to assume (purchasing-power risk, credit or business risk, interest-rate risk, market risk), the rational equity investor will invest in that equity security which promises the highest possible return for that level of risk. This minimum acceptable return is his cost of capital. It perhaps could be stated as his opportunity cost.

The Investor in Debt

The third group we have identified is composed of the investors who purchase debt securities. The debt investor, like the equity investor, must likewise identify the degree of total risk he is willing to assume. In general, the more risk he is willing to assume, the higher return he will expect from his investment in the form of interest. Earnings per share are of interest to him only insofar as the firm has the ability to pay the periodic fixed-interest charges and to return his principal at maturity. In essence, like the equity investor, within the appropriate risk parameters of the individual debt investor, the "cost of capital" for the debt investor is likewise his "opportunity cost." The phrase "opportunity cost" as used in our definitions has some implications we should recognize.

As Shakespeare once said, "One man in his time plays many parts." Likewise, an equity investor may shift to the position of a debt investor and vice versa, or one individual may be an equity and a debt investor at the same time. That is to say, he may hold a portfolio of both debt and equity securities. His goal, however, will be unchanged in that he will still be demanding the highest return possible for the composite risk which he is willing to assume.

The minimum rate of return or "cost of capital" we could expect the informed debt (or equity) investor to settle for would be the return on United States government obligations. These obligations are secured by the credit of the United States government, carry the minimum risk in the short run, and are readily salable. (The equity investor could always sell his equity shares and purchase the government obligations.) The rate of interest paid on government securities does fluctuate according to market demand. However, if these secure government issues paid 3, 5, or 7 percent, one could expect this rate to be the absolute minimum total return any investor would accept on any other security. That is to say that the interest rate paid by United States government obligations would serve as a bench mark for any type of investor's "cost of capital."

If great numbers of investors switch to the government securities (or any other type of debt), the increased demand for debt capital could be expected to drive the interest rate down, and the equity rate of return could become more attractive! Therefore, the interests and "opportunity costs" of one group will vitally affect the interests and "opportunity costs" of another group as well as members of the same group. We would not, however, be accurate nor would it be feasible to combine the interests and opportunities of the several groups into a single definition of the "cost of capital," and we have not. They are interdependent at times, but they are not identical.

In short, then, the cost of capital for any firm is that rate which must be earned by the firm in order to attract investment funds. This rate also dictates the minimum return which must be earned by the firm on its internal investments. This internal rate must be such that the returns demanded by investors can be met.

PROBABLE VALUE OF FIRM'S STOCK

Within the frame of reference we have established, we can now attempt to combine our "cost of capital" concepts with the problem of determining an appropriate but hypothetical market value and cost of capital for the Jones Electronic Corporation stock. Our investment banker has advised that we might well need this estimate for two reasons. First, it may be necessary to place the Jones stock with a trustee as collateral for a debt issue; second, it may be necessary to sell additional shares of the Jones stock. We may need a combination of debt and equity in order to raise the $4 million required to purchase ADCO.

Comparison with Other Firms

The banker indicated that our first problem would be to find several firms about the same size as Jones Electronic Corporation with about the same risk factors. It was suggested that an analysis of certain financial ratios of the firms selected would or could lead to some idea of a probable value of the Jones stock.

As a point of departure, the investment banker recommended to us the X Corporation and the Y Corporation. The market price and the earnings per share for the X Corporation currently are $25 and $2.50, respectively. The Y Corporation stock is currently selling at $50 per share and is earning $4 per share. The banker stated that further examination of the X Corporation's and the Y Corporation's recent financial statements indicates that the market price for each of the two companies can be expressed in the following multiples:

	X Corporation	**Y Corporation**
Times earnings per share, 1971	10	$12\frac{1}{2}$
Times earnings per share, 1966–1971	14	14.6
Times dividends per share, 1971	20	25
Times dividends per share, 1966–1971	22	29.2
Times book value per share, 1971	1.4	1.3
Market price per share, 1971	$25	$50

The data for X Corporation and Y Corporation could be presented in another way:

	X Corporation	**Y Corporation**
$\text{Price-earnings ratio} = \dfrac{\text{market price}}{\text{earnings after taxes (1971)}}$	$\dfrac{\$25}{\$2.50} = 10 \text{ times}$	$\dfrac{\$50}{\$4} = 12\frac{1}{2} \text{ times}$
$\text{Current earnings yield} = \dfrac{\text{earnings after taxes (1971)}}{\text{market price}}$	$\dfrac{\$2.50}{\$25} = 10\%$	$\dfrac{\$4}{\$50} = 8\%$
$\text{Current dividend yield} = \dfrac{\text{dividend (1971)}}{\text{market price}}$	$\dfrac{\$1.25}{\$25} = 5\%.$	$\dfrac{\$2}{\$50} = 4\%$

These figures indicate that present equity investors in X Corporation are currently receiving a 10 percent return on their investment as measured by the earnings-yield ratio and a 5 percent return based on the dividends yield (X paid 50 percent of earnings as a dividend). Stockholders of Y Corporation receive currently an 8 percent return on their investment as measured by the earnings-yield ratio and a 4 percent return as measured by the dividend yield (50 percent of earnings paid out as dividends).[1]

The current 1969 earnings per share for the Jones Corporation are $3.42, based on the present 50,000 shares outstanding. The average earnings for the period 1968–1971 were $3.25 per share. The Jones book value per share is currently approximately $6.50 per share. If we would apply the X Corporation and the Y Corporation multiples as indicated above, the probable market value of the Jones Electronic Corporation stock could be calculated as follows:

PROBABLE VALUE OF JONES ELECTRONIC CORPORATION STOCK

	Based on	
	X Corporation	Y Corporation
Based on 1971 earnings	$34.20	$42.75
Based on average earnings, 1968–1971	$32.50	$39.625
Based on dividends, 1971	None	None
Based on average dividends, 1968–1971	None	None
Based on book value, 1971	$4.79	$4.45

We must be careful before we arrive at too many conclusions concerning the probable market value of the Jones stock from the results above. As with most, if not all, of our analyses, there is an implicit assumption involved! The general manager put his finger directly on the point when he said, "Wait a minute, I never invest my money on what a company has done; I'm only interested in what it is going to do!" He is absolutely right! Our analysis based on 1971 earnings can be valid only if we assume that the X Corporation and the Y Corporation will continue to earn exactly $2.50 and exactly $4 per share indefinitely and that the Jones earnings will be exactly $3.42 per share indefinitely. The same observation is true if we use the average earnings for the 1968–1971 period. Investors, as we know, may have very different expectations. In short, when analysts use historical data to arrive at the probable value of a given stock, they are using history only as a point of departure to estimate future earnings! As a matter of fact,

[1] The willingness of rational investors to accept a lower return on their investment in Y Corporation is related to a number of factors such as a difference in the risk associated with X's returns to Y's returns or different assumptions with respect to future performance, that is, accepting a lower current return on Y in anticipation of higher future returns. These problems will be explicitly considered later in this and the following chapter.

have we not proved about three times already that the market value (present value) of any investment is nothing more than future anticipated earnings discounted back to the present time? Stated another way, isn't the current market value of any stock simply the present value of an annuity (annual earnings per share or annual dividends per share or both) discounted at an "appropriate" rate of interest (the investor's "cost of capital")? The answer to all these questions is yes!

We can now translate the Jones data into the following form:

$$\text{Price-earnings ratio} = \frac{\$34.20}{\$3.42} = 10 \text{ times}$$

$$\text{Earnings-yield ratio} = \frac{\$3.42}{\$34.20} = 10\%$$

Dividend-yield ratio = none

If the Jones stock were selling at $34.20 per share, one would be tempted to say from the Jones ratios that investors who are interested in the degree of risk the Jones Corporation offers are at present demanding a 10 percent return on their investment. It could be argued that this is evident by the fact that they are willing to pay 10 times estimated future earnings. Don't you say it! Consider the results if investors immediately estimated future earnings to increase one-third to $4.56 per share while current earnings remain at $3.42 per share. If the investor's cost of capital remained at 10 percent, the market price could be expected to increase to $45.60, calculated as follows:

1. $$\frac{\text{Market price}}{\text{Anticipated earnings}} = \frac{\$45.60}{\$4.56} = 10 \text{ times}$$

$$\frac{\text{Anticipated earnings}}{\text{Market price}} = \frac{\$4.56}{\$45.60} = 10\%$$

The ratios, after the market price of the stock increased to $45.60 per share, would appear as follows:

2. $$\frac{\text{Market price}}{\text{Current earnings}} = \frac{\$45.60}{\$3.42} = 13.3 \text{ times earnings}$$

$$\frac{\text{Current earnings}}{\text{Market price}} = \frac{\$3.42}{\$45.60} = 7.5\%$$

Future earnings would be discounted at 10 percent, and the current earnings yield (perhaps temporarily) would drop to 7.5 percent! Some equity investors in the Jones stock would, if they held their stock, thus be willing to accept a current yield of 7.5 percent in return for anticipated future earnings yielding 10 percent. We must remember that no meaningful analysis is generally this simple. Nor is this one!

Other less well-informed investors may anticipate no increase in earnings and still be perfectly satisfied with a 7.5 percent return (item 2 above)! If earnings do increase to $4.56 per share, it is possible for the "7.5 percent investor" to receive "economic profits," or those profits that were above and beyond what is necessary to keep his funds invested in Jones stock, at least temporarily. However, what would you expect to happen to the market value of the Jones stock if other "7.5 percent investors" learned of the anticipated earnings per share or the anticipated earnings yield and decided to buy the stock? Their decision to purchase the shares would indicate that they believed 7.5 percent was an adequate payment for the risks involved. The market price could be expected to increase in these circumstances to a value of $60.80.

$$\frac{\$4.56}{\$60.80} = 7.5\%$$

If the market value of the Jones stock were "pushed" to $60.80 and the "10 percent investor" anticipated no further increase in the future earnings per share, he could be expected to sell his stock. The increased supply of Jones stock on the market may or may not cause the market price to fall. It would depend upon whether there were enough "7.5 percent investors" willing to buy the stock. Normally, however, the market price of the Jones stock could be expected to fall at least slightly, if only temporarily.

The same movements in the market price of the Jones stock could be expected (1) if a large portion of the present Jones stockholders were not willing to wait for the future 10 percent return and, in fact, see the opportunity to earn a current 10 percent return via another investment; or (2) if the current stockholders simply do not share the optimistic outlook; or (3) if the current stockholders elect to take advantage of the capital gain opportunity and decide to sell their present holdings. These shares would then be offered on the market. If the number of shares offered by present stockholders were numerous enough, the supply could exceed the demand and the market price of the Jones stock could be expected to retreat to somewhat lower levels. If the market price fell to $40 and if the present earnings remained at $3.42 per share, the investor's current earnings yield might slip back to 8.55 percent.

$$\frac{\text{Market price}}{\text{Current earnings}} = \frac{\$40}{\$3.42} = 11.66 \text{ times earnings}$$

$$\frac{\text{Current earnings}}{\text{Market price}} = \frac{\$3.42}{\$40} = 8.55\% \text{ current earnings-yield ratio}$$

As indicated, this market-price retreat may well be temporary. If informed, rational investors still anticipate a $4.56 earnings per share in the future and continue to demand a 10 percent return (because other investment opportunities with relatively equal risks offered no more than an anticipated 10 percent return), the Jones stock could be expected to move back up toward the former $45.60 market price. (Continue to keep in mind that we are still talking about a first approximation!)

It would seem at this point that we have learned our lesson, which is that the probable market value for the Jones stock is only remotely (if at all) related to the historical data for the X Corporation and the Y Corporation. We as investors are primarily interested in future earnings.

Having disposed of the X Corporation and the Y Corporation as a basis for a probable value for the Jones stock, we must move on in our efforts to determine a probable market price for the Jones stock.

In order to put the analysis that follows in the proper frame of reference, we must restate our definition of the firm's cost of capital set forth earlier (that rate of earnings per share and/or dividends per share that will not dilute the value of the present stockholders' equity). You have perhaps noticed that we have been referring to earnings per share and/or dividends per share. At this point, we want to briefly zero in on the "and/or." As indicated earlier, not all equity investors' aims and goals may be the same. One type of investor may be interested in earnings per share and growth of the firm with the implied capital gains opportunity. A second type of equity investor may be interested in the payout received in the form of dividends per share. A third type of equity investor may be interested in both dividends and earnings. One firm cannot be all things to all people at the same time, nor can our analysis! As the financial executive of the Jones Electronic Corporation contemplating a possible public offering of Jones stock, your first problem will be to define the "financial market" (the type of equity investor) we hope to attract. Our aim, of course, is to appeal to the greatest market segment possible in order to obtain the highest price possible for the shares we intend to offer. As always, there are alternatives. In broad perspective, the alternatives boil down to (1) the "earnings group," (2) the "dividends group," or (3) the "dividend and earnings group." We will deal with the "earnings group" first, the "dividends group" second, and finally, the "dividends and earnings" group.

Probable Value to Earnings Group

As a point of departure, we need the net worth section of the latest Jones Electronic Corporation balance sheet.

Net worth

Common stock	50,000 shares issued 500,000 shares authorized		$ 85,833
Retained earnings			
Beginning-of-year balance		$240,917	
Profit for year (net of taxes)		192,775	433,692
Total net worth			$519,525

Book value per share $\frac{\$519{,}525}{50{,}000 \text{ shares}} = \$10.39+, \text{ or } \$10.40$

Earnings per share last year $\frac{\$192{,}500}{50{,}000 \text{ shares}} = \$3.85+, \text{ or } \$3.85$

Net worth at beginning of year

Common stock	$ 85,833
Retained earnings	240,917
	$326,750

Return on net worth

$$\frac{\text{Earnings } \$192{,}500}{\text{Net worth } \$326{,}750} = 58.99\%, \text{ or } 59\%$$

It is clear that Jones earned 59 percent on net worth this past year. Does this mean that the Jones "cost of capital" is 59 percent? Must we continue to earn 59 percent on net worth in order not to dilute stockholders' equity? The answer is no. (Recall your definition of the cost of capital.) This observation is clearly correct and can be demonstrated by adding the $192,500 earned during the year to retained earnings and then calculating the rate of return on net worth.

$$\frac{\text{Earnings } \$192{,}775}{\text{Net worth } \$519{,}525} = 37\%$$

Examine the same ratio one year later, assuming the same dollar earnings:

$$\frac{\text{Earnings } \$192{,}775}{\text{Net worth } \$712{,}300} = 27\%$$

Clearly, the earnings-to-net-worth percentage relationship does not reflect accurately the firm's cost of capital.

As an example, let us assume that we sold 50,000 shares of Jones stock for $4 million. If we insist upon a 27 percent return on net worth on this new investment, the required earnings for the new acquisition will be \$1,080,000 per year (\$4 million × 27 percent × \$1,080,000). This sum would equal earnings per share for the new stock of \$21.60. The present stock, 50,000 shares, would thus pick up a windfall, if present equity or operations earned the same \$3.85 per share during the same period based on the original 50,000 shares outstanding.

50,000 shares presently outstanding	× \$ 3.85	=	\$ 192,500
50,000 shares new issue	× 21.60	=	1,080,000
			\$1,272,500

$$\frac{100{,}000 \text{ shares}}{\$1{,}272{,}500} = \$12.73 \text{ new combined earnings per share!}$$

If investors are anticipating no growth, the new share must earn only \$3.85 per share, or a total of \$192,500 if the intrinsic value of the Jones stock is to remain constant. Any earnings per share above this amount would increase this value, and any lesser amount would have the contrary effect.

As indicated, we could express the required earnings per share as a percentage without any difficulty. If the additional stock issued for \$4 million increased capital by 50,000 shares and the required earnings were \$192, 500 (\$3.85 per share), we could say that the firm's marginal "cost of capital" (for this one transaction) was 4.819 percent, or 4.82 percent. The low rate of 4.82 percent should lead us to believe that investors would not be purchasing historic earnings alone, but rather are anticipating some growth in earnings.

$$\frac{\$192{,}500}{\$4{,}000{,}000} = 4.82\%$$

However, as we have seen, the percentage will change as the data are changed. The required *earnings per share,* however, *remain constant* for any number of new shares of capital stock if the growth assumption is valid.

As always, the analysis is not quite as simple (but almost) as indicated above. Consider the same 50,000 shares for the same \$4 million, but include the flotation costs (the expense involved in marketing the stock). The investment banker indicated that it would cost about 5 percent, or \$250,000, to market the stock. This means we would receive \$3,750,000 and the rate of earnings on the new capital must be 5.14 percent in order to equal \$3.85 per share.

$$\frac{\$192{,}500}{\$3{,}750{,}000} = 5.14\%$$

Have the required earnings per share changed? No, we still need $3.85 per share. However, these same earnings per share translate to very different expressions as rate percents. This is why we prefer to express the firm's "cost of capital" in terms of earnings per share. It is clear, concise, constant, and understandable!

Significance of Financing Mix on Cost of Debt and Equity Capital

The cost of debt capital is considerably easier to calculate. We are not directly concerned with earnings per share, nor would we be concerned with the cost of any prior debt issues. Again, we are concerned with a marginal decision. Quite simply, if the present market rate of interest for long-term debt, with total risks comparable to those of the Jones organization, is 8 percent, the effective or after-tax interest rate to Jones will be 4 percent (assuming a 50 percent marginal tax rate). The after-tax cost of debt is used in order to make the data consistent. You will recall that the cost of common equity has been covered in terms of earnings per share. As such, this cost is an after-tax cost. Thus, the cost of debt must be considered on the same basis. Flotation costs, again, would raise the rate somewhat. If these costs totaled $250,000, Jones would receive $3,750,000. Interest would equal $320,000 on $4 million. The interest would be allowed as a tax deduction so that the effective cost of the debt capital would then be 4.26 percent.

$$\frac{\$160{,}000}{\$3{,}750{,}000} = 4.26\% \text{ or } \$160{,}000 \text{ per year to cover annual interest expense}$$

Since the debt investor does not participate in earnings beyond the interest received, any earnings above 4.26 percent on the $3,750,000 in funds received would thus increase the present shareholders' earnings per share. A quick answer to the Jones problem would be "finance with debt." (Another significant consideration would be that the debt would be paid in 15 or 20 years, depending upon the terms of the loan, while the dividends to the new stockholders would go on forever.)

Calculated cost of $4 million in equity	5.1405%
Calculated cost of $4 million in debt	4.2666%
Saving when financed with debt	0.8739%

Which means that the $3,750,000 ($4 million minus flotation costs) acquired by equity financing must earn 5.14 percent in order to produce $3.85 per share, and that the $3,750,000 acquired by debt financing must earn 4.26 percent in order not to dilute the present earnings of $3.85 per share.

It can be noted that should President Jones choose to acquire ADCO in exchange for Jones stock in what is known as a tax-free exchange, ADCO would have to earn $3.85 per share, just as Jones Electronic stock would, in order not not to dilute the earnings of the present Jones Corporation stockholders. On the other hand, if President Jones should choose to acquire ADCO in exchange for Jones bonds, ADCO would have to earn only $160,000 (after taxes) in order not to dilute the earnings of the Jones corporate stockholders. For emphasis, the stock deal must earn $3.85 per share after taxes; the bond deal requires earnings of only $160,000 after taxes. This is so because interest on bonds (with an exception to follow) is a deductible business expense.

We conclude, then, that in order not to dilute the $3.85 earnings per share that the existing stockholders of the Jones company presently realize on the 50,000 shares of stock they now hold:

1. The $3,750,000 net proceeds from the issuance of 50,000 additional shares of stock must generate earnings of $385,550 less federal income tax thereon of $192,775, a net of $192,775.
2. The $3,750,000 net proceeds from the issuance of $4 million per value of bonds must generate $160,000 in order to meet the yearly deductible interest charges of $160,000 (4 percent of $4 million after taxes).

   The difference between the amounts required to be earned by equity financing ($385,550) and by debt financing ($160,000) is $225,550.

In addition to the above consideration, you are keeping firmly in mind the fact that if ADCO can be acquired by debt financing, the 4.26 percent on $3,750,000 ($160,000) will revert to the present stockholders as an addition to earnings per share when the debt has been retired. This is in contrast to the fact that dividends to the new equity owners from earnings will be a continuous obligation of the firm.

It is apparent that there is an advantage to be gained by debt financing. The tax factor produces the advantage that interest on debt is tax-deductible, while dividends are not. It should be pointed out that the advantage of debt financing extends to a corporation using borrowed funds for acquiring its own outstanding stock. The acquisition increases the earnings per share of the corporation's shares still outstanding. This in turn generally produces a favorable effect on the prices of these shares. Further, if the treasury shares are later sold at a profit, the profit may be tax-free to the corporation.

After carefully studying these figures, you were convinced—finance with debt—but you did have some mixed emotions. You have been forcefully reminded again and again that almost every analysis is not as simple as it appears. You did, however, phone for an appointment to visit with the investment banker again.

You were right, it is just not that simple! After listening on the phone to your general analysis and ideas, the banker agreed that in principle you were relatively accurate. He also agreed that if the Jones and ADCO stock were placed with a trustee under a bond indenture,[1] you could probably raise the $4 million via debt. However, he did call attention to one assumption you had made, and that was the 8 percent interest rate. He asked that you delay your visit until the first of next week so he could do a little homework.

We tried to play golf over the weekend, but your score was almost as high as the numbers you kept talking about! I didn't think you would make it until Monday—but you did. You arrived on time for your appointment. After some preliminary conversation, you were soon examining the following schedule indicating the investor's required cost of capital.

Straight Debt Financing		Equity Financing	
Amount	Required Effective Interest Rate to Maturity	Amount	Required Return
$1,000,000	8%	$3,000,000	8%
2,000,000	10	2,000,000	7
3,000,000	15	1,000,000	15
4,000,000	20	—0—	

The banker explained that our assumption of 8 percent would be valid within a limited range of debt financing. As the amount of debt increased, the business or credit risk alone would balloon the interest requirements if the debt were to be salable. In addition, the banker advised that he probably could place a new Jones stock issue privately. A major insurance company had expressed interest. He explained further that the potential equity investor would pay a premium for the shares if some debt were present in the capital structure. Such debt would allow the firm to use financial leverage for the benefit of the equity

[1] An indenture is a document which details the responsibilities of the corporation or issuer to the purchasers of its debt securities. It also establishes procedures to be followed by the trustee should the issuing firm fail to meet its responsibilities to the bondholders.

The number of new shares to be issued to be used in step 2 was not so readily obtained. It is necessary to determine the number of shares that would be issued at a calculated market price that would bring the Jones organization approximately $3 million after the sale. The number of shares to be sold will depend upon the calculated market price! The calculated market price, as you will see, will in turn depend upon the number of shares necessary to raise the $3 million! That may sound complicated, but the example worked out rather nicely by trial and error. As an example, the authors originally estimated 35,000 shares would have to be sold, and the analysis appeared as follows:

Original estimation:

2. New shares	35,000
Present shares	50,000
Total shares	85,000

Step 3 simply takes the total income after taxes that is available to equity and determines the earnings per share.

$$\frac{\text{Available for equity}}{\text{Total shares}} = \frac{\$570{,}000}{85{,}000} = \$6.70 \text{ earnings per share}$$

Step 4 capitalizes the earnings per share at the equity investor's cost of capital to arrive at a maximum probable market price.

$$\frac{\text{Earnings per share}}{\text{Capitalization rate}} = \frac{\$6.70}{0.08} = \$83.75$$

However, when we multiply $83.75 by 35,000 shares, we would only have raised $2,931,250 before the expense of the sale. The estimated 35,000 shares were arbitrarily raised to 40,000 shares, and the results were that we would raise $3,008,175 after the expense of the sale.

Steps 5 and 6 indicate the net proceeds to Jones for the sale of 40,000 shares.

The exact number of shares and the price per share can be accurately determined algebraically by the use of the following formula (X is the number of additional shares required to be issued for the $3 million):

$$\frac{\text{Total estimated income to equity } \$570{,}000}{\text{Present number of shares outstanding } 50{,}000 + X} \text{ multiplied by } X$$
$$= \$240{,}000 \text{ (8\% return on \$3,000,000)}$$

Therefore $X = 36{,}363$ shares.

$$\frac{\text{Amount received for shares}}{\text{Number of shares issued}} = \frac{\$3{,}000{,}000}{36{,}363} = \$82.50 \text{ market price per share}$$

Step 7 determines the cost of the debt and equity capital expressed as a percentage.

Step 8 weights the cost of the debt and equity capital required for the $4 million needed for the ADCO acquisition according to the 25 to 75 percent proportion.

ALTERNATIVE 2

50% Straight Debt, $2,000,000 at 10%
50% New Equity, $2,000,000 at 7%

---

1. ADCO marginal income after taxes, as estimated (assumes no growth) $450,000
   Less two times annual interest requirements (½ of 10%) × $2,000,000 × 2* 200,000
   $250,000
   Add Jones normal income (rounded) 200,000
   $450,000

2. New shares 25,000
   Present shares 50,000
   Total shares after new issue 75,000

3. $\dfrac{\text{Available for equity}}{\text{Total shares}} = \dfrac{\$450{,}000}{75{,}000} = \$6.00$ earnings per share

4. $\dfrac{\text{Earnings per share}}{\text{Capitalization rate}} = \dfrac{\$6.00}{0.07} = \$85.71$ *maximum* probable market price

5. $ 85.71 Market price
   25,000 New shares
   $2,142,750 Gross funds provided by new equity

6. $2,142,750 Gross funds
   107,137 Less 5% flotation costs
   $2,035,613 Net funds to Jones

7. Effective cost of new funds:

   Debt: $\dfrac{\text{Required annual interest}}{\text{Net proceeds from debt}} = \dfrac{\$100{,}000}{\$1{,}900{,}000\dagger} = 5.26\%$

   New equity: $\dfrac{\text{Required earnings, new shares } (25{,}000 \times \$6.00)}{\text{Net proceeds, new equity capital}} = \dfrac{\$150{,}000}{\$2{,}035{,}613} = 7.368\%$

8. Weighted cost of new capital:
   Debt: 50% × 5.26% = 2.63%
   Equity: 50% × 7.368% = 3.68
   6.31%

---

* By using two times the annual interest requirements, there is built into our estimated calculations a margin of safety which will result in a somewhat lower, more conservative maximum probable market price.

† $2,000,000 less $100,000 flotation costs.

ALTERNATIVE 3

75% Straight debt, $3,000,000 at 15%
25% New equity, $1,000,000 at 15%

---

1. ADCO marginal income after taxes, as estimated (assumes no growth) $450,000
   Less two times annual interest requirements (½ of 15%) × $3,000,000 × 2 450,000
   —0—

There is little point in carrying this analysis any further. The marginal income from ADCO would barely cover the interest requirements! Now we must build a framework for further analysis of the ADCO acquisition.

Alternative	No. of New Shares	Maximum Selling Price	Required Earnings per Share	Annual Interest Expense	Firm's Weighted Cost of Capital	Average Earnings per Share All Shares
1	40,000	$79.16	$6.33	40,000	7.36%	$6.333
2	25,000	85.71	6.00	100,000	6.31	6.000
3	None					

A significant aspect we must not overlook is the immediate increase in the book value of President Jones' stock (and yours!).

Present book value per share	$10.40
Present net worth	$ 519,525
Add new equity (alternative 2)	2,035,613
Total net worth	$2,555,138

$$\frac{\text{Total net worth } \$2{,}555{,}138}{\text{Number of shares } 75{,}000} = \$34.07 \text{ (rounded) new book value}$$

BOOK VALUE

	No. of Shares	Old Book Value	New Book Value	Increment
President Jones' stock	45,000	$468,000	$1,533,150	$1,065,150
Your stock	5,000	52,000	170,350	118,350

More important, consider the market value of your present holdings.

MARKET VALUE

	No. of Shares	Anticipated Market Value per Share	Anticipated Total Market Value
President Jones' stock	45,000	$85.71	$3,856,950
Your stock	5,000	85.71	428,550
Total market value	50,000		$4,285,500

The basic question now is, What is the significance of what we have now that we have it? There is little point in examining alternatives 3 and 4 in any detail. The rate of interest is just too high, and ADCO earnings will not cover these requirements. In addition, the risk to the equity shareholder would be so high that the shares could not be sold regardless of price. However, we can make several observations.

Our framework shows that if our decision between alternatives 1 and 2 were made on the basis of the lower cost of capital, alternative 2 would be the choice. Alternative 2 requires that Jones issue 25,000 shares instead of the 40,000 shares indicated by alternative 1. This means that future income must be split among only 75,000 shares instead of 90,000 shares under alternative 1! Further, the indicated selling price for alternative 1 is $79.16 as compared with $85.71 under alternative 2. The significance of this difference would be reflected in a lower immediate increase in both the book and the market value of the present shares. Required earnings per share under alternative 2 would be *$6.00* as compared with *$6.33* under alternative 1 in the short run. Any future additional earnings above the calculated amount of net income available to equity would be split, as indicated, with 25,000 instead of 40,000 new shares! It was precisely this latter point, plus the fact that the present 50,000 shares would control two-thirds (50,000 shares/75,000 shares) of the common-stock votes and thus could effectively control the board of directors, that would cause President Jones to favor alternative 2.

Significance of Increased Sales Volume to Earnings per Share

President Jones had pointed out that he could see continued growth of sales at about 10 percent per year for at least five years and then, perhaps, sales would level off. (Our market-value calculations, thus far, have been based on the assumption of "no growth.") What is the significance of this? Does this mean that earnings per share will grow as follows?

Present earnings per share	= $6.00
First year	$6.00 + 10% = $6.60
Second year	$6.60 + 10% = $7.26
Third year	$7.26 + 10% = $7.98
Fourth year	$7.98 + 10% = $8.78
Fifth year	$8.78 + 10% = $9.66

Don't you ever believe it! Why? Let me ask you a couple of questions. First, do you have the additional capacity to handle the increase? Second, are you presently earning a profit? (The authors would like to leave three blank pages while you think about that! We're really back to Chapter 3, aren't we?)

Our analysis of the additional earnings per share for the next five years would be calculated as follows:

1. Sales at the present mix of 225,000 units of "normal" sales (56.25%) at $7.20 each and 175,000 units to Allied (43.75%) at $6 per unit indicate an average contribution to profit as follows:

	Normal Sales		Allied Sales
Selling price	$7.20		$6.00
Less variable cost	1.00		1.00
Contribution to profit	$6.20		$5.00
	×56.25%		×43.75%
Weighted contribution	$3.4875	plus	$2.1875 = $5.675 per unit

2. Increase in profit to equity with 10 percent increase in sales with constant sales mix.
Anticipated first-year sales—400,000 units.

Year	10% Increase in Units	Weighted Profit per Unit	Total Additional Profit	Additional Profit per Share per Year (Rounded) (75,000 Shares)
2	40,000	$5.675	$227,000	$3.02
3	44,000	5.675	249,700	3.33
4	48,400	5.675	274,670	3.66
5	53,240	5.675	302,037	4.03
6	58,560	5.675	332,328	4.43

Therefore, earnings per share would appear as follows:

Earnings per share first year	$ 6.00
Second year ($6.00 + $3.02)	9.02
Third year ($9.02 + $3.33)	12.35
Fourth year ($12.35 + $3.66)	16.01
Fifth year ($16.01 + $4.03)	20.04
Sixth year ($20.04 + $4.43)	24.47

SIGNIFICANCE OF PRESENT-VALUE ANALYSIS TO MARKET VALUE OF STOCK

As a matter of interest, we can discount these earnings at 8 percent (the equity investor's cost of capital) and decide how much the investment in ADCO is really worth to Jones and/or potential stockholders. We will deal with the potential new stockholder first. (We are moving into an area that really belongs as part of the subject matter of the more advanced course in finance. However, let's take a quick look at the general problems. Furthermore, President Jones wanted to see a five-year projection—without dividends!)

Year	Earnings per Share	Present-value Factor 8%		Present Value (75,000 Shares)
2	$ 9.02	0.926	=	$ 8.35
3	12.35	0.857	=	10.58
4	16.01	0.794	=	12.71
5	20.04	0.735	=	14.73
6	24.47	0.681	=	16.66
				$63.03+

Plus what? Plus some value for the stock after the five-year growth period. If we assume no further growth and that after the five years, growth earnings will remain at $24.47 per share indefinitely, we must discount this indefinite flow of earnings at 8 percent and bring this sum back five years.

$$\frac{\$24.47}{0.08} = \$305.87(0.681) = \$208.97$$

Therefore, the pattern of earnings outlined above capitalized at 8 percent is worth a total investment per share of $208.97 + $63.03, or $272! This indeed could be a glamour stock and could follow the pattern of glamour stocks that have gone before, which means the stock could sell 60, 70, 80, or 100+ times earnings!

President Jones reviewed your calculations and indicated that if you were even 50 percent too optimistic, it was clear to him at this point that he did not want to sell additional shares, if possible. The Jones organization, or rather, you and the president, were in a difficult position. If you could tell the story of your projected earnings, you might well sell your stock to that group of equity investors who either would be willing to anticipate earnings beyond the five-year period you have used as a cutoff date or would anticipate an even faster rate of growth. However, to do so, that is, to make public your knowledge of the ADCO potential, might only invite competitors or even persuade

Allied itself to make more of an effort to operate ADCO! For the moment, you could only sit tight.

You prepared for the president a summary of cumulative earnings per share and book value per share. These figures were based on the assumption that ADCO was purchased entirely by using borrowed funds in the amount of $4 million at 20 percent interest. The calculations further assume a 10 percent per year growth for five years following the year of acquisition.

	Total Earnings after ADCO Acquisition (after Taxes)	Less Interest on $4,000,000 at Effective Rate of 10%	Balance to Retained Earnings	Cumulative Balance Retained Earnings
Retained earnings balance				$ 519,525
First year + additional profit	$ 650,000*	$ 400,000	$ 250,000	769,525
	227,000			
Second year + additional profit	877,000	400,000	477,000	1,246,525
	249,700			
Third year + additional profit	1,126,700	400,000	726,700	1,973,225
	274,670			
Fourth year + additional profit	1,401,370	400,000	1,001,370	2,974,595
	301,910			
Fifth year + additional profit	1,703,280	400,000	1,303,280	4,277,875
	332,328			
Sixth year	2,035,608	400,000	1,635,608	5,913,483
Total	$7,793,958	$2,400,000	$5,393,958	

* ADCO Marginal Income	After Taxes	$450,000
Jones Company normal Income		200,000
		$650,000

Year	Earnings per Share (50,000 Shares)	Book Value per Share (50,000 Shares)
Last	$ 3.85	$ 10.40
Current (est.)	5.00	15.39
2	9.54	24.93
3	14.53	39.46
4	20.03	59.49
5	26.06	85.56
6	32.71	118.27

Productivity of retained earnings is equal to the change in EPS divided by the change in book value per share:

	$32.71		$118.27	
	−3.85		−10.40	
Change in EPS	$28.86	Change in book value	$107.87	$\frac{\$28.86}{\$107.87} = 26.75\%$

→ Growth of earning change in EPS ÷ Change in book value.

Probable Market Value to Earnings-Dividends Group

With this information now available, we can develop two concepts at the same time. We can examine the interests of the equity investor who is concerned with both dividends and earnings. In addition, we can drop the assumption of "no growth" as we estimate the probable intrinsic value of the Jones stock as expressed by a projected market price per share. This market price per share will be developed from an objective and rational frame of reference. We will not be concerned with the day-to-day psychological and/or illogical factors that may influence the short-run movements in the market price of equity securities. (One word of caution before we begin: More sophisticated applications of some of the principles we are about to develop are available. However, our present purpose is to develop concepts and ideas upon which we can build in more sophisticated studies of financial management in advanced courses.)

With this understanding we can now proceed through the several steps of our analysis, assuming that 50,000 shares are oustanding and no new shares will be issued.

1. The Jones Electronic Corporation plans to follow a no-dividend policy for the five-year growth period and is conservatively estimating no further growth in earnings per share beyond this five-year period. (No further growth is perhaps unrealistic, but is conservative—and enables us to leave the matter of further growth to the advanced course.)
2. Under the assumptions in item 1 above, the book value of one share of Jones stock would grow from $10.40 to $118.27 over the five-year period. This represents an increase of $107.87.
3. Still under the assumptions of item 1 above, the earnings per share would increase from $3.85 annually to $32.71 annually. This is an increase of $28.86.
4. On the average over the six-year period, the productivity of the Jones retained earnings was, therefore, 26.75% (during the growth period). At the end of the sixth year, the retained earnings were producing at the rate of 27.65%.

$$\frac{\$32.71}{\$118.27} = 27.65\%$$

5. Therefore, if we can assume that the Jones sales and costs will continue indefinitely at the level attained at the end of the sixth year—and this is quite an assumption—and that the equity (dividend and earnings) investors' cost of capital is 10 percent,

we can say that the Jones stock is producing 2.765 times the market capitalization rate.

6. We can now capitalize the dividends and the weighted earnings to arrive at a probable market value for the Jones stock (assuming the six-year period of growth and then stability after that period).
7. After the six-year period, two-thirds of the yearly earnings will be distributed as dividends.
8. Market value per share is $518.56.

$$\frac{\text{Dividend} + \text{productivity of retained earnings}}{\text{Market capitalization rate}} = \frac{\$21.81 + 2.765\,(32.71 - 21.81)}{0.10}$$

$$= \frac{\$21.81 + \$30.14}{0.10} = \frac{\$51.85}{0.10}$$

$$= \underline{\underline{\$518.56}}$$

Significance of Stock Splits and Stock Dividends on Market Value of Stock

As President Jones reviewed this analysis, allowing for a margin of deviation as the estimated 10 percent annual sales increase is compared with reality over the six-year period, he was more determined than ever that we should try to arrange some form of debt financing to acquire ADCO. If stock eventually had to be sold, he would prefer to sell the stock after the six-year period of growth! At that time, if not now, it would probably be wise for the Jones board of directors to arrange for perhaps a five-to-one stock split or perhaps a stock dividend or a series of stock dividends. For our purposes, either the stock split or the stock dividend would accomplish the same goal, which would be to increase the number of shares and thereby lower the market value per share so that we could create a broader base of potential equity investors.[1]

As an example, a five-to-one stock split would mean that present stockholders would return their stock to the corporation and the corporation would promptly issue to them five shares for every one share surrendered. (President Jones would then hold 225,000 shares instead of his present 45,000 shares, and you would hold 25,000 shares instead of your present 5,000 shares.)

A stock dividend would accomplish the same purpose (that is, a lower value per share). Each year earnings would be transferred by the corporation from the retained earnings account to the common stock account, and additional shares would be issued to the present stockholders equal to the amount transferred. If the five-to-one stock-split

[1] For example, if the number of shares were not increased by stock splits or stock dividends when the market price is $518.56, the smaller investor often would not be attracted by this stock. He would need $51,856 for 100 shares.

route were followed, the market value per share would be calculated in the same manner, except that the earnings per share and the dividends per share would be divided by 5 to reflect the five-to-one stock split.

$$\text{Market value} = \frac{\$4.36 + 2.765(\$2.18)}{0.10} = \frac{\$4.36 + 6.03}{0.10}$$

$$= \frac{10.39}{0.10} = \underline{\underline{\$103.90}}$$

The book value of the present Jones Electronic Corporation stockholders would appear as follows at the end of the six-year period before and after the stock split:

	Shares	Book Value		Total Value
	BEFORE STOCK SPLIT			
President Jones	45,000	$118.27	=	$5,322,150
Your stock	5,000	118.27	=	591,350
	AFTER STOCK SPLIT			
President Jones	225,000	$23.654	=	$5,322,150
Your stock	25,000	23.654	=	591,350

Providing the six-year sales forecast is relatively accurate and the stock split is arranged, the market value of this same stock would appear as follows:

	Shares	Calculated Market Value		Total Value
President Jones	225,000	$103.90	=	$23,377,500
Your stock	25,000	103.90	=	2,597,500

SUMMARY

The potential purchase of ADCO requires us to consider our cost of capital in explicit terms. When we acquire ADCO, we will be adding assets to the left-hand side of our balance sheet. We will also be adding claims to the right-hand side. The structure of the firm's assets largely determines its earnings, while the structure of its claims determines the ultimate distribution of those earnings. We know that the firm offers its products and its securities in competitive markets and both must meet the market test. Thus, as we approach investors and ask them to exchange their savings for the securities we offer, we must be prepared to compensate these institutions and individuals in an adequate manner. The immediate question which arises is, of course, what is adequate?

Adequate compensation, at a minimum, is a level of return which compensates investors for the risk incurred in holding our securities. Thus, our potential bondholders would require a competitive level of return, protection against purchasing-power risk and interest-rate risk, etc.

The cost of capital is an outgrowth of this risk-return relationship which exists between the firm and the investment community. It is the level of this cost which will determine whether or not the ADCO proposal can offer a return which is equal to or greater than the cost of the capital to be employed. As you began your consideration of the cost of capital of Jones Electronic Corporation, you considered three points of view. They were:

1. The existing cost of capital to the firm as seen by professional management.
2. The cost of capital made available by new equity investors.
3. The cost of capital furnished by new creditors or debt holders.

Common to all three groups was the concept of minimum acceptable return. The firm then may view its cost of funds as the minimum return which must be provided in order to secure investment capital. In order to quantify this level of return, you were forced to consider the returns being offered by firms similar to the Jones Electronic Corporation. You studied two such firms and used a price-earnings ratio to determine their cost of equity capital. This proved to be a generally unsuccessful approach in that it failed to consider the potential growth of current earnings. You then began to construct a hypothetical price for Jones Electronic shares. Your calculations involved discounting current and potential earnings at some interest rate which provided investors with an acceptable rate of return. This approach showed real promise, and a first approximation of the cost of equity capital was reached.

The cost of debt capital was a good deal easier to compute. It was simply that rate which investors demand for like securities of equivalent risk. This gross rate was then adjusted to reflect the tax deductibility of interest payments. At this same time you postulated several series of debt and equity combinations in order to determine what combination of debt and equity would yield the lowest aggregate cost of capital to the firm. You noted that the introduction of additional quantities of low-cost debt should lower the firm's overall cost of funds. However, as debt levels increased to the point where the firm's solvency became suspect, costs began to rise rapidly and the firm's cost of funds was then adversely affected by any increase in total debt. This increase in the total cost of capital was determined to have two sources:

1. The increased interest rate required by lenders
2. The deterioration in the quality of our earnings available to common shareholders

At the conclusion of this analysis you were ready to approach yet another approximation of the firm's cost of capital. This time you viewed the return provided to equity investors as having two forms. The first form of return was predicted earnings and/or dividends for a specified period of time. The second form of return was the receipt of the market value of the share at the end of the time period. These returns were then discounted and a present value of the stock was calculated. It was in this final approach that you refined your cost of equity capital concept and related it to the proposed purchase of ADCO. You were then in a position to evaluate the proposal with reference to the promised return and the cost of funds to be employed.

QUESTIONS FOR DISCUSSION

1. What is meant by the term "agio"? Why has it been argued that an agio is necessary?
2. What are the sources of loanable funds? How is interest elasticity involved in the supply of loanable funds from each source?
3. What role does government play in the supply of loanable funds?
4. Why, in Jones' situation, will the interest rate be a relatively minor consideration in the decision concerning the ADCO stock purchase?
5. What are the various types of risks that investors assume as their funds are invested in debt or equity? What is the significance of these risks with respect to the expected yield?
6. What is meant by the term "cost of capital"? Be explicit in your answer.
7. What is a firm's intrinsic value?
8. How does "supply and demand" relate to the "cost of capital"?
9. What problems are encountered when we attempt to establish a probable market value for a given company's stock by comparing the "operating results" of the company with the "operating results" of several other companies?

10. What basic assumption is involved when the price-earnings ratio and/or the dividend yield are used as the basis for the market value of a given stock?

11. Why is it difficult to express the firm's "cost of capital" in terms of a percentage?

12. What is the significance of the chart on page 368?

13. What basic assumptions are involved in the analysis of alternative 1 beginning on page 370 and alternative 2 beginning on page 372?

14. What are the significant differences between alternatives 1 and 2 from President Jones' point of view?

15. What immediate benefits would the present Jones stockholders receive if alternative 2 were adopted?

16. Why were alternatives 3 and 4 not considered?

17. Why would an annual increase in sales of 10 percent not result in an earnings-per-share increase of 10 percent?

18. What is the significance of the analysis on page 375, which indicates that earnings per share will increase from $6 to $24.47 over a five-year period?

19. What is the significance of the $208.97 calculated on page 376?

20. What is the significance of the analysis on page 377?

21. What is meant by "productivity of retained earnings," and how is it calculated?

22. What basic assumptions are involved in calculating the probable market value of Jones stock on page 379?

23. Explain carefully the rationale for using each number in the calculation.

24. What is a stock split?

25. What is a stock dividend?

26. Distinguish between the two terms in Questions 24 and 25.

PROBLEMS

1. The Long Company is currently earning $5 million per year with 1 million shares outstanding. It is anticipated that earnings will increase 10 percent per year for five years and will then remain constant. Dividend payout is expected to be 50 percent. Long Company is currently selling at a multiple of 10. J. J. Swift currently has funds invested, earning an 8

percent return, and is considering selling his present holdings and buying the Long stock on the open market. Mr. Swift intends to hold his shares for five full years and sell them on the fifth anniversary of their purchase. What is the maximum he would rationally pay for the Long stock based on the factors above?

2. Assume the same facts as in Problem 1, but at the end of the five-year 10 percent growth period, the growth rate of the Long stock would be 5 percent indefinitely. How much would Swift rationally pay for the Long stock on the open market based on the facts above?
3. A firm is financed totally with common stock. It is currently earning $5 per share, and no growth in this earnings figure is anticipated. The market price for its shares is $75.
   a. What is this firm's cost of equity capital stated as a rate percent?
   b. If 20,000 new shares were issued without flotation costs to finance a new investment, what annual level of after-tax earnings would be required if the value of all shares were to be maintained at $75?
4. Using the facts in Problem 3, assume that the firm is financed in the following manner:

Bonds payable	$20,000,000
Common stock	40,000,000

   The bonds are 4 percent 20-year debentures, and they are currently selling at par.
   a. Calculate the cost of capital for the firm and state your answer as a rate percent.
   b. Would the altered financial structure change your answer to 3b above?
5. Assume that the firm described in Problems 3 and 4 has changed its capital structure and now presents the following picture:

Accounts payable[1]	$ 3,000,000
5% Notes payable	2,000,000
Bonds payable, 4%	20,000,000
Common stock	40,000,000

   Calculate the weighted average cost of this new capital structure.
6. Using the information provided in Problem 5 above, assume that the earnings of the firm are currently $5, but have been growing at a compound annual rate of 8 percent for the past few years. Investors have no reason to believe that this growth will not continue.

   Calculate the weighted average cost of capital to include this anticipated growth.
7. Using the information presented in Problem 6 above, recalculate the weighted average cost of capital, giving effect to the fact that bonds of equal risk are currently selling to yield 6 percent.

[1] The firm takes advantage of all discounts for prompt payment.

8. a. In 1959 ATT split existing capital stock 3 for 1. Before the split, the capital accounts were as follows:

Common Stock, par value $100	$7,000,000,000
Authorized, 100,000,000 shares	
Outstanding, 70,000,000 shares	
Capital Surplus	2,200,000,000
Retained Earnings	1,900,000,000

The split was handled in such a manner that no capitalization of surplus or retained earnings occurred. Demonstrate, using the same accounts as above, how this was done.

b. In 1961 Magnavox split its common stock on a 3-for-1 basis. Par value remained unchanged, and no retained earnings were capitalized. Before the split the capital accounts were as follows:

Common Stock, par value $1	$ 2,400,000
Outstanding, 2,400,000 shares	
Capital in Excess of Par Value	16,800,000
Retained Earnings	13,000,000

What would the balances in these accounts be after the split?

REFERENCES

Archer, Stephen H., and LeRoy G. Faerber: Firm Size and the Cost of Equity Capital, *Journal of Finance,* vol. XVI, pp. 69–84, March, 1966.

Arditti, Fred D.: Risk and the Required Return on Equity,'' *Journal of Finance,* vol. XXII, pp. 19–36, March, 1967.

Barges, Alexander: ''The Effect of Capital Structure on the Cost of Capital,'' Prentice-Hall, Inc., Englewood Cliffs, N.J., 1963.

Baxter, Nevins D.: Leverage, Risk of Ruin and the Cost of Capital, *Journal of Finance,* vol. XXII, pp. 395–403, September, 1967.

Ben-Shahar, Haim: The Capital Structure and the Cost of Capital: A Suggested Exposition, *Journal of Finance,* vol. XXIII, pp. 639–653, September, 1968.

——— and Abraham Ascher: Capital Budgeting and Stock Valuation: Comment, *American Economic Review,* vol. LVII, pp. 209–214, March, 1967.

——— and Marshall Sarnat: Reinvestment and the Rate of Return on Common Stocks, *Journal of Finance,* vol. XXI, pp. 737–742, December, 1966.

Beranek, William: ''The Effects of Leverage on the Market Value of Common Stocks,'' University of Wisconsin, Bureau of Business Research and Service, Madison, 1964.

Bierman, Harold, Jr., and Richard West: The Acquistion of Common Stock by the Corporate Issuer, *Journal of Finance,* vol. XXI, pp. 687–89, December, 1966.

Blum, Walter J., and Wilbur G. Katz: Depreciation and Enterprise Valuation, *University of Chicago Law Review,* vol. XXXII, winter, 1965; reprinted in James Van Horne (ed.), "Foundations for Financial Management," pp. 593–599, Richard D. Irwin, Inc., Homewood, Ill., 1966.

Boness, A. James: A Pedagogic Note on the Cost of Capital, *Journal of Finance,* vol. XIX, pp. 99–106, March, 1964.

Bosland, Chelcie C.: The Valuation of Public Utility Enterprises by the Securities and Exchange Commission, *Journal of Finance,* vol. XVI, pp. 52–64, March, 1961.

Brewer, D. C., and J. Michaelson: The Cost of Capital, Corporation Finance, and the Theory of Investment: Comment, *American Economic Review,* vol. LV, pp. 516–524, June, 1965.

Brigham, Eugene F., and Myron J. Gordon: Leverage, Dividend Policy, and the Cost of Capital, *Journal of Finance,* vol. XXIII, pp. 85–103, March, 1968.

——— and James L. Pappas: Duration of Growth, Changes in Growth Rates, and Corporate Share Prices, *Financial Analysts Journal,* vol. XXIV, pp. 157–162, May-June, 1966.

——— and Keith V. Smith: The Cost of Capital to the Small Firm, *The Engineering Economist,* vol. XIII, pp. 1–26, fall, 1967.

Briscoe, G., J. M. Samuels, and D. J. Smyth: The Treatment of Risk in the Stock Market, *Journal of Finance,* vol. XXIV, pp. 707–713, September, 1969.

Cohen, Jerome B., and Sidney M. Robbins: "The Financial Manager," chap. 22, Harper & Row, Publishers, Incorporated, New York, 1966.

Cragg, J. G., and Burton G. Malkiel: The Consensus and Accuracy of Some Predictions of the Growth of Corporate Earnings, *Journal of Finance,* vol. XXIII, pp. 67–84, March, 1968.

Crockett, Jean, and Irwin Friend: Capital Budgeting and Stock Valuation: Comment, *American Economic Review,* vol. LVII, pp. 214–220, March, 1967.

Durand, David: Costs of Debt and Equity Funds for Business: Trends and Problems of Measurement, reprinted in Ezra Solomon (ed.), "The Management of Corporate Capital," pp. 91–116, The Free Press, New York, 1959.

Edwards, Charles E., and James G. Hilton: High-Low Averages as an Estimator of Annual Average Stock Prices, *Journal of Finance,* vol. XXI, pp. 112–115, March, 1966.

Elton, Edwin, and Martin Gruber: The Effect of Share Repurchase on the Value of the Firm, *Journal of Finance,* vol. XXIII, pp. 135–149, March, 1968.

Fama, Eugene F.: Risk, Return and Equilibrium: Some Clarifying Comments, *Journal of Finance,* vol. XXIII, pp. 29–40, March, 1968.

Farrar, Donald E., and Lee L. Selwyn: "Note on Taxes, Corporate Financial Policy and the Cost of Capital to the Firm," working paper, Massachusetts Institute of Technology, Sloan School of Management, Cambridge, Mass., 1967.

Fisher, Lawrence, and James H. Lorie: Rates of Return on Investments in Common Stock: The Year-by-Year Record, 1926–65, *Journal of Business,* vol. XLI, no. 3, pp. 291–316, July, 1968.

Haley, Charles W.: A Note on the Cost of Debt, *Journal of Financial and Quantitative Analysis,* vol. 1, pp. 72–93, December, 1966.

Helwing, R. C.: "The Valuation of Small Bank Stocks," Bureau of Business and Economic Research, Michigan State University, East Lansing, Mich., 1966.

Holt, Charles C.: The Influence of Growth Duration on Share Prices, *Journal of Finance,* vol. XVII, pp. 465–475, September, 1962.

Kaplan, Seymour: Computer Algorithms for Finding Exact Rates of Return, *Journal of Business,* vol. XL, no. 4, pp. 389–392, October, 1967.

Keenan, Michael: The State of the Finance Field Methodology Models of Equity Valuation: The Great Serm Bubble, *Journal of Finance,* vol. XXV, pp. 243–273, May, 1970.

Lerner, Eugene M.: The Integration of Capital Budgeting and Stock Valuation, *American Economic Review,* vol. LIV, September, 1964; reprinted in James Van Horne (ed.) "Foundations for Financial Management," pp. 327–346, Richard D. Irwin, Inc., Homewood, Ill., 1966.

Lintner, John: Dividends, Earnings, Leverage, Stock Prices and the Supply of Capital to Corporations, *Review of Economics and Statistics,* vol. XLIV, pp. 243–269, August, 1962.

———: The Cost of Capital and Optimal Financing of Corporate Growth, *Journal of Finance,* vol. XVIII, May, 1963; reprinted in James Van Horne (ed.), "Foundations for Financial Management," pp. 460–478, Richard D. Irwin, Inc., Homewood, Ill., 1966.

Litzenberger, Robert H.: Equilibrium in the Equity Market under Uncertainty, *Journal of Finance,* vol. XXIV, pp. 663–671, September, 1969.

Mahoney, John J.: Earnings per Share and the Insensitive Denominator, *Management Accounting,* July, 1970, p. 15.

Malkiel, Burton G.: Equity Yields Growth, and the Structure of Share Prices, *American Economic Review,* vol. LIII, pp. 467–494, December, 1963.

Mao, James C. T.: The Valuation of Growth Stocks: The Investment Opportunities Approach, *Journal of Finance,* vol. XXI, pp. 95–102, March, 1966.

Miller, M. H., and Franco Modigliani: Cost of Capital to Electric Utility Industry, *American Economic Review,* vol. LVI, pp. 333–391, June, 1966.

Modigliani, Franco: The Cost of Capital, Corporation Finance and the Theory of Investment: Reply, *American Economic Review,* vol. IL, pp. 655–669, September, 1958; Taxes and the Cost of Capital: A Correction, *American Economic Review,* vol. LIII, pp. 433–443, June, 1963; Reply, *American Economic Review,* vol. LV, pp. 524–527, June, 1965.

——— and M. H. Miller: The Cost of Capital, Corporation Finance and the Theory of Investment, *American Economic Review,* vol. XLVIII, pp. 261–297, June, 1958.

Myers, Stewart C.: A Time-State-Preference Model of Security Valuation, *Journal of Financial and Quantitative Analysis,* vol. III, pp. 1–34, March, 1968.

Ortner, Robert: The Concept of Yield on Common Stock, *Journal of Finance,* vol. XIX, pp. 186–198, May, 1964.

Resek, Robert W.: Multidimensional Risk and the Modigliani-Miller Hypothesis, *Journal of Finance,* vol. XXV, pp. 47–51, March, 1970.

Robichek, Alexander A., and John G. McDonald: The Cost of Capital Concept: Potential Use and Misuse, *Financial Executive,* vol. 33, pp. 2–8, June, 1965.

———, ———, and R. C. Higgins: Some Estimates of the Cost of Capital to Electric Utilities, 1954–1957: Comment, *American Economic Review,* vol. LVII, pp. 1278–1288, December, 1967.

——— and Stewert C. Myers: Risk Adjusted Discount Rates, *Journal of Finance,* vol. XXI, no. 4, pp. 727–730, December, 1966.

——— and ———: Valuation of the Firm, Effects of Uncertainty in a Market Context, *Journal of Finance,* vol. XXI, pp. 215–227, May, 1966.

Sarma, L. V. L. N., and K. S. Hanumanta Rao: Leverage and the Value of the Firm, *Journal of Finance,* vol. XXIV, pp. 673–677, September, 1969.

Sarnat, M., and H. Ben-Shahar: Reinvestment and the Rate of Return on Common Stocks, *Journal of Finance,* vol. XXIII, no. 1, pp. 737–742, December, 1966.

Sauvain, Harry: "Investment Management," 3d ed., chapters 6–8, Prentice-Hall, Inc., Englewood Cliffs, N.J., 1967.

Schwartz, Eli: Theory of the Capital Structure of the Firm, *Journal of Finance,* vol. XIV, pp. 10–18, March, 1959.

——— and J. Richard Aronson: Some Surrogate Evidence in Support of the Concept of Optimal Financial Structure, *Journal of Finance,* vol. XXII, pp. 10–18, March, 1967.

Soldofsky, Robert M.: The Return on Common Stock: Growth Yield or Current Yield, *Quarterly Review of Economics and Business,* vol. II, pp. 21–30, May, 1962.

———: The History of Bond Tables and Stock Valuation Models, *Journal of Finance,* vol. XXI, pp. 103–111, March, 1966.

——— and Roger Biderman: Yield-Risk Measurement of the Performance of Common Stocks, *Journal of Financial and Quantitative Analysis,* vol. III, pp. 103–111, March, 1968.

——— and James T. Murphy: "Growth Yields on Common Stock: Theory and Tables," State University of Iowa, Iowa City, Iowa, 1963.

Solomon, Ezra: Measuring a Company's Cost of Capital, *Journal of Business,* vol. XXVIII, pp. 240–242, October, 1955.

———: Leverage and the Cost of Capital, *Journal of Finance,* vol. XVIII, pp. 273–279, May, 1963.

———: "The Theory of Financial Management," chap. 3, Columbia University Press, New York, 1963.

Vickers, Douglas: Elasticity of Capital Supply, Monopsonistic Discrimination, and Optimum Capital Structure, *Journal of Finance,* vol. XXIII, pp. 1–9, March, 1967.

———: The Cost of Capital and the Structure of the Firm, *Journal of Finance,* vol. XXV, pp. 35–46, March, 1970.

Wendt, Paul F.: Current Growth Stock Valuation Methods, *Financial Analysts Journal,* vol. XXXIII, pp. 3–15, March-April, 1965.

West, Richard R., and Harold Bierman, Jr.: Corporate Dividend Policy and Preemptive Security Issues, *Journal of Business,* vol. XLI, no. 1, pp. 71–75, January, 1968.

Weston, J. Fred: A Test of Cost of Capital Propositions, *Southern Economic Journal,* vol. XXX, pp. 105–112, October, 1963.

——— and Eugene F. Brigham: "Managerial Finance," 3d ed., chap. 11, Holt, Rinehart and Winston, Inc., New York, 1969.

Wippern, Ronald F: Financial Structure and the Value of the Firm, *Journal of Finance,* vol. XXI, pp. 615–633, December, 1966.

Chapter Thirteen
LONG-TERM FINANCING

CHARACTERISTICS OF LONG-TERM FINANCING

At the next meeting of the Jones executive committee, President Jones indicated that he had had several meetings with the Allied "high command," and they were pushing for some sort of commitment concerning the ADCO property. He was quite pleased that you had reviewed the cost of capital aspects and requested that you check and recheck, test and retest, your forecast of future sales prospects. In addition, he asked that you proceed with financing possibilities. While it did appear that it would be quite possible, if not probable, that the ADCO acquisition could be financed from retained earnings over the first five or six years. We must secure some type of financing to secure the funds to buy the company to earn the profit in order to pay the debt from retained earnings.

It would be impossible to state categorically that all bonds and/or other evidence of long-term debt have definite characteristics. The ingenious mind of man can and does meet all contingencies and circumstances.

1. A bond is nothing more than the written evidence of a contract whereby funds are advanced by the creditor to the borrower in return for a promise to repay the funds at maturity.
2. A fixed rate of interest must be paid at intervals agreed upon for the use of the borrowed funds.

3. Bondholders have a claim prior to the stockholders on both income (up to the amount of the interest payment) and the assets in general up to the amount of the debt in the event of default.[1]
4. Bonds generally contain clauses and restrictions that reflect the relative financial strength of the borrower and lender and the judgment of the lender as to the risk involved in advancing the funds.

The four characteristics listed above are typical of most bonds and so do not make meaningful distinctions between the two basic varieties of bonds. For the most part, bonds can be described as either secured or unsecured obligations of the issuer.

Secured Bonds

Secured bonds are obligations with specific claims to particular corporate assets. They can be, for example, first mortgage bonds which have a prior claim to the property of the corporation which is mortgaged under the provisions of the indenture. The provisions of the indenture specifically designate the mortgaged assets and the excluded assets. Below is an example of such an indenture provision relating to a $100 million first mortgage bond issue of the Jones and Laughlin Steel Company sold in 1965 and due in 1991.

> The Bonds are secured by the indenture which, by its terms, constitutes, except as to *permitted liens* and the exceptions hereinafter noted, a first mortgage lien upon all the property, real, personal and mixed, owned by the Corporation. . . .[2]
>
> Certain types of property are excepted from the lien of the indenture . . . principally: (1) cash, securities, receivables, patents, choices in action and other intangible rights, other than such as are required by the express provisions of the indenture to be subjected to the lien thereof, (2) merchandise and supplies acquired for resale and property consumable in operations, (3) manufactured products, materials in process of manufacture, and materials intended for use in manufacture, (4) minerals which have been or shall be mined, quarried or extracted as permitted by the Indenture, (5) motor vehicles and railway rolling stock not used exclusively within plants, and boats and other marine equipment, aircraft, and office furniture and fixtures, (6) tools, machinery, equipment and like personal property not affixed, actually or constructively, to real property or plants and which are not essential to the operation of the plants, (7) short-term leases, (8) property in Louisiana or

[1] Bond indentures specify numerous responsibilities which the issuer must fulfill over the life of the contract. His failure to fulfill certain of these responsibilities, i. e., payment of interest when due, constitutes a default. Normally in the event of a default the due date of the debt is accelerated and the principal is due immediately.

[2] *Granting Clauses.*

> outside the continental United States, (9) residential, warehouse or store property acquired after January 28, 1966, where the fair value, including the fair value of improvements, does not exceed $250,000, office leases executed after such date and other leases executed after such date where the annual rental is less than $25,000 and the fair value of improvements does not exceed $250,000, and (10) buildings and equipment used for the generation of gases (including compressed air) employed in processing iron and steel which are not owned by the Corporation even though affixed actually or constructively to real property or plants of the Corporation.
>
> The Series E Bonds will be secured, equally and ratably with the outstanding Bonds of all other Series aggregating $119,433,000 principal amount, by a valid and direct first mortgage lien, subject only to *permitted liens* and the exceptions, reservations and exclusions set forth in the granting and 'under and subject' clauses of the Indenture, (i) on all fixed properties owned by the Corporation on December 31, 1965 (except properties in the State of Louisiana or located outside the continental United States), (ii) all the outstanding capital stock of all *subsidiaries* of the Corporation, and (iii) all indebtedness owed by *subsidiaries* to the Corporation at the end of the calendar month next preceding the date of issuance and sale of the Series E Bonds, maturing more than one year, or not intended to be paid within one year, after the incurrence thereof, or which has remained unpaid for more than one year prior to such date. In the Indenture, the Corporation covenants to maintain the Indenture as a first lien upon all the mortgaged property, subject only to *permitted liens* and the exceptions, reservations and exclusions set forth in the granting and 'under and subject' clauses of the Indenture, which clauses permit purchase money or existing liens on property acquired not exceeding $66\frac{2}{3}\%$ of the cost of the property subject thereto, and the renewal and refunding thereof.[1]

In reading the provisions you note that the bonds have a general claim to all the assets except those which have been excluded by specific enumeration. You may have also noted that the bonds being issued are Series E. Some investigation will reveal that there are, in fact, other series of bonds outstanding, and all outstanding series were issued under a single indenture written in 1947. In such cases the original indenture, with the Mellon National Bank and Trust Company as the trustee, was created to finance particular property additions. The bonds, Series A, issued at that time were secured to these properties. New series bonds are issued by the borrower from time to time as new properties are acquired and new bond issues floated to finance them.

Because of this open-ended feature, the final paragraph in the quoted material states that Series E bonds share equally and ratably with all other series. Thus, if a default were to occur and the property

[1] Under and Subject Clauses; Section 4.12.

were sold, all bondholders would share equally and ratably in the liquidation proceeds derived from those assets. If, at that time, their claim had not been satisfied 100 cents on the dollar, these secured creditors would join the other general creditors of the firm and receive a portion of the proceeds derived from the liquidation of the remaining unmortgaged assets.

The protection of the bondholders which is afforded by the mortgage reduces the risk on the bonds secured thereby. Consequently, investors normally require a rate of interest on such bonds which is lower than the rate they would require on unsecured obligations.

Unsecured Obligations—The Debenture

The unsecured bond is usually called a debenture. It differs from the mortgage or secured obligation in that it is dependent for its repayment on the general credit and operating capabilities of the issuer. This is the type of bond that does not have any specific assets pledged as security that could be seized and sold to satisfy the claims of the bondholders. In the event of default and liquidation, debenture holders join the other general creditors of the corporation and seek restitution as one of many creditors of equal standing. In short, they have no exclusive or original claim to any particular assets which can be liquidated for their sole benefit. In the event of bankruptcy, the holders of these securities would have the same claim as other unsecured creditors.

An example of this distinction between a secured and an unsecured obligation is provided by the July 1, 1969, issue to $100 million of debentures by the National Cash Register Company.

> The Debentures are limited to $100,000,000 principal amount, but the Indenture does not limit the amount of other securities, either secured or unsecured, which may be issued by NCR.
>
> If NCR or any Domestic Subsidiary[1] shall mortgage or pledge as security for any indebtedness any plant used primarily for manufacturing operations in the United States of America or any investment in any Domestic Subsidiary, whether owned at the date of the Indenture or thereafter acquired, NCR will secure or cause such Domestic Subsidiary to secure the Debentures equally and ratably with all indebtedness secured by such mortgage or pledge. This covenant does not apply to (a) any mortgage existing on such property at the date of the Indenture, (b) any mortgage in favor of NCR or a Domestic Subsidiary, (c) purchase money mortgages or mortgages of other liens existing on property at the time of its acquisition, whether or not assumed, provided the indebted-

[1] The term "Domestic Subsidiary" as defined in the Indenture excludes a subsidiary engaged primarily in financing the sale of products of NCR or a subsidiary. (Section 1.01.)

> ness secured thereby does not exceed 75% of the lesser of the cost or fair value of such property or (d) certain renewals of or substitutions for any mortgage permitted under (a), (b) or (c). (Section 4.06.)
>
> If, upon any consolidation or merger of NCR with or into any other corporation, or upon any sale or conveyance of substantially all of its properties, or upon any acquisition by NCR of all or any part of the property of another corporation, the property of NCR owned immediately prior thereto would by reason of an after-acquired property clause of other similar provision thereupon become subject to a mortgage, lien, pledge, charge or encumbrance, NCR, prior to such event will secure the Debentures (equally and ratably with any other indebtedness of NCR then entitled thereto) by a lien on all such property of NCR prior to all liens, charges and encumbrances other than any theretofore existing thereon. (Section 11.03.)

You note immediately that the unsecured obligations of NCR in no way encumber its existing properties until such time as a mortgage or second issue would be floated. It should also be noted that if such properties were previously mortgaged, they would be unavailable to provide security for the debentures being issued currently. Investors who desired to purchase the debentures would require a higher level of compensation for risk under these circumstances than if the issue had been secured.

Since debenture bonds are unsecured, the bond indenture will usually contain a clause stating in effect that the borrower will not pledge assets as security to other creditors without the expressed consent of the indenture holder. This is understandable. The pledging of assets to secure another creditor would weaken the position of the original debenture holder by inserting a superior claim to the assets in the event of default. The indenture may likewise provide that the borrower may not enter into other indenture agreements for the same reason, or the indenture may provide that any additional debentures must be "subordinate debentures" and thus have only a second claim on assets behind existing claims which include the first debenture.

Debentures are unsecured by specific property. In addition, their claim to liquidation proceeds may also be subordinated to the claim of senior debt holders. Debentures of this type are called subordinated debentures. Below you can see an indenture provision describing such a subordination of claim. In June of 1969, Fisher Foods offered $18 million of subordinated debentures. The indenture describes the subordination in these terms:

> Upon any distribution of assets of the Company upon any dissolutionment, winding up, liquidation, or reorganization, the payment of the principal of, premium, if any, and interest on the Debentures is to be

> subordinated to the extent provided in the Indenture in right of payment to the prior payment in full of all Senior Indebtedness. Subject to certain exceptions provided for in the Indenture, in the event and during the continuation of any default in payment of Senior Indebtedness beyond any applicable period of grace or an event of default permitting the acceleration of Senior Indebtedness, no payment on account of principal, premium, if any, or interest may be made on the Debentures (Sections 3.01, 3.02 and 3.03), but the obligation of the Company to make payment of principal, premium, if any, or interest on the Debentures will not otherwise be affected. (Section 3.04.) The Debentures will be subrogated to the rights of the holders of Senior Indebtedness to the extent of payments made on Senior Indebtedness upon any distribution of assets in any such proceedings out of the distributive shares of the Debentures. (Section 3.03.) *By reason of such subordination, certain general creditors of the Company may, in the event of insolvency, recover more, ratably, than holders of the Debentures upon any such distribution of assets.* [Emphasis added]
>
> Senior Indebtedness is defined in the Indenture as the principal of, premium, if any, and unpaid interest on (a) Indebtedness, for the payment of which the Company is responsible or liable, whether outstanding on the date of execution of the Indenture or thereafter created, incurred, guaranteed, or assumed, which is for money borrowed from, or the payment of which is guaranteed to, others and (b) renewals, extensions, and refundings of any such indebtedness, unless, in the instrument creating or evidencing the same or pursuant to which the same is outstanding, it is provided that such indebtedness, or such renewal, extension, or refunding thereof, is not superior in right of payment to the Debentures. (Section 1.01.)

In short, the result of the emphasized subordination provision could be that other senior creditors may receive full or partial payment of their claims, while subordinated debenture holders could receive no payments whatever.

In addition to the clauses noted above as applicable to the debenture bond, it may be well to observe that indentures can be long-drawn-out documents. Various restrictions and protective clauses designed to protect the bondholder in the event of default or threat of insolvency may be part of the agreement. Most certainly, pledged assets and/or collateral descriptions will be included. The Jones and Laughlin indenture quoted in the beginning of the chapter presents a good illustration of such collateral descriptions.

The banker explained the "open-end" features as well as the "closed-end" features of the various mortgage or trust arrangements. An "open-end" mortgage provides that additional funds may be obtained by mutual agreement with the same collateral or security without the necessity of a new bond issue. A "closed-end" debt issue means exactly what it says. That is, no additional funds can be secured by the assets pledged with equal priority.

An "after-acquired" property clause may be included in an indenture to provide that all property acquired subsequent to the mortgage or trust agreement would automatically become additional security for the mortgage or trust. A combination of these latter two clauses could effectively limit our future borrowing power.

The right to pay off the bonds prior to full maturity is sometimes termed a payoff privilege or a "call provision." Under this provision, the borrower reserves the option to call part or all of the outstanding bonds in for payment in full plus premium to the lender. The amount of the premium normally varies directly with the length of time remaining until maturity. It can be as high as 5 or 6 percent if the bond is called early in its life. This premium is designed to compensate the lender for the expense and trouble of finding alternative investments. This call provision can be significant to the borrower.

The investment banker showed you the following call provision from a current issue of first-mortgage bonds:

> *Optional Redemption.* The Series E Bonds will be redeemable, upon 30 days' notice as provided in the Fifty-Eighth Supplemental Indenture, at any time or from time to time, either as a whole, or in part in the principal amount of $1,000,000 or any multiple thereof, upon payment of the applicable redemption price (expressed in percentages of principal amount) set forth below during the respective 12-month periods ending on the first day of February in the years set forth below:

1967	104.00%	1977	102.00%
1968	103.80%	1978	101.80%
1969	103.60%	1979	101.60%
1970	103.40%	1980	101.40%
1971	103.20%	1981	101.20%
1972	103.00%	1982	101.00%
1973	102.80%	1983	100.80%
1974	102.60%	1984	100.60%
1975	102.40%	1985	100.40%
1976	102.20%	1986	100.20%

Bond maturities characteristically run for periods of 10, 20, or 30 years or longer. The interest rate is a function of the supply of and the demand for loanable funds, which includes a judgment factor reflecting the lender's judgment of the risks involved.

The annual interest rate agreed upon by the lender and the borrower is a calculated risk for both parties. For example, a 30-year bond issue with a 4 percent annual interest rate negotiated 10 years ago would be a tremendous bargain for the borrower if the interest rates increased to 8 percent per year. In this case, the lender would be pleased to have his money returned so that he could reinvest it at 8 percent. Conversely, an 8 percent interest rate at this time might well reverse the position of the two parties 10 years from now if interest rates fall. Quite often, the "calculated risk" will be expressed in terms of the repayment provisions. As an example, the borrower may, by agreement, obligate himself to retire (to pay in full) a certain percentage of the outstanding bonds annually after a given period (for example, five years) and periodically thereafter. On the other hand, the borrower may be required to deposit periodic payments into a "sinking fund," which may earn interest, so that funds will accumulate to pay the full amount required at maturity. Planning for repayment can be a significant point in reaching an agreement between the lender and the borrower.

As an example of such a sinking fund, the investment banker showed you a provision which was a part of an existing debenture issue of a large manufacturing concern.

> The Debentures will also be redeemable on similar notice through the operation of the Sinking Fund on July 15, 1976, and on each July 15 thereafter to and including July 15, 1993, at 100% of principal amount together with accrued interest to the date fixed for redemption. The Sinking Fund will provide for the retirement of $5,000,000 principal amount of Debentures on each such sinking fund date. In addition, NCR may retire in any year, pursuant to the Sinking Fund, an additional principal amount of Debentures not exceeding the principal amount required to be retired under the mandatory provisions of the Sinking Fund. The optional right to retire, if not exercised. does not accumulate. NCR may, at its option, receive credit against Sinking Fund payments by surrendering Debentures acquired through purchase or with respect to Debentures redeemed other than for the Sinking Fund. (Sections 3.01, 3.04, 3.05 and 3.06.)

With this minimum amount of knowledge you made another appointment with the investment banker. He is familiar with the factors which make for the success or failure of bond issues. He will also have his finger on current and anticipated interest yields. It is hoped that with his advice we can include or exclude specific bond features that would contribute to the success of our proposed bond issue should we have one!

Public versus private placement. We were advised that bonds or other forms of debt may be sold publicly or placed privately. Quite frequently, if the bonds are of sufficient quality and involve a sufficiently large amount of money, they can be sold or placed with individual foundations, insurance companies, or other financial institutions. Bonds in smaller amounts may, on occasion, be placed with private individuals without a public sale. This procedure involves direct negotiations between the lender and borrower concerning the terms and conditions of the transactions and generally saves the expense of the sale, but may carry higher coupon rates of interest.[1]

When bonds are sold publicly, an investment bank or a group of banks may agree to purchase the entire issue as an investment or for resale to the public at large. Additional expense and lower net proceeds to the issuer may result because of commissions and fees. (We must explore these implications later, if a bond issue appears feasible in our case.) If the bonds are sold publicly, part of the bond contract (indenture) will provide for the appointment of a "trustee." The function of the trustee is to enforce the terms of the indenture. (In the event of a failure to comply with the agreed terms, it would be the duty of the trustee to act upon the "default" and to seek remedy for the benefit of the bondholders.) This may or may not mean the seizure and sale of property, depending upon the type of bond and the terms of the indenture.

Significance of Trust Indenture Act of 1939. Most bond issues are subject to the Trust Indenture Act of 1939 and must be registered with the United States Securities and Exchange Commission. As a matter of curiosity, we looked up this act and found the following:

1. Trust indentures for all corporate issues in excess of $1 million sold to the public in interstate commerce must be "qualified" with the Securities and Exchange Commission.
2. The trustee must qualify as a financially responsible institution.
3. The instrument must require adequate performance of the trustee in performing his duties on behalf of bondholders.
4. There must be no conflict between the trustee's interest as trustee and any other interest he or it may have.
5. There must be provision for reports to bondholders by the trustee.

The investment banker advised us that in order to market our bonds, we must compete in the money markets with other borrowers for loanable funds. Our banker continued by discussing some of the various types of bonds that have been sold. The first of these was the mortgage bond, with which we were somewhat familiar already. His discussion of this and other bonds may be summarized as follows.

[1] See Direct Placement of Corporate Debt, *Economic Review,* March, 1965.

Mortgage Bonds

Specific assets or all the firm's assets may be pledged as security or collateral to the bondholders. In the event of default in the payment of interest or principal, it becomes the duty of the trustee to legally seize the pledged property and to either liquidate the same for the benefit of the bondholders or take other steps as may be necessary. For example, the trustee may use the power of sale, if granted in the indenture, as a lever against other creditors in determining the future of the business organization. Other creditors may be delayed or dissuaded from pressing claims too strongly if a mortgage bondholder holds the power of sale over vital assets. Other creditors may relax the urgency of their claims if they are aware of the fact that if they press too hard the result could mean total loss to the creditors not protected by a pledge of specific assets. The trustee may not, however, in good judgment, force an immediate sale when such a sale results in a loss to his bondholders.

In the event a sale is necessary under the mortgage agreement and the funds received were inadequate to satisfy the bondholder's claims, the bondholder would become an unsecured creditor to the extent of the deficiency. On the other hand, any excess received by the trustee from the sale of the pledged assets would be made available to unsecured creditors, if any, on a pro-rated basis, or would accrue to the original borrower. It is clear that in the event of default, insolvency, or bankruptcy of the business, the priority of claims to the assets is quite significant to all creditors, secured or unsecured. This priority may likewise be expressed in terms of first-mortgage bonds, second-mortgage bonds, and the like.

Equipment Trust Certificates

Equipment trust bonds are generally sold to a lender by a trustee acting for the issuer. The trustee then purchases the equipment for the issuer. The trustee, however, retains the legal title to the equipment. The equipment, for example, aircraft or railroad rolling stock, is generally the type that can be used by other operating companies and is considered quite attractive as security by lenders.

The high investment standing of these certificates is an outgrowth of two factors:

1. If the issuer fails to make the payments required, the lenders can claim the equipment easily since they hold legal title to it. Furthermore, the equipment can be quickly resold. For example, a Boeing 747 is used by all air carriers; therefore, its reclamation and placement with another airline is entirely feasible.

2. Payment schedules normally are such that the depreciated value of the equipment exceeds the balance due on it. Thus the reclaimed asset would be worth substantially more than the outstanding debt.

The equipment trust certificate is extremely popular in railroad financing. Its strength is an outgrowth of the dismal record of railroad defaults on bonded debt in the past. Thus, the fact that the strongest form of security is evolved by the weakest of issuers should not come as a surprise. Investors' demands for protection must be met before financing can be successfully undertaken.

Collateral Trust Bonds

Bonds secured by marketable securities of other corporations (for example, stocks and bonds) are called collateral trust bonds. These securities could be issued by firms which hold the securities of other firms as a part of their assets. The collateral trust certificates are secured to these assets, and the holders of the certificates can lay claim to them in the event of default.

Income Bonds

The significant feature of this type of bond is that the payment of interest is contingent upon earnings. Interest is, therefore, not a fixed charge per year. However, interest is ordinarily cumulative for three years and must be paid at maturity. In all other respects, the income bond can have all the features of an ordinary bond. In the event of default at maturity, legal action can be brought to enforce payment.

Income bonds are typically found in the capital structure of railroads. They originate during a reorganization when the carrier attempts to scale down fixed charges in line with its reduced revenues. As a result of such actions, certain bondholders are forced to accept these contingent return securities in lieu of the bonds they formerly held in the bankrupt firm.

Convertible Bonds

The "calculated risk" may likewise be expressed in terms of a convertible feature. This provision gives the lender the option of carrying the bond to maturity or of converting the bond into a stated number of shares of the borrower's common or preferred stock at a stipulated rate in order to share in the borrower's growth as reflected generally in the appreciation of the common-stock values. As an alternative to the convertible feature, the bonds may be sold with "warrants attached." This gives the purchaser of the bond the option of keeping the bond and, in addition, of purchasing a given number of shares of stock of the issuing company at a specified price within a specified time period. The warrants may thus have value in themselves and can be exercised (that is, turned in for the purchase of the stock) or can be sold to another investor. The significant factor in determining the value of the warrants will be the movement or the expectations of movement in market price of the underlying common stock. If the market price of the stock moves above the exercise price specified in the warrant or if an investor expects the price to move upward, the warrant will obviously have value. If the market price of the stock falls below the specified purchasing price or if investors think it will fall below that price, the warrant will have little or no value.

The banker indicated that he would be pleased to look into long-term financing possibilities for us. Our problem, briefly stated, is that the Jones Electronic Corporation has no collateral nor assets that can be pledged as security for long-term financing unless the ADCO assets are pledged in the mortgage agreement. Our annual-earnings history and prospects appear to be excellent. However, we really do not want to talk about future earnings in detail at this time!

As we returned to the office, the matter of the convertible bond kept pushing into our thoughts. Our first consideration is why the Jones organization would choose to use the convertible bond for long-term financing. You could think of at least three solid reasons. First, we want to raise additional capital by using debt. However, the financial structure of the Jones Electronic Corporation may or may not lend itself to a straight debt issue at a reasonable interest rate. A bond issue of $3 million or $4 million with an 8 percent interest rate may thus have to be sold by Jones at a discount if the 15 percent yield previously estimated is in fact demanded. The discount itself creates probems, not the least of which is that more 8 percent bonds will have to be sold to raise the required $4 million! As an example:

1. A $1,000 bond at 8 percent will require an $80 interest payment each year.
2. The maximum any investor should pay for a stream of income of $80 for 20 years discounted to 15 percent if held to maturity would yield $561.84. This is so because the $80 per year can be treated as an annuity. We calculate the present value of an annuity of $80 at 15 percent for 20 years and the present value of $1,000 discounted 20 periods at 15 percent as follows:

$80 × 6.2593 (P.V. of annuity of $1 20 periods at 15%) =	$500.744
$1,000 × 0.0611 (P.V. of $1 discounted 20 periods at 15%) =	61.10
	$561.844

3. The current yield would be 14.242 percent:

$$\frac{\$80}{\$561.844} = 14.242\%$$

Thus, at a selling price of $561.844 per bond, the yield would be 15+ percent if held to maturity, or a 14.242 percent current yield. Even more significant, it would be necessary to sell approximately 7,475 $1,000 bonds to raise the required $4 million and cover the 5 percent flotation costs.

	$4,000,000
Plus 5% flotation cost	200,000
	$4,200,000 ÷ $581.844 = 7,475 bonds

Annual interest at 8 percent would be an effective annual interest rate to the Jones Electronic Corporation of 4 percent (50 percent tax rate) and would total $299,000; and $7,475,000 would be due and payable in 20 years. This is quite a price to pay!

On the other hand, by using the convertible feature, we may be able to reduce the effective rate of interest to 10 percent or even 8 percent. A 10 percent effective rate would increase the funds received by the sale of the debt as follows:

$80 × 8.514 (P.V. of annuity of 20 periods at 10%) =	$681.12
$1,000 × 0.149 (P.V. of $1 discounted 20 periods at 10%) =	149.00
Selling price of bonds	$830.12

Now we need sell only 5,060 bonds. Annual effective interest would be $202,400, and $5,060,000 would be payable at the end of 20 years, if the bonds had not been converted to stock by that time.

If the convertible "sweetener" would enable us to sell the bonds at par ($1,000), to yield 8 percent we could sell 4,200 bonds. The annual effective interest would be 4 percent after taxes and would total $168,000; and $4 million would be payable at the end of 20 years, if the bonds had not been converted to stock. The difference between the discounted bond prices we calculated above at 15 and 10 percent and the par value of the bonds is called the *investment premium* to the buyer of the bonds. Therefore, the convertible feature added to the straight debt might save the Jones Corporation all or a considerable part of the investment premium that must be paid to market the bonds.

Second, President Jones does not really want to sell additional stock at this time, but if stock has to be sold to raise the additional funds, the convertible bond may well be a way to force the sale of the stock at a higher price than could be obtained on the market at this time. This is especially probable if we continue our policy of not disclosing estimated future income so as not to create the possibility of attracting competition or planting ideas with Allied about retaining ADCO. Why is this so? We'll answer this question via the following example (assuming we can market the bond at par with the convertible feature).[1]

Figure 13-1 graphically portrays the following assumptions:

1. The bond will be sold at par ($1,000) with an 8 percent annual coupon rate, callable at 110 within five years.
2. Without the convertible feature, the bond would sell for $562 (rounded).
3. The Jones Corporation retains the right to call the bonds (pay the par value plus any accrued interest to the date of the call) at any time within five years of the issuing date. If such a call is made, a redemption premium of $100 per bond must be paid to the bondholders.
4. In addition, let us further stipulate that at the end of six years and within ten years from date of issue, or any time thereafter until ma-

[1] Hypothetical model of a convertible bond. Source: Eugene F. Brigham, An Analysis of Convertible Debentures: Theory and Some Empirical Evidence, *Journal of Finance,* vol. XXI, p. 37, March, 1966.

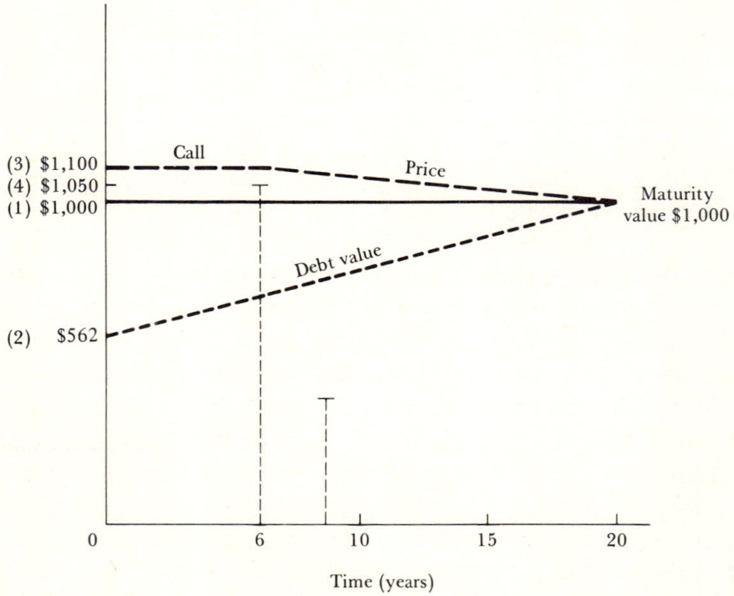

Figure 13-1

turity, the bondholder has the option of surrendering his bond to the Jones Corporation in return for that number of shares which will equal a value of $1,050. The value of each share will be calculated in one of two ways:

a. Market value
b. Book value per share the sixth year capitalized at the average earnings-to-net-worth yield over the six-year period.[1]

If the conversion to common stock is made within the specified time limits, the number of shares determined at the end of the fifth year shall be the number of shares issued upon subsequent conversion without regard to book or market value at that time. In short, then, the determination of the number of shares to be issued will be made at the end of the fifth year.

President Jones requested that you make an analysis of the significance of the convertible bond issue under the following conditions:

1. The bonds would total $5 million plus $60,000 in flotation costs.
2. Effective interest would be 4 percent.
3. There would be a 10 percent increase in sales volume after the first year ADCO was acquired and an additional 10 percent for the next five years (see page 377).

Your analysis is shown in the table at the top of page 404.

One observation is at once clear; that the Jones organization will be able to pay off the $5,060,000 convertible bond issue at the end of the sixth year from retained earnings. This will be true if the estimates are sound and if the proper liquidity is maintained.

Approximately two shares of stock per bond would be issued, if the bonds were sold at par and converted on a basis of $1,050 per bond. Five thousand and sixty bonds must be sold to cover the $5 million needed

[1] The conversion feature which you have proposed differs somewhat from the normal stipulations of publicly held convertible bonds. In the more typical case there already exists a market price for the firm's shares, and their shares are actively traded. For example, suppose that the current market price per share is $40 and convertible bonds are issued in denominations of $1,000. The conversion feature could be described in terms of either a conversion price or a conversion ratio. Thus the feature could stipulate that each bond is convertible in common stock at $50 per share. You could then convert your $1,000 bond subsequently to 20 shares of common stock. You would do so of course only if the market value of the stock rose from its current level to some value in excess of $50. The conversion feature could also be described in terms of a ratio, in this case 20 to 1. You could convert your $1,000 bond into 20 shares of common stock. You would as before be paying the equivalent of $50 per share.

Since no public market exists for the Jones stock at this time, you are forced to write a conversion feature which sets a conversion formula rather than a conversion price.

	Total Earnings after ADCO Acquisition (after Taxes)*	Less Interest on $5,060,000 at Effective Rate of 4%	Balance to Retained Earnings	Cumulative Balance Retained Earnings
Retained earnings balance				$ 519,552
First year + additional profit	$ 650,000	$ 202,400	$ 447,600	967,125
	227,000			
Second year + additional profit	877,000	202,400	674,600	1,641,725
	249,700			
Third year + additional profit	1,126,700	202,400	924,300	2,566,025
	274,670			
Fourth year + additional profit	1,401,370	202,400	1,198,970	3,764,995
	301,910			
Fifth year + additional profit	1,703,280	202,400	1,500,880	5,265,875
	332,328			
Sixth year	2,035,608	202,400	1,833,208	7,099,083
Total	$7,793,958	$1,214,400	$6,579,558	

* Same as page 377.

Year	Earnings per Share (50,000 Shares)	Book Value per Share (50,000 Shares)
Current	$ 3.85	$ 10.40
1	8.95*	19.34†
2	13.49	32.83
3	18.49	51.32
4	23.98	75.30
5	30.02	105.32
6	36.66	141.98

Productivity of retained earnings is equal to the change in EPS divided by the change in book value per share:

Change in EPS: $36.66 − 3.85 = $32.81 Change in book value: $141.98 − 10.40 = $131.58

$$\frac{\$32.81}{\$131.58} = 24.94\%$$

Earnings to net worth six-year average yield = 24.94%.
Net worth per share, end of sixth year = $141.98.

$$\frac{\$141.98}{24.94\%} = \$569$$ estimated value per share at time of earliest possible conversion—end of sixth year.

* $\frac{\text{Balance to retained earnings}}{\text{Number of shares}}$ or $\frac{\$447,600}{50,000 \text{ shares}} = \$8.95$

† $\frac{\text{Cumulative balance, retained earnings}}{\text{Number of shares}}$ or $\frac{\$967,125}{50,000 \text{ shares}} = \$19.34$

plus the flotation costs that can be converted to approximately 11,200 shares of stock. This would be a loss of 18.30 percent in stock ownership in return for $5 million and the opportunity for growth.

Jones	45,000 shares	=	73.53%
You	5,000	=	8.17
New stock	11,200	=	18.30
	61,200 shares	=	100.00%

After reviewing your analysis, President Jones was more convinced than ever that he would make every effort to effect the ADCO purchase with the convertible-bond feature and would attempt to call the bonds in at $1,050 on or before the end of the sixth year.[1] The $50 premium would be a small price to pay for 18.30 percent of a business entity with the opportunities for growth that appeared probable. If we use as an example the earnings of the sixth year of $1,833,208, this amount would then be divided into 61,200 shares instead of 50,000. Earnings per share would not only drop from $36.66 to $29.954, but the new minority interests would receive $335,440, or 18.3 percent of the $1,833,208. The total bond-call premium would amount to only $253,000! This amount would be allowed as a deductible expense. Thus, the maximum cash outlay would be $126,500 (assuming a marginal tax rate of 50 percent). The 18.3 percent new minority interest would last indefinitely, and the call premium would occur only once. There is no contest. The bonds must be called prior to the end to the sixth year. Perhaps at that time the financial strength of the Jones Electronic Corporation will support a regular debt issue if needed. It should.

EFFECT OF LONG-TERM FINANCING ON RETURN TO EQUITY—LEVERAGE

President Jones then asked you what impact the proposed bond issue would have on the projected market value of the stock when the firm decided (1) to sell its shares publicly and (2) to float additional debt to provide for the conversion of the bond on the basis of a theoretical market value for the shares. This you realized was a difficult question to answer since so many variables were involved.

Your previous discussions of leverage can provide a point from which to begin your consideration of the impact of leverage on the market price of the firm's common stock. Will the introduction of debt capital

[1] Since the bonds become freely convertible after the sixth year, any attempt to call them after that time would probably result in the bondholders' electing to convert their bonds. At that point, the firm has no choice but must accept the tendered bonds and issue the required number of shares to each bondholder.

into the firm's financial structure result in a higher or lower market price for the outstanding shares? Let us consider each of the main capital components and determine how they will react to increases in total debt.

The firm which currently utilizes no long-term debt has in most instances an unused borrowing capacity. In short, it could attract borrowed funds if it so desired. As such a firm increases the percentage of debt in its capital structure from zero to some higher level, we could anticipate the rate of interest paid to rise after the debt level had passed a certain point.

As indicated by Figure 13-2, the cost of debt capital K_i remains constant over a range of values, but as the debt burden begins to place a strain on the firm's ability to service debt, lenders will require increased compensation for the higher level of risk incurred. A good example of this relationship was evident in the progressively higher interest costs which we would have been required to pay if we were to acquire ADCO under any of the four alternatives considered in Chapter 12.

The conservative use of debt or financial leverage must also have an impact on the expectations of equity investors. As bonds are incorporated into the financial structure, they provide the basis for increases in the size and quantity of assets. These assets will in turn occasion higher levels of revenue and income which will be available to the common shareholders, who have not increased in number. Furthermore, the bondholders who have provided the funds used in the expansion have contracted to accept a stipulated return such as 5 percent without regard to the actual return earned on the new assets. Thus, if a 10 percent return is earned on new investment and bondholders receive only 5 percent, the difference is available in the form of increased earnings per share to the equity holders.

As debt is added, the claim of equity investors to earnings becomes subordinated to the claim of bondholders. In addition, the firm has

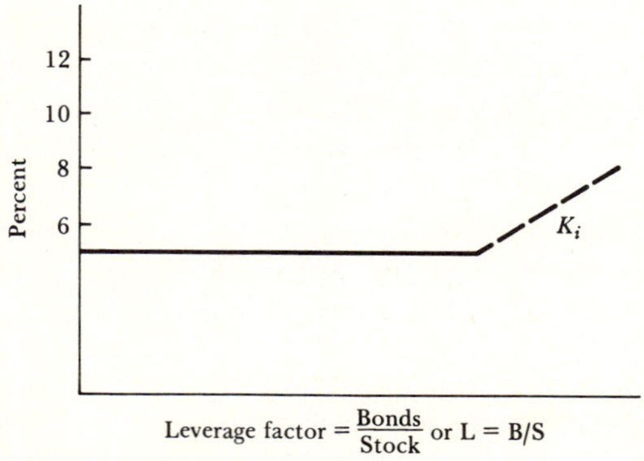

Figure 13-2

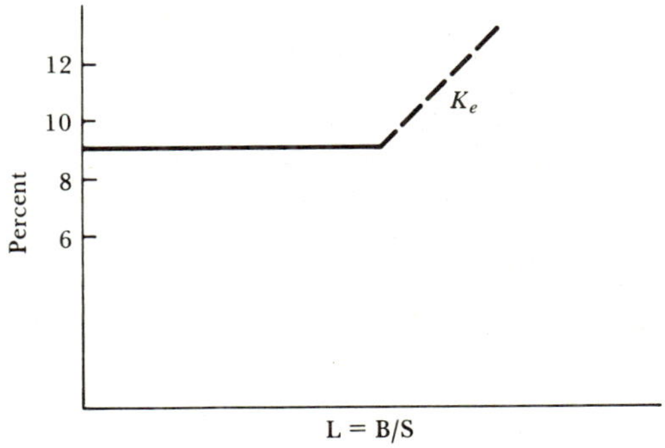

Figure 13-3

increased its risk of legal failure and its susceptibility to financial failure and reorganization.

The cost of equity capital K_e or the return demanded by investors should increase as the corporation adds debt to its capital structure. Figure 13-3, however, indicates that the return demand by investors does not increase as risk increases over a certain range. How can this be true if investors are as a group rational men?

In answer to this question you have only to recognize the fact that within certain limits the increase in risk occasioned by the introduction of debt is compensated for by an increase in the investor's anticipations with respect to the returns he will derive from holding the shares. However, this situation can persist only if corporate debt is maintained within the limits of the firm's ability to safely service that debt. Thus when that ability is in doubt, the return demanded by equity investors will increase, as will the cost of obtaining new equity capital.

If the relationships described above have any validity, the effect of increases in debt on the firm's overall cost of capital K_o may be portrayed as shown in Figure 13-4.

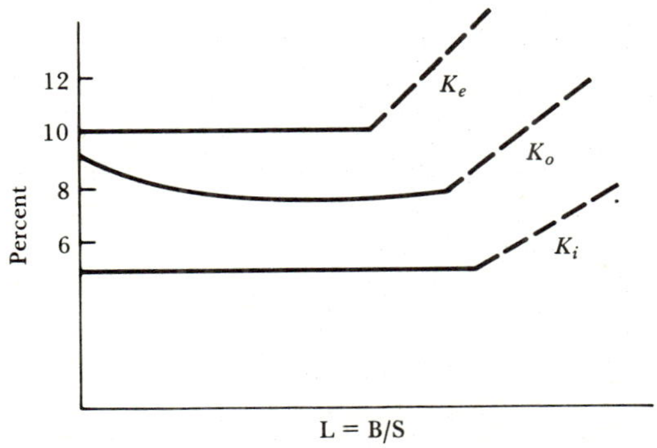

Figure 13-4

Initially, as low-cost debt K_i is floated and the cost of equity K_e remains unchanged, the firm's overall cost of the combined bundle of financing, K_o, must fall. Thus it would appear that there exists for any firm a particular combination of financing which is optimal or lower in cost than alternative combinations. The financial manager in striving to achieve this combination is attempting to minimize the overall cost of capital to the firm. If he is successful, he will, in effect, be maximizing the value of the firm, as represented by the price of its securities, for a given quantity of capital employed.

MARGINAL COST OF DEBT

From a marginal point of view the true cost of incremental debt financing is something more than the interest rate which must be paid. The true cost of such financing is a combination of the cost of the increased interest paid and any change in the value of the equity which occurs as a result of the increase in debt. Diagrammatically, we could show that at the margin the true cost of debt exceeds the interest paid on that debt (see Figure 13-5).

The curve *M,* the marginal cost of debt, differs from K_i in that it includes as a cost of new debt the deterioration in the value of the equity caused by the increase in the risk of liquidation.

In answer to President Jones' specific question relating to the impact of callable, convertible bonds which, it is hoped, will be issued to acquire ADCO, you can render an answer only in the most general terms. Currently, Jones Electronic employs no debt and earns an extremely high return on its equity. Theoretically, investors will pay a price for its shares which represents the anticipated earnings on the shares discounted at some rate to allow for their inherent risk. If we

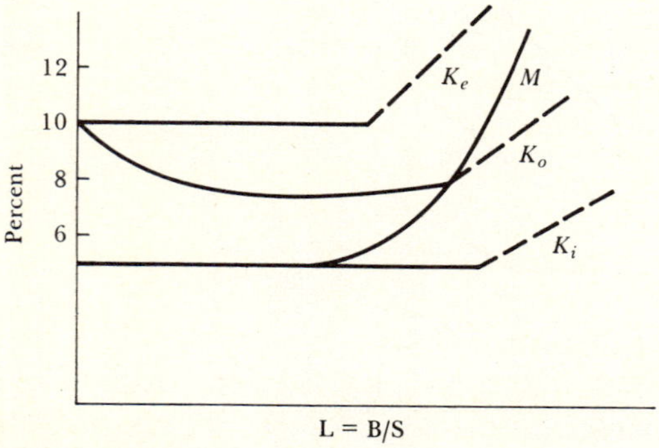

Figure 13-5

add low-cost debt to our capital structure in order to acquire new assets which promise to deliver a high rate of return, we are in effect increasing the level of earnings which can be anticipated by holders of our shares. Furthermore, if the amount of debt issued can be safely serviced, we have not increased the basic risk with respect to those earnings. The result should be higher stock values.

With specific reference to our valuation formula

$$\text{Price} = \frac{\text{Dividends} + \text{productivity of retained earnings}}{\text{Market capitalization rate } (K)}$$

we are increasing our numerator, anticipated earnings, without increasing our risk factor K. In this way it can be seen that attempts to evolve an optimal financial structure are consistent with and focal to the realization of our goal of maximizing the value of our outstanding shares. Thus if we have been successful in maximizing this latter value, fewer shares will have to be issued upon conversion of the bonds when and if bondholders elect to convert.

President Jones paused for a moment and simply said, "It will be a great deal if you can pull it off!" You noticed the emphasis on the word "you" and simply replied, "Why not?" The answer was, "Go ahead, get it done!"

Now—I am going to the golf course—now. You worry about that one!

After several days of reflective thinking, you called Allied for an appointment with the executive officers to discuss the preliminary details of the ADCO acquisition. The meeting was arranged and you arrived on time as scheduled. You found that you were surrounded by several officials, including the president and chairman of the board, as well as the chief legal counsel, his assistant, and the assistant's assistant. You had made your presentation as analyzed earlier. However, your offer was for a total price of \$3 million instead of \$4 million. You expected some adjustment in the selling price! The result was dead silence for what seemed like forever. (It was only two or three minutes.) The meeting lasted slightly less than one hour, with the remaining time spent in informal question answering and detailed explanations of the intent of your proposal and its terms. The meeting ended on a note of cautious optimism. The Allied attorneys asked that the discussions be adjourned for a week while they studied the proposal.

You returned to your office and began to think about possible reasons why Allied and the other shareholders should not accept your offer. A big plus is the fact that Allied approached President Jones with the offer to sell ADCO and is presently seeking a commitment to do so. In addition, from a financial point of view, the offer would seem to be attractive. You decided to summarize the total picture for President Jones. Your analysis appeared as follows:

1. Allied would receive the benefit of the capital loss discussed in Chapter 11, dealing with the analysis of financial statements. This saving alone would amount to $574,000, calculated as follows:

Allied's investment in ADCO	$5,000,000
Selling price of ADCO (60% to Allied)	2,400,000
Capital loss	$2,600,000

   This capital loss can be offset against the capital gain of $2 million which has already been realized and recognized in the same taxable year on the sale of Apex stock (discussed in Chapter 11). For 1970, 28.7 percent (28 percent plus surcharge of $2\frac{1}{2}$ percent on 28 percent, or 0.7 percent) of the earlier gain would be the maximum tax if the ADCO loss were not incurred. The capital gains tax on this basis would be $574,000.
2. Our best estimate of Allied's earnings from the sale of raw material to ADCO was approximately $250,000 annually before taxes. The $4 million offer we are prepared to make for ADCO was calculated by discounting an annuity of this amount for 15 years at 6 percent.

$250,000 × 9.712 = $2,428,000 rounded to $2,400,000 (60 percent of $4 million)

3. Your next calculation made you feel even better about whether or not Allied and the officers owning 40 percent of ADCO should accept a $4 million offer. If the offer were accepted, Allied would receive interest at the rate of 8% on the indebtedness but would lose the income earned on the present sale of raw material to ADCO. Allied would receive $192,000 per year in interest as compared with their present earnings of approximately $250,000. However, this loss of income would be offset by the risk that ADCO's sales would continue to decrease. In this event, Allied's profits from ADCO transactions would likewise decrease. On the other hand, the $192,000 interest income would be a relatively sure thing and would be secured by a mortgage on the ADCO property (and probably the Jones property as well). Furthermore, the loss in income of $29,000 ($250,000 − $192,000 = $58,000 at 50% tax rate = $29,000) would be a rather small item compared with the other advantages of the sale.
4. The sale would mean considerably more to the officers of Allied who were given 40 percent of ADCO stock as a bonus several years ago. They have been receiving no dividends and could now claim capital gains on their share of the selling price ($1,600,000—40 percent of $4 million). They would collectively receive the annual interest of $128,000 versus no current return whatsoever from ADCO! The Allied officials made it quite plain that there would

be no "conflict of interest" on their part, and they were dealing strictly for Allied's best interest. We are, therefore, going to have to meet Allied's 60 percent requirement, and the 40 percent will take care of itself. However, a capital gains tax must be paid.

Unfortunately, the actual receipts of the sale would not be received until at least six years and possibly 20 years from that date! This could be a financial burden that could force the sale of the Jones bonds immediately at a possible discount with the subsequent loss of interest income to the bondholders during the term of the bonds! However, Section 453 of the IRS Code provides that if an installment provision is written into the bond indenture, the capital gains tax will not have to be paid until each installment is received and must be paid only on the gross-profit portion of the amount received.

As an example, if we assume that the selling price for all the Allied stock was $4 million, then each shareholder (each holding a 10 percent interest in Allied) would receive $400,000 of Jones bonds on the exchange for their Allied stock. These bonds would be paid off $200,000 in 1977 and $200,000 in 1978.

If this taxable exchange were to qualify as an installment sale, it would result in no tax for 1971 and a maximum capital gains tax of $50,000 for 1977 and $50,000 for 1978, computed as follows:

Installment sale in 1971:	
Selling price	$400,000
Basis of ADCO stock to shareholder	0
Long-term capital gain	$400,000
Ratio of gross profit to selling price	100%
Amount received in 1971	0
Income tax for 1971	
Taxable years 1977 and 1978:	
Selling price received in each year	$200,000
Gross-profit ratio	× 100%
Long-term capital gain recognized in each of the years 1977 and 1978	$200,000
Maximum tax for each of the years 1977 and 1978:	
25% of $50,000	$ 12,500
25% of $150,000[1]	37,500
	$ 50,000

[1] Technically, the Internal Revenue Code provides (for years beginning in 1972 and thereafter) no alternative tax with respect to a net long-term capital gain exceeding $50,000. But, after applying to the excess the 50 percent deduction (which applies to all long-term capital gains including the amounts in excess of $50,000), the remaining 50 percent is subject to ordinary income tax treatment. Thus, since there is a maximum 50 percent rate on the ordinary income of individual taxpayers, it can be said that the excess of long-term capital gains over $50,000 is subject to a maximum tax rate of 25 percent.

The results would be the same as above if half the bonds were to mature in 15 years (in 1987) and the other half in 16 years (in 1988).

The preceding tax calculation illustrates a very significant feature of the installment sale. If the installment sale feature were included in the bond indenture, the officers of Allied would not be required to pay the tax on their gain until the installments were received. (Allied would pay no tax in any event because of the capital loss incurred.) This is significant. Without the installment feature the tax on the gain must be paid in the taxable year of the sale and might create a liquidity problem for each of the directors. In fact, some of the bonds received might have to be sold in order to pay the tax. With the installment feature the tax must be paid but at least not until the bonds are redeemed and the cash is received.

A split second after you had finished explaining the tax advantages that would accrue to the 40 percent individual sellers of ADCO stock if the transaction were arranged to qualify as an installment sale, you were bombarded by both the attorney and the accountant.

"Ho, ho, ho—beautiful—before the tax reform act of 1969—but unworkable today."

The 1969 act contained amendments to the Internal Revenue Code (called anticonglomerate provisions) which were aimed at discouraging acquisitions by fast-moving conglomerate corporations through the use of tax-favored debt instruments (commonly referred to as "funny money"). Actually, what was happening was that the conglomerate purchasing the controlling stock of another company in exchange for the conglomerate's convertible bonds was able to finance the acquisition partly through the tax savings resulting from having the interest on the bonds allowed as a tax deduction. The transaction was arranged as an installment-sale device to shelter the tendering selling shareholders from an immediate taxable transaction. (A tax-free exchange of stock for stock would have made the sellers of the absorbed company equity owners in the conglomerate. Thus, dividends to them would not be deductible by the conglomerate.)

The 1969 amendments reduced the tax advantages to both the buyers and the sellers.

The provisions affecting the sellers (the 40 percent individual owners of ADCO stock) limited the availability of the installment method of reporting. Ordinarily, the installment method of reporting gain on the casual sale of personal property (where the price exceeds $1,000) is available only if payments received in the year of sale (called "initial payments") do not exceed 30 percent of the sales price. Obligations of the seller are normally not considered as "initial payments." Thus, prior to the 1969 act, the conglomerates were making their stock acquisitions for debt attractive to the selling stockholders by deferring 70 percent or more of the sales price through debenture bonds payable in two or more installments. Under the 1969 act, the amount of certain bonds or other corporate evidence of indebtedness must be treated as payable in the year of sale, thereby disqualifying many transactions of installment reporting where such bonds are used. Under the new rules, the bonds or other evidences of indebtedness which must be taken into account for purposes of the 30 percent limitation are those payable upon demand or issued by a corporate or governmental entity with interest coupons attached, or in any form designed to render the bonds readily tradable in an established security market. Thus, in the Jones case, the installment method of reporting gain on the sale of ADCO stock for convertible bonds of the Jones Corporation will not be available.

As to the provisions of the 1969 act designed to limit the advantages to the buyers of the stock (Jones Corporation in our case), the new provisions provide briefly as follows: Where a corporation acquires stock or two-third of the assets of another corporation in exchange for its convertible bonds, interest expense in excess of $5 million per year, generally, will not be tax-deductible. Thus, in our case, the new law does not come into play (the interest deduction each year will be less than $5 million), and the interest expense would be deductible.

The accountant also added that the 1969 act limited the amount of the deduction for the premium paid by a corporation on repurchase of its convertible bonds to an amount not in excess of the normal call premium for nonconvertible corporate indebtedness. Thus, if a corporation repurchased its convertible bond issued at $1,000 for $1,500 (market value), the premium paid is *$500.* The increase in market value was partly due to the conversion feature. The amount deductible will be limited to an amount not in excess of a normal call premium for nonconvertible corporate indebtedness unless the corporation can prove that a greater amount had to be paid because of the cost of borrowing.

The attorney commented that in his opinion, the major purpose of the foregoing corrective legislation in the corporation acquisition area was to blunt the increasing concentration of economic power through acquisitions which fall outside the antitrust laws. To this end, the reduction in the installment method appears to miss the target. The corrective legislation will extend to transactions never intended to be reached and thereby create new inequities. Take our case—the Jones Corporation is hardly a conglomerate seeking to devour large corporations for the purpose of restricting competition. Yet our proposal may not be acceptable because of the hardships that will be imposed on the ADCO stockholders selling their 40 percent interest on the installment basis. After all, they will be called upon to make a payment of a tax before they receive the proceeds of sale, since our bonds may not be readily marketable. However, the attorney continued, there may be a safety hatch in the law. The Congressional Committee Reports indicates that ordinary promissory notes are not to be included as "initial payments." This leaves possible room for changing the type of instruments that would be issued by Jones for the ADCO stock. If this proves unworkable, we would just have to pay to each 10 percent owner a cash down payment large enough to take care of the tax which they will be called on to pay because the installment sale does not qualify for deferred tax treatment.

The attorney (and also the accountant) commented that we should not count on any loss carry-forwards that were caused by the high costs and low selling prices of ADCO's products. He pointed out that Sections 482 and 269 and a number of court cases cast considerable doubt about using the loss carry-over after the change in ownership and the change in ADCO's method of doing business. At best, we could be buying a lawsuit should we attempt to reap any tax benefits from the unused loss carry-forward. He advised that for the purpose of estimating future flow of funds, we assume that no tax benefits will be derived from the ADCO operating loss carry-forward. Likewise, we should not give any consideration in the purchase price to any value for the loss carry-forward. (Fortunately, we did not and now we will not!)

In general, he felt our total position was sound, if our future sales estimates were reasonably accurate (50 percent or more—but we knew that). However, he did call attention to the possibility that Allied could induce us—in fact, would probably require us—to include as collateral not only the ADCO plant but also the Jones plant and equipment in the mortgage indenture and then conceivably could refuse to purchase their requirements from us. (What a rude awakening this was!) A little reflection indicated that you could arrange this whole financing package, purchase ADCO, and then Allied would be in a position to force Jones into financial difficulties by failing to buy the number of units anticipated (or any number of units from the Jones firm). Allied might then be in a position to foreclose on the mortgage, and the complete package could be Allied's once again, including the entire Jones operation! This possibility may seem remote, but at times, "business is business." He suggested that a collateral agreement be made with Allied stated that Allied would be committed to purchase *X* number of units each year for the next five or six years. (As you may recall, this is the precise reason or possibility that prompted President Jones to insist that our normal market not be neglected.)

The meeting with Allied was scheduled for the next morning. President Jones and the attorney accompanied you. The same battery of experts represented Allied. The Allied officials had done their homework well. They insisted that they must have $3,250,000 as payment for Allied's 60 percent interest in ADCO. They had arrived at this figure by capitalizing at 10 percent the annual income of $325,000 which they stated had been earned from sales to ADCO. They asked that officers of Allied who own the remaining 40 percent interest in ADCO receive a proportionate price for their interest, namely, $2,167,000, so that the total purchase price for 100 percent of Allied would be $5,417,000.

We indicated that we were not willing to assume that the ADCO operation will or would have earned $325,000 annually indefinitely. Rather, the only way Allied could place a value on the ADCO operation was to discount the stream of income over the remaining economic life of the plant and equipment with reasonable allowance for the risk of technical obsolescence. We indicated that, in our judgment, Allied had cleared approximately $250,000 per year before taxes on the ADCO operation. If we could do as well for 15 years while earning a 6 percent return, the present value of $250,000 would be $2,400,000 (as we calculated earlier). The Allied spokesman countered that we would do much better, that is, earn far more profit annually, considering the reduction in cost per unit for our present production with the more efficient equipment. He stated that, in his judgment, we would earn between $600,000 and $700,000 before taxes annually. By discounting this stream at 10 percent for 10 years, the plant would be worth $3,687,000 to $4,301,500 ($600,000 × 6.145 = $3,687,000, or $700,000 × 6.145 = $4,301,500) plus the margin on increased sales to Allied. He further stated that the sales contracts held by Allied at this time would guarantee the Allied's purchases from the Jones Corporation would increase at least 50 percent each year for at least five years. With this you did a quick mental calculation (although you scribbled the annual increases on a pad) while you listened to the next sentence.

		50% Increase in Units	Total Units
Present Allied contract for the coming year	40,000 units		
First year		20,000	60,000
Second year		30,000	90,000
Third year		45,000	135,000
Fourth year		67,500	202,500
Fifth year		101,250	303,750

He continued that, in his judgment, this volume should warrant a reduction in unit cost to Allied, as he was certain we would pass the breakeven point. (Shades of Chapter 3!) You responded with a deadpan expression as he continued and as you recalled that your own forecasted sales volume increase was but 10 percent per year. Using this

10 percent forecast, you had predicted your ability to pay off the bonds within a six-year period. You compared your sales forecast below with Allied's forecast above.

	10% Increase in Units
Second year	40,000
Third year	44,000
Fourth year	48,400
Fifth year	53,240
Sixth year	58,560

He then asked for your reaction. It was lunchtime, and it was suggested that the Jones delegation would perhaps like to discuss the latest developments at lunch. The meeting could be continued at 2 p.m.

The discussion during lunch was long and serious. Very little of the food was consumed. The maitre d' expressed his concern that the quality of the food may not have been up to the usual fine standard. You suspected that his real concern was about the size of the gratuity! But with several millions of dollars in the balance within the next several hours, food was relatively unimportant. Your discussions with President Jones and your tax attorney can be summarized as follows.

It is most significant and essential that the Jones Corporation obtain from Allied a firm commitment concerning Allied's purchases from Jones during the next five or six years. Total sales to Allied per Allied's estimate could be as follows:

	Units
Next year	40,000
First year	60,000
Second year	90,000
Third year	135,000
Fourth year	202,500
Fifth year	303,750

Allied had suggested a reduction in price because of this increase in volume purchased. We are going to counter that rather than reduce the price to Allied, we will add to the price that we will pay for ADCO. We do not want to reduce our selling price as a matter of policy. Allied had suggested a price reduction of $1 per unit. Over the six-year period, total Allied purchases from Jones are estimated to be 831,250 units. If the price per unit to Allied were reduced $1 per unit, the reduction would increase Allied's profits before taxes by $831,250 over a six-year period, or $415,625 after taxes. If the price paid for the ADCO stock were increased to $4,500,000 from $4,000,000, Allied's 60 percent share would be $2,700,000; and if the price for ADCO were increased to $5,000,000, Allied's 60 percent share would be $3,000,000.

Recalculating Allied's capital loss indicates the following:

	$4,000,000 Price	$4,500,000 Price	$5,000,000 Price
Investment in Allied	$5,000,000	$5,000,000	$5,000,000
Proceeds of sale of 60% of ADCO stock	2,400,000	2,700,000	3,000,000
Capital loss	$2,600,000	$2,300,000	$2,000,000

Allied needs a $2 million capital loss this year to offset the $2 million capital gain earned on the sale of the Apex stock earlier this year. Any price for ADCO that will net Allied less than $3 million will result in an excess capital loss over and above the $2 million loss that is needed. However, we must continue to keep in mind that any of the three proposed prices for the ADCO stock will result in a $574,000 capital gains tax savings to Allied. The Allied officials could well take the position that this savings is not our concern, and they would be correct except that we can't help thinking about the $574,000 capital gains tax savings as an increase in the proceeds to be received by Allied as a result of the sale of the ADCO stock to Jones.

President Jones indicated that if worse came to worst, he would pay the $5 million on a convertible-bond basis as outlined earlier in return for a firm purchase contract from Allied. You advised him to sit tight on the $4,000,000 or the $4,500,000 offer until the last minute. It would not be possible to earn $574,000 any easier. Stated another way, Allied would have to earn $1,148,000 from operations to realize $574,000 after taxes (assume the tax rate is 50 percent). Of course, Allied is thinking exactly the same way.

You indicated that it would be desirable if the Jones Electronic Corporation actually controlled Allied. This would ensure that Allied would purchase all their requirements from Jones. You even suggested, with an air of jest, that perhaps we should buy out or absorb the entire Allied operation at this time instead of just purchasing ADCO from Allied. A flash of light, or something, seemed to flash across everyone's face. You know that ". . . many a true word has been spoken in jest." However, this idea was dismissed as being impractical at this time. The biggest problem would be the lack of bargaining power. We know the amount of earnings we anticipate over the next five or six years. However, these are anticipated earnings and would only serve to suggest that perhaps ADCO's only real problem is inadequate management. It was decided to proceed with the final arrangements as quickly as possible.

After considerable give and take over the next nine hours, without an adjournment for dinner, a memorandum of agreement was signed by all parties. The price for ADCO was determined to be $4,750,000. Allied agreed to purchase all raw-material requirements from Jones or ADCO insofar as we could deliver the desired quantities promptly. However, no guarantee of an annual specific quantity was included.

The convertible-bond issue and the installment-payment feature of the bond were accepted by Allied as proposed. No comment was made by either side about the sale's not qualifying as an installment sale. We assumed that this was one of the factors which gave rise to the higher settlement price than we had anticipated earlier. It was the end of a long, hard, yet pleasant day. The entire day was pleasant because both Jones and Allied would benefit from the ADCO transaction.

The meeting adjourned about 11:30 p.m. with everyone almost too tired for dinner. However, President Jones invited you and the Jones attorney to have dinner with him at the exquisite "Round Tree Room." During the dinner, he likewise invited you and your family (if any) to spend the weekend with him in Buenos Aires, Argentina. You were on cloud nine. I watched as your plane took off in the early morning hours on Thursday.

SUMMARY

The previous chapter pursued the proposed acquisition of ADCO in relation to its investment merit. This chapter also deals with the purchase of ADCO but is primarily concerned with the financing of the acquisition. Your initial consideration involved the flotation of debt securities. You examined the common characteristics of debt instruments and pointed out to President Jones that while basic contractual provisions were similar, debt securities were highly flexible financial vehicles. They could be secured or unsecured, subordinated or prior claim. Their life cycle might be fixed or flexible, and repayment could take a variety of forms. In addition, special securities like equipment trust certificates and convertible bonds were available for asset financing.

Your next considerations were related to yields and market prices. A bond, you recalled, contains at least two contractual promises, the payment of interest and the repayment of principal. The market value of the bond is, then, nothing more than the present value of these two contractual dollar flows. The discount rate applied to these flows will be determined by the general level of riskless interest rates and the level of risk associated with the particular payments in question.

The use of bonds in the corporate claim structure was then discussed. You were quick to note the relationship which existed between the use of leverage and the cost of capital. The most significant calculation which you made involved the determination of the true marginal cost of new debt. This cost is a composite one and includes both the increased interest paid and also an allowance for any increase in the cost of equity capital which was related to the additional debt financing.

At the conclusion of the analysis you were prepared to sit down with Allied and talk turkey. Again, the tax framework became a critical factor in your analysis and in the determination of the final price to be paid for ADCO. The preparation which you made before the Allied meeting bore fruit in that the final agreement was not a "horse trade" but a reasoned settlement with financial advantages for each party.

QUESTIONS FOR DISCUSSION

1. What are the basic characteristics of bonds and/or other evidence of long-term debt?
2. What is the significant difference between secured and unsecured obligations?
3. What is the significance of a first-mortgage bond?
4. What is an "open-ended feature" with respect to long-term financing?
5. What is the significance of the "open-ended feature"?
6. What is a debenture?
7. What is an indenture?
8. What is the basic difference between placing bonds for sale privately and offering them for sale to the public at large?
9. What are equipment trust certificates?
10. What are collateral trust bonds?
11. What are income bonds?
12. What is an "after-acquired" clause that may be included in an indenture?
13. What is a "payoff privilege"?
14. What is a "call provision"?
15. What is the significance of the convertible bond?

16. Why was the Jones organization reluctant to discuss future profitability with respect to the proposed long-term debt?

17. What is a bond discount? Illustrate.

18. What is a bond premium? Illustrate.

19. What economic factors would give rise to the bond discount or the bond premium?

20. Why would the Jones organization consider marketing convertible bonds?
    a. What are the advantages?
    b. What are the disadvantages?

21. What is financial leverage?

22. What is the significance of financial leverage to equity investors?

23. What is the marginal cost of debt?

24. Why should Allied accept the Jones offer to finance the acquisition of ADCO by way of convertible bonds?

25. What are the tax advantages of the convertible feature to the owners of the ADCO stock?

26. What advantages would the installment repayment of the long-term debt have to the ADCO stockholders prior to the 1969 Tax Reform Act?

27. What advantages would the installment repayment of the long-term debt have to the ADCO stockholders after the 1969 Tax Reform Act?

28. What tax advantages would there be to the Jones organization if they arranged the repayment of the convertible bonds by the installment method prior to the 1969 Tax Reform Act?

29. What tax advantages would there be to the Jones organization if they arranged the repayment of the convertible bonds by the installment method after the 1969 Tax Reform Act?

30. Why did the Allied officers insist that they must have $3,250,000 as payment for Allied's interest in ADCO?

31. Why was the Jones organization unwilling to accept the $3,250,000 price?

32. Upon what basis did the Jones organization offer $2,400,000 for Allied's interest in ADCO?

33. What was the significance of the sales contract between Allied and the Jones organization with respect to the sale of the ADCO stock?

34. Why was the Jones organization unwilling to sell their product to Allied at a reduced price?

35. What alternative to the reduction in price did Jones offer to Allied?

36. What was the significance of the final agreement whereby Jones acquired all the capital stock of ADCO?

PROBLEMS

1. Your firm has decided to offer a debenture bond. The proceeds of the issue will be used to finance new plant construction. The firm already has first-mortgage bonds in your capital structure. The bonds are secured by a general lien on all the existing buildings and properties of the firm. You have been asked to write a summary of the security available to the new debenture holders and to explain their rights and priorities in the event of liquidation.
   a. Write such a description.
   b. How would the security of the debenture holders be affected if the indenture describing the first-mortgage bonds contained an after-acquired property clause.

2. Gone Corporation has fallen upon hard times and is forced into a liquidation proceeding. Total liquidation proceeds were $400,000. The right-hand side of the balance sheet is made up of the following claimants:

Trade Creditors	$100,000
First Mortgage Bonds	400,000
Common Stock and Retained Earnings	500,000

   a. How would the liquidation be divided if the assets to which the mortgage bondholders were secured had netted $100,000 of the total $400,000 realized on the liquidation?
   b. How would the price proceeds be divided if all the creditors had been ranked equally, that is, none were secured?

3. Your firm is preparing to offer a convertible debenture. You intend to specify a coupon rate of 5 percent. The bonds will be issued in $1,000 denominations and will be outstanding for 20 years. Other bonds of equivalent risk and duration are currently offering a yield of 7 percent.
   a. If your bonds were sold as straight debt instruments, what selling price could you expect?
   b. What premiums are you asking investors to pay for the convertibility feature?
   c. Write a detailed conversion feature in terms of both a conversion price and rates. Use your own figures.

4. Below you can see the income statement of Worthy Corporation.

Sales	$2,000,000
Cost of Sales	1,000,000
Gross Profit	1,000,000
Interest	200,000
Profit before Tax	800,000
Tax 50%	400,000
Profit after Tax	400,000
Shares Outstanding	200,000
Market Price per Share	$60

The firm's convertible securities will be called. The result of this action will be the issuance of an additional 100,000 shares and a reduction of $150,000 in annual interest charges.

a. What will be the impact of conversion on earnings per share?
b. What impact will conversion have on the market price?
c. What factors did you consider in arriving at your answer to (b) above?

5. You are asked to present a graphic depiction of the introduction of leverage into a firm's financial structure. Your presentation should include your concept of the impact of leverage on the cost of both debt and equity capital.

REFERENCES

Baumol, William J., Burton G. Malkiel, and Richard E. Quandt: The Valuation of Convertible Securities, *Quarterly Journal of Economics,* vol. LXXX, pp. 48–59, February, 1966.

Bladen, Ashly: "Techniques for Investing in Convertible Bonds," Salomon Bros. & Hutzler, New York, 1966.

Bowlin, Oswald D.: The Refunding Decision, *Journal of Finance,* vol. XXI, pp. 55–68, March, 1966.

Brigham, Eugene F.: An Analysis of Convertible Debentures: Theory and Some Empirical Evidence, *Journal of Finance,* vol. XXI, pp. 35–54, March, 1966.

Broman, Keith L.: The Use of Convertible Subordinated Debentures by Industrial Firms 1949–1959, *Quarterly Review of Economics and Business,* vol. III, pp. 65–75, spring, 1963.

Carleton, Willard T.: An Analytical Model for Long-range Financial Planning, *Journal of Finance,* vol. XXV, pp. 291–315, May, 1970.

Cohen, Jerome B., and Sidney M. Robbins: "The Financial Manager," chaps. 11, 24, Harper & Row, Publishers, Incorporated, New York, 1966.

Donaldson, Gordon: New Framework for Corporate Debt Policy, *Harvard Business Review,* vol. XL, pp. 117–131, March–April, 1962.

Fischer, Donald E., and Glenn A. Wilt, Jr.: Non-convertible Preferred Stock as a Financing Instrument 1950–1965, *Journal of Finance,* vol. XXIII, pp. 611–624, September, 1968.

Gupta, Manak C.: The Effect of Size, Growth, and Industry on the Financial Structure of Manufacturing Companies, *Journal of Finance,* vol. XXIV, no. 3, pp. 517–529, June, 1969.

Herzog, John P.: Investor Experience in Corporate Securities: A New Technique for Measurement, *Journal of Finance,* vol. XIX, pp. 46–62, March, 1964.

Johnson, Ramon E.: Term Structures of Corporate Bond Yields as a Function of Risk of Default, *Journal of Finance,* vol. XXII, pp. 313–345, May, 1967.

Lerner, Eugene M., and Willard T. Carleton: Financing Decisions of the Firm, *Journal of Finance,* vol. XXI, pp. 202–214, May, 1966.

McKenzie, Robert R.: Convertible Securities, 1956–1965, *Quarterly Review of Economics and Business,* vol. VI, pp. 41–48, winter, 1966.

Miller, G. R.: Long-term Business Financing from the Underwriter's Point of View, *Journal of Finance,* vol. XVI, pp. 280–290, May, 1961.

Poensgen, Otto H.: The Valuation of Convertible Bonds, parts I and II, *Industrial Management Review,* vols. VI and VII, pp. 77–92 and 83–98, fall, 1965, and spring, 1966.

Robichek, A. A.: Problems in the Theory of Optimal Capital Structure, *Journal of Financial and Quantitative Analysis,* vol. 1, pp. 1–35, June, 1966.

Schwartz, Eli: The Refunding Decision, *Journal of Business*, vol. XL, no. 4, pp. 448–449, October, 1967.

Skelly, William S.: "Convertible Bonds: A Study of Their Suitability for Commercial Bank Bond Portfolios," Salomon Bros. & Hutzler, New York, 1959.

Solomon, Ezra: "The Theory of Financial Management," chap. 3, Columbia University Press, New York, 1963.

Weil, Roman L., Jr., Joel E. Segall, and David Green, Jr.: Premiums on Convertible Bonds, *Journal of Finance,* vol. XXIII, pp. 445–464, June, 1968.

Williams, B. S., and Marvin Letwat: Underwritten Calls of Industrial Convertible Securities, 1950–1961, *Quarterly Review of Economics and Business,* III, pp. 71–77, winter, 1963.

Chapter Fourteen
MERGERS AND ACQUISITIONS

Quite a few years have passed since the ADCO acquisition. You were able to follow the "game plan"; and the convertible bonds issued to Allied have been retired. Jones sales and profits have increased steadily, and you have created the image and are being regarded as something of a financial genius. Needless to say, your annual compensation has increased threefold. You appeared to enjoy your newfound success. However, the enjoyment was only on the outside. On the inside you were troubled. You saw the following headline in the Wall Street Journal:

AEROSPACE CRISIS

Subcontractors Suffer
As Big Defense Firms
Cancel Their Orders

Many Failures, Bankruptcies
Are Caused by Dependence
On the Prime Contractors

But Some Find Other Buyers

You were concerned about Allied, the major purchaser of Jones' production. Allied is in the aerospace business! President Jones' inquiries to Allied about future requirements from Jones have resulted in vague answers. Fortunately, President Jones has always insisted upon constant development of "other sales," that is, other than Allied. However, Allied still constitutes about 25 percent of total sales. Financially, Jones is in a relatively strong position. However, a loss of 25 percent of total sales could be quite a jolt.

As you have said many times before, "The biggest problem in any one problem is knowing what the problem is!" The problem at hand is easily identified. The solution will require a little more study. The basic problem is to retain at least your current earnings per share and hopefully to continue Jones' rate of growth. If Allied sales were significantly cut back, one alternative would be a deeper penetration into the "other sales" market. Further detailed discussion on the broad aspects of the problems would be a waste of time at this point. You have no real or meaningful notion as to the size of the potential market. Jones simply does not have a marketing research staff nor market data from any other source. There are several alternatives:

1. Conduct the research yourself.
2. Develop a marketing research staff.
3. Retain a marketing consulting firm to do the job.

You decided upon the last-mentioned alternative. You also decided to set forth some guidelines to establish the type of information you would like to have available. These guidelines, or the establishing of these guidelines, would be your first task.

GUIDELINES FOR MARKET RESEARCH

The following morning you meet with the consulting firm. You want to know:[1]

1. *Total industry sales potential,* which means optimum sales to all potential customers of products currently being produced or products which could be produced. In order to reach the optimum sales level, we may be talking about educational advertising or the use of greatly expanded sales forces by all producers. Industry sales potential implies all possible sales by all producers.
2. *Current total industry sales potential,* which means that calculations would be limited to those products being produced and currently being sold by all producers.
3. *Industry market penetration rate,* which involves a determination of the extent to which producers have exploited or developed potential markets for existing products. In short, if the industry as a whole

[1] The approach followed herein can be found in a more extensive form in Robert S. Weinberg, Strategic Planning for Acquisitions and Mergers, in G. Scott Hutcheson, "The Business of Acquisition and Mergers," chap. 6, pp. 62–78, Presidents Publishing House, Inc., New York, 1968.

has saturated the potential market, Jones by necessity must look to item 1 above, which means Jones may or may not be able to develop new products and thus new markets. It would depend upon how well the industry has penetrated this potential. Hopefully, in the short run, it would be discovered that Jones can, with its current plant and equipment, create new markets without the capital expenditures of the type we dealt with in Chapter 5, Capital Budgeting. If this latter course of action is not possible, Jones may have to look elsewhere. These considerations lead to item 4 below.

4. *Jones' market potential,* which means, given the limitations or restraints of Jones' current plant capacity, sales force, and product mix, what percentage of potential industry total sales could Jones expect or hope to capture? The degree to which Jones would be successful would indicate Jones' *market penetration rate.*

We can then express Jones' share of the market in terms of *units, dollars,* or *a percentage* of total industry sales. Once we arrive at the units and dollars involved in potential sales, it will be necessary to consult the flexible budget, or to construct a new one, to reflect the new product or products, if any. The flexible budget (Chapter 4) will provide Jones with some information relating tc production limitations. (Jones cannot profitably produce at any level where marginal cost exceeds marginal revenue.) From this information, projected profit and loss figures, cost-profit-volume relationship, and some cash-flow data, at least the outflow can be estimated.

In essence, the examination will operate like a TV camera that looks at potential market conditions from a distance, zooms in for a close-up involving cost analyses, and then backs away again as far as the flexible budget and/or prudent capital expenditures for new plant and equipment will permit, if any. Capital expenditures must be balanced against other investment opportunities or the opportunity cost of the funds involved.

The potential market problem can be clearly illustrated by Figure 14-1 on page 428.

However, sales are one thing, profitable sales are quite another. As indicated earlier, the flexible budget must be consulted and possible capital budgeting implications must be considered. Nevertheless, as a first step, the executive committee authorized the retention of a marketing research firm in order to get the sales potential picture.

After some weeks of uncertainty the research report was ready. Briefly, the report indicates that the market involves total industry potential of some 1,150,000 units on an annual basis. The current industry penetration rate was estimated at about 26 percent with full development some 10 years in the future. An orderly annual growth rate would be about 300,000 units. You quickly calculated that this would be at an

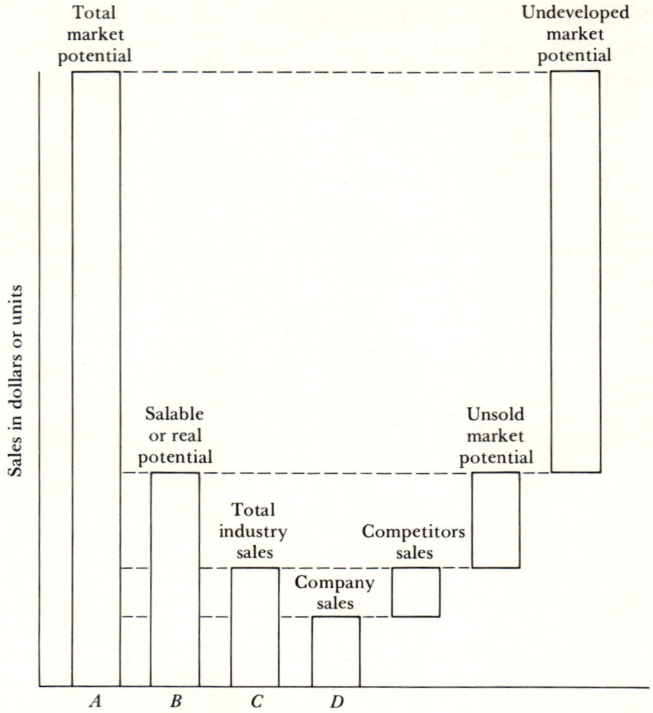

Market development rate: $\frac{B}{A}$

Market realization rate: $\frac{C}{B}$

Competitive impact factor: $\frac{D}{C}$

Figure 14-1

annual rate of 13 percent compounded annually. (How did you arrive at the 13 percent?) If you can't answer this question, try finding the percentage figure from the compound sum of $1, page 486, that will give you the factor which when multiplied by 300,000 equals 1,150,755!

Year	Base	Growth Rate	Potential Units Shipped
1	300,000	1.13	339,000
2	339,000	1.13	383,070
3	383,070	1.13	432,869
4	432,869	1.13	489,142
5	489,142	1.13	552,730
6	552,730	1.13	624,585
7	624,585	1.13	705,781
8	705,781	1.13	797,532
9	797,532	1.13	901,211
10	901,211	1.13	1,018,368

$$\frac{1{,}150{,}755}{300{,}000} = 3{,}835$$

or

approx. 13%

The figures on this table assume that the development rate will be 100 percent. You just do not think that all factors and circumstances will jell at the right time, so you adopted an 80 percent development rate and constructed the following table:

CHART

Year	Yearly Output	×	Growth Factor	=	Potential Units Shipped	×	Market Realization Rate	=	Probable Shipments of Units for Industry
1	300,000	×	1.13	=	339,000	×	0.80	=	271,200
2	339,000	×	1.13	=	383,070	×	0.80	=	306,456
3	383,000	×	1.13	=	432,869	×	0.80	=	346,295
4	432,790	×	1.13	=	489,142	×	0.80	=	391,314
5	489 052	×	1.13	=	552,730	×	0.80	=	442,184
6	552,630	×	1.13	=	624,585	×	0.80	=	499,668
7	624,471	×	1.13	=	705,781	×	0.80	=	564,625
8	705,652	×	1.13	=	797,532	×	0.80	=	638,026
9	797,387	×	1.13	=	901,211	×	0.80	=	720,969
10	901,047	×	1.13	=	1,018,368	×	0.80	=	814,694

Company Sales in Units

The calculation of company sales during the forecasting period will be the result of multiplying total industry sales by a ***competitive impact factor.*** The competitive impact factor is a measure of the firm's share of the total market vis-à-vis our competition. Jones has, for all intents and purposes, a single competitor, Apex Corporation. If Jones is to realize a rate of growth in sales which exceeds that of the industry, it will be necessary to increase its competitive impact factor at the expense of its chief competitor, Apex. Currently, Jones controls approximately 75 percent of the market and Apex the remaining 25 percent. If this current situation were to remain unchanged throughout the forecast period, Jones would realize a growth in annual unit shipments of the following magnitude:

Year	Probable Industry Shipments, Units	×	Competitive Impact Factor	=	Jones Shipments, Units	×	Weighted Price	=	Total Sales
1	271,200	×	0.75	=	203,400	×	$6.90	=	$1,403,460
2	306,456	×	0.75	=	229,842	×	6.90	=	1,585,910
3	346,295	×	0.75	=	259,721	×	6.90	=	1,792,075
4	391,314	×	0.75	=	293,485	×	6.90	=	2,025,046
5	442,184	×	0.75	=	331,638	×	6.90	=	2,288,302
6	499,668	×	0.75	=	374,751	×	6.90	=	2,585,782
7	564,625	×	0.75	=	423,469	×	6.90	=	2,921,936
8	638,026	×	0.75	=	478,519	×	6.90	=	3,301,781
9	720,969	×	0.75	=	540,727	×	6.90	=	3,731,016
10	814,694	×	0.75	=	611,020	×	6.90	=	4,216,038

Given Jones' level of projected shipments in units, we can now convert this figure into annual sales revenues.

Company Sales in Dollars

Jones, as you know, uses a dual price system. Sales to Allied are made at $6 per unit and other sales at $7.20. Allied purchases about 25 percent of total production and other customers account for the remaining 75 percent. The most recent income statement shows that Jones shipped 203,400 units. The average selling price per unit, given our sales distribution to Allied and others, is as follows:

Total shipments		
Allied shipments	203,400(0.25) =	50,850
Other shipments	203,400(0.75) =	152,550
Total shipments		203,400
Total sales in dollars		
Sales to Allied	50,850($6) =	$ 305,100
Sales to others	152,550($7.20) =	1,098,360
Total sales		$1,403,460

$$\text{Weighted average selling price} = \frac{\$1,403,460}{203,400} = \$6.90$$

The report then determined Jones' probable sales revenues over the forecast period by multiplying unit shipments by weighted average price. You were quick to notice that this projection of total revenue depends on the assumption that the Allied sales continue to be 25 percent of total sales. The validity of this assumption is at the root of our present discussions. However, you continued with the report as is, feeling that projections could be made later without this basic assumption. However, you did feel uneasy.

Year	Forecasted Shipments by Jones Corporation	×	Weighted Average Selling Price	=	Projected Sales
1	203,400	×	$6.90	=	$1,403,460
2	229,800	×	6.90	=	1,585,620
3	259,674	×	6.90	=	1,791,750
4	293,430	×	6.90	=	2,024,667
5	331,578	×	6.90	=	2,287,888
6	374,682	×	6.90	=	2,585,305
7	423,390	×	6.90	=	2,921,391
8	474,681	×	6.90	=	3,275,298
9	540,627	×	6.90	=	3,730,326
10	610,911	×	6.90	=	4,215,285

Given these estimates of Jones' probable sales figures, we then calculated company profits and earnings per share.

Company Costs and Expenses

The calculation began with an examination of Jones' latest income statement for a complete year's operations.

Jones Electronic Corporation
Projected Statement of Profit and Loss
For the Year October 1, 1971, to September 30, 1972
(Excluding ADCO Operations)*

Sales		
180,000* units at $6.90		$1,242,000
Cost of Goods Sold		
180,000 units at $2.80		504,000
Gross Profit		$ 738,000
Less		
General and Administrative Expenses		147,846
Net Profit before Taxes		$ 590,154
Income Tax—22% × $ 25,000 =	5,500	
48% × $565,154 =	271,274	276,774
		$ 313,380

* For planning purposes we have treated ADCO as a distinct division and have not considered its products or costs of production. We will continue to exclude its assets and sales, with the exception of those assets which will be employed directly in the production of the primary product.
† Industry sales this past year were 240,000; Jones' share of that figure was 0.75(240,000) = 180,000.

The income statement shown above could be used to show the relationship between sales and costs at our current level of production and our present selling price. In many instances this is done by taking each expense item as a percentage of sales and then simply projecting this same relationship at a series of sales levels. While this percentage-of-sales method has the advantage of simplicity of calculation, it is in reality very seldom useful. Its inherent drawback, of course, is its failure to recognize the fact that costs will change with production levels in a variable rather than a fixed percentage relationship. As you can see, we are back to our cost curves and flexible budget again! At this point a new flexible budget was prepared in order to forecast product costs over the planning period.

The cost information generated by the flexible budget with the anticipated rate of growth in projected earnings per share and the stream of future income is as follows:

Year	Sales	−	Costs	=	EBT*	−	Tax	=	EAT†	EPS (50,000 Shares)	Growth Rate in EPS
1	$1,403,460		$1,185,500		$ 217,960		0.50		$108,980	$ 2.17	0.359
2	1,585,620		1,290,000		295,620		0.50		147,810	2.95	0.308
3	1,791,750		1,405,000		386,750		0.50		193,375	3.86	0.090
4	2,024,667		1,530,500		421,167		0.50		210,583	4.21	0.211
5	2,287,888		1,677,000		610,888		0.50		305,444	6.10	0.224
6	2,585,305		1,837,500		747,805		0.50		373,902	7.47	(0.212)
7	2,921,391		2,332,750		588,641		0.50		294,320	5.88	0.209
8	3,275,298		2,563,750		711,548		0.50		355,774	7.11	0.194
9	3,730,326		2,854,250		849,076		0.50		424,538	8.49	0.240
10	4,215,285		3,161,750		1,053,535		0.50		526,767	10.53	
											0.18, or 18% Approx. average rate of growth in EPS

* Earnings before taxes.
† Earnings after taxes.

The diversification gap. All the information which we have processed thus far has revealed that Jones' operations will provide a rate of growth in earnings per share of approximately 18 percent. As soon as you arrived at the earnings-per-share figure, and especially the growth rate, you put down your pencil and looked point-blank at me and stated, "We're not going to make it, even with Allied." You were visibly shocked. I said, "What are you talking about?" You then called my attention to the firm's cost of equity capital.

As a part of our analysis in Chapter 13, it was determined that the rate of growth in EPS was a function of the productivity of retained earnings. It was demonstrated there that Jones' earnings were growing at a compound annual rate of 26 to 27 percent. In short, investors were willing to assign a higher value or price to our shares in part because of the firm's potential rate of growth in earnings.

Our analysis of market potentials has revealed to us that we will, in all likelihood, be unable to meet investors' anticipation with respect to increases in earnings per share (26 to 27 percent), even with the unlikely assumption that Allied's sales remain firm. The consequences

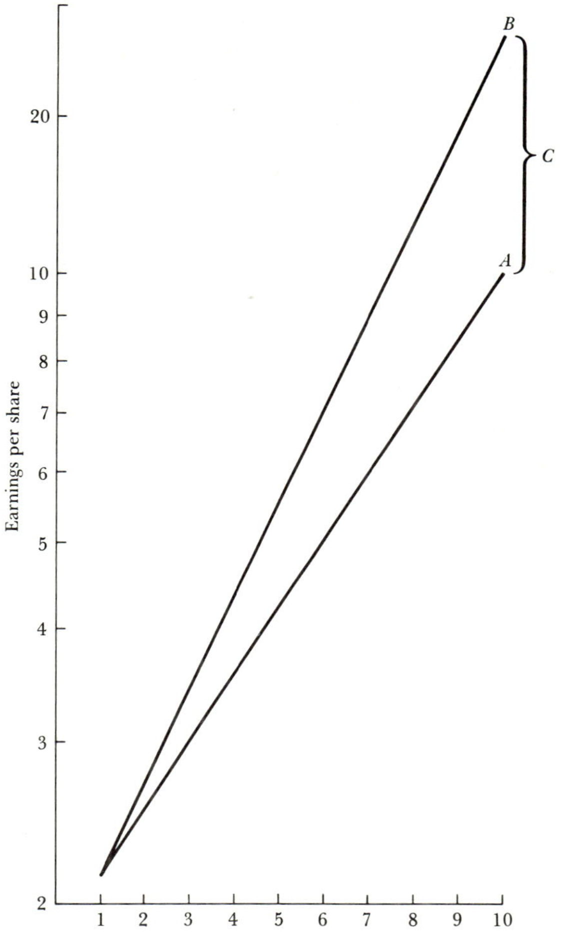

Figure 14-2

of this failure would, of course, be reflected in declining stock prices. Graphically, this dilemma would look something like Figure 14-2.

Line *A* on the graph above shows our projected rate of growth in earnings per share. Line *B* depicts that rate of growth in Jones' earnings per share which investors assume will be realized. The bracket labeled *C* can be designated as the gap which exists between probable corporate performance and investor anticipations. The implication of our analyses should now be clear. Jones' present industry and product line do not offer those growth opportunities which are consistent with the expectations of the investment community. No wonder you felt a shock wave. You had just assumed that growth would continue. The marketing report was worth every cent you paid for it. Success builds the ego, which in turn leads to complacency.

As the financial manager of Jones, Inc., it has been and will be your task to resolve this discrepancy in such a manner that Jones' stock values will not suffer a significant decline.

INTERNAL DIVERSIFICATION

After attending to routine business for several days, you had developed several alternatives (as usual). It was obvious to you that the Jones firm could simply reorient the thrust of its capital budgeting efforts in order to purchase the assets required to enter new and more profitable product lines. Another alternative would be to merge with or acquire an existing firm. This has been discussed at executive committee meetings. In fact, at an executive meeting, when the general subject of mergers and acquisitions was discussed, one member of the committee inquired why the Jones Electronic Corporation would even think about merging with, or acquiring, another business. In fact, he stated, "Why don't we grow our own?" You answered that, generally, it seemed to you, moving into a new endeavor could be accomplished considerably more cheaply and less painfully by an acquisition than by starting from scratch. Jones would be able to avoid the problems of market acceptance, of overcoming known and unknown hazards, and of obtaining acceptable profit levels without the initial periods of losses that a new enterprise could expect to encounter.

In addition, you pointed out that while the Jones organization may have developed a successful management team in the electronics business, this same team may or may not function as well in an entirely different endeavor. Secretly you were wondering how much of the Jones' success was the result of the president's ability to produce a stable, superior product; and perhaps, luck had a little to do with it, that is, being in the right place at the right time (for example, the ADCO acquisition). But luck is usually 90 percent preparation, so let's share the success with President Jones.

DIVERSIFICATION THROUGH MERGERS AND ACQUISITION

Consider the question "is the Jones organization interested in industrial capitalism or financial capitalism?", or, in other words, "is Jones interested in growth via increased sales and lower costs, or are you about to embark upon a course of action in which growth is the result of steps taken to secure financial control over other firms?" Your primary interest would be to maintain a continuous growth in earnings per share. That's not really an answer—but you are interested in both increased efficiency and growth by financial means.

There can be a great deal of difference in the management responsibility or degree of control exercised by the acquiring corporation. As an example, the Jones group could get extensively involved in the management of subsidiaries; or it could limit its supervision to the financial functions of budgeting and monitoring of performance. The acquired division or subsidiaries, in the latter case, would be relatively free to make operating decisions within the broad framework set down by the "home office."

As discussed in an earlier chapter, the goal and objective of professional management and, indeed, the responsibility of professional management is at least to maintain the firm's relative position in the industry or industries within which the firm operates and, in a broader measure, in the economy as a whole. The general public, and thus the financial community, judges management's performance, rightly or wrongly, by the losses or profits expressed as earnings or deficits per share. Acquisitions and mergers can significantly contribute to earnings per share. It is within this frame of reference that the term "financial capitalism" takes on meaning.

If you intend to embark on a course of financial rather than operating acquisitions, you should examine, define, and understand the significance of the several options open to the "merger engineer." You've got some work to do.

TYPES OF MERGERS

Your research has indicated that there are several kinds of mergers. You know that the term *vertical* merger describes a situation whereby a business organization acquires a customer or a supplier. As an example, a steel fabricator might acquire its supplier of raw material or a customer. This type of merger is *vertical* in the sense that the fabricator is reaching down to its source of supply or up to its customers. You also know that a *horizontal* merger takes place when a business entity acquires its competitor. Thus, the steel fabricator could acquire or merge with other steel fabricators.

A *conglomerate* merger can best be described as neither of the above! This definition is not very meaningful except to imply that there are all shades and fashions of conglomerate mergers. A pure conglomerate merger would be illustrated if the steel fabricator were to acquire or merge with a radio or television station. In essence, the pure conglomerate merger takes the form of a combination of totally unrelated business entities. However, what is related or unrelated can be, and is, a matter of judgment, and this fact leads to various opinions and shades of opinions. This latter factor would be totally immaterial if it were not for the governmental regulatory agencies' interest in the prevention of monopoly and the preservation of a competitive economic environment. Therefore, as we shall see, the interpretation of what is or is not a related field is not only fuzzy but also significant.

Clearly, not all mergers and acquisitions are illegal, per se. You know that it will be very important, however, that you consult your attorney when a merger or acquisition is contemplated. This is especially good advice since Jones Electronic is already engaged in an oligopolistic industry with few competitors. Therefore, it might be well for you to do a bit more research on the legal and antitrust aspect of the subject.

You will learn very quickly that statutes and words that would appear to be quite explicit and succinct take on meanings and connotations that are quite different from the original prose. You will likewise learn that the law is what the judges say it is! As judges are called upon to rule and write opinions that interpret the law, the law can be construed narrowly or broadly. Further, judges may, and do, differ among themselves, even in the Supreme Court of the United States, as to what is the law of the land. You will discover that the political and economic philosophy of the political party in office will influence the regulation and enforcement of given statutes. As you well know, from time to time a national election can abruptly change this political and economic philosophy.

Significance of Antitrust Laws

It might serve a useful purpose at this time to indicate some high spots in the development of the antitrust law as it applies to mergers and acquisitions. As you begin your research, you will become involved with the Sherman Antitrust Act of 1890. Section I of this law, in essence, makes it unlawful "to engage in agreements, combinations, and conspiracies in restraint of trade." Section 2 of the act, in essence, makes "any attempt to monopolize any part of interstate or foreign trade unlawful." Therefore, what is meant by "restraint of trade" or "monopolize" can be very significant indeed.

As an example, the Supreme Court of the United States in 1895 held that it was not unlawful for the American Sugar Refining Company to increase their control of the sugar refining business from 65 to 98 percent by a series of horizontal mergers. The rationale for the court decision was simply that the American Sugar mergers involved production and manufacturing rather than commerce. Following this decision, many important and significant mergers took place in the production sector of the economy until by 1903, 26 corporations controlled 80 percent or more of the production in their respective fields. One might ask, are production and manufacturing not commerce? These decisions, obviously, interpreted the word "commerce" quite narrowly. They said it was not.

Various attempts were made by the government to close this "loophole" in the Sherman Act. In 1911 the Supreme Court held that agreements, combinations, and conspiracies were illegal only if they were "unreasonable."[1] What does the word "unreasonable" mean?

In 1920 the Supreme Court held that mere size or unexerted economic strength did not evidence unreasonableness, per se.[2] In 1914 Congress passed the Clayton Act, which defined several practices, including mergers, to be unlawful "where the effect would be to *lessen competition or tend to create a monopoly.*" This act was narrowly interpreted by the courts so as not to apply to the *purchase* of the assets of another company; rather, it was limited to those mergers created by the acquisition of the *capital stock* of another corporation. In addition, no attempt was made to enforce the law against horizontal mergers because it was believed that the Clayton Act applied only to vertical mergers. You can imagine what happened between 1925 and 1930! There were many, many horizontal mergers.

In 1950 Section 7 of the Clayton Act was amended by enactment of the Celler-Kefauver Act to include the acquisition or purchase of assets, per se. The amendment applied to *"all mergers and acquisitions* which had the effect of *substantially 'lessening competition or tending to create a monopoly.'"* This new statute was vigorously applied, and over 800 mergers were attacked by the government from 1950 through 1960. Businessmen and corporate officers reacted by turning away from large horizontal mergers toward the conglomerate type of merger.

While, as indicated earlier, a precise definition of a conglomerate appears to be impossible, it might be helpful to say that a conglomerate is a firm that operates in a few, several, or many different economic areas that may or may not be directly related. With respect to the law and this type of business organization (conglomerate), a Congressional Committee report expressed the intention of the new Section 7 of the Cellers Act, in essence, as follows: "[Any combination that tends to] . . . increase . . . the relative size of the enterprise, making the acquisition to such a point that its advantage over its competitors threatens to be decisive . . . [is illegal]."[3] What do these words mean? Well, they have been the subject of litigation ever since. The point is, again, that the law is what the judges say the law is as litigation comes before the court. The court may at times appear to be slow and overcautious. At other times, they may appear to act or react with too much speed. However, sooner or later, legal history shows, the courts do reflect the social, political, and economic philosophy and the social mores of the majority of the electorate, at least of those who vote! Therefore, you must consult your attorney and he will give you

[1] *Standard Oil Co. v. United States*, 221 U.S. 1 (1911).
[2] *United States v. United States Steel Corp.*, 251 U.S. 417 (1920).
[3] *H. R. Rep.* 1191, at p. 8.

his opinion as to how the court will react to a given set of facts, and that is the very best he can do. It is all that you can expect.

If you feel a bit uneasy about all this—you should! There are some broad guidelines that you can follow. The term "broad" is used because the language is broad and the interpretation varies. However, as indicated earlier, Congressional Committee reports indicate that the legislation was directed at those mergers and acquisitions which tend to:

1. *Eliminate potential competition,* which means that even though one firm may not now be competing with another firm, if the acquired firm has the potential to do so, any merger between the two has been considered illegal as a restraint of competitive forces on the market.
2. *Create the opportunity for reciprocal dealing,* which means that if one firm produces a product another firm needs, and the second firm produces a product that the first firm needs, clearly the two firms could be expected to deal with each other—especially since, in essence, they are now one company. The combination would thus eliminate competition—rightly or wrongly. The combination could equally be expected to reduce the number of independent firms conducting research and developing competitive new ideas.
3. *Create oligopolistic conditions and eliminate competitive zeal for fear of retaliation.* It might be useful to examine several examples.

In *United States v. El Paso Natural Gas Co.*[1] the Supreme Court held that it would be a violation of antitrust laws for El Paso to acquire Pacific Northwest. Pacific Northwest operated in a contiguous market selling natural gas. The basis for the decision was the elimination of a potential competitor. (The case could also have been decided on the basis that the acquisition would have been a significant horizontal merger.) Another example involving a potential competitor was the *Federal Trade Commission v. Proctor & Gamble Co.*[2] Proctor & Gamble, the largest seller of household cleaning products, acquired Clorox, which had about 50 percent of the household bleach market. The court held the merger to be illegal because Proctor, with its tremendous marketing strength, was a most likely entrant into the household bleach field. A merger between the two firms would lessen potential competition.

The difficulty in defining terms or phases such as "tending to lessen competitive forces" is clearly illustrated by a court decision to issue a preliminary injunction involving *Allis-Chalmers Manufacturing Co. v. White Consolidated Industries.*[3] The basis for the preliminary injunction

[1] 376 U.S. 651 (1964).
[2] 386 U.S. 568 (1967).
[3] 414 f(2nd) 506 (3rd Clr 1960).

was the fact that after the merger, Blaw-Knox, a White subsidiary, would be the only firm in the industry that would be capable of designing, producing, and installing a complete rolling mill. It was argued that this capability would be injurious to competitors.

It is clear that the Federal government and the courts have taken a dim view with respect to the concentration of economic power. In fact, as we have seen, businesses related only by *common distribution methods* (Clorox), and those combinations which would eliminate *potential* competitors, have been challenged. Other things being equal, there would be little point in Jones buying an antitrust lawsuit at this point, when other opportunities may be available.

But why should Jones Electronics get involved in a merger or an acquisition?

1. *Increased leverage.* The ability and willingness to attract debt is seriously lacking in many companies. We have examined the advantage of a reasonable amount of leverage earlier. In short, if you could borrow money at $7\frac{1}{2}$ percent or so, and in turn earn 15 percent, you would do so as long as prudence and the market would permit. Many firms have an innate fear of debt financing.
2. *Lower cost of debt capital.* In all probability a larger company would have more sources of funds and probably at more reasonable rates. However, each case must be examined individually.
3. *More efficient capital rationing.* A larger firm, again, should have more investment opportunities and a better-trained capital budgeting staff. Further, the larger firm could probably cross industry lines more readily than smaller firms.
4. *Better allocation of human resources.* Human resources can be allocated perhaps more efficiently as opportunities for advancement become more numerous. This factor is significant as top managerial talent is being developed.
5. *Better use of Jones' staff facilities.* Better and more efficient use of national advertising, research and development departments, computer operations, and financial management services, among others.
6. *More, and more efficient, accountability.* Divisional managers and cost center management may be more responsive to firm policy with respect to cost and operating controls. Divisional managers are not accountable to distant stockholders, but they are directly responsible to headquarters!

On the other hand mere size does not guarantee any of the above. However, the opportunity for all the above could well exist.

Finally, you would expect a definitely larger increase in earnings per share than would be available without the merger. There would be little point in buying a reduction in earnings per share on a long-term basis.

THE MERGER CANDIDATE

The natural question would be, What should you be looking for in terms of a candidate for merger or a new acquisition?

1. *Unused tax shield.* We have already seen in the previous chapter that a loss carry-forward can provide the funds to cover a significant part of the purchase prices, provided, of course, that the new venture can be turned around—earn a profit.
2. *Incompetent management.* Likewise, the ADCO acquisition illustrated how incompetent management, and perhaps stockholder dissatisfaction, could contribute to a take-over possibility.
3. *Closely held corporations.* Closely held corporations could be susceptible to a take-over because of the lack of a widespread public market for the stock and possible estate-tax problems.
4. *Excess liquidity.* It is sometimes possible to finance a take-over with the acquired firm's own cash or borrowing power.
5. *Unproductive plow-back by the acquired corporation.* The acquired corporation could possibly have exhausted its investment opportunities for their cash-flow plow-back within its present corporate structure. Therefore, more productive investment and, therefore, higher earnings per share would be available to the present stockholder of the merger candidate if he becomes part owner of another corporation. This situation may or may not imply inept financial management by the present corporate officials.
6. *Implications of accelerated depreciation methods.* As you have seen, accelerated depreciation methods can generate cash flows that can be manipulated via the mechanics of the merger while book profits can be quite modest. A significant factor causing the low book earnings could be the accelerated depreciation expense. You know it, I know it, but others may not know it!

MECHANICS OF MERGERS AND ACQUISITIONS

Our next consideration would involve the implications of the mechanics of the merger and/or acquisition. The *buyer* or acquiring corporation should be interested in several factors:

1. The basis for the future depreciation of the acquired assets
2. The measurement of gain should the assets be sold or transferred to another by subsequent sale

The seller or acquired corporation should likewise be interested in the manner in which the transaction is effected. This will involve the following:

1. Whether or not any gain is subject to taxation.
2. Whether or not any loss can be apportioned to the stockholders as individuals.
3. If the transaction does result in a gain to the acquired corporation, the question is whether the gain is taxed at ordinary income tax rates, or whether the transaction will be treated as a capital gain with the more favorable rates. (See Chapter 2.)

As far as depreciation and the buyer are concerned, it is obvious that the higher the depreciation base, the larger the tax deductions and the larger the cash flow the corporation can expect over the years. (See Chapter 7.) The net effect of depreciation on earnings per share can likewise be calculated by using the material covered earlier in the depreciation chapter. The measurement of the gain for the present buyer upon a subsequent sale will, to a significant extent, be determined by the depreciation base and the method of depreciation employed after the acquisition. However, consider carefully the following:

Depreciation Recapture

Sections 1245 and 1250 of the Internal Revenue Code require that when certain property is sold at a gain, some of the depreciation expense that had previously been charged off to expense—thereby lowering taxable income for the previous period—may be regarded as ordinary income and taxed accordingly at the time of the sale.

Section 1245 relates to personal and other property, but explicitly exempts depreciable real estate. As an example, assume the following:

Cost of asset	\$100
Accumulated depreciation	50
Adjusted basis or book value	\$ 50

If the asset is sold for \$75, it is obvious that the asset is worth \$75, not the \$50 calculated. Any asset is worth the amount a willing buyer will pay a willing seller. Depreciation rates for prior periods were too high by \$25. Therefore, the \$25 is taxed at ordinary income rates at the time of the sale. This is termed depreciation recapture.

1. If the asset sold for \$50, there is no gain, no depreciation recapture.
2. If the asset sold for \$90, the asset that originally cost \$100 has,

for practical purposes, depreciated $10 while $50 in depreciation has been charged in prior periods. Therefore, $40 would be treated as ordinary income.

3. If the asset sold for $120, there is $50 depreciation recaptured and $20 taxed as a capital gain. (In fact, the asset had not depreciated. The depreciation taken in prior years would be now taxed as ordinary income—depreciation recapture—plus $20 taxed as a capital gain.)

Section 1250 deals with depreciable real estate. The key date to remember is December 31, 1969. After this date, depreciation recapture on depreciable real estate is treated in much the same manner as Section 1245 property. Prior to that time, depreciation recapture did not apply to depreciable real estate.

Tax Consequences

Corporate acquisitions are broadly classified as (1) tax-free reorganizations or (2) taxable transactions. (Again, we have no intention of exhausting this subject, but it will no doubt be helpful if you understand the basic elements of the tax consequences so that you can recognize a problem when you see one.)

Tax-free Reorganizations

Briefly, *for tax purposes,* there are three types of tax-free mergers, categorized as follows: *A* mergers, *B* mergers, and *C* mergers.

The *A* merger is termed a statutory merger. This type of merger involves the combination of two or more firms, with one of the former independent firms retaining its identity as the continuing entity. The shareholders of the acquired corporation (seller) must have a continuing interest in the acquiring corporation's (buyer's) voting capital stock, at least equal in value to a major part of the shareholders' interest in the corporation that is being acquired. Should a shareholder of the corporation being acquired sell his stock upon receipt from the buyer, this stock will not be counted in determining whether or not the old shareholders have received the value required above. Thus, the actions of one shareholder, if he holds a substantial interest, could possibly cause the acquisition to be disqualified as an *A*-type merger. We will return to the significance of this possibility later.

A *B* merger takes place when one firm acquires at least 80 percent of the capital stock of another firm in return for the stock of the buyer. Both firms retain their separate legal identities. This type of merger creates a parent-subsidiary relationship.

A *C* merger takes place when one firm acquires all, or substantially all, of the *assets* of a second firm in return for the voting stock of the buyer. The selling firm may or may not remain as a corporate shell without assets.

Taxable transaction. It can be noted that in a type *A* merger *property* can be transferred as part of, or all of, the consideration for the acquisition of the seller's assets. Not so with *B* or *C* reorganizations (for all practical purposes). Therefore, a *B* or *C* reorganization can be made a taxable transaction merely by including some property in the total consideration. Your question, immediately, was, "Why should anyone want a taxable transaction when it could be free?" Now, you are back to depreciation and subsequent sale considerations.

To understand the significance of the last sentence, you must understand the significance and implications of a merger carried out as a "taxable transaction."

The tax consequences of a "taxable transaction" include the following:

1. No gain is recognized by the selling corporation, provided the seller sells stock to the buyer to give him the required interest in *B* mergers (80 percent) *or* if the selling corporation continues to exist but is completely liquidated within one year, at which time the individual stockholders will be taxed on any gain.
2. If the merger is a taxable transaction, the buyer can set up the assets on its books for depreciation and resale purposes at a value equal to the *total purchase price,* provided the assets are transferred forthwith at the time of the merger, or if the selling corporation continues pursuant to a plan of liquidation adopted within two years of the acquisition.
3. Shareholders of the seller in a tax-free reorganization are taxed on the gain, if any, in a tax-free reorganization in the year in which they sell the stock, or upon liquidation of the selling corporation.
4. The implications of installment sales were thoroughly covered in Chapter 13, and you may review these provisions there.

Now, is it clear to you why the buyer could be interested in a taxable transaction, and the seller might prefer a tax-free reorganization? If not, you have been reading instead of studying. Go back and try it again!

Do you understand how the tax consequences to the seller's shareholders can be changed if a substantial shareholder decides to sell the stock of the buyer he has received in the transaction? If not, you have been reading, not studying. Go back!

Significance of the Accounting Method

In general, a merger or acquisition can be treated for accounting purposes as (1) a purchase or (2) a pooling of interest. There is quite a difference between the two.

Purchase accounting. The transaction is recorded on the books of the buyer as a purchase of the net assets of the seller. The liabilities of the seller may likewise be assumed. So much of the purchase price as is reasonable is assigned to each asset purchased, and the amount assigned to each asset becomes its depreciation base, if applicable, for the buyer. As an example, assume Company A acquired the assets of Company B. Company B had depreciated the assets down to a book value of $1,000. Company A paid $5,000 to B for the assets. Assume further that the reasonable, fair market value of the assets was $3,000. The excess paid by A to B, or $2,000, would be recorded as goodwill. If A were able to purchase the assets for $500 (book value $1,000), the assets could be recorded on A's books at the $1,000 value and an entry would be made on A's books to explain the difference between the $1,000 value and the $500 paid as negative goodwill, or excess equity over cost of asset purchased. The transaction probably sounds innocent enough. However, in case of goodwill's being recorded, one of three things must happen:

1. Goodwill, in some circumstances, can remain as an asset on the books of A indefinitely. On most occasions, federal regulatory bodies will not allow this to happen.
2. Goodwill is written off over a short, or longer, period of time.
3. Goodwill is written off at one time against A's retained earnings at the time of purchase.

The significance of goodwill is simply that if the account is written off periodically, earnings per share are reduced in an amount equal to the write-down. The financial manager interested in earnings per share would not welcome this action. The amortization of goodwill is not a deductible expense for tax purposes. This makes goodwill doubly painful. On the other hand, in the relatively rare instance where negative goodwill is involved, since the assets were recorded at a valuation higher than the purchase price, the negative goodwill is amortized periodically over the life of the asset. Earnings per share would thus be increased by the periodic amortization. In the hypothetical case cited above, if the life of the asset were five years and $500 was the negative goodwill, $100 would be added to income after taxes annually for five years. Thus for the five-year period earnings per share would be increased.

A second factor is involved, depreciation of the assets purchased. With the same five-year period, an assigned valuation of $3,000, and no salvage value, income would be reduced $600 per year for the five-year period. Earnings per share would likewise be lowered. The tax consequences would be beneficial, but the financial manager interested in earnings per share may not prefer this treatment. On the other hand, the investment of the excess depreciation plus the tax savings might well cause the earnings per share to equal or exceed their pre-write-off levels. (See Chapter 7. Research into this area indicates that this later observation is seldom discussed in the financial literature. In our view, it can be significant.)

One other consideration should be mentioned. If shares of A's stock are given in exchange for the assets of B, the fair market value of the stock transferred is the price paid by A for B's assets. Otherwise the results of a purchase for cash or shares are identical with the above analysis.

Pooling accounting. In general—and we leave the details for the accountant—the pooling transaction involves:

1. The transfer of voting stock of the buyer in return for the assets of the seller
2. Retention of the interest of the former owners of the selling corporation in the combined entity
3. An intent by the sellers to retain the shares of the buyer (the new stockholder can dispose of 25 percent of the buyer's stock in the year following the sale, an additional 25 percent the second year, and the balance at any time thereafter)
4. A continuation of the seller's management in the combined enterprises
5. The retention by the buyer of the business of the seller for a reasonable period of time

If these qualifications are met, the transaction may qualify as a "pooling of interest" for accounting purposes.

The significance of this treatment is threefold:

1. The seller's assets and liabilities are transferred and combined or pooled with the buyer's assets at whatever value the assets are carried on the books of the seller. No adjustments are made.
2. The pooling takes effect retroactively. Thus it is possible to reflect income for the entire current year of merger even though the merger did not take effect until December 31, that is, the last day of the year.

3. No goodwill can be involved because the assets and liabilities are just combined without regard to the considerations paid. (The accountant must make several adjusting entries, but in essence this is the result.)

Your imagination and/or logic can readily see the possible impact the pooling option gives to earnings per share. These include the fact that the amortization of goodwill is no problem—there isn't any; depreciation expense may be lower, resulting in higher reported income in the future.

THE TOOLS OF ACQUISITIONS AND MERGERS

As you have seen, earnings per share can be affected by the choice of the accounting method to be employed in a campaign of acquisition activity. In like manner, resultant earnings per share for the acquiring corporation can be affected or managed on the basis of the securities issued by the acquiring corporation. You indicated that you realized that earnings per share could be manipulated within the acquisition framework; however, you wanted to be a little more specific.

FORMS OF PAYMENT AND RESULTANT EPS

Let us demonstrate the effect on resultant earnings per share of three different forms of payment which could be employed by the acquiring firm. In the following simulated financial take-over, we can utilize common stock, cash, or convertible debentures as a form of payment.[1] The corporation which is diversifying via an acquisition will be designated as Firm A, while the potential target corporation will be called Firm B. The financial information listed below for Firms A and B will be used in each of the three situations to follow:

Firm A

After-tax profits for 1965	= $4,000,000
Common stock outstanding	= 4,000,000 shares
EPS	= $1
Multiple	= 15
Market price of common	= $15
Cash dividend per share	= $0.30
Debentures outstanding	= 0
Preferred stock outstanding	= 0
Expected after-tax profits for 1966	= $4,000,000

[1] Henry B. Reiling, EPS Growth from Financial Packaging; Conglomerate Mergers and Acquisitions: Opinion and Analyses. 44 *St. John's L. Rev.*, special ed., 1970.

Firm B

After-tax profits for 1965	= \$1,000,000
Common stock outstanding	= 1,000,000
EPS	= \$1
Multiple	= 15
Market price of common	= \$15
Cash dividend per share	= \$0.30
Debentures outstanding	= 0
Preferred stock outstanding	= 0
Expected after-tax profits for 1966	= \$1,000,000

Acquisition by Common Stock

If Corporation B's shareholders were to accept an exchange of common stock on the basis of either earnings per share or market value, Firm A would acquire Firm B by issuing an additional 1 million shares of A's common to the holders of B's common. The resultant EPS for A's consolidated earnings in 1966 would be neutral, given the fact that the acquisitions were accounted for as a pooling of interest. In short, then, after-tax profits would have increased 25 percent, but outstanding shares would have also increased by this amount.

On the surface, it would appear that A's diversification had been without any real value to the original owners. Such may indeed be the case. On the other hand, it is quite possible that the combined firms would now be more attractive to investors on the grounds that the combination has resulted in the addition of some significant organizational, financial, or operational strengths. If this were true, we could envision the possibility of the market's ascribing some higher multiple to the shares of the combined firms. In such a situation, stock prices may well increase in response to what appears to be a financially neutral acquisition.

In the situation where initial earnings multiples differed, the combination could also result in an increased value for the combined earnings of the two firms. For example, if A's multiple had been 30 times and the exchange of shares had been made on the basis of market prices, the final value of total shares could be computed as follows:

	Market Price	Terms of Exchange	No. of shares of A issued
A	\$30	Two shares of B for one share of A	500,000
B	\$15		

Combined Earnings	Resultant EPS	Market Price for Resultant Shares
\$5,000,000	$\frac{\$5,000,000}{4,500,000} = \$1.11$	\$31.11

The increase in the market value of the resultant shares is a direct consequence of the fact that the two firms possessed very different initial price-earnings ratios or multiples. In fact, during the 1960s, much of the increase in value of the shares of conglomerates had this very source.

Acquisition by Cash

In comparing the effects of an acquisition by the use of common stock with the use of cash, let us recall that, barring the introduction of exogenous factors, our initial illustration involving common stock was financially neutral. Had Firm A used cash to purchase B, a beneficial effect on earnings could easily be envisioned. Firm A would simply purchase all outstanding shares of Firm B at a price of $15 million. Those shares would then be retired, and Firm A's earnings would be the combined earnings of the two firms. Outstanding shares, however, would remain at the original 4 million. Resultant EPS would then be $1.25. Again, the market value of Firm A's shares could be expected to reflect the earnings increase. You can now see that, while the share-for-share exchange of common stock which we discussed initially was a "value neutral" acquisition, the exchange for cash is a "value positive" transaction.

Acquisition by Convertible Debentures

Acquisitions utilizing convertible debentures or other similar instruments were extremely popular during the decade of the 1960s. These financial instruments were used and misused so extensively by growth-oriented firms that the American Institute of Certified Public Accountants, in a series of opinions, has restructured the manner in which earnings-per-share figures may be computed when convertible securities are issued as a form of payment.[1]

Prior to 1967, earnings-per-share calculations ignored the potential for dilution which exists inherently when convertible securities are outstanding in a firm's capital structure. Consequently, if Firm A had acquired Firm B and issued convertible debentures rather than common stock, the net effect on the resultant EPS would be approximately the same as if a purchase for cash had been effected.

1966 Earnings = $5,000,000 (after tax + interest costs)

Shares outstanding = 4,000,000

Approximate EPS = $1.25

[1] Accounting Principles Board No. 49; Accounting Principles Board No. 15; Accounting Principles Board No. 9.

However, you will note that no provision for the potential increase in the number of shares which would be outstanding upon conversion of the debentures has been made. If such potential dilution is ignored by the market, we could anticipate a substantial increase in the price of Firm A's shares. For example, if A's existing multiple of 15 were fully applied to the increment earnings of 25 cents, the price of A's shares could increase from $15 to $18.75.

In order to better inform investors and to foster increased disclosure within the financial statements, the Accounting Principles Board formulated "Opinion No. 9." The gist of this opinion was to require a computation of earnings per share to give effect to the dilution effect of all shares which would be outstanding if those securities which derived a large part of their value from their convertibility features were in fact converted into common shares. In this context, the earnings per share which Firm A would report could well be $1 rather than the $1.25 reported previously.

In response to some problems of implementation with respect to computing which convertible securities were in fact common stock equivalents, the Accounting Principles Board issued "Opinion No. 15." The effect of this opinion was twofold:

1. It determined the following standard test for investment value and common stock equivalency. If a convertible security has a cash yield which is less than 66⅔ percent of the current bank prime rate of interest at the time of issuance, it will be considered a common stock equivalent for purposes of computing EPS.

   On this basis, then, if Firm A had issued a convertible debenture (to Firm B), and its interest rate was less than 66⅔ percent of the current prime bank rate, this convertible debenture would have been a common stock equivalent. The effect of this determination would be to force the inclusion of those shares into which the debenture could be converted into the calculation of EPS for the combined company.
2. In addition to the above, Opinion No. 15 also prescribed that the common stock equivalency of a convertible security would be determined only once during its life, and this determination would be made at the time of issuance. This one-time-only rule would prevent undue fluctuations in the denominator of the EPS ratio from year to year.

The effect of this most recent opinion on our hypothetical firms is not easily determined from the available facts. At worst, however, resultant EPS could be $1, or at best $1.25, depending on the actual terms of the conversion and the relationship between the interest rate of the debentures and the current bank prime lending rate.

As we now approach our own merger and acquisition activities, we are conscious of the facts that:

1. EPS figures which result from merger and acquisition are in part determined by the method of accounting which the firm employs, that is, purchase method versus pooling method.
2. EPS figures are also in part determined by the form of security and basis of exchange which are employed.

You feel ready to tackle Jones' acquisition activities. You begin with a restatement of the problem. Jones Corporation has in the past maintained a high rate of growth in both sales and earnings. Ultimately, we hope to make a public offering of our shares and benefit from the high price-earnings multiples which the market ascribes to superior growth-oriented equities. However, we have become aware that the maintenance of our past growth record will be impossible if we remain bound to our narrow product base. In addition, we have come to recognize the high level of risk to which we are exposed in any industry which is so highly dependent on the uncertainties of federal budget commitments.

Consequently, we seek to diversify for two purposes:

1. To ensure that our prior growth record can be maintained
2. To become more broadly based by entry into an unrelated industry

THE SEARCH FOR ACQUISITION CANDIDATES

In our search for an acquisition which will meet our needs we have several sources of information which are potentially available. We may learn of the existence of acquisition candidates by means of:

1. Internally generated leads, which result from company-sponsored letters of inquiry; or candidates may be discovered by our own salesmen and field representatives.
2. Externally generated leads, which may result from contacts with business brokers, bankers, attorneys, etc.
3. Information published in the financial press regarding merger situations.

You began your search for acquisition candidates in concert with your banker, who over the years has become familiar with your firm and its development. Several additional confrences were held, and a screening technique was developed. This screening procedure involves several steps.

Step 1. *Investigate the seller's motivation.* Why is the firm available for sale? In almost every case imaginable the seller's motivation will result from the fact that he feels the firm will be less valuable to him in the future. This does not mean that the firm will not be valuable to us. For example, the seller may simply foresee personal estate problems with which his current firm is ill equipped to cope. Thus, the firm is less valuable to him now than it was in the past. In like manner, he may feel that the size of his firm restricts his managerial scope. In the future he would like to become associated with a larger enterprise as the result of an acquisition. In still other instances, publicly owned firms may well desire to be acquired in order to ease their problems of capital acquisition. Regardless of the situation, however, we as potential purchasers must fully understand the seller's motivation. A failure to do so can lead to either our unsuccessful bid or, even more meaningfully, a successful proposal but an unhappy and unprofitable corporate marriage.

Step 2. *Assess the seller's current and potential compatibility with both your current organization and the organization you plan to develop.* If we have embarked on a planned program of acquisition or mergers, we should be fully aware of our needs. In addition, we must be capable of examining the operations, both current and potential, of a merger candidate in order to determine whether or not the firm can contribute significantly to the achievement of our predetermined goals. For example, our own plans may require that we generate certain managerial or marketing strengths in addition to those which we already possess. In this situation a potential acquisition should be screened with these factors in mind in addition to the more normal financial measures which are employed.

Step 3. *Formulate the exact financial package of cash and/or securities which will effect the combination of the firms.* In this regard an attempt must be made to create a financing arrangement which is desirable from the seller's point of view. However, it is more important to finance the acquisition in a manner consistent with the purchaser's limitations since you, the purchaser, ultimately must live with the resultant capitalization.

Step 4. *Make detailed plans to supervise post acquisition operations.* In this way immediate attention will be given to those areas of the combined operation which are considered critical. Responsibility and reporting channels should then be related to each of these critical areas. Finally, standards of measurement should be created and applied in order to determine the success or failure of each post merger activity.

Using this technique, you have been able to screen several firms and are now considering one potential acquisition very carefully.

DESCRIPTION OF KIDCO

From its inception until 1955 KIDCO was known principally for its musical toys. Since that time KIDCO has substantially increased the number and diversity of its toys and other products while emphasizing its market and promotional efforts and developing worldwide manufacturing and distribution facilities. During the past 10 years KIDCO has increased its annual sales from approximately $260,000 to more than $2 million, primarily through the continuous introduction of new products and improvement of established products. Over this period KIDCO has successfully introduced such items as fashion dolls and accessories, talking and walking large dolls, educational and preschool toys, miniature dolls, and cars. KIDCO's toys and other products have varied over the years, and the diversity of its line limits its dependence of any particular toy or other product. KIDCO estimates that during its fiscal year ending January 30, 1974, sales of miniature cars will account for approximately 25 percent of net sales, and no other category of toys will account for more than approximately 12 percent of net sales. This was also true for the 1973 projection.

Most of KIDCO's products are designed by its research and design staff, and many of them include patented or proprietary mechanisms and materials. The toys which it now produces appeal to boys and girls from two years through early teens. The majority of KIDCO's products retail at prices ranging from 75 cents to $15.

KIDCO's marketing organization has been significant in the company's development. This organization is responsible not only for sales but for market research and advertising. Market research is intended to decrease the uncertainty of acceptance of new products and to suggest improvements for products already sold by the firm. Most of KIDCO's product lines receive substantial consumer advertising, including network television advertising to establish brand and trade name identification. KIDCO hopes to create, in addition to its sales force, a field merchandising group which covers retail outlets to assist in the merchandising of KIDCO's products and to provide the firm with information regarding market acceptance of new products.

KIDCO uses contract manufacturers to assemble a significant portion of components and finished toys in the Far East and Mexico for United States and foreign distribution.

Typical of the toy industry, KIDCO's business has been seasonal, with a substantially greater portion of shipments occurring during the last six months of each year. KIDCO has initiated marketing programs intended to encourage its customers to make more purchases during the first half of the year. KIDCO believes that earlier shipments resulting from these programs will enable it to utilize its production facilities more efficiently. KIDCO expects, however, that its business will continue to be largely seasonal.

In recent years KIDCO has extended its business beyond the toy industry to other products used by young people in their leisure time, including playground equipment, pet supplies, cassettes, and magnetic tape. In 1974 the company will begin, through a joint venture, to produce and distribute family motion pictures. To date, each of these activities has contributed less than 10 percent of the net sales of KIDCO.

In addition to this general description of KIDCO's activities, you have been able to complete a thorough analysis of the firm's financial statements. You have also applied the market and earnings model developed earlier for Jones to KIDCO. The results as shown below were very encouraging.

Year	Sales	—	Costs	=	EBT*	—	Tax	=	EAT†	EPS (100,000 Shares)	Growth Rate in EPS
1	$2,000,000		$1,600,000		$ 400,000		$ 200,000		$ 200,000	$ 2.00	0.365
2	2,268,000		1,722,000		546,000		273,000		273,000	2.73	0.322
3	2,532,000		1,810,000		722,000		361,000		361,000	3.61	0.111
4	2,622,000		1,820,000		802,000		401,000		401,000	4.01	0.239
5	3,044,000		2,050,000		994,000		497,000		497,000	4.97	0.270
6	3,472,000		2,210,000		1,262,000		631,000		631,000	6.31	0.181
7	3,790,000		2,300,000		1,490,000		745,000		745,000	7.45	0.301
8	4,463,000		2,525,000		1,938,000		969,000		969,000	9.69	0.220
9	5,238,000		2,874,000		2,364,000		1,182,000		1,182,000	11.82	0.332
10	6,448,000		3,298,000		3,150,000		1,575,000		1,575,000	15.75	

* Earnings before taxes.
† Earnings after taxes.

Several decisions regarding the acquisition of KIDCO remain to be made. The first is the selection of the most favorable accounting treatment for the acquisition. In short, should we use a purchase or a pooling-of-interest technique? The second decision which must be reached is the determination of the form of payment. You are fully aware that each of these decisions will affect the resultant earnings per share of the combined enterprise.

You now bring the balance sheets of the two firms together. Below you can see the firms as single entities.

ACQUISITION OF KIDCO (PURCHASE)

If these two balance sheets were brought together under a purchase method using cash as a medium, the combined firms would appear as shown below.

ACQUISITION OF KIDCO (PURCHASE METHOD)

	Jones	KIDCO	Adjustments		Jones, Inc.
ASSETS					
Cash	$ 100,000	$1,500,000	$9,000,000*	$9,000,000†	$ 1,600,000
Accounts Receivable (Net)	1,345,000	1,025,000			2,370,000
Inventories	50,000	500,000			550,000
Prepaid Expenses	5,000	200,000			205,000
Fixed Assets (Net)	6,500,000	4,775,000			11,275,000
Goodwill			1,000,000†		1,000,000
Total					$17,000,000
LIABILITIES					
Current					
Notes Payable	$ 35,000	$ 600,000	600,000†	4,500,000*	$ 4,535,000
Bonds Payable				4,500,000*	4,500,000
Accounts Payable	65,000	1,000,000	1,000,000†		65,000
Income Taxes Payable	25,000	200,000	200,000†		25,000
Deferred Income Taxes	50,000				50,000
Current Installments of Long-term Debt		400,000	400,000†		
Accrued Expenses		200,000	200,000†		
Long-term Debt		500,000	500,000†		
EQUITY					
Common Stock, Jones	$ 200,000				200,000
Common Stock, KIDCO ($1 par)		$ 100,000	100,000†		
Additional Pair-in Capital, KIDCO		4,000,000	4,000,000†		
Retained Earnings, KIDCO		1,000,000	1,000,000†		
Retained Earnings, Jones	7,625,000				7,625,000
Total Claims					$17,000,000

* Jones sells $4.5 million in bonds at par, simultaneously borrowing $4.5 million from the bank.
† Jones pays $9.0 million to acquire the net assets of KIDCO. This cash is first used to pay creditors, the balance going to stockholders.

Jones, Inc.
Consolidated Balance Sheet
of December 31, 1975

Assets		
Cash		$ 100,000
Accounts Receivable	$1,380,000	
Less Allowance for Doubtful Accounts	35,000	
Net Receivables		1,345,000
Inventories		50,000
Prepaid Expenses		5,000
Total Current Assets		$1,500,000
Fixed Assets at Cost	9,500,000	
Less Accumulated Depreciation and Amortization	3,000,000	
Net Fixed Assets		6,500,000
Total Assets		$8,000,000
Liabilities		
Current Liabilities		
Notes Payable	$ 35,000	
Banks	25,000	
Other	10,000	
Total Notes Payable		$ 35,000
Accounts Payable		65,000
Federal Income Taxes		25,000
Total Current Liabilities		125,000
Deferred Federal Income Taxes		
Accelerated Depreciation Deducted for Tax Purposes		50,000
Stockholders Equity		
Common Stock, No Par Value		
Authorized 500,000 Shares Out 70,000		200,000
Retained Earnings		7,625,000
Total Stockholders Equity		7,825,000
Total Claims		8,000,000

KIDCO, INC.
BALANCE SHEET
December 31, 1975

ASSETS

Current Assets		
Cash		$1,500,000
Receivable	$1,050,000	
Less Allowance for Doubtful Accounts	25,000	
Net Receivable		1,025,000
Inventories		500,000
Prepaid Expenses		200,000
Total Current Assets		$3,225,000
Fixed Assets at Cost	$5,500,000	
Less Accumulated Depreciation and Amortization	1,000,000	
Net Fixed Assets		4,500,000
Other Assets		
Net Leasehold Acquisition Cost		275,000
Total Assets		$8,000,000

LIABILITIES

Current Liabilities		
Notes Payable	$ 600,000	
Banks	400,000	
Total Notes Payable		$1,000,000
Current Installments of Long-term Obligations		
Accounts Payable		$1,000,000
Accrued Expenses		200,000
Federal Income Taxes		200,000
Total Current Liabilities		$2,400,000
Long-term Obligations		500,000
Stockholder Equity ($1 par, 100,000 shares)		100,000
Additional Paid-In Capital		4,000,000
Retained Earnings		1,000,000
Total Liabilities and Net Worth		$8,000,000

If our acquisition of KIDCO were handled for cash as shown above, the impact on Jones' earnings over our planning period would be significant. You took this opportunity to prepare the following exhibit for the executive committee.

	Earnings of Jones	Predicted Jones EPS	Earnings of KIDCO	Total* Earnings after Cash Purchase	EPS† after Cash Purchase
1	$108,980	$ 2.17	$ 200,000	$ 308,980	$ 6.17
2	147,810	2.95	273,000	420,810	8.41
3	193,372	3.86	361,000	554,372	11.08
4	210,583	4.21	401,000	611,583	12.23
5	305,444	6.10	497,000	802,444	16.04
6	373,902	7.47	631,000	1,004,902	20.09
7	294,320	5.88	745,000	1,039,320	20.78
8	355,774	7.11	969,000	1,324,774	26.49
9	424,538	8.49	1,182,000	1,606,538	32.13
10	526,767	10.53	1,575,000	2,101,767	42.03

* You have ignored added interest charges and amortization of goodwill for this illustration.
† 50,000 shares.

ACQUISITION OF KIDCO (POOLING)

An alternative approach to the purchase of KIDCO for cash would involve the acquisition of this firm using securities as a form of payment and accounting for the merger by the pooling-of-interests method. You recalled from our earlier discussion that the pooling-of-interest method can be likened to the coming together of two rivers to form a third. The resultant firm is simply the sum of the two components, and no goodwill is created.

If Jones were to acquire KIDCO on the basis of an exchange of two shares of KIDCO for one share of Jones, the resultant firm would have 100,000 shares outstanding. Jones' current EPS is $2.17, while KIDCO's is $2. The exchange of shares on a two-for-one basis appears to be quite generous in Jones' favor. However, you are confident that an exchange on these terms could be negotiated if the terms included employment contracts for KIDCO's current management, who are also its sole shareholders.

If such an exchange were successfully negotiated and the pooling-of-interest method were applied, the Jones acquisition would evolve a financial statement as illustrated below:

ACQUISITION OF KIDCO (POOLING METHOD)

	Jones	KIDCO	Adjustments		Jones, Inc.
ASSETS					
Cash	$ 100,000	$1,500,000			$ 1,600,000
Accounts Receivable	1,345,000	1,025,000			2,370,000
Inventories	50,000	500,000			550,000
Prepaid Expenses	5,000	200,000			205,000
Fixed Assets (Net)	6,500,000	4,775,000			11,275,000
Total	$8,000,000	$8,000,000			$16,000,000
LIABILITIES					
Notes Payable	$ 35,000	$ 600,000			$ 635,000
Bonds Payable					
Accounts Payable	65,000	1,000,000			1,065,000
Income Taxes Payable	25,000	200,000			225,000
Deferred Income Taxes	50,000				50,000
Current Installments of Long-term Debt		400,000			400,000
Accrued Expenses		200,000			200,000
Long-term Debt		500,000			500,000
EQUITY					
Common Stock, Jones	200,000			$4,100,000*	4,300,000
Common Stock, KIDCO ($1 par)		100,000	$ 100,000*		
Additional Paid-in Capital, KIDCO		4,000,000	4,000,000*		
Retained Earnings, Jones	7,625,000			1,000,000†	8,625,000
Retained Earnings, KIDCO		1,000,000	1,000,000†		
Total Claims	$8,000,000	$8,000,000			$16,000,000

* KIDCO's common stock account is debited in the amount of $100,000 and the stock is retired. KIDCO's additional paid-in capital account is also debited with $4 million and closed. The capital stock account of Jones is credited in the amount of $4,100,000 to show the consideration received for the newly issued 50,000 shares of Jones common stock.

† The retained earnings account of KIDCO is debited for $1 million and Jones' retained earnings account is credited with a like amount to reflect the transfer of balances.

The form of payment used in conjunction with the pooling-of-interest accounting method has a real effect on resultant EPS. You will make a point of this result when you give your report to the executive committee.

After some agonizing moments and with a great deal of mixed emotion you recommended to the Jones board of directors that the merger

JONES CORPORATION PROJECTED EPS

Year	Purchase by Cash	% Increase, Purchase by Cash	Purchase by Common Stock	% Increase, Purchase by Common Stock
1	$ 6.17		$ 3.08	
2	8.41	.36304	4.20	.36363
3	11.08	.31747	5.54	.31904
4	12.23	.10379	6.11	.10288
5	16.04	.31152	8.02	.31260
6	20.09	.25249	10.04	.25187
7	20.78	.03434	10.39	.03486
8	26.49	.28873	13.24	.27430
9	32.73	.23556	16.06	.21299
10	42.03	.28414	21.01	.30821
Average rate of growth		.24345		.24226

with KIDCO be consummated. After several weeks of detailed analysis of the information you had presented, the merger was approved. Good luck!!!!

SUMMARY

The complex financial problems which arise in almost every merger cannot be fully discussed in a single chapter, nor even in a single volume devoted solely to corporate mergers and acquisitions. Consequently, the instructional goals of this chapter are severely limited ones. The Jones Corporation has become aware of the potential risks which are inherent in its position as a single-product subcontractor in the aerospace industry. The firm undertakes an independent audit of its market potential, both current and long-term. Utilizing a market back approach, this potential is translated into projections of costs, revenues, and earnings per share over the forecast period.

This study proves to be revealing indeed. The Jones Corporation's potential growth in earnings per share is restricted by the current and future potential of our basic markets. In short, our markets and product mix will no longer support the rate of growth in EPS that has made Jones' stock a high-multiple growth-oriented equity security. The difference between our rate of growth as internally perceived and investor assumptions about our potential rate of growth is critical.

If we are unable to close this gap quickly, the market value of Jones' stock will decline. Since the task of the financial manager is to maximize the value of the firm's equity securities, we begin the task of closing the gap between investors' anticipations and market potential.

Certain problems which are inherent in internal diversification lead us to adopt a course of action involving diversification through the process of mergers or acquisitions.

As we initiate our activities in this area, we become aware of the types of mergers which are possible and the various accounting techniques which are employed. The legal framework within which the financial executive must operate with respect to merger activity must also be considered at the outset since court-enforced divestitures are the expensive and time-consuming results of poorly initiated programs of acquisition.

Once the financial executive has developed his expertise in these areas, the actual process of acquisition may begin. Jones Corporation must be conscious of the impact of any acquisition on current and future EPS. It is this concern which will dictate the terms of purchase and the type of security issued. In addition, we must be especially conscious of the accounting method employed. All these factors influence resultant EPS for the combined firm. The ultimate purchase of KIDCO was negotiated with all the above constraints in mind. The immediate and long-run consequences of the acquisition were compatible with our goal of maximizing the value of Jones' equity securities.

It is important to reemphasize that we have had only a brief and elementary introduction to merger planning. The development of real talent in this area is the result of study and long experience.

QUESTIONS FOR DISCUSSION

1. What are the guidelines for a market research problem for a given firm?
2. What is the significance of each of the above?
3. What is meant by the term "competitive impact factor"?
4. Outline the steps necessary to convert the market research information as illustrated by the text into a probable impact on earnings-per-share?
5. What is the "diversification gap"?
6. What is the significance of this gap?
7. What is internal diversification?
8. What are the hazards of internal diversification?
9. Compare and contrast "financial capitalism and industrial capitalism."
10. What is the goal, objective, and responsibility of professional management?
11. What are the characteristics of the several types of mergers?

12. Trace the development of the antitrust law with respect to mergers and acquisitions.
13. What are the benefits a firm might expect from a merger and/or an acquisition?
14. What possible criteria could be used in the search for a merger candidate?
15. What factors would be of interest to the acquiring corporation with respect to the mechanics of the merger?
16. What factors would be of interest to the seller with respect to the mechanics of the merger?
17. What is the significance of "depreciation recapture"?
18. Compare and contrast a *tax free reorganization* and a *taxable transaction.*
19. What is the broad significance of a purchase versus the pooling of assets?
20. What is the significance of the method of payment to the seller by the buyer of an acquisition?
21. What sources of information concerning possible merger candidates are available?
22. What screening procedure is available?
23. What is the significance of each procedure in question 22 above?

REFERENCES

Alberts, William W., and Joel E. Segall (eds.): "The Corporate Merger," The University of Chicago Press, Chicago, 1966.

Ansoff, H., Igor, and J. Fred Weston: Merger Objectives and Organization Structure, *Quarterly Review of Economics and Business,* vol. II, pp. 49–58, August, 1962.

Barr, Andrew: Accounting Aspects of Business Combinations, *Accounting Review,* vol. XXIV, pp. 175–181, April, 1959.

Bock, Betty: "Mergers and Markets," National Industrial Conference Board, Inc., New York, 1962–1964.

"Business Combinations," Opinion of The Accounting Principles Board, No. 16, American Institute of Certified Public Accountants, New York, 1970.

Butters, J. Keith, John Lintner, and William L. Cary: "Effects of Taxation, Corporate Mergers," Division of Research, Graduate School of Business Administration, Harvard University, Boston, 1951.

Crane, Roger R.: The Place of Scientific Techniques in Mergers and Acquisitions, *Controller,* vol. 29, July, 1961; reprinted in James Van Horne (ed.), "Foundations for Financial Management," pp. 581–592, Richard D. Irwin, Inc., Homewood, Ill., 1966.

Folz, David F., and J. Fred Weston: Looking Ahead in Evaluating Proposed Mergers, *NAA Bulletin,* vol. 43, pp. 17–27, April, 1962.

"Intangible Assets," Opinion of the Accounting Principles Board, No. 17, American Institute of Certified Public Accountants, New York, 1970.

Jaenicke, Henry R.: Management's Choice to Purchase or Pool, *Accounting Review,* vol. XXXVII, pp. 758–765, October, 1962.

Kaplan, A. D. H.: The Current Merger Movement Analyzed, *Harvard Business Review,* vol. XXXIII, pp. 91–98, May-June, 1955.

Kelly, Eamon M.: "The Profitability of Growth through Mergers," The Pennsylvania State University Press, University Park, 1967.

Kinard, Hargett Y.: Financing Mergers and Acquisitions, *Financial Executive,* vol. 31, pp. 13–16, August, 1963.

McCarthy, George D.: Premeditated Merger, *Harvard Business Review,* vol. 39, January-February, 1961; reprinted in James Van Horne (ed.), "Foundations for Financial Management," pp. 565–580, Richard D. Irwin, Inc., Homewood, Ill., 1966.

Mace, Myles L., and George G. Montgomery, Jr.: "Management Problems of Corporate Acquisitions," Division of Research, Graduate School of Business Administration, Harvard University, Boston, 1962.

Michaelson, A. M.: Business Purpose and Tax-free Reorganization, *Yale Law Review,* vol. LXI, pp. 14–44, January, 1952.

Mosich, A. N.: Retroactive Poolings in Corporate Mergers, *Journal of Business,* vol. XLI, no. 3, pp. 352–362, July, 1968.

Mossin, Jan: Merger Agreements, Some Game-Theoretic Considerations, *Journal of Business,* vol. XLI, no. 4, pp. 460–471, October, 1968.

Reilly, Frank K.: What Determines the Ratio of Exchange in Corporate Mergers? *Financial Analysis Journal,* vol. 18, pp. 47–50, November-December, 1962.

Sapienza, S. R.: Pooling Theory and Practice in Business Combinations, *Accounting Review,* April, 1962.

———: Business Combinations—A Case Study, *The Accounting Review,* vol. XXXIX, pp. 91–101, January, 1963.

Silberman, Irwin H.: A Note on Merger Valuation, *Journal of Finance,* vol. XXIII, pp. 528–534, June, 1968.

Smalter, Donald J., and Roderic C. Lancey: P/E Analysis in Acquisition Strategy, *Harvard Business Review,* vol. 44, pp. 85–95, November-December, 1966.

Tincher, William R.: Yardsticks for Evaluating Corporate Acquisitions, *Management Review,* October, 1964, pp. 33–45.

Chapter Fifteen

REORGANIZATION AND BANKRUPTCY

With the merger with KIDCO accomplished, you were perfectly prepared to sit back and concentrate on the general operations and growth of the Jones organization. However, this was not to be. The phone rang and the company attorney requested that you have lunch with him the following day. He needed your advice and/or help in a matter totally unrelated to the Jones organization.

The attorney's client held $4 million subordinated 8 percent debentures, maturity date September 30, 1989. It appeared quite probable that for the third time the debtor would be unable to meet the semiannual interest payments when due. The senior $6\frac{1}{2}$ percent mortgage bondholders had been and are talking about foreclosure. The attorney was concerned about what position his client should take. He was relatively unfamiliar with the practical problems involved but did, of course, understand the legal implications.

During the phone conversation you requested that the attorney secure and bring along with him the latest financial statements of the debtor. Your purpose was to examine the capital structure. You were interested in the type and amount of debt financing the debtor had accumulated and the debt-to-equity ratio of the company.

During lunch the following day, the attorney produced the balance sheet of the debtor.

Southeastern Corporation
Balance Sheet
May 31, 1972
(In Millions)

Current Assets	$ 2.75
Net Property	17.00
Miscellaneous Assets	0.25
Total Assets	$20.00
Accounts Payable	$0.75
Taxes Payable	0.50
Notes Payable, 8%	1.25
Other Current Liabilities	0.50
6½% First Mortgage Bonds, Due 1989	9.00
8% Subordinate Debenture, Due 1989	4.00
Common Stock ($10)	3.00
Paid-in Capital	3.00
Retained Earnings	(2.00)
	$20.00

The profit and loss statement indicated a $685,000 profit *before interest* and *taxes* for the last 12-month period. Interest payable for the same period was as follows:

Notes Payable	1.25	8%	$ 100,000
Mortgage Bonds	9.00	6½%	585,000
Subordinate Debentures	4.00	8%	320,000
			$1,005,000

THE LEGAL RIGHTS OF INTERESTED PARTIES

Clearly, Southeastern is in trouble. Something must be done. At this point, what should or could be done is not so clear because there are several classes of interested parties that have divergent interests. The present stockholders are interested in protecting or salvaging as much of their investment as possible. The creditors want to be paid; and not all the creditors have the same legal rights or the same interest.

1. The 6½ percent mortgage bondholders could simply attempt a foreclosure on the mortgage. In effect, this could ultimately mean a seizure of the company plant. The mortgaged equipment could be

sold, if the foreclosure were successful; and the net proceeds (after the expense of the sale) would be used, first, to pay the accrued interest and principal on the bonds. After the bondholders were paid, any excess would be added to the general assets of the company and would be available to general creditors. The plant is listed at a book value of $17 million. However, what price the plant would bring at a forced sale might be another matter.

2. The 8 percent subordinate debenture holders are not as fortunate. The term "subordinate" means inferior or below. The term "debenture" is almost always used to indicate only a promise to repay without specific collateral or security. This feature involves more risk than secured debt and carries a higher interest rate. Therefore, in effect the subordinate debenture holders stand with the general creditors in the event of a forced sale.
3. The taxes and wages payable would stand with the general creditors in the event of a mortgage foreclosure, but would carry the first priority in the event of a formal bankruptcy.
4. The general unsecured creditors are just that—unsecured.
5. Finally, the preferred stockholders (Southeastern doesn't have any) would receive the par value of their stock, with the common stockholders last in line.

Therefore, if the bondholders' move to foreclose were successful, and if the plant could be sold under the mortgage for $9 million plus the expense of the sale, the bondholders could come out whole. The subordinate debentures and general creditors would then be forced to look to the remaining assets for recovery. In the instant Southeastern case, total remaining assets would be $3 million. However, the "other assets" in the amount of $0.25 million represent primarily prepaid items such as insurance and operating supplies inventory. These items would in fact bring very little as the insurance policies are canceled and the supplies are sold. In reality the subordinate and general creditors could look to an amount slightly in excess of the $2.75 million in current assets to cover unsecured liabilities totaling $7 million dollars. These creditors could at best expect to receive approximately only 39+ percent of the amount due. The investment of the common stockholders would be lost in total. It is therefore quite obvious that the different classes of investors do have different interests.

The luncheon was over, but the discussions would continue the next day. When you arrived, there were three of you there. The attorney had invited the Southeastern financial vice-president to join you. At your first opportunity you ask the vice-president, "Why?" Why the liquidity problem and why so much debt with the fixed interest payments? As for the liquidity matter, the answer was simple. Some $2.25 million in accounts receivable was tied with prime defense contractors that were themselves on the verge of bankruptcy proceedings caused by contract cancellations and cutbacks. Their funds were tied up in unfinished inventory.

THE EFFECT OF HIGH DEBT-TO-EQUITY RATIO

The high debt-to-equity ratio was in hindsight a serious if not fatal error. However, the vice-president indicated that Southeastern's projected internal rate of return was something like 16 percent after taxes. The use of leverage, that is, borrowing money at $6\frac{1}{2}$ percent, or $3\frac{1}{4}$ percent after taxes, at a 50 percent tax bracket and subordinate debenture money at 8 percent, or 4 percent after taxes, would be advantageous if Southeastern could earn 16 percent on these same funds. Debt was attractive also because bondholders, or any type of debt holder, do not participate in the management of the organization. The interest expense is deductible for tax purposes, and as we learned earlier, a "call provision" in the bonds can provide flexibility as events unfold and conditions change.

The Southeastern vice-president stated that he had learned a valuable lesson involving why and when. Why debt should be issued and when debt should be issued can be two entirely different questions. When not to use debt is made perfectly clear by the Southeastern problem. A company cannot afford to use debt when sales and, more specifically, income are not stable and relatively predictable. Clearly, if income is reasonably anticipated to increase, the use of leverage with a fixed interest rate is attractive and useful. Earnings per share will increase by the difference in the interest rate and the rate of earnings provided by the debt funds.

An ancillary question is why anyone should invest in debt securities. Again, Southeastern provides an example of when one should not buy particular debt securities. One normally invests funds to secure an income and/or appreciation in value. Debt securities do not appreciate in value except during periods of deflation when the value of the dollar is increasing. (In a healthy, growing economy this result is unlikely except for short periods of economic adjustment.) Therefore, the attractiveness of debt securities is the fixed steady income. Debt securities may contain a conversion feature that permits the holder, at his option, to convert the debt into capital stock of the issuer. This later provision provides an opportunity to participate in any increase in the issuer's growth.

In Southeastern's case, it is a lack of sufficient earnings to service the debt—pay the interest—that is the root of the problem. There is simply too much debt outstanding. This latter factor really contributed significantly to the liquidity problem. The bankers would not lend additional short-term funds to Southeastern when the debt-to-equity ratio was so high. More specifically, the problem was the earnings-to-fixed-charge ratio. If Southeastern could not pay the interest on the bonds, how could they be expected to pay the interest on the loan, not to mention the principal?

The question then switched to the 8 percent subordinated debt. The vice-president stated that when additional funds were needed, the subordinated debt was issued as a result of a specific provision in the $6\frac{1}{2}$ percent bond issue. These provisions stated that if additional senior debt was to be acquired by Southeastern, the written consent of the trustee under the bond indenture was required. When additional funds were needed, this consent was refused on the basis that additional bonds would impair the security of the first issue. Southeastern, therefore, had to go the subordinated debenture route and was thus forced to pay the higher interest rate. The higher interest rate was attractive to investors at that time, but now the subordination feature is significant. As indicated, the subordinated debt has no claim to any assets until the mortgage bondholders are paid, and then it must assume the same risk as general creditors. (This latter feature is not always so. The subordinated indenture could have been written to provide priority over general creditors. General creditors—accounts payable—would not have been consulted.) The degree of subordination is determined by the terms of the subordinate indenture. As an example, the mortgage terms could have required subordination to the extent of 50 percent of the senior bonds. That is, upon liquidation each senior bondholder would receive 50 percent of the amount due before the subordinated debt would share in the distribution of Southeastern's assets. The subordinated debentures here were 100 percent subordinated.

While some insight has been gained as a result of the discussions with the vice-president of Southeastern, very little has been added toward a solution of the attorney's problem. It still isn't clear what position his client should take with respect to his $4 million in Southeastern's subordinate debt.

As always, there are several alternatives, which can be summarized as follows:

1. Southeastern can request an *extension* of time within which all classes of creditors will demand payment.
2. Creditors can agree to a *composition* whereby all creditors receive a reduced percentage of their claims.
3. The business can be reorganized and a new and different capital structure created.
4. The business can be liquidated either voluntarily or otherwise.

The attorney recognizes that the choice of alternatives does not lie exclusively with the bondholders. Each class of the interested parties has legal rights that are not mutually exclusive. That is, no group—the (1) general creditors, (2) wage earners, (3) governmental bodies to which the taxes are due, (4) secured bondholders, (5) holders of the subordinate debt, and/or (6) stockholders—can take a course of action that will not affect the rights and claims of the other parties. It can reasonably be expected that "for every action there will be a reaction."

The secured bondholders are in a preferred position. However, this position does not mean that the bondholders can dictate a solution to the problem. As indicated, other interested parties have rights. These rights can be protected or enforced. The key to the protection is legal insolvency.

The attorney indicated that in order for a firm to be legally insolvent, one of two conditions must exist:

1. Total liabilities must exceed the fair value of the firm's assets.
2. The firm must be unable to meet its financial obligations as they become due.

A quick glance at Southeastern's current balance sheet indicates that if book values reflect *fair value,* liabilities do not exceed assets. However, the second condition is obviously present. Southeastern is unable to meet its obligations as they become due. The fact that Southeastern is legally insolvent opens up some interesting possibilities, and none of them appear to be good. The most serious possibility is bankruptcy—voluntary or involuntary.

VOLUNTARY BANKRUPTCY

When bankruptcy occurs and is properly adjudicated by the courts, two things may happen: (1) the company may be reorganized or (2) the company may be liquidated. Therefore, if the stockholders and/or management feel that reorganization is in their best interests, vis-à-vis, some of their equity may be saved, Southeastern can file a voluntary petition in bankruptcy. This petition serves to stop all legal proceedings until the entire matter receives court review and adjudication. Bankruptcy may, therefore, be the only course of action available to the equity owners. Thus, any action by the bondholders to foreclose might result in a voluntary petition in bankruptcy being filed by Southeastern. This voluntary petition by Southeastern will hold in abeyance all legal actions and will protect the subordinated debt, general and other creditors, and the stockholders, until the matter is resolved by the courts.

INVOLUNTARY BANKRUPTCY

Should Southeastern fail or not choose to file the bankruptcy petition, general creditors (or any class of creditors for that matter) could file an involuntary bankruptcy petition for court review and adjudication if the following conditions were met:

1. Total debts are $1,000 or more.
2. There were 12 or more creditors (any three of them with valid claims equal to $500 or more can file the involuntary petition).
3. There were less than 12 creditors (any one of them can likewise file if the petitioner's claim is $500 or more).
4. The creditor had committed one or more of the following acts of bankruptcy as set forth by the Federal Bankruptcy Act.

ACTS OF BANKRUPTCY

1. *Concealment or fraudulent conveyance of assets.* Concealment means the hiding of assets with the intent to defraud creditors. A fraudulent conveyance is the transfer of assets to a third party with the intent to defraud.
2. *Preferential transfer.* A preferential transfer is a transfer of assets or a payment to a creditor that would enable the preferred creditor to receive all his claim or a larger percentage of his claim than would be received upon liquidation.
3. *Legal lien.* Should an insolvent debtor permit a creditor to obtain a legal lien on the debtor's assets or fail to discharge or pay the lien within 30 days, he has permitted preferential treatment per se, and other creditors, as recited above, would be entitled to file an involuntary petition in bankruptcy against the debtor.
4. *Assignment.* Should the insolvent debtor assign specific property to a given creditor in full or partial satisfaction of the creditor's claim, he has likewise permitted preferential treatment.
5. *Appointment of a receiver or trustee.* Should the insolvent debtor permit the appointment of a receiver or trustee to operate the business, this likewise is an act of bankruptcy.
6. *The admission of insolvency in writing.* The written admission of insolvency is an act of bankruptcy. An insolvent debtor, therefore, must be very careful about what is put in writing.

It is clear that the act was designed to prevent fraud and to provide protection to all creditors during liquidation. Other provisions provide for an equitable distribution of assets that will recognize the priority of claims among the various classes of claimants. In addition, once discharged by the bankruptcy court proceedings, the insolvent debtor is free to begin anew, if he is able to do so, without the burden of the prior debt.

Therefore, the sole choice of action in Southeastern's case does not lie with the bondholders. Other parties have interests that will be protected by the courts. The next question that presents itself is, What could the various interested parties expect to receive if a voluntary or involuntary petition in bankruptcy were filed?

Once a petition is filed and if the facts are clear, the court will generally adjudge the debtor as bankrupt. The next step is to safeguard the bankrupt's property while hearings are held to determine final disposition. As indicated earlier, the court has two alternatives. The first is to effect a reorganization, and the second is to liquidate the assets and to distribute them to the interested parties on an equitable basis.

In order to determine the best course of action, the court will appoint a disinterested party to act as referee between the various claimants. As soon as possible, the referee will call a meeting of all creditors to validate the claims against the bankrupt. The bankrupt will be required to furnish a schedule of all assets and liabilities. At this point the creditors have the right to elect a trustee who shall take control of the business entity. If the selection of a trustee is not immediately agreed upon by the various classes of creditors and claimants, the court may appoint a receiver to take custody of the insolvent's property until the trustee is elected.

The next problem is for the trustee to place some value on the firm's assets. This valuation will be made from two points of view. First, what funds would be available for payment to the creditors if the firm were liquidated? Second, what would be the ability of the firm to pay fixed debt charges and dividends as a going concern if it were reorganized?

The valuation of the assets upon liquidation is simply what someone would pay for them at a public sale. The valuation in terms of the ability to pay fixed debt charges and dividends is nothing more than the present value of the expected stream of income before interest and dividends but after taxes. This latter problem is tricky because the taxes to be paid will be determined in part by the interest to be paid.

Thus, during the valuation process, the trustee does find himself in a dilemma. First, he is attempting to find the present value of the firm after interest expense in order to arrive at a new capital structure. The new capital structure will determine the amount of the new debt issue. Worse yet, the amount of the new debt to be issued will determine the annual interest expense, which in turn is significant in determining the amount of debt to be issued in the first instance! However, the problem must be faced.

At this point the attorney began to take a keen interest. His thoughts were turning to the problem of liquidation versus reorganization. He glanced at the $17 million book value of net property on Southeastern's balance sheet. The claim of the $6\frac{1}{2}$ percent first mortgage bonds amounts to $9 million. He was thinking that foreclosure might not be in the best interests of his client. While book value may not reflect the true value of the assets, property sold by foreclosure at a forced sale rarely brings the true value.

The first step would be to secure a discreet appraisal of Southeastern's assets, and the second step would be to estimate Southeastern's future earnings. The attorney emphasized the "discreet" part of his analysis because he did not want to "rock the boat" until he had some basis for a decision for his client. The Southeastern vice-president was more than willing to help because he did not want a liquidation. He preferred a reorganization that might salvage some of the equity in the short run and all of it in the long run if the firm was successful. He felt quite responsible because of the excess debt financing he had arranged. In summary, the real question is whether the firm is worth more dead or alive. This was the question the attorney asked you to determine.

THE VALUATION PROBLEM

As indicated, the valuation of the firm must be made from two points of view (you added the possibility of a third):

1. The liquidation value at a forced sale
2. The value as a going concern for the purpose of reorganization
3. The value the firm has as a merger candidate under somewhat forced conditions

Your guess was that neither the equity nor the unsecured creditors would fare very well upon liquidation. Southeastern's plant is more or less specialized, and the market for the same is rather limited. The Southeastern vice-president, with the approval of his president and board of directors, was quite helpful. After several weeks of discreet inquiry, the best estimate of the plant value at a forced sale was 40 percent on the dollar, or about $6,800,000, perhaps $7,500,000. The $6\frac{1}{2}$ percent mortgage bondholders held the entire plant as collateral for the debt and would thus receive all these funds.

At the best figure, $7,500,000, the bondholders would be forced to join the subordinate and general creditors to recover the last $1,500,000 of the $9,000,000 in bonded debt outstanding. Total remaining assets equal $3 million to satisfy $7 million in general and unsecured claims plus the $1,500,000 6½ percent bond deficiency. Total unrecovered claims would be $8,500,000. The best estimate of the liquidation value of the remaining assets is approximately $1,500,000 after the expense of the sale, or a 17.7 percent return to the creditors. The equity would be lost in toto. The attorney's client would thus receive 17 percent of the $4 million investment, or $680,000 less attorney's fees.

The vice-president estimated future annual earnings to be $1,800,000 before interest and taxes, would be about the best one could expect without a complete change of direction for the Southeastern firm.

The next question to be investigated would be the total amount of securities, debt and equity, the firm could reasonably be expected to support based on the annual income after taxes but before interest. After juggling the figures about with several combinations of debt and equity, you decided upon some basic premises for the development of the valuation of Southeastern as a going concern:

1. You would like to retain the 6½ percent interest rate on the first mortgage bonds and the 8 percent interest rate on the subordinate debentures.
2. Return to equity would be at about 8½ percent on book value. (You winced at the use of book value, but really there was nothing better at this time vis-à-vis no realistic market value—market value had dropped drastically with the previous failures to pay interest.)
3. You adopted the estimated annual income of $1,800,000 before interest and taxes.
4. A review of the capital structure of other companies in the industry indicated about a 65 to 35 debt-to-equity ratio. There is no real reason that Southeastern should adopt an industry average or should copy another firm's debt-to-equity ratio if a better one can be justified. However, it might be a good place to start.
5. Total capitalization should be about two-thirds of the present $17 million, or approximately $12 million. With a 35 percent debt figure, a reorganization of the capital structure based on the ability of the firm to support the same would be as follows:

Debt	$ 4,200,000
Equity	7,800,000
	$12,000,000

You jotted down some figures to try for size:

$6\frac{1}{2}\%$ mortgage bonds	\$ 4,200,000
8% subordinate debentures	2,400,000
Capital stock	5,400,000
	\$12,000,000
Annual interest on the above basis:	
$6\frac{1}{2}\%$ mortgage bonds	\$ 273,000
8% subordinated debentures	192,000
Total annual interest expense	\$ 465,000
Annual tax expense:	
Estimated annual income	\$1,800,000
Less estimated interest	465,000
Income before taxes	\$1,335,000
Taxes at 50%	667,500
Available to equity	\$ 667,500

Return to equity would be 12+ percent:

$$\frac{\$667{,}000}{\$5{,}400{,}000} = 12.3\%$$

The return to equity looked a bit high. However, the return to equity should be somewhat higher than the return to debt. The subordinates would earn 8 percent.

Using the above figures as a basis, you next reexamined the capital structure you had adopted. Based on earnings, the total capital structure appeared to be reasonable.

Estimated annual income	\$ 1,800,000
Estimated taxes	465,000
	\$ 1,335,000
Present value of an annuity at 12% for 25 years	9.077
Total value of supportable securities	\$12,117,795
	or
	\$12,000,000

You have made several big assumptions. As an example, why did you discount the income for 25 years? Why not 20 years or 30 years? There really is no good reason. Probably you used 12 percent as the discount rate because that was approximately the calculated return to equity. However, at least you have a start. The next problem is who gets what. There really isn't much of a choice. Legally, you must recognize the priority of the claims against Southeastern, which means that the secured creditors must be satisfied in full in any reorganization before the unsecured creditors are included.

You know that any reorganization must be approved by the court handling the jurisdiction of the bankrupt. The court will insist on the basic doctrine of fairness, which means that any reorganization must recognize all claims in the order of their legal and contractual priority. It is clear that if only $4,200,000 in new mortgage bonds are issued, it would be impossible for the $9 million worth of bonds to receive the same protection they had with the senior mortgage bonds. These bondholders no doubt would be forced to accept some junior securities. From the highest priority down to the debt, the reorganized capital structure might be expected to be as follows:

The $6\frac{1}{2}\%$ mortgage bonds would receive the total of in mortgage bonds, and	$ 4,200,000
The $6\frac{1}{2}\%$ mortgage bondholders receive $\frac{1}{2}$ of balance due in 8% subordinate debentures, and	2,400,000
$\frac{1}{2}$ of balance due in common stock	2,400,000
The 8% subordinate debt would receive common stock	3,000,000
	$12,000,000

Wrong—! Why?

Had the subordinate debentures been secured in any way, such as a second mortgage on the plant and equipment behind the senior $6\frac{1}{2}$ percent mortgage bondholders, you would have been correct. However, as a general creditor you must take only your share of the $3 million. This means that instead of receiving all the $3 million in stock, the attorney's client will receive only four-sevenths of $3 million, or approximately $1,290,000 in common stock for the $4 million investment in 8 percent subordinate bonds. This is so because there is a total of $7 million in unsecured debt and the 8 percent subordinates represent only $4 million of that total. The present stockholders lose 100 percent.

Clearly, based on the above considerations, the firm is worth more alive, to the attorney's client at least, than it is dead.

While all the above has been going on, Southeastern's entire management group has been making the same sort of study. It was clear to them that Southeastern's current stockholders stood to lose their entire investment, and management themselves would no doubt lose their positions. It is not very hopeful to be an ex-official of a bankrupt business organization.

In retrospect, it is true that the company's (Southeastern's) debt to equity, 80 to 20, was probably too high and there was too much of it. The earnings were really not that bad. The biggest problem was the liquidity problem. Accounts receivable were tied up, although suits had been filed on Southeastern's behalf to give as much protection as possible. However, Southeastern stands in about the same position with respect to their debtors as Southeastern's unsecured creditors. In fact, Southeastern, by filing the suit to recover their accounts receivable, might be the straw that broke the camel's back. Southeastern may have forced their customers' hands into preferential treatment. As indicated earlier, should Southeastern's customers not remove Southeastern's lien against them within the prescribed time, this failure alone would be an act of bankruptcy. Southeastern's management and directors were seriously considering withdrawing the lawsuits until the water had cleared a bit. They requested their attorney to do so.

In the meantime, a slim ray of light for Southeastern was available. The Southeastern vice-president, at his board of directors' direction, personally was visiting each of the general unsecured creditors with three different propositions. The first was requesting an extension of time for payment. He explained that it would appear that all unsecured general creditors as well as equity would lose 100 percent if the firm were liquidated or if the $6\frac{1}{2}$ percent bondholders were successful in foreclosure. This, of course, might relieve the immediate pressure from one quarter but would not solve the real problem. Most, if not all, of the general creditors agreed that this approach would be only temporary. The vice-president agreed further that all purchases would be on a cash basis during the interim until conditions cleared up with respect to Southeastern's receivables. He confessed that this latter agreement was shaky if the Southeastern receivable situation was prolonged.

The vice-president's second proposition was a request that all general creditors agree to a composition, that is, that all creditors agree to take only a percentage of their liability in full settlement. Several of the creditors reminded him that this agreement alone would not solve anything except to partially relieve the liquidity problem. This second idea was not so well received.

To sweeten the second idea that vice-president suggested a combination of a percentage payment in cash and the balance in preferred or common stock. To issue preferred stock would not violate the restriction in the $6\frac{1}{2}$ percent mortgage indenture with respect to no additional long-term debt. While it might appear the creditors were really in no position to dicker in view of the probable outcome of a bankruptcy, several held out until some settlement or understanding was made with the bond and debenture holders.

In reality, the general creditors did have some strength now that the matter of a possible bankruptcy was out in the open. You will recall that unsecured creditor's claims amounted to \$1.25 million plus the 8 percent note payable and the taxes payable. Any three of them could force bankruptcy. Several smaller ones were threatening to do just that after hearing the "news." Calmer heads prevailed for the most part, and to avoid a preferential payment by Southeastern, one of the larger creditors actually "bought" two smaller claims totaling $7,500 to temporarily eliminate the possibility of a quarter of a million total loss to the purchasing firm. Smaller creditors do have remedies. The bigger creditor was forced to buy his claim. To the creditor with the quarter of a million dollar possible or probable loss, an additional $7,500 may be a good investment. At best it would cost him $3,750 after the tax writeoff in the event of a total loss. He thought it was a good "bad" investment, and he knew that it was bad "good" investment.

Part of the vice-president's earlier strategy of complete cooperation was about to pay off. At least you and the attorney were involved! He requested to meet with you again. In short, he suggested that the attorney accept for his client $4 million in preferred 8 percent stock in return for the subordinate debentures outstanding and agreed to sweeten the deal to $5 million in 8 percent preferred instead of $4 million, a 25 percent bonus. The attorney agreed to discuss the matter with his client. On the way back to the office, both you and the attorney almost simultaneously stated that there was little reason to accept that deal. You'd still have the same old management, the same liquidity problem.

There followed a series of phone calls and at least one meeting—perhaps there were two—from and with the $6\frac{1}{2}$ percent bondholders' committee that had been formed to protect their mutual interests. They likewise had been calculating and had arrived at about the same conclusion that you had reached. The time had arrived to come to grips with the alternatives available. We had skirted the edges of some alternatives and discussed others, but now that the word of Southeastern's problems was out, specific action was needed.

It was decided that all creditors should come together on an informal basis to discuss common interests. This was a calculated risk because fireworks could easily erupt. It is quite apparent that someone will probably lose, and no one could be expected to volunteer to do so. However, it was time to lay the cards on the table. The attorney suggested, with the approval of President Jones (which somewhat puzzled you), that you be the "take charge guy." You accepted.

You decided that if you were going to take charge, you would take charge. There was only one problem. Not all parties had agreed to your new role, and some probably never would. However, the Southeastern vice-president had paved the way a little by his discussions with the general creditors. At least all parties know that there is need for some action—formal or informal. Your first line of attack would be that an informal approach could be less expensive and could result in preserving more assets in both the short and the long run until some course of action was determined. Southeastern's management was obviously uneasy about the whole matter but had every incentive to carry on as efficiently as possible.

A meeting of general unsecured creditors was called. Some 80 percent of the claims were present. The purpose of this meeting was to organize a creditors' committee that could speak for and protect the interests of the general creditors. There were more attorneys present representing creditors than there were creditors. It was a stormy session at first. People were angry. Threats of bankruptcy petitions were made over and over. Many of the creditors could afford the loss and were determined to punish Southeastern. Others could not and would not. After a full day of listening, you requested about 4:00 p.m. that the group recess until 7:30 p.m. Your rationale was that a good dinner and a little time might calm things down and bring some order out of obvious chaos. The group agreed.

At the evening meeting, you did take charge at the outset. In your opening remarks you indicated the results of your study of the situation. The possibility of the significant losses sobered the conversations considerably. You wondered whether you could have saved time if you had brought the facts to light earlier in the day. You concluded that the therapy of exposing the anger and emotions was worth the time. In order to avoid words and phrases that would be difficult to retract, Southeastern's management was not invited. Anyway, a committee of three creditors was elected, with all present agreeing to hold tight until further developments. Phone calls the next day to the absentees brought creditor participation to almost 100 percent. Unfortunately, the creditors you were unable to reach could still upset the applecart before there were any apples to sell. The committee took over the task of contacting the remaining creditors and securing agreement. This they did. Working with the $6\frac{1}{2}$ percent first mortgage bond committee was considerably easier, and the attorney represented all the 8 percent subordinate debt. Considerable progress had been made.

A second meeting of all interested parties except management was called. There were eight people present—three each for general unsecured creditors and the bondholders, the attorney, and yourself. All present were attorneys except you. In order to get started, you again outlined possible procedures. The possibilities were as follows:

1. Receivership or trusteeship
2. Reorganization
3. Liquidation
4. Merger

Clearly, a voluntary settlement, reorganization, or merger would be significantly less expensive and less time consuming. The net results could be less loss for all creditors concerned. This was the real objective of the meeting of the parties, if possible. Legal leverage, or what could happen if legalistic procedures were followed, could serve as a club to drive the various parties together. The group inquired as to whether or not, in your opinion, a reorganization was feasible.

Feasibility refers to the practicality of the reorganization plan. If the plan is unworkable because of failure to alleviate the financial difficulties of the old organization, the new plan will only invite the same problems with additional losses to interested parties. You have done your homework well, because the next step is to place a value upon the new securities to be issued if the firm is reorganized. This you have done or at least estimated. However, the test is yet to come.

If the matter goes the formal bankruptcy route, and the plan is presented, the court will then authorize and direct that a public sale of the corporate assets take place. Outside bidders may come in at this point but must pay cash to the old corporation if the valuation price is met or exceeded. Usually if the valuation is realistic, no cash bidders will match or exceed the valuation price. This is not always the case. However, it is no real problem since the purpose is not to reorganize just to reorganize. The purpose is for creditors to receive as much value as possible. Many would prefer the cash from a sale that could be reinvested elsewhere rather than receive new but fewer securities from the old firm. Dissenters from the reorganization plan theoretically would receive their claims in cash provided the reorganization plan is realistic and new investors could be found to put cash in the firm. However, if a substantial creditor dollar interests dissent from the plan and new money is not forthcoming to pay off the dissenters, the reorganization may well fail. If this is so, liquidation will be the only answer. However, dissenters must weigh their actions very carefully. Liquidation may provide a return of zero. Again, you have done your homework well. All creditors know the facts and have been given the opportunity to get angry and reconsider.

ALTERNATIVES TO BANKRUPTCY

How to accomplish the objectives of reorganization was the subject of some discussion. Several suggestions were offered:

1. Request that unsecured creditors trade their debt obligations for noncumulative preferred stock. This would mean that instead of payment and interest on the debt, if any, the creditors would receive a higher priority upon liquidation than common stockholders but less priority than both secured and unsecured debt. Income would be received if and only if the board of directors of the new firm declared dividends to the preferred stock. This is so because of

the noncumulative nature of the proposed stock, which means that all preferred dividends for prior years need not be paid in full before the common stock receives a dividend payment. If any dividend is declared, the preferred stock receives priority. There would appear to be little incentive for a creditor to accept the noncumulative feature except as a last resort. Cumulative preferred stock may be more attractive, which means that all preferred dividends—current and for prior years—must be paid before common dividends are declared.

2. Request the consent of the fixed-charge bond and subordinate debenture holders to accept new debt with a contingent interest clause. This could mean that interest would be paid only if the firm's income reached a given level.
3. Receive consent to reduce annual sinking-fund requirements by providing for payment over a longer period of time.
4. Receive consent to reduce the interest rate on outstanding interest-bearing debt.

At first a hard-nosed attitude erupted again. The $6\frac{1}{2}$ percent bondholders took the position that foreclosure would make them whole. Clearly, other interested parties would not permit this to happen, and a petition in bankruptcy would be filed. The subordinate debenture holders represented by the attorney urged reorganization. Southeastern stockholders and management could be expected to challenge the valuation figure of $12 million. Unsecured general creditors could be expected to challenge everything.

As tempers cooled again, the most sensible thing to do appeared to be to push for a voluntary reorganization.

If Southeastern is reorganized, a very serious problem will be the raising of cash to meet the need for:

1. Adequate working capital
2. New equipment that may be necessary
3. Possible court costs, trustee or receiver and other legal fees
4. Settlement of dissenting creditors' claims

All these matters present serious problems and require serious review of all possible solutions. Then came the nitty-gritty matters as the group considered the alternatives. They received again your earlier studies with respect to the forced sale value of the assets, the reasonable capital structure the firm could be expected to carry, the anticipated annual earnings of the firm, and the effect all these would have on the various interested parties. Things looked very glum indeed when you were called from the meeting to answer an urgent phone call.

The Southeastern vice-president was requesting an immediate meeting with the committee. He arrived in 30 minutes. Southeastern had been busy trying to protect its own interest, that is, the interest of the equity holders and management. Southeastern had received a firm offer that was substantially as follows:

1.	The $6\frac{1}{2}$ percent mortgage bondholders were to receive in cash all accrued interest, and the buyer would assume the bond obligation. This consideration would equal (three semiannual interest payments + the $9 million face value of the notes).	$ 9,877,500
2.	All taxes would be paid.	500,000
3.	All other creditors would immediately receive 50 percent of the amounts due in the buyer's common stock discounted 5 percent from the current market price of $108 per share.	3,350,000
4.	Equity owners should receive nothing at this time. However, the buyer did agree to establish a fund consisting of all earnings averaged over the next five years calculated with the new debt interest obligations, in excess of an annual 12 percent return before taxes on their investment of $13,627,500. The fund would be used first to repay the creditors in item 3 the remaining 50 percent of their claims, and then the firm's common stock would be issued to current equity holders pro rata for the balance in the fund. After the 5-year period, no futher obligation would remain. Thus the equity holder would receive a *certificate of contingent interest.*	
		$13,627,500

It took very little discussion for the $6\frac{1}{2}$ percent mortgage bondholders to agree. Southeastern already had agreed, and general creditors, including the attorney for the subordinate debt, were not too reluctant. Everyone wanted to know the name of the buyer. No one could really agree until they knew whose stock they might own. Southeastern stated that a first-class firm was involved. However, an arrangement in principle was necessary before the name could be revealed.

The agreement was quickly given. There were no dissenters, so court action was unnecessary. The name of the firm was Northeast Industries, Inc., a AAA firm listed on the big board. The deal was consummated within 10 days. You were offered the presidency at $180,000 per year plus a bonus arrangement and stock options. Did you take it?

SUMMARY

A debtor is technically bankrupt if either (1) the value of his liabilities exceeds the fair value of his assets or (2) he is unable to pay his obligations as they become due. Being technically bankrupt is one thing—being legally bankrupt is something else.

Before a debtor can be legally bankrupt, a petition in bankruptcy must be filed with the federal court. The petition may be voluntarily filed by the debtor, or the petition may be filed by certain creditors. This latter petition is known as an involuntary petition in bankruptcy. Prior to the filing of a petition in bankruptcy the courts have no jurisdiction over the debtor. When a firm is technically insolvent, several classes of parties are involved: (1) secured creditors, (2) unsecured creditors, (3) wage earners, (4) governmental taxing bodies, and (5) the stockholders.

Bankruptcy proceedings are basically designed to protect all interested parties by maintaining the status quo until the court can determine the fair and equitable thing to do with respect to the debtor's assets. No suits may be filed, nor can legal liens be enforced during the bankruptcy proceedings. However, not all the interested parties have the same interest, and some of the interested parties cannot afford the "protection" of the bankruptcy law. Each class of interested party must weigh carefully the probable outcome of formal bankruptcy proceedings. Informal settlements on agreemnts may well be the better of the two evils.

However, formal bankruptcy proceedings may be the only relief the debtor or creditor may have if a settlement is undesirable. Formal bankruptcy proceedings involve two general courses of action, with the possibility of a third:

1. Liquidation of the firm
2. Reorganization of the capital structure of the firm
3. A merger with a financially sound firm

Upon liquidation of a firm it is seldom that the stockholders of the bankrupt receive anything. The court will insist upon reorganizing the legal priority of claims, which means that all secured debt holders will receive their claims in full after taxes and certain wages and the expense of the sale of the firm's assets are paid. General unsecured creditors are next in line for payment, followed by preferred stockholders, if any; finally, common stockholders receive any balance of the proceeds.

Upon reorganization the same priority will follow. Reorganization generally takes place when the firm is worth more alive than dead or there is a chance for a larger recovery as a going concern. The reorganization must be feasible; that is, the capital structure and, more specifically, the debt-to-equity ratio must be such that debt interest can be paid plus a reasonable return to equity. Former senior debt owners may be required to accept all or part of their interest in junior securities and/or preferred or common stock. Whether or not former equity owners retain an interest in the reorganized firm depends upon the present value of future earnings discounted at the market capitalization rate. The market capitalization rate depends upon the opportunity cost of investors willing to accept the level of risk involved in the reorganized firm.

While the legal rights of the various parties are clear, the practical implication of these legal rights is not or may not be so clear with respect to any given party. Utmost care and caution must be exercised in situations where the debtor is insolvent. As a wise man once said, "Never let your education interfere with common sense!"

QUESTIONS FOR DISCUSSION

1. Compare and contrast insolvency and bankruptcy.
2. What is the significance of the difference between the two?
3. What is the significance of a high debt-to-equity (or vice versa) ratio in a bankrupt situation?
4. What are the alternatives available to an insolvent firm's management prior to bankruptcy?
5. What are the specific acts of bankruptcy?
6. Distinguish between voluntary and involuntary bankruptcy.
7. When would a firm seek voluntary bankruptcy?
8. Distinguish between the duties and responsibilities of (*a*) a referee in bankruptcy, (*b*) a trustee in bankruptcy, and (*c*) a receiver in bankruptcy.
9. What valuation problem is present in a bankruptcy proceeding and why is it important?
10. Assume that you are a trustee in bankruptcy faced with a valuation problem.
    (a) What valuation problem would you have in the event of liquidation?
    (b) Would the problem be the same if the firm is to be reorganized? Why or why not?
11. Assuming a reorganization, what is the basic valuation problem?
12. Who would normally be the interested parties in a bankruptcy proceeding, and what are the legal rights of each?

13. What leverage do general creditors have, if any, in an informal reorganization?

14. What cash requirement does a firm seeking formal reorganization face?

SUGGESTED READINGS

Allocation of Corporate Reorganizations between Chapters X and XI of the Bankruptcy Act, *Harvard Law Review,* vol. 69, pp. 352–362, December, 1955.

Allocation of Securities in Corporate Reorganization: Claims Measurement through Investment Value Analysis, *Yale Law Review,* vol. LXI, pp. 656–685 May, 1952.

Altman, E. I.: Financial Ratios, Discriminant Analysis, and the Prediction of Corporate Bankruptcy, *Journal of Finance,* vol. XXIII, pp. 589–609, September, 1968.

Billyou, D. F.: Priority Rights of Security Holders in Bankruptcy Reorganizations: New Directions, *Harvard Law Review,* vol. LXVII, pp. 553–590, February, 1954.

Blum, Walter J.: Full Priority and Full Compensation in Corporate Reorganization: A Reappraisal, *The University of Chicago Law Review,* vol. XXV, pp. 417–444, spring, 1958.

Calkins, Francis J.: Feasibility in Plans of Corporate Reorganizations under Chapter X, *Harvard Law Review,* vol. LXI, pp. 763–781, May, 1948.

———: Corporate Reorganization under Chapter X: A Post Mortem, *Journal of Finance,* vol. III, pp. 19–28, June, 1948.

Guthmann, H. G.: Absolute Priority in Reorganization, *Columbia Law Review,* vol. LXV, pp. 739–754, September, 1945.

Hirsch, Geroge J., and Sidney Krause: "Bankruptcy and Arrangements," 3d ed., Practicing Law Institute, New York, 1964.

Krause, Sidney: Chapters X and XI: A Study in Contrasts, *Business Lawyer,* vol. 19, pp. 511–526, January, 1964.

O'Leary, P. M.: The Role of Banking Groups in Corporate Reorganizations, *American Economic Review,* vol. XXVIII, pp. 337–344, June, 1939.

Walter, James E.: Determination of Technical Insolvency, *Journal of Business,* vol. 30, pp. 30–43, January, 1957.

Weintraub, Benjamin, and Levin Harris: "Practical Guide to Bankruptcy and Debtor Relief," Prentice-Hall, Inc., Englewood Cliffs, N.J., 1964.

APPENDIX

TABLE A-1: COMPOUND SUM OF $1

Year	1%	2%	3%	4%	5%	6%	7%	8%	9%	10%	12%	14%	15%	16%
1	1.010	1.020	1.030	1.040	1.050	1.060	1.070	1.080	1.090	1.100	1.120	1.140	1.150	1.160
2	1.020	1.040	1.061	1.082	1.102	1.124	1.145	1.168	1.188	1.210	1.254	1.300	1.322	1.346
3	1.030	1.061	1.093	1.125	1.158	1.191	1.225	1.260	1.295	1.331	1.405	1.482	1.521	1.561
4	1.041	1.082	1.126	1.170	1.216	1.262	1.311	1.360	1.412	1.464	1.574	1.689	1.749	1.811
5	1.051	1.104	1.159	1.217	1.276	1.338	1.403	1.469	1.539	1.611	1.762	1.925	2.011	2.100
6	1.062	1.126	1.194	1.265	1.340	1.419	1.501	1.587	1.677	1.772	1.974	2.195	2.313	2.436
7	1.072	1.149	1.230	1.316	1.407	1.504	1.606	1.714	1.828	1.949	2.211	2.502	2.660	2.826
8	1.083	1.172	1.267	1.369	1.477	1.594	1.718	1.851	1.993	2.144	2.476	2.853	3.059	3.278
9	1.094	1.195	1.305	1.423	1.551	1.689	1.838	1.999	2.172	2.358	2.773	3.252	3.518	3.803
10	1.105	1.219	1.344	1.480	1.629	1.791	1.967	2.159	2.367	2.594	3.106	3.707	4.046	4.411
11	1.116	1.243	1.384	1.539	1.710	1.898	2.105	2.382	2.580	2.853	3.479	4.226	4.652	5.117
12	1.127	1.268	1.426	1.601	1.796	2.021	2.252	2.518	2.813	3.138	3.896	4.818	5.350	5.936
13	1.138	1.294	1.469	1.665	1.886	2.133	2.410	2.720	3.066	3.452	4.363	5.492	6.193	6.886
14	1.149	1.319	1.513	1.732	1.980	2.261	2.579	2.937	3.342	3.797	4.887	6.261	7.076	7.988
15	1.161	1.346	1.558	1.801	2.079	2.397	2.759	3.172	3.642	4.177	5.474	7.138	8.137	9.266
16	1.173	1.373	1.605	1.873	2.183	2.540	2.952	3.426	3.970	4.593	6.130	8.137	9.358	10.748
17	1.184	1.400	1.653	1.948	2.292	2.693	3.159	3.700	4.328	5.054	6.866	9.276	10.761	12.468
18	1.196	1.428	1.702	2.026	2.407	2.854	3.380	3.996	4.717	5.560	7.690	10.575	12.375	14.463
19	1.208	1.457	1.754	2.107	2.527	3.026	3.617	4.316	5.142	6.116	8.613	12.056	14.232	16.777
20	1.220	1.486	1.806	2.191	2.653	3.207	3.870	4.661	5.604	6.728	9.640	13.743	16.367	19.461
25	1.282	1.641	2.094	2.666	3.386	4.292	5.427	6.848	8.623	10.835	17.000	26.462	32.919	40.874
30	1.348	1.811	2.427	3.243	4.322	5.743	7.612	10.063	13.268	17.449	29.960	50.950	66.212	85.850

Year	18%	20%	24%	28%	32%	36%	40%	50%	60%	70%	80%	90%
1	1.180	1.200	1.240	1.280	1.320	1.360	1.400	1.500	1.600	1.700	1.800	1.900
2	1.392	1.440	1.538	1.638	1.742	1.850	1.960	2.250	2.560	2.890	3.240	3.610
3	1.643	1.728	1.907	2.067	2.300	2.515	2.744	3.375	4.096	4.913	5.832	6.859
4	1.969	2.074	2.364	2.684	3.036	3.421	3.842	5.062	6.544	8.352	10.498	13.032
5	2.288	2.488	2.932	3.436	4.007	4.653	5.378	7.594	10.486	14.199	18.896	24.761
6	2.700	2.986	3.635	4.398	5.290	6.328	7.530	11.391	16.777	24.138	34.012	47.046
7	1.085	3.583	4.508	5.629	6.983	8.005	10.541	17.086	26.844	41.034	61.222	89.387
8	3.759	4.300	5.590	7.206	9.217	11.703	14.758	25.629	42.950	69.758	110.200	169.836
9	4.435	5.160	6.931	9.223	12.166	15.917	20.681	38.443	68.720	118.588	198.359	322.688
10	5.234	6.192	8.594	11.806	16.060	21.647	28.925	57.665	109.951	201.599	357.047	613.107
11	6.176	7.430	10.657	15.112	21.199	29.439	40.496	86.498	175.922	342.719	642.684	1164.962
12	7.288	8.916	13.215	19.343	27.983	40.037	56.694	129.746	281.475	582.622	1156.831	2213.314
13	8.599	10.699	16.386	24.759	36.937	54.451	79.372	194.619	450.360	990.457	2082.295	4203.297
14	10.147	12.839	20.319	31.691	48.757	74.053	111.120	291.929	720.576	1683.777	3748.131	7990.065
15	11.974	15.407	25.196	40.565	64.359	100.712	155.568	437.894	1152.921	2862.421	6746.638	15181.122
16	14.129	18.488	31.243	51.923	84.954	136.97	217.795	658.84	1844.7	4866.1	12144.0	28844.0
17	16.672	22.188	38.741	68.461	112.14	186.28	304.914	985.26	2951.5	8272.4	21859.0	54804.0
18	19.673	26.623	48.039	85.071	148.02	253.34	426.879	1477.9	4722.4	14063.0	39346.0	104130.0
19	23.214	31.948	59.568	108.89	195.39	344.54	597.630	2216.8	7555.8	23907.0	70824.0	197840.0
20	27.383	38.338	73.864	139.38	257.92	468.57	836.683	3325.3	12089.0	40642.0	127480.0	375900.0
25	62.669	95.396	218.542	478.90	1033.6	2180.1	4499.880	25251.0	126700.0	577060.0	2408000.0	9307600.0
30	143.371	237.376	634.810	1645.5	4142.1	10143.0	24201.412	191750.0	1329200.0	8193500.0	45517000.0	230470000.0

TABLE A-2: PRESENT VALUE OF $1

Year	1%	2%	3%	4%	5%	6%	7%	8%	9%	10%	12%	14%	15%
1	0.990	0.980	0.971	0.962	0.952	0.943	0.935	0.926	0.917	0.909	0.893	0.877	0.870
2	0.980	0.961	0.943	0.925	0.907	0.890	0.873	0.857	0.842	0.826	0.797	0.769	0.756
3	0.971	0.942	0.915	0.889	0.864	0.840	0.816	0.794	0.772	0.751	0.712	0.675	0.658
4	0.961	0.924	0.889	0.855	0.823	0.792	0.763	0.735	0.708	0.683	0.636	0.592	0.572
5	0.951	0.906	0.863	0.822	0.784	0.747	0.713	0.681	0.650	0.621	0.567	0.519	0.497
6	0.942	0.888	0.838	0.790	0.746	0.705	0.666	0.630	0.598	0.564	0.507	0.456	0.432
7	0.933	0.871	0.813	0.760	0.711	0.665	0.623	0.583	0.547	0.513	0.452	0.400	0.376
8	0.923	0.853	0.789	0.731	0.677	0.627	0.582	0.540	0.502	0.467	0.404	0.351	0.327
9	0.914	0.837	0.768	0.703	0.645	0.592	0.544	0.500	0.460	0.424	0.361	0.308	0.284
10	0.905	0.820	0.744	0.676	0.614	0.558	0.508	0.463	0.422	0.386	0.322	0.270	0.247
11	0.898	0.804	0.722	0.650	0.585	0.527	0.475	0.429	0.388	0.350	0.287	0.237	0.215
12	0.887	0.788	0.701	0.625	0.557	0.497	0.444	0.397	0.356	0.319	0.257	0.208	0.187
13	0.879	0.773	0.681	0.601	0.530	0.469	0.415	0.388	0.326	0.290	0.229	0.182	0.163
14	0.870	0.758	0.661	0.577	0.505	0.442	0.388	0.340	0.299	0.263	0.205	0.160	0.141
15	0.861	0.743	0.642	0.555	0.481	0.417	0.362	0.315	0.275	0.239	0.183	0.140	0.123
16	0.853	0.728	0.623	0.534	0.458	0.394	0.339	0.292	0.252	0.218	0.163	0.123	0.107
17	0.844	0.714	0.605	0.513	0.436	0.371	0.317	0.270	0.231	0.198	0.146	0.108	0.093
18	0.836	0.700	0.587	0.494	0.416	0.350	0.296	0.250	0.212	0.180	0.130	0.095	0.081
19	0.828	0.686	0.570	0.475	0.398	0.331	0.276	0.232	0.194	0.164	0.116	0.083	0.070
20	0.820	0.673	0.554	0.456	0.377	0.319	0.258	0.215	0.178	0.149	0.104	0.073	0.061
25	0.780	0.610	0.478	0.375	0.295	0.233	0.184	0.146	0.116	0.092	0.059	0.038	0.030
30	0.742	0.552	0.412	0.308	0.231	0.174	0.131	0.099	0.075	0.057	0.033	0.020	0.015

Year	16%	18%	20%	24%	28%	32%	36%	40%	50%	60%	70%	80%	90%
1	0.862	0.847	0.833	0.808	0.781	0.758	0.735	0.714	0.667	0.625	0.588	0.556	0.526
2	0.743	0.718	0.694	0.650	0.610	0.574	0.541	0.510	0.444	0.391	0.346	0.309	0.277
3	0.641	0.609	0.579	0.524	0.477	0.435	0.398	0.364	0.296	0.244	0.204	0.171	0.146
4	0.532	0.516	0.482	0.423	0.373	0.329	0.292	0.260	0.198	0.153	0.120	0.095	0.077
5	0.476	0.437	0.402	0.341	0.291	0.250	0.215	0.186	0.132	0.095	0.070	0.053	0.040
6	0.410	0.370	0.335	0.275	0.227	0.189	0.158	0.133	0.088	0.060	0.041	0.029	0.021
7	0.354	0.314	0.279	0.222	0.178	0.143	0.116	0.095	0.059	0.037	0.024	0.016	0.011
8	0.395	0.266	0.233	0.179	0.139	0.108	0.085	0.068	0.039	0.023	0.014	0.009	0.006
9	0.263	0.226	0.194	0.144	0.108	0.082	0.063	0.048	0.026	0.015	0.008	0.005	0.003
10	0.227	0.191	0.162	0.116	0.085	0.062	0.046	0.035	0.017	0.009	0.005	0.003	0.002
11	0.195	0.162	0.135	0.094	0.066	0.047	0.034	0.025	0.012	0.006	0.003	0.002	0.001
12	0.168	0.137	0.112	0.076	0.052	0.036	0.025	0.018	0.008	0.004	0.002	0.001	0.001
13	0.145	0.116	0.093	0.061	0.040	0.027	0.018	0.013	0.005	0.002	0.001	0.001	0.000
14	0.125	0.099	0.078	0.049	0.032	0.021	0.014	0.009	0.003	0.001	0.001	0.000	
15	0.108	0.084	0.065	0.040	0.025	0.016	0.010	0.006	0.002	0.001	0.000		
16	0.093	0.071	0.054	0.032	0.019	0.012	0.007	0.005	0.002	0.001	0.000		
17	0.090	0.080	0.045	0.026	0.015	0.009	0.005	0.003	0.001	0.000			
18	0.069	0.051	0.038	0.021	0.012	0.007	0.004	0.002	0.001	0.000			
19	0.050	0.043	0.031	0.017	0.009	0.005	0.003	0.002	0.000				
20	0.051	0.037	0.026	0.014	0.007	0.004	0.002	0.001	0.000				
25	0.024	0.016	0.010	0.005	0.002	0.001	0.000						
30	0.012	0.007	0.004	0.002	0.001	0.000							

Periodic equal amounts

TABLE A-3: SUM OF AN ANNUITY OF $1 FOR *N* YEARS

Year	1%	2%	3%	4%	5%	6%	7%	8%	9%	10%	12%	14%
1	1.000	1.000	1.000	1.000	1.000	1.000	1.000	1.000	1.000	1.000	1.000	1.000
2	2.010	2.020	2.030	2.040	2.050	2.060	2.070	2.080	2.090	2.100	2.120	2.140
3	2.030	3.060	3.091	3.122	3.152	3.184	3.215	3.246	3.278	3.310	3.374	3.440
4	4.060	4.122	4.184	4.245	4.310	4.375	4.440	4.596	4.573	4.641	4.770	4.921
5	5.107	5.204	5.309	5.416	5.526	5.637	5.751	5.867	5.985	6.105	6.353	6.610
6	6.152	6.308	6.468	6.633	6.802	6.975	7.153	7.336	7.523	7.716	8.115	8.536
7	7.214	7.434	7.662	7.898	8.142	8.394	8.654	8.923	9.200	9.487	10.089	10.730
8	8.286	8.588	8.892	9.214	9.549	9.897	10.260	10.637	11.028	11.436	12.300	13.233
9	9.389	9.755	10.159	10.583	11.027	11.491	11.978	12.488	13.021	13.579	14.776	16.085
10	10.462	10.950	11.464	12.006	12.578	13.181	13.816	14.487	15.193	15.937	17.549	19.337
11	11.567	12.169	12.808	13.486	14.207	14.972	15.784	16.645	17.560	18.531	20.655	23.044
12	12.883	13.412	14.192	15.026	15.917	16.870	17.888	18.977	20.141	21.384	24.133	27.271
13	13.809	14.680	15.618	16.627	17.713	18.882	20.141	21.495	22.953	24.523	28.029	32.069
14	14.947	15.974	17.086	18.292	19.599	21.091	22.550	24.215	26.019	27.975	32.393	37.581
15	16.097	17.293	18.599	20.024	21.579	23.276	25.129	27.152	29.361	31.772	37.280	43.842
16	17.258	18.639	20.157	21.825	23.857	25.673	27.888	30.324	33.003	35.960	42.753	50.980
17	18.430	20.012	21.762	23.698	25.840	28.213	30.840	33.750	36.974	40.545	48.884	59.118
18	19.615	21.412	23.414	25.645	28.132	30.906	33.999	37.450	41.301	45.599	55.750	68.394
19	20.811	22.841	25.117	27.671	30.539	33.700	37.379	41.446	46.018	51.159	63.440	78.969
20	22.019	24.297	26.870	29.778	33.006	38.785	40.995	45.762	51.160	57.275	72.052	91.025
25	28.243	32.030	36.459	41.046	47.727	54.865	61.249	72.106	84.701	98.347	133.334	181.871
30	34.785	40.568	47.575	56.085	66.439	79.058	94.461	113.283	136.308	164.494	241.333	356.787

Year	16%	18%	20%	24%	28%	32%	36%	40%	50%	60%	70%	80%
1	1.000	1.000	1.000	1.000	1.000	1.000	1.000	1.000	1.000	1.000	1.000	1.000
2	2.160	2.180	2.200	2.240	2.280	2.320	2.360	2.400	2.500	2.600	2.700	2.800
3	3.506	3.572	3.640	3.778	3.918	4.062	4.210	4.360	4.750	5.160	5.590	6.040
4	5.066	5.215	5.368	5.684	6.016	6.362	6.725	7.104	8.125	9.256	10.503	11.872
5	6.877	7.154	7.442	8.048	8.700	9.398	10.146	10.846	13.188	15.810	18.855	22.370
6	8.977	9.442	9.930	10.980	12.136	13.406	14.799	16.324	20.781	26.295	33.054	41.265
7	11.414	12.142	12.916	14.615	16.534	18.696	21.126	23.853	32.172	43.073	57.191	75.278
8	14.240	15.327	16.499	19.123	22.163	25.678	29.732	34.395	49.258	69.916	96.225	136.500
9	17.518	19.086	20.799	24.712	29.369	34.895	41.435	49.153	74.887	112.866	167.983	246.699
10	21.321	23.521	25.959	31.643	38.592	47.062	57.352	69.814	113.330	181.585	286.570	445.058
11	25.733	28.755	32.150	40.238	50.399	63.122	78.998	98.739	170.995	291.536	488.170	802.105
12	30.850	34.931	39.580	50.985	65.510	84.320	108.437	139.235	257.493	467.458	830.888	1444.788
13	36.786	42.219	48.497	64.110	84.853	112.303	148.475	195.929	387.239	748.933	1413.510	2601.610
14	43.672	50.818	59.196	80.496	109.612	149.240	202.926	275.300	581.850	1199.293	2403.968	4683.914
15	51.660	60.965	72.035	100.815	141.303	197.997	276.979	386.420	873.788	1919.869	4087.745	8432.045
16	60.925	72.939	87.442	126.011	181.87	262.36	377.69	541.99	1311.7	3072.8	6950.2	15179.0
17	71.673	87.068	105.931	157.253	233.79	347.31	314.66	759.78	1968.5	4917.5	11816.0	27323.0
18	84.141	103.740	128.117	195.994	300.25	459.45	700.94	1064.7	2953.8	7868.9	20089.0	49182.0
19	98.603	123.414	154.740	244.033	385.32	607.47	954.28	1491.6	4431.7	12591.0	34152.0	88528.0
20	115.380	146.628	186.688	303.601	494.21	802.86	1298.8	2089.2	6648.5	20147.0	58059.0	159350.0
25	249.214	342.603	471.981	898.092	1706.8	3226.8	6053.0	11247.0	30500.0	211270.0	824370.0	3011100.0
30	530.312	790.948	1181.882	2640.916	5873.2	12941.0	28172.0	60501.0	383500.0	2215400.0	11705000.0	56896000.0

TABLE A-4: PRESENT VALUE OF AN ANNUITY OF $1 FOR *N* YEARS

Year	1%	2%	3%	4%	5%	6%	7%	8%	9%	10%	12%	14%	16%	18%	20%	24%	28%	32%	36%
1	0.990	0.980	0.971	0.962	0.952	0.943	0.935	0.926	0.917	0.909	0.893	0.877	0.862	0.847	0.833	0.806	0.781	0.758	0.735
2	1.970	1.942	1.913	1.886	1.859	1.833	1.808	1.783	1.759	1.736	1.690	1.647	1.605	1.566	1.528	1.457	1.392	1.332	1.276
3	2.941	2.884	2.829	2.775	2.723	2.673	2.624	2.577	2.531	2.487	2.402	2.322	2.246	2.174	2.106	1.981	1.868	1.766	1.674
4	3.902	3.808	3.717	3.630	3.546	3.465	3.387	3.312	3.240	3.170	3.037	2.914	2.798	2.690	2.589	2.404	2.241	2.096	1.966
5	4.853	4.713	4.580	4.452	4.329	4.212	4.100	3.993	3.890	3.791	3.605	3.433	3.274	3.127	2.991	2.745	2.532	2.345	2.181
6	5.795	5.601	5.417	5.242	5.076	4.917	4.766	4.623	4.486	4.355	4.111	3.889	3.685	3.498	3.326	3.020	2.759	2.534	2.339
7	6.728	6.472	6.230	6.002	5.786	5.582	5.380	5.206	5.033	4.868	4.564	4.288	4.039	3.812	3.605	3.242	2.937	2.678	2.455
8	7.652	7.325	7.020	6.733	6.463	6.210	5.971	5.747	5.535	5.335	4.968	4.639	4.344	4.078	3.837	3.421	3.076	2.786	2.540
9	8.566	8.162	7.786	7.435	7.108	6.802	6.515	6.247	5.985	5.759	5.328	4.946	4.607	4.303	4.031	3.566	3.184	2.868	2.603
10	9.471	8.983	8.530	8.111	7.722	7.360	7.024	6.710	6.418	6.145	5.650	5.216	4.833	4.494	4.193	3.682	3.269	2.930	2.650
11	10.368	9.787	9.253	8.760	8.306	7.887	7.499	7.139	6.805	6.495	5.988	5.453	5.029	4.656	4.327	3.776	3.335	2.978	2.683
12	11.255	10.575	9.954	9.385	8.863	8.384	7.943	7.536	7.161	6.814	6.194	5.660	5.197	4.793	4.439	3.851	3.387	3.013	2.708
13	12.134	11.348	10.635	9.986	9.394	8.853	8.358	7.904	7.487	7.103	6.424	5.842	5.342	4.910	4.533	3.912	3.427	3.040	2.727
14	13.004	12.106	11.296	10.563	9.899	9.295	8.745	8.244	7.786	7.367	6.628	6.002	5.468	5.008	4.611	3.962	3.459	3.061	2.740
15	13.865	12.849	11.938	11.118	10.380	9.712	9.108	8.559	8.060	7.606	6.811	6.142	5.575	5.092	4.675	4.001	3.483	3.076	2.750
16	14.718	13.578	12.561	11.652	10.838	10.106	9.447	8.851	8.312	7.824	6.974	6.265	5.669	5.162	4.730	4.033	3.503	3.088	2.758
17	15.562	14.292	13.166	12.166	11.274	10.477	9.763	9.122	8.544	8.022	7.120	6.373	5.749	4.222	4.775	4.059	3.518	3.097	2.763
18	16.398	14.992	13.754	12.659	11.690	10.828	10.059	9.372	8.756	8.201	7.250	6.467	5.818	5.273	4.812	4.080	3.529	3.104	2.767
19	17.226	15.678	14.324	13.134	12.085	11.158	10.336	9.604	8.950	8.365	7.368	6.550	5.877	5.316	4.844	4.097	3.539	3.109	2.770
20	18.046	16.351	14.877	13.590	12.462	11.470	10.594	9.818	9.128	8.514	7.469	6.623	5.929	5.353	4.870	4.110	3.546	3.113	2.772
25	22.023	19.523	17.413	15.622	14.094	12.783	11.654	10.675	9.823	9.077	7.843	6.873	6.097	5.407	4.948	4.147	3.564	3.122	2.776
30	25.808	22.397	19.600	17.292	15.373	13.765	12.409	11.258	10.274	9.427	8.035	7.003	6.177	5.517	4.979	4.160	3.569	3.124	2.778

GLOSSARY

GLOSSARY

Accruals: Continually recurring short-term liabilities. Examples are accrued wages, accrued taxes, and accrued interest.

Accrued interest: Interest accrued on a bond since the last interest payment was made. The buyer of the bond pays the market price plus accrued interest. Exceptions include bonds that are in default and income bonds.

Aging schedule: A report showing how long accounts receivable have been outstanding. It gives the percent of receivables not past due and the percent past due by, for example, one month, two months, or other periods.

Amortization: A generic term that includes various specific practices such as depreciation, depletion, writeoff of intangibles, prepaid expenses, and deferred charges.

Annuity: A series of payments of a fixed amount for a specified number of years.

Assets: Everything a corporation owns or is owed: cash, investments, money due, materials, and inventories, which are called *current assets;* buildings and machinery, which are known as *fixed assets;* and patents and goodwill, called *intangible assets.*

Assignment: A relatively inexpensive way of liquidating a failing firm that does not involve going through the courts.

Balance sheet: A condensed statement showing the nature and amount of a company's assets, liabilities, and capital on a given date. In dollar amounts the balance sheet shows what the company owned, what it owed, and the ownership interest in the company of its stockholders.

Balloon payment: The final payment larger than the preceding payments when a debt is not fully amortized.

Bankruptcy: A legal procedure for formally liquidating a business carried out under the jurisdiction of courts of law.

Bearer bond: A bond that does not have the owner's name registered on the books of the issuing company and that is payable to the holder.

Bond: Basically an IOU or promissory note of a corporation, usually issued in multiples of $1,000, although $100 and $50 denominations are not uncommon. A bond is evidence of a debt on which the issuing company usually promises to pay the bondholders a specified amount of interest for a specified length of time and to repay the loan on the expiration date. In every case a bond represents debt—its holder is a creditor of the corporation and not a part owner as is the shareholder.

Book value: An accounting term, book value of a stock is determined from a company's records by adding all assets (generally excluding such intangibles as goodwill), then deducting all debts and other liabilities, plus the liquidation price of any preferred issues. The sum arrived at is divided by the number of common shares outstanding, and the result is book value per common share. Book value of the assets of a company or a security may have little or no significant relationship to market value.

Breakeven analysis: An analytical technique for studying the relation between fixed cost, variable cost, and profits. A breakeven *chart* graphically depicts the nature of breakeven analysis. The breakeven *point* represents that volume of sales at which total costs equal total revenues (that is, profits equal zero).

Callable: A bond issue all or part of which may be redeemed by the issuing corporation under definite conditions before maturity. The term also applies to preferred shares that may be redeemed by the issuing corporation.

Capital budgeting: The process of planning expenditures on assets whose returns are expected to extend beyond one year.

Capital gain or capital loss: Profit or loss from the sale of a capital asset. A capital gain, under current federal income tax laws, may be either short-term (six months or less) or long-term (more than six months). A short-term capital gain is taxed at the reporting individual's full income tax rate. A long-term capital gain is taxed at a maximum of 25 percent, depending on the reporting individual's tax bracket. Up to $1,000 of net capital loss—incurred when securities are sold at a lower price than was paid for them—is deductible from the individual's taxable income during the year reported. If the capital loss is more than $1,000, as much as $1,000 annually is deductible annually thereafter until all of the loss has been deducted. The amount of capital loss which may be deducted is reduced by the amount of any capital gain.

Capital stock: All shares representing ownership of a business, including preferred and common.

Capitalization: Total amount of the various securities issued by a corporation. Capitalization may include bonds, debentures, and preferred and common stock. Bonds and debentures are usually carried on the books of the issuing company in terms of their par or face value. Preferred and common shares may be carried in terms of par or stated value. Stated value may be an arbitrary figure decided upon by the directors or may represent the amount received by the company from the sale of the securities at the time of issuance.

Capitalization rate: A discount rate used to find the present value of a series of future cash receipts; sometimes called *discount rate.*

Cash budget: A schedule showing cash flows (receipts, disbursements, and net cash) for a firm over a specified period.

Cash cycle: The length of time between the purchase of raw materials and the collection of accounts receivable generated in the sale of the final product.

Cash flow: Reported net income of a corporation *plus* amounts charged off for depreciation, depletion, amortization, and extraordinary charges to reserves, which are bookkeeping deductions and not paid out in actual dollars and cents. A yardstick used in recent years because of the larger noncash deductions appearing to offer a better indication of the ability of a company to pay dividends and finance expansion from self-generated cash than the conventional reported net income figure.

Collateral: Securities or other property pledged by a borrower to secure repayment of a loan.

Collateral trust bond: A bond secured by collateral deposited with a trustee. The collateral is often the stocks or bonds of companies controlled by the issuing company but may be other securities.

Common stock: Securities that represent an ownership interest in a corporation. If the company has also issued preferred stock, both common and preferred have ownership rights, but the preferred normally has prior claim on dividends and, in the event of liquidation, assets. Claims of both common and preferred stockholders are junior to claims of bondholders or other creditors of the company. Common stockholders assume the greater risk but generally exercise the greater control and may gain the greater reward in the form of dividends and capital appreciation. The terms *common stock* and *capital stock* are often used interchangeably when the company has no preferred stock.

Compensating balance: A required minimum checking account balance that a firm must maintain with a commercial bank. The required balance is generally equal to 15 to 20 percent of the amount of loans outstanding. Compensating balances can raise the effective rate of interest on bank loans.

Consolidated balance sheet: A balance sheet showing the financial condition of a corporation and its subsidiaries.

Convertible: A bond, debenture, or preferred share that may be exchanged by the owner for common stock or another security, usually of the same company, in accordance with the terms of the issue.

Correspondent: A securities firm, bank, or other financial organization that regularly performs services for another in a place or market to which the other does not have direct access. Securities firms may have correspondents in foreign countries or on exchanges of which they are not members. Correspondents are frequently linked by private wires. Member Organizations with offices in New York City also act as correspondents for out-of-town Member Organizations that do not maintain New York City offices.

Cumulative preferred: A stock having a provision that if one or more dividends are omitted, the omitted dividends must be paid before dividends may be paid on the company's common stock.

Cumulative voting: A method of voting for corporate directors that enables the shareholder to multiply the number of his shares by the number of directorships being voted on and cast the total for one director or a selected group of directors. A 10-share holder normally casts 10 votes for each of, say, 12 nominees to the board of directors. He thus has 120 votes. Under the cumulative voting principle he may do that or he may cast 120 (10×12) votes for only one nominee, 60 for two, 40 for three, or any other distribution he chooses. Cumulative voting is required under the corporate laws of some states, is permissive in most others.

Current assets: Those assets of a company which are reasonably expected to be realized in cash, or sold, or consumed during the normal operating cycle of the business. These include cash, U.S. government bonds, receivables and money due usually within one year, and inventories.

Current liabilities: Money owed and payable by a company, usually within one year.

Debenture: A promissory note backed by the general credit of a company and usually not secured by a mortgage or lien on any specific property.

Depletion: Natural resources, such as metals, oils and gas, and timber, which conceivably can be reduced to zero over the years, present a special problem in capital management. Depletion is an accounting practice consisting of charges against earnings based upon the amount of the asset taken out of the total reserves in the period for which accounting is made. A bookkeeping entry, it does not represent any cash outlay, nor are any funds earmarked for the purpose.

Depreciation: Normally, charges against earnings to write off the cost, less salvage value, of an asset over its estimated useful life. It is a bookkeeping entry and does not represent any cash outlay, nor are any funds earmarked for the purpose.

Director: Person elected by shareholders at the annual meeting to establish company policies. The directors appoint the president, vice-presidents, and all other operating officers. Directors decide, among other matters, if and when dividends shall be paid.

Discounting: The process of finding the present value of a series of future cash flows. Discounting is the reverse of *compounding.*

Diversification: Spreading investments among different companies in different fields. Another type of diversification is offered by the securities of many individual companies in consequence of the wide range of their activities.

Dividend: The payment designated by the board of directors to be distributed pro rata among the shares outstanding. On preferred shares, it is generally a fixed amount. On common shares, the dividend varies with the fortunes of the company and the amount of cash on hand, and may be omitted if business is poor or the directors determine to withhold earnings to invest in plant and equipment. Sometimes a company will pay a dividend out of past earnings even if it is not currently operating at a profit.

Double taxation: Short for "double taxation of dividends." The federal government taxes corporate profits once as corporate income; any part of the remaining profits distributed as dividends to stockholders is taxed again as income to the recipient stockholder.

Earnings report: A statement—also called an *income statement*—issued by a company showing its earnings or losses over a given period. The earnings report lists the income earned, expenses, and the net result.

EBIT: Abbreviation for "earnings before interest and taxes."

EPS: Abbreviation for "earnings per share."

Equipment trust certificate: A type of security, generally issued by a railroad, to pay for new equipment. Title to the equipment, such as a locomotive, is held by a trustee until the notes are paid off. An equipment trust certificate is usually secured by a first claim on the equipment.

Equity: The ownership interest of common and preferred stockholders in a company. Also refers to excess of value of securities over the debit balance in a margin account.

Ex-dividend: A synonym for "without dividend." The buyer of a stock selling ex-dividend does not receive the recently declared dividend. Open buy and sell stop orders and sell stop limit orders in a stock on the ex-dividend date are ordinarily reduced by the value of that dividend. In the case of open shop limit orders to sell, both the stop price and the limit price are reduced. Every dividend is payable on a fixed date to all shareholders recorded on the books of the company as of a previous date of record. For example, a dividend may be declared as payable to holders of record on the books of the company on a given Friday. Since five business days are allowed for delivery of stock in a "regular way" transaction on the New York Stock Exchange, the Exchange would declare the stock "ex-dividend" as of the opening of the market on the preceding Monday. That means anyone who bought it on or after Monday would not be entitled to that dividend.

Ex-rights: "Without the rights." Corporations raising additional money may do so by offering their stockholders the right to subscribe to new or additional stock, usually at a discount from the prevailing market price. The buyer of a stock selling ex-rights is not entitled to the rights.

Face value: The value of a bond that appears on the face of the bond, unless the value is otherwise specified by the issuing company. Face value is ordinarily the amount the issuing company promises to pay at maturity. Face value is not an indication of market value. Sometimes referred to as *par value.*

Financial leverage: The ratio of total debt to total assets. There are other measures of financial leverage, especially ones that relate cash inflows to required cash outflows. The debt–total asset ratio is generally used to measure leverage.

Fixed charges: A company's fixed expenses, such as bond interest, that it has agreed to pay whether or not earned and that are deducted from income before earnings on equity capital are computed.

Gilt-edged: High-grade bond issued by a company that has demonstrated its ability to earn a comfortable profit over a period of years and pay its bondholders their interest without interruption.

Goodwill: Intangible assets of a firm established by the excess of the price paid for the going concern over its book value.

Government bonds: Obligations of the U.S. government, regarded as the highest-grade issues in existence.

Growth stock: Stock of a company with prospects for future growth—a company whose earnings are expected to increase at a relatively rapid rate.

Guaranteed bond: A bond that has interest or principal, or both, guaranteed by a company other than the issuer. Usually found in the railroad industry when large roads, leasing sections of trackage owned by small railroads, may guarantee the bonds of the smaller road.

Guaranteed stock: Usually, preferred stock on which dividends are guaranteed by another company, under much the same circumstances as a bond is guaranteed.

Holding company: A corporation that owns the securities of another, in most cases with voting control.

Income bond: Generally, income bonds promise to repay principal but to pay interest only when earned. In some cases unpaid interest on an income bond may accumulate as a claim against the corporation when the bond becomes due. An income bond may also be issued in lieu of preferred stock.

Indenture: A written agreement under which debentures are issued, setting forth maturity date, interest rate, security, and other terms.

Interest: Payments a borrower pays a lender for the use of his money. A corporation pays interest on its bonds to its bondholders.

Investment: The use of money for the purpose of making more money, to gain income or increase capital, or both. Safety of principal is an important consideration.

Investment banker: Also known as an *underwriter.* He is the middleman between the corporation issuing new securities and the public. The usual practice is for one or more investment bankers to buy outright from a corporation a new issue of stocks or bonds. The group forms a syndicate to sell the securities to individuals and institutions. Investment bankers also distribute very large blocks of stocks or bonds—perhaps held by an estate. Thereafter the market in the security may be over-the-counter or on a regional stock exchange, the American Exchange, or the New York Stock Exchange.

Leverage: The effect on the per share earnings of the common stock of a company when large sums must be paid for bond interest or preferred stock dividends, or both, before the common stock is entitled to share in earnings. Leverage may be advantageous for the common stock when earnings are good but may work against the common stock when earnings decline. Example: Company A has 1,000,000 shares of common stock outstanding, no other securities. Earnings drop from $1,000,000 to $800,000 or from $1 to 80 cents a share, a decline of 20 percent. Company B also has 1,000,000 shares of common but must pay $500,000 annually in bond interest. If earnings amount to $1,000,000, there is $500,000 available for the common, or 50 cents a share. But earnings drop to $800,000 so there is only $300,000 available for the common, or 30 cents a share—a drop of 40 percent. Or suppose earnings of the company with only common stock increased from $1,000,000 to $1,500,000. Earnings per share would go from $1 to $1.50, or an increase of 50 percent. But if earnings of the company that had to pay $500,000 in bond interest increased that much, earnings per common share would jump from 50 cents to $1 a share, or 100 percent. When a company has common stock only, no leverage exists because all earnings are available for the common, although relatively large fixed charges payable for lease of substantial plant assets may have an effect similar to that of a bond issue.

Liabilities: All the claims against a corporation. Liabilities include accounts and wages and salaries payable, dividends declared payable, accrued taxes payable, and fixed or long-term liabilities such as mortgage bonds, debentures, and bank loans.

Line of credit: An arrangement whereby a financial institution (bank or insurance company) commits itself to lend up to a specified maximum amount of funds during a specified period. Sometimes the interest rate on the loan is specified; at other times it is not. Sometimes a commitment fee is imposed for obtaining the line of credit.

Liquidation: The process of converting securities or other property into cash. The dissolution of a company, with cash remaining after sale of its assets and payment of all indebtedness being distributed to the shareholders.

Liquidity: The ability of the market in a particular security to absorb a reasonable amount of buying or selling at reasonable price changes. Liquidity is one of the most important characteristics of a good market.

Marginal cost: The cost of an additional unit.

Mortgage bond: A bond secured by a mortgage on a property. The value of the property may or may not equal the value of the so-called mortgage bonds issued against it.

Municipal bond: A bond issued by a state or a political subdivision, such as county, city, town, or village. The term also designates bonds issued by state agencies and authorities. In general, interest paid on municipal bonds is exempt from federal income taxes.

Negotiable: A security title to which is transferable by delivery.

Noncumulative: A preferred stock on which unpaid dividends do not accrue. Omitted dividends are, as a rule, gone forever.

Opportunity cost: The rate of return on the best *alternative* investment that is available. It is the highest return that will *not* be earned if the funds are invested in a particular project. For example, the opportunity cost of *not* investing in common stocks yielding 8 percent might be 6 percent, which could be earned on bonds.

PAR: In the case of a common share, par means a dollar amount assigned to the share by the company's charter. Par value may also be used to compute the dollar amount of the common shares on the balance sheet. Par value has little significance so far as market value of common stock is concerned. Many companies today issue no-par stock but give a stated per share value on the balance sheet. Par at one time was supposed to represent the value of the original investment behind each share in cash, goods, or services. In the case of preferred shares and bonds, however, par is important. It often signifies the dollar value upon which dividends on preferred stocks and interest on bonds are figured. The issuer of a 3 percent bond promises to pay that percentage of the bond's par value annually.

Participating preferred: A preferred stock that is entitled to its stated dividend and, also, to additional dividends on a specfied basis upon payment of dividends on the common stock.

Payback period: The length of time required for the net revenues of an investment to return the cost of the investment.

Pooling of interest: An accounting method for combining the financial statements of two firms that merge. Under the pooling of interest procedure, the assets of the merged firms are simply added together to form the balance sheet of the surviving corporation. This method is different from the "purchase" method, in which goodwill is put on the balance sheet to reflect a premium (or discount) paid in excess of book value.

Preferred stock: A class of stock with a claim on the company's earnings before payment may be made on the common stock and usually entitled to priority over common stock if company liquidates. Usually entitled to dividends at a specified rate—when declared by the board of directors and before payment of a dividend on the common stock—depending upon the terms of the issue.

Premium: The amount by which a preferred stock or bond may sell above its par value. In the case of a new issue of bonds or stocks, premium is the amount the market price rises over the original selling price. Also refers to a charge sometimes made when a stock is borrowed to make delivery on a short sale. May refer, also, to redemption price of a bond or preferred stock if it is higher than face value.

Price-earnings ratio: The current market price of a share of stock divided by earnings per share for a twelve-month period. For example, a stock selling for $100 a share and earning $5 a share is said to be selling at a price-earnings ratio of 20 to 1.

Principal: The person for whom a broker executes an order, or a dealer buying or selling for his own account. May also refer to a person's capital or to the face amount of a bond.

Pro forma: Projected. A *pro forma* financial statement is one that shows how the actual statement will look if certain specified assumptions are realized. *Pro forma* statements may be either future or past projections. An example of a backward *pro forma* statement occurs when two firms are planning to merge and show what their consolidated financial statements would have looked like had they been merged in preceding years.

Record date: The date on which you must be registered on the books of a company as a shareholder in order to receive a declared dividend or, among other things, to vote on company affairs.

Refinancing: Same as *refunding.* New securities are sold by a company, and the money is used to retire existing securities. The object may be to save interest costs, extend the maturity of the loan, or both.

Registered bond: A bond that is registered on the books of the issuing company in the name of the owner. It can be transferred only when endorsed by the registered owner.

Rights: When a company wants to raise more funds by issuing additional securities, it may give its stockholders the opportunity, ahead of others, to buy the new securities in proportion to the number of shares each owns. The piece of paper evidencing this privilege is called a right. Because the additional stock is usually offered to stockholders below the current market price, rights ordinarily have a market value of their own and are actively traded. In most cases they must be exercised within a relatively short period. Failure to exercise or sell rights may result in actual loss to the holder.

Serial bond: An issue that matures in relatively small amounts at periodic stated intervals.

Sinking fund: Money regularly set aside by a company to redeem its bonds, debentures, or preferred stock from time to time as specified in the indenture or charter.

Split: The division of the outstanding shares of a corporation into a larger number of shares. A 3-for-1 split by a company with 1 million shares outstanding would result in 3 million shares outstanding. Each holder of 100 shares before the 3-for-1 split would have 300 shares, although his proportionate equity in the company would remain the same, since 100 parts of 1 million are the equivalent of 300 parts of 3 million. Ordinarily, splits must be voted by directors and approved by shareholders.

Stock clearing corporation: A subsidiary of the New York Stock Exchange that acts as a central agency for security deliveries and money payments between member firms of the Exchange.

Stock dividend: A dividend paid in securities rather than cash. The dividend may be additional shares of the issuing company or shares of another company (usually a subsidiary) held by the company.

Transfer: May refer to two different operations. One is the delivery of a stock certificate from the seller's broker to the buyer's broker and legal change of ownership, normally accomplished within a few days. The other is the recording of the change of ownership on the books of the corporation by the transfer agent. When the purchaser's name is recorded on the books of the company, dividends, notices of meetings, proxies, financial reports, and all pertinent literature sent by the issuer to its securities holders are mailed direct to the new owner.

Transfer agent: A transfer agent keeps a record of the name of each registered shareowner, his or her address, and the number of shares owned and sees that certificates presented to his office for transfer are properly cancelled and new certificates issued in the name of the transferee.

Voting right: The stockholder's right to vote his stock in the affairs of his company. Most common shares have one vote each. Preferred stock usually has the right to vote when preferred dividends are in default for a specified period. The right to vote may be delegated by the stockholder to another person.

Warrant: A certificate giving the holder the right to purchase securities at a stipulated price within a specified time limit or perpetually. Sometimes a warrant is offered with securities as an inducement to buy.

Working capital: A firm's investment in short-term assets—cash, short-term securities, accounts receivable, and inventories. *Gross working capital* is defined as a firm's total current assets. *Net working capital* is defined as current assets minus current liabilities. If the term *working capital* is used without further qualification, it generally refers to gross working capital.

Working control: Theoretically, ownership of 51 percent of a company's voting stock is necessary to exercise control. In practice—and this is particularly true in the case of a large corporation—effective control sometimes can be exerted through ownership, individually or by a group acting in concert, of less than 50 percent.

Yield: Also known as *return*. The dividends or interest paid by a company expressed as a percentage of the current price—or, if you own the security, of the price you originally paid. The return on a stock is figured by dividing the total of dividends paid in the preceding twelve months by the current market price—or, if you are the owner, the price you originally paid. A stock with a current market value of $40 a share that has paid $2 in dividends in the preceding twelve months is said to return 5 percent ($2.00 ÷ $40.00). If you paid $20 for the stock five years earlier, the stock would be returning you 10 percent on your original investment. The current return on a bond is figured the same way. A 3 percent $1,000 bond selling at $600 offers a return of 5 percent ($30 ÷ $600). Figuring the yield of a bond to maturity calls for a bond yield table.

Sources: "The Language of Investing," New York Stock Exchange, January, 1968.

Fred J. Weston and Eugene F. Brigham, "Essentials of Managerial Finance," Holt, Rinehart and Winston, Inc., New York, 1968.

INDEX

INDEX

Accelerated-depreciation methods, 294
Accounts receivable as source of short-term financing, 240
Accounts receivable policy, 252–262
Accumulation of earnings, improper, 46–48
Acquisitions, 425
  Accounting Principles Board Opinion No. 9 and No. 15, 449
  by common stock, 447, 448
  by common stock convertible debentures, 448
  criteria for search for candidates, 450
  earnings per share, 450
  economic power, 439
  framework for, 316
  mechanics of, 440
  pooling vs. purchasing, illustrated, 452
  reasons for, 439
  significance of form of payment, 446
  tax considerations, 442
  tools of, 446
Act(s):
  of bankruptcy, 469
  Federal Securities, 34
  Federal Securities Exchange, of 1934, 34
  Model Business Corporation, 30
  Ultra vires, 31
Activity ratios, 324–325
Add-on interest, 170–171
Adjusted gross income, 23
  deductions from, 24
Administered prices, 306–308
Agio, 344
Agreements, repurchase, 226–227
Annuity:
  compound sum of, 69–73
  due, 71
  ordinary, 70
Anticipation, investor, and common stock prices, 369
Antitrust Laws, 436
Articles of Incorporation, illustrated, 48
Asset appraisal, significance of, 333
Authority of partnership, 27
Average revenue, significance of, 303, 304
Average tax rate, 24
  corporations, 36
  illustrated, 25
Average total costs, 63

b formula, 99
Balance sheet, 86
  projection, 229
Bank financing, 164–167
  use of present value concepts, 164
Bank loans, requirements for, 166
Bank reconciliation, 217
Bankers' acceptance, 223–224
Bankruptcy:
  acts of, 469
  alternatives to, 478
  composition, 467
  effect of high debt-to-equity rates, 466
  extension of time, 467
  insolvency, 468
  legal rights of parties, 464–465
  liquidity, 466
  remedies, 467–469, 477
  reorganization, 467

Bankruptcy:
valuation problem, 471
voluntary, 468
"Blue-sky laws," 34
Board, Federal Reserve, The, 34
Bonds:
calculation of yield, 400
call provision, 395
collateral trust, 399
convertible, 399
income, 399
indenture, 393
mortgage, 397–398
open end, 392
public vs. private placement, 396
secured, 389
Series E, 391
sinking fund, 396
subordinate, 393
types of, 398–399
unsecured, 392
Book value, 33
Breakeven analysis, 94
illustrated, 95
Budget:
cash receipts, 231–232
flexible, 88–93
production, 306
Budgeting, capital (*see* Capital budgeting)
Business failures, causes of, 3
Business organizations, forms of: corporation, 19, 29–31, 35
individual proprietorship, 17–19, 21, 22, 24
partnership, 26–28
single proprietor, 17–19, 21, 22, 24
Business trust, 29
Buy vs. lease, 175–181
earnings per share, 175, 204
effect of depreciation method, illustrated, 202

Calculation of yield on bonds, 400
Call provision bonds, 395
Capital:
cost of, 343, 356
debt investor, 357
to the firm, 356
and investment risks, 355
new equity investor, 357
Capital:
cost of: significance of financing mix, 366
gain (*see* Capital gain)
loss (*see* Capital loss)
Capital budgeting:
applied, 116
importance of, 117
defined, 113–116
estimation of costs and benefits, 114
evaluation of risk, 114–115
fixed budget, 151
generation of proposals, 114
open end budget, 151
postaudit, 116
reevaluation, 116
selection of proposals, 115–116
Capital gain:
long-term, 37, 328
net long-term, 37
net short-term, 37
short-term, 37
Capital gains and losses, 37, 328, 329
corporate taxpayers, 39
definitions of, 37
illustrated, 39, 40, 330
individual taxpayers, 37–39
offset applied, 410, 417
Capital loss:
long-term, 37
net long-term, 37
net short-term, 37
short-term, 37
Capital stock, 33
Capitalization rate, 9
factors determining, 9
Carrying costs, inventory, 266
Cash:
internal control of, 216–221
profitability of, 214–216
Cash discounts, effect of, 238
Cash-flow:
analysis, 227–232
illustrated, 231
summary, illustrated, 233
Cash funds, 221
Cash receipts budget, illustrated, 231–232
Cash-to-cash cycle, 212
Casual sale, installment method, 42–43
Chattel mortgage, 165
"Check kiting," 220

Classical theory of interest, 344
Closed end debt, 394
Collateral trust bonds, 399
Collection expenditures, 260–262
Commission:
  Federal Power, 35
  Securities and Exchange, 34
Common-law trust, 29
Common stock, 32
  investor anticipation and prices, 369
Company, joint stock, 29
Compound amount, 68
Compound interest, 67
Compound sum:
  of an annuity, 69–73
  of an annuity due, illustrated, 72
  of $1, illustrated, 68
  of an ordinary annuity, illustrated, 71
Comptroller (*see* Controller)
Consolidation of corprations, 31
Control of inventories, 262–264
Controller, functions of, 4
Convertible bond, 399
  illustrated, 402
Corporate management, 35
Corporate savings, 345
  reasons for, 345
Corporate shares:
  regulation of, 34
  tax implications, 36
  tax rates, table, 36
Corporate stock, 32
  probable value of, 358
    illustrated, 370, 375
    to investors seeking both dividends and earnings, 378
    to investors seeking dividends, 366
    to investors seeking earnings, 363
    present value analysis, 375
  registration of, 34
  stock splits and stock dividends, 379
  transfer of ownership, 33
Corporate tax rate, table, 36
Corporate tax treatment, 44
Corporate taxpayers, capital gains and losses of, 39
Corporations:
  consolidation of, 31
  directors of, 31, 35
  dissolution of, 30–31
  fringe benefits, 19
  implied powers of, 31
Corporations:
  legal implications of, 29
  management of, 31, 35
  merger of, 31
  officers of, 35
  payment of tax, 45
  requirements to form, 30
  stockholder's rights, 31
  taxed as partnership, 47
Cost of capital, 343, 356
  debt investor, 357
  to the firm, 356
  and investment risks, 355
  new equity investor, 357
  significance of financing mix, 366
Cost of credit policy, 252, 253, 261
Cost curves, illustrated, 48, 92
Cost-profit centers, 332
Cost-profit-volume relationship, 95–96
Cost push and inflation, 293
Costs:
  average total, 63
  differential, 93–94
  fixed, 59, 307
  and inventories, 264–269
  joint, 332
  marginal, 63, 93–94, 302
  production, 275
  semi-variable, 100
  stock-out, 276–277
  variable, 60, 307
Credit:
  and billing procedures, 236–238
  Dun and Bradstreet report, illustrated, 256–257
  extension of, 258–260
  external information, 255
  framework for decision, 258–260
  information: internal, 255
    sources of, 255–258
  investment, 294
  period, 253
  policy: cost of, 252, 253, 261
    marginal cost vs. marginal revenue, 252, 254
Cumulative preferred stock, 32
Curve, demand, 301
    elasticity of, 301, 333
    oligopolistic, 309
Customer goodwill, 276
  inventory policy, 276
Cycle, cash-to-cash, 212

Dealer paper:
  finance, 224
  industrial, 223
Debt:
  closed end, 394
  financing, 2
  intermediate-term, 160
  investor in, cost of capital, 357
  long-term, 160
  marginal cost of, 408–418
  open end, 395
  short-term, 160
Decision making, financial: goal of, 11, 12
    interdisciplinary nature of, 5, 6
    role of accounting, 12
Declining balance, 192–194
Deductions:
  from adjusted gross income, 24
  from gross income, 23
  standard, 23
Deflation, 293
Demand curve, 301
  elasticity of, 301, 333
  oligopolistic, 309
Demand poll, inflation, 292
Dependency exemption, 24
Dependent variable, 100
Deposit, negotiable certificates of, 224–225
Depreciation:
  accelerated, 294
  methods of, 187
    and the flow of funds, 185–207
      evaluation of, 188, 189, 195
      tax implications, 186–187
    net income and earnings per share, 189–190
    straight-line, 188
  recapture, 141–142
Differential costs, 93–94
Directors of corporations, 31, 35
Diseconomies of scale, 61–62
Dissolution:
  of corporations, 30–31
  of partnership, 27
Diversification:
  internal, 434
  through merger and acquisition, 434–435
Diversification gap, 432

Dividends, 329, 330
  liquidating, 329
  received, 44
    corporate tax treatment, 44
    individual tax treatment, 44
  yield, 359, 361
Dun and Bradstreet credit report, illustrated, 256–257

Earnings per share, 444
  buy vs. lease, 175, 204
  convertible bond financing, 404
  effect of leverage, 405
  and increased sales volume, 374
  and sales volume, 374
  tax shield, 198
Earnings yield, 359, 361
Economic environment, 289–296
  government activity, 295
  role of investment, 291
  time lag, 290
Economic order quantity, 265–269
  critique of, 267–268
Economies of scale, 61–62
Elasticity:
  of demand curve, 301, 307
  of interest rate, 344
Equipment trust certificates, 398–399
Equity funds, 2
Exchange Commission, Securities and, 34
Executive:
  financial, 10
  goal of, 10
Exemptions, dependency, 24
Expenditures, collection, 260–262
External credit information, 255
External funds, 160

Failures, business, causes of, 3
Federal Power Commission, 35
Federal Reserve Board, The, 34
Federal Securities Act, 34
Federal Securities Exchange Act of 1934, 34
Finance, mathematics of, 66
Finance function, 2
  interdisciplinary nature of, 5–6
Finance paper, prime sales, 223

Financial decision making:
  goal of, 11, 12
  interdisciplinary nature of, 5–6
  role of accounting, 12
Financial executive, 10
  functions of, 5
  goal of, 10
Financial management, goal of, 6–9
Financial ratios:
  critique, 326
  industry data, 327
  value of internal data, 327
Financial responsibility, division of, 3
Financial risk, 352
Financing:
  bank, 164–167
  debt, 2
  manufacturer, 167–170
Financing mix, significance of cost of capital, 366
Firm's stock, probable value of, 358
Fixed costs, 59, 100, 307
Fixed-variable cost relationship, significance of, 96, 103
Flexible budget, 88–93
  illustrated, 90
Float time, 237–238
Formation of corporations, requirements for, 30
Forms of business organizations (*see* Business organizations, forms of)
Formula, *b*, 99
Framework for acquisitions, 316
Fringe benefits:
  corporations, 19
  individual proprietorship, 19
  single proprietor, 19
Function, finance, 2
  interdisciplinary nature of, 5–6
Functions:
  of controller, 4
  of financial executive, 5
  of treasurer, 4
Funds:
  cash, 221
  effective use of, 3
  equity, 2
  external, 160
  investment, sources of, 345
  liquidity, 221
  loanable vs. supply of money, 349
Funds:
  operating, 221
  source of, 159–164
  supply of, 344

Gain, capital (*see Capital gain*)
General partner, 26
Goals:
  of financial executive, 10
  of financial management, 6–9
Goodwill, 444
Gross income, 23
Gross profit on installment sale, illustrated, 42
Guidelines for marketing research, 426

Hedging, 280

Implied powers of corporations, 31
Improper accumulation of earnings, 46–48
Income:
  adjusted gross, 23
    deductions from, 24
  gross, 23
    deductions from, 23
  taxable, 24
Income bonds, 399
Income taxes, payment of, 44–45
Incorporation, articles of, illustrated, 48
Increased sales volume and earnings per share, 374
Indenture:
  after acquired property, 395
  bonds, 393
Independent variable, 100
Individual payment of tax, 44
Individual proprietor:
  fringe benefits, 19
  legal implications of, 17–18
  limitations of, 19
  tax implications of, 18, 21, 22, 24
Individual tax rates, tables for: married:
      joint, 21
      separate, 20
    unmarried, 22
Individual tax treatment, 44
Individual taxpayers, capital gains and losses of, 37–39

Inflation:
cost push, 293
demand poll, 292
Installment method, casual sale, 42–43
Installment sales, 41, 411
effects of Tax Reform Act of 1969, 412
Interest:
add-on, 170–171
classical theory of, 344
compound, 67
simple, 67
on unpaid balance, 171–172
Interest rate:
and loanable funds, significance of, 344, 347, 349
regulatory tool, 348
and risk, 450
Interest rate risk, 222, 351
Intermediate-term debt, 160
Intermediate-term loans, sources of, 161
Internal control:
of cash, 216–221
of inventories, 277
Internal credit information, 255
Internal diversification, 434
Internal rate of return, 125–127
Inventory:
carrying costs, 266
control of, 262–264
and costs, 264–269
customer goodwill, 276
internal control of, 277
and liquidity, 263
ordering costs, 268
policy, 272–276
and production budget, 272–274
and sales budget, 272
and sales and production budget, 272
ratios: critique, 271
turnover, 269–272
and risk, 263
valuation of, 278
valuation method, significance of, 278–279
Investment credit, 294
Investment funds, sources of, 345
Investment risks and the cost of capital, 355
Investment tax credit, 45–46
Investor:
debt, cost of capital, 357
new equity, cost of capital, 357
Investor anticipation and common stock prices, 369
Involuntary bankruptcy, 469

Joint costs, 332
Joint stock company, 29
Joint venture, 29

"Lapping," 220
Laws:
Antitrust, 436
"Blue-sky," 34
Lead time and safety stock, 276
Lease vs. buy, 175
illustrated, 176–177
Leasing, 173–175
Least squares, 101
Legal implications:
of corporations, 29
of individual proprietor, 17–18
of partnership, 26
of single proprietorship, 17–18
Leverage, 405
operating, 103–104
Leverage ratios, 322–323
Limitations:
of individual proprietor, 19
of single proprietorship, 19
Limited partnership, 28
Liquidating dividend, 329
Liquidity, 3
and inventories, 263
Liquidity funds, 221
Liquidity ratios, 321–322
Liquidity responsibility, 211–214
Loanable funds:
significance of interest rate and, 344, 347, 349
vs. supply of money, 349
Lockbox system, 237
Long-term capital gain, 37, 328
Long-term capital loss, 37
Long-term debt, 160
Long-term financing, characteristics of, 389
Loss:
capital (*see* Capital loss)
net operating, 40
illustrated, 41

Management:
  corporate, 35
  of corporations, 31, 35
  financial, goal of, 6–9
  of short-term investments, 221–227
Manufacturer financing, 167–170
Marginal cost, 63, 93–94, 302
  of debt, 408–418
Marginal revenue, 303, 307
Marginal tax rate, 24
  corporations, 36
  illustrated, 25
Market risk, 354
Market structure:
  and prices, 296–300
  significance of, 308
Market value, 33
Marketable debt of the United States government, 223
Marketing research, 426
  applied, 427
  guidelines for, 426
Massachusetts trust, 29
Mathematics of finance, 66
Mechanics:
  of acquisitions, 440
  of mergers, 440
    and acquisitions, 440–446
Merger candidate, 440
  criteria for search for, 450
Mergers, 425
  Accounting Principles Board Opinion No. 9 and No. 15, 449
  acquisition: by common stock, 447–448
    by common stock convertible debentures, 448
  and acquisitions, mechanics of, 440–446
  antitrust considerations, 437
  of corporations, 31
  earnings per share, 450
  economic power, 439
  mechanics of, 440
  pooling vs. purchasing, illustrated, 452
  reasons for, 439
  significance: of accounting method, 444
    of form of payment, 446
    of goodwill, 444
  tax considerations, 442
Mergers:
  tools of, 446
  types of, 435
Model Business Corporation Act, 30
Money, loanable funds vs. supply of, 349
Monopolistic competition, 297
Monopoly, 300
Mortgage, chattel, 165
Mortgage bond, 397–398

Negotiable certificates of deposit, 224–225
Net:
  long-term capital gain or loss, 37
  operating loss, 40, 331
    illustrated, 41, 329
  present value, 127–140
  short-term capital gain or loss, 37
New equity investor, cost of capital, 357
No-par value stock, 32
Nominal partner, 26

Officers of corporations, 35
Oligopolistic demand curve, 309
Oligopoly, 298–300
  types of, 299
Open end bonds, 392
Open end debt, 395
Operating funds, 221
Operating leverage, 103–104
Opportunity cost, 58
Ordering costs, inventory, 268
Ordinary annuity, 70
Organizations, business, forms of (*see* Business organizations, forms of)
Ownership of corporate stock, transfer of, 33

Par value, 32
Participating preferred stock, 32
Partners:
  authority of, 27
  dormant, 27
  duties of, 27
  general, 26
  nominal, 26

Partners:
remedies of, 27
secret, 27
silent, 26
types of, 26–27
Partnership, 26
authority of partners, 27
dissolution of, 27
duties of partners, 27
legal implications, 26
limited, 28
remedies of partners, 27
types of partners, 26–27
Payment of tax:
corporation, 45
income, 44–45
individual, 44
Perfect competition, 297
Perimeters for price changes, 305
Personal savings, 345
reasons for, 345
Plans for growth, 319
Pooling accounting, 445–446
Power Commission, Federal, The, 35
Powers of corporations, implied, 31
Preemptive right, 33
Preferred stock, 32
Present value:
analysis: market value of corporate stock, 375
of probable value of corporate stock, 375
of an annuity due, illustrated, 78
cash flow (annuity), 129
of $1, illustrated, 74
of an ordinary annuity, illustrated, 76
and purchase price, 334–336
of a single sum, 73–75
Price changes, perimeters for, 305
Price-earnings ratio, 359–361
Price-volume relationship, 301–303
Prices:
administered, 306–308
investor anticipation and common stock, 369
and market structure, 269–300
transfer, 332
perimeters for, 305
Pricing, 300–306
target, 306
Prime sales finance paper, 223
Probability analysis, 145
Probable value:
of corporate stock, 359
comparison with other firms, 359
illustrated, 370, 375
to investors seeking both dividends and earnings, 378
to investors seeking dividends, 366
to investors seeking earnings, 363
present value analysis, 375
of firm's stock, 358
Production budget, 306
and inventory policy, 272–274
Production costs, 275
Profitability, 3
Profitability ratios, 325
Project selection, 122
average return on the average annual investment, 123–124
payback period, 122–123
Projection, balance sheet, 229
Proprietor, individual: fringe benefits, 19
legal implications of, 17–18
limitations of, 19
tax implications of, 18, 21, 22, 24
Proprietorship, single: fringe benefits, 19
legal implications of, 17–18
limitations of, 19
tax implications of, 18, 21, 22, 24
Proxy solicitations, 34
Purchase accounting, 444–445
Purchase price and present value, 334–336
Purchasing power:
risk, 351
significance of, 289

Rates:
average tax, 24
capitalization, 9
factors determining, 9
interest: elasticity of, 344
regulatory tool, 348
risk and, 450
marginal tax, 24
tax: corporations, 36
average, illustrated, 25

Rates:
tax: corporations: marginal, illustrated, 25
tables: corporate, 36
corporate shares, 36
individual: married: joint, 21
separate, 20
unmarried, 22
Ratio(s):
activity, 324–325
analysis, 321
inventory turnover, 269–272
leverage, 322–323
liquidity, 321–322
price-earnings, 359–361
profitability, 325
Reconciliation, bank, 217
Registration of corporate stock, 34
Regression analysis, 99
Regulation of corporate shares, 34
Regulatory tool, interest rate as, 348
Remedies of partners, 27
Repurchase agreements, 226–227
Requirements:
for bank loans, 166
to form corporation, 30
Reserve Board, Federal, The, 34
Responsibility, division of financial, 3
Retaliation, 299
Return, internal rate of, 125–127
Revenue, marginal, 303, 307
Rights:
preemptive, 33
of stockholders, 31
Risk:
financial, 352
interest-rate, 351
and interest rate, 450
and inventories, 263
investment, and the cost of capital, 355
market, 354
purchasing-power, 351

Safety stock, 262
and lead time, 276
Sales:
budget and inventory policy, 272
forecast, illustrated, 231–232, 306
and sales pattern, 275–276
Sales:
installment, 41
pattern and sales forecast, 275–276
volume and earnings per share, 374
Savings:
corporate, 345
source of, 346
governmental, source of, 347
personal, 345
source of, 345
reasons for, 345
Scale:
diseconomies of, 61–62
economies of, 61–62
Secret partner, 27
Secured bonds, 390–392
Securities and Exchange Commission, 34
Semi-variable cost, 100
Sensitivity:
analysis, 140–145
and probability combined, 145–153
Series E Bonds, 391
Service-life methods, 190–191
Shares, corporate, regulation of, 34
Short-term capital gain or loss, 37
net, 37
Short-term debt, 160
Short-term investments, management of, 221–227
Short-term tax-exempt bills, 225
Silent partner, 26
Simple interest, 67
Single proprietorship:
fringe benefits, 19
legal implications of, 17–18
limitations of, 19
tax implications of, 18, 21, 22, 24
Single sum, present value of, 73–75
Sinking fund bonds, 396
Small Business Administration (SBA), 163
Solicitations, proxy, 34
Sources:
credit information, 255–258
funds, 159–164
internal, 160
tax shield, 195
intermediate-term loans, 161
investment funds, 345
savings: corporate, 346

Sources:
savings: governmental, 347
personal, 345
short-term financing, accounts receivabe, 240
Standard deduction, 23
Statement of source and application of funds, 234–236
work sheet, illustrated, 234
Stock:
capital, 33
common, 32
company, joint, 29
corporate, 32
probable value of, 358
cumulative preferred, 32
dividends and stock splits, 379
no-par value, 32
option, 315–316
participating preferred, 32
preferred, 32
safety, 262
splits and stock dividends, 379
treasury, 31
Stock-out costs, 276–277
Stock-outs, 263
Stockholder's rights, 31
Subordinate bonds, 393
Subordinated indenture, 393
Sum-of-the-years-digits, 194–195
Supply:
and cost, 57–58
of funds, 344
of money vs. loanable funds, 349
Syndicate, 29

Target pricing, 306
Tax:
average rate, 24
implications: corporate shares, 36
of individual proprietor, 18, 21, 22, 24
of single proprietorship, 18, 21, 22, 24
marginal rate, 24
rates: average, 24
corporations, 36
illustrated, 25
corporate, table, 36
individual: joint returns, table, 21
separate returns, table, 20
unmarried, table, 22
Tax:
rates: marginal, 24
corporation, 36
illustrated, 25
shield: accelerated methods, 196
applied, earnings per share, 198
service-life methods, 196
straight-line method, 195
tables, corporate shares, 36
treatment: corporate, 44
individual, 44
Tax-exempt bills, short-term, 225
Tax-free reorganizations, 442
Taxable income, 24
Taxpayers:
corporate, capital gains and losses, 39
individual, capital gains and losses, 37–39
Theory of interest, classical, 344
Tools:
of acquisitions, 446
of mergers, 446
Transfer of ownership, corporate stock, 33
Transfer prices, 332
Treasurer, functions of, 4
Treasury stock, 31
Trust:
business, 29
common-law, 29
Massachusetts, 29
Trust Indenture Act of 1939, 397

Ultra vires act, 31
United States government marketable debt, 223
Unpaid balance, interest on, 171–172
Unsecured bonds, 392

Valuation of inventories, 278
Value:
added, 332
book, 33
of corporate stock, present value concepts applied, 415
market, 33
net present, 127–140
no-par stock, 32

Value:
  par, 32
  probable, of firm's stock, 358
Variable:
  dependent, 100
  independent, 100
Variable costs, 60, 307
Venture, joint, 29
Voluntary bankruptcy, 468

Yield:
  dividend, 359, 361
  earnings, 359, 361